RED SCARE

RED SCARE

MEMORIES OF THE AMERICAN INQUISITION
AN ORAL HISTORY

GRIFFIN FARIELLO

I.C.C. LIBRARY

AVON BOOKS ◆ NEW YORK

Excerpt on pp. 17-19 from Cedric Belfrage, *The American Inquisition* (New York: Bobbs-Merrill, 1973; reprinted Thunder's Mouth Press, 1989). Copyright © 1973 by Cedric Belfrage. Reprinted by permission of Susan Bergholz Literary Services, New York. p. 337 Lewis Allan & Earl Robinson, "The House I Live In" (Los Angeles: Warner/Chappell Music, Inc., 1942). Copyright © 1942 Chappell & Co. (renewed). All rights reserved. Reprinted by permission. p. 366 Leon Rosselson, "The World Turned Upside Down." Reprinted by permission of Leon Rosselson. p. 374 Lee Hays & Walter Lowenfels, "Wasn't That a Time" (New York: Sanga Music, Inc., 1957). Copyright © 1957, 1966 by Sanga Music, Inc. All rights reserved. Reprinted by permission.

AVON BOOKS
A division of
The Hearst Corporation
1350 Avenue of the Americas
New York, New York 10019

Copyright © 1995 by Griffin Fariello
Published by arrangement with W.W. Norton & Company, Inc.
Library of Congress Catalog Card Number: 94-25859
ISBN: 0-380-72711-0

The Norton edition contains the following Library of Congress Cataloging in Publication Data:
Fariello, Griffin.
   Red scare : memories of the American Inquisition : an oral history / Griffin Fariello.
     p. cm.
Includes bibliographical references and index.
1. Anti-Communist movements—United States—History. 2. Internal security—United States—History—20th century. I. Title.
E743.5.F34   1995
973.92—dc20   94-25859

First Avon Books Trade Printing: May 1996

Printed in the U.S.A.

QPM 10 9 8 7 6 5 4 3 2 1

For Mimi,
the fellow traveler of my heart
and
in memory of
Joe Passen,
a proud member of the working class

As someday it may happen that a victim must be found,
I've got a little list—I've got a little list
Of society offenders who might well be underground,
And who never would be missed—who never would be missed!
The task of filling up the blanks I'd rather leave to you,
But it really doesn't matter whom you put on the list,
For they'd none of 'em be missed—
They'd none of 'em be missed!

—Ko-Ko, Lord High Executioner, *The Mikado*

RED
SCARE

Contents

ACKNOWLEDGMENTS 15

PRINCIPAL FEDERAL HERESY TRIBUNALS AND LAWS 17

FIRST AND FIFTH AMENDMENTS TO THE CONSTITUTION 21

PREFACE 23

INTRODUCTION 27

Red Diapers 47

ROBERT MEEROPOL 47   GENE DENNIS 54

ROBBIE BRIDGES 58   CHRIS TRUMBO 63

BECKY JENKINS 69

The Peekskill Riot 74

IRWIN SILBER 75   BOB BLACK 78

Hounds 81

M. WESLEY SWEARINGEN 84   HARVEY JOB MATUSOW 97

HERBERT BROWNELL, JR. 108   ROY BREWER 112

PETER SZLUK 122

The Purge of the Civil Service 127

JERRY AND SYLVIA MANHEIM 131   JOSEPH RAUH 137

AL BERNSTEIN 141

A Graveyard of Careers 144

ALGER HISS *146*   CARL MARZANI *152*

JOHN STEWART SERVICE *158*   JOHN MELBY *165*

ANTHONY GEBER *170*

Atom Bomb Spies 175

MORTON SOBELL *181*   HELEN SOBELL *189*

STEVE NELSON *195*

The Fall of the Communist Party 199

STEVE NELSON *204*   LORETTA STARVUS *212*

DOROTHY HEALEY *219*   JUNIUS SCALES *226*

Five Minutes to Midnight 236

JUNIUS SCALES *239*   ARCHIE BROWN *241*

HON BROWN *243*   SYLVIA THOMPSON *247*

JOE PASSEN *249*   FAY BLAKE *251*

The Hollywood Blacklist 255

RING LARDNER, JR. *260*   FRANCES CHANEY *266*

HOWARD KOCH *272*   PAUL JARRICO *276*

JEFF COREY *284*   JOHN SANFORD *289*

EDWARD DMYTRYK *294*   DAVID RAKSIN *305*

Arts and Entertainment 315

MARK GOODSON *320*   FRANK TARLOFF *326*

KAY BOYLE *331*   JOSEPH RAUH *338*

ARTHUR MILLER *340*   JOHN RANDOLPH *345*

ANGUS CAMERON *352*   MELVIN BARNET *355*

Troubadours of the Left 362

PETE SEEGER *363*   FRED HELLERMAN *367*

RONNIE GILBERT *370*

Breaking the Working Class 375

CLINTON JENCKS *380*   JOE SACHS *390*

CLAIRE HARTFORD *395*

On the Waterfront 402

BILL BAILEY *405*   JACK O'DELL *413*

Red-ucators 419

Universities 426

LINUS PAULING *426*   OSCAR SHAFTEL *429*

CHANDLER DAVIS *434*   ROBERT COLODNY *440*

M. BREWSTER SMITH *444*

Labor Schools 447

DAVE JENKINS *447*   HERBERT APTHEKER *451*

Public Schools 455

RUTH GOLDBERG *455*   FRANCES EISENBERG *459*

JEAN WILKINSON *464*

Fighting Jim Crow 469

ANNE BRADEN *472*   SYLVIA THOMPSON *482*

VIRGINIA DURR *487*   LEE LORCH *489*

JACK O'DELL *500*

The Peace Movement　507

LINUS PAULING　*509*　　　　　EDITH JENKINS　*515*

The Fight Against HUAC　521

RICHARD CRILEY　*521*　　　　FRANK WILKINSON　*528*

JEAN WILKINSON　*537*　　　ARCHIE BROWN　*540*

HON BROWN　*543*

The Arlington Case　544

SYLVIA THOMPSON　*544*

SOURCES　*549*

INDEX　*557*

Acknowledgments

A book of this sort is never a solo effort. I wish to express my deepest thanks to all those who gave willingly of their time and energy to this project.

As a scribbler without an agent is a lost soul these days, I certainly appreciate one of the best, Sandra Dijkstra, along with Katherine Goodwin and everyone else at the Dijkstra Literary Agency. Their support was invaluable.

At Norton, Rose Kernochan, Dan Conaway, and Amy Cherry provided the best of editorial support. A special thanks to Dan, who saw the project to completion. Not only has he become a good friend, but over the years he has been a fount of encouragement and sage advice. Thanks also to my editorial assistant Ellen Umansky, who provided timely assistance. Another debt of gratitude to W. H. Ferry for his generous financial aid.

Walter LaFeber and Howard Zinn were kind enough to read portions of the manuscript and offer their suggestions and corrections. Curt Gentry kindly furnished a much-needed list of connections. Attorney Jerome Garchik provided access to Kay Boyle's FBI file. Joan Cohen of Legwork spent long hours contacting the Hollywood veterans. Bill Bailey, Joe Passen, Joseph Rauh, Joe Sachs, Morton Newman, and others too numerous to list were more than helpful in providing the names of interviewees. The interviews, of course, required able transcribers; Helen Harvey of Word-Works and Elaine Blanchard carried most of the load, with Inga Khoury and Avivah Ernst supporting.

The support of my parents and immediate family was of immeasurable help, and I am indebted to them for it. Among the many friends who listened with great forbearance and encouragement to my endless tales of the Red Scare, I express particular gratitude to David and Sheila MacDonald, Simone and Mary Jane Di Piero, Jim Steck and Sandy Dutro,

Daniel Woodrell and Kathrine Estill, Kathleen McNulty, Damian Sharp, Ira Sandperl, and Steve Cohen. Nancy Clark's affection and friendship is a cherished support. Janet Reed, another marvelous companion, was there at the inception, and her enthusiasm for the project kindled my own.

Nearly 150 interviews were taped over the life of this this project, less than half of which are included. With few exceptions, I left each encounter certain I held another vital piece of the mosaic. But somehow cuts had to be made.

So for all those who so generously shared their lives, I offer my gratitude. The time spent with you was an honor and an education.

Principal Federal Heresy Tribunals and Laws

HOUSE COMMITTEE ON UN-AMERICAN ACTIVITIES (HUAC)[1]—1938–75

Preceded by the Dies Committee, HUAC became in 1945 the first permanent committee established to investigate "subversive" and "un-American" propaganda and activities, and also the most powerful. From 1945 to 1957, HUAC held at least 230 hearings, at which more than three thousand persons testified, of whom more than one hundred were cited for contempt. Chairmen: Martin Dies (Texas), 1938–44; John S. Wood (Georgia), 1945–46; J. Parnell Thomas (New Jersey), 1947–48; Wood again, 1949–52; Francis E. Walter (Pennsylvania), 1955–64; Edwin P. Willis (Louisiana), 1965–68; Richard H. Ichord (Missouri), 1969–1975.

LOYALTY BOARDS (for federal employees; established nationwide under Truman's loyalty order)—1947

From 1947 to 1953, 26,236 persons were referred to the loyalty boards for investigation. More than four thousand hearings were held, and nearly thirteen thousand interrogatories and letters of charges were issued.

SENATE INTERNAL SECURITY SUBCOMMITTEE (SISS)—1951–76

Chairmen: Pat McCarran (Nevada); William E. Jenner (Indiana); James O. Eastland (Mississippi); Thomas J. Dodd (Connecticut).

SUBVERSIVE ACTIVITIES CONTROL BOARD (SACB)—1950–73

Established by the Internal Security (McCarran) Act. Five full-time members appointed by the President. Sole purpose was to determine which organizations would be required to register as "Communist-action," "Communist-front," or "Communist-infiltrated." Those groups com-

---

[1]Renamed the House Internal Security Committee in 1969.

pelled to register would be required to disclose membership and sources of funding. All literature or airwave material would have to be stamped "Disseminated by _____, a Communist organization." Members of such organizations would not be allowed to apply for a passport or renew an old one.

Permanent Subcommittee on Investigations of the Senate Committee on Government Operations

Chairmen: Joseph R. McCarthy (Wisconsin), 1953–54; John L. McClellan (Arkansas), 1955–60.

Smith Act (1940)

Made it a crime "to knowingly or willfully advocate, abet, advise, or teach the duty, necessity, desirability, or propriety of overthrowing any government in the U.S. by force or violence," or "to print, publish, edit, issue, circulate, sell, distribute, or publicly display any written or printed matter advocating, advising, or teaching the duty, necessity, desirability, or propriety" of overthrowing any such government. It was also illegal to belong to, organize, or help organize any organization, or "assembly of persons" who advocated or encouraged the same. The penalties were ten years in prison and a $10,000 fine.

Taft-Hartley Act (1947)

Antilabor bill largely written by the National Association of Manufacturers (NAM). Among many labor restraints, Section 9(h) compelled all elected union officials to file yearly affidavits swearing they were not members of the Communist Party. Penalties for noncompliance included union decertification. Perjury charges awaited those accused of filing falsely.

Internal Security (McCarran) Act (1950)

Set forth as its thesis a Communist conspiracy to establish a "totalitarian dictatorship in the countries throughout the world." Title II established concentration camps for use in national emergencies (this clause stayed on the books until 1971).[2] Set up SACB (see above).

Immigration and Nationality (McCarran-Walter) Act (1952)

Tightened previous restriction on aliens and heavily reduced immigration from nonwhite countries. Allowed for the denaturalization and depor-

---

[2]J. Edgar Hoover kept his own roundup lists before the McCarran Act and maintained them after its repeal. Ironically, Senator Paul Douglas, coauthor of Title II, was marked for pickup.

tation of citizens deemed "subversive," as well as the deportation of resident aliens for political activity. Removed deportation case from the courts by setting up own boards unhampered by due process.

COMMUNIST CONTROL ACT (1954)

An attempt to exclude the Communist Party from the ballot and deny it access to the courts to enforce contracts. While not directly outlawing the Party, this act (sponsored by Hubert Humphrey) stripped it of "all rights, privileges, and immunities attendant upon legal bodies." It also forbade any member of a "Communist-action" or "Communist-infiltrated" organization from holding office or employment with any labor organization.

First and Fifth Amendments to the Constitution

Preface

> The struggle of man against power is the struggle of memory against forgetting.
> —MILAN KUNDERA

This book of memories spans the two decades from 1945 to 1965, an era largely connected in American recall with tail fins and rock and roll, and with the last time a middle-class family of four could be supported on a single income. But it was also a time of political upheaval, when the question "Are you now or have you ever been a member of Communist Party?" was prologue to personal ruin, life in exile or on the blacklist, a shattered family, imprisonment, suicide, and for some even a violent death. For many who faced that question, the consequences of their answer still haunt them today.

"It was a watershed event in Hollywood—the hearings and the blacklisting and the informing. The memories die hard, although the people involved are dying. We're talking about forty years ago for those of us who were called in '51, and more for the Ten who were called in '47. There are only two of them left." Back then, he was a young screenwriter active in the Communist Party. With a dozen films to his credit, the future looked promising. He would be blacklisted for nearly twenty years.

The memories die hard—yet for many Americans, only the barest sketch of the era remains, or nothing at all. In 1992, a man of thirty, doing well in a San Francisco publishing firm, told me what he knew of the Red Scare: "It was Joseph McCarthy, and he went after Hollywood actors for the sake of publicity. Richard Nixon was in on it." One woman of thirty-five demanded, "When did all this happen?" Another of the same age, after confusing "Reds" with her favorite baseball team,[1] came back astonished: "America *had* a Communist Party?"

Studs Terkel, in his introduction to *"The Good War,"* laments America's fast-fading memory. "It appears that the disremembrance of World War Two is as disturbingly profound as the forgettery of the Great Depres-

---

[1] In the 1950s, the dangers of semantic association were not lost on the Cincinnati Reds, who to avoid any confusion briefly changed their name to the Redlegs.

sion—World War Two, an event that changed the psyche as well as the face
of the United States and of the world." The Red Scare was another sort of
war—one against dissent and nonconformity. It changed the psyche and
face of the United States as surely as did World War Two.

Our collective amnesia is partly a token of that grim spree; for many
years, just to present a comprehensive record of the period would have
been "controversial," and to be "controversial" invited suspicion. Thus in
popular culture and education we hand the era to Joseph McCarthy, the
one man almost everyone agrees was up to no good: let him be the flaw in
our seamless weave. Yet McCarthy was only the opportunistic creature of
larger events.

*"Everything changed at the end of the Second World War. The ally Russia
became the enemy. Anybody who had sympathy became suspect. Because I was
local Party chairman, because I had studied in Moscow and fought in Spain,
I was the devil himself."* He was just hitting middle age then, a Party
organizer with a family, a couple of kids. He would face twenty-five years in
prison.

The Red Scare was Truman's Cold War come home to roost. When the
shooting stopped in 1945, the United States stood untouched among the
ruined nations of the globe. At that point we were the most powerful
country on earth; yet our moral and intellectual life seemed dominated by
the existence of a foreign nation. In a 1949 essay,[2] Archibald MacLeish
explained the phenomenon: "American foreign policy was a mirror image
of Russian foreign policy: whatever the Russians did, we did in reverse.
American domestic policies were conducted under a kind of upside-down
Russian veto: no man could be elected to public office unless he was on
record as detesting the Russians, and no proposal could be enacted, from a
peace plan at one end to a military budget at the other, unless it could be
demonstrated that the Russians wouldn't like it."

Led by a reactionary Congress, and with considerable aid from Harry
Truman, the media trumpeted the alarm: encircled by the Soviets and
betrayed from within, our nation was endangered. This fear dominated
national life; steps were taken to discipline the citizenry. Loyalty oaths
became the order of the day. First it was government employees who were
affected, then teachers; soon Americans of all varieties were mumbling
oaths of fealty. Even Las Vegas got into the act, swearing a troupe of

[2]"The Conquest of America," reprinted in *Atlantic Monthly,* March 1980.

strippers to a solemn vow that they had never conspired to overthrow the government.

State and federal investigators grilled suspected citizens on their reading habits, voting patterns, and church attendance. Support for racial equality became evidence of subversive leanings. Heretical literature was banned from public and school libraries; some communities even held book burnings. Hollywood scoured its films for the subversive taint. Neighbors informed on neighbors, students on their teachers. Readers of "questionable" works hid their leftist tomes or buried them in the back garden. Seven war-era concentration camps were dusted off, and lists prepared of the radicals to fill them.

By the early 1950s, nearly all of America's radicals had been identified by the FBI. But the Inquisition demanded a public accounting. Witnesses before the investigating committees were expected not only to repent their past heresies but to name their former comrades. The pressure to collaborate was enormous. The full weight of government and society hung by a thread over each reluctant individual. One's livelihood depended on one's willingness to inform; and many times, so did the avoidance of a prison sentence. Federal agents were known to threaten the uncooperative with internment in the newly established camps, with the removal of their children, with the deportation of aging relatives. All one had to do was cooperate and life would be restored. It was a seductive whisper: repent, ask forgiveness, give a few names. Of course, those named would in turn suffer. But might they not anyway? Hadn't they already been identified? Could anyone know for sure?

Many Americans did collaborate; a number quite eagerly, others in daring the line between ruinous defiance and complete cooperation, still others only after time on the blacklists, a few even from their prison cells. But many more refused, and they paid dearly for their principles.

Here then is an attempt to rescue a chapter of history from our habitual "forgettery," a mosaic of voices from both sides of the Great Fear. Here are ordinary men and women—Communists, progressives, and New Dealers alike—as they recall their lives under the Inquisition. Here also are the hounds that hunted them—the Attorney General, the union boss, the FBI agent, the security officer, and the professional informer.

From the hunted who cooperated, there are regrets and confusion, and earnest explanations. After more than forty years, they still struggle to be understood. From those who resisted, there is pride in having behaved well in difficult times. There is anger and sorrow aplenty for the friendships betrayed, the lives and careers cut short, and the resulting years of struggle.

Laughter comes into play too, as dark as it may be, for every Inquisition is at its core an enormous absurdity, and the relief of humor is as evident today as it was then. Ultimately, however, this is a story of America at midcentury when, at the pinnacle of national strength, we turned in fear to strike down our own.

Introduction

There are today many Communists in America. They are everywhere—in factories, offices, butcher stores, on street corners, in
private businesses. And each carries in himself the germ of death
for society.

—J. Howard McGrath,
Attorney General under Harry Truman, 1949

Today we call it the McCarthy Era. While convenient, the tribute is not
without reason. McCarthy's villainy was so plain that his name became a
malediction in the very year of his ascendancy.[1] Characterized by one
historian as "crass and unprincipled, an unimaginative opportunist, and
a distinctly second-rate politician," McCarthy was also a "shrewd judge of
public attitudes and temper." The blend made him a formidable adver-
sary.[2]

Elected to the Senate in 1946, McCarthy was almost invisible on the
public scene until February 1950. It was then, in Wheeling, West Virginia,
that he stumbled upon his cause. The *Wheeling Intelligencer* reported his
remarks the next day. "I have here in my hand a list of 205 that were known
to the secretary of state as being members of the Communist Party and
who, nevertheless are still working and shaping the policy of the State
Department."

His timing was propitious: his charges followed upon guilty verdicts in
the Alger Hiss and Judith Coplon cases, the disclosure of the first Soviet
atomic explosion, and the arrest of nuclear scientist Klaus Fuchs as a Soviet
spy, as well as the victory of the Chinese Communists the previous year.
Backed with seemingly solid evidence and a certain convincing sincerity,
McCarthy explained these unsettling developments to a disturbed America.
Communists, subversives, and fellow travelers, he said, had occupied posi-

[1]On March 29, 1950, Herblock, a political cartoonist with the *Washington Post*, portrayed a
struggling GOP elephant being dragged and pushed by right-wingers toward a stack of dripping
tar buckets topped by a barrel labeled "McCarthyism." The term caught on immediately and
soon entered dictionaries. According to Thomas C. Reeves in *The Life and Times of Joe
McCarthy* (New York: Stein & Day, 1982), McCarthy was privately stung by the term and
despised it, but publicly exclaimed that "McCarthyism" was a synonym for "Americanism" and
that he welcomed the new word.

[2]Athan Theoharis, *Seeds of Repression: Harry S. Truman and the Origins of McCarthyism*
(Chicago: Quadrangle Books, 1971).

tions of power in the government and betrayed America's vital interests to the worldwide Soviet conspiracy.

For the next five years, McCarthy's shrill accusations dominated public life, influenced foreign and domestic policy, and held two Presidents hostage. He waged a guerrilla war against the establishment, accusing the State Department, the Democratic Party, the U.S. Army—even Truman and Eisenhower themselves—of treasonous pro-Communist behavior.

Within time, McCarthy's increasingly reckless charges and suspect methods wearied his reactionary supporters in Congress. The 1954 Army–McCarthy hearings finally sent them scurrying. By the end of the year, McCarthy was a spent force, censured by the Senate and ignored by the press. By 1957, he was dead.

But the elements of "McCarthyism"—defined in *Merriam-Webster's Collegiate Dictionary* as the use of "indiscriminate allegations" and "unsubstantiated charges"—were hardly McCarthy's alone, nor did he usher them into America's mid-century war against the Left, nor did they diminish after his fall. Joe McCarthy was just one (and certainly not the brightest) of the many Inquisitors who adorned American life in those dreary days. He was not nearly as resourceful as J. Edgar Hoover, whose harmful doings were not fully exposed until after his death; nor was he as cunning as Richard Nixon, an early McCarthy tutor,[3] who paved his way to the White House (and to eventual public disgrace) with equally bad intentions. While McCarthy made the notion of security risks in the federal bureaucracy a national obsession from 1950 to 1954, the ground in which he flourished had been well prepared before his arrival.

On the afternoon of April 12, 1945, a stroke ended the life of Franklin Roosevelt. On the following day, the man who succeeded him spoke with the press. "Boys, if you ever pray, pray for me now . . . when they told me yesterday what had happened, I felt like the moon, the stars, and all the planets had fallen in on me." It was with good reason that Harry Truman felt this weight, for he was woefully unprepared for the job. A compromise candidate for the vice presidency, Truman knew little of foreign affairs and had been viewed with indifference by Roosevelt. Truman was told nothing of the crucial deliberations at Yalta, or of the existence of the atom bomb, or of Roosevelt's plans for the postwar world. In fact, Truman had met

---

[3]For several months following the Wheeling, West Virginia, speech, Nixon met privately with McCarthy, attempting to educate him in the politics of anticommunism. Nixon recalled later that he had constantly urged restraint, but that McCarthy did not listen (Reeves, *Life and Times*, pp. 246–47).

with the President only two or three times during the eighty-two days of his vice presidency. Harry was the first to admit his own ignorance. "They didn't tell me anything about what was going on here," he complained a month after the succession.[4]

Just as Harry's new job was largely a cipher to him, so was Harry a puzzle to nearly everyone else. In those first few days, the men who had served Roosevelt could do little more than speculate about the unknown Missourian. "No one knows what the new President's views are—at least I don't," observed Secretary of War Henry Stimson.

One thing was certain: Harry Truman was no Franklin Roosevelt. While Roosevelt was an internationalist—urbane, worldly, and long used to the subtleties of power—Truman was a domestic politician, devoutly religious and parochial, in many ways a holdover from nineteenth-century America. Raised to maturity in a turn-of-the-century neofrontier society, largely self-educated, and politically bred in the rough-and-tumble of Missouri machine politics, Truman carried with him all the weaknesses and strengths of the "self-made man." Critics and admirers alike have tended to depict him as a straightforward and simple personality, decisive, energetic, and optimistic. In dedicating a volume of his memoirs to Truman, Dean Acheson, his Secretary of State, referred to him as "the captain with the mighty heart" and portrayed the man as an inspirational and inexhaustible leader "deeply trained in the moral values of Graeco-Judaic-English thought . . . sturdy and confident . . . alert and eager to gain additional knowledge and new insights."[5]

But other writers have pointed to the limitations of the Truman personality. "When he was finally confronted with foreign policy questions," wrote Daniel Yergin of Truman's first months in office, "all he had as background was his storybook view of history and a rousing Fourth of July patriotism. He tended to see clearly defined contests between right and wrong, black and white. Neither his personality nor his experience gave him the patience for subtleties and uncertainties."[6] In a similar vein, David McCullough contrasted Truman with his patrician predecessor. "Roosevelt loved the subtleties of human relations. . . . He was sensitive to nuances in a way Harry Truman never was and never would be. Truman, with his rural

[4]Daniel Yergin, *Shattered Peace: The Origins of the Cold War and the National Security State* (Boston: Houghton Mifflin, 1978), p. 70.

[5]Dean Acheson, *Present at the Creation: My Years in the State Department* (New York: Norton, 1969), pp. 927–30.

[6]Yergin, *Shattered Peace,* p. 72.

Missouri background, and partly too, because of the limits of his education, was inclined to see things in far simpler terms, as right or wrong, wise or foolish. He dealt little in abstractions."[7]

Alonzo Hamby, another Truman biographer, has indicated darker shades, depicting him in part as a man "who felt constantly unappreciated and harassed by others, was frequently suspicious of many of those around him . . . vindictive, seething with unfocused hostility," a man whose negative experiences left him with a lifelong "sense of insecurity and frustration" that called forth "recurrent fears of failure and feelings of anger, and leading to frequently bungling attempts at compensation"—perhaps explaining Truman's at times almost overwhelming "need to show the world who was boss."[8]

All are reasons that travel well in explaining why Truman held little appreciation for the idealists, liberals, and radicals who were the spurs of the New Deal. Many of them were Ivy League intellectuals, eager to promote bold new ideas, at ease in a world shaded with gray. "Crackpots and the lunatic fringe" was Truman's characterization of the men who had surrounded Roosevelt. Nor did he care for the terms "progressive" and "liberal," and he made it clear he believed the American people wanted a "rest from experiments."[9]

Under Truman, the New Dealers drifted away; the ones who remained would either be fired or forced out. In searching for comfort at the White House, Truman reached out to the familiar and surrounded himself with cronies, a number of whom would later involve his administration in a series of debilitating scandals. I. F. Stone, always a sharp observer of the capital scene, described the new crowd in the White House as "big-bellied, good-natured guys who . . . saw Washington as a chance to make useful 'contacts,' and were anxious to get what they could for themselves out of the experience. . . . The Truman era was the era of the moocher. The place was full of Wimpys who could be had for a hamburger."[10]

Roosevelt was a hard act to follow, and that could only have aggravated Truman's flagging confidence. For twelve years, FDR had imbued the nation with his own exuberant courage and confidence. No one was more

---

[7]David McCullough, *Truman* (New York: Simon & Schuster, 1992), p. 325.

[8]Alonzo L. Hamby, "An American Democrat: A Reevaluation of the Personality of Harry S. Truman," *Political Science Quarterly,* Vol. 106, No. 1 (1991), pp. 33–55.

[9]Yergin, *Shattered Peace,* p. 241.

[10]I. F. Stone, *The Truman Era: 1945–1952* (Boston: Little, Brown, 1972), p. xxi.

aware of that fact than Truman himself. "There have been few men in all history the equal of the man into whose shoes I am stepping," Truman remarked to a newsman on the first morning of his new job. "I pray God I can measure up to the task." Truman entered the White House a highly insecure man, at a point when the world was changing radically. To compensate for that insecurity, he was determined to establish that he was in fact in charge. He would be as tough as the toughest. There would be no "appeasement." Within twenty-four hours of taking office, he announced to an aide that it was time to "get tough" with the Russians.[11]

Another group Truman held in little regard was the American Communist Party. He made no secret of his conviction that they were a "despicable minority," and he would voice similar opinions throughout his life. As early as the fall of 1946, Truman was confiding to his diary the motif that would mark his era: "The Reds, phonies and the parlor pinks seem to be banded together and are becoming a national danger. I am afraid they are a sabotage front for Uncle Joe Stalin."[12]

On March 12, 1947, President Truman appeared before a joint session of Congress to request support for a global war against communism. It was the unveiling of the Truman Doctrine, the foundation of our foreign policy for the next three decades. Wherever aggression threatened peace or freedom, Truman intoned, America's security was involved, and it would be necessary to "support free peoples who are resisting attempted subjugation by armed minorities or outside pressures." Although the Soviet Union was never mentioned by name, the inference was plain: America was challenged by a worldwide campaign of Communist subversion and Soviet expansion.

The underlying, and almost reflexive, assumption was that the Soviet Union had replaced Nazi Germany as the implacable expansionist foe. As Averell Harriman, the U.S. ambassador to the Soviet Union, had warned Truman on April 20, 1945, America was faced with a "barbarian invasion of Europe." To Harriman's delight, Truman replied that he was "not afraid of the Russians" and intended to be "firm."

While the Second World War bequeathed superpower status to the Soviet Union and the United States, it is difficult to overstate how much the postwar power of the United States overshadowed that of the war-ravaged

[11]Walter LaFeber, *America, Russia, and the Cold War, 1945–1975,* 3d ed. (New York: Wiley, 1976), p. 17.

[12]Richard M. Freeland, *The Truman Doctrine and the Origins of McCarthyism: Foreign Policy, Domestic Politics, and Internal Security, 1946–1948* (New York: Schocken, 1974), p. 140.

Soviets. For decades, the Soviet Union would view its need for secure borders through the searing lens of the German blitzkrieg.[13]

"Economically the Soviets are exhausted," reported U.S. Naval Intelligence in January 1946. The following year, State Department consultant John Foster Dulles contended that war was "one thing which Soviet leadership does not want and would not consciously risk."

Nevertheless, mistrust between the two powers flourished in the chaos of the postwar world, with both nations securing spheres of control. Stalin, desperate to shield his western borders with a buffer of friendly or subservient states, viewed with intense suspicion any efforts by the United States and Britain that might allow anti-Soviet forces to predominate in Eastern Europe. Truman and his colleagues, morally repelled by Soviet police-state tactics and burdened with a reflexive anticommunism that presumed the Russians were bent on world revolution and hegemony, were either unable or refused to distinguish between the Soviets' revolutionary rhetoric and Stalin's essentially conservative and nationalistic aims. A Soviet sphere in Eastern Europe was only the first step to world conquest, they reasoned, conveniently ignoring America's own sphere of control.[14] When they tried to break the Russian sphere, the Soviets only moved to strengthen their grasp.

Truman saw the Soviet hand everywhere, and ascribed to Stalin motives and powers of influence over European Communists and leftists that were greatly exaggerated. From this ingrained misconception, as played out during the Greek crisis of 1947, came the Truman Doctrine, which by conjuring a world divided into irreconcilable realms of good and evil committed

---

[13]The United States suffered more than 400,000 dead during its four years of war, but was virtually unscathed in any other measure. At war's end, its economy was booming with a gross national product that had more than doubled. With 6 percent of the world's population, the United States held three-fourths of the world's invested capital and two-thirds of its industrial capacity. In contrast, the Soviet Union, which had taken the brunt of the Nazi effort, suffered an estimated 20 to 25 million war dead, nearly half of the war's total. The German army had completely or partially destroyed fifteen large cities, 1,710 towns, and 70,000 villages, leaving 25 million homeless. The invaders destroyed 31,850 industrial concerns, 65,000 kilometers of railroad track, 90,000 bridges, 10,000 power stations, 98,000 collective farms, and immense quantities of livestock and poultry—in all, an estimated $128 billion worth of property. As a result, Soviet industrial output had dropped 42 percent from its 1940 level. Lawrence S. Wittner, *Cold War America: From Hiroshima to Watergate* (New York: Holt, Rinehart & Winston, 1978), pp. 8–9.

[14]While decrying the lack of political democracy in the Axis nations newly liberated by the Soviet Union, the United States firmly controlled its own sphere. To confound the growing popularity of the Community Party in Italy, for instance, the American military government banned political activity, imposed press censorship, jailed antifascists, and relied on fascist institutions and personnel to run the bureaucracy. To achieve the same aims, the United States intervened massively in Italy's 1948 elections. Gabriel Kolko, *The Politics of War: The World and United States Foreign Policy, 1943–1945* (New York: Random House, 1990), pp. 55–57.

the United States for a generation to a policy of containment and global intervention.[15]

The roots of the Greek crisis lay in the Second World War, when the German occupation had been opposed with great success by the People's Liberation Army (ELAS), the military arm of the National Liberation Front (EAM). EAM, spearheaded by the Greek Communists, was a coalition of six parties. According to American historian W. H. McNeil, who was in Greece during the war: "By the time of liberation, the EAM numbered about two million members, out of a population of seven million. They were incomparably superior to all rivals in their organization and enthusiasm."[16]

When the British landed in 1944, upon the evacuation of the Germans, they found EAM with control over nearly four-fifths of Greece. C. M. Woodhouse, a staunch conservative, and the British commander of the Allied Military Mission in Greece at the time, characterized the Communists within EAM as "a tiny numerical minority," while London estimated nine-tenths of ELAS members were non-Communist.[17]

Churchill's decision to reinstate the discredited King George II,[18] rebuild a Greek army loyal to the monarchy, and disarm ELAS soon led to fierce fighting in Athens between EAM and British troops—the only battle during the Second World War in which a resistance movement fought the West.

Churchill would later comment that "getting peace restored in Greece . . . involved the killing of large numbers of Communists."[19] Stalin, who had agreed to Churchill's free hand in Greece for similar freedom of his own in Rumania and Bulgaria, held "strictly and faithfully" to the agreement and uttered not a word of protest.[20] Roosevelt was made well aware of the agreement, as he was of Stalin's subsequent neutrality in Greece.[21]

In February 1945, the Varkiza Agreement ended the conflict. EAM agreed to surrender its arms and the three-fourths of Greece it still con-

---

[15]Daniel Yergin, "Harry Truman—Revived and Revised," *New York Times Magazine,* October 24, 1976.

[16]Wittner, *Cold War,* p. 31.

[17]Kolko, *Politics of War,* pp. 172–75.

[18]The king's popularity had been damaged by his support of military dictator General John Metaxis, whose reign lasted from 1936 until the German takeover in 1941.

[19]Yergin, *Shattered Peace,* p. 295.

[20]Winston S. Churchill, *Memoirs of the Second World War* (Boston: Houghton Mifflin, 1959), pp. 885–904.

[21]Warren F. Kimball, *Churchill and Roosevelt: The Complete Correspondence,* vol. 3 (Princeton, N.J.: Princeton Univ. Press, 1984).

trolled to the British and their royalist allies in exchange for recognition of EAM and the Communist Party, elections, a constitutional plebiscite, an end to reprisals against resistance fighters, and a purge of profascist elements from the Greek army and police.

With the royalists firmly in power, however, the agreement proved to hold little substance. The Greek government and its rightist allies soon launched a campaign of terror against the Left, which included torture, beatings, mass arrests, the destruction of printing presses, the assassination of journalists,[22] and massacres. By late 1946, bands of angry EAM veterans, perhaps ten thousand in all, had taken to the mountains and resumed their armed struggle.

On February 21, 1947, Dean Acheson received startling news from the British ambassador. Britain could ill afford its commitments in the Balkans and would withdraw in six weeks. His Majesty's Government devoutly hoped that the United States could assume the burden of both Greece and Turkey. Joseph Jones of the policy planning staff noted the implications: "Great Britain had within the hour handed the job of world leadership, with all its burdens and all its glory, to the United States."[23]

Truman and the State Department were elated at the prospect of replacing the British in Greece. Congressional leaders, however, were hardly as eager. As Republican conservatives, they balked at what most feared would prove to be a largely inflationary entanglement.

Two weeks before the President announced his doctrine, Truman and his top advisers held a meeting with congressional leaders to warm the path for his initiative. The reception was cool, until Dean Acheson spoke up. He declared that Soviet success in Greece "might open three continents to Soviet penetration. . . . The corruption of Greece would affect Iran and all the east. It would also carry the infection to Africa through Asia Minor and Egypt and to Europe through France and Italy, already threatened by the strongest Communist parties in Western Europe. The Soviet Union [is] playing one of the greatest gambles in history at minimal cost. . . . We and we alone [are] in a position to break up the play."[24]

Actually, internal conditions and indigenous support made the play al-

---

[22]Among the eventual casualties was CBS correspondent George Polk. In May 1948, his corpse was found in Salonika Bay. Bound hand and foot, he had been shot in the back of the head. The subsequent cover-up, in an effort to maintain American public support for the rightist regime, threw the blame onto the leftist guerrillas Polk was attempting to contact for a story. Edmund Keeley, The Salonika Bay Murder: Cold War Politics and the Polk Affair (Princeton, N.J.: Princeton Univ. Press, 1989).

[23]Howard Zinn, Postwar America (Indianapolis: Bobbs-Merrill, 1973), pp. 43–44.

[24]Acheson, Present at the Creation, p. 293.

most entirely a Greek affair. Stalin, maintaining his end of the Anglo-Soviet bargain, wavered between indifference and hostility toward the Greek Communists. Earlier, he had attempted to reassure Truman on the matter, writing to the new President that the Soviet Union "understands the whole importance of . . . Greece for the security of Great Britain."[25]

Nevertheless, Truman chose to present the Balkan imbroglio as a bold move in the Soviet gambit for control of the free world. With this, the alarm of falling dominoes first sounded in postwar politics, and the congressmen responded. Senator Vandenberg encouraged Truman to speak just as forcefully to the nation, and suggested that he "scare hell out of the American people."

The President took Vandenberg's advice to heart. In a speech on March 6 at Baylor University in Texas, Truman declared that if the expansion of state-controlled economies did not stop, and if an open world market for private business was not restored, then severe depression would return and the government would have to intervene massively in society. Americans might then lose their traditional economic and personal freedoms. "Freedom of worship—freedom of speech—freedom of enterprise," Truman observed. "It must be true that the first two of these freedoms are related to the third," for "peace, freedom, and world trade are indivisible." He concluded, "We must not go through the thirties again."[26]

Much of the same thinking animated early drafts of the Truman Doctrine. Presidential adviser Clark Clifford promoted a draft asserting that "continued chaos in other countries and pressure exerted upon them from without would mean the end of free enterprise and democracy in those countries and the disappearance of free enterprise in other countries would threaten our economy and our democracy."

According to Truman, the early drafts "made the whole thing sound like an investment prospectus."[27] Framed in these terms, the speech would have little popular appeal. "The only way we can sell the public on our new policy," noted one memorandum, "is by emphasizing . . . Communism vs. Democracy" as the "major theme."[28]

Truman characterized the reaction to his speech in his *Memoirs:* "All over the world, voices of approval made themselves heard, while Communists and their fellow travelers struck out at me savagely."[29] Actually, Tru-

[25]Wittner, *Cold War,* p. 6.

[26]LaFeber, *America, Russia,* p. 55.

[27]Harry S. Truman, *Memoirs,* vol. 2 (Garden City, N.Y.: Doubleday, 1956), p. 106.

[28]Wittner, *Cold War,* p. 33.

[29]Truman, *Memoirs,* vol. 2, p. 106.

man's speech met immediate criticism from a broad spectrum of Americans, more than a few from within the President's camp.

Columnist Walter Lippmann warned that the United States was "not rich enough to subsidize reaction all over the world or strong enough to maintain it in power." Senator Taft, an archconservative, assailed it as an attempt to divide the world into Communist and anti-Communist spheres. "If we assume a special position in Greece and Turkey," he said, "we can hardly . . . object to the Russians continuing their domination in Poland, Yugoslavia, Rumania, and Bulgaria."[30] Secretary of State Marshall was caught off guard by the exaggerated weight of the "anti-Communist element of the speech" and cabled Truman rather tactfully that the speech "was overstating the case a bit." The President replied that from "all his contacts with the Senate, it was clear that this was the only way in which the measure could be passed." Presidential adviser Bernard Baruch put the case more bluntly, calling the speech "tantamount to a declaration of . . . an ideological or religious war."[31]

Less than two weeks later, President Truman brought his anti-Communist war home to America. On March 25, 1947, he put his signature to Executive Order 9835 and launched the Federal Employees Loyalty Program, the most sweeping loyalty inquiry in the nation's history.[32] E.O. 9835 authorized investigations into the beliefs and associations of all federal employees. This first such peacetime program was so vaguely worded that in time every aspect of an employee's personal life would be opened to federal scrutiny. Moreover, the accused would not have the right to confront the accuser or, in almost every case, even be privy to the accusation.

Included in E.O. 9835 was what David Caute characterized as "the most destructive departure in postwar domestic politics"—the Attorney General's list of subversive organizations with its catch-all notion of "sympathetic association."[33] For the most part, the list of seventy-eight organizations[34] was a grab bag of left-wing political parties, peace groups, relief organizations, defense committees, and labor schools. High on the list, of

[30]Wittner, *Cold War*, p. 33.

[31]Freeland, *Truman Doctrine*, pp. 100–1.

[32]Previous loyalty programs existed during both world wars, but neither approached the scope of Truman's peacetime effort.

[33]David Caute, *The Great Fear: The Anti-Communist Purge Under Truman and Eisenhower* (New York: Simon & Schuster, 1978), p. 269.

[34]Thirty-two more were added in May 1948. By November 1950, the number was up to 197. Under Eisenhower, an additional 62 were tagged on, bringing the total to 254. At the same time, the House Un-American Activities Committee kept its own separate and equally potent list. By 1950 it numbered 624 organizations.

course, was the Communist Party, USA. Membership in or association with any of the listed groups was the spark for an investigation and, in the majority of cases, dismissal.

With a stroke of his pen, Truman had sowed the ground from which would spring the worst excesses of the Red Scare. The Attorney General was not required to hold hearings before listing an organization; nor was there any provision for appeal or judicial review. The list was quickly adopted by state and local governments, defense-related industries, and schools; it became a qualifying test for passports, occupancy of federal public housing, and even tax exemptions. Within time, it became the yardstick of loyalty in almost every area of American life and operated, in effect, as a presidentially approved blacklist.

Writing in his *Memoirs* years later, Truman would lamely defend his loyalty program as having started out as fair as possible "under the climate of opinion that then existed." Privately, however, he would concede it had been a terrible mistake.[35]

Clark Clifford, who, as counsel to the President, met with Truman every day, spoke of the motives behind the loyalty program in a 1978 interview with Carl Bernstein. "We never had a serious discussion about a real loyalty problem. . . . the President didn't attach fundamental importance to the so-called Communist scare. He thought it was a lot of baloney. . . . It was a political problem. . . . [Truman] had to recognize the political realities. He'd gotten a terrible clobbering in 1946 in the congressional elections. We gave a good deal of thought to how to respond. We had a presidential campaign ahead of us and here was a great issue, so he set up this whole kind of machinery."[36]

Historians continue to debate Truman's motives for issuing the order, and in doing so, his culpability for what followed. His supporters have it that he acted out of necessity; had he not moved first, the newly elected 80th Congress, many of whom had campaigned on charges of subversion in high places, would have pushed through a program far worse.

Some of his detractors hold that he acted not to waylay reactionary appetites, but to ensure passage of the Truman Doctrine. The argument follows that Truman surely understood the role increased international tensions would play in producing demands for action against domestic "subversives." If he did not preempt the field at home, then Congress,

[35]McCullough, *Truman*, p. 553.

[36]Carl Bernstein, *Loyalties: A Son's Memoir* (New York: Simon & Schuster, 1989), pp. 197–200.

tightfisted and isolationist, would have used this cudgel to attack his program against subversion abroad. Thus, the inevitability of the loyalty program lay in Truman's presentation of his foreign policy in the crisis-laden rhetoric of an international crusade.[37]

There is evidence that Truman was aware of the salutary effects a domestic Red Scare might have on his foreign policy. In June 1945, the State Department completed a top-secret study on the "Possible Resurrection of the Communist International, Resumption of Extreme Leftist Activities, Possible Effect on United States," and sent it to Truman for his careful consideration. The study offered a word of advice: "Decisive action against the American Communists would be a convincing demonstration to Stalin of the inherent strength of this country and would strengthen relations between the two countries."[38]

The Clifford-Elsey Report submitted in late September 1946, which provided the core of the Truman Doctrine, also made a pressing argument for a loyalty program: "The Soviet Government, by utilizing the membership of the Communist Party in the United States, has thousands of invaluable sources . . . in various industrial establishments as well as in the departments of the Government. . . . Every American Communist is potentially an espionage agent . . . requiring only the direct instruction of a Soviet superior to make the potentiality a reality." In its final recommendations, the report urged that "within the United States, Communist penetration should be exposed and eliminated" and cited the "armed forces, government agencies, and heavy industry" as the "principal targets for communistic infiltration."[39]

It is not unlikely that all of these considerations played a role in Truman's

---

[37]See Freeland, *Truman Doctrine*.

[38]Kolko, *Politics of War*, p. 447.

[39]In his memoirs, *Counsel to the President* (New York: Doubleday, 1991), Clark Clifford characterizes the extent of this argument within the report as "a paragraph" and hands the authorship to Attorney General Tom Clark and J. Edgar Hoover. Clifford writes that it "hinted at the rationale for a loyalty program, although we did not realize it at the time." Referring to it as "the most unfortunate section of the Clifford-Elsey Report," he goes on to say that there were no grounds to believe the government to be "riddled with Reds" but that the assertion was included in the final report only because "it represented the deeply held views" of Clark and Hoover. Actually, the argument extends over several pages and begins with the assertion that the "Soviet Government is actively directing espionage and subversive movements in the United States." Its open inducement to expose and eliminate "Communist penetration" is surely more than a hint at a rationale, and suggests that Clifford, in advance of the disastrous 1946 elections, may have already been inducing Truman to seize the initiative against Communists at home. Clifford-Elsey Report quoted form Arthur Krock, *Memoirs: Sixty years on the Firing Line* (New York: Funk & Wagnalls, 1968), pp. 472–475, 481.

thinking. Faced with domestic political pressures and congressional resistance to his dramatic change in foreign policy, and inured by his own antipathy for radicalism to the dire consequences of unleashing a Red Scare, Truman may recklessly have chosen the most expedient route.

But in those years, it must have been difficult to determine which face Truman presented on this issue, for in an effort to seize the anti-Communist banner from his congressional opponents, he ran his 1948 campaign with a dual policy on Red-baiting—his was good, the Republican's was bad—and maintained it throughout his remaining years in office.

In late September, Truman campaigned for the Catholic vote in Boston: "All this talk about Communism . . . is in the pattern with [Republican] appeals to religious prejudice against Al Smith in 1928. . . . I want you to get this straight now. I hate Communism." This was the essential Truman tactic: to disparage Republican anti-Communist rhetoric as a threat to Catholics, while exploiting Catholic anti-Communist passions for his own gain.

Not long after, Truman derided those who were "much wrought up about the Communist bugaboo," but then allowed his Justice Department to indict twelve leaders of the Communist Party under the Smith Act four months before the election.[40]

To isolate the third-party candidacy of former Vice President Henry Wallace, Clark Clifford recommended that "every effort must be made . . . to identify him in the public mind with the Communists." Truman followed suit faithfully. "I do not want and will not accept the political support of Henry Wallace and his Communists," pronounced Truman in accents of McCarthy to come. "These are days of high prices for everything, but any price for Wallace and his Communists is too much for me to pay."

In a successful attempt to shore up sagging union support, Truman vetoed the antilabor Taft-Hartley Act, as it conflicted "with important principles of our democratic society." Yet, after his veto was overridden, he never instructed his Solicitor General to press the courts for a ruling on Taft-Hartley's constitutionality. After the election, his administration then used the act's anti-Communist provision to persecute those unions that had opposed Truman's foreign policy and supported Henry Wallace. In fact, Truman invoked Taft-Hartley more times in 1948 alone than Eisenhower did in eight years.

In May 1950, Truman wrote to the national commander of the Veterans

[40]Caute, *Great Fear*, pp. 33–35.

of Foreign Wars, "All this howl about organizations a fellow belongs to gives me a pain in the neck," while forgetting that he himself had codified the Attorney General's list.

In January 1951, Truman voiced fears that his loyalty program was infringing on civil liberties. Three months later, he amended his program for the worse. With the signing of Executive Order 10241, he altered the basis for dismissal from "reasonable grounds" for belief in disloyalty to "reasonable doubt" as to loyalty, thus shifting the burden of proof onto the accused.[41]

The public, rather than question the loyalty program, naturally assumed the existence of the disloyal and the subversive—for why else would there be a program to uncover them? Far from being placated, congressional reactionaries, now armed with the President's admission of subversive dangers, wrested the initiative from Truman and called for more purges and investigations. Given this opportunity, Joe McCarthy emerged to join in the vilification of the State Department.

With the Eisenhower administration came new twists in the loyalty game and a new Republican determination to ferret out the "traitors." Ike scrapped Truman's program, criticizing it for ignoring the security threat from loyal employees. Now the nation was endangered by "bad tendencies." Eisenhower's Executive Order 10450 mandated immediate suspension without pay for "any behavior, activities, or associations which tend to show that the individual is not reliable or trustworthy." No provisions for hearings were made, leaving it up to the discretion of the agency or department head. A few months later, Eisenhower added exercising an article of the Bill of Rights to the criterion for automatic dismissal. Now employees would be summarily sacked for pleading the Fifth Amendment before a congressional committee.

By 1954, the Emergency Civil Liberties Committee warned that "the threat to civil liberties in the United States today is the most serious in the history of our country." It was indeed a desperate time. Following the lead of the federal government, thirty-nine states had made it a criminal offense to advocate violent governmental change, *or to join any organization so advocating*. The determination of which organization was advocating what was left to the discretion of prosecutors. More than three hundred federal, state, and local laws had been passed prohibiting "subversive activities." In Texas, membership in the Communist Party was worth twenty years in

[41]For Truman's statement that he would do just the opposite, see Joseph Rauh under "The Purge of the Civil Service."

prison. In Michigan, the act of "writing or speaking subversive words" was good for life imprisonment. Tennessee punished "unlawful advocacy" with the death penalty. Virginia also proposed execution for anyone caught "lurking with intent to spy."

Beginning in May 1952, the State Department officially curtailed freedom of travel. Hundreds of suspected heretics were denied passports, including Supreme Court Justice William O. Douglas. It was the boast of Scott McLeod, the State Department's new chief of security, that no one who had criticized American foreign policy would be allowed to leave the country. It was just as difficult to get into the country: from 1947 on, entry visas were denied to anyone with beliefs outside the newly narrowed margins of American thought.

In 1954, Samuel Stouffer of Harvard University attempted to measure the breadth of that thought with a national poll. His findings revealed that 73 percent of the respondents would turn in their neighbors or acquaintances "whom they suspected of being Communists." Seventy-seven percent of those polled wanted to strip admitted Communists of their citizenship, while 51 percent were in favor of imprisoning them.

Yet only 3 percent of Mr. Stouffer's respondents had ever met an admitted Communist, even though 10 percent harbored suspicions about certain acquaintances. "He was always talking about world peace," responded a housewife from Oregon. "I saw a map of Russia on a wall in his home," said a locomotive engineer from Michigan. "I just knew. But I wouldn't know how to say how I knew," from a Kansas farmer. "She had more money to spend and places to go than seems right," reasoned a woman from Iowa. "He had a foreign camera and took so many pictures of the large New York bridges," from another housewife in New York.

Nevertheless, these statistics may well reflect the shallow roots of the Red Scare, measuring only the uncritical ease with which many Americans take on the attitudes evinced by politicians and the media. For when asked, "What kind of things do you worry about most?" 80 percent responded in terms of personal or family problems, with the largest block expressing concern over business and economic problems—less than 1 percent worried about the threat of Communists in the United States. In fact, 30 percent of Stouffer's sample could not even identify Senator McCarthy.

While the majority of Americans were concerned with paying their rent and medical bills, government committees were ferreting out heretics by quizzing them on their reading habits (*The Nation* and *The New Republic* were suspect), on their sexual habits ("When did you first reach an understanding with your wife?"), their voting patterns ("Did you vote for Henry Wallace?" "How did you feel about a fourth term for FDR?"), their political opinions ("You have been heard criticizing the Korean War effort"), or for even having political opinions at all ("You have been accused of belonging to a group that engages in political discussions").

The loyalty contagion spread from the government and military into private business and the professions, and then into entertainment and communications. It hit assembly-line workers, plumbers, and telephone operators; merchant seamen and dock workers. Even the defenders of civil liberties capitulated; the NAACP and the ACLU purged their ranks of the suspected, and several leaders of the ACLU dutifully informed the FBI on the politics of their members. Recreation-minded citizens signed loyalty oaths to acquire fishing licenses, high school students signed them to receive their diplomas, and tenants of public housing projects handed them over with their rent.

A private industry sprang up that specialized in security investigations. Dun and Bradstreet offered corporate America a Personnel Security Service on a subscription basis, as did the Better America Federation, the Western Research Foundation, and Fidelifax, Inc., staffed by forty-five former FBI agents in thirty cities. But towering above all the firms specializing in the listing, monitoring, and surveillance of radicals was the American Security Council. Founded in 1955 by former FBI agents and servicing such major corporations as GE, Honeywell, Motorola, Lockheed, and U.S. Steel, the ASC by 1961 boasted of over one million Americans in its files.

No one knows exactly how many Americans fell under the shadow of the loyalty investigations. By 1956, it was estimated that 13.5 million Americans were required to undergo some form of loyalty test or investigation as a condition of employment. But this figure only reflects the workforce at a given moment and does not take into account high job turnover, nor the continued activity after 1956. The actual number might well be twice as high.

How many Americans lost their jobs or were blacklisted as a consequence of the Red Scare? Those figures are difficult to determine. Many who were about to be fired chose to resign rather than risk adverse publicity. Others were fired on any available pretext (as management associations openly recommended in those days).

A tally of the suicides and premature deaths is equally difficult. No doubt they were more numerous than the occasional references in the literature would lead us to believe. To be targeted as a Communist or a subversive was to endure enormous pressures. One could face unrelenting harassment from the FBI, the loss of one's livelihood, impoverishment, vilification in the press, estrangement from friends and family, physical attacks, and, many times, imprisonment. The hounding that drove Professor F. O. Matthiessen out a high window, actor Philip Loeb to a lethal dose of sleeping pills, and scientist William Sherwood to take poison just as surely took the lives of actor John Garfield and economist Harry Dexter White from heart attacks.

As the anti-Communist purges mounted and were condoned and applauded, societal restraints loosened, and a number of Red Scare victims met with violent deaths. Robert Now, chairman of the Charleston Wallace-for-President committee, was stabbed to death in 1948 by a rabid anti-Communist. In 1961, John Farmer, having read that Thomas Parkinson, a Berkeley poet and Yeats scholar, was both a Communist and a homosexual, burst into Parkinson's campus office and shot him in the face at close range and killed his teaching assistant, Stephen Thomas. Both William Remington and Bob Thompson were put in prison by the Red Scare, and both died as a result of violence suffered there, so they too enter the lists.

As a nation we paid a hard price as well: the loss of political diversity, of the Old Left community of labor schools and progressive unions; the mechanical rejection of any notion that smacks of "socialism"; and the straitjacket of "responsible opinion" that has narrowed our public discourse to the breadth of a child's hand.

Playwright Arthur Miller, himself a target of the witch hunts, once noted that "an era can be said to end when its basic illusions are exhausted." The worst of the persecution was not over until 1960, and even then it limped on for another five years or so. The government attacks against the antiwar movement during the late 1960s, in particular the persecution of Students for a Democratic Society (SDS) and the destruction of the Black Panthers, were a more violent continuation of policies begun during the Cold War against an earlier radical group—the Communist Party of the United States.

During the 1980s, the Reagan administration attempted to silence its critics with Red-baiting tactics. The President charged that "pro-Soviet agents" were spreading "disinformation" in the media and Congress. Out of the Interior Department came charges that "extreme environmentalists" were a "left-wing cult" hostile to "our very form of government" and that the Sierra Club and the Audubon Society were "infiltrated" by Communist sympathizers. The President attacked the nuclear freeze movement as "Soviet-inspired," lamented the passing of the House Un-American Activities Committee, and sent the FBI to hound the detractors of his policy in Central America. Reagan also greatly expanded the powers of the FBI and the CIA in domestic surveillance and dusted off the McCarran-Walter Act to exclude critics of the United States from entering the country. Even films were deemed "anti-American" and excluded.[42]

During the 1988 presidential campaign, George Bush's daily reminder that Michael Dukakis was "a card-carrying member of the ACLU"[43] turned "liberal" into a synonym for subversive. Even more recently, Tara O'Toole, a Clinton appointee, was attacked by two Republican senators because the feminist study group to which she belonged had used the word "Marxist" in its name two years before she became a member. In 1993, *Fortune* magazine reached back forty years to assail the father of Clinton nominee Lani Guinier as "a devotee of Joe Stalin" for his associations with the American Labor Party and the United Public Workers.[44]

Even though the debate is unresolved, the passage of nearly fifty years since the unveiling of Truman's loyalty program has blessedly diminished the hunt for the "enemy within," but the residual remains clear. While the Communist Party of the United States was the first victim of the repression, the nation as a whole suffered the consequences.

[42]Richard Fried, *Nightmare in Red: The McCarthy Era in Perspective* (New York: Oxford Univ. Press, 1990), pp. 199–200.

[43]According to Haynes Johnson, a number of North Carolina voters said they believed Dukakis to be a Communist after viewing Bush commercials naming him as a member of the ACLU with a close-up of a card reading: "ACLU, American Communist Labor Union." *Sleepwalking Through History: America in the Reagan Years* (New York: Norton, 1991), p. 398.

[44]"Lani's Father," *Fortune,* July 12, 1993.

RED SCARE

Red Diapers

ROBERT MEEROPOL

In the summer of 1950, Ethel and Julius Rosenberg were arrested and charged with masterminding the plot to steal the secrets of the atomic bomb. They were convicted in March 1951 of "conspiracy to commit espionage" and died in the electric chair at Sing Sing Prison on June 19, 1953. Robert, their youngest son, is the founder of the Rosenberg Fund for Children. "I've set up this fund to provide for the educational and emotional needs of children whose parents have either been killed or injured or lost jobs or been harassed because of their progressive activities. They're enduring the kind of a nightmare that I endured, and the way we provide help is to provide a safe haven for them. It took me a long time to get around to it, but it's a direct outgrowth of what happened to me as a child."

I remember visiting my parents, but not clearly. I'm told that we visited them at least a dozen times from about the fall of 1951 right up until two days before the execution. So that was an eighteen- or twenty-month period in which we visited them maybe once a month or once every six weeks. I remember, but it's all like one visit. I remember driving in this big old Buick with plush back seats. I remember driving up the Henry Hudson Parkway along the Hudson River and I remember this sense of danger and foreboding, and yet it was like this fun excursion. I don't really remember the prison so much. I guess that's what you block. I remember seeing them in a room and I remember things being ordinary. I remember playing with them, playing word games, and talking with them, and eating a candy bar. I just remember it being kind of ordinary. I don't remember it being histrionic, I don't remember it being upsetting. But then again maybe that was part of my whole defense mechanism, and theirs too. I know from their letters and from talking with my brother that they worked very hard to keep things on an emotionally even keel.

That's my memory of it. You know, it's very pedestrian. But that's the way it is. When I think about Hollywood movies and trying to make something dramatic of all this, it didn't seem dramatic to me. Or maybe the very understatement is the drama.

I often start with the story of my parents' arrest, but the fact of the matter is I don't remember the actual arrest. All I can repeat is what my brother has told me. The arrests took place in July and August of 1950. I was just barely over three years old at that point. But my very first memory that's directly related to the period is also one of the first memories I have at all.

You see, my father was arrested first, and then my mother went to testify before the grand jury in July of 1950. When she completed her testimony that day, she was arrested as she left the grand jury room. She had left my brother and me with a baby-sitter, and the baby-sitter didn't know what to do with a three-year-old and a seven-year-old. So the baby-sitter took us around the corner and a few blocks down on the Lower East Side of New York City to my grandmother's house.

My grandmother was trying, with the government's help, to coerce my mother into cooperating. See, the government had offered my aunt and uncle, David and Ruth Greenglass, a deal, which was if you cooperate and name others, then the wife will not be arrested and she'll be able to stay home and take care of the children, and the husband will get a prison sentence but won't be killed.

They took the deal and then cooperated by naming my parents, and my parents were supposed to take a similar deal and cooperate by naming others. And my mother's mother, who was siding with my mother's brother, went to my mother in prison and said, "Why don't you back up David's story?" And when my mother refused, my grandmother said, "Well then, I'm going to put the kids in an orphanage." She was using the threat of putting us in an orphanage to coerce my mother. And while I can't say for certain that the government was putting her up to it, I believe that to be the case.

One of my first memories is my grandmother following through on that threat and telling us we couldn't live there anymore and she was going to put us in an orphanage. But she didn't have the heart to say, "I'm doing this because your mother's not listening to what I say." She had to make up a story, and that's where my first memory comes in. She said this is a cold-water flat and the toilet freezes in the wintertime, and it's not a safe place for children to live. So I remember going into the bathroom and peering down into the toilet to try to find some ice and of course there was no ice, it wasn't yet winter anyway.

That's one of my very first memories, and it's in the context of being placed in an orphanage. We were in this place where we couldn't leave, with a whole bunch of other kids. The relatives would come and take us out on weekends. My parents were in prison, and here I was, a little three-year-old in this orphanage which I equated with prison. My very earliest memories were of that. Throughout this entire period, there was this sense of foreboding, that something was terribly wrong and frightening. As a four- and five-year-old, I didn't follow my parents' trial. Adults tended not to talk about it—they tried to protect us.

Finally, after nine months, we got out of the orphanage and we went to live with my father's mother on Laurel Hill Terrace in upper Manhattan, and I remember it as a very isolated time. My brother went to school. My memory was of staying in the house and playing and really not doing anything else. I don't remember seeing other kids, and I guess this was part of feeling that we were somehow in hiding.

My brother was harassed in elementary school. He talked about who his parents were, and his friends' parents found out. He was thrown out of somebody's house with the mother screaming at her son, "I don't want you playing with your Communist friends anymore!"

So when things like that started happening, it was decided that we should be moved to rural New Jersey, to Toms River, where some friends of my parents lived. This was rural chicken-farm country, and there was a progressive Jewish community in that area. We lived in semisecrecy. We still had the name Rosenberg, but we never talked about it. We very quickly learned to shut up.

In fact, I learned that in general. I learned very early on that if I acted upset, adults fussed over me. But it never did any good. It never brought my parents home, it never changed the circumstances of this dread-filled atmosphere that I lived in. Instead, if I pretended I didn't understand what was going on and acted dumb, then everybody would be relieved. And that made life easier for me. So I quickly developed this defense mechanism of not understanding and of also forgetting. And it was very easy as a five- and then six-year-old to just be focused on playing outside.

I remember one of the myths that in part was perpetrated probably unintentionally by *The Book of Daniel*,[1] the novel and then the movie, is that my brother and I were manipulated by the people who sought to save my parents in order to gain sympathy for my parents. That we were brought

[1] By E. L. Doctorow (New York: Random House, 1971).

out to rallies, and that we were callously used without thought for how this might affect us. That's just totally untrue. We were not put on public display. We were protected. I remember we went to one rally[2] at the very end in Washington at the White House, where my brother delivered the clemency letter to Eisenhower.[3] We were really shielded. That was important to us, and yet the shielding was incomplete in the sense that I still felt the fear and apprehension that surrounded us in a gut way, even if I couldn't in an intellectual way.

For instance, I remember the period just before the execution, which was in June of 1953. I was six then. A special stay of execution was issued by Justice Douglas during the last week of my parents' lives. I remember hearing on radio that the executions had been put off. Then the Supreme Court was reconvened in special session and the stay was overturned, the executions were set for the very next day. And though I pretended not to, I also remember knowing—on some level I can't specifically find—that they were executed.

I remember I made up this story, figuring out in my own six-year-old way why this could happen. I believed that their attorney was asked by the Supreme Court to come up with ten reasons why their lives should be saved, and because the attorney succeeded in doing that, the executions were then stayed. And then the Supreme Court asked for an eleventh reason, and the attorney was unable to come up with an eleventh reason and so the executions were then carried out. That's what I believed as a six-year-old.

I started the first grade in the fall of 1953. After four months we were pulled suddenly out of school and sent back to my grandmother's house in New York, where I then started going to another school. This really bothered me. I hated constantly being the new kid everywhere—every situation I was in seemed temporary and unstable and strange. It was as if my life constantly changed during that period and somehow it was all because of this trouble, but it was never really explained to me.

What I later found out happened was that the school board of Toms

[2]Meeropol remembers only one, but actually attended two others: one in 1952, at which his older brother, Michael, against the wishes of the adults, pulled Robert onto the stage; another in 1953, where the boys remained largely unnoticed in the audience.

[3]Eisenhower was convinced that a pardon without an admission of guilt would be a political-warfare victory for the international Communist movement, leaving America to appear "weak and fearful" in the face of subversion. In response to a clemency letter penned by ten-year-old Michael that was delivered to the White House two weeks before his parents' execution, Eisenhower wrote that "they have even stooped to dragging in young and innocent children in order to serve their own purposes" (Cook, p. 162).

River, New Jersey, found out who we were and said that we couldn't attend New Jersey public school 'cause we weren't residents of the State of New Jersey. So I was kicked out of the New Jersey public schools at the age of six. In fact, to this day, I think of it as the sort of official version of the friend's mother saying, "I don't want you playing with your Communist friends anymore."

We went to a Christmas party that year, not a Hanukkah party but a Christmas party. We came into this room and there was this giant Christmas tree and all these kids around it. I didn't know any of the kids. It turned out that this party was for Michael and me, and all the presents, this huge pile of presents, were for us! I couldn't understand why there were all these kids, but all the presents were for me. I remember being totally dumbfounded by it all. At that party was this couple, Abel and Ann Meeropol, who drove us home and said that we were going to come to live with them and would we like that. I remember sort of liking them, so I said, sure.

We moved in with them. They lived about twenty blocks from my grandmother's house on Riverside Drive in New York City. I remember our parents' attorney, Manny Bloch, coming to visit, and things seemed to be very smooth. And then one evening when I was getting ready for bed, there was a knock on the door. It was a policeman. I don't remember exactly what happened, but the next day we were packed up and taken off to another orphanage in Pleasantville, New York.

What happened was that a conservative group, the Jewish Board of Guardians, had filed a petition with the children's court saying that we were being abused by the Meeropols.[4] That this was a case of political abuse, that we were being taken to rallies, where we were forced to listen to grisly descriptions of executions, that we were being taught to hate our country. None of this had ever happened, it was completely false. But the judge issued the order and the police came to seize us. And that night an argument developed, so the judge was prevailed upon to stay the execution of the order till the next morning. Then we were taken away to an orphanage.[5] So once again there was this weird uprooting. And once again we were in

[4]The petition was actually filed by the New York Society for Prevention of Cruelty to Children and joined by the Jewish Board of Guardians.

[5]Throughout the night the police guarded the street, the corridor outside the apartment, and even the roof. The next morning a phalanx of officers escorted the family to court, where the children were secretly remanded to an institution. The Meeropols were forced to file a writ of habeas corpus to discover where the children had been taken and to have them placed instead with their grandmother. According to Evelyn Williams, the probation officer assigned to the case by the children's court, Judge Jacob Panken threatened her with dismissal unless she recommended that the children be institutionalized.

school with a new set of kids and not really understanding what this was all about, but knowing somehow it was all connected.

A legal custody battle developed, and we ultimately ended up back with the Meeropols. But for a while we had to sleep at Grandma's house but we could eat dinners with the Meeropols. A long, complicated set of arrangements that didn't really all get straightened out until 1957, when the adoption was finalized.

I remember being eight, nine years old, playing on the streets of New York City, and the conversation coming up around what newspaper your parents read. The Meeropols, my parents, didn't read the *Daily Worker*, they read the *Guardian*. But I was very nervous about any paper, so I was scared to say that they read the *New York Times*, which is what they normally read, because I thought maybe that was bad too because it seemed different from what the street kids were reading. I couldn't say they read the *Daily News* because I knew that was the real conservative bad paper, but I thought the *New York Post*, which was kind of shaped like the *News* and somewhat like it, would be more acceptable. That was all part of the cover.

I remember at one point, rumors came around that the House Un-American Activities Committee was coming to New York and my father[6] was going to be called. He didn't want the focus on the family, so we pulled up and moved to a friend's vacant apartment in the Bronx for six weeks. I remember my parents saying, "If someone tries to talk to you, ignore them because they might give you a subpoena." I didn't know what a subpoena was, but I just knew not to talk to people and if some strange man wanted to ask me some questions about something I was to ignore him. I remember somebody following me down the street to the subway and me just walking faster and faster and quick running into the subway.

I remember being very nervous when I would be at friends' houses and there were news programs that recounted the early fifties. I would always try to go to the bathroom or do something to be away when my parents' case came up. My solution was to try to not be there, to put as much distance as I could between it and me, because it was very unsettling and bad things were associated with it, like being thrown out of school, or being put in an orphanage, or being thrown out of somebody's house. Throughout there was always the sense that something might happen, that's probably the best way I can describe it, something might happen. We don't know what it is—but it's bad. And the only protection you have is to be quiet.

[6]Abel Meeropol, his adopted father.

That's my own little personal horror story. But there are two sides to it. You see, my parents' attorney set up a trust fund for Michael and me. This fund enabled us to become children of the movement. It enabled us to live, to become secure and safe. He traveled around the country raising money for us. In fact, in Detroit in the fall of 1953, he described the fund that he was setting up, that it would be another Rosenberg fund for the children. Which I find to this day ironic that I'm now doing something called the Rosenberg Fund for Children, even though when I set it out, I didn't pattern it on that.

Abel Meeropol was a blacklisted songwriter who wrote under the name Lewis Allan. He wrote "Strange Fruit" and "The House I Live In"[7] and a number of other songs. He was in New York with no work, with no money. This fund enabled us to attend alternative high school. I attended the Little Red School House and Elizabeth Irwin High School in Greenwich Village in New York, progressive alternative schools. People like Angela Davis, Kathy Boudin, Arthur Miller's kids went there, Norman Mailer's daughter was there. It was a school at which my parents' beliefs were not considered extraordinary, and they might be considered heroes rather than villains.

Nobody talked about who we were, but people knew. In fact, there was this charade—we would pretend that no one knew so we could all act normal. In fact, this occurred throughout our entire lives until we became public figures in the 1970s. A friend described the way people used to refer to my brother when he was at the University of Wisconsin in the late sixties—he used to be described as Michael Meeropol You-Know-Who-His-Parents-Were. But nobody would ever say that to him or me, because it was considered impolite, I guess, or maybe that we were still undercover and they didn't want to intrude. So that gave us some space and actually it was very good.

I didn't tell anybody who I was, even my closest friends. There were times when I became close to someone and would want to tell them who I was, and I never would.

I was going to get married, and before my future wife came to live with me, I said to her, "Before you do this, you oughta know." I finally got myself to tell her, and it turned out she already knew. A mutual friend of ours had sat her down and said, "Hey, do you know who Robby is?" Which is exactly how my best friend found out. But she never mentioned it,

[7]Recorded by Billy Holiday and Paul Robeson, respectively. For lyrics to "The House I Live In," see Kay Boyle, footnote 11, under "Arts and Entertainment."

because she felt it was important for me to be the one.

That kind of thing happened a lot. I suppose it was like being in the closet—well, who knows and who doesn't know? You could be more open with people who knew. There were people who you really wished knew, and it was always a relief when they did.

GENE DENNIS

A husky man of medium height, soft-spoken and gracious, Dennis was a longshoreman for twenty years until he was injured on the job. His father, Eugene Dennis, was the general secretary of Communist Party of America and in 1949 was indicted under the Smith Act along with other top leaders of the CPA. He was imprisoned for four years in the Atlanta Federal Penitentiary.

Some of my earliest childhood memories are of being at Party conferences, conventions, rallies, May Day parades. There's an excitement in all that, this constant "You must be so proud of your daddy; you're going to wear your daddy's shoes when you get older." All these people adored him or respected him or were proud of him. I can remember feeling, well, I'm glad they're proud of him 'cause I'm proud of him, but I don't know about wearing his shoes! [Laughs.]

I was five or six when I knew something was really wrong. There was a lot of tension at home, and there were photographs in the newspapers. Around '47, my father was called before the House Committee on Un-American Activities, and he refused to answer questions.[1] He was in the headlines, and the talk around the house was about prison and what might happen and what might happen to my parents' friends. I felt we were under siege.

It wasn't yet a time of great fear for me, because I was surrounded by other Party adults who were all involved in this big struggle together—us against them. And I was on a scholarship to a progressive school in New

---

[1]Dennis refused to appear. He was convicted of contempt of Congress and sentenced to one year in prison.

York City. So the community that I lived in and went to school in was sort of a sanctuary, but I had this feeling that out there dark clouds were gathering. That was my sense of it, up until the Smith Act indictments[2] came down.

Around that time, I went with my mother to the movies to see *Ivanhoe* with Robert Taylor; and the second feature was a film about the Red Menace, and I was feeling kind of uncomfortable and anxious while it was on. And then came a big shot of my father and the other Party leaders who were indicted, coming down the Foley Square courthouse steps. Then came the anger and fear in this dark movie house. I was glad it was dark. It was one of the first times I had felt that kind of public venom directed at my father. That made me feel the vulnerability that we were in at that time.

When several of the Party leaders went underground,[3] the whole issue of surveillance became paramount in a way that it hadn't before. Children and spouses of Party leaders, people who were friends of people who had gone underground, were being followed in a way that hadn't happened before. I knew that it hadn't happened before, 'cause everybody was talking about it. I was given strict instructions on watching behind me, watching out as I was going to and from the playground, or the school bus, or whatever, to see if people were following me. For my own safety—not that I was a child courier or anything like that! [Laughs.] It became a part of my life to be watching out for strangers who were the FBI, who were out to harass us or to try and get the goods on our friends. That's when the fear started, that whole posture of literally looking over my shoulder. And as I got older, closer to nine or ten, which brings us up to '51, '52—my father's already in prison—I felt hunted, because I was out in the world more myself, it wasn't just from home to first grade anymore. It was being involved in after-school activities, and going to friends' houses and moving around New York City by myself. And when I was alone like that, it was scary.

I was followed. There were times I knew that clearly. The older I got, the better I got at identifying these guys. Once, on the street, they flashed a badge and said, "We want to ask you some questions," and I split. Ran all the way home, and it was a long way.

Friends of mine, other red diaper babies, we tried at times to make sport of it. We knew, for example, our telephones were tapped. I knew this

---

[2]On July 28, 1948, twelve members of the National Board of the Communist Party were indicted on two counts of "teaching and advocating the violent overthrow of the government."

[3]Immediately after the Supreme Court upheld the convictions, four of the Party leaders, acting on the collective decision of the leadership, jumped bail and disappeared, accompanied by thousands of Party members. For more on the Communist underground, see "Five Minutes to Midnight."

signal—from toddlerhood probably—hand in the air, making circles, pointing up to the ceiling. Adults would make that gesture to say "We are being listened to by the government" and "We just don't talk, we don't name names and we don't talk sensitive politics here in this place." And so now and then, my friends and I, we would play games with that. One time I called up a friend of mine and said, "I have an envelope for your dad from Gil." Referring to Gil Green,[4] one of the Party guys. "We'll meet at 160th and Riverside Drive." So a couple hours later we hopped on the bus and we went by there, and there were feds all over the place! It was hysterical, it was a kick then. We could take it and turn it into some juvenile gang thing, in the cause of the Revolution, or something like that! So it wasn't all fearful. There were ways I could find amongst kids my own age, and certain adults, a comfort and a humor during that time. But I cannot remember feeling relaxed. I could feel momentarily safe, but never relaxed.

I didn't visit my dad in prison every time. That was real hard, especially in the beginning. It was hard for me to see him locked up. But I did go. My mother went every month. I think visiting privileges were once a month, and I went maybe every other, or every third. The Party continued to pay his paycheck to us, and then there was some aid through the Smith Act Families Defense Fund or whatever the committee was, which was an ongoing legal-defense and family-support committee that went on all through those years that the various leaders were in prison or underground. So it was always tight for us. By the time my father was national chairman of the Party in '59, he was making seventy-five dollars a week, which was very, very tight.

I remember when my father was in prison that all kinds of people from outside the Party—at least that's the way I thought of them, from different unions, ministers, neighbors—went out of their way to take care of us. Not any expression of political solidarity, but just, "We want you to have this television set. We want you to have this money to take a week's vacation. We want to help young Gene to go to school." Or "Have some clothes," or "Here's some food." I don't mean a bag of groceries, but like a cake or casserole. There were just lots of ways that people outside the Party were doing this. Now, they may have been in the Party for all I know, but that was not the way they acted; it's not the way my mother reacted to them. It was surprise and gratitude that there were people who had respect for my father and sympathy for what our family was going through and expressed that in very nurturing kinds of ways. And that mattered to me. That was

[4]One of the convicted Party leaders who had jumped bail.

something that stayed with me. Even when I was in a lot of tenuous situations politically over the years, I always had the sense that it's not just us against them.

Two things had changed by the time my dad got out of prison. One was that he had become real thin and all white-haired. And I had seen that transformation while he was in prison. It wasn't a graceful aging that I saw. I saw a tension in him and a tiredness. I was twelve and a half when he got out, I was becoming a teenager. These two things were going on: my dad's getting old and I'm becoming a man. And we didn't have much time to sort all that out. I was proud of him. I was proud of him for having survived. I always had the feeling that terrible things had happened to him in prison that he never told us about.

My memories of before prison were not of any golden years, so I didn't harken back to some wonderful time in our family that had suddenly been disrupted. It was always hard. And Dad coming home was another chapter in that. He was under restrictions because of parole, and he was frustrated. Within a few years he was seriously ill. He died in '61, so it was barely five years that he was out of prison before he died. And that all seemed to go quickly. Still, there was a celebration of his coming out of prison, of us being back together, getting away, having some brief vacations together, out of the city.

When I was getting ready to graduate from high school, I decided that I was not going to sign the loyalty oath that you had to sign to get your diploma in the State of New York. I was called on the carpet before the principal—me and at least one other student. We decided on our own, and my parents were a little concerned [laughs] about jeopardizing my high school graduation, but I wasn't going to sign that damned thing. And we went on our own to the ACLU and the newspapers and all that. So the principal called me on the carpet and said that I was going to discredit the school and I had to think about my future. And I said, "If my future has to be built on violating the Constitution of the United States, I don't want any part of it!" [Laughs.]

I always felt that people like my parents were the real Americans, and this didn't come from any education in Marxism-Leninism, anything like that. I didn't get that kind of education at home; the doors were open to me to read and to experience all points of view—political, religious, and everything else. My parents wanted me to make up my own mind about things. But I felt compelled somehow to learn more about what had really happened in this country and who was really trying to implement the Bill of Rights and the promises of the American Revolution or the Emancipation Proclamation. I wanted to find out, and I felt that the Left really was. By the time I was halfway through high school I felt there was no doubt that not only things weren't gonna get better without us—"us" meaning the Left—putting up a fight, but that they were going to get a whole lot worse. My father got out of prison, and shortly after the Smith Act was thrown out for being unconstitutional, but I felt that the guys' coming out of prison and what seemed to be a loosening of the persecution was going to be temporary. That we couldn't count on anything, we just had to keep up the good work, keep the faith so to speak, and keep fighting.

ROBBIE BRIDGES

Robbie Bridges's father was Harry Bridges, the legendary leader of the International Longshoremen's and Warehousemen's Union (ILWU). Suspected of being a secret Communist, Harry was brought to trial four times in twenty years. The Supreme Court was so repelled by the government's 1945 attempt that Justice Murphy denounced it from the bench: "The record in this case will stand forever as a monument to man's intolerance of man." Robbie Bridges has worked for the fire department of Bay Area Rapid Transit for more than two decades. A tall man, composed and articulate, he speaks of his father with great pride.

In 1954, when I was about seven, my parents got a divorce and my mother moved from San Francisco back to New York. I was uprooted from my father and became very saddened by that. It was a very difficult time. As far as I can remember they were always fighting—over the phone, during visits—and yet, my mother, having been with my father during his trials and his battles with the government, with all her anger with him, still made me realize that an important person he was and the important things he had done.

I was put in New Lincoln, a progressive school which I don't think exists anymore. I was very lucky, my friends' parents were very labor-conscious, very social-minded, and a lot of them were in the same boat. I went to school with Zero Mostel's[1] children. A good friend's father was Martin Luther King's lawyer. Susan Sontag's children were there. A lot of them were friends of my father, which is probably one reason I was there.

At times, it could be embarrassing, because I was expected to be a labor expert. When any question came up of who Walter Reuther[2] was or John L. Lewis[3] or anybody like that, my teachers always singled me out to answer the question—and I had no idea what they were talking about. I wasn't that interested in labor, although I was always interested in what my father was doing.

I always respected my father, considered him one of my heroes, and his heroes became my heroes. I remember in 1959, when John Kennedy was such a great hero to the other kids, and to me he was a real antihero. He had said publicly he was going to get my father, and so had Bobby Kennedy, and I didn't appreciate that.

I had heroes that nobody else seemed to have, like Fidel Castro and Jimmy Hoffa.[4] It was kind of confusing. I understand why my father felt that way. He recognized the qualities these people had, that the press totally negated. He believed the important thing was to try and find work for people and to improve everybody's life. He believed that Castro and Hoffa, with all the bad things about them, still had that as their main goal.

When I was growing up in New York, he would come back for business and meetings. I was lucky that he had that opportunity, or else I would never have seen him. He was very casual, he always stayed in cheap hotels, he traveled on weekends to save money. There was nothing extravagant about him. People had all kinds of crazy ideas. They always assumed he lived in a big house in Hawaii, which of course he never did. He never had a big house anywhere. Never made a lot of money, made a point of always making as much as the highest-paid longshoremen—who were probably making more than him with their overtime.

I had friends who laughed at me for not realizing that my father had

---

[1]Zero Mostel (1915–77), comedic actor best remembered for his portrayal of Tevye in *Fiddler on the Roof*, was blacklisted from 1951 to 1966.

[2]Walter Reuther (1907–77) was an influential labor leader, instrumental in the rise of the United Auto Workers.

[3]John Llewellyn Lewis (1880–1969) was the longtime leader of the United Mine Workers. He founded the CIO in 1935 (it was expelled from the AFL in 1936) and remained as its president until 1940.

[4]James Riddle Hoffa (1913–75) was the controversial leader of the Teamsters Union. Convicted under various charges of corruption, Hoffa was imprisoned from 1967 to 1971, when his thirteen-year sentence was commuted by President Nixon. He disappeared four years later, presumably murdered.

people killed because of the powerful man he was. Friends I quickly dropped the friendship with. They thought I was real naive. I was just incredulous, I couldn't believe with the knowledge that people had about my father that they would think that. I heard a lot of ideas from friends who were way off the beam.

Other times, I would come out to the West Coast and stay with my father. One time in the late '50s, he was telling me about a battle that ensued when he was at Sally Stanford's[5] restaurant. I was pretty young, and when I think back to how impressionable I was, it wouldn't be the kind of thing I would tell my children. [Laughs.] He was in the rest room apparently, and was attacked by a couple of men—goons, he called them—who tried to gouge his eyes out. He was very specific about that, and to this day I wonder why he would tell me. I guess he wanted to impress upon me how serious people were. It turned out that Sally came into the rest room to help him out.[6]

I wasn't sheltered, I knew he was facing danger. My mother always warned us that people were tapping the phones and people were following us. I was always careful asking who was at the door. I always assumed the phone was tapped, although I certainly wasn't afraid of what we could be talking about.

In 1976, I went to a friend's wedding. Her stepfather had been a CIA agent, and he confided in me that years ago, he had tried to kill my father, taken a shot at him. I remember he was laughing about it—not that it was funny, but it was just amazing to him that here he could tell Harry Bridges's son this.

Of course, I asked my father about it, and he just shrugged it off, like "Nah, it never happened." I think it *did*, and he just didn't want to worry me. The funny thing was, I heard another story about it later, that it happened in a rest room again and they assumed my father was standing up and apparently he was sitting down and that's why they didn't hit him.

I left New York very happily in 1966 to go to Berkeley, and got thrown into the middle of all the antiwar demonstrations. That caused some problems with my father. He didn't support the war in Vietnam, but any position he

[5]Sally Stanford (1903–82) was a celebrated madam of prewar San Francisco. With the close of World War Two, she sensed the end of San Francisco's freewheeling ways and opened the Valhalla, a plush Sausalito restaurant richly furnished from her defunct bordello. In 1976, she was elected mayor of Sausalito; she served one term.

[6]According to Bridges's biographer Robert Cherny, this incident occurred in the early 1950s. The two thugs were from the right-wing Sailors Union of the Pacific, headed by Bridges's nemesis, archreactionary Harry Lundeberg.

took he saw as the union's position.[7] He felt most of the longshoremen supported the war. He didn't think it was correct to go against the police—he felt there was more important things to protest.

· In those summers I was working down on the docks as a casual clerk and was in an interesting position with my long hair and being looked upon as a hippie. In the morning the guys would give me a hard time, they would wonder what I was doing down there. And then by lunchtime, when they found out who I was, it was all backslapping and having a great time: "Your father's a great guy." So I was in a very strange position. I'd come upon graffiti that said bad things about my father and I'd rub it out.

He was very much a pacifist. Growing up, it was difficult for me to be interested in model airplanes. All my father would say when he saw them was, "That's a weapon of war, you shouldn't be interested in that." I still have a fascination with airplanes. I go to air shows and I can't help but feel a little guilty.

I learned that I had a family name to uphold. A lot of people didn't understand that. But throughout my life I always felt there was a certain image to uphold, and it was difficult. I kept a level head about my working-class background. I didn't have expectations of becoming a rich person. Probably the most important thing I remember my father talking about is to have the security of a job for life, and his goal was to see that people had that.

I consider myself lucky today. I have a house. I've got a good job, probably for the rest of my life—which is important to me and I credit that to values I got from my father. I think it is important to do a good job and to do an honest job. That certainly was one thing I heard over and over and over—that and his feeling that the Soviet Union was never our enemy. He impressed upon me that he was always communicating with Soviet labor leaders, that the workers in Russia were in power and that they always assured him there would never be any more war, especially with the United States, and that was important to him.

I wonder what he would think today.[8] I don't think he would be too impressed with what happened to the Soviet Union. He probably would point to Yugoslavia and all the problems there and say, "That's what happens when you don't have a strong system. That would have never happened under Communism."

[7]In 1965, the ILWU convention overwhelmingly passed a resolution calling for a cease-fire, withdrawal of troops, and negotiations. This sentiment was years ahead of its time, especially in labor circles. That same year the AFL-CIO heartily resolved to support the war.

[8]Harry Bridges died on March 30, 1990, at the age of eighty-nine.

He was pretty blind to problems in the Soviet Union. I remember when he went to Rumania, he had a few complaints about his treatment, but all in all he had nothing but praise for the system. No inflation in the Soviet Union, everybody's got a job, everybody gets an education, everybody gets medical care. He was their champion. You couldn't pin him down on that one. His gripes were with this country and the problems we have here.

For years, we had a pretty rough relationship. We never saw eye to eye on anything. No way you were going to talk him out of a position. It was like negotiating a labor contract. I had the same trouble everybody did—his ex-wives, his counterparts across the negotiating table—he was a tough person to deal with, very stubborn, very principled. He would take a position and that was it.

But our relationship changed rapidly in the late '70s. I wrote him a letter explaining how proud I was of him as my father and as a person, and put down a few things in writing I had always wanted to say. That seemed to break the ice. Soon after, I got married and started a family. I guess he felt that I was being responsible enough and was proud I had a stable marriage, which, of course, didn't last too long. My marriage ended in a terrible divorce, so I guess things tend to repeat themselves. I was kind of saddened by all that. I wanted to prove to him how stable my life could be. Afterward, when we talked about my divorce, he and I would compare notes and I tried to learn from the problems he had with my mother and not to repeat the same mistakes.

I was having enough problems just dealing with my marriage falling apart, I couldn't imagine having the pressures he must have had. He was separated from his children and had a continuous battle with my mother, and on top of that, the persecution from the government, problems with the union, and on and on.

Being the son of Harry Bridges, I did run into some flak. I remember in 1968, I was dating a girl whose father was a wealthy doctor. He called me in one evening and said, "I don't approve of who your father is," and that was the end of that relationship. I was kind of surprised. He warned me he would send the police after me if I continued to see his daughter. I think deep down I kind of enjoyed it. I wasn't totally in love at that point, and found it interesting that my father still stirred people up after all that time.

But that was pretty rare. Most people idolized him and appreciated what he had done. But a lot of people had no idea. He kept a low profile, he never advertised who he was, wasn't on TV much. If you weren't aware of the labor scene, you didn't really know that much about him. Most people, even today, think I am related to either Art Bridges, who sells cars, or Lloyd Bridges, the actor. Very rarely will they ask me if Harry was my father. Most of the time they think he was a car salesman. Around labor circles, of course, people know. At work I never mention it. Usually other people point it out and say, "You're kidding," and I have to tell them it's not something you make up.

I've always tried to memorize the trials and all that. He was in court so much that it is hard to remember, and every time you read about it in the newspapers they change it around—now is it three times to the Supreme Court? Actually, two times in all. But he's never given too many interviews. There's not too much written about it, because he didn't feel they would get it right. John L. Lewis once told him, "You will never be able to tell the story, because no one will believe the truth." So he was very careful about that.

I've tried to teach my children about their grandfather. He was pretty much bedridden when they were younger, but they are aware of what he did, and now they are under the microscope in school. The teachers know who they are, and the kids seem to handle it real well. They speak about their grandfather, and they brought to school a videotape of one of the documentaries that was done on him. They are very proud of him and they still miss him.

CHRIS TRUMBO

Chris Trumbo's father was Dalton Trumbo, screenwriter and novelist, who served a jail term as one of the Hollywood Ten.[1] As a blacklisted screenwriter, Dalton Trumbo wrote eighteen cut-rate scripts under various pseudonyms. Using the name Robert Rich, he garnered an Academy Award for The Brave One, to the utter embarrassment of the industry.

[1] In 1947, the Hollywood Ten became the first of filmland's many artists and workers called before HUAC. Electing to defy the Committee, the Ten relied on the protection of the First Amendment and refused to reveal whether they had ever been members of the Communist Party. They all served time for contempt of Congress. For more on the Ten, see Ring Lardner, Jr., and Edward Dmytryk under "The Hollywood Blacklist."

My sister and I were both aware of what was going on right from the beginning. It was hard to keep information away from us It was the first time the Committee had gotten involved in Hollywood, and there was the Committee for the First Amendment,[2] which was strongly in support of the Ten, up to a point. So the hearings were all over the papers and in the newsreels.

Around 1947, because of the hearings, my parents decided they would explain to us what these things were about, rather than have it be a mystery. I was seven at the time. They described communism as "from each according to his capacity, to each according to his contribution." Capitalism was one man hiring another man as cheaply as possible to sell a product for as much as possible. My sister took to Communism, but I kind of liked the idea of capitalism! [Laughs.] It seemed to me that in the struggle between the Right and the Left, the Right was winning and we were on the wrong side somehow. [Laughs.]

I caught flak from peers—that was unavoidable. At least it was for me. We moved from Beverly Hills to a place we had in the mountains to get away from what my parents thought might be tough times for us in the big city. But it was unavoidable, no matter where we went.

When my father was writing for the black market, he had different names for different producers. You'd answer the phone and deliver messages, and he was a different name for everybody. He also had a series of different bank accounts for each of them. He'd set up the accounts, but he didn't like the idea of driving around all over the place simply to deposit money when you have a son who's able to do these things. So I'd go and deposit checks for all the different accounts. They were mostly to protect the producer from any kind of casual inquiry. Any serious inquiry into the matter would've exposed the whole scheme. But that would have involved the federal government and income tax records.

When *The Brave One* won an Oscar and there was a missing writer, my father decided that he could make political capital out of the situation. Not through a legal or philosophical exposition, but by making fun of the Academy, by making the blacklist an object of ridicule. And that's what he

---

[2]The CFA was a civil liberties defense group that sprang up in reaction to the persecution of the Hollywood Ten. It was composed of such prominent Hollywood artists as Humphrey Bogart, Lauren Bacall, John Houston, and Edward G. Robinson. CFA members flew to Washington to support the Ten, but within weeks, the group was flying for cover as the Red smear threatened to tinge their own careers. "I'm No Communist" headlined the article Bogart published in *Photoplay* magazine in March 1948, although the actor admitted that he was a "dope."

was able to do. His theory was that people really don't like solemn arguments about "Gee, how you have injured me. This is a terrible thing you've done to me." But that they would find it amusing that people were secretly writing and producing scripts and as hard as the studios tried to blacklist them, they would surface in odd ways.

We moved to Mexico in 1951. My sisters and I went to a private American school there, in Mexico City. We didn't speak the language. It was difficult. As far as I was concerned, we were on the run, in hiding. This was not a choice, not a matter of "Well, let's go live in Mexico, what a pleasant place. The people are friendly and you can learn a foreign language in your spare time." It was by economic necessity. Albert Maltz[3] was already in Mexico. So was Gordon Kahn.[4] There was a community of American writers and artists, and there was a feeling among them that they could make a living in the Mexican film industry. Some of the blacklisted managed to stay in Mexico and do all right for a while—George Pepper and Hugo Butler produced one or two documentaries that were really quite good. But for my father, that didn't work out. It also happened to a number of other people who tried living in Mexico. Ian Hunter,[5] and Ring Lardner, Jr., and John Bright[6] was there for a while. None of them found it satisfactory. People who went to London and to Paris found it much easier. We came back in 1954. We were under observation, but I never paid attention. I was never overly watchful about it. It doesn't pay. There's nothing you can do about it.

The blacklisting changed our family lifestyle. But it's hard to say how, because what happens is it becomes your present. For instance, wherever we moved or wherever we went, someone would eventually discover the name and make the links. That was inevitable. The responses varied. In *Additional Dialogue*[7] there's a long letter to the principal of my little sister's grammar school outlining the outrages that were more or less committed against her, which was ostracism. Being put in Coventry, as it were. The teachers got involved in the process also.

[3]Screenwriter, one of the Hollywood Ten, blacklisted from 1948 to 1969.

[4]Screenwriter, identified in 1947 as one of the Hollywood Nineteen, the original group to be called before HUAC, out of which were culled the Ten. Kahn had twenty-eight screen credits from 1937 to 1949, then none.

[5]Ian McLellan Hunter, screenwriter, blacklisted from 1953 to 1969.

[6]Screenwriter, twelve screen credits from 1937 to 1951, then two abroad, none in the United States.

[7]Dalton Trumbo, *Additional Dialogue: Letters of Dalton Trumbo, 1942–62* (New York: Evans, 1970).

There was an award for each grade in high school, and I was nominated for the tenth-grade English award. I was told of this by a teacher who was as new as I was at the school. She didn't know any better and discovered later she wasn't supposed to have told me. I asked a couple months down the line what had happened, and she said, "Well, I'm really sorry." They had given it to somebody else because of my family background. Unfortunately, I had told my father about this potential award, and he eventually inquired what had happened! [Laughs.] So I had to tell him. He went down and spoke to the principal. He wanted to know what was wrong with our family background, considering they'd never met us. Eventually, we shared the award! [Laughs.] But I always regretted having mentioned it to my father. You just can't bring in your parents. You have handle those things by yourself, one way or the other.

There was the day in junior high when I was suddenly swept off my feet by some kids and thrown in the furnace. It was on at the time, and they closed the door behind me. I was all the way inside. I remember thinking, "Jesus, here I am inside a goddamn oven! What the hell's going on?" I got out when the teacher arrived. [Laughs.] It burned my eyebrows, and the eyelashes were missing. It also burned a pair of hands.

Things like that made me angry, not fearful. I wasn't afraid to go to school the next day. My mother remembers me coming home, singed, burned, changing my clothes, being really angry, and going back to school. She never asked! [Laughs.] She thought, "Well, I guess he's handling whatever's going on." It's something I never mentioned to anybody until years later.

My father broke the blacklist in 1960. What happened was that two pictures came out with his name on them. One was *Exodus* and one was *Spartacus*. Strange things happened. Organizations like the American Legion would boycott pictures of people that they disapproved of, if their names were on them. They set out to boycott *Exodus*, which opened in Boston, and found themselves picketing the picture along with the Nazi Party, which was there because the film was nice to Jews. Ironies like that were constantly cropping up. Opposition to him and to his working continued in the industry. If you look at the *Hollywood Reporter*, you'll find objections to him working on *Hawaii*, and on and on. So it was a constant battle for him, and then it stopped. But the blacklist continued for other writers.

To get unblacklisted was not difficult at that point. You merely signed a letter saying that you weren't currently a member of the Communist Party.

That's all you had to say. The more they wanted you, the less you had to do. They just wanted symbolic capitulation.

There were a number of people who never did it. And there were a number of people who did do it. But that was a personal choice. And there were a number who did do it without ever naming anybody else's name. Which was the fine point there. It was only people like my father and Ring Lardner, Jr., and Waldo Salt that were unwilling to go that far even, because they felt the government had no right to compel this in any way and neither had their employer. So they just wouldn't move an inch. And that was the ethical decision that they made.

In 1963, I was in New York with some people at an all-night restaurant across the street from Columbia. I was going to school there at the time. One of my friends started talking about how he had been up at Sarah Lawrence and had met Norman Cousins's daughter. This guy, Mike, who I didn't know, said, "So what? Dalton Trumbo's son goes to Columbia." My friends and I looked at each other, and said to him with one voice, "Who's Dalton Trumbo?" [Laughs.] He gave us the whole rundown on him, the Stalinist screenwriter. Then I asked, "What is his son like?" He says, "Oh, he belongs to a Southern fraternity and hates his old man." Peculiar, never had that opportunity again. I think Mike was a member of the Progressive Labor Party[8] and later he turned out to be a stool pigeon. So I wasn't welcome in the New Left either because my father was somehow a Stalinist! [Laughs.]

My parents' politics really had to do with American populism and almost nothing with Communism itself. They both came from poor backgrounds. My mother was part of a kid vaudeville act, then she was a carhop. My father worked in a bakery. Their experience was not middle-class, not hopeful. During the Depression, they were at the mercy of an economic system that didn't give a shit about you. Basically they were more in opposition to what they considered to be the horrors of American government than they were in adherence to a philosophical political system.

Most of my parents' friends were Communists. And the Party provided my father with intellectual stimulation. He went to college at various points, but never got a degree, never considered himself to be educated.

[8]Early New Left group identified as Maoist in persuasion. Although Maoists would not view the designation of "Stalinist" in a negative light, a Trotskyist certainly would. Perhaps Mike was a member of the Socialist Workers Party, an anti-Stalinist splinter of the Socialist Party founded by Leon Trotsky in 1938 and still active in the 1960s.

The Party had a lot of intellectuals in it, and he respected that. In those days, in the forties in Hollywood, it was a very dynamic group.

I remember these people coming over to the house, once a week. My older sister and I were teenagers, and we always wondered why these people were coming over, since we knew that my parents didn't care for them personally. One week my sister says, "They're walking down the driveway to father's study," and I burst out laughing and say, "Guess what? It's a cell meeting!"[9] I had figured it out! This was just their regular meeting. It wasn't a secret, but they had never told us. When I said, "That's what you're doing," they said, "Sure!" I don't think they called them "cell meetings," I must have picked those things up from *I Led Three Lives,*[10] or something. [Laughs.]

My parents believed that organized social action was the only way to get anything done. And that's why my father was interested in helping to form the Screen Writers Guild and labor movements in general. Our family never had a great identification with Mother Russia. When the Khrushchev revelations occurred, they didn't startle me. But they bothered my father, they bothered him a great deal.

My father didn't join the Party until 1943, and then quit several years later. Later, he got angry at the shoddy treatment of the California Smith Act victims and wrote *The Devil and the Book,* a pamphlet in their defense, and rejoined the Party. Then he quit again sometime in the fifties. There was an [laughs] impulsiveness that ran through it all. The idea of him taking direction from the Party was laughable. He wasn't that kind of person.

I don't think he left the Party with rancor. He believed absolutely in their right to exist and would do what he could to support their existence. He disliked a lot of people in the Communist Party, but a lot of people outside the Party as well.

How did all this affect me? At one time I would have said the blacklist didn't affect me at all. Later on, I said, "Oh, wait a second, I just didn't know it." I'm not particularly social and forthcoming. I'm just not that open to new acquaintances. You tend to learn, at least I did, that you will go to a new school or a new neighborhood, you will make some friends,

---

[9]The designation of "cell" to describe a local group was abandoned by the Communist Party in 1920 in favor of "branch" or "club." The popular media, however, along the FBI and its allies, held to the earlier term for an extra dash of the sinister.

[10]A nationally syndicated television show based on Herbert Philbrick's lurid memoirs of life as an FBI mole in the Communist Party. Soaked with all the melodrama of a B-movie thriller, *Three Lives* was sent to Europe, where bewildered viewers, long used to pluralism in politics, weren't sure if they were to take it seriously.

and then months later, suddenly those people aren't your friends anymore. They've learned who you are. "Don't you know that's so-and-so?"

BECKY JENKINS

A dark blond woman with strong features, Becky Jenkins, now in her fifties, is the granddaughter of Maynard Dixon (a Western painter) and the daughter of Dave Jenkins (see under "Red-ucators").

I can't remember when I became aware that we were different. But it was really early. When I was very little, my parents had a policy of not telling me that they were in the Communist Party. They believed there was too much danger and the less I knew, the safer I would be. There is no question that on some level I knew it. But when I asked the direct question "Are you members of the Communist Party?" they did some sidestep and actually said, "We're not going to tell you." So it was perfectly clear.

I was very political when I was a little girl. My father's prominence in the movement impressed me a lot, and I was crazy about him. In the forties, he was the director of the California Labor School,[1] a hub of great activity during the heyday of the Old Left. I had a sense of being a part of an embracing community of people who shared a worldview and who were my friends.

The labor school was an incredible phenomenon. I've often wanted to figure out some way to duplicate it, without the dominance of Party politics, of course. I took dance lessons there as a little girl. There was an active theater and an art department, endless other classes. It was the combination of art and politics.

As the witch hunt heated up, my father resigned as the director of the labor school and he began to fly around the country doing defense work for various unions, Left unions, that were under siege. These were men and women who had devoted their lives to working people. Many of them were in the Party, I'm sure, but a lot of them weren't.

[1]For more on the California Labor School, see under "Red-ucators."

Also it was a time of terrible sexism. Even though these people were way in advance of other sections of the population, and even though there were some exceptional women leaders, men had the focus and dominated the leadership. I figured out years later how deeply that affected me as a little girl. I think it explains some of the bitterness of many women from the Old Left who were in less significant positions of power.

I was terrified when it really started to heat up. Quite often, the FBI were parked in front of our house, sometimes to serve subpoenas on my parents. My parents were both summoned in front of the California Burns Committee,[2] and I don't know what other committees. The grown-ups will have to tell you! [Laughs.]

The FBI was a presence. There was no question the phone was tapped. The phone would go dead, you'd get the head operator by mistake, things like that. We made jokes about it. Once my father demanded to speak to a phone company supervisor and said, "Look, if you're going to tap the phone, just do it correctly, so my calls aren't interrupted."

There were periods when people went underground, people would disappear. Friends of my parents would just be gone. There was pressure not to see psychiatrists because of the fear of telling things that would be used against you. Paranoia was rampant, most of which was justified. The job of sorting out the real fears from the imaginary ones was a terrible strain. There was this sense of being isolated and misunderstood by the people around us. On top of that, we were Jews but we weren't religious. We were atheists, which would have been enough to ostracize us in our lower-middle-class white neighborhood. And then we were secret Communists but public radicals, although everyone knew or suspected the truth. It was a mess of confused identities, secrets, and danger.

Then there were times when my parents appeared before committees, when their names were in the newspapers. While my father was escaping a subpoena, he ran over some rooftops and fell through a glass skylight into the Yellow Cab garage! I mean, things like that were news. [Laughs.] There was no way to be anonymous.

In retrospect, I did things that were pretty obnoxious. I would stand up every day in my seventh-grade class and report on the Harry Bridges trial. I was educating my classmates. I must've been just a frightful drag. Kids would be encouraged to bring in newspaper reports, and I would bring in

[2]California's little HUAC, under the chairmanship of Senator Hugh H. Burns, a former undertaker.

big political news. I feel two ways about it—that I was a pain in the ass to my contemporaries, and that it was a terrible burden on me, as a little person, to feel so obligated to change the world.

I was the oldest one in the family. I think my brothers and sisters remember this period quite differently, although my sister Margie, who's a dancer, just told me an interesting story. She was being sued by a disgruntled dancer in her company. She'd just been served with some papers. And she said that after some tough old lady came and gave her a subpoena, she went upstairs and sobbed. She realized that it frightened her and it reminded her of her childhood.

There was no doubt I was alienated from other kids. Our house was full of books, paintings, and music. We all took dance and music classes. I was not one of the gang. I always had friends, but I think I was considered strange. I certainly felt strange. There were all the problems of just being an adolescent. With my big body and big Russian face, there was no way I was going to fit that fifties standard of beauty. But there was a small group of friends and teachers who I liked and who seemed to appreciate me, and they saved my life.

When I was in high school, things got even more terrifying. I was in high school from 1950 to 1954, which was the height of McCarthyism as well as the collapse of the Left in America. My community began to disintegrate around me. The whole thing moved into a really emotionally dark and catastrophic period.

When I was in my first year in high school, the Korean War was going on. In a social studies class, I said something about it being a civil war and America should stay out of it. The teacher responded with "That's the position of the Communists!"[3] and the class started to laugh and scream and hoot at me, yelling "Commie!" I ran home from school sobbing, just humiliated. My father came to school the next day and insisted on a meeting with the principal, the boys' and girls' deans, and the teacher, Miss Keeley, and said to them, "I'm a taxpayer. I want my child protected in school. I know all of you have signed the loyalty oath, and these are frightening times, but you may not persecute my kid."

There was no question that among a certain group of teachers I was labeled a Communist, and I was treated accordingly. Various friends would tell me over the proceeding years that teachers would take them aside and

---

[3]The official version follows a simple sequence: in June of 1950 the North Koreans, at Stalin's order, suddenly attacked an innocent and defenseless Republic of Korea. The Left, however, believed the conflict to be a civil war provoked by South Korea with the cooperation of the United States.

say, "Becky Jenkins, look out for her. She's a Communist. You can tell she's a Commie; she has so many black friends."

I hung out a lot with black kids, and that was a combination of things. One was my politics, right? I was obsessed with black oppression. And also black men really liked and appreciated me. Their aesthetic included big women—big bodies and big personalities. I have to be completely honest, it was sexy and more fun to be around them. Also the black kids tended to be more politically sophisticated. Their instincts were to go for the under-dog. They were a very important part of my life and development as a person.

Anyway, it was a nightmare for me. When I had my sixteenth birthday party the football team came and broke up the house looking for signs I was a Communist. My father was out of town fund-raising at the time. There was no defense against these guys. They tore out lighting fixtures in the bathroom and wrote on the walls. It was terrifying. It all had the patina of the Red Scare, that we were Commies, we were bad, and anything that happened to us we deserved. When I went to my twenty-fifth high school reunion, a lot of people came up and apologized to me. Came up and said, "You know, I've thought about you often. I'm really sorry." That was very, very nice.

Add to that this adolescent alienation; I didn't know who I was or what I was doing. And the heat was on around my parents. But I had a group of friends who were the children of radicals. We hung together in a group, so there was some support outside of school. There were some people in the neighborhood who were quite heroic, and liked us in spite of how different we were. Those few stood out.

Eventually, the Left couldn't withstand the pressure, and it became even more sectarian. A lot of its problems and weaknesses intensified as it got more isolated. There seemed to be a direct ratio between the pressure from the outside and the foolishness inside the Party. This is from my perspec-tive. My father—I don't think I realized this at the time—was in trouble with the Party a good deal of the time. He thought a lot of Party policy was crap, and because of that he was being kicked out and then asked to come back.

Then the Khrushchev report[4] came out. I was a freshman at State and I

---

[4]At the Twentieth Party Congress of 1956, with Stalin safely three years in his grave, Premier Khrushchev officially exposed the crimes committed under the direction of the former dictator.

remember it was as if the whole world shifted on its axis. My parents left the Party, as did most of their friends. I was involved in the Labor Youth League.[5] I left and hit the bars. I started to hang out in North Beach and got involved in the Beat scene in earnest, I felt safe there. I wasn't a band chick, but I was close. I worked as a waitress and went to jazz clubs. And again, black people were a refuge for me. At one point I sought out prostitutes and burlesque musicians who worked in the strip joints along Pacific Avenue. There was a feeling of wanting to hit the bottom, look around, and not operate out of any of the old premises.

And again, it corresponded with a period in my life where I didn't know who I was or what I wanted to be when I grew up—and it was not all right in my family to not want to be *something*. I had a sense of falling out of my extended community, a world community of socialists, good people that were fighting for social justice. It was gone. Feeling a part of a world community is hard to explain to people, although I suppose Catholics must feel it, as do most Jews.

All kinds of things happened in my parents' extended community. People got divorces, friendships ended, people left their jobs. It was fascinating to watch, in a horrible way. The personal and political were absolutely connected. Secrets were revealed, secret love affairs, acrimonious divorces. The whole fabric of life rearranged itself. I realized many people had been living lives they didn't like in the name of political commitments they suddenly no longer had to keep. The net holding them all together disappeared. For some it was a tragedy and for others it was a new freedom.

The report stunned the Communist world and effectively dismantled the American Communist Party by sparking a mass exodus of disillusioned and embittered members. Ironically, this was an event the FBI and its allied forces purportedly had wished to accomplish for more than a decade.

[5]The Labor Youth League was formed in 1949 as a successor to the Young Communist League. With two hundred chapters and up to five thousand members, the LYL opposed the Korean War, the Cold War, and racism and supported the eighteen-year-old vote, more school funding, and a higher minimum wage. The Party dissolved the LYL in 1957 amid the upheaval provoked by the Khrushchev report.

The Peekskill Riot

The single most violent confrontation of the era took place over two days in August and September 1949, in the town of Peekskill, New York. The inhabitants of this tiny burg relied on the summer trade for their livelihood, but increasingly resented the seasonal influx of thirty thousand New Yorkers, many of them Jewish, and the regular arrival of Communists who held conferences at the area's residence camps. Paul Robeson[1] had headlined annual fund-raising concerts in the area dating back to 1946. His return in 1949 set off a bloody riot.

If the fracas needed a spark, it was the publicity surrounding a speech Robeson made in Paris earlier that year. Seizing upon a remark in the speech, the nation's press roundly attacked him as a traitor who had renounced his allegiance to the United States in favor of the Soviet Union. What the man had actually said was "It is unthinkable that the Negro people of America or elsewhere . . . would be drawn into war with the Soviet Union."

When the concert was announced, the *Peekskill Evening Star* cried "subversive" in three-column headlines and stated flatly, "The time for tolerant silence that signifies approval is running out." Joining in the call for mass action against the concert was the Peekskill Chamber of Commerce, the Junior Chamber of Commerce, the assistant county district attorney, the American Legion, the Veterans of Foreign Wars, and the Catholic War Veterans.

The rioting that ensued marked the opening volley of popular state-sanctioned violence against the Left. Governor Dewey's

---

[1] Paul Leroy Robeson (1898–1976) was a world-famous African-American singer and actor. A courageous leader in the civil rights movement and an unbending spokesman for many left-wing causes, Robeson was hounded for more than twenty years.

investigating committee and grand jury exonerated and praised the nine hundred state troopers and local police that actively participated in the violence. One immediate effect of the praise was to mobilize hate groups along the Eastern Seaboard. From Staten Island to Tallahassee, effigies of Paul Robeson hung from burning crosses. In the Bronx, a church meeting to protest the violence was attacked by a mob of two hundred. The police did not respond.

Back in Peekskill, the atmosphere thickened. Bumper stickers were distributed: "Communism Is Treason. Behind Communism Stands the Jew! Therefore: For My Country—Against the Jews!" Jewish residents received threatening letters and phone calls. In a neighboring village, a Jewish home was stoned by a mob, while anti-Semitic remarks were screamed at the mother and child within. Four firebombings were attempted on the home of Stephen Szago, the owner of the concert grounds, and his front door was riddled with bullets. On September 6, the *Peekskill Star* compared the perpetrators of the two riots to the patriots of the Boston Tea Party.

The attacks left 215 concert-goers injured, of which 145 were hospitalized; twenty-five were arrested.

IRWIN SILBER

In 1949, Irwin Silber was the executive director of People's Artists, Inc., the sponsor of the Peekskill concert. Silber is the editor of more than twenty song anthologies, including *Lift Every Voice, Songs of Independence,* and *The Folk Singer's Wordbook.*

I remember 1938 was the first time I was in a May Day parade.[1] It was impressive, there must've been a quarter of a million people marching along

[1] Observance of May 1 as an international labor holiday first began in the United States in 1886, when it was the date of a nationwide strike for the eight-hour day. But it was Chicago's Haymarket Square riot on that first May Day and the two hundred workers killed or wounded by the police that memorialized the date. Over the years, May Day as a labor holiday has become almost exclusively identified with the Left. During the Red Scare, May Day parades were routinely photographed by the FBI for later identification of the heretics participating in this "Red Holiday."

Eighth Avenue in New York City, with people hanging out the buildings cheering you on. And I remember the last big May Day parade in '50 or '51. There was ten thousand of us—maybe. It was dangerous, people really dumping on you, throwing rocks and garbage and all kinds of stuff at the parade. And the cops were not interested in protecting you. After a while it got reduced to just holding a rally in Union Square without a parade,[2] then it was not possible to hold even those anymore. It was all very sad.

That was the beginning of the big decline of the Left, and Peekskill was one of the last gasps. The Peekskill concert was sponsored by my organization, People's Artists, which published *Sing Out!*[3] We were responsible for the actual program. In fact, my ex-wife sang "The Star-Spangled Banner" at the second Peekskill concert, the one that wasn't broken up. You know, there were two concerts. Well, the first one didn't get held. There was a riot. Then a week later, everybody went back and put on a concert.

See, this was an annual event. It was held for the benefit of the Civil Rights Congress.[4] Paul Robeson, who was a founding director and charter member of our organization and a friend of mine, would sing at these every summer. They raised a lot of money. People would come from all over the summer resort area in upstate New York for this concert. But this was 1949, shortly after Robeson, at the height of his prestige, made this speech in Paris saying that there was no reason for American blacks to fight in a war that the United States might cook up with the Soviet Union. People were furious with him. So a bunch of American Legionnaires in a peace delirium organized a protest against the concert. They whipped up a tremendous amount of fervor for about a week before the concert. So when we all drove up there it was an incredible traffic jam. They blocked the entrances to the concert grounds; nobody could get through. These people had actually captured the concert stage area and were blocking all the roads and nobody could go forward or back.

We didn't know what was going on. My wife got out of the car and went wandering off—for some crazy reason—to find out what was happening. She ran into six or eight guys, who began tossing her around like a football.

[2]In April 1953, the New York State Supreme Court upheld a mayoral ban on the Eighth Avenue May Day parade because, as the police commissioner put it, the marchers were "puppets of the Soviet government." However, they were allowed to gather in Union Square.

[3]*Sing Out!* was a magazine of folk, labor, and civil rights songs published by People's Artists—the Party-oriented successor to People's Songs, the entertainment arm of the Left labor movement founded by Pete Seeger and Woody Guthrie.

[4]A legal defense organization active from 1946 to 1956, the CRC was called the most successful "Communist front" of all time. Utilizing mass organization tactics to further their legal efforts, the CRC fought against Jim Crow laws and for civil liberties.

They just kept shoving her around and feeling her up and so on. She finally got away from them, but she was shaken by that. Some other people got beaten up[5] and finally everyone made their way home.

People were furious. They really wanted to put on this concert. A large number of people knew that this was the beginning of serious harassment of the Left, and a lot of us felt, "Okay, this is the way fascism probably looked in its earliest stages, and if we don't make a stand now, we're all gonna be in trouble." In the intervening week it was decided to fight back. So people in the left-wing trade unions, and the Communist Party, and a lot of blacks in Harlem decided to get together and put this concert on again. One of the stories they tell is that the leading black gangster in Harlem came up to Paul Robeson and said, "Listen, you want us to go back up to Peekskill with you and take care of you during this concert? I'm prepared to bring one hundred guys with me who'll let these people know where it's at if they mess with you." And Robeson said, "Well, I really appreciate that, but that's not quite what we had in mind." We wanted to do it a little bit more politically than that.

Anyway, we went back to Peekskill with about fifteen hundred people armed with baseball bats to guard the concert.[6] They surrounded this big open field—furriers, wholesale workers, wherever the Left was strong in the unions. A lot of people turned out—about twenty-five thousand. It was quite an event. Very impressive.

After the concert, when the people left on the buses, they were attacked. The mobs were waiting a little further down the road. Some of the bus drivers refused to drive, and people who were at the concert who'd never driven buses before drove the buses out of the place. Bricks and stones were thrown at the buses—with the cooperation of the police.[7] The state police turned their backs. The pictures showed big beefy policemen pretending as though they wanted to hold back the crowd, and people just throwing—it was an open scandal. A couple hundred people were injured. One guy I knew lost his eye. He got hit by a stone.

Getting Robeson out was hair-raising. That was one of the big security problems they had to solve. They got a relatively large car, but still inconspicuous, and he lay on the floor, rolled in a blanket. So it looked like just one other car. But they had a ring of cars around him, with people who

[5]At this first incident, fourteen concert-goers were injured before the police intervened.

[6]Other sources put the number of guards at 2,000 to 2,500.

[7]Many of the nine hundred policemen present actively participated in the violence, smashing windows and dragging people from their cars to run a gauntlet of club-swinging officers.

were prepared to deal with any contingency, in case he got spotted. But he was smuggled out of the place. Later, there was an investigation, but all phony. Nothing happened. I think eventually the commission concluded that the riot was provoked by the people who ran the concert.[8] [Laughs.]

The aftermath was painful. I think it was a victory of a kind, but it was mixed. We never could do another concert there again. It was part of the last gasp of the Left before the fifties.

[8]On September 14, Governor Dewey characterized the concert-goers as "followers of Red totalitarianism" and ordered a grand jury investigation to determine whether the concert was "a part of the Communist strategy to foment racial and religious hatred." Not surprisingly, the grand jury report of June 1950 absolved the police and local officials of all blame, while tagging the hapless picnickers as "the shock troops of a revolutionary force."

BOB BLACK

In 1949, Bob Black was a young musician with People's Folksay, a spin-off of People's Songs that provided folk singers, political satirists, and performers for union meetings and political action groups. Since 1979 he has been on the faculty of the Native American studies program at the University of California at Berkeley.

The day before the second concert, I was driving up to Pete Seeger's house with a friend. Pete lived in Beacon, New York, and we were going to spend the night there, then go back for the concert the next day. On our way, we stopped in Peekskill for a cup of coffee. I remember sitting in a booth and listening to the people behind us. One of these guys was saying to the other, "You coming to our riot tomorrow? We're going to show these Commies." When we got to Pete's house I told him, "They are getting ready for a big one—they're really organizing."

The next day, we went back through Peekskill, and there was a big banner across the main street, "Wake up, America—Peekskill did!" In other words, they had shown up the threat of the left-wingers and this was a clarion call to America to be on the alert for subversion. They had people in the streets. One guy was throwing handbills into cars, parodies on popular songs of the day. One I remember, there was a popular song "He's Too Fat for Me" and the parody was "He's Too Red for Me."

Out on the concert grounds, the union guys had the whole performance area double-ringed. The inside ring contained the performers. Robeson was well protected by bodyguards. I got to talking to Woody Guthrie, Pete asked me to come on the stage. We did a group number together and we just had a great time. It was a real picnic affair. Off in the distance, the VFW, and the American Legion were marching with banners and shouting. You could see them on the road. They did not try to break through. Of course, they couldn't, the whole area was ringed. I later found out that all of the union guys had baseball bats hidden in the grass around the area. Later, during the confusion and the attacks, the police moved in and arrested a lot of the guys for carrying weapons, i.e., the baseball bats.[1]

So we spent a very pleasant day. I remember it was just a wonderfully harmonious time. Nobody paid any attention to all of the commotion going on at the edge of the area.

The problem was, there was only one road in and out of the grounds. Toward the end of the day, we were getting ready to leave. I was in a car with a friend and two other people. Seeger was in another car, a little station wagon. One of the union guys came over and said, "Better roll your windows up—they're throwing sand." We rolled the windows up and we left through that one road.

As soon as we got on the road, you would see the state police directing traffic. It was one-lane and it was very slow and you had to stop and wait because everyone had to get out the same way. At least, this is what we were told. On both sides of the road were locals, the American Legion, Veterans of Foreign Wars. They were shouting[2] and then they started throwing rocks. I do not know how many people were hit but quite a number of cars had their windows smashed.[3] A rock about eight or nine inches in diameter busted the window of the car I was in, hit the driver on the side of the head, and knocked him out.

A fat state policeman, I can still see his protruding belly, walked up with his hand on his gun and said, "You goddamn Commie Jews. If you don't get out of here, I'm going to kill you." I was in the backseat, the guy was knocked out in the front seat—more and more rocks were hitting the car.

[1]As the last of the cars pulled off the concert grounds, the police drew their revolvers and charged the remaining union guards. The guards were clubbed, arrested, and forced to march to the police compound with their hands held over their heads. The baseball bats were handed over to the mob.

[2]Eyewitness reports have it that among the epithets of "Dirty Jew!" "Nigger!" and "Commie Jew!" was the chant "We're Hitler's boys—out to finish the job!"

[3]Fifty buses and cars had their windows smashed, fifteen were overturned.

This friend of mine jumped into the front seat, pushed the other guy off to the side, and started driving. We were hiding in the back down on the floor and we moved slowly out. Pete was in the car in front of us with his wife, Toshi, and one or two of his kids. His windows were smashed out too.

Throughout this, the state police did absolutely nothing. Actually, they egged them on. There was no attempt to protect the cars. Some people were blinded and quite a number of people were hurt very seriously, had to go to the hospital. We made it out of there by the skin of our teeth. We went out to Pete's house, took out the broken glass from the car windows and buried it. Pete was worried about the locals, he wanted to keep it as quiet as possible.

There was a little progressive camp nearby, in a community called Woodland Park. We all got together there that night. Pete spoke about Peekskill and all of us sang "We Shall Overcome." The next day we drove back to New York City in Pete's car without any glass and it was colder than hell.

Hounds

The most relentless force in the war against the Left was J. Edgar Hoover's FBI. The Bureau was at the heart of the Red Scare, sending and receiving muddied streams of rumor and misinformation through a network of professional informers, security officers, law enforcement agencies, anti-Communist pressure groups, and newsmen around the country.

Hoover's skillfully created (and largely false) public image as top crime fighter and domestic watchdog allowed him to inflate an equally false image of the Red Menace. Decrying that "cowardly, slithering mass of humanity, too evil and slinking to assume their true identities," that " 'ism' scum . . . seeking to engulf Americanism," he greatly expanded the power and numbers of his beloved agency. In 1939, Hoover had 785 agents; by 1952, he had more than 7,000, the vast majority of whom earned their pay prowling for homespun subsersives. Hoover's vision for America was bleak and monotheistic—a puritanical triumvirate of Christianity, Big Business, and the FBI. Armed with a massive publicity machine, his secret files, and an army of agents, he attempted to enforce nationwide conformity in belief, thought, and action.

Hoover called upon neighbor to inform on neighbor, schoolchildren to inform on their teachers—and for everyone to shun the Left. He blackmailed those who challenged his power—including at least one President.[1] Agents burgled, tapped, and bugged, suborned perjury, intimidated and blackmailed. During this period, the Bureau stockpiled

[1]In 1941, an FBI agent was assigned to follow suspected Nazi spy Inga Arvad, a former Miss Europe. The agent captured her on tape making love with a young naval officer named John Fitzgerald Kennedy. This was the beginning of Jack's FBI file, which expanded to include any number of White House liaisons—including one affair with a gangster's moll. Hoover kept Kennedy well aware of this information, and in turn Kennedy kept Hoover.

more than 25 million files on American citizens. From 1941 to 1975 virtually every civil rights group, left-of-center labor union, and left-wing political organization (approximately 13,500 in total) was monitored by the FBI.

By 1956, with the Communist Party down to less than five thousand members, one out of every three members was an FBI informant. So riddled was the CP that informers named other informers, and many a meeting was held where the majority worked for the government. In order to maintain their viability, a number of informers recruited friends and acquaintances into the Party, only to turn them over to the FBI.

But the professional witnesses' main job was to identify political heretics, and once their well ran dry, they plucked personalities from newspaper columns, branded their critics as subversives, and recycled rumors from Hoover's files. Those named were required to prove their innocence, yet to be named was a burden almost impossible to overcome. Admitted membership in the Communist Party was considered conclusive of subversive intent; even to hold a parallel belief with the Party was to be guilty of the same. Claims of innocence were scorned as cynical manipulations of the judicial system, while evidence of a rock-ribbed establishment life merely revealed the cunning of the Communist intrigue.

With Truman's loyalty program came the rise of the security officer. Every department and agency of the Executive Branch was required to "develop and maintain . . . a staff specially trained in security techniques." In 1952, the State Department alone staffed 322 security officers to police the thoughts of its eleven thousand stateside employees, with a proportionate number assigned to monitor its nine thousand overseas employees.

These men commanded enormous authority, empowered as they were to scrutinize the personal behavior, associations, and sex lives of employees in their departments. "They relish the collection of derogatory information," wrote S. A. Goudsmit, chairman of the physics department of Brookhaven National Laboratory. "Their job is an outlet for their frustrated hatred of men. They are biased against intellectuals and anyone who reads a book." Journalist Elmer Davis once acted as a reference for a woman who had applied for civilian employment at the Navy Department. When visited by a security officer from Naval Intelligence, Davis praised the woman's mental capabilities. The officer commented, "These intelligent people are very likely to be attracted to communism."

Soon nearly every corporation and university in the country secreted a security officer somewhere in its bowels; many were former FBI agents who remained loyal emissaries of Hoover's empire.

On May 3, 1972, with Hoover safely expired for at least twelve hours, the *WashingtonStar* commented, "Hoover suffered neither fools nor Attorneys General gladly, and occasionally he confused the two." During the half century of Hoover's dominion, he served under sixteen Attorneys General. Indeed, Hoover's power was such that it was difficult to determine who worked for whom, especially in the years after World War Two.

Tom Clark, Truman's first Attorney General, showed no interest in supervising Hoover and rubber-stamped his every request. Clark rarely read the reports Hoover sent him and turned over all wiretap requests to an assistant, as he "didn't want to know who was tapped or who wasn't tapped." Clark would later claim that he was much less concerned with the Communist menace than was Hoover, and would dismiss most of the cases as "somewhat squeezed oranges," but he prosecuted them anyway. Hoover repaid this accommodation by presenting his boss with one of his used bulletproof limousines, after Clark had okayed Hoover's purchase of a new one.

But the apex of Hoover's power was achieved during the Eisenhower years. William Sullivan, a former assistant director of the Bureau, believed Ike to be a "very gullible man," explaining that Eisenhower "blindly believed everything the director told him, never questioned a word. . . . Hoover soon had him wrapped around his finger." Richard Nixon had also long been enthralled with the director, and as Vice President he dutifully phoned Hoover twice a day.

Attorney General Brownell, whose story is included here, gave Hoover free rein, although he probably had little choice. "I have full confidence and admiration for Mr. Hoover," Brownell once remarked, "I like to stress that whenever possible." By now, Hoover was helping to shape White House policy, particularly in law enforcement, internal security, and civil rights. The AG and his subordinate clashed on only one substantive issue. Brownell had proposed new civil rights legislation (the first since Reconstruction) to create the Civil Rights Commission and to give federal courts the power to enforce voting rights. As Sanford Ungar has noted, Hoover's opposition on rather narrow-minded and bigoted grounds was "probably a major factor in President Eisenhower's decision not to push for the Brownell civil rights program."[2]

[2]Sanford Ungar, *The FBI* (Boston: Atlantic Monthly Press, 1976).

But more often than not, the Attorneys General were the White House bulldogs on the hunt for Reds. In 1948, Tom Clark—later appointed by Truman to the Supreme Court—clearly expressed his sentiments on political dissent: "Those who do not believe in the ideology of the United States, shall not be allowed to stay in the United States."

In 1954, speaking at the request of President Eisenhower, Herbert Brownell called for a "stepped-up anti-Communist program" designed to "utterly destroy the Communist Party U.S.A. and its activities." The package included elimination of the Fifth Amendment by compelling testimony under "immunity," widening the definition of perjury, legalized wire-tapping, power to outlaw labor unions, the removal of citizenship from native-born citizens, and the death penalty for peacetime espionage. He also proposed the formation of an "anti-treason" division within the Justice Department which would devote itself to cases of spying, treason, and the loyalty of federal employees. Even the conservative *Wall Street Journal* thought some of the proposals to be extreme, but Brownell went on television to assure the nation there would be no "McCarthyist taint." Two months previously, he had set the stage for the package by announcing the discovery of twenty thousand documents on spies in government "lost" by the Democrats.

M. WESLEY SWEARINGEN

A special agent of the FBI from 1951 to 1977, Swearingen was assigned to Chicago for ten years, where he did "political" work on the internal security detail. His duties included surveillance, illegal break-ins, and maintenance of the Security Index—a list of Americans to be placed in concentration camps during time of "declared national emergency." For more on the FBI, read Swearingen's *FBI Secrets* (South End Press).

For about five years, from shortly after I arrived in Chicago, I was doing illegal break-ins—bag jobs, as we call 'em. At that time we picked on the leaders of the Communist Party. When a few of them were indicted under the Smith Act and went underground,[1] then we started picking on people we thought might be contacts, members of the family, relatives, and people we thought might be couriers.

First we'd get permission from Washington to do a survey. That amounted to finding out where the person lived, whether it was an apartment building or a private residence, whether the landlord or superintendent was cooperative, and whether we knew the hours that the person would be away from their apartment—and how many people lived there. If someone was sharing an apartment with someone else then we'd have to do an investigation on them also. Then if everything looked good, we usually got permission from Washington. I don't know if it actually came from Hoover or not, but everything theoretically came from him. It could have come from Clyde Tolson[2] or someone in the Domestic Intelligence Division. We'd go ahead, and if we found something we would photograph it, and if we didn't we'd go on to the next one. But if we found something important, then we might do it again a month later.

We tried to be careful. If there were papers we'd make little sketches, measure the distance of the papers from the edge of the desk and make notes. It became a little easier when Polaroid developed the instant camera. We could take a picture, wait sixty seconds, and we had a picture of how things were arranged on the desk.

We found things like membership lists, or what could be construed as membership lists, and correspondence to some of the fugitives who were in the underground. But never any evidence of anything illegal. Well, of course, the Communist Party was considered subversive—but we never found any evidence of any crimes, it was all political.

I was counting bag jobs for a while. Not all of them involved my going inside, because you take turns. If the case is assigned to you, you have to go inside. You can't dump that on somebody else. There were different kinds of assigned positions—you can be lookout man or you could be involved in surveillance. I figured I was involved in about five hundred bag jobs myself, and that doesn't involve other agents who were doing jobs at the same time. Sometimes our squad had bag jobs going on at the same time, one in one spot and one in another spot. Then there were times that I did as many as three in one day—and quite often. I don't know whether it was

[1]For stories of life in the Communist underground, see "Five Minutes to Midnight."

[2]Clyde Tolson was the assistant director of the Bureau and Hoover's longtime and almost inseparable companion.

my attitude, you know, I was fairly calm, cool, and collected, and I was younger than just about anybody on the squad.

We had a group of twenty-four agents on the squad, and we'd split up in teams of twelve. So if a bag job involved a large family, like William Sennett, for instance, who was married and had two kids, then we would have to follow him to work, and we'd have to follow his wife to work, and we'd have to follow the two kids to school. The two kids went to different schools—one kid went to grade school and the other one was in junior high. We had to make sure that both kids went to school, and that involved at least four agents, two on one and two on the other, and four on the wife and four on Bill, so we got twelve right there. Then you need two or three to go inside and one on the outside, so we're now using men from the other team. If what's left of the other team could do a relatively small bag job, then they could go out and do one while we're doing one on Sennett.

Then there was one person who at times would disappear on us—he would get up early in the morning, or leave at all hours of the day and night—and when we wanted to do a bag job on him, we'd find out that he wasn't home. So we would spread twelve or fifteen agents at the ends of the street, at the subway entrances and exits, and at the various bus stops that he could get off at. We'd do a bag job on his place not knowing where in the hell he is. Which is really touchy, because he could suddenly appear and he's got two minutes to walk from the bus stop or the elevated station to his apartment and so we've got two minutes to collect our papers and get out of there. That was a real tense situation, and not too many people wanted to go in there. Some of the agents turned into alcoholics, a couple of them had real bad cases of ulcer.

Most of us rather enjoyed the excitement. I know I did. You could get an adrenaline high that was fantastic—the thought of doing this without getting caught. We'd go in without our guns and badges and credentials. If we got caught we couldn't say who we were, that was an added thrill. And if we got caught we'd probably be fired. At least that was what we were told, but some of us thought, "We've got twenty-four guys out here, how's Hoover going to fire us?" We were pretty naive, because he'd have fired twenty-four of us without batting an eye and claimed that was a rogue operation out there in Chicago.

None of us worried too much about the illegality, because most of us were veterans from World War Two. Gee, all you had to do is wave a flag and we'd stand up and salute and do all kinds of things. And after the indoctrination we got in training school about communism and the Communist Party and how they were trying to overthrow us, it was like war all over again, just that no one was shooting at anybody yet. We all thought, "This is great, we're defending the country and nobody knows anything about it."

One of the things you'd do on your survey for a bag job, or if you're going to verify a person's employment, is a full field investigation on their neighbors. If we found that the neighbor was a World War Two veteran, we had it made. All we had to do is tell somebody who served in World War Two that the guy next door is a member of the Communist Party and that's all she wrote. The guy would probably go over and help us on a bag job. Any World War Two veteran was one hundred percent, and if he belonged to AMVETS, boy, it was cinched. If we found that the neighbor on the other side of the house had been to a few demonstrations, then we wouldn't even bother approaching him, because we figured the first thing he would do is go tell his neighbor.

SURVEILLANCE

There were two families in Chicago that we had twenty-four-hour surveillance on for a while—relatives of some of the fugitives we were looking for. That was the wives of Fred Fine and Gil Green.[3] I'm sure New York and Los Angeles must have had operations like that too.

Twenty-four-hour surveillance involved a combination of wiretaps on the telephone and a bug in the apartment. If someone left the house at eleven o'clock and they were going to meet someone downtown for lunch at twelve o'clock and then do something else, we would usually go ahead and move into where they were going to have lunch rather than just follow them from the house to downtown, so the surveillance would be more discreet.

In most instances they knew they were being followed. I don't recall ever following any of these Communist Party members who didn't make a U-turn. They'd drive about three or four car lengths and make a U-turn, which shakes everybody up because we're all set up to go in one direction and someone will have to make a move to stay with them. But after a while we got used to that. We just figured that they were going to make a U-turn and set up accordingly.

[3]Fine and Green were two members of the CP leadership convicted and sentenced to prison under the Smith Act. After their appeals were turned down, they were ordered by the Party to jump bail and go underground. Five years later, they surrendered peacefully, again on orders from the Party.

I recall one instance, a real top-secret meeting, where a man got on a subway—actually he was with an informant of ours—and we tried to follow him but we lost him on the subway. Later, the informant said this guy got on and off the subway so many times he lost count.

THE ARREST OF CLAUDE LIGHTFOOT

Claude Lightfoot was the chairman of the Communist Party of Illinois in Chicago. He had been indicted by a grand jury under the Smith Act. I arrested Claude in 1954.[4]

All of our surveillance didn't do anything, it was a stroke of luck that we found Claude. Two agents were driving home one night. They lived over in Hammond, Indiana. They saw this gray Plymouth that we had surveilled for months, maybe even years, that was owned by Sam Kushner, but Bill Sennett and just about anybody would be driving it at different times. Anyway, they recognized the car, so being the good agents that they were, they said we're not going home yet. They made a U-turn and followed it to the south side of Chicago and lost it in traffic. That was a Friday night. Saturday morning we called in the whole security section of the office, about one hundred and twenty-five agents out of two hundred and fifty.

We were paired off and given quadrants, and what we did was drive up and down the alleys and streets until we found the car. After about an hour we found it parked on the south side. We set up a surveillance. About five o'clock that afternoon in the middle of summer, Claude finally came up to the car and got in and drove away. At that time, I had been sitting in a panel truck with no ventilation. It was about ninety degrees outside and about a hundred and fifty in the truck. It got so damned hot that we stripped down to our shorts. We were soaking wet. We called and said, "We can't take this anymore, you're liable to find a couple of corpses in here." So our supervisor came over and drove us down to the gas station, and just about that time Claude hopped in the car and drove away.

Claude was pulled over by the agents near a housing development. So we hop back in the van and run down there. Claude is black, and about the time I get there he's surrounded by all these white agents. We didn't have any black agents back then, only chauffeurs in Washington and a chauffeur who was a clerical employee in Chicago that was black, but he wasn't an

[4]In January 1955, Lightfoot was convicted of being a member of the CP while knowing it advocated the violent overthrow of the government. His sentence of five years in prison and a $5,000 fine was upheld by the Supreme Court in 1956, then dismissed in a second appeal in 1961.

agent. Anyway, Claude is standing there in this housing development and they're having a little discussion. I walk up and say, "What's going on?" [Chuckles.] Claude is a fugitive—you don't stand around and discuss the time of day with a fugitive, you throw those handcuffs on him. Claude turned to me and said, "These guys said that I looked like somebody who just left an apartment where there was a burglary."

I couldn't believe it. I pulled out my credentials and said, "Claude, I'm Special Agent M. Wesley Swearingen. You're under arrest for violation of the Smith Act." Claude just kind of wilted. I handcuffed him and we marched him off to a car and took him to the office.

One of the things you were supposed to do is search him. I searched Claude in the housing development to make sure he didn't have a gun or a knife. When we got back to the office, I made him empty his pockets, took everything out, and wrote up an inventory. Agents were standing around like it was some kind of a news event, and I wasn't getting too much assistance. I was a relatively young agent, but all these guys that had been sniffing around watching Communists all these years were afraid to let anybody know who they were, that's how paranoid they were. They were afraid the Communist Party would get their name. I don't know what they were afraid of, maybe that the Communist Party was going to do some of the things to them that we were doing to the Communist Party, like go down and break into their house or maybe threaten their kids. When I signed the inventory, the dollars and cents and everything that was in Claude's wallet, I needed a witness. I turned around and I couldn't get another agent to witness that thing.

There must have been half a dozen agents there who had witnessed everything, because it was a big event in their life—it was the first time they had ever arrested anybody. At that point I was fairly disgusted. Claude could see right away how things were going and he says, "Gee, I think you're short . . ." I forget how much he said. I said, "Come on, Claude, this is between you and me. You decide how much money you had when you came in here, and I'll change it, then I'll go ahead and take the money out of my pocket, but you and I are going to sign this thing even though we can't get anybody else in here to sign it." And he laughed, he said, "Okay, that's the right dollar amount."

HARASSMENT OF REDS

COINTELPRO[5] started in 1956, and some guys felt that since they had a badge and were doing what Hoover wanted them to do, they could do just about anything. Some of the guys on surveillance would put sugar in the gas tank, which really louses it up. I never wanted to do that, because you screw up somebody's car and all they're going to do is break down and sit there and then *you* have to sit there. So I thought that was kinda dumb. But this is the kind of sick, sadistic thing that some guys would like to do.

I would do what you would consider COINTELPRO. If I had someone working someplace and it was a fairly good job, if I had the inclination I might get them fired. But then again, if it was a place that was fairly secure and I knew where they were, I might just decide to leave them there. We had requirements when someone changed their employment—we'd have to go and find them again, and that's always a problem. They might stay for five or ten years in a good-paying job.

And there were those subjects who worked in what was considered national security plants. Most of the major corporations that had government contracts fell into that category. I felt it was better to have someone working where you could check on them through security. In those large corporations, the security agents were usually former FBI agents. So you had a perfect source who could watch this person.

We would tell security that so-and-so is a member of the Communist Party, but we don't want you to fire him. We'd like you to keep an eye on him and if we get word that he might try to sabotage something, we'll let you know right away. Most of the time I would do that. Of course, if you got someone who was just a miserable personality—antisocial and antiestablishment: he didn't like Hoover, didn't like the FBI, didn't like the U.S. government—then you might pick on him and get him fired all the time. Every time he gets a new job you go in and tell them that this guy's really

---

[5]Hoover's counterintelligence program gave official sanction to "disrupt, disorganize and neutralize" chosen targets. The first was the CPUSA, practically moribund by this date with fewer than five thousand members, some fifteen hundred of whom were FBI informants. The many tactics used included planted news stories alleging criminal conduct; anonymous letters and phone calls disseminating derogatory information, real or manufactured; hang-up calls, lockstep surveillance, and intrusive photography; on-the-job-site interviews; the questioning of teachers (if the target had children) and the questioning of the parents of the children's friends; IRS audits; and planted evidence which would result in arrests. As new perceived threats emerged—the civil rights movement, the New Left, and black nationalism—COINTELPRO grew more violent, with talk of poisoning children, the sanctioning and encouragement of assassinations, and even murder.

dangerous and if anything happens he's liable to sabotage the plant. That's all they have to hear and they'll figure out some way to get rid of him.

I felt, and most of the agents felt, that Communists were the scum of the earth. Our attitude was if they don't like it here they can go someplace else, and that was that. But after a while, when I was following Bill Sennett around and looking in his place all the time, I thought to myself—and even mentioned to others after a few years—"You know, if he quit and went to work, he could really make a lot of money because he's a hard worker." The hours he put in for the Communist Party were just unbelievable, and he was intelligent and made a good appearance.

Then later on, when we weren't doing so many bag jobs and I was a case agent on Richard Criley[6] and Claude Lightfoot and Bill Sennett and a bunch of the others, I'm reading their speeches and what they write and listening to what they say, and I'm thinking, "Gee, this isn't all that bad. They want equal rights in the union for minorities and blacks and equal pay for women. What the hell is wrong with this?" And I couldn't find that anybody was breaking any laws. Maybe someone would get a parking ticket, but that happens to anybody, except Hoover, because he didn't drive his own car so he was never responsible for overtime parking. As far as I could see, they just wanted to have things a little bit better and that's all.

That was the start of my disillusionment. And as it went on, I thought I'd better not say anything to anybody because they're going to look at me cross-eyed. Once in a while I might get a sympathetic ear and then somebody would say, "Yeah, but they're still trying to overthrow the government by force and violence." But I could never see where their force and violence was coming from. There was never any evidence of it. They didn't go out and march and demonstrate like the Weathermen did in 1969 in Chicago.[7] It would be easy to believe that they might do something like that, but the police departments could pretty well handle just about any small groups. So in a practical sense they weren't about to overthrow anybody. Get themselves thrown in jail was about the extent of it.

[6]Richard Criley was a founding member of the National Committee to Abolish HUAC. See his story under "The Fight Against HUAC."

[7]What is now known as the "Days of Rage" began on October 8, 1969, when in reaction to the previous year's police riot at the Democratic convention, up to three hundred of the renegade Weatherman faction of Students for a Democratic Society gathered in Chicago's Lincoln Park. Armored in protective clothing and armed with clubs and pipes, the Weathermen set out to do battle with more than two thousand of the city's tough and reactionary police force. When the dust settled four days later, six of the radicals had been shot, 250 arrested, and most of them soundly clubbed. Seventy-five cops were injured.

INFORMANTS

There were a couple of real good ones. Morris Childs[8] was the best informant in Chicago. He was said to be the courier between Moscow and the Party. In fact, he was such a high-level informant that if we got word over the wiretaps that somebody like Claude Lightfoot was going to meet with him, we had to discontinue the surveillance. We were not permitted to go anywhere near Childs on surveillance. It made him nervous, and we didn't want anyone to know we were aware of him.

He was being paid more as an informant than I was as an agent! In fact, I think he was paid double what my salary was. In '52, '53, I was making about fifty-five hundred dollars, which wasn't too bad. I think he was probably making ten or eleven thousand dollars a year, or maybe twelve, as an informer. Childs was definitely reliable, and one of the ways that we could check would be information from other informants. Of course, when you couldn't corroborate it, you had to just hope he's not giving you a con job.

We had a program developing informants, and it got so that at one point we had three informants in a three-man cell[9] in Chicago. We had informants reporting on informants. It was ridiculous. Of course, when that cell met with another cell and there was only one informant in the other cell, then we had four informants we could compare information on. When six people met or if a dozen people met, we might have seven or eight informants and we could see how accurate they were. So if we had one informant that was giving us a bunch of crap, then we'd just discontinue him and go someplace else.

I'd say toward the late fifties—along about 1960 and from then on—probably close to fifty percent of the Chicago Party were FBI informants. It went way up, about three out of five in the higher levels of the Party. I'm not going to mention any names, 'cause I'm not allowed to. So you can guess from here on out.

Starting after World War Two, I'd say for thirty years, we knew everything that was going on inside the Party, except maybe when somebody

[8]For twenty-eight years, Jack and Morris Childs, double agents extraordinary, fed information to the FBI. As couriers between the American CP and the Soviet Union, they reportedly channeled $1 million of Soviet funds a year into Party coffers.

[9]When selected elements of the Party went underground in 1950 and 1951, those in hiding were organized into units of three to five members, with only one member having knowledge of the membership in the next-higher unit. For more on the Communist underground, see "Five Minutes to Midnight."

goes to the bathroom. I'm being ridiculous at this point, but whatever's going on in the Party, we knew.

HOOVER'S FANTASY

You have to understand that Hoover was obsessed with what he called "commonism," and he couldn't even pronounce the word properly. When someone is that fanatic, if you want to keep your job, you just go along with it. You tell him what he wants to hear, make him happy. A lot of agents weren't going to do that, so they were quitting. One time in the mid to late fifties when Hoover gave the percentage of turnover in the FBI, I sat down and figured out if no one else in the FBI quit except the ones that I knew were quitting in Chicago—which was one or two a week—the figure would be larger than what Hoover was giving in Congress. And I knew that agents were leaving New York like crazy, because New York was one of the offices you could get to after about a year or two in the FBI. So if there were that many vacancies being filled in New York and the New York agents weren't going to Memphis or Louisville or other places, then they must be resigning.

It was a period of such hysteria. I think it was all generated by Hoover and his sycophants who wanted to rise in the Bureau and would do whatever he wanted. Of course, we had an indoctrination and training school—they gave us practically two weeks of lectures about the Communist threat. So everyone was adequately brainwashed. The only ones who didn't believe it, I guess, were the ones doing criminal work—they could care less.

They thought a lot of that was bullshit. Like Bill Roemer, who has written two books on the Mafia. We used to do bag jobs together, from 1954 to about 1957. He was thoroughly disgusted. He wanted to get on the Top Hood program[10] and start putting these gangsters in jail, which he did. There were others that transferred. In fact, I'd say about seventy-five percent of what ended up being the Top Hood squad in 1959 came from

[10]The Top Hoodlum program was inaugurated in November 1957, just days after Hoover had been disastrously upstaged by a state trooper in Apalachin, New York. The attentive trooper had noted an unusual number of long black limousines pulling into the gates of a nearby estate. What he had detected, and later disrupted, was a convocation of more than one hundred of the most powerful organized crime figures in America. For more than three decades, Hoover had assured America that no such organization existed. Not only did the Bureau not know the mobsters were going to meet, they didn't even know who they were. The FBI could not identify any of the sixty-two arrested, including Vito Genovese, Joseph Bonanno, and Santos Trafficante.

the Security Division, because guys were just fed up with Hoover's imaginary Communist Party.

But some people, you give them a gun and a badge and they'll work for nothing. It's a little bit like . . . how can I describe it? How can I describe a sheriff in the South who's so fat he can't get his gun belt on, enjoying beating blacks on the side of the head? I don't understand it, but there were agents like that, who just enjoyed it. They had the full backing of Hoover and the FBI, and they were getting paid for it. Some guys are that way. How do you explain people in the Gestapo?

SECURITY INDEX

When I got to Chicago in the summer of '52, the Security Index was already well under way—that was a list of people to arrest in case of some national emergency.[11] And you know a national emergency could have been just about anything that somebody like Richard Nixon wanted to make. Then Eisenhower signed Executive Order 10450, which put a lot of people on the Security Index who were members of the Communist Party—although 10450 doesn't say that, that's the way it was interpreted—and the Attorney General's list of organizations. So we had a writing project that took us away from bag jobs for a few months because we were literally putting thousands of people on the Security Index.

You know, when FBI officials testified before the Church Committee[12] they said, "At one point we had fifteen thousand people on the Security Index." Expressing it like that you get the feeling that at one point we had as many as fifteen thousand. But that's like saying that when you're filling up Soldier Field for a football game, at some point you have fifteen thousand in the stadium. But wait a few minutes and you've got several thousand more. This is the way the FBI gives the information to Congress, and Congress doesn't know what the hell they're saying. They think: "Well, at

[11]A secret Hoover kept from Congress and the public, the Security Index dated from 1939 and was originally dubbed the Custodial Detention list. Along with aliens and citizens of "German, Italian, and Communist sympathies," radical labor leaders, writers and journalists critical of the administration and the FBI, and certain members of Congress all graced Hoover's austere atlas. In 1943, Attorney General Biddle discovered its existence and ordered Hoover to abolish it. Hoover did so by changing its name to the Security Index, then ordered that it be kept a secret from the Justice Department. Later, Congress provided Hoover a patina of legality with the passage of the Internal Security Act of 1950. Along with other draconian provisions, the act provided for concentration camps in times of national emergency to detain without trial anyone who had been a member of the CP since January 1, 1949.

[12]The Senate Select Committee on Intelligence Activities, 1975–76, chaired by Frank Church (D–Idaho).

some point that's the maximum that we had," which is not true. At some point we had fifteen thousand—leading up to a hundred thousand.

If we did a bag job and we came across a list of names that didn't say "membership" at the top but you could interpret it as possibly membership, then to be on the safe side we'd say, "Yeah, this is probably membership," and we'd go with it from there. Or we'd say something like T-1, of known reliability, advises on such-and-such a date that so-and-so's name was in possession of the Communist Party. And if we had positive information like Morris Childs saying that so-and-so is a member of the Communist Party, that's good, he gets on the Security Index and he's on there forever.

During the Church Committee hearings, one of the senators asked James Adams, who was then associate director of the FBI, how long a person would stay on the Security Index. I think they were talking about one individual who had been on there something like twenty or twenty-five years. And the senator said, "Did you have any information that he was still a member of the Communist Party?" And Adams's response was, "We didn't have any information that he was *not* a member of the Communist Party." Which means that if some informant doesn't tell us that this guy dropped out of the Communist Party, then we'd keep him in there and we'd keep him on the Security Index. Sometimes we would get information that someone did drop out of the Communist Party, but we wouldn't believe it anyway. Bill Sennett stayed on the Security Index almost ten years after he quit the Party because no one would believe it.

We had what was considered an active Security Index, then we had a Reserve Index. We had a list of about a hundred thousand people just in Chicago. The Reserve Index was a list of people who had been around for a long time but we didn't have anything real current on them. In order not to get the Security Index so large that we couldn't handle it, we'd put them on the Reserve Index. After we round up all the ones that were considered a real threat, then we'd go after these other people.

How many in the country altogether? I suppose there was an equal number on both lists in San Francisco, Los Angeles, maybe close to the same number in Detroit, maybe double or triple the number in New York City. Altogether, possibly close to a million people, if we really got down to the nitty-gritty. But the practical point of view is that we couldn't have put a million people anyplace. But we probably had names on or information on that many people that we could have, but that was one of the reasons that we watched the size of the actual Security Index in Chicago, because we knew that it would be a matter of logistics. You can't go out and arrest a hundred thousand people. There weren't enough FBI agents and police officers in Chicago to do that. So we had to keep the Security Index at a reasonable level.

We knew definitely we would be rounding people up when Khrushchev was banging his shoe on the table. During the Cuban missile crisis, we were within a hairbreadth of actually activating a roundup. We knew darn well that when the first missile comes flying from Cuba, we're going to be out there throwing people in a camp. We didn't have any orders, it was just the general atmosphere, and of course if a national emergency had been declared, then we would not have waited for anything else. It would have just been a matter of getting a phone call from someone like Alan Belmont in the Domestic Intelligence Division to put the Security Index program into effect, which meant that we'd pull all the cards from the geographical areas; we'd get hold of the local police officers and we'd go out and start arresting people. I don't know where in Chicago we were going to throw them. One time, I figured out the only place we could put so many people would be in Soldier Field.

The government still has a form of this program which they now call the Administrative Index, which was created out of the pressure exerted from Congress and the Church Committee. The legal authority for the Security Index expired in 1971, or something like that, but the FBI was not going to give it up. Then when the Church Committee started their investigation, headquarters realized, uh-oh, we've got problems, so we had better take these people off the Security Index and call this something else. So when Kelley was director,[13] we had a program of culling the names of what you might call the most revolutionary from the Security Index and putting them on the Administrative Index, the ADEX. The Attorney General ordered the remaining names from the Security Index destroyed, but they weren't.

The agent that testified before the Church Committee that there was no way that they could make up a list of the names that had been deleted perjured himself, because what we did was take the names from the Security Index, stamp them "Canceled" with a date, and put them in a different file cabinet. So we didn't throw any of the cards away, they were just in the file cabinet next to the ADEX, and if anything happens, all we have to do is go pull them out.

And of course Congress didn't know that we had those, because they

---

[13]Clarence Kelley, a twenty-one-year veteran of the Bureau (1940–61), was the third permanent director after the death of Hoover in 1972.

assumed that they were all destroyed. We were playing the same old game that Hoover was doing back in the forties and fifties with the Attorney General, he didn't tell him anything. So when we were canceling the Security Index, we didn't tell Congress that we took them out of one drawer and put them in another. Congress would have had a fit had they known it—and they still don't know it now.

WHAT WAS GAINED

In Chicago, fifty percent of our work was political. We had two hundred and fifty agents. Half of them were on the security squads and half of them were on the criminal squads. We had five security squads and five criminal squads, so there are about twenty-five men per squad, it was right down the middle.

I can't think of anything we uncovered during those ten years that was worthwhile in terms of national security. About the most productive thing I did was arrest Claude Lightfoot, and then the Supreme Court said the Smith Act was unconstitutional, so what was that? During all that time that was the only arrest I made. It strikes me now, and it struck me then after a few years, that it was a waste of time and a waste of taxpayers' money. But it contributed to my total years of retirement and pension, so you look back and it's not all that bad, because I have a real nice retirement. But that's about the only benefit I can see out of it. Of course, some people say we kept the Communist Party in check; well, I don't know if we did that.

HARVEY JOB MATUSOW

Three years after he joined the Communist Party in 1947, Harvey Matusow dropped a nickel into a public phone and dialed the FBI. He offered to become an informer. He was soon one of the Justice Department's top professional witnesses, with a flair for publicity that brought him national celebrity. He campaigned for Senator Joe McCarthy, dined at the Stork Club with J. Edgar Hoover, and even married a millionaire. Less than three years later, Matusow publicly confessed that the testimony which had damned so many had been a complete fabrication. The Justice Department struck back, charging Matusow's recantation to be a Communist plot to malign the professional witness program. Eventually, Matusow was convicted of perjury—not for his previous falsehoods, but for his disavowal of them. He served four years in Lewisburg Federal Penitentiary. He now runs a private shelter for the homeless in Tucson, Arizona.

We had an association of professional witnesses, the Federation of Former Communists, literally a club where we could get together—for mutual protection, really.[1] A good part of society didn't like what we did in a very heavy way. So it was a question of fighting off the attacks. Let's say that Paul Crouch[2] was being attacked by so-and-so because of some stuff on the stand. So we'd get together, "Oh, so-and-so, yeah, I knew him." And we'd figure out how we could counterattack and help each other.

I was not as well known nationally as Herbert Philbrick,[3] because he had the TV series *I Led Three Lives,* and Matt Cvetic[4] had *I Was a Communist for the FBI,* the film and TV series. They were the superheroes because movies were made about them, but I was the only young informer.[5] The government witnesses of the time were all in their forties, fifties, and sixties. And here I came along, a young war veteran who served well during World War Two. My field was mainly youth. It was what people wanted to hear about, youth—and the media, because I'd been a member of the Newspaper Guild. Nobody until I came on the scene talked about the Communist entrapment of youth. Which was all rubbish anyway.

[1]But also with an eye to achieving higher status, recognition, and fees.

[2]Paul Crouch, who claimed to have left the Party in 1942 after seventeen years, was one of the more brazen liars in the business. Claiming to be a confidant of the Soviet Union's top military leaders, Crouch entranced gullible congressional investigators with tales of an anticipated Red Army landing in Florida and his own complicity in a Russian plot to subvert the entire U.S. military establishment. It was this astonishing revelation, according to Roy Cohn, that set off McCarthy's Fort Monmouth investigation.

[3]Herbert Philbrick was perhaps the best-known of the professional ex-Communists. After years as an FBI mole, he surfaced in 1949 at the first Smith Act trial to help convict eleven members of the Party leadership. His television series was taken from his autobiography of the same title and portrayed the Communists as plotting to sabotage factories, smuggle drugs, and subvert America's youth. Up to a few years before his death in 1993, Philbrick continued to lecture on such topics as "The Red Underground Today" and "Christianity versus Communism."

[4]Matt Cvetic joined the Communist Party in 1943 on behalf of the FBI and emerged in 1950. He was destined to appear as a witness at least sixty-three times and name more than five hundred people. See Steve Nelson under "The Fall of the Communist Party" for more on Cvetic.

[5]Matusow was twenty-four in 1950.

My attacks on Pete Seeger and the Weavers,[6] the whole folk song movement, you know, "It's a way of trapping the youth." Nursery rhymes, folk songs, square dances, I never believed what I was doing. The stuff's not believable. But the McCarthy forces, and particularly the Hearst newspapers, took advantage of it and made a media blitz of it.

There were high school assemblies that were convened for me to talk about Communism and young people. We were media heroes. I remember in Montana I spoke at a drive-in movie between the films. I was the advertised guest speaker. They had me on the microphone and they were showing the film *My Son John*,[7] with Robert Walker. In 1952, television was not that big; I did a tremendous number of radio talk shows across the country. So among the informers, I was very well known.

I was very easily attracted to the Communist movement. When I came home in '46, a year after the war ended, the Communist movement took all the altruistic feelings I had and directed it in a way that I felt comfortable. But it wasn't long before I discovered that the Communist movement was as weird as any other movement, and politics was politics, whether it was Communist, Republican, or whatever. And when the witch hunt started in '47, and '48, when the first indictments came down on the Communist Party, I found it inconceivable that I was asked to go underground.[8] I didn't believe in it, and that was where my break with the Communist Party came. Basically, that's why Joe McCarthy and I got on well, because we had that same morality. If you're going to be something, be up front about it, or don't be it at all.

In 1950, when I contacted the FBI and became a double agent, I was a street kid covering my bet on both sides. That's another way of looking at it, and I can detach and see that. Here also I was this very bright dyslexic kid who was totally miserable because I couldn't make it to college. The frustration that I had at that point in my life was beyond belief. When I was a kid in high school my IQ was 150 and I couldn't write an English sentence.

---

[6]For another view of Matusow, see Fred Hellerman and Ronnie Gilbert under "Troubadours of the Left."

[7]An amusing but deranged Hollywood melodrama made in 1952. The beloved son of an all-American family is revealed to be a secret Communist. Through the love of his careworn mother, he sees his errors and sets off to confess to the FBI—only to be gunned down by vengeful Red agents. Director Leo McCarey, himself a friendly witness before HUAC in 1947, headed a movement to have all members of the Directors Guild sign a loyalty oath.

[8]The Party sent dedicated elements of its secondary leadership underground. According to his book and others' accounts, Matusow's Party work appears to have been confined to circulating petitions and selling the *Daily Worker*. See "Five Minutes to Midnight" for more on the Communist underground.

The only way I got out of high school in 1943 was to join the Army in my senior year. I was failing everything.

This was also one way for acceptance in the higher plane of American life. I'm a twenty-four-year-old high school dropout and the leaders of the country are getting advice from me as to how to run the country? I had U.S. senators, members of the cabinet, coming to me for advice. It was surreal. I lived in a house in Washington with twenty-six rooms that's now the German ambassador's residence. Every week we had leaders of the country coming to our dinners. A few years earlier, I'd been working for a bookie in the Bronx and now I'm dealing with the power brokers of America and the world? As long as I played this charade, I had access to this power, and it was hard to walk away from.

But another thing happened—and this was not part of *False Witness*.[9] The Communists talked about the underground movement in France, how they had infiltrated the Nazis and worked to undermine them. And these discussions sat heavy on my heart and my intellect. I had a Walter Mitty fantasy that I was going to gather material on the right wing by infiltrating it as the French Communists had infiltrated the Nazis. When I contacted the McCarthy forces and all the people I'd worked for on the Right, I used to take stuff from their files, and that's how I was able to write *False Witness*. I collected this huge amount of documentation because I knew someday I was going to drop the shoe. Now, I can't say now whether that fantasy was a moral justification that I gave myself for what I did. I don't know, because the mind is a strange thing, and I can't really go back and say, "This is exactly what I did," because I was a kind of free spirit. I still am, that's the one consistency in my life. I think the total amount I got paid in all the time I was an informer was under two thousand dollars.[10] But remember, I married a woman who had millions of dollars.[11] I didn't need that money. The money I got as an informer I usually gave away. I never did it for the money. I did it for psychological reasons. I don't do anything for money.

I met Hoover a couple of times, had dinner with him one night at the

[9]Attacked by Attorney General Brownell as a Red plot, *False Witness* (New York: Cameron and Kahn, 1955) is Matusow's chronicle of his intrigues and fabrications as a professional witness. For more on *False Witness*, see Angus Cameron under "Arts and Entertainment."

[10]Matusow testified at the trial of Clinton Jencks that in 1952 he had made $10,000 as a professional ex-Communist. This would be the equivalent of $47,000 today.

[11]His bride was Arvilla Bentley, a wealthy contributor to Joe McCarthy's anti-Communist campaign, who was subpoenaed concerning a $10,000 donation that purchased soybean futures instead of a Red-free America. At the request of McCarthy, Harvey spirited the woman out of the country.

Stork Club, with Roy Cohn[12] and Walter Winchell.[13] I used to hang out with Winchell a lot and ride around in his Caddy when he went out chasing police calls. But that dinner was surreal. I guess we were talking about Communists and anti-Communists and all that garbage. The conversation was nothing, all stereotypes and clichés. I had a social life with Cohn. I used to go out on double dates with him. He was more than just the attorney, you know, we were two kids from the Bronx.

See, Hoover and Cardinal Spellman[14] and Cohn were part of a kind of closet gay group. Cohn's rise to political power came because of his gay relationship with Cardinal Spellman. It was a high-level group of closet gays who kind of kept to themselves. If you look at Nazi Germany, there was a similar group in Germany that built the Nazi Party.

There were three different parts to my job. There was the category "Who did you know to be a Communist? We want their name and your associations with them." Then there was "We're going to feed stuff into the record through you, even though you had no knowledge of it." And three, be an investigator and just sort of dig up stuff and find other witnesses for them.

I made a rule of thumb. I never volunteered a name they didn't already have. And it was very easy to give testimony, like when the FBI called me in and they'd say, "Do you know John Doe?"

"John Doe?"

"Yeah, he hangs around in the Tompkins Square area."

"Oh yeah, I know John Doe."

"Do you know Mary Doe?"

And then they'd give me a little background. Of course I knew John and Mary Doe. But unless I knew they knew the people, I didn't know them. There are many people who I never named, 'cause my rule was only tell them what they knew.[15] It was easy to con them into believing that I was

[12]Equally loathed and respected, Roy Cohn began his career with his role in the Rosenbergs' trial, as chief counsel for Joe McCarthy, and through his friendship with J. Edgar Hoover. Notorious as a power broker to a host of media barons, mobsters, politicians, and glitterati, Cohn's habitual disregard for ethical niceties led to numerous indictments and professional misconduct charges. He was finally disbarred shortly before his death from AIDS in 1986.

[13]Walter Winchell was an inveterate Red-baiter and one of America's most fabled newspapermen. His gossip column and radio show were conduits for much misinformation leaked by his friend J. Edgar Hoover.

[14]Francis Cardinal Spellman stood at the head of the American Catholic hierarchy. The cardinal frequently taxed the Truman administration with "appeasement" of the American Communists.

[15]Matusow is credited with turning over 216 names to the Justice Department. While he

giving them fresh information. They were naive. At one time I said I knew ten thousand Communists, and nobody knew ten thousand people as Communists. But they never questioned it. When I said there were one hundred and twenty-five Communists working for the Sunday *Times,* and the Sunday *Times* only employed ninety-two people, they never questioned it. I was able to give them the names of seven or eight Communists that I knew, 'cause I'd been in the Newspaper Guild, but they had those names anyway.

A good example: because I was involved in youth, the committee wanted to get headlines; so they found out that in 1926, the year I was born, the Communist Party had set forth a plan to infiltrate the Boy Scouts. They had some documentation, some leaflets and other bullshit, and that's all there was. So the House Committee on Un-American Activities research director, Benjamin Mandel, gave me the documents. He said, "We want to enter this into the record." So when I testified and committee members asked me about the Boy Scouts, I pulled out the documents and said, "Well, the Communists attempted to infiltrate the Boy Scouts." Now the next day, there were headlines across the country, stating that the Communists are infiltrating the Boy Scouts. And nowhere in those stories did it make reference to the fact that this was something that happened a quarter of a century earlier.[16]

The committee used witnesses like me to help beat the drums and bring the tempo up to where people would be afraid. So the naming of names was almost a minimal part of your testimony. It was more working with the committee counsels—people like Roy Cohn or Donald T. Appel, the committee investigator who found the Pumpkin Papers[17]—in bringing up stuff

---

claims to have named only those the FBI already knew, his book *False Witness* suggests differently. "My first reports were oral. They . . . included names, addresses, and telephone numbers of college students, working youth, secretaries, and others. . . . The FBI wanted the physical descriptions of my friends. . . . I took pictures of individuals and identified them at the FBI office." (p. 30)

[16]"Witnesses Bare Red Plot to Infiltrate Boy Scouts" was the headline on the *Syracuse Herald-Journal* of August 13, 1952. The only documents mentioned are pamphlets from 1930 promoting the Young Pioneers as a rival organization to the Scouts. Matusow named Don West, a Baptist clergyman and "Communist organizer" who had organized Scout troops in his churches—thus "infiltration."

[17]The Pumpkin Papers were the bombshell of the Alger Hiss espionage case. They turned up in a superb bit of theatrics one night in December 1948. Whittaker Chambers, Hiss's accuser, led HUAC investigators across his farm to a hollow pumpkin, and from it he extracted five rolls of microfilm. They were said to be secret government documents passed to Chambers by Hiss. Richard Nixon, who cut his teeth on the case, hailed the microfilm as "conclusive proof of the greatest treason conspiracy in this nation's history." Twelve of the documents were released a

that the committee members could use to get headlines, like the Boy Scouts.

When I said I knew ten thousand people by sight as Communists, that was an out-and-out lie. But it was never really the question of the out-and-out lie, it was the innuendo, the half-truth, that you built upon. The Mother Goose Rhymes was part of the whole bit. You see, the trade union movement in a couple of campaigns had these nursery rhymes:

"Jack be nimble / Jack be quick / Don't let the poll tax / Make you sick."

"Jack and Jill / Have had their fill / Of congressmen who spurn them / They're making notes / To cast their votes / For men who really earn them."

"Jack Sprat could eat no fat / His wife could eat no lean / Because the Congress done them in / And picked their pockets clean."

Those were the three I quoted. So, instead of saying it was the trade union movement, I said, "The Communists have written these nursery rhymes to corrupt our children." And that made headlines.

The government was naive. They didn't know anything. But look at the government agent, some FBI agent who had trained at Quantico, Virginia, who had no reality to the world. He naively believed whatever any witness told him, 'cause he wanted to believe it. This came out during the Senate hearings in Salt Lake City in the first week of October '52. There was a strike at Kennecott Copper, so in Salt Lake City they arranged to hold hearings of the Senate committee investigating the Mine Mill Smelter Workers Union, and that's where this whole thing came about.

Clinton Jencks[18] had been a Communist. I mean, I never saw his Communist Party card, but Jencks was a Communist.[19] But I used the Jencks case to set the government up. Because in all my contemporaneous reports to the FBI, I said, "I never knew Jencks to be a Communist. I think he's a Communist, but I have no knowledge of it." And then when he went to trial, I said, "I knew him to be a Communist."[20] The result was the Jencks

---

week later, and found to be rather anticlimactic; the rest were not published or produced at Hiss's trial for "security reasons." See Alger Hiss under "A Graveyard of Careers."

[18]Clinton Jencks was an organizer for the International Mine, Mill and Smelter Workers Union in northern New Mexico. See his story under "Breaking the Working Class."

[19]In front of a grand jury, Matusow testified that during a stay at a vacation ranch in New Mexico, Jencks had revealed to him his Party membership, thus Jencks was liable for perjury on his Taft-Hartley oath. On the strength of Matusow's testimony, Jencks was convicted and sentenced to five years in prison. There is no evidence that Jencks was a Communist.

[20]In a hearing on the motion for a new trial after his recantation, Matusow did tell the trial judge that his original reports to the FBI would show that he never identified Jencks as a Party

case, the Supreme Court decision which was the first thing that opened up the door for Freedom of Information and the mandatory disclosure of evidence held by the prosecution that might help the defendant.[21]

This thing about sabotaging the Korean War effort by going on strike in the copper mines, that was kind of fabricated. Oh, Jencks and I did talk about stuff like that, you know, if there's a strike the Korean War effort could be sabotaged.[22] It was just small talk. And the committee wanted me to say that. It didn't come from Jencks. It was the desire of the committee for me to say that the Communists planned to have a copper strike to sabotage the Korean War effort. We'd be sitting down, having dinner or coffee, and just talking.

"Well, how can you do it?"

I'd say, "Well, obviously they want to sabotage the war effort."

"Well, say it."

Just as when Cohn was preparing the Smith Act case against Trachtenberg,[23] who was head of International Publishing, and he wanted to introduce the book *The Law of the Soviet State* by Vishinsky.[24] He said, "Did you ever discuss it with him?" And I said, "Well, we discussed every book that they published." He said, "What do you mean?" Well, I worked in the bookstore and Trachtenberg would come in at least twice a week and since I was one of the clerks he'd ask me, like any publisher, "How's our book selling?" So I discussed the book with him, and on that we built a fabrication that he discussed the book with me. And that was all Cohn needed to introduce the book into evidence. Because Vishinsky in the book talked about the force that will overthrow the government—that was the basis of convicting Trachtenberg.[25]

---

member. Yet in *False Witness* (p. 192) he quotes a statement he gave to the FBI in October 1951, prior to his first public testimony: "Jenks [sic] told me he was a party member." He goes on to say that he lied to the FBI.

[21]Armed with Matusow's recantation, Jencks appealed for a new trial and was denied. The Supreme Court later ordered a new trial at which the original FBI reports were to be opened to the defense.

[22]Matusow made front-page headlines with this fabrication: "Charge Jencks Hit War Effort"; "Ex-Spy Vows Red Bosses Ordered Copper Strike." In his interview, Jencks denies talking to Matusow about much of anything.

[23]Alexander Trachtenberg, owner and publisher of International Publishers, a press close to the Party, on trial in the second round of Smith Act cases.

[24]Andrei Vishinsky, Soviet diplomat and author of a reportedly leaden tome. Vishinsky first came to international attention as the chief prosecutor in the Great Purge trials of 1934–38.

[25]Matusow testified that Trachtenberg had urged him to promote the sale of Andrei Vi-

See, I didn't lie. He did discuss the book with me. And that's why Trachtenberg was one of the two defendants to get released, get a new trial. The people who my testimony was material to all were released. The reality is, I'm the only person that went to jail for anything I did. Nobody else.[26]

The president of Queens College, John Jacob Theobald,[27] came to my house, and I would talk to him about how the Communist teachers worked. It was all bullshit, but he wanted to hear it. I'm sure he used it to fire some people.[28] But even to this day, I have to tell you, I don't see economic deprivation as pain. I don't see that as being hurt. I mean, if you're hung up on the material world, then it's pain. If your world isn't based on that, they can't hurt you with it. And mine has never been based on the economy, because it's a charade. That's why I can live the way I do now, communally. I'm still a Communist, 'cause I believe communal living is the finest thing that we can do.

During the '52 primary campaign, McCarthy was ill. He'd ruptured his diaphragm and had this operation. And his staff was panicked because they really wanted some people to feed the flames. I think it was somebody at the Hearst organization who suggested to the McCarthy staff that I go out and fill in for most of his major speaking engagements in Wisconsin.[29] I was contacted and went down to Washington and met some of his staff people, his wife-to-be, Jean Kerr, and they set up a series of speeches for me. My first one was to be in Green Bay, that was the test, and the McCarthy people were out to monitor how the speech was received, and it was very

shinsky's *The Law of the Soviet State,* asserting it contained directives for the overthrow of capitalism. Thus, the prosecution was able to tie the hapless publisher to an expression for the need to "overthrow," therefore conspiracy, and hence convict and sentence him to three years in prison.

[26]In the second Smith Act trial of April 1952, discussed above, Matusow appeared as one of three professional witnesses against the Party leaders. His job, according to *False Witness,* was to implicate "each defendant." These thirteen people did indeed go to jail. They received sentences ranging from one to five years. Three years later, on the weight of Matusow's confession, only two, Trachtenberg and George Charny, were granted new trials. Both were again convicted.

[27]Theobald once explained to a discharged teacher, "The Board of Higher Education does not discharge teachers; rather the teacher by his own act in refusing to testify thereby brings about a termination of his employment."

[28]See Oscar Shaftel under "Red-ucators."

[29]According to *False Witness,* it was Matusow, swelled with his success at the Smith Act trial, who went to McCarthy's campaign headquarters and volunteered his services to Jean Kerr. As McCarthy was already out of the hospital, there was no need for Matusow to fill in Joe's speaking engagements.

well received. After that I spoke in Madison and Milwaukee and Wausau and Ashland and all over the state. The speeches were very successful, and the McCarthy people attributed a lot of the energy toward helping him win that primary to my work.

I'd never met McCarthy at this point; he was in the hospital.[30] So one day his campaign manager, Urban Van Siesteran, said, "Would you like to meet Joe? He's coming out of the hospital." He said, "We'll be at the hotel. Why don't you come by at three o'clock?" What I didn't know when I got to the hotel was that McCarthy didn't like other people to answer his phone. He always answered his own phone. And frequently he'd put on a voice and make believe it wasn't him, it was just one of his ways. So I called the room and asked for Urban Van Siesteran and I recognized McCarthy's voice. He said, "Who wants to speak to him?" and I said, "This is Harvey Matusow." "Are you the Harvey Matusow making speeches for Joe McCarthy?" "Yeah, I'm making speeches for that fascist son of a bitch!" And he broke up laughing. "He called me a fascist son of a bitch!" He repeated that about three or four times. He couldn't stop laughing.

The very first day I met McCarthy, he told me to my face, he said, "You're just like me, Harvey. You're a practical joker, and someday you'll turn on me." After I recanted, he sent word to me—he wouldn't see me directly—in essence, he said, "I know why you're doing it, and it's okay. I don't hate you." He knew why I was doing it.

All right. How did it all end? Well, I was getting bored with it. I had married Arvilla and we talked about it and felt it was best if I pull out. My conscience was starting to get to me, and I started to feel strongly that I had to stop. One day I was real depressed and was sitting in Central Park on Fifth Avenue, near the Jewish Theological Seminary, and engraved up in stone on the wall was the biblical quote "Do justly, love mercy, walk humbly with thy God." It touched me, and I felt that that's what I had to do.

I called up the *New York Times* and met with their correspondent Gladman Hill, and gave them an affidavit saying that I had lied. Now they could have broken the case then, instead of waiting for *False Witness* to come out, but they put my affidavit in their safe and never did anything with it. Then I called up *Time* magazine and gave them a similar affidavit and then I called up the *New York Post* and gave them an affidavit. None of these papers acted on any of my information. I then went to the Communist Party

---

[30]Actually, Matusow met McCarthy on the first day he volunteered at campaign headquarters.

attorneys and said, "I'd like to do something," but they wouldn't talk to me. I went to see Bishop Oxnam,[31] and he finally talked about it. I went down to Washington, where I'd been very friendly with Drew Pearson. I wrote the sample chapter of *False Witness* plus the outline on Jack Anderson's[32] typewriter. Jack Anderson actually helped me with proofreading and stuff.

The fact that I had been to the *New York Times* and *Time* magazine and the *New York Post* and had written the first chapter of the book on Jack Anderson's typewriter long before I met Cameron and Kahn, that undermined any attempts of the government to get a conspiracy indictment against them,[33] which is what they were trying to do.

I believe the FBI wanted to kill me. Hoover wanted me dead. They would've killed me if they'd found me walking down the road. I would've ended up in the desert somewhere.[34] Hoover's had more people killed than you've got fingers on your hands. You ask me what proof I have; I don't have proof. But I know that the FBI was looking for me and every agent in the United States—and in every office, there was a bulletin to find me. The fact that I got to Taos, New Mexico, and I left Taos and the FBI was in Taos looking for me within three hours of my departure.

We could trace it down, and the FBI records show this. They were always: "Where is he? Find him!" I was not wanted for any crime, but Hoover wanted me.

I went to prison because I said Roy Cohn had suborned perjury, that Cohn and I had worked together at fabricating the story of Trachtenberg and *The Law of the Soviet State*. Which is true, Cohn and I did it together. But the government couldn't allow the charge to stand that Cohn had suborned

[31]Bishop G. Bromley Oxnam was a well-known libertarian. He revealed Matusow's recantation in June 1954 at a Baltimore conference of the Methodist Church. After the press picked up the story, Matusow was called before HUAC and questioned. He then backed off, calling Oxnam "a dishonest man."

[32]Drew Pearson and Jack Anderson worked together on Pearson's column, "Washington Merry-Go-Round."

[33]The Justice Department attempted to prove that Angus Cameron and Albert Kahn had bribed Matusow into a conspiracy to recant. *False Witness*, which was published by Cameron and Kahn, was supposedly the fruit of that conspiracy.

[34]After Matusow wrote that first chapter in Anderson's office, he abandoned his book and set off on an eight-hundred-mile bicycle trip across Texas and into New Mexico. By this time, Cameron and Kahn, having heard of Matusow's desire to write a book from the Oxnam report, were trying to reach him through his parents. "But I was in no hurry," wrote Matusow, "and I didn't care if I ever wrote a book."

perjury or had knowledge of my perjury at the stand, so they prosecuted me on perjury charges for saying that. I was innocent of what I went to prison for. Not that I had not committed perjury, but I was completely innocent of that specific act. Cohn knew I'd been lying through my teeth about Trachtenberg, no question about it. He also suborned perjury when he was chief counsel at the McCarthy Committee and he knew I was bullshitting when I said I knew one hundred and twenty-six people working for the *New York Times* who were Communists when only ninety-two people worked on the staff. Today, with Cohn's reputation being what it is, who'd deny my charge? The government never would have prosecuted.

I don't think the McCarthy period is going to be understood until everybody's dead. The Germans still can't look at Hitler, and America has a difficult time looking at the McCarthy period. My friend Bill Duffy said to me three weeks ago, "It makes no difference, anybody who has worked for McCarthy will always be a villain to many people." And I suspect that's true—regardless of what I do and how well I do it, there will be people who totally discredit me. I suspect that long after I'm dead, there'll still be a tremendous amount of hatred toward me. I run into it all the time.

HERBERT BROWNELL, JR.

An attorney at Lord Day & Lord, Barrett Smith for sixty years, Brownell served as campaign manager for Eisenhower's 1952 presidential run and then as Attorney General until 1957.

It was a tough assignment, being Attorney General at the height of the Cold War. I got used to being accused by both sides of being on "the other side" in the continual battles over national security matters. I think McCarthy accused me of Communist tendencies.

There were some excesses in infringing individual rights that had to be stopped. But I think the government had to have a program against Communist aggression. I was convinced of that at the time, given the situation that the Soviets were subsidizing the American Communist Party in cash every month,[1] and no doubt were using people in the government to get classified information—that was proven in a number of cases. The government had to do something to try and stop that kind of infiltration into government circles. It just was an impossible situation where we had to take some defenses. They were tapping our embassies and all that sort of thing, and subverting government employees.

You don't need it today, I don't think, but at that time you had people like Alger Hiss[2] and Harry Dexter White,[3] high government officials who were sending classified information to Russia, and that's pretty serious. But, thank God, with the collapse of communism and all, I can't believe that there's any internal danger anymore from Communist agents.

It's hard to recreate the atmosphere that there was in the forties and fifties. The FBI was into it, committees of both Congresses were in on it, their constant investigations and so forth. It became a political issue, which it never should have, of course, but it did. So by the time the Eisenhower administration got in, it had been one of the great issues in the presidential campaign of '52. It was politicized and was complicated by the fact that McCarthy was so irresponsible and was blowing it up for political purposes. I think he was trying to run for President on it. I always thought so, anyway.

Everybody was relieved when Harvey Matusow recanted.[4] He got himself into a position where, instead of being a witness, paid by the hour or

[1]Communist Party records seized in Moscow in 1991 apparently reveal that from 1960 to 1989 the American Party received up to $2 million a year. For reported Moscow financing in earlier years, see M. Wesley Swearingen, footnote 8, earlier in this chapter.

[2]In 1950, Alger Hiss, a high-ranking and distinguished State Department official, was convicted of two counts of perjury on espionage charges raised by Whittaker Chambers, a former Party member and the sole witness against him. Hiss was sentenced to five years in prison. The case quickly became a totem of the domestic Cold War. See Alger Hiss under "A Graveyard of Careers."

[3]The most senior government official named by Whittaker Chambers was Harry Dexter White, assistant secretary of the Treasury and principal architect of the International Monetary Fund and the World Bank. In 1948, White appeared voluntarily before HUAC and denied all allegations. Three days later, he died of a heart attack. In 1953, Brownell, then Attorney General, publicly charged that Truman had promoted White to the IMF, even though the FBI had informed him that White was a "Communist spy." This exaggeration (Hoover had only referred to unsubstantiated allegations) set off an angry dispute with Truman, who answered with misstatements of his own.

[4]At the time, Brownell proclaimed Matusow's recantation to be part of a "Communist plot" to discredit the Justice Department's "campaign against subversion." In February of 1954, he convened a grand jury to uncover the conspiracy. See Harvey Job Matusow earlier in this chapter and Angus Cameron under "Arts and Entertainment."

something of that sort, he was really on the government payroll.[5] He testified in many of the cases and became somewhat of a stooge of the prosecution. I personally put a stop to that.[6] After I found out what was happening, we never again used him as a witness in any government cases.[7] Some of the convictions his testimony figured in were overthrown on that basis, as they should have been.

The FBI counterintelligence program was set up under an executive order of Franklin D. Roosevelt.[8] There were many civil liberty questions involved. For example, FDR didn't limit the FBI as to the methods it was entitled to use in carrying out his executive order.[9] They went ahead and wiretapped, as it hadn't up to that time been declared illegal. But they went too far in their enforcement tactics, in my opinion, and so when I came in as Attorney General, I tried to get court decisions which would give instructions to the FBI and to all the government agencies as to what means they could use in fighting government subversion and what fair procedural rules there should be, like facing your informers and not using anonymous information to convict anybody.[10] It gradually worked out, but it took maybe five years or

[5]Scores of professional witnesses were on the government payroll, and even bargained for higher pay. One assistant attorney general, seeking more funds before the House Appropriations Committee, complained, "We have to negotiate with them and shop around. That expert witness business is really killing when you consider the rates these fellows charge today."

[6]In April 1954, Brownell announced that the Justice Department would discontinue the employment of informer-witnesses as full-time "consultants." Instead of regular salaries, they would henceforth be paid only for their specific services.

[7]The Justice Department ceased using Matusow as a witness in midsummer of 1954, but only at Matusow's insistence. Up to that date, Brownell claimed, there were no grounds for doubting Matusow's veracity, even though almost a year earlier Matusow had given the *New York Times* an affidavit attesting to his habit of lying as a government witness. Although Brownell may not have been aware of it, the law firm that represented the *Times* in obtaining the affidavit was Lord Day & Lord, Brownell's own firm until his appointment as Attorney General.

[8]In a 1939 press release, Roosevelt instructed the FBI to "take charge of investigative work in matters relating to espionage, sabotage, and violation of the neutrality regulations." A year later, in a memo to Attorney General Jackson responding to a Supreme Court decision banning wiretaps, Roosevelt okayed the "limited" use of "listening devices" in cases of "suspected subversive activities."

[9]FDR's 1940 memo stipulated that the Attorney General must approve and authorize each wiretap "after investigation of the need in each case" and further limited the practice to aliens, "insofar as possible." Hoover, as was his wont, brushed over these restrictions.

[10]Actually, it was Brownell, with his directive of May 20, 1954, on microphone surveillance, who gave J. Edgar Hoover carte blanche to bug whomever he chose, by any means he found necessary: "Considerations of internal security and the national safety . . . compel the unrestricted use of this technique in the national interest." Brownell later testified in the 1981 court case *Socialist Workers Party v. Attorneys General:* "There never was any definition of the methods that were to be used in carrying out the directive. The methods were left to the discretion of

so for the courts to get around to lay down those rules. It was a period of chaos and confusion in the area of internal security. Later on, too, Congress passed legislation curbing the use of certain enforcement methods.

There was strong support for outlawing the Communist Party. It was a very divisive issue for a long time. Civil libertarians thought that the Communist Party had as much right to run candidates for office and to speak up as anybody else, and I agreed.[11] The Supreme Court said when Communists conspired to overthrow the government by force and violence, however, then that was a statutory offense and they could be sent to jail, as they were. In other words, I prosecuted those who so conspired. A big trial before Judge Harold Medina was conducted in the 1940s and the court upheld the statute and a lot of the leaders of the American Communist Party were sent to jail.

Harold Stassen advocated outlawing the Party, and he debated Governor Dewey on it. Dewey took the civil rights position that it should not be done, that that was the wrong way to attack the Communist menace. After that debate he defeated Stassen for the Republican nomination for President, so that sort of killed off the idea.

Eisenhower never had to take a stand on that particular issue—it was settled really before he came into office. I don't think anybody after 1948 seriously contended that the Communist Party had no rights.[12] The individual leaders of the Communist Party were American citizens and they had the right to speak their piece, and people had a right to vote against them or their candidates and all that sort of thing. But to outlaw them was wrong.

There was no doubt there was a spirit of fear created by some of these wild charges of McCarthy and innocent people got hurt. But there were no rules, so prosecutors or committees could go pretty far in badgering these witnesses. But we finally got the courts to draw the guidelines, so I think those things were corrected eventually. But it was a period of pretty difficult

the FBI." In 1955, Brownell, along with Hoover, insisted that national security depended on keeping informers secret in loyalty cases.

[11]In a televised report to the nation on April 9, 1954, Brownell announced a massive effort to destroy the Communist Party in the United States. He characterized Party members as "scheming and devious men and women dedicated to the destruction of our government and our way of life."

[12]Eisenhower, in his 1954 State of the Union Address, proposed depriving American Communists of citizenship. Later that year, he signed into law the Communist Control Act, which stripped the CP of "all rights, privileges, and immunities attendant upon legal bodies."

problems for the government and for government employees.

Considering the conditions at that time, I think I would've done some things differently in tactics. I realized the necessity for an employee security program,[13] but in the absence of guidelines from the courts, I think we used some tactics that were shortsighted. On the government employee program, for instance, I think we could have confined it to people whose job was to handle security information instead of examining all government employees.

Since the FBI's counterintelligence program was established by executive order of FDR and was not changed by Truman or Eisenhower or the Congress in any material respect, I limited my efforts in the internal security field largely to getting definitive court rulings on where to draw the line between the needs of national security and the constitutional rights of individuals.

[13]Brownell refers to the Federal Employees Loyalty Program, initiated by Truman and expanded and hardened under Eisenhower. See under "The Purge of the Civil Service."

ROY BREWER

A member of the International Alliance of Theatrical Stage Employees (IATSE) since 1927, Roy Brewer came to Hollywood in 1945 as international representative to resolve a jurisdictional dispute with the left-wing Conference of Studio Unions (CSU). As an officer of the Motion Picture Alliance for the Preservation of American Ideals (MPA), Brewer allied himself with HUAC and the American Legion, rising to unprecedented power in the movie industry. He scrutinized film projects and careers alike for the fatal Red taint, and his word could stop both in their tracks. Brewer became a studio exec for Allied Artists in 1953.

Historically, this was a country of honest people. We didn't have too many disciplinary problems because most people did the right thing. If a law was passed it was their obligation to obey the law, even if they didn't like it. But, the Communists started on an entirely different premise. First of all, they think any belief in God is an instrument to deceive the people and therefore it's their duty to destroy that influence. And with them, *right* is what the Communist Party *says* is right; it has no relation to fact so far as the

Communists are concerned. The extreme example is that the Communists built their structure in this country as anti-Hitler, that's how they got recruits in the early part of the twentieth century. But when it served their purpose, they went to bed with Hitler.[1]

The failure of the American people to understand was considerable, because if a man swears to you he's telling the truth, and he has any *semblance* of integrity, Americans tend to believe him. The Communists play on this. You can't use a lie detector test on a Communist because a lie detector test is a way to detect a subconscious guilt feeling. Since they feel no guilt when they lie, because it is their duty, the test passes them with flying colors!

It's a very interesting and a very long story. I'll try to at least touch the highlights because this book you're doing tends to serve the Communist purpose. Understand now, the person that is going to read this will give the same credence to a Communist who's programmed and *trained to lie* as a man like myself who'll tell you the *truth*! The public has either believed or been confused by the lies to the point that we have had no defense. And we have no defense today against the secret underground Communist apparatus. They have completely intimidated Congress to the point that they won't even mention the name on the floor. I say this, because I've been through it. I'm one of the very few survivors. I never was fooled, I attacked them right from the beginning.

You see, in 1934, the Soviet Union dispatched funds to certain American Communists in order to finance the takeover of the motion picture industry. The idea was to use motion pictures as propaganda to soften the peoples of the world toward communism.

Not long after, two people showed up on the scene, Jeff Kibre[2] and John Howard Lawson.[3] Kibre was to organize the trade unions, but he was

[1]Brewer refers to the Hitler-Stalin pact of 1939–41, which called for the cessation of war preparations by each side against the other and divided Eastern Europe into two spheres of influence. The pact came as a shock to everyone in the American Left, as did the Party's abrupt retreat from its rigid antifascism. While still holding both sides responsible for the war, the *Daily Worker* reserved its sternest criticism for the Allies and consistently absolved the Nazis of any special culpability. In reaction, Left sympathizers distanced themselves from the Party while Popular Front groups crumbled as their membership fled.

[2]A 1931 graduate of UCLA, Jeff Kibre came from a family of Hollywood set decorators. By 1938, he was an open member of the Communist Party and the head of the IATSE progressives, a splinter group opposed to the mobster-dominated reign of union leaders George Browne and Willie Bioff. In fact, it was Kibre's complaint to the NLRB of corrupt union practices that eventually led to Browne and Bioff's downfall.

[3]A New York playwright, John Howard Lawson made his first Hollywood foray as a screenwriter in 1928. By 1934, he was a full-time resident of the film colony and a member of the

rather quickly exposed through some letters that he had written to the California CIO, which was controlled by Communists at the time, and dropped out of sight by the late '30s. But Lawson was much more successful. His job was to organize the creative artists, the intellectuals of the community. He organized and led the Screen Writers Guild, which became the center of Communist influence in the industry. Lawson was the commissar of Hollywood and influential in other guilds, unions, and Communist front organizations—that is, up until the House UnAmerican Activities Committee hearings of 1947, after that they were pretty much exposed.

In the early '40s, the Hollywood AFL unions came under attack from Herbert Sorrell and his Conference of Studio Unions.[4] Sorrell was picking up where Kibre left off, there's no doubt about that. The Communists realized they had made a mistake by having such an easily identified Communist as Jeff Kibre head this drive, so they had Sorrell cancel his membership with the understanding that he would not have to follow Party discipline as far as his union and the building treades went, but otherwise he would support the Communist program.[5]

Through this attack the Communists infiltrated and undermined the leadership of the AFL unions. The main target was my union, the International Alliance of Theatrical Stage Employees, which was the largest union in the industry. That's how I got involved, and I've been fighting the Communists ever since.

On March 12 of 1945, the SCU called a wildcat strike over whether the set decorators, who were represented by IATSE, would go over to the Painters Union, which was affiliated with Sorrell and the CSU. At the time, we thought this was just a minor jurisdictional affair, but it blew up into a major conflict. Out of this came the Hollywood investigations and the disclosures that shocked the world.

I showed up in Hollywood about six hours after the strike began. My original job was to study these jurisdictional problems and come up with a

---

Communist Party. A cofounder of the Screen Writers Guild, he was elected its first president in 1933. His career ended in 1947, when, as the leading member of the Hollywood Ten, he refused to answer questions before HUAC.

[4] A flat-nosed ex-prize fighter, Herbert Sorrell had long been active in the Hollywood unions opposed to IATSE's dominance. By 1941, he was the business agent for the Moving Picture Painters and the head of the CSU. By 1945 the CSU, with nearly ten thousand workers, was a clear threat to IATSE with its sixteen thousand members.

[5] Whether Sorrell, an extremely independent exponent of union democracy, was ever a member of the Communist Party is still unclear, but ideologically he was close to the Party and accepted its help when offered. Brewer asserts that Sorrell admitted his membership before his death.

solution. Well, that changed pretty fast. The strike was against my union and I had to do what I could to break it. That meant keeping the studios running at all costs. I had to decide whether a studio could operate or not, or whether a picture could be finished or had to be shut down. It wasn't a job I was prepared for, but the responsibility was mine. It wasn't long before I discovered that our union was in an all-out fight for survival against the Communist apparatus! If we didn't destroy them, they'd destroy us. So we began a program of attack and exposure that eventually paid off. It wasn't easy, there was great deal of bitterness and violence. For a while, we had guards around my home, and for about six weeks my daughter went to school with a bodyguard.

One thing I learned during that period is this: the communists don't know how to fight when they're on the defensive. Their program is nothing but lies, deceit, and deception. Without the opportunity to choose the time and the issue so they can appeal to the emotions and frustrations of the people, they're exposed for the liars they are and they lose face.

One of the main groups fighting the Hollywood Communists was the Motion Picture Alliance.[6] The MPA was not an organization of reactionaries. It was strictly a group that was fighting the infiltration of the Communists into the motion picture industry. I knew that only a small part of these were real Communists. I realized that many of them had been tricked into the Party and then couldn't get out.

First of all, we laid down a code that would protect the interests of Americans from *hidden* Communists. Everybody knew that there were some Communists in Hollywood—but who were they? And so, we had a program of separating the hard-core Communist from those who were duped into going along. Once they were isolated and people knew them, then they were no problem. It was a controversial program, very few people understood it. But it was a sound program one we hoped to carry off successfully! As links showed up, the MPA would publicize them. For example, if something surfaced that proved a certain person was a Communist agent, we would simply expose it. That's all you needed to do. Once they were exposed, they couldn't work. Any man that admitted that he was a Communist during that period would've been fired. And there was no blacklist, in its true sense.

Now, one of the most honest accounts of this period is John Cogley's

---

[6]The Motion Picture Alliance for the Preservation of American Ideals (MPA) was founded in 1944 by a prominent group of Hollywood conservatives, foremost among them was its first president, Sam Wood. A successful director and zealous anti-Communist, Wood's will specified that no heir, with the exception of his widow, could inherit unless they filed an affidavit swearing they "are not now, nor have ever been, Communists."

book financed by the Fund for the Republic.[7] Although he criticizes the so-called blacklisting, he also documents the screenplays written by Communists. He had this to say about my role: "Brewer was careful not to make errors. Though he was quick to charge others with being 'soft on communism,' he was slow to charge anyone with actual Party membership. This was known to the studios and in the anti-communist power centers, where Roy Brewer had become a name to be reckoned with."

I didn't mind if the Communists would come out in the open and say, "I think this is a better system." I wouldn't say a word. But they lie about being Communists and try to seduce people. Every person that's decent and honest ought to object to that. The evil was the secrecy of it, the deception. You can't have a decent world that's built with people who lie in order to try to use other people.

Look what they did to John Garfield.[8] They got him married to a Communist woman so they could control him. The poor little guy. He was not an intellectual, but he had acting talent, and they used his talent. Early on, Garfield was scheduled to be called before the committee, they had his card number and his wife's card number. He wanted his wife to go with him; he wanted to tell everything and get it off his chest. She wouldn't let him and he argued with her.

Garfield did appear before HUAC, but he didn't tell the truth.[9] He didn't admit that he'd ever been in the Party, and I knew he had been. Then he couldn't get a job anyplace. Nobody would touch him with a ten-foot pole, because they had evidence he *was* a Party member and he denied it. Then I started getting signals—"Louis Nizer[10] would like to talk to you." Garfield wanted out and Louie Nizer was going to set him free. Nizer had a file of all the things Garfield had done; he'd been to the Boy Scouts and all this, he couldn't be a Communist. I looked at what Louie Nizer had and said, "It won't work," because he was denying the facts. Now Garfield was in the Party. His wife got him in and she wouldn't let him out.

[7]Cogley, John. Report on Blacklisting, 2 vols. *The Fund for the Republic*, 1956.

[8]John Garfield (1913–52) was a popular film star of the forties who made his career portraying the tough, defiant young man from the wrong side of the tracks.

[9]Once a member of the Young People's Socialist League and active in a number of leftist organizations in the thirties and forties, Garfield desperately insisted before HUAC in 1951 that he couldn't name any Communists because he didn't know any. The committee sent his testimony to the Justice Department for possible perjury prosecution. He went to pieces under the strain and died of a heart attack in May 1952.

[10]Louis Nizer was one of the top attorneys during this period. He later successfully represented John Henry Faulk in his libel suit against Aware, Inc.

Well, I found out that Nizer didn't want my advice, he just wanted my approval. He got kind of short with me, because I was this upstart. All we wanted Garfield to do was tell the truth: "I got in the Party. There's the reason I got in." We'd expect him to say, "I made a mistake by getting in, but here's what happened." And who helped you? We insisted that he had to come clean. Name names? Absolutely! Because they had no right to be secret. Do they have a right to maintain a secret organization and victimize people in the interests of the foreign policy of a country which is an enemy of ours? A thief doesn't have a right not to expose his accomplices. These men are criminals in my book. They're still a part of the conspiracy if they conceal it—that's the theory, and I think it was absolutely right. If they want to be Communists, let 'em be Communists. And you can judge them on the basis of the truth. But if they conceal the truth so they hurt somebody else, no society can tolerate that.

I met with Garfield before he died. I went to dinner with Garfield and Victor Riesel,[11] and we were going to help him get out. Garfield died before he could clear himself. He had a heart attack.

I did not want Communists making our motion pictures, I'll tell you that! I would've fought them if they were in the open, because they did put propaganda in our films. But the trouble is most people didn't know propaganda when they saw it. I'll tell you a scene they put in *The Best Years of Our Lives,* one of the finest pictures of that period. It was released in 1946, before we discovered that the Soviets were not going to be our allies.

Now Dick Walsh[12] and I went to see the premier of that picture, and he didn't see anything wrong with it. But here's the scene. Two of the characters are gathered around the bar. Dana Andrews[13] was the soda jerk who was being mistreated. Because he could not get a job that was commensurate with the skills he had displayed in the military, he had to settle for being a soda jerk. Harold Russell was sitting at the counter—you remember him, the fellow who lost his hands.[14] In walks this man you've never seen before,

[11]Hearst columnist and professional anti-Communist.

[12]Richard Francis Walsh was the international president of IATSE at the time of this anecdote.

[13]Dana Andrews's career reached its peak in the mid-forties with *Laura* (1944), *A Walk in the Sun* (1946), *The Best Years of Our Lives* (1946), and *Boomerang* (1947). He continued to find work as a leading man and supporting player for the next three decades.

[14]As a World War Two paratrooper, Russell lost both hands in a hand-grenade explosion. He was picked out of an Army documentary by director William Wyler for *Best Years* and won 1946 best supporting actor for portraying an amputee struggling to adapt to civilian life, as well as a second, special Academy Award "for bringing hope and courage to his fellow veterans." He is the only actor to win two Academy Awards for the same role.

and he says something about the lousy Russians. Andrews says, "What did you say?" "Oh," the man says, "it looks like we fought the wrong people." Andrews says, "What? You say all of our sacrifices were in vain? Why, you dirty louse!" He grabs him and punches him in the nose. He falls down and Harold Russell picks the American flag out of his lapel button with his mechanical hand. Thus it created the image of the American "firster" who later became the basis of the Communist attack to discredit anyone who tried to question Russia's place in the world scene.

Now, I thought: "Millions of people are going to see that!" I said to Walsh, "Boy! They got their licks in on that scene!" And Dick Walsh said, "What are you talking about?" I said, "That scene there, identifying as anti-American everybody who criticized the Russians. That's really what it did. They pulled the flag out of his lapel." "Oh, well," he says, "if that's the best they can do." [Laughs.] That was Dick Walsh. He was my boss. But let me tell you something; that was a tremendous scene. How did it get in there? It wasn't in the original script. We don't know for sure who put it in. Willie Wyler[15] was the director. Willie was not a Communist, but he was soft. He didn't like the charges against people. He got his neck out on the Committee for the First Amendment.[16] But the associate producer of that picture was a man by the name of Lester Koenig. He was a Communist. He'd been identified.[17]

You can tell we didn't go half-cocked on these things at all. Now, I never made an issue of that movie, because it was such a fine picture that it took so much explaining to get people to understand, and if my own boss didn't understand it . . . But nonetheless, it may have delayed our recognition of the Soviet betrayal for quite a while.

Edward Dmytryk is a fine man.[18] He had a brilliant mind and worked his way up to being a director. He had this guilt complex that a lot of 'em had. His father was a trade unionist and he wanted to do something for the programs that his father fought for. Now whether his father had any Communist leanings or not, I don't know. But as far as I know, Dmytryk didn't

[15]William Wyler (1902–81) was a three-time Oscar-winning director, nicknamed "Ninety-Take Wyler."

[16]A founder of the CFA, Wyler continued to lobby against the blacklist long after many of the other CFA liberals had jumped ship.

[17]Lester Koenig, who appeared before the committee in September of 1951 as an unfriendly witness, testified that he was not a member of the Communist Party.

[18]Edward Dmytryk, director and one of the Hollywood Ten, later cooperated with the committee. See his story under "Hollywood Blacklist."

distinguish between them. He thought they were working for the same things his father did.

After he got out of prison, he had time to think it through and he looked at himself and said, "What am I doing? I am not a Communist!" Dmytryk went to Ike Chadwick[19]—Ike was the head of what they called the Poverty Row producers—and he said, "I've made a fool of myself. I haven't been a Communist since '46. I want a chance to prove to the toughest anti-Communists in town that I'm not a Communist." And so Ike brought him to me. I called a meeting of the MPA and we set up a committee to talk to him, because, to be honest about it, we didn't believe his story. Here he'd been running with Communists and going to jail with them, but he wasn't a Party member? That didn't make any sense, but it proved to be true. We had a split in the MPA over that. I said, "If these people are telling the truth and want out, it's our duty, not only to get the ones that are wrong, but to help the ones that have been victimized." I think it was the most important decision that I ever made in the whole thing.

There were fourteen people on that committee. Among them was Ronald Reagan and Art Arthur, a writer, later secretary of the Motion Picture Industry Council. We set up this meeting and we listened to his story. We began to see maybe he is telling the truth. So we said, "Well, you made the record, you have to unmake it. But we'll help you unmake it." So we had this fellow Murphy, who was a member of the MPA and a writer for *The Saturday Evening Post*. We asked him if he could get a story in the *Post* in which Dmytryk would tell the story that he told us.

If Dmytryk was willing to have his story told in the *Post*, we figured it must be true and we would help him. So he did, and did the Party come down on him. They ran this double-page spread saying he was a liar and he was no-good and everything else.[20] So we went to bat for Dmytryk, and we got him restored. And the minute we did that, then Dick Collins[21] broke. He wanted help to get out so we agreed to help him also. He really opened

[19]Chadwick was also a member of the Motion Picture Industry Council. Formed by Brewer in 1949, the MPIC was created to bring the "Communist problem" to the attention of studio execs and to "clear" repentant Communists.

[20]After the *Post* article, "What Makes a Hollywood Communist," was published on May 10, 1951, the *Hollywood Reporter* printed a scathing retort by Albert Maltz, also one of the Hollywood Ten. This in turn brought an answering salvo from the MPIC (again in the *Hollywood Reporter*), entitled "You Can Be Free Men Again!"

[21]Richard Collins was a ten-year veteran of the Party (1938–48) and coauthor of the wartime heresy *Song of Russia*. He became one of the Unfriendly Nineteen subpoenaed by HUAC in 1947. He appeared before the committee in 1951 and named twenty-one of his former comrades, including Paul Jarrico, his longtime writing partner.

it up. His information brought on new hearings that shocked the world. Those hearings established that a number-two official of one of the major studios was a dues-paying member of the Communist Party.[22] The Dmytryk case was important because it isolated the hard-core Communists and broke the lines of communication between them and their dupes.

The only one that really lied to us was Lee J. Cobb.[23] He told us he never was in the Party. We didn't have the proof at the time, but later on we discovered he'd lied to us. He named names afterwards, but he lied first. That made it doubly hard for him, because once he lied to us we didn't care whether we helped him again.

Then there was the case of the screenplay called *The Hook,* which had been written by Arthur Miller.[24] It dealt with a story of corruption in the Longshoremen's Union on the East coast. This union was bitterly anti-Soviet and at times had refused to unload Russian ships. The script clearly indicated that the union was under control of the racketeers. It was offered to two studios as a package with Elia Kazan, who at that time was a Communist,[25] for no money up front, which was an unheard of arrangement because normally this package would have been worth about a quarter of a million dollars for talent of this quality.[26] They first sent it to RKO. The head of RKO said to me, "I got this script here that's got a union angle. I'd like to have you look at it and see if you think we should try to make it." So I said I'd take a look for him. After I read it I called him back and said, "You not only have a union problem, you have a Communist problem because Harry Bridges[27] has announced that he is going to file a

---

[22]Richard Collins named Martin Berkeley who in turn named Sidney Buchman, a writer-producer and assistant to Harry Cohn, head of Columbia Pictures. By September 1951, when Buchman refused to name names, he had been out of the Party for six years.

[23]Lee J. Cobb (1911–76), outstanding character actor of the stage, screen, and television, appeared before HUAC in 1953 and named twenty actors and writers. See Jeff Corey under "Hollywood Blacklist."

[24]See Arthur Miller under "Arts and Entertainment."

[25]While this story takes place in 1950, Kazan's Party membership extended from 1934–36.

[26]As Miller tells the story in Timebends (New York: Harper & Row, 1988), the downbeat script was tough to place, they went to Cohn because he was from the same rough dockside neighborhood as the film setting. Cohn agreed to make the film provided that Kazan make another picture for him, and that the two would receive no money until the film was in profits.

[27]Harry Bridges (1901–1990), Australian-born leader of the West Coast International Longshoremen's and Warehouseman's Union. Many on the Right, Brewer included, believed Bridges to be under the control of the CP. Harry, tough-minded and fiercely independent, freely admitted his sympathies toward Marxism and the Soviet Union, but always denied membership in the Party. For more than twenty years, the government unsuccessfully tried to prove he was a member. See Robbie Bridges under "Red Diapers."

petition to try to gain representation for the employees on the East coast waterfront and the picture could play an important role in convincing them to join with Bridges."

So, RKO says, "Well, Harry Cohn at Columbia just bought it." So I called the head of labor relations at Columbia and stated my concern. He in turn called Cohn and Cohn said, "Well, you don't have to worry, we'll change it." I made it clear that I was not objecting to any exposé of corruption in the waterfront unions, but I was not going to stand by and see a Communist union take over the members in New York if I could help it.

I told him that I couldn't see how changes could be made because the problem was inherent in the timing of the picture and the union election. I told Cohn that I thought the motive for making the picture now and giving them the script for such extraordinary terms was an attempt to influence the East coast longshoremen, who had been traditionally anti-Communist. He still insisted that he thought he could change it. Well, I didn't agree.

I didn't hear anything more, until one day I had a call from the labor relations director that Cohn wanted to see me. I walked into his office and there was Kazan and Miller. I was supposed to tell them how I wanted the script changed. Well, I realized this was a pretty big order and one for which I was unprepared. They asked me what I objected to in the script and I told them, "You have this progressive fellow being kicked around by the gangsters and it almost parallels the claims of a Communist character that was operating right here in Hollywood in my own union."

Miller suggested that maybe we could have him accused of being a Communist and he could deny it. I laughed and said, "Look, if he was asked that question and he didn't deny it, they'd kick him out of the Party, so that's no solution." The truth is, the Communists had a rule that the minute you were asked if you were a member, you were automatically expelled from the Party and then you could say, "No, I'm not a Communist."[28]

So then I got an inspiration. I said, "Well, maybe if we had the representatives of the *People's Worker* come down here"—that was a contraction of

[28]As a result of legal prohibitions and popular prejudice, thousands of leaders of public, civil, political, and trade union organizations who privately adhered to Communism were unable to make this affiliation publicly known. For to do so would jeopardize their leadership in those areas which the Party had concentrated for years. Out of this dilemma arose two catagories of membership: those who were openly known as Party members, and those in positions of influence who participated on a semiclandestine level, known in Party argot as "submarines." While this duality was viewed by many on the Right as evidence of a conspiracy, the Party was actually following the path of least resistance. Whether the Party protected its influential adherents with such Byzantine extremes as outlined by Brewer is dubious.

the *People's World* and the *Daily Worker*—"and offer their services to help lick these gangsters, and this fellow would tell him, "Get off the waterfront! You're worse than the gangsters!" [laughs] My suggestion was a way of counteracting Miller's ridiculous solution to the problem of establishing this man as an anti-Communist.

Miller says "Well, I'm not sure that would be a very good thing. I don't know." The meeting broke up, and the next thing I knew, Miller had pulled out of the deal.

I didn't believe Communists had any business writing our screenplays. If they were going to take dictation from a foreign country as to what to put in our screenplays so as to prejudice our interests against the enemy, they had no right there. That was my position, and I still think I was right. And I make no apologies for that at all.

Everybody that helped them should go kneel and pray for forgiveness, because we may be coming to the time when all this is coming to an end. The course of events are moving toward the basic line of the prophecies perhaps right now. I am not a rabid church-going man, but I believe the Bible is true. You find that most of the basic things are coming true. Don't forget that the conflict right now is shaping up between the legitimate sons of Abraham and the illegitimate sons of Abraham. Did you realize that? [Sighs.] Yeah, it's a funny thing.

PETER SZLUK

From the late forties to 1962, Szluk was a State Department security man, the special assistant to the director of personnel. As with many in the civil service, his home is furnished with memorabilia of his travels. Framed on the wall is a letter from J. Edgar Hoover thanking him for a job well done.

The fingering would usually start by somebody sending in a letter—without a name or anything—to our security office in the State Department. It might just say that so-and-so was a registered member of the Communist Party in such-and-such a time. We would turn it over to a fella by the name of Jack. I'm not gonna mention his last name because he's still around and I don't want to use the name of somebody that was involved in some really bad stuff. Anyway, Jack and his gang would take the letter and I don't know how the hell they did it, but they would eventually get to the guy that wrote it. You'd be surprised, just by examination of the envelopes, the ink, they could pinpoint it right down where they can say that's the guy. Jack and his people were able to do this.

Next, we would interrogate that person, "Now prove what you said about so-and-so." And ninety-nine percent of the time, it was a bunch of crap. That was my job—especially during the period of that awful Joe McCarthy and those two kikes, Cohn and Schine. Keep in mind that because of my network of informants, I was in a position to know all of the secret vices and leanings of all of these people in government, from the White House right down to the janitor in the State Department. McCarthy was scared of me because he knew I had stuff on him, which I can't go into. He knew, of course, that I had stuff on Cohn and Schine.

You know, I built this network up by myself, because before I assumed that job of hatchet man for the State Department, well, it was easy come, easy go. But I cleaned house! [Laughs.] I got rid of the people that were undesirable and I cleared those whose name had been besmirched by sons of bitches. So I had a twofold project going all the time: to get those that deserved to be kicked out, and to clear those who had been maligned by vicious, no-good sons of bitches. You'd be surprised how rotten people are to one another, simply because maybe some guy wouldn't drop his pants for some woman or a man, I'm telling you!

Keep in mind that if they were guilty, the son of a bitch had to go. And if I had any suspicion that this was a besmirching job or somebody was out to get this guy because of some difference between he and she or he and he, I would do everything possible to clear this guy. If he didn't clear, bang, out he'd go. To this day, nobody knows who some of the people were that I got rid of because they were sodomites.[1] I would protect it, particularly because so many of them had families. The only thing I regret in my campaign to rid the State Department of that type of individual was when within minutes, and sometimes maybe a week, they would commit suicide,

---

[1]In 1953 alone, 425 employees were summarily dismissed from the State Department as a result of "allegations of homosexuality." U.S. intelligence agencies were unanimous in their belief that "sex perverts in government constitute security risks," as they were said to be susceptible to blackmail. It was J. Edgar Hoover that proved this to be true, by blackmailing them himself. Nevertheless, in the history of espionage, there were very few gays trapped by their sexual preference compared to the number of heterosexuals lured by the charms of the opposite sex.

yeah. I'd tell them, "You're finished." The toughest part would be that. One guy, he barely left my office and he must've had this thing in his coat pocket—and boom!—right on the corner of 21st and Virginia. That was our office, on 21st and Virginia. Of course, nobody knew that he had been in to see me. It remained a mystery except to me and the security people.

The gay was a pretty large percentage of them.[2] But it was all sorts of things, selling secrets to the enemy, any human frailty, we had it. And if it got out of hand, we obviously could not tolerate it, because the Foreign Service was the cream of the crop. You were supposed to be spotless. And if you did anything, regardless of how small or insignificant it might seem to somebody on the outside, to us it meant you've had it.

Maybe I would go to the Secretary or the personnel director, but there was no formal hearing. Hearings . . . what the hell for? That was a waste of time! No, I was the hatchet man. Szluk's got it. Szluk says the son of a bitch is a queer, out he goes! I was a power unto himself. Nobody bothered me because they didn't dare. Although I had a pretty good reputation among the top people in the department, that I was not the sort of person that would just out of malice grab somebody and get rid of them, because I wasn't. They trusted me. If anyone deserved to leave the State Department either because of policy, habit, inclination; all right, he had to go. But if it came to my attention that somebody was trying to get rid of this man because of a turndown or disagreement or whatever, then once I was satisfied, the shoe would be on the other foot and sometimes the informant would be given his walking papers.

Leftists were suspect, although I probably leaned towards them, because I believed in free expression. As long as it was not anything that you did or thought that would harm the State Department or our country. Past membership in the Communist Party would be negative but not necessarily a factor which would result in departure from the department, because it would depend upon what had been done. Now keep in mind if the membership was back in the thirties—we are now in the forties, fifties, and

[2]For many conservatives, homosexuality and communism were indistinguishable. In the 1950 and 1952 elections, GOP stalwarts blasted the Truman administration for "harboring sexual perverts." Thousands of suspected guys were purged from federal jobs. *Washington Confidential,* a 1951 scandal sheet in book form, touted the State Department's Homosexual Bureau, manned by "former counterespionage agents, whose duties are to ferret out pansies in Foggy Bottom." The frenzy scaled lunatic heights with the call of Senator Wherry of Nebraska to guarantee "the security of seaports and major cities against sabotage through conspiracy of subversives and moral perverts." He, and others, believed in the existence of a "world list" of gays who could be enlisted for espionage, sabotage, and terrorism. Supposedly compiled by Adolf Hitler, the list had reportedly fallen into the hands of Joseph Stalin.

sixties—and if this person had demonstrated by an adherence to a major political party a clean bill of health insofar as association, or associations with people and organizations, during that intervening period, no way did I take into account what they had done in their early days. Because I took the position that all young men and all young women commit some indiscretion in the early formative days of their growing up, and this should not be forever after held against them. Don't you think that was a pretty good philosophy or belief?

But if they were still party members, or kept those associations—*out*. Then they were blackballed. You know what blackballing means? They'd end up on the breadline somewhere, and I didn't give a hoot. Blackballed everywhere—we could do it, yessiree, boy. Keep in mind that this is a country that believes in freedom, and these sons of bitches were trying to besmirch that. So I had no tolerance for them, and if we caught them, and if they were Grade A, and I mean Grade A, they were sold on it one hundred percent—get rid of that son of a bitch. Put him on a breadline. And we did.

I didn't think leftists were a threat to the nation, no way. Because if I had believed that, I would have killed them, literally. Any man that would do anything to harm this country, yessiree. I thought they were jokes. I just thought that they were sad sacks. During Joe McCarthy and that period, which is a sad period in our American history, I never worried that there was a Communist takeover. I thought it was a laugh. Of course, in today's world we're buddy-buddy with those people, and I think the danger of their taking over is greater now than it might've been back in my time. Back in those days the CP worked behind the scene, and that's what killed them, but today they're more out in the open and you don't know what the hell they're planning.

I recall on one occasion I met secretly with this high-level official of the department at the New Yorker Hotel. He was still in the Party, but he wasn't active. But if you were able to show that there was a membership card issued in his name, that was enough. His departure was announced in the press at that time—and I'm not going to mention the year either. It was made to appear that because of some unusual family developments, an illness of some kind among the immediate family, he had decided to leave the service. And he was on his way up from the ambassadorial level into the upper echelons of the department.

He admitted that he'd been conned into it. I said, "You were a young man when you took up with the sons of bitches. Why the hell have you kept this line straight and narrow—narrower with every year—but you still have that line into Moscow?" You see, he had joined the Party like a lot of young people did, back in the Depression. And some of the people that joined retained that strong belief in that philosophy within them and they carried it into adult life. It was a time between their youth and their adult life, when everything was promising. And because they had moved up the ladder, they somehow linked the promise with the moving up the ladder. Which of course was all wrong, because they had moved up simply because they had the talent and the perseverance and the potential which was developed within the department of the Foreign Service. And the only answer he could give was "I don't know."

Yeah, a depression could do it, an unfortunate love affair could do it. It always surprised me how many men would go off the deep end into some other dangerous activity that required my eventual attention, simply because of unrequited love.

The Purge of the Civil Service

Since 1884, the federal government had been forbidden by law to inquire into the "political or religious opinions or affiliations of any applicant" for civil service employment. During World War One, however, the Civil Service Commission (CSC) conducted nearly four thousand loyalty investigations. On the eve of World War Two the Hatch Act was passed, forbidding the employment of any person with "membership in any political party or organization which advocates the overthrow of our constitutional form of government." But even during the war years, the CSC forbade its investigators to inquire into any question of reading habits, union affiliations, sympathy for Loyalist Spain, or membership in a number of other organizations that under Truman and Eisenhower would be considered incompatible with federal employment.

The great hunt during the postwar years was, of course, for Communists in government. During World War Two a few hundred Communists had been employed in the new war agencies. The Office of Strategic Services (OSS) actively recruited Communist veterans of the Spanish Civil War as commandos. By all accounts, those Communists in the field were highly effective and courageous soldiers; similarly, those working in Washington were reported to have performed commendably. Within a year after war's end nearly all of them had moved on. The process of easing out the remainder was fairly quiet, at least until 1947 and the advent of Truman's loyalty program. After 1948, virtually no Communists were uncovered in the federal civil service.

It is worth noting that during the entirety of Roosevelt's wartime employee security program there were few more than one hundred dismissals and some thirty resignations—a great contrast to what was to follow.

In November 1946, Harry Truman, faced with a newly elected reactionary Congress and under pressure from Tom Clark, his Attorney General, established the President's Temporary Commission on Employee Loyalty. Chairman A. Devitt Vanech, Clark's special assistant, set the tone by informing the commission of "the serious threat which *even one* disloyal person constitutes to the security of the United States." Equally ominous was that most of those summoned to testify were from the FBI, Military Intelligence (G-2), and other investigating agencies. As historian David Caute notes, they were men who "by profession and cast of mind were obsessed not only by the need for total vigilance but also possessed by hatred for the New Deal." One lieutenant colonel from G-2 testified, "A liberal is only a hop, skip, and a jump from a Communist. A Communist starts as a liberal."

Truman inaugurated his Employees Loyalty Program on March 25, 1947. Along with it came the Attorney General's List of Subversive Organizations. The starting point of the program was the immediate fingerprinting and processing of loyalty questionnaires from more than two million federal employees. With this information, investigators ran a "national-agency name check" through the files of the FBI, the Civil Service Commission, all military intelligence branches, and the House Un-American Activities Committee. The object of this search was "derogatory information," which was defined as anything that bore, directly or indirectly, on the question of "reasonable doubt" as to loyalty. All affiliations with suspect organizations, associations with suspect persons, and reports of behavior, expression, and opinions that might indicate some degree of sympathy with communism were extracted.

Within a few years, another development intensified the repressive nature of the program. In 1950, Congress passed Public Law 733, which permitted the suspension of an employee, without due process, for reasons of "national security." A security risk was not necessarily disloyal, but might be someone whose character, habits, and associations made him or her potentially liable to disclose classified information, or vulnerable to blackmail. This opened personal beliefs and behavior to investigation. One woman, for instance, found herself deemed a security risk because her child arrived "too soon" after her marriage. Scott McLeod, the State Department's chief security man, put it succinctly: "There can be no proof [of security risk], since future events are not susceptible to proof."

As the loyalty-security apparatus grew more extensive, with ever more files and investigations, chances increased that *something* might turn up that could be considered derogatory—which routinely led to a "full field investigation." By 1952, more than forty thousand federal employees had undergone full-scale investigations, which entailed the interviewing of friends, neighbors, fellow students, fellow employees, former teachers and colleagues, even one's grocer or hairdresser. This set off another round of name-checking, as all these associates had to be checked for derogatory information as well. After 1953, the Eisenhower program mandated a full investigation for every "sensitive" position, which was defined so loosely that, for example, every single position in the State Department fell under this heading.

If an employee was so unlucky as to be charged with disloyalty, he met his inquisitors at one of the two hundred agency loyalty boards[1] established under the Truman program. An employee who lost out at this level was afforded an appeal to one of the fourteen regional boards, and above that to the twenty-five members of the Loyalty Review Board. These "distinguished and stalwart" men, as the *Herald Tribune* described them, were largely conservative and Republican, as this was Truman's shield against right-wing criticism. Liberal intellectuals were considered too "naive" for service on any of the boards. However, as many of the charges made clear, naiveté was not the function of one's political outlook.

This was amply demonstrated when Charles Bohlen's confirmation as Eisenhower's ambassador to the Soviet Union temporarily ran aground. One of the principal derogatories in his loyalty-security file was a statement by a stenographer who claimed she could detect immorality in men with her "sixth sense." Accordingly, Bohlen's vibrations were not on the straight and narrow. In another case, a Pentagon bootblack was accused of having donated ten dollars to the Scottsboro Defense Fund.[2] The man underwent seventy FBI interviews before he was judged loyal enough to polish military shoes—even though the alleged offense occurred before he was born.

Neither the Truman nor the Eisenhower program ensured that once investigated and cleared an employee would stay cleared. With every new transfer or promotion came a new investigation. As every new law and executive order imposed increasingly stringent criteria, old cases

---

[1]The military and the Veterans Administration handled their loyalty problems separately, with more than five hundred loyalty boards of their own.

[2]On March 25, 1931, in Scottsboro, Alabama, nine young black men were framed on rape charges, quickly tried, and sentenced to death. The Communist Party's spirited defense through the seven-year legal battle crystallized black support for the Party. In 1937, four of the defendants were released; the remaining five endured long prison sentences—the last defendant was not released until 1950.

were reviewed in light of new standards. Numerous employees found themselves investigated and cleared seven or eight times, only to be finally suspended without pay or dismissed on the same charges.

The reaction of government employees was fear and suspicion. "Loyalty Issue Keeps U.S. Employees Jittery," announced the *Herald Tribune* in June 1950. In 1952, two psychologists, Marie Jahoda and Stuart Cook, published a study of the effects of the loyalty and security programs on seventy federal employees from more than a dozen agencies. Some spoke of "Gestapo methods," "just like in Germany." A number of those approached refused to participate, fearing an FBI ruse. Others begged off, concerned that "in an investigation I might be asked why I participated."

The universal aim was to avoid investigation at all costs, for even if the final result was clearance, the punishment of suspension without pay, loss of reputation, and the burden of legal fees started long before the investigation was completed. Extreme caution was the only deterrent. "Why lead with your chin?" asked one respondent. "If Communists like apple pie and I do, I see no reason why I should stop eating it. But I would." One's reading habits were considered crucial. One man explained, "If there is only a rumor that a person reads Marx, nothing will happen to him. Of course, if the rumor turns out to be true, this is a different matter." Others prudently limited their magazine reading to *Collier's* and *The Saturday Evening Post.* Another person recalled moving into a new home only to find a stack of *New Masses*[3] in the basement. "I didn't know what to do with it. It seemed dangerous. So in the end I burned it."

Involvement in any organization concerned with social reform or the spread of ideas was automatically suspect. It was better not to join any organizations at all, as one could never be sure what group might appear on the Attorney General's list. For a short period, even the Consumers Union, publishers of *Consumer Reports,* was listed as subversive. Whether at work or in a social setting, controversial discussions were to be avoided. Taboo topics included admitting Red China to the UN, atomic energy, religion, and civil rights. One respondent so desired to avoid conversation that he chose to take an earlier bus to work because he had overheard some regulars on his original bus discussing politics.

By the summer of 1955 the liberal press was agitating against the abuses of the security programs, giving heart to the liberal elements in

[3] *The New Masses* was the dominant radical literary journal from its founding in 1926 to its demise in 1948. Among the artists and writers featured were Reginald Marsh, Ernest Hemingway, Erskine Caldwell, Theodore Dreiser, and Langston Hughes.

Congress. But the power of the conservatives was far too great to permit any meaningful corrective legislation. The most effective challenges came in the late 1950s, as the Supreme Court began to restore the rights of due process, including the right to cross-examine hostile witnesses. These rulings restored more than one hundred employees to their jobs and forced proceedings to be dropped against more than seventy-five others.

Between six thousand and nine thousand government employees were fired under the Truman/Eisenhower loyalty programs. At least eight thousand were forced to resign. Three went to prison (William Remington was murdered there), one died of a heart attack, and at least seven others were driven to suicide.[4]

[4]The tallies of firings, forced resignations, mortalities, etc. that conclude these chapter introductions are necessarily often educated guesses derived from a number of secondary sources. Ralph Brown's *Loyalty and Security: Employment Tests in the United States* (New Haven: Yale Univ. Press, 1958) is the best-known of these, but only covers the period up to 1956. David Caute's *The Great Fear: The Anti-Communist Purge Under Truman and Eisenhower* (New York: Simon & Schuster, 1978) attempts a more accurate count.

JERRY AND SYLVIA MANHEIM

In 1950, Jerry Manheim was a young and gifted physicist at IT&T. He enjoyed the defense work he was involved in and looked forward to a promising career. The promise was cut short when he was accused of being the head of a Communist ring within the laboratory. He was not cleared for nearly six years. In 1960, CBS aired *The Pieces,* a cautionary drama based on his experiences.[1]

JERRY: I was brought up in Chicago in a very middle-class home. I had no information about anything left of the Democratic Party until college. I think I was a sophomore when I saw a sign for a Socialist Study Club

[1]In an irony perhaps emblematic of the times, the actor who portrayed Manheim most likely had to be approved first by CBS's own security officer. At this time, CBS still maintained its own blacklist of actors, writers, and technicians. See Mark Goodson under "Arts and Entertainment" for more on the television blacklist.

meeting. I didn't know what that meant, so I went, and was very impressed with the philosophical position the group was espousing. I joined. I was drafted probably within a year of that meeting. I met Sylvia at a dance for servicemen at Local 65, and started seeing her regularly. She was working at the time as a switchboard operator at the Communist Party headquarters in New York. She arranged for me and a friend of mine to have a meeting with V. J. Jerome, who was the chief theoretician of the Communist Party at that time.

SYLVIA: Also the editor of *The New Masses.*

JERRY: So my friend and I went up and had this meeting with him at Communist Party headquarters. It was verbally violent. My friend was afraid they were going to throw us out the window. After we left, they told Sylvia if she wanted to keep her job, she should stop seeing me, because I was a . . . what was I?

SYLVIA: You were a "left-wing deviationist and Trotskyite."[2]

JERRY: And Trotskyite? I didn't even know I was a Trotskyite, but apparently that's what I was. When the war ended, I attended the University of Illinois. Sylvia also went there, and we continued going to the Socialist Study Club. In 1946 we were married. Around 1949, I got a job in research and development with IT&T in New Jersey. I was working on what they called the "strip line," which was the precursor of the printed circuit. We were also doing work on a system for a missile.

I had been there approximately ten months when I was called into the security office. They came and got me out of my lab. When I got to the office, they informed me that I was a security risk. They wouldn't give me any information, except that I had to be out of there immediately. A security man followed me back to my office while I cleared out my radio and lunch bucket. I couldn't even go by myself because I was such a terrible risk. [Laughs.] I was on leave without pay until it was resolved. There I was, out on my ass.

The very first thing I did was to call up the ACLU. I was a member. I told them what happened. Those were in the good ol' Morris Ernst days. He was head of the ACLU back then. Sometime after he died, they found

[2]A follower of Leon Trotsky, the archrival of Joseph Stalin, and therefore in opposition to the American Communist Party. The Trotskyists, as they preferred the term, believed the Soviet Union had degenerated under the leadership of Stalin and favored a return to the Leninist regime, which they believed was more internally democratic and internationally revolutionary. In 1941, while exiled in Mexico City, Trotsky was murdered with a mountaineering ax. The deed had been ordered by Stalin.

his private papers, and there were a whole bunch of letters that began, "Dear Edgar, What can I do for you now?"[3] They said, "We can't help you at all." I was dumbfounded. So I said to the ACLU person, "Well, what are the names of the organizations on the Attorney General's list?"—figuring I might've belonged to one of them. They said, "We won't tell you that." They wouldn't even give me a list of the organizations.

I went to see this attorney, Murray Gordon, of the same firm that represented David Greenglass,[4] and I liked him very much. He said he would take my case.

We found out that IT&T claimed that I was head of a Communist ring there. That was the main accusation and that's why they fired me. Years later, through my FBI files, I discovered that I was also supposed to be the head of the Communist Party in Hartford, Connecticut. I had been to Hartford exactly once for two hours to go to the veteran's hospital for a test.

Because IT&T was involved with the Department of Defense, the hearing was held at the Pentagon. We collected people who would go down and testify on my behalf. Of course, asking someone to testify presents a risk of sorts for them, some of it real and some imagined. People responded in ways which I never would have predicted. There were those who said, "I don't want to have any more conversations with you, just don't call me anymore." Some of my close friends responded that way. Others, like a young person I knew, a member of the Young People's Socialist League and in a defense industry, had no qualms about coming. Of all the people who went, he put himself at what I'd consider maximum risk. I don't think I even asked him.

The hearing was held before a board of military people. The chairman was a civilian, as I recall, and the rest were all big brass from the Army, Navy, Marine Corps, and Air Force. They were mainly colonel rank, or the equivalent, and they had been tapped and told, "Your next three-month assign-

---

[3]Morris Ernst was not only a giant of civil liberties and the general counsel of the American Civil Liberties Union (1930–54), but also J. Edgar Hoover's personal attorney and friend, a fanatic champion of the FBI, and an informant. Ernst neutralized criticism of the FBI within the ACLU, turned over privileged communications to the Bureau, and even offered to become the attorney for the Rosenbergs, so as to better assist the FBI. Irving Ferman, director of the ACLU Washington office from 1952 to 1959, was also an FBI informer. Ferman regularly sent in names of ACLU members for security checks, turned over internal documents, and informed on persons critical of the FBI.

[4]David Greenglass was the central prosecution witness in the Rosenberg atom spy case. His testimony ensured the convictions of his sister, Ethel, and her husband, Julius. See under "Atom Spies."

ment is to sit in Washington and listen to security cases." They had no training in this at all. Some of them had very minimal education.

They brought up the fact that when I was in the Army, I was a member of the orientation team for our company. They said, "As a member of the orientation team, you said such-and-such about the Russians."

I said, "That's true, I did."

They said, "That's real Communist stuff."

"I didn't have any option. We were given all the material by the Army. My job was to pass it on to the troops at the orientation meeting."

They said, "That's a lie. The Army would never say that about the Russians."

"Well, can I have some time to find the pamphlet and send you a copy of it?" They agreed to give me two weeks.

They also said that I was a member of the Party, that I was in charge of the ring at IT&T, and that they had evidence for this. None of it was true. They pointed to the fact that I had a book in my house called *Political Economy* by an economist named Leontiev. That was right. I picked it up for a quarter at a used-book sale. I thought it would be interesting, but I never had read it. Sylvia also testified at the hearing.

SYLVIA: I was very nervous. Colonel Rounds, who was sitting in the back, a rather rotund colonel with red cheeks, got up and said, "Mrs. Manheim, what organizations does your son Carl belong to?"

I said, "My son is five years old. He belongs to the Cub Scouts. That's a crazy question."

He said, "Well, I have to tell you, Mrs. Manheim, that Communist parents indoctrinate their children at young ages." At that point, I knew in my soul that we didn't have a chance. With that kind of reasoning, I knew it was over.

They asked me what newspapers I read. I told them that I read the *New York Post*, which was a good newspaper in those days, and that I occasionally read the *New York Times*. They said, "Why don't you read the *Journal American?*" which was just one of these scandal sheets. They also asked, "Do you frequent a movie house called the Little Carnegie?" They said they saw me attend a Russian movie there. I said, "Well, yes, I like foreign films." They also noticed that I belonged to a drama reading group, that we had a black friend, that people of other colors came to visit us. All these things fit together on a profile of a really subversive couple.

JERRY: Of course, they brought up the fact that Sylvia had worked as a switchboard operator at the Communist Party headquarters, which in their eyes was tantamount to being in the hierarchy.

That was the end of the hearing, and then I had two weeks to find the pamphlet. I went to Columbia University and found the pamphlet in the library. I wasn't allowed to take it, as it was classified. But I cut out the pages I needed. It was that important to me. The same day that I sent in this evidence showing that what I had said was accurate, I got the verdict. They had no interest in it. The decision from the security board was that I was a security risk.

We had no idea who had accused me in the first place. They wouldn't tell me. They protected their confidential sources. We spent a long time wondering who saw that book *Political Economy* in the house. It turned out that it was probably the black fellow that used to come to our house! [Laughs.] That would be ironic. We couldn't figure anybody else that could've done that.

When we got the verdict, I was thrown out on my ear. I had a friend, an engineer, who was selling televisions out of his house and putting up antennas. He hired me for something like fifty dollars a week. It was an obscenely low salary. I was putting antennas up and practically killing myself in the winter, sliding off the roofs. I wasn't that agile. I worked with him for quite a while, from '50 to the end of '52. Then I worked with another fellow who was trying to start an engineering company. I worked in his basement, soldering and doing various other things. After that, I got a job with a company that did some defense work. They wanted to know what my clearance level was. So I had to say, "I don't want to do any defense work," and I quit. This happened a couple of times. Everyone was doing defense work, so I was only around for a few months at a time. I felt like a pariah, like I was lurking around society as a shadow. It was terrible.

During this time, the FBI was always around. Sometimes they'd get into our car and talk to us, which was better than getting in their bugged car to talk to them. They were always asking about other people, and I never told them anything. But sometimes, I would be stupid and engage them in conversation. I remember them talking about Einstein, and everything they said about him was wrong. After all, I do know something about physics. It was just crazy.

SYLVIA: They even went to our neighbors and asked if we borrowed anything and if we didn't return it. Remember the time they came to my house and asked about my mother? These two lovely young FBI men— they all came in pairs wearing three-piece suits, gray with a little vest— knocked on my door. I invited them in. They said to me, "We know that you worked for the Communist Party, and if you don't give us the names of the people that you worked with, your mother could be deported. We know she became a citizen illegally." They gave me twenty-four hours to make up my mind. I didn't sleep all night. They came back the next morning, the same handsome men in their three-piece suits, and I invited them in, offered them coffee. All I said to them was, "I have to look in the mirror in the morning and face myself. I can't give you names."

I said, "The only people that I do remember are Elizabeth Bentley and Louis Budenz."[5] Of course, everybody knew them. So I said, "Those are the two people that I know worked for the Party, but the other people, it's been ten, fifteen years, I have no idea. What do you want me to do?" That was it, and they left.

JERRY: I was just going from job to job, feeling awful. Finally, I got a job teaching at Cooper Union. I worked in the math department in the engineering school. It was now '55, and the climate had changed. We knew that if we got some new documentary evidence, we could reopen the case. Sylvia found some of the letters I'd written her when I was overseas in the Army, telling her my opinion of the Communist Party. I had an attorney friend who told me, "I think you ought to try to get Joseph Rauh to handle your case."

I'd received a telegram from Roy Cohn to appear at Foley Square to testify, so I went to Rauh and his partners to discuss the situation. When they asked what I was planning on doing, I said, "I'm going to take the Fifth Amendment."

Rauh said, "Why are you going to do that?"

"Because it's nobody's business what my politics are."

Rauh responded, "That's really nifty. Don't you know they want people like you, Fifth Amendment Communists?[6] How many Communists do you know?"

I said, "I don't know anybody that I can say for sure is a Communist."

"And you're going to take the Fifth?"

They really leaned on me, saying that this was a stupid thing to do, and that it was very selfish of me. I understood their argument, but I wasn't ready for it. That weekend, Rauh went to Washington. He was having lunch in some restaurant when Joe McCarthy came over and said, "Oh boy, we're going to have your man Manheim on the stand, a Commie, and

---

[5]Bentley and Budenz were well-known ex-Communists and FBI informers.

[6]Pleading the Fifth Amendment was the only sure way an unfriendly witness could avoid prison and at the same time avoid testifying about his beliefs or acquaintances, who would certainly be forced to undergo the same ordeal. Pinning the tag of "Fifth Amendment Communist" to a witness was designed to leave a perception of conspiratorial activity, which would generate more sensational headlines.

we're going to run him into the ground." He was gloating about the fact that they were getting me to Foley Square.

Rauh said, "He's going to be wonderful. Manheim's not taking the Fifth."

"What do you mean, he's not taking the Fifth?"

"That's exactly what I'm telling you. He's not taking the Fifth."

McCarthy was absolutely flabbergasted. The next day I got a telegram canceling my appearance at Foley Square. Rauh was absolutely right, all they wanted were Fifth Amendment Communists. [Laughs.]

So Rauh collected data and we decided to have another hearing. This time it was in New York, in some federal office. These were civilians. They said, "We want to tape-record this conversation. Just to make sure there are no errors. You'll have an opportunity to read the transcript to make any corrections you want." They asked about being a member of the Party. I told them I was not, nor had I ever been, a Communist. I'd never been pro-Communist.

This time, my clearance was restored. Afterwards, I decided to sue the government for the money that I lost, since I was never a risk. I had been receiving extraordinary raises when I was at IT&T, but all I could claim were the statutory raises. At this point, I was teaching for thirty-six hundred dollars; at IT&T I had been making seven thousand dollars. With just the statutory raises, they would owe me something like forty thousand dollars, a huge amount of money. The government's position was, no, they only owed me the difference between what I made and what I would've made had I not received any raises. We settled on their terms. We got two thousand dollars, and the attorneys took a third. I ended up with fourteen hundred dollars, my payment for all of this agony.

Getting my clearance was very important to me psychologically, but it didn't matter in terms of employment. I didn't have the stomach for going back into industry. I never did.

JOSEPH RAUH

As founder and national chairman of the liberal Americans for Democratic Action (ADA), Rauh was known as anti-Communist and anti-McCarthy.

One of America's foremost defenders of civil liberties and civil rights, he represented many of the government employees trapped in the Employees Loyalty Program.

Whatever one might say to justify the Red-baiting battles in the forties, the fight was over by the time McCarthy came in 1950. The Communists had no strength left by '48. Whether one wants to feel it was a significant war, whether one feels the Communists were never very strong, I've got to leave that to the experts. But I don't think McCarthy is the most important guy in the world. He just hurt people. There was nothing there by the time he got there. He built a demagogic, synthetic machine against an enemy that didn't exist.

I became known as a loyalty lawyer because of the '47 Truman program. I'm against the idea of testing anybody's loyalty. If you have access to the hydrogen bomb, you may want to have cautionary procedures. I don't question that. But to have this kind of procedure applying to all government employees, it was just outrageous. There was no possible justification for the Truman executive order. So I handled as many cases as I could.

I spent at least ten years of my life trying to knock out Hoover's position on the loyalty security order. He would not put up the names of his informants except when they agreed, and generally they didn't agree. So you knew what was said, but you didn't know who the hell said it. You could have somebody that you had insulted say something about you that wasn't true. You could have somebody you'd had a fistfight with say something that wasn't true. The people running the program didn't realize how outrageous not having confrontation was. You can't be fined for a traffic ticket without the policeman that gave it to you, and if you want to say the policeman was drunk, you've got a right to say it. But you could have your loyalty impugned and lose your job without ever knowing who said what about you. It was an absolute disgrace.

In one case I handled, a federal employee was accused of having received regular shipments of Communist literature at his home. Although we didn't know it at the time, the government witness was also the accuser. He was my client's ex-landlord. I asked him, "You said earlier it was Communist material. How did you know it was Communist material?" He said, "Any literature that brings up the names of Karl Marx and Lenin is not about football games. When you see these names in literature you know what it is about." Then I said, "So the literature could have been labeled as anti-Communist?" He said, "I didn't know, it could have been. It might have been anti-Communist material."

Well, the case was over. But it was an accident that I blew their case up, sheer accident that the government was silly enough to put on a guy that they hadn't even questioned to see if he had the right answers.

I guess I won Hoover's enmity. Hoover would leak my file of the cases to his senators. In 1950, Max Lowenthal published a hostile book on the FBI[1] and the *Washington Post* decided it was too hot to handle with just one review, so they had two. Father Walsh[2] of Georgetown was the pro-Hoover, and I was nominated to write the anti-Hoover review. It ran on a Sunday, and that morning the phone rang at eight o'clock. It was Justice Frankfurter.[3] He said, "Joe, you really gave it to that swine Hoover!" He hated Hoover's guts. At noon the next day, Senator Bourke Hickenlooper of Iowa gave a full-dress review of my FBI file on the Senate floor. All about my loyalty cases, how I'd once been the counsel for some Polish relief operation after World War Two. Everything you could think of. The object of putting this out on the Senate floor was to discredit me, to show that I was pro-Communist.

In 1951, Charlie Murphy[4] called me up and said that the President would like to see a few leaders of the ADA to talk about next year's campaign. Truman hadn't decided whether he was going to run in '52. So I had a roundup of about nine or ten of us and we went over to Blair House, where he was living at the time. Each of our people had a chance to say what they thought of the Truman administration. I had arranged to go last. I said, "Mr. President, as far as I'm concerned the loyalty program is a disaster," and I told him the story about the supposed Communist literature. Truman turned to Charlie Murphy and Dave Lloyd,[5] two staff people he'd brought

---

[1]Lowenthal's *The Federal Bureau of Investigation* (New York: William Sloane, 1950) was the first book to hit the stands that was critical of the FBI. To make sure it would be the last, Hoover developed a web of informants in publishing. Among them were Henry Holt and Bennett Cerf, who may have been instrumental in delaying by six years the publication of a later critique. In the meantime, both Lowenthal and his publisher found themselves grilled by HUAC; the book was denounced on the floor of the House and Senate; planted editorials condemned it and Hoover's favored columnists trashed it; Hoover's agents were instructed to discourage booksellers from stocking it. The author was publicly and privately smeared—he never published another book.

[2]Father Edmund Walsh, the Georgetown University dean who first suggested that Joe McCarthy might want to use Communists in government as his campaign theme.

[3]Supreme Court Justice Felix Frankfurter, for whom Lowenthal had once been a law clerk.

[4]Charles Murphy, who succeeded Clark Clifford as special counsel, was one of Truman's principal advisers.

[5]A presidential assistant and speechwriter, David Lloyd was also a founding member of the anti-Communist ADA. In 1947, Joe McCarthy accused him and his wife of being "members of Communist-front organizations" and claimed that Lloyd had "a relative who had a financial

with him, and said, "Is Joe telling the truth? Is that really happening?" Both Charlie and Dave said, "Yes, Mr. President, we're afraid there are cases like Joe has mentioned." Truman said, "We've got to do something about it." Now, either I didn't get through or somebody lied to him about what they were doing, because three weeks later he signed an order that tightened the law and made it worse.[6] God knows, he might have been play-acting with me. But how do you know when a President's play-acting?

People were allowed legal representation when in front of the loyalty board, but there was only so much a lawyer could do. How can you cross-examine a piece of paper? That's exactly what my job was. You had the charges and a witness that didn't show up. So you always had to ask for the witness, and when they didn't appear, make an argument that this proves the witness is lying.

The best example of that was the William Remington[7] case. I always refer to that as my little Hiss case. Remington worked in the Commerce Department and was trained as an economist. Miss Elizabeth Bentley[8] was his accuser. She was this roly-poly thing. She was always portrayed as a Mata Hari, but if she was Mata Hari, I feel sorry for those guys that slept with her. She had called Bill a Communist on *Meet the Press.* We had no choice but to sue or give in. So we sued for libel, and eventually won, settling out of court.

At the same time, Remington was called before the loyalty board. Remington was rather an egotistical fellow and thought he could handle the

---

interest in the *Daily Worker.*" The source for the charges was the files of the State Department's personnel security program. One week later, Lloyd revealed that he and his wife had belonged to a few left-wing organizations "a long time ago" and that the relative in question was his great-aunt, who had died in 1941.

[6]In April 1951, responding to congressional cries of "soft on communism," Truman tightened the criteria for dismissal with Executive Order 10241, only three months after he publicly voiced fears that his loyalty and security program was infringing civil liberties. Whereas under E. O. 9835 an employee would be retained if there was reasonable doubt of disloyalty, the new amendment mandated dismissal. Thus Truman reversed the burden of proof; civil servants would now have to prove their innocence. By March 1952, of the 9,300 employees who had been cleared, 2,756 were again under investigation in light of the new criterion.

[7]A hapless government employee whose 1936 undergraduate sabbatical as a messenger boy for the Tennessee Valley Authority included roommates who were, or may have been, Communists.

[8]Elizabeth Bentley, billed by the press as the "Blond Spy Queen," worked within the Party as an FBI informer from 1945 to 1947. She then went on to become one of the more sensational professional witnesses of the period. In 1948, she accused Remington of having given her government documents to pass on to the Russians during the war.

loyalty hearing himself. He lost in the lower board. We appealed and just hammered on having Bentley come for cross-examination. The board asked Bentley to come, but they didn't have subpoena powers and she didn't show up, and we won.

Then the grand jury indicted him for perjury, for saying he wasn't a member of the Communist Party. It was incredibly biased; the foreman of the grand jury was writing a book with Bentley and the prosecuting attorney had been Bentley's personal lawyer.[9] He was convicted and then the court of appeals reversed it. Then they reindicted him for things he said when he took the stand defending himself. They claimed that he denied knowing of the existence of the Young Communist League when he was at Dartmouth. He was convicted for a second time. The Supreme Court wouldn't grant him a review. He was sent to a hard-core prison, Lewisburg, and given no protection there despite their awareness of anti-Communist rough talk. Bill worked at night and slept in the daytime, so it was easy to get at him. He was murdered by three car thieves.[10] They crushed his brain with a sock with rocks in it. One of them was heard saying, "I'm going to get me a Commie."

The Remington case is the best illustration of how bad the climate had become. It shows the degree of governmental wrongdoing. The government's actions are much worse than anything Remington, a lowly employee in the Commerce Department, could possibly have done.

Joseph Rauh died on September 3, 1992, at the age of eighty-one.

---

[9]In a 1990 article that reviewed the case, Rauh wrote, "Working together, they [the foreman and prosecutor] called Remington's estranged wife before the grand jury and forced her—by threatening statements, harsh and misleading questions, and denial of food—to change her earlier story that she and her husband had never been members of the Communist Party." Joseph L. Rauh, Jr., "An Unabashed Liberal Looks at a Half-Century of the Supreme Court," *North Carolina Law Review* 69, no. 1 (November 1990), p. 224.

[10]Remington was killed on November 22, 1954, nine months into his three-year sentence.

AL BERNSTEIN

Among the three unions representing government workers, the left-wing United Public Workers of America was alone in its stand against

Truman's loyalty program. Membership in the UPWA quickly became incompatible with federal employment. To Al Bernstein fell the job of defending union members summoned before the loyalty boards.

My job had a fancy title—it was called director of negotiations. In those days the issues were primitive. Government workers had really no rights. For example, some of the big issues at the time was just posting vacancies on bulletin boards, and setting up grievance procedures. The bulk of our membership consisted of blue-collar workers—prison guards, veterans' hospitals—and they had a tough time of it. Prison guards especially were at the mercy of wardens. When I was in San Francisco I organized the prison guards on Alcatraz. And it wasn't that difficult, because their conditions were awful. They couldn't get leave—they were in the same spot as the prisoners except they got paid!

When the Executive Order 9835 came down, I slid into the business of representing our members who were brought up on charges. The reason being that part of my duties also had been to handle grievances—and these were grievances. It wasn't long before my office resembled the waiting room of a very successful physician. I had a good fellow working for me named Art Stein, who was the secretary-treasurer at the time. He had to give me a hand just in screening the cases. There were hundreds of them, literally. For a couple of years I was deluged; I worked day and night.

At my home people would be coming at night hauling these envelopes they had received which were called interrogatories. These interrogatories had no substance to them, they were statements that you're accused of this, this, and this. These people were scared to death, livelihood at stake, their neighbors being quizzed about them, their position in the community—win, lose or draw—never the same.

I soon found out what the process was about; these were kangaroo courts. No cross-examination of witnesses—in fact, no witnesses. Not only no witnesses, but no evidence. And because of that the cases became extremely difficult. The prevailing rule was guilt by association. If you ever had the courage to speak out on an issue like segregation, you were a marked man. The members of the boards would read from documents which would state, T-17[1] stated that so-and-so belonged to such-and-such of an organization, or T-17 stated that the employee's brother was a mem-

---

[1] The T designation, perhaps derived from the last letter of "informant," was used by the FBI to conceal the source of information, which might have been an informer, a wiretap, or a bug. See M. Wesley Swearingen under "Hounds."

ber of the Communist Party, that was the extent. Some of the stuff you could identify as wiretaps. This was unadulterated, raw stuff that the FBI had turned over to the loyalty boards. They had no way of knowing whether it was any good or not.

It's unbelievable what went on in those days. Anybody who took a stand on civil liberties or intellectual pursuits like the Washington Bookshop here in D.C.—a meeting place for people who enjoyed intellectual get-togethers—my job was to defend them. The charges were all the same. They ran from associating with your parents, if they were under suspicion, to going to this bookshop. It was something ironical—the woman who was the head of the bookshop at this time was an employee of the Interior Department, a well-respected woman, and she got hit with the charges. I represented her and we won! But the bookstore continued to be a source of charges. I'd win the case, I'd have to go in again and defend someone else for going into it.

What you did was put them on the stand and tried to deal with these questions. In practically every case you got character witnesses from their bosses, their fellow workers. That was all you could do. We were successful in many of them. Successful in the fellow didn't lose his job, but what happened was they finally couldn't get promotions, so they'd quit. You couldn't win.

Of course, the union was under attack[2] at the same time, and I came into my share of it. It was terrible; the wife gets affected, your kids get harassed at school. When the union blew up I was really unemployable and I knew it, so I opened a laundromat. I stayed there about five years. The FBI would stop us on the street long after I had ceased to be a union functionary. They'd show me their credentials and I would tell them, "I have nothing to say." I later discovered that they followed me around in automobile surveillance. Here I was running a laundromat and they were following me around!

[2]For another look at the assault on the United Public Workers, see Joe Sachs under "Breaking the Working Class."

A Graveyard of
Careers

Of all the government agencies affected by the loyalty and security program, none was so battered as the State Department. Reactionary elements of Congress who despised the New Deal and the wartime alliance with the Soviet Union tarred State as a coterie of Communists, fellow travelers, homosexuals, Ivy League intellectuals, and traitors.

The attack began with the *Amerasia* case of June 1945 and the Marzani case of the following summer. But in 1948, Whittaker Chambers, a self-described Communist spy, came forward with charges of espionage against Alger Hiss. The resulting drama riveted the nation and provided the turning point for the ascendancy of the far Right.

Hiss was the consummate New Dealer. A brilliant lawyer educated at Johns Hopkins and Harvard Law, clerk to Justice Oliver Wendell Holmes, and a fervent supporter of Roosevelt's reforms, he represented everything the Right hated. On the other hand, Chambers was a slovenly wreck of a man, given to suicide attempts and sensational tales of espionage. In the ensuing legal battle, Hiss was convicted of perjury and sent to prison. Whether he was really guilty or the victim of a psychopathic liar whose story suited the designs of ambitious politicians—most notably Richard Nixon—is as hotly argued today as it was more than four decades ago.

The Hiss case provided the Right with a handy cudgel to batter the State Department New Dealers. So when China went Communist in 1949, it was no surprise that the Right painted the two events with a seamless Red stoke. The defeat of Chiang Kai-shek's Nationalist forces by the Communist armies of Mao Tse-tung was no surprise to State Department and academic experts. They had long warned that the corrupt and inefficient leadership of Chiang's Kuomintang Party (KMT) would lead to a Communist victory.[1] But to the Republican Party and the

[1]The Chinatown purges resulted from this furor. Chiang had long been unpopular among the Chinese in San Francisco and New York. To stifle this criticism, the KMT formed the

China Lobby,[2] the "loss" of China could only have occurred through the treachery of the Alger Hisses in Washington.

Accordingly, the main villains in the plot were the China Hands. These were the Foreign Service's Far Eastern experts, men with decades of experience in China. They had correctly predicted the defeat of Chiang, but now were accused of having willed the event. Such was the purge that followed that of the twenty-two Foreign Service officers assigned to China before the war, only two remained in 1954. The rest had been either dismissed or scattered around the globe; one officer with eighteen years of Far Eastern experience found himself stamping visas in Guayaquil, Ecuador.

Using the China furor as a stepping-stone, Joe McCarthy made a leap to national prominence with his 1950 Wheeling, West Virginia, speech charging that 205 people known by the Secretary of State to be Communists were still working in the State Department. Even though McCarthy juggled the numbers from day to day and refused to open his "list" to scrutiny, the controversy was such that Truman finally authorized a Senate Foreign Relations subcommittee to investigate the charges. After much testimony and perusal of loyalty-security and FBI files, the subcommittee, under Senator Millard Tydings, characterized McCarthy's allegations as "the most nefarious campaign of half-truths and untruths in the history of this republic." Unfortunately for those publicly named by McCarthy, this slap in the face did little to cool the ardor of conservative reaction. By January 1953, eighteen of the thirty-four had been forced out of government.

During the Eisenhower years, State Department employees suffered a reign of terror under a former FBI agent named Scott McLeod. Hired by Secretary of State Dulles to appease J. Edgar Hoover and Joe McCarthy, McLeod headed the Bureau of Security and Consular Affairs, and soon ran personnel as well. With him came two dozen ex-agents to augment the hundreds of security officers already in place. McLeod informed his staff that he hated Commies, Comsymps, liberals, intellectuals, and fairies

---

Chinatown Anti-Communist League. To be anti-Chiang was to be branded pro-Communist. FBI agents prowled the alleys, subpoenas were issued, and nearly one hundred Chinese were deported. Eugene Moy, editor of the *China Daily News,* was imprisoned under the Trading with the Enemy Act for accepting an ad from the Bank of China.

[2]The China Lobby originated in the Chinese embassy during World War Two. The lobby coordinated pro-Kuomintang propaganda and reportedly subsidized its expenses by smuggling narcotics. In the postwar period, it was transformed into a high-profile pressure group through the support of wealthy conservatives who believed Truman was betraying China to the Communists.

(reportedly in those exact words)[3] and found no difference between them. The ex-agents put their training to work: they rifled desks and file cabinets, opened employee mail, tapped phones, grilled employees on their reading habits, kept them under surveillance, and burglarized their homes. Suspect employees were informally notified that an investigation would begin in forty-eight hours, but they were free to resign without charges in the interim—provided they not defend themselves or attempt to return to government service.

With its members regularly whipped in public as homosexuals, bunglers, and Communists, the Foreign Service became known as a graveyard of careers. In 1950, the post of assistant secretary of state went begging through thirty-two men before the thirty-third accepted it. Officers in the field became extraordinarily cautious, even staging mock hearings to anticipate harsh interrogations. Theodore White commented that America now had "a Foreign Service of eunuchs." As late as 1960, one State Department official confided to a researcher that it had been eight years since he had read an overseas report that he personally disagreed with but nevertheless felt was worthy of study.

ALGER HISS

In 1948, Hiss was a highly respected New Deal lawyer and State Department official, the newly elected president of the Carnegie Endowment for International Peace. That was also the year he became the target of Whittaker Chambers, who had confessed to a lurid career as a Communist spy. Chambers's accusations eventually put Hiss behind bars for nearly four years. He has fought his case for more than forty-five years.

My case was largely a political issue, an attempt of the Republicans to damage the Democratic tradition. Almost all New Dealers were attacked by the Right. In fact, before the House Un-American Activities Committee there was the Dies Committee, and someone appearing before that had even called Mrs. Roosevelt a Communist.

[3]Curt Gentry, *J. Edgar Hoover: The Man and the Secrets* (New York: Norton, 1991), p. 409.

While I was at the State Department, I was involved with the founding of the United Nations and I attended the Yalta Conference.[1] The right wing was very glad to have me as a target. There is no doubt about that. They used my case to attack the New Deal and Roosevelt's foreign policy mercilessly.

J. Edgar Hoover, who at that time was considered a laudable public servant, was trying to ingratiate himself with what he thought would be the incoming Republican regime. At that time a lot of people hoped that Truman would not be reelected, and as you know, Hoover stayed in office for a long, long time by devious methods, which, years later, included the actual blackmailing of Kennedy.[2]

We New Dealers had discovered that Hoover was not loyal to the New Deal program,[3] and this was reported to Roosevelt. We made no secret of our belief that J. Edgar Hoover was disloyal to the President, so he had it in for all of us.

Whittaker Chambers first told his story to Adolf Berle[4] in 1939. He named various people as Communists in the government, some of whom obviously were unjustly accused, including myself and my brother, who was also in the State Department at the time. Nothing ever came of the charges against my brother.

Not one of the accusations against me was ever alleged by anyone other than Chambers and the people who repeated Chambers's charges. They were continuously recycled until there seemed to be many sources, but they had all come from the FBI, which leaked Chambers's statements.

In 1946, I was in London attending the first meeting of the United Nations as an adviser to the American delegation. When I returned to Washington, Secretary of State Byrnes let me know that several Republicans in Congress were claiming I was a Communist. He said the rumors had come from the FBI, and suggested I go see Hoover to clear the matter up.

Hoover wouldn't meet with me, but passed me along to one of his assistants. As I recall, he asked me a series of rather perfunctory questions

[1]Conference of Roosevelt, Churchill, and Stalin held over eight days in February 1945 in the Soviet town of Yalta. The right wing habitually criticized the decisions reached there as "selling out" Eastern Europe to the Soviets.

[2]See "Hounds," footnote 1.

[3]From March 1933 to July 1934, Hiss served as counsel to the New Deal's Agricultural Adjustment Administration (AAA). There he became aware that FBI field agents were operating in direct opposition to the liberal AAA policies: openly siding with critics of the program and actively harassing members of farm organizations who supported New Deal programs.

[4]Adolf Berle (1895–1971) was a member of Roosevelt's Brain Trust and assistant secretary of state (1938–44).

about whether or not I knew various people. Some I did, some I didn't. He seemed satisfied, and I thought that was the end of it.

Two years later, when I was at the Carnegie Endowment, the charges came up again. The source was revealed as a man named Whittaker Chambers. He had asserted before HUAC that I had been a Communist some twelve years before and that we had been friends.

The name Whittaker Chambers didn't mean a thing to me. He looked vaguely familiar from the news photos, but I couldn't recognize him. I wanted to confront him personally. This was in the beginning of August 1948. Two days later, I appeared voluntarily before the committee to rebut the charges. Unfortunately, Chambers wasn't there. I told the committee his name meant absolutely nothing to me. I answered all their questions and everything seemed to go fine.

Unbeknownst to me, Richard Nixon convinced the committee otherwise.[5] They called an executive session for a few days later. It was only then that I finally met Chambers. He had changed a lot, but I recognized him. I knew him under the name George Crosley, and only for a couple of years in '35 and '36, while I was with the Nye Committee investigating the munitions industry.[6] Back then, he claimed to be a freelance journalist, and we had struck up a sort of haphazard relationship. I sublet our old apartment to him, as the lease wasn't up, and he borrowed money from me; small amounts, nothing much. He never paid any of it back, but would come around asking for more. This went on for a while, and I did him favors. I gave him an old Ford that was going to waste, and a few other things. Then I came to my senses, realized this guy was just a deadbeat, and I cut the thing off. That was in 1936 and I hadn't had any contact with him until this executive session. I challenged him to repeat his accusations in public, so I could sue him for libel.

Some time later, he did so on *Meet the Press*, and I followed with a suit. In the course of the libel suit, he expanded his accusation to include espionage, which he had previously denied under oath. He backed this up with a

[5]Nixon was concerned that if the committee backed out of the case, its reputation would be destroyed for good. At this point, Nixon also knew what Hiss and the rest of the committee didn't, that a dozen years earlier, Chambers had gone by another name.

[6]In his investigation of war profiteering, Senator Gerald P. Nye, a leading isolationist, was operating on the theory that business profits lead to foreign entanglements. Hiss made a number of enemies through his performance as counsel, among them Irénée and Pierre Du Pont and Bernard Baruch, the highly respected "adviser to Presidents" who had been chair of the War Industries Board during World War One. Baruch, incensed by Hiss's zealous questioning of his finances, made no secret of his belief that Hiss must be a Communist.

sheaf of State Department documents, all dated in 1938, that allegedly I had passed to him. Before a grand jury, I denied doing any such thing, then found myself indicted on two counts of perjury. They couldn't charge me with espionage, as the statute of limitations had run out on that, so they charged me with denying espionage! [Laughs.] There were two perjury counts, one alleging that I had given Chambers documents, the other alleging that I had known him after 1936.

There were many documents, none of which were of any particular importance. Some of them had passed through my department, but we showed that only three of the many documents would've gone through my office.[7] Those had my initials on them. And if indeed I was engaged in espionage for Chambers, it is hardly likely I would've initialed something before giving it to him. [Laughs.] The great bulk of the documents we proved passed through different offices. They were also available to a man named Wadleigh,[8] who admitted he had given papers to Chambers and who at times came into my office because his division was under the supervision of my chief, Mr. Francis Sayre. When Wadleigh was put on the stand as a government witness, he said he didn't know whether he had given Chambers these particular documents. So it was never absolutely clear that's where they came from. Then the prosecutor argued that I might have gone out to Wadleigh's division to appropriate the papers.

The other evidence they used against me were documents Chambers had put on five rolls of thirty-five-millimeter film and hidden in a hollowed pumpkin on his farm. He did this the morning before he rather dramatically revealed them to the press. After that, they became known as the Pumpkin Papers.

Two rolls of film had dull nonsensitive State Department documents about routine trade negotiations with Germany. The other three rolls weren't released until 1975, when my lawyer got them under the Freedom of Information Act. One of these was blank, and the other two had inconsequential Navy Department memos, including one about the proper

[7]At Hiss's second trial, Walter Anderson, chief of the State Department's record branch, testified that routinely twenty-five to fifty copies of each document were distributed through twenty-two offices, where at least 250 people had access to them. The pressroom received "a great many" of these documents. No records were kept of the destruction of extra copies.

[8]Henry Julian Wadleigh confessed to passing hundreds of documents to Chambers in the late thirties. He also testified that he knew nothing of Hiss's alleged involvement with Chambers and went on to describe Hiss as "a very moderate New Dealer with strongly conservative instincts."

painting of fire extinguishers. Documents that were available through any government library. If I had been a spy, I was giving him pretty lousy information.

My old Woodstock typewriter came into play, as some sixty of the documents had been copied on a machine believed to be a Woodstock. Chambers claimed that my wife had typed the copies and I had turned these over to him. It hardly makes sense that a spy would spend long hours retyping documents, instead of just photographing the originals. But you have to remember the hysteria of the times made fantastic charges seem acceptable.

We had disposed of the Woodstock back in 1937. After a long search we found it. It was introduced into evidence by my counsel because we believed that it had been our typewriter. It was only later we discovered that it could not have been our typewriter as its serial number did not fit the dates when my father-in-law acquired his typewriter,[9] which is the one that came to me through my wife.

Much later, we discovered FBI documents that showed the FBI knew the typewriter in court was not my typewriter and reported to Hoover that the dates were off. So the prosecution, including Hoover, misled the court, misled the defense, and of course, misled the jury.

Obviously, Richard Nixon had much to gain if he could manipulate Chambers. And very clearly the FBI did manipulate, because they took him to various places I had lived, so he could identify them in court. As it happened, one house in particular had been extensively remodeled since I knew him. He described it in court as it stood in 1948, not 1935. Years later we discovered that his pretrial statements to the FBI contradicted the statements he made in court.[10]

Nothing produced in the trial was independent of Chambers. Under perjury rules, the prosecution's evidence must be asserted by two independent witnesses. Not only were there not two independent witnesses, there was no documentary evidence that wasn't dependent on Chambers's word.

[9]Apparently, Hiss's father-in-law had acquired the machine in 1927. Thus its serial number would fall between 145000 and 204500. The Woodstock introduced in court was number 230098, which would have been manufactured in 1929.

[10]Over the years, Chambers had given a variety of dates for his break with the Communist Party: 1935, early 1937, at the end of 1937, in the spring of 1937, early 1938, and late February 1938. Yet all the documents supposedly passed to Chambers by Hiss were dated between January 5 and April 1, 1938. Several weeks after he leveled espionage charges against Hiss, Chambers changed his story again, saying he had left the Party on April 15, 1938. The FBI then suppressed most of his earlier conflicting statements.

A number of important people came to my defense.[11] Supreme Court Justices Frankfurter and Reed both appeared as character witnesses for me. I did not ask them to appear at the second trial because the right wing was so critical of them for having helped me at the first trial. Adlai Stevenson was also a character witness. None of them ever backed off. In fact, when I applied for readmission to the Massachusetts bar, Justice Reed, who had since retired, wrote a letter saying he still supported me. Frankfurter was dead by that time.

I was tried twice. The first trial ended in a hung jury. After which, Nixon spoke of impeaching the judge because he had not been a hanging judge. There was so much hysteria in the country that it wasn't possible to get a fair-minded jury for the second trial. After I was convicted, we appealed the case and were eventually turned down for a hearing by the Supreme Court. You need four votes to gain a hearing. Frankfurter and Reed had testified for me and therefore couldn't vote. Douglas and Black did want to take the case and voted for it. If Frankfurter and Reed had been able to vote, the court would have taken the case. In his book, *Go East Young Man,* Justice Douglas says that no court could have sustained the conviction as there was no independent witness to corroborate Chambers's story.

I was in prison for forty-four months. Once I was released I immediately started to try and clear my name. The Justice Department was none too happy about it, but that is not surprising. But again a lot depends on what judge you get. When I filed my coram nobis petition[12] for a new trial, I got a judge who had been appointed by Richard Nixon. But I have continued and I have firm support.

I would like to add that in September of 1992, General Dmitri Volkogonov, a high-ranking Russian official, reported that a review of the KGB and other Soviet archives revealed not a single document supporting the charges against me. I take that as a complete exoneration.[13]

[11]Another longtime supporter was Secretary of State Dean Acheson. On the day of Hiss's sentencing, Acheson was asked at a press conference for a comment on the case. The Secretary responded, "Whatever the outcome of any appeal . . . I do not intend to turn my back on Alger Hiss." The resulting outcry (Nixon labeled the statement "disgusting") moved Acheson to submit his resignation to Truman, who turned it down.

[12]A petition for writ of error, coram nobis concerns errors so egregious that they command the attention of the courts no matter how many years have passed. Filed in 1978, this was Hiss's last legal move for vindication. The case was assigned to Judge Richard Owen, a Nixon appointee, who Hiss felt had demonstrated his bias against him in a earlier suit under FOIA. In 1983, Owen denied the petition. The court of appeals affirmed, and the Supreme Court again declined to hear his case.

[13]"Mr. Hiss had never and nowhere been recruited as an agent of the USSR. Not a single document, and a great amount of materials have been studied, substantiates the allegation." General Volkogonov claimed he had searched KGB and military archives and was in the midst of

reviewing the Presidential archives. In conversation with John Lowenthal, a Hiss case historian, the general further stated that while he could not give a 100 percent guarantee "that something wasn't destroyed . . . if [Hiss] was a spy then I believe positively I would have found a reflection in various files." (*New York Times*, October 29, 1992) Some weeks later, in the midst of the commotion set off by his claims, Volkogonov hedged his bet with the assertion that he was "not properly understood," that if such evidence did exist "there's no guarantee that it was not destroyed, that it was not in other channels." (*New York Times*, December 7, 1992) But he did not retract his original statement. Two years later, as of this writing, no documents contradicting the general's original statement have been forthcoming.

CARL MARZANI

The first federal employee to be persecuted, Carl Marzani is a veteran of the Spanish Civil War and a former member of the Communist Party (1939 to 1941). After serving with distinction with the Office of Strategic Services (OSS) during World War Two, Marzani was transferred to the State Department. He resigned his post in October 1946. Three months later, he was indicted under eleven counts of fraud for denying past Party membership before the Civil Service Commission. He spent three years in prison.

The FBI wanted to know who sent me to the OSS. Well, nobody sent me. What happened was a friend of mine had a friend named Barton in the OSS. My friend said to Barton, "Boy, Marzani would be terrific for you." I went to see him and he hired me on the spot. But then I had to be cleared. I told him, "Look, I'm going to have trouble with the FBI." I said to him specifically, "You ask me any question you want, but there are some questions you don't ask me. But whatever you ask me, I'll tell you the truth." I wanted him to be able to deny he knew I had been a Communist. He said, "We'll have no problem."

The next day he told me that the guy who was the very top of OSS research and analysis was Baxter, my college president from Williams. His assistant was my history professor, Birdsell. Birdsell had considered himself a Left liberal, and I had told him I had been a member of the Communist Party. So I said to Barton, who hired me, "There'll be no problem because Birdsell is my friend." The next day Barton said, "Boy, if that's your friend, God help you in your enemies." He said, "Birdsell is going around the top echelon saying Marzani's a Communist and you shouldn't hire him."

Then Barton and his superior figured out a way to beat the FBI. They said we need Marzani right away, so while the FBI does the checking, we're going to check with Navy Intelligence, and G-2, Army Intelligence, and if he's clear, we'll hire him. Of course, there was nothing in ONI and G-2. Donovan[1] said okay, so they hired me. After you're hired, the FBI can't do fuck-all. The Civil Service Commission can fire me; Donovan can fire me only with the Civil Service Commission approval.

The FBI pushed the Civil Service Commission not to hire me, and they had a hearing. Donovan sent his personal attorney to represent me. I lost that one. We immediately appealed, and on the appeal, Donovan's attorney was saying, "We need this guy," and the commission approved me.

Truman didn't like the OSS—he thought it was a Gestapo and he didn't like Donovan.[2] After the war, he broke up the OSS.[3] A big piece of it went to the State Department to set up an intelligence group. The State Department didn't want it, because the State Department was constructed so that every country had a desk officer who controlled everything. If you get an intelligence outfit, there'd be dualism.

I was transferred from OSS to the State Department without having any say on the subject. I was simply part of the outfit that was shifted over. After Churchill's Fulton, Missouri, speech I realized that Truman was really bent on a Cold War and I resigned, but I didn't do it right away because I had an enormous amount of leave. In the five years I was in the OSS and the government, I had never taken one day leave. So I decided, with the agreement of my boss, that I would take three months off before I resigned. So I actually resigned in October of '46. But when I was indicted on January 1st, I discovered that the government had scratched that October date out and wrote in December, indicating that they had caught me while I was still in the State Department. They were stupid, because there was a stamp on my resignation papers which was not legible, but with infrared it was brought out and it was marked "Accepted" with the original date.

[1]Major General "Wild Bill" Donovan (1883–1959) emerged from World War One as the most decorated soldier in American history. He founded the American Legion, served as U.S. assistant attorney general, 1925–29, and headed the Office of Strategic Services, 1942–45.

[2]Actually, Truman didn't know much about the OSS or Donovan. Denied access to wartime intelligence reports, Truman relied instead upon information provided by OSS critics. Among them was J. Edgar Hoover, who leaked to Truman information regarding one of Donovan's extramarital affairs, which deeply offended Truman, a devout family man.

[3]The OSS was abolished in September 1945, one month after the surrender of Japan.

My case represented three different strains coming together. One was the FBI hatred of the OSS—Donovan and Hoover hated each other.[4] I heard Donovan say that Hoover was a fascist, just like that. And Hoover, of course, thought the OSS was full of Reds.[5] Another strain was the loyalty oath, which was then being debated and went into effect about a month after I was indicted. But the indictment was part of that, to show what they would do to anybody who had been a Communist. The third was a film I made while on leave, during the summer of '46, for the United Electrical Workers, CIO. *Deadline for Action* was the first work saying that the Cold War is the responsibility of Truman. General Electric, the company that employed the majority of UE members, was shown in the film to have worked with Nazi Germany, to have lied to the government, indicted and found guilty, and had settled out of court. They spent millions of dollars to block this, and here I come with a big film, which got tremendous distribution. GE was just burned like hell.

Several months after I was indicted, there was a public relations convention at the Waldorf Astoria, and one of the people present was an ex-Red, Saul Mills, who had been a CIO state official. But he now was in public relations with a private firm. And GE public relations said, "There are different ways of skinning a cat. For example, take the case of Carl Marzani. We pointed out that he was a Red and now he's in jail, and that's one way of solving problems."

They indicted me for fraud, for taking my salary without revealing that I'd been a member of the Communist Party. You see, during World War Two, Congress passed a law that the statute of limitations, which is three years,

[4]The Hoover-Donovan feud dated back to the 1920s, when Donovan served as Hoover's immediate superior in the Justice Department. Hoover resented what he considered to be Donovan's meddling in FBI affairs; Donovan, for his part, carelessly dismissed Hoover as a mere bureaucrat and a "detail man"—a misjudgment that haunted his career. Hoover, in waging war against the OSS, leaked derogatory information about Donovan, infiltrated the organization with his own agents, and ran surveillance on many OSS agents. Ruth Shipley, Hoover's ally in the Passport Office, took to stamping "OSS" on the passports of Donovan's supposedly secret operatives, until a complaint to the President stopped the practice.

[5]In 1941, with the war in full swing, Donovan was unconcerned with the political beliefs of his agents. He needed recruits who were fluent in foreign languages, familiar with partisan warfare, and able to work effectively with foreign resistance movements, many of which were led by Communists. The OSS recruited a number of agents from the most likely source—the American Communist Party. When the FBI showed Donovan files on three Communist veterans of the Abraham Lincoln Battalion engaged in covert operations in Europe and demanded they be fired, Donovan reportedly snapped, "I know they're Communists, that's why I hired them!"

would be suspended for fraud against the government. That's to block the armaments manufacturers from doing what they did in World War One, which was rip us off and then you could never collect because of the statute of limitations. Now they suspended the statute so that for fraud the statute of limitations would be three years from the end of the war rather than three years from the time it was committed.

So they prosecuted me. Now they had the original FBI interrogation in which they asked, "Were you a member of the Communist Party?" I said no, which was a lie. They could have prosecuted me for perjury, but the statute of limitations had run out on perjury. So by prosecuting me for fraud, they were able to bring in all the evidence that I had been a member. Then to be covered, they had a guy from the State Department testify that towards the end of 1945, he had asked me had I been a member of the Communist Party and I said no, which of course was absolutely untrue. The guy was lying, the prosecutor knew he was lying. And the judge must have known they were lying.

I worked with the Joint Chiefs of Staff, I worked with General Marshall[6] directly. I didn't go around saying I used to be a member of the Communist Party, but everybody knew I was radical. I never made any secret of it. We weren't bullshitting anybody. It was known that I had been a Red. When I told my boss, "Ask me any question, but there's some questions you shouldn't ask," I'm giving him deniability, as they say, as Poindexter said for Reagan. But it was evident, he knew that that's what I was saying.

During the clearance process, I was pretty much told by my superiors, "Look, just deny you're a Communist." But I couldn't quite prove that, but as people kept dying off—Donovan died, Barton died—I suddenly realized that if I don't get something on paper, it'll be my word against the FBI. So I wrote to Edward Mason, who was the very top guy, next to Donovan, for our outfit. He was the OSS representative on the Joint Intelligence Conference of the Joint Chiefs of Staff. I said I'm writing my memoirs, and I'm writing the recollection of how I was hired and I'm sending you a copy and I would appreciate it if it checks out with your recollection or whether there are differences. And I laid out all the details, and how it was all done. He wrote back, "To the best of my recollection, you're quite accurate, this is the way I remember it." This was a number of years ago, I think he's dead now. He was in nineties then.

[6]George Catlett Marshall (1880–1959) served as Army Chief of Staff, 1939–45; originated the European Recovery Program, known as the Marshall Plan; later became Secretary of State and Secretary of Defense; and was awarded the Nobel Peace Prize in 1953.

I was indicted on eleven counts. The first nine: had I ever been a member of the Communist Party, had I ever given money to the Communist Party, had I ever worked for the Communist Party, had I ever distributed leaflets for the Communist Party, etc. In other words, the counts were always the same thing, I'm a Communist. Since the government used the fraud stat-ute, the appeals court said that the statute of limitations applied, so the first nine counts were thrown out. The court of appeals upheld the last two counts. It went up to the Supreme Court, and they split four to four, with Douglas abstaining.

We petitioned for a rehearing. In the whole history of the United States, there were only eight rehearings. Mine was the eighth. In our brief we said that whatever reason Douglas had for abstaining, we had complete confi-dence in his integrity and would waive any question, that we thought it was important that there should not be a four-to-four decision. But Douglas abstained again and they split four to four. A split court means that the lower court stands.

Anyway, I got three years and I served thirty-three months. Ordinarily, with good behavior, you only serve twenty-seven months and twenty days out of thirty-six months. But in jail I started writing a book on my case and tried to smuggle the manuscript out. They took five months good time away for that. The day before, a guy had been caught with a knife and they only took three days off his good time.

They didn't want us to write, they didn't want us to read. In other words, they treated us like the political prisoners we were. But to this day, the government will not accept that we were political prisoners. They're all criminals that broke the Smith Act, they defrauded the government, and so on. So you find yourself in a situation where you have to fight within their terminology.

In fact, every goddamn rule that the jails had was broken, did not apply to the political prisoners! Prisoners are allowed to write—but we weren't allowed to write. Prisoners were allowed to get *anything* to read—we couldn't get anything that had the word "Russia" in it, even if it says "We hate the Russians."

The fundamental rules of the jail are designed, number one, to prevent your escape; number two, not to get any weapons in; number three, to prevent homosexuality. Those are the major problems. In the meantime you can write, you can teach. They help you get a high school equivalency degree, so they need teachers. Here I am, a graduate of Williams and Oxford, with degrees in three or four different disciplines. They wouldn't use me because I'm a Red.

There was one exception. The guy who was teaching American history was sick one day. He had been a teacher somewhere. He was in for molesting and taking a small girl across state lines. So the deputy warden called me and asked if I would take over this class on the American Revolution. He said, "No Red stuff now." I said, "No Red stuff." So when I teach that evening, the son of a bitch sits in the front row to make sure. I thought, "I'll show you."

I started off by saying, "I don't want to go into too much detail about the American Revolution, but I want to talk about what it takes to make a revolution." I started to quote Lenin—but he didn't know it was Lenin—on the three conditions for revolution. Number one, you have to have a deeply held population-wide resentment on something, and generally speaking the most prevalent ones were independence, like the American Revolution, or overthrow of a tyranny, like the French Revolution, or losing a war, like the czar did. The second condition was to have a group of people who are willing and able to run a revolution, like the American Committees of Correspondence, the Jacobins in France, the Bolsheviks in Russia. And I said the third, you must have a bunch of nincompoops on top, like George the Third, like the czar. That night, I gave them a first-class lesson in Marxism, and the deputy warden's there nodding, nodding.

Parnell Thomas was in jail with me for taking kickbacks of a dollar and a half or two dollars a week from his secretary.[7] He got a year and a day. I was in jail with him and the Hollywood guys, Ring Lardner and Lester Cole, and with one of the directors of the Joint Anti-Fascist Refugee Committee, Jacob Auslander. As a matter of fact, Auslander and Thomas came face to face in the chow line. I was there. I was watching Auslander, he was Viennese, very cultured. He was trembling with anger and he looks at Thomas and finally he says, "You . . . you . . . *cocksucker!*" It was the worst thing he could think of!

By the way, Thomas got paroled on the very first day he was eligible. I didn't get paroled three times, even though the first name on my parole petition was Albert Einstein, the second name was Thomas Mann, the third name was General Donovan, and then came the names of more than fifteen hundred professors, heads of departments at Harvard and other universities. Not a peep from the parole board, nothing. I did all my time.

The tragedy in my case was that my wife was very ill with multiple sclerosis and ended up in a wheelchair. That made it very tough. She got multiple

[7]J. Parnell Thomas (born John Feeny), a Republican from New Jersey, was the pugnaciously reactionary chairman of HUAC from 1947 to 1948. Thomas was charged with illegally receiving about $4,000 for expense vouchers and $7,000 in staff kickbacks.

sclerosis before I went in but after I was indicted. They didn't give a damn. It's such shittiness that people find it difficult to believe.

On the other hand, I was lucky because I was the first case and there was lots of money. Hollywood used to send us donations. By 1947 the government had just started its Red Scare, but McCarthy wasn't there yet, so the hysteria wasn't as bad. By the time you get to 1950 and McCarthy, there were too many people in need. At the time I was the only one, so the money came in and my wife was taken care of.

I had two little children. One was a year old when I went in, and the other was around three or four. They suffered, they really did. You don't realize it. When I got out, my daughter would come and sit close, but the moment I'd acknowledge it, the moment I put out my hand, she'd run away. Obviously, what had gone into her head was don't show too great a love for your father because he might go away again.

JOHN STEWART SERVICE

Service was with the Foreign Service in China from 1933 to 1945. When the Nationalist government fell to the Communist forces, he and other China Hands were accused by Joe McCarthy of "selling China out." In 1950, Service was fired by the Loyalty Review Board in connection with espionage charges that he had been cleared of six times previously. He fought his case for reinstatement to the Supreme Court and won. After retiring in 1962, he spent ten years at the Center for Chinese Studies at the University of California at Berkeley.

The loss of China to the Communists in 1949 really brought the State Department China specialists under fire. In those days, America considered herself omnipotent, and China was supposed to be our great friend. The public couldn't understand how this could have happened; all the wonderful things that the U.S. had done for the Chinese people.[1] We had the

---

[1] The Republican Party in particular had long regarded China with a proprietary zeal. "With God's help," exclaimed Senator Kenneth Wherry, "we will lift Shanghai up and up, ever up, until it is just like Kansas City."

missionaries there; we protected China's integrity with the Open Door policy—never mind that it was primarily to make sure American business-men didn't lose out to British and other businessmen. How could this happen? Never mind that China was a big country that wasn't ours to lose! There must be treachery, a conspiracy somewhere, that betrayed China to the Communists.

At first, most of us thought it was just a passing phase. We didn't expect the catastrophe that happened; there was no precedent for anything like this hysteria. Sure, I was an obvious target because of the *Amerasia* case,[2] but then pretty soon Davies was attacked, then Vincent, then Clubb.[3] Gradu-ally we realized that we were all under attack because of our views in reporting on China. The Kuomintang, Chiang Kai-shek's party, certainly did their part; their secret police kept us under surveillance and probably pilfered some papers. In Washington all our telephones were tapped.

I first "got into trouble," you might say, in June of 1945 when I became involved in the *Amerasia* case. Philip Jaffe, the editor-publisher of a maga-zine on the Far East called *Amerasia,* was discovered to be getting copies of U.S. government documents.[4] They were apparently supplied to him by a man named Larsen who worked for the State Department. Jaffe was either a Communist or very close to it.[5] His magazine was anti–Chiang Kai-shek and was the only specialist magazine dealing with the Far East. Originally it was very good. Later on it became, shall we say, more devoted to a particu-lar point of view.

The FBI had already raided Jaffe's office[6] and were watching him when I came home on leave from China in April '45. When Jaffe looked me up, they thought, "Oh boy, this all fits together!" I allowed Jaffe to see some

[2]This was the case in which Service was charged with espionage. See below.

[3]John Paton Davies, was suspended on security charges, cleared, reinvestigated, then cleared again, only to be grilled by the McCarran Committee and threatened with a perjury indictment. John Carter Vincent was dismissed as a "loyalty risk" after having been cleared four times. O. Edmund Clubb, Jr., was recommended for dismissal on security grounds, cleared by the Secre-tary of State, and demoted, at which point he resigned.

[4]The documents discovered were from the State, War, and Navy departments, many of which were classified Confidential. Later, Assistant Attorney General James McInerney testified that the documents "were very innocuous . . . a little above the level of teacup gossip in the Far East," and that the classifications were "nothing short of silly."

[5]Years later, Jaffe admitted to being a "close fellow traveler," but never actually a member.

[6]Actually the FBI burgled the offices, planted bugs, and tapped the phones, and performed the same services on a half-dozen other locations as well. The raid, along with the arrests, came later; they seized some eight hundred documents in the raid.

personal copies of my reports about China.[7] But that was customary. I allowed many members of the press to see them for background information. But the copies that were found in his files were not from me, they were from Larsen.

I was arrested in June, along with five other people, and charged with espionage. They anticipated that after the arrest they would get more information. They searched my apartment and seized the contents of my desk, but they didn't find any smoking gun.

The case against me was very thin. I don't think anybody knows what all was in back of it. But the FBI was working in China, along with the Office of Naval Intelligence. ONI had a working agreement with the head of Chiang Kai-shek's secret police. I was the chief villain as far as the Chinese secret police were concerned, because of my contacts with the Chinese Communists. My guess is that the FBI people in China had already had some communication about me with the FBI in the States.

Originally the charges were laid under the Espionage Act. I don't think they ever had any evidence of espionage against Larsen.[8] The thing never got very far. Three were indicted by the grand jury; Jaffe, Emannuel Larsen, and Andrew Roth. Three were not indicted. The FBI had made a lot of illegal searches, and the evidence was tainted. So the government finally settled for a much lesser charge—illegal possession of government documents. Jaffe paid a fine, Larsen pled nolo contendere, and Roth went to England. But they never actually made any very serious efforts to bring him to trial.[9] I was cleared. The grand jury refused to indict me—twenty to nothing. But dropping the charges didn't end the business, because the case was continually picked up and recycled.

The State Department reprimanded me for being indiscreet. I said, "Sure, I've been indiscreet. I'm willing to acknowledge that." I felt that our policy of backing the Chinese Nationalists was a hell of a mistake. I was talking fairly freely about the need for an evenhanded policy in a rather hotheaded, youthful way—I was what, thirty-five, thirty-six? I thought what was going to happen in China was a disaster. Well, it was a disaster. Civil war was starting in China, and we knew a civil war would end in

---

[7]Among these were a report of an interview with Mao Tse-tung, eight or ten personal copies of memoranda on China that did not contain any discussions of U.S. political or military policy, and an unclassified transcript of a radio broadcast out of Yenan, the Chinese Communist capital.

[8]There was no evidence that the documents had been passed on to a foreign power or used for anything other than background for scholarly articles.

[9]Jaffe's fine amounted to $2,500; Larsen's was $500; Andrew Roth, a Navy officer, was discharged from the service the day before the arrests. His indictment was dropped in February 1946.

Communist victory. It was going to make things a lot worse. We hoped a civil war could be avoided or made much shorter.

The professional Red-hunters always alleged that the case had been suppressed. There were also people who were in the House—a man named Dondero[10] and several others—who kept bringing up charges that the case had not been properly prosecuted. And then Patrick Hurley used that as background for his charges against me when he resigned in November '45 as ambassador to China. He had failed in his mission to bring about a conciliation between the Communists and the Kuomintang. He was looking for a scapegoat, so he blamed me and some other people for having not supported him in China.[11] The charges were a lot of hogwash, but they gave me a lot of unfavorable publicity. Of course, the China Lobby people kept pushing it as well.

Then in 1949 the State Department published a China White Paper in an effort to prove that they had tried to support Chiang, but it was his failings and the corruption of the Kuomintang government that lost China. In the White Paper they published an appendix showing that Davies, myself, and some others in China had correctly predicted the downfall of the Chiang government. Unfortunately, this involved excerpting a lot of our reports, which laid open that we had been critical of Chiang Kai-shek. The State Department thought this was a good idea, but it was disastrous for us, because it publicized that we had advocated some cooperation with the Chinese Communists in the war against Japan. We argued for a Tito policy: we supported Tito in Yugoslavia, and we said we should do the same in China. And so this fed into the developing public hysteria about the loss of China.

And then McCarthy started in February of 1950.[12] He was fed by a newspaperman[13] a list of people who were being investigated in the State

[10]Ultraconservative Republican George Dondero of Michigan, whose greater fame rests on the battle he led against the "Red art termites" of abstract expressionism. All modern art is Communist, an "instrument and weapon of destruction," reasoned Dondero, "because it does not glorify our beautiful country, our cheerful and smiling people." Its creators and promoters "are our enemies."

[11]Hurley's letter of resignation read in part: "The professional foreign service men sided with the Chinese Communist armed party and the imperialist bloc of nations whose policy it was to keep China divided against herself. . . ."

[12]The infamous Wheeling, West Virginia, speech, in which McCarthy claimed to possess a list of 205 secret Communists working in the State Department.

[13]Ed Nellor, a McCarthy speechwriter on loan from the *Washington Times-Herald*. He had passed on a report from Robert E. Lee, a former FBI man, who had become chief of staff to the House Committee on Appropriations. The report was not a list of Communists, but 108 case summaries of what Lee called "incidents of inefficiencies" in the State Department's personnel security program.

Department. Well, most of these were people who had worked for the Office of War Information or the OSS, and after the war they were discontinued and the remnant staff was temporarily taken over by the State Department. These people were being phased out. Most of them had no connection with State.

Any rate, McCarthy's bluff was called by the Senate and they set up the Tydings Committee,[14] a subcommittee of the Foreign Relations Committee, to investigate his charges. McCarthy was up a tree—most of his hoorah was about people who weren't on his original list. I wasn't on his original list. He had nothing; most of his charges were baseless. So I got involved after the China Lobby, and to some extent the FBI, came galloping to his rescue with more charges. Those were based on the fact that I had been in Yenan and had a lot of contact with Chinese Communists, was favorably impressed by them, and figured that the United States ought to maintain an evenhanded policy in China because they were going to win.

McCarthy's charges are always very vague. He had all these roundabout ways of saying you were a Communist without actually coming out and saying it. It was mostly innuendo—"He was a Communist stooge." If you said anything good about Communists in those days, then you were as good as a Communist. So that if Owen Lattimore[15] was accused of being a Communist, and you knew Lattimore, you were a Communist. If the Communists advocated deposing the Japanese emperor and you thought the emperor institution wasn't very good, why, you also were a Communist. All sorts of tenuous connections created these allegations.

After the grand jury had refused to indict on the *Amerasia* case, I had a hearing before a personnel board in the State Department and they cleared me on the same charges. Then after the loyalty program was set up, there were several investigations just on the file. But after McCarthy made his charges, the State Department had to institute regular full hearings on the same thing, and that went on for a long time. We went into everything that anybody had said; every charge that had been flung around by a China Lobby man or anybody else. The State Department cleared me. Then they changed the standards and they cleared me again, and then there was more

[14]Chaired by conservative Democrat Millard Tydings of Maryland, chairman of the Armed Services Committee.

[15]An eminent China scholar with unorthodox views, Lattimore was the director of the Walter Hines Page School of International Relations at Johns Hopkins University. Even though Lattimore had been only briefly connected to the State Department during the war, McCarthy nevertheless denounced him as "the chief architect of our Far Eastern policy" and the top Soviet espionage agent in the United States. He was finally cleared after five years of fighting the Justice Department on the flimsiest of perjury charges (i.e., did his lunch with the Soviet ambassador ten years earlier take place before or after the Nazi invasion of Russia?).

evidence submitted, which was real hokum. Because once you get enough publicity, there are crackpots who come to the FBI with all sorts of allegations—that I had a police record in New York for homosexuality and all sorts of nutstuff.

The State Department kept clearing me, but this did not satisfy the Loyalty Review Board, which was the top board. So they said, "Well, we're going to have our own hearing." They had a one-day hearing—a kangaroo court. In those days, you didn't have to find anybody disloyal, all you had to do was find what they called "reasonable doubt of loyalty." It's a very hard thing to disprove. They instructed the State Department to fire me. The State Department checked with the White House. But Truman had created the Loyalty Review Board, and it was a hot political potato at the time. The White House said, "Well, there's nothing you can do. If they say fire him, then fire him." I was dismissed on twenty-four hours' notice, at the close of business the next day.

There were some people in sensitive positions, certainly, who had to break off contact, but none of our China friends or the people we knew well. I had trouble renting an apartment in New York. The only question they asked was "Is this the same man who was fired by the State Department? Sorry." I was even turned down for life insurance. I wanted to get term insurance, because I'd lost my Foreign Service insurance. The guy said, "Well, how do we know? You may jump out a window." By this time there had been one or two people who were under attack and had committed suicide. So from a life insurance point of view, maybe the guy had a point.

We exhausted all the administrative remedies. The Loyalty Review Board was presumably under the Civil Service Commission, so we asked them first that the Loyalty Review Board would have a reconsideration, that they'd not considered all the evidence, and they turned us down. Then we asked the Civil Service Commission to have a reconsideration, and they refused. We went to the White House, and the White House refused. So then we went to court. We had a terrible time just getting our case heard, because the government fought to have the courts reject it. We finally got a complaint accepted and we worked our way through the courts. It took a long time, seven years. We lost in the district court and we lost in the court of appeals. Finally, in 1957, we won unanimously in the Supreme Court, eight to nothing!

When the Supreme Court came down with its decision, I was riding the subway in New York. Every paper had my picture on the front page. I felt conspicuous as hell, because here I was in this damned crowded subway train with my picture on the paper. But no one recognized me! [Laughs.]

Not a single person. By then, sentiment toward the loyalty program had gradually changed, and most of the headlines reflected that, except for *Time* magazine, which had always been against the critics of Chiang Kai-shek. *Time* said that the Supreme Court had ruled that the State Department didn't follow its own regulations, so "now that you know what to do, do it the right way and fire him!" [Laughs.] But *Time* was out alone.

It was frustrating, years and years, the whole business of getting through the courts. But eventually I won, and so I did as I'd planned to do: I went back to the government, much to the government's horror! [Laughs.] I was a political embarrassment, as far as they were concerned. They were going to send me to Germany, but that fell through. The German government was tired of being a dumping ground for security cases. They'd had several already, so they didn't want another one. They ended up sending me to the American consulate in Liverpool, England. Liverpool was a bit of a Siberian backwater with no work of any importance. Mainly, the office just issued visas. After three years there, I realized there wasn't a prayer for a worthwhile assignment or promotion. So what the hell, why stay around? I'd made my point. So I retired at fifty-two.

During those years the State Department got rid of a lot of people with a more balanced point of view. Others were apt to be conservative, or pro-Kuomintang—and a lot of people in State were pro-Kuomintang. Because of that, I'm sure the reporting was hampered. If you read the White Paper, you can see that the reporting, by and large, was pretty straight. The conservatives didn't come out and say the good things about Communists that we'd been saying: that they had popular support, that their policies benefited the farmer, and so on. But nonetheless, they were critical. Practically all Americans with any real contact in China, even Wedemeyer,[16] wrung their hands about the corruption in Chiang Kai-shek's government.

Where the real pinch came down is not so much on the reporting from the field, but on limiting the type of people who go into the Foreign Service. The security program has discouraged a lot of the best and the brightest from even considering the Foreign Service. Look what happens. Once you decide you want to take the Foreign Service exam, you're at the mercy, without any knowledge or appeal, of a security clearance procedure which is run by policemen. A lot of them not very bright policemen. And

[16]In July 1947, Lieutenant General Albert Wedemeyer, a staunch ally of the Nationalist Chinese, was sent by Truman to China and Korea on a fact-finding mission to appraise "the political, economic, psychological, and military situations—current and projected." His confidential report asserted that the Kuomintang's "reactionary leadership, repression, and corruption has caused a loss of popular faith in the Government."

they're not going to take any chances on someone who attended a rally or signed a petition. So anyone that has shown any liberal or radical political activity will be blackmailed by the security people, and they will never know why they didn't get clearance. So what do you have left? Certainly not the best and brightest! [Laughs.] I'm not trying to say that it's the dregs, by any means. But most of the people that come into the Foreign Service now are pretty conventional. They haven't done very much, certainly in the political line, or even shown very much interest in anything like that.

JOHN MELBY

In 1951, John Melby was considered a brilliant Foreign Service officer with impeccable anti-Communist credentials. In September of that year, he was charged with being a security risk for having "maintained an association" with playwright Lillian Hellman. In 1953, after seven loyalty-security hearings, Melby was fired.

My problem in the McCarthy period concerned exclusively my association with Lillian Hellman,[1] whom I had met in Moscow during the war. We had quite an affair, and it continued, in one sense or another, up until the time she died. In September 1951, I received a letter from the Security Office, with a series of questions which I was requested to answer. Most of them just the usual garbage. Although there were a couple on Lillian in there, I didn't think that was particularly serious. I still thought what was bugging them was me in China and the China White Papers, because after all I'd really written that White Paper. But no, that wasn't so. So I answered the original interrogatory, particularly the questions on Lillian. And this on the advice of a lawyer in New York, who said, "Look, you can't possibly remember all the times you've seen her. Just pick out a representative selection of the times and frequencies."

So I answered those two questions that way. Then in November they came back at me with a second interrogatory that concerned Lillian exclu-

---

[1]Lillian Hellman (1905–84), playwright and screenwriter, was well known for her leftist politics and thirty-year association with writer Dashiell Hammett. Hellman was blacklisted in Hollywood from 1952 to 1961.

sively. And there they said the department has information that you spent a weekend with Miss Hellman, who is alleged to be a member of the Communist Party, at her farm in Westchester County. Well, it so happened that it was true and it was one of the times that I had not mentioned. All I could do was say, "Yes, it's quite true. I was there. I spent a whole weekend with her. There wasn't anybody else there, just the two of us.[2] She had let the servants go for the weekend, and the farmer was away. So, sure, I was there, so what?" Well, this clearly did not satisfy them, and this was followed in April by formal charges: having associated with one Lillian Hellman, who is a member of the Communist Party.[3] A date was set for a hearing, July 19, 1951. The last hearing ended eighteen months later.

They started out with "Are you a Communist?" My lawyers at that time saying, "Let's go on the record, he is not and never has been a member of the Party." They knew that and they didn't pay any attention to it. It was a question of association with somebody who is alleged to be a member of the Party.

The way the system worked in those days, you were given charges but you were not told who had made them. You were not permitted to confront the accuser, and you were not permitted to answer him directly. You couldn't refer to files or anything else.[4] I, frankly, had accepted some bad advice from some friends, who said, "Look, this thing is a lot of nonsense. Get the most conservative lawyer you can find, and do exactly what he wants you to do. Then forget it and it'll be all over."

Well, that was a mistake, because my lawyer, who practiced before the Federal Communications Commission, was a good enough lawyer, but he didn't know anything about this area of the law—he didn't claim to. He didn't know what to do when they'd throw these questions at me.[5] He

[2]As neither of them had told anyone about the visit, it was Melby's first rather unnerving realization that one or both of them were being watched by the FBI.

[3]In mid-May, Melby received an amended letter of charges: there were two new ones. One was that while serving in China he had carried on an affair with a woman friendly to the Communists. The other was that he had been a regular reader of the *Daily Worker* while in El Paso in 1937. Largely window-dressing, neither of these charges received more than a passing reference during the hearings. The focus was always Lillian Hellman.

[4]It is worth noting that the allegations against Hellman of Party membership and subversive activity were based on the flimsiest of associations and the unreliable testimony of Louis Budenz, a professional witness, and Martin Berkeley, a Hollywood canary for HUAC. But Melby was not allowed to inspect or know the source of the "evidence" against his former lover, and was uncertain as to its reliability. Under the constant grilling, his confusion grew.

[5]From Robert Newman's account, *The Cold War Romance of Lillian Hellman and John Melby* (Chapel Hill: Univ. of North Carolina Press, 1989), it appears that for the most part, Melby's attorney was an able performer. The syllogistic trap Melby found himself in was inescap-

couldn't believe what he was hearing. In the end they found against me. Fortunately, none of this ever got any publicity. Largely because I knew a great many newspapermen in Washington. Some of them came to me privately and said, "We understand you're in trouble. Do you want some publicity on the thing?" And I said "No, I don't," so they laid off.

That was very fortunate, because in May, Lillian was to testify before the House Un-American Activities Committee. She was very concerned about two things. One: would my name be brought up in the hearing? And two: Averell Harriman was beginning to run for President, and she had been a house guest of his in Moscow.[6] You can imagine, in the McCarthy period, what could be made of this alleged Communist as a houseguest of a candidate for the highest office in the land. You can imagine the scare headlines in the tabloids. As it turned out, nothing was said about either Harriman or me. We were all amazed. But so much of this was done on a buckshot approach. Fire the buckshot, and if you happen to hit somebody, go after 'em. It is entirely possible that they didn't even know.

As a matter of fact, after I'd been terminated in 1953, Father McGuire, who'd been a friend of mine in China with National Catholic Welfare, a very liberal kind of guy, went to Scott McLeod, who was then director of security[7] under John Foster Dulles. Father McGuire was prospecting to see what could be done about my troubles. And what McLeod said to him was "Look, my advice to you is keep your hands off this case, because if you don't, we're going to turn Melby's files over to Senator McCarthy. He doesn't know about it yet." So McGuire then phoned me and said, "Look, John, what do you want me to say on this?"

I said, "Oh my God, the last thing I want is McCarthy getting his sticky fingers on this thing. I've got two sons who are getting to be military age, and they're planning to apply for a commission in the Army. Furthermore, there's the question of Lillian, who says we can go to court on this, but I cannot ask her to testify, which she would have to do. I don't think she realizes what would be involved if she had to testify about me and her. I just cannot do this to her, any more than I could turn on her."

------

able: Hellman was bad; Melby associated with Hellman; therefore Melby was bad. No number of stellar character witnesses (and there were many, including Dean Rusk), no amount of lawyerly skills, could break this implacable logic.

[6]Hellman was the guest of Harriman during World War Two, when he had been the U.S. ambassador to Moscow. Melby and Hellman met during this stay.

[7]Scott McLeod, friend of Joe McCarthy and former FBI agent, created a police-state atmosphere in the State Department. At the end of his first year of tenure, he proudly announced that 484 employees had been removed without a single hearing.

Which is what they wanted me to do in my hearings. The main thing they were after me to say was "I have made a terrible mistake. I am ashamed of myself. I will never again have anything to do with her or anybody like her." What I told them was "I can't do that. I have no reason to believe she's a Communist. A left-wing radical, sure. So am I, in a sense. But a member of the Communist Party, I do not believe it." They kept hammering, "Will you promise that you will never again see her?" I said, "I will not do that. I have to live with myself."[8]

Those who were on the loyalty-security board who were trying me were a bunch of slobs, except on the appeal hearing. The chairman of that was a fairly well known Foreign Service officer, Joe Satterthwaite. And Joe said, "Look, Mr. Melby, let me ask you. Considering the atmosphere today, do you think you have any right to associate with anyone who might by any interpretation be construed by anyone as undesirable?" I just looked at him, I said, "Mr. Chairman, I don't have any answer to that." The counsel for the board once asked me the question "We have a report that you've been seen in hotel lobbies in Washington a good deal recently. Do you think it's a good idea for you to be seen in public while this is going on?" I said, "A hotel lobby is a public place and I'll go anyplace I want to."

But that was the atmosphere. The people who were not of my vintage, or Jack Service's, have a hard time visualizing the atmosphere of terror, really, it was terror, that pervaded everything. People whom you've known most of your life would see you coming down the street and they would cross the street so they wouldn't have to pass you.

Well, I appealed my suspension and I got a new lawyer. The man I got was Joe Volpe, who had been general counsel to the Atomic Energy Commission and had handled all the security matters for them. Joe had also been Oppenheimer's lawyer. Joe was as good as they come in that business. He did a beautiful job on it, but it was hopeless. Finally in May, I was terminated. The only notification I got was a letter from the undersecretary for administration, who merely said, "The Secretary has determined that your continued employment is no longer in the national interest." So, I guess I was the highest-ranking officer in the Foreign Service to be fired.

[8]At the time, under the incessant hammering of seven protracted hearings, Melby appears understandably to have been more diplomatic than defiant. While resisting a categorical promise never to see Hellman again under any circumstances, Melby twice went so far as to affirm that he had "no intention" of seeing her again. Finally, at the end of a long day of grilling, he capitulated further: "Had I the slightest suggestion . . . of this kind of activity and views that have come out here, the association would have been discontinued permanently, automatically, and right then and there."

It took me two years to find another job. Not that my potential employers knew anything about my hearing, but in those days the mere fact that you had worked for the State Department Foreign Service was enough. Everybody was scared of it—a bunch of Communists.[9] In fact, the reputation of the service was such that even though there was normally between five and ten thousand applicants a year to the Foreign Service, that second year when I was still looking for a job, there was none.

I finally got a job at Yale University, as a research associate in Southeast Asian studies. Yale apparently decided that, State Department or no State Department, the question was, does he know anything about Southeast Asia? After a while it got where nobody paid much attention to my State Department background.

When Kennedy became President, I thought, well, here at last, we got a good Democratic president, and Dean Rusk is the Secretary of State. I'd worked for Dean in the department. I went around to see him. He said, "I know this is terrible. Just leave it with me, and I'm going to straighten things out." Nothing happened. Additional queries, and nothing happened. So finally I go to see Roger Jones, who had taken a postretirement job as undersecretary for administration of the State Department. Jones said to me, "I'm going to tell you what did happen. I'll probably get fired for telling you, but I don't care." The chairman of the House Un-American Activities Committee had served notice on Rusk that "if you attempt to get anyone on our list promoted or advanced, or if you bring anybody else to us who is on our list,[10] the State Department is going to have one hell of a bad time with its appropriations. It's up to you." In other words, he was blackmailing Rusk.

But I did get cleared. That happened in 1980, in the last months of the Carter administration. I realized that if I was going to get anything done, this administration was probably my last chance. So I went again to Averell Harriman, who was very close to the Carter administration. I told him I thought this was the last chance, and he said, "You're absolutely right, and we're going to do something about it." And he did. I'd been at it for some thirty years.

John Melby died at age seventy-nine on December 18, 1992.

[9] Two years before his 1953 firing, Melby in his capacity as a Foreign Service officer gave a speech in St. Louis. Afterward, he overheard two astonished ladies appraising his performance: "He sounds like a normal American."

[10] According to Jones, HUAC maintained a list of persons it did not wish promoted and of persons it did not wish to be reemployed. Melby's name was on the list.

ANTHONY GEBER

Anthony Geber's problem with the Foreign Service security apparatus
began when his parents were imprisoned by the Communist government
in Hungary. We meet at his home in a suburb outside of Washington,
D.C., a neighborhood of ranch-style houses and sloping lawns.

I was born in Budapest, Hungary, in 1919 and came to the United States as
a student in 1938. I was drafted into the Army in 1943 and they sent me to
Berlin two years later. I was anxious to visit my parents, who still lived in
Budapest. I hadn't seen them for seven years. It wasn't easy, but finally, the
Russians, who were occupying Budapest, opened up and allowed American
military personnel who had close relatives in Hungary an entry permit.
When I got back, there was a call from a colonel who was planning an
official trip to Hungary and Rumania. He asked if I was interested in going
again, and I said yes. That answer decided my fate. In order to go, because
I was about to be discharged and shipped back to the States, I had to either
sign up for another six months in the Army or become a civilian employee
of the military government. I chose the latter, and this is how I became a
bureaucrat.

In April 1946 I was stationed in Berlin. Military governors came and
went, but I stayed. Eventually, I became a Foreign Service staff officer.
During the blockade, things got so bad the government couldn't afford to
feed us, so we were sent to the Zone: first to Nuremberg, then Bad Nau-
heim, and eventually I got back to Berlin. In 1952 I went to Bonn, working
for the Office of Political Affairs. That's when my troubles started.

The Stalinist regime in Hungary started deportations of thousands of people, mostly of the middle class. They were deporting them to small villages
in eastern Hungary, miserable places. Among them were my parents. It was
a rather cruel procedure, and I know of numerous examples where it was
evident that their primary objective was cruelty against the "bourgeois"
rather than any rational policy objective.

But through either foresight or luck, my parents got the attention of the
Dutch minister in Budapest. He found them a refuge, inviting them to
move up to a house rented by the Dutch in Budapest. The very same night

my parents moved, the political police came to drag them out of the house. But luckily and with great foresight, the Dutch minister who lived next door stayed up that night and when the political police arrived he told them they could not enter the premises, which were under diplomatic protection. So they left, and there my parents lived. (Incidentally, the Dutch minister was commended by his queen and the story of my parents became quite well known.) At first they didn't dare to move out of the house or the garden. Later on, they took short walks around the premises. But their situation became increasingly tenuous.

The minister wrote me that it was not a permanent solution, that one would really have to do something about it. First of all, if Hungary asked for extradition, he could not protect them, because they were Hungarian citizens. Second, he expected to be transferred in the near future and this was an action he had taken on his own and he would prefer not to burden his successor with the problem.

I tried a great number of things to get them visas. They each needed an exit permit from the Hungarians and an entrance visa from the U.S. The exit permit was the more difficult of the two to get. There were stories that if one paid five thousand dollars at the Hungarian consulate in New York, one could get an exit visa. But nothing worked.

Finally, I contacted a man who used to be counsel for the Hungarian National Bank before escaping to Austria. Now he spent most of his time trying to get others out. He offered me a rather iffy proposition. There was this Hungarian farmer who lived in Vienna. Before the war he had smuggled flint for lighters and saccharine. Now he was smuggling people, so he was a very experienced smuggler. He had already brought out groups of twenty or thirty people, some of whom I knew by name and could ascertain that this had happened.

It was risky and involved things like marching through fields. My father was seventy-four, in good condition and good health, a strong man; but my mother was rather frail. I really didn't know what I could or should do. But finally, I decided that I had to leave it up to my parents. I deposited a certain amount of money in escrow in a bank that would be his if the plan was a success. I never dealt with him directly, you understand, it was all through the lawyer.

Well, toward the end of 1952, he went off. We hoped my parents would get to Vienna in time to celebrate Christmas together. He went and he came back, and there were various stories as to why he came back, but then he went out again. He didn't arrive by December '52, and nothing was heard of my parents. Then in March came rumors that something went wrong, that my parents had been arrested. It was much later that I found out the details.

The smuggler had contacted my parents. They did not think they could or should undertake this very risky flight, but they wanted to think it over for a day or two. Then the smuggler got arrested. Under torture, he apparently gave out the names of people he had contacted. Just at that time, my parents got a call that my father's younger brother had a stroke and was probably in his last hours. They decided to take the risk and go to town to see him. But that telephone conversation had been tapped. They were arrested by the political police a couple of blocks away from the house where they lived.

On May 21, 1953—it's a date relatively easy for me to remember because it's the day my oldest child was born in Bonn—I got a letter from a lawyer in Budapest. He explained how my parents had been arrested, how he had very good connections in the appropriate circles in Hungary and he could do them some good, but for that we should meet somewhere. The signature was illegible, it gave an office and street address. The whole thing sounded rather phony. I consulted my superiors, friends of the family. I checked with the CIA representatives, as to what they could do to safeguard me against possible kidnapping.

In the end, I decided to send a telegram saying that I was willing to meet with him at the Bristol Hotel in Vienna, which was under U.S. Army control, on two days' advance notice. I also added to please give my parents the news that their first grandchild was born. He wrote back saying unfortunately the possibility for him to come to Vienna was out, and I probably had more of a possibility of moving around freely. He asked me if I could suggest another place, the implication being why don't I come to Budapest. He also said he transmitted my message to my parents, and there was a slip of paper that was obviously detached from something else, in my father's handwriting, saying congratulations. I learned later that the slip was the bottom part of a letter in which my father, contrary to the wishes of his jailers, cautioned us against any dealings with the Hungarians.

Shortly after that, a fairly high-ranking police officer from Hungary escaped and was interrogated in Vienna. He knew about my parents' case and told those who interrogated him that they were all right, considering the circumstances. They had gotten a year in jail. He also said that the Hungarian intelligence services would try to contact me in the form of a so-called lawyer, which, of course, had already happened. This information was cabled to intelligence in Bonn, and I was told about it. It also went to Washington. This is when our security people got interested in me.

Because my parents were in jail behind the Iron Curtain, it was decided that I was not supposed to handle classified material, or I could handle it only "under control." I had two responsibilities in Bonn's political office—Berlin relations and the Saar relations.

Doing it "under control" meant that my boss called me in the morning, showed me the classified telegrams, and asked me to draft answers. When I finished, I took them back and he stamped them "Confidential and Secret." It was a farce. This went on for a while. Then I was dismissed.

No one ever sat me down and questioned me about my parents. Everything I had ever done to get them out was aboveboard. My superiors knew. They still fired me because of it—because my parents were in jail, because the Hungarian intelligence services evidently made an effort to contact me, succeeded in contacting me. But first and foremost, I was fired because there was Senator McCarthy in Washington. The State Department was under attack, and security people throughout the government were shaking in their boots and were not going to take any risks if they could avoid it.

I never had a loyalty-security hearing. First of all, I was a temporary employee, as most of us were still at the time. I went through two committee interviews for getting into the Foreign Service, but I was a staff officer. I had no employment rights.

I soon learned that my mother had died, about ten days before she would have been released from jail. They let my father out on December 23, just in time to go to my mother's funeral. I informed the administrative and security people in the department that there was a change in the situation with my parents, and my security question was submitted to a review.

I became a test case in the department. It was decided that people who have relatives behind the Iron Curtain should not be automatic dismissal cases. I was cleared. In the end, I got my clearance from no less than the security chief in the department, Mr. McLeod.

Then my problem of getting gainful employment with the government started. It coincided with the reduction in force in the early days of the Eisenhower administration—people who had tenure were bumping each other off. It was very difficult to find a job. But from the moment I got the official notification that I had been cleared, I was never without at least two job offers in various organizations. But nothing ever seemed to work out.

I was pleased to get a job offer with the Foreign Aid office in Tehran, but they gave it to somebody who'd originally had a security problem, but had now been cleared. I was rather indignant that they would even talk to someone who had had a security problem. [Chuckles.] Then Foreign Aid Administration offered me a job to go to Indonesia, which seemed a very remote place, but I told them to put in my name. The next thing I heard was they could not give me a security clearance. I asked why not. After all, the only thing I did have during that crazy time was a clearance, fresh and hot off the press from the great Mr. McLeod, who wasn't known to be very generous with them.

Luckily I had a friend who was a former security officer. He found out that just because my department had given me clearance didn't mean others were going to accept it. Each agency had its own security procedures and didn't tolerate anybody else's intervention.

I got a phone call from the Operations Control Board that they had a job for me. They said, "Go home, we will call you in a couple of days." A couple of days went by and there was no phone call. Finally, I called and they said, "We have some problem." I asked if it was security. They wouldn't tell me over the phone. They said it would take another couple of days. I again called my friend and told him that something was going on. This was early in the morning, and he said, "Go have a drink." I said, "I don't usually start drinking this early, but if you insist, I will. Just tell me what is going on." He said, "They're getting cold feet, but rest assured, you will get the job." When I asked, "What are you doing about it?" he said, "I'm warming their feet." The job never came through.

Just about that time, I had a call from Howard P. Jones, who was head of the high commissioner's office in Berlin while I was there. I didn't report directly to him, but he knew me quite well. He told me, "I have been appointed mission director of the aid organization in Indonesia. Would you like to come with me as program officer?" I said, "Howard, you probably must have heard how that job was offered to me before, but I was turned down for security reasons." But Howard did his magic, and within two days I was sworn in for the job. After my assignment in Indonesia, I reverted back to the State Department, became a Foreign Service officer, and had a successful and rewarding career.

My father came out of jail in December 1953. I never was able to get him out of Hungary. I wasn't permitted in and he wasn't permitted out. The next time I was issued a visa to enter Hungary was in 1962 to attend his funeral.

Atom Bomb Spies

In the early morning hours of August 29, 1949, the Soviet Union detonated its first atomic weapon. America's nuclear monopoly was over.

When President Truman announced the event on September 23, he sought to calm the nation. "Ever since atomic energy was first released by man, the eventual development of this new force by other nations was to be expected. This probability has always been taken into account by us." General Eisenhower took the news in stride, characterizing it as "a development that was anticipated years ago." The *New York Times* commented, "There is no valid reason for surprise at this development . . . . Only those Americans who failed to pay attention to what was said of the atomic bomb by the men who knew most about it—namely, the men who built it—could ever have believed that we possessed a permanent and exclusive monopoly."

Apparently, the ranks of the inattentive included many journalists and politicians. A few days after the explosion, *Atomics,* a scientific journal, described the resulting outcry: "The news has already rocked the nation; it is being screamed from banner headlines in every newspaper from Los Angeles to Portland, Maine, and radio commentators have worked themselves into a minor panic, many of them have the country practically at war with Russia." Almost immediately, Capitol Hill conservatives deduced that America's atomic "secrets" had been stolen and cried "treason." Senator Karl Mundt laid the onus on "earlier and prevailing laxity in safeguarding this country from Communist espionage." Richard Nixon spoke up from the House Un-American Activities Committee charging the Truman Administration with "hastening" Russia's atomic know-how by its failure to act against Red spies. The widely publicized estimates of nuclear scientists in 1945—that there were no secrets and Russia would have the bomb in five years or less—had not been given much credence by American policy makers.

The truth, as often happens, did not lie entirely in either camp. During the Second World War, the Soviets launched a major effort to penetrate the American nuclear project. Stalin wanted the bomb as quickly as possible and duplicating the American plutonium device appeared to be the surest route. This, even though one of his own scientists, Georgii Flerov, had the calculations for a uranium-235 bomb as early as 1941, a design successfully tested in 1951. By the best estimates of the time; the fruits of their intelligence saved the Soviets one to two years in developing the plutonium device exploded in 1949.

The estimates made by many politicians, and even Edward Teller, of ten to twenty years before a Soviet bomb was possible underestimated Soviet scientists and the ability of the Stalinist command economy to create an atomic industry in a war-torn nation. The main obstacle for the Soviets lay in the availability of raw materials. David Holloway makes the point in *Stalin and the Bomb:*[1]

> The length of time the Soviet Union needed to develop the bomb was determined more by the availability of uranium than by any other factor . . . . The first production reactor was built as soon as there was enough uranium for it. The physicists were ready to assemble and test the bomb as soon as plutonium had been extracted from uranium irradiated in the reactor and fabricated into two metal hemispheres. It was this path, rather than the design and development of the weapon itself, that determined how long it took the Soviet Union to build the bomb.

The public search for spies, however, preceded the Soviet bomb test. In 1948, the House Un-American Activities Committee charged that the Berkeley Radiation Laboratory had been infiltrated by Communists, who had passed atomic secrets to the Soviet Union early in the war. They pointed to a group of talented young physicists who had flirted with communism in the late thirties and early forties, all proteges of J. Robert Oppenheimer.[2]

Oppenheimer, who supported many a radical cause, was a friend of Steve Nelson, a high-ranking and open member of the Communist Party. Nelson, in turn, held some degree of acquaintance with Oppenheimer's

[1]David Holloway. *Stalin and the Bomb: The Soviet Union and Atomic Energy 1939–1956.* (New Haven: Yale Univ. Press, 1994).

[2]J. Robert Oppenheimer (1904–1967) directed the building of the atom bomb during World War II. Later appointed the top government adviser on nuclear policy, he was suspended as a security risk in 1953, charged with close associations with Communists and obstructing the development of the N–bomb.

students. That alone was enough to damn the entire group. In the minds of HUAC and its allies, any connection between a scientist and a Communist could only mean espionage. With this, HUAC seized upon physicist Joseph Weinberg and publicized the case of "Scientist X," with Nelson as the "master-spy."

It is likely that Nelson was involved in an effort to garner information. At the time, Army security officers testified to "highly confidential sources" that placed a scientist named "Joe" at the home of Steve Nelson offering to give "highly confidential information." Surveillance placed Nelson meeting with the Soviet Vice Consul in a park and handing him an envelope. In the years since, the "source" has been revealed to be FBI taps and bugs.[3]

While HUAC was busy making headlines in the Old House Office Building, more productive investigations were underway on the campus of Arlington Hall, a former junior college in suburban Virginia. There, the Army Signal Intelligence Service was painfully decrypting a stockpile of cables intercepted between Moscow and the Soviet consulate in New York from 1943 to 1945. The cables contained KGB and other Soviet intelligence traffic, as well as diplomatic and trade exchanges. Codenamed JADE, then BRIDE, and finally VENONA, the project would uncover Klaus Fuchs, the most effective Soviet agent in the Manhattan Project.[4] It would also lead to the senseless deaths of the only two Americans ever executed for espionage.

On June 19, 1953, Julius and Ethel Rosenberg, the parents of two young sons, were put to death in the electric chair at Sing Sing prison. Charged with conspiring to pass the "secrets" of the atomic bomb to the Soviet Union, they were sentenced as if they had been convicted of treason. In the docket with the Rosenbergs was codefendant Morton Sobell. Sobell was labeled by the press as an "atom spy," although the prosecution made no such claim. In fact, the Justice Department never presented any clear-cut evidence that he had committed espionage of any kind. Nevertheless, Sobell was given a thirty-year sentence and dispatched to Alcatraz Federal Penitentiary.

[3]See Anthony Cave Brown and Charles B. MacDonald, *On a Field of Red: The Communist International and the Coming of World War II* (New York: Putnam, 1981), pp. 620–22; also Curt Gentry, *J. Edgar Hoover: The Man and the Secrets* (New York: W. W. Norton, 1991), p. 312.

[4]In 1946, another British scientist, Alan Nunn May, had been arrested for espionage after Igor Gouzenko, a cipher clerk at the Soviet embassy in Ottawa, Canada, defected with a suitcase of files on Soviet activities in Canada. May was sentenced to ten years at hard labor and served six. Klaus Fuchs was sentenced to fourteen years and served nine.

The bitter debate over the guilt or innocence of the Rosenbergs has endured longer than the Cold War itself. In unquiet graves, they became icons of the conflict itself. For many on the Left they were innocents sacrificed in the game of nations. For those on the Right, certain of their guilt, the Rosenbergs exemplified the treachery of the Communist Party, the enemy within. Others took the opinion that Julius was guilty of espionage, but that Ethel was only peripherally involved.

Forty-nine VENONA intercepts, decoded largely between 1947 and 1952, were released in July 1995, the first of more than two thousand to be declassified over the following year. No doubt the cause of much pain and sadness, they show Julius Rosenberg to have been the head of a spy ring gathering and passing defense information to the Soviet Union.

According to Robert Lamphere, the chief FBI agent on the case,[5] the trail to the Rosenbergs began in the spring of 1948. A decoded intercept from July 1944 reported: "ANTENNA[6] visited his school friend Max Elitcher . . . . He has access to extremely valuable material on guns." The message gave detailed information on Elitcher and his wife and requested that Moscow "check Elitcher and communicate your consent to his clearance." Through Naval Intelligence, Lamphere learned that Elitcher had attended an anti-draft rally in 1941 with Morton Sobell. A background check revealed that the two had been fellow engineering students at CCNY and had roomed together after graduation. Lamphere claims that around the same time another message fragment named Joel Barr as a potential recruit for the KGB.[7] A third decoded intercept reported background information on a then-unknown woman: "Information on LIBERAL's wife, Surname that of her husband, first name ETHEL, 29 years old. Married five years. Finished secondary school . . . . Knows about her husband's work . . . . In view of delicate health does not work."

While these leads temporarily ran aground, a cable partially deciphered

[5]Robert J. Lamphere and Tom Shachtman, *The FBI–KGB War: A Special Agent's Story* (New York: Random House, 1986). As Lamphere published in 1986, well before the intercepts were declassified, he apparently relied on memory to reconstruct details of the messages. Therefore, the cable referring to ANTENNA contacting Elitcher refers to a meeting in July, not June as he states in his book, and no code-name for Elitcher appears to have been assigned.

[6]Hundreds of code names were used in the encrypted messages to disguise the identities of Soviet intelligence officers and agents, as well as organizations, people, or places discussed. Thus KAPITAN was President Roosevelt, BABYLON was San Francisco, ENORMOZ was the Manhattan Project, REST was Klaus Fuchs, and ANTENNA/LIBERAL was Julius Rosenberg.

[7]While none of the intercepts mention Joel Barr in this context, a decoded cable of May 5, 1944 discusses the recruitment of Alfred Sarant, "a lead of ANTENNA's." Throughout the intercepts, investigators are uncertain whether the codenames HUGHES and METER refer to Barr or Sarant, perhaps leading Lamphere, relying largely on memory, to confuse the two.

in mid-September 1949 proved to be of more immediate import. The message revealed the partial title of a report on the gaseous diffusion process received from an agent codenamed REST, part of the British contingent to the Manhattan Project. Within a short time, the author of the report was discovered to be Klaus Fuchs, one of the top British scientists. The following January, under interrogation by British Intelligence, Fuchs began to confess. Eventually he would reveal that he had passed vast amounts of classified information to the Soviets during and after the war, including detailed sketches of the bomb's design.

In May 1950, Fuchs identified a Philadelphia chemist named Harry Gold as his courier.[8] Gold in turn implicated another source inside Los Alamos. This person was unknown to Fuchs, a machinist with a tenth-grade education named David Greenglass.[9] Arrested in June, Greenglass confessed and identified his brother-in-law, Julius Rosenberg, as the head of the spy ring. In time, other deciphered cables would corroborate elements of these confessions. One such cable from September 1944 discusses LIBERAL's recommendation to recruit "the wife of his wife's brother, Ruth Greenglass" as her husband "is a mechanical engineer and is now working at the ENORMOUS plant in Santa Fe, New Mexico." Other cables, using codenames OSA for Ruth and KALIBR for David, detail further approaches to the couple and their eventual compliance.

VENONA settles questions, but raises disturbing ones as well. The messages do not confirm key elements of the atomic spying charges against Julius. The cable that reports the January meeting during which David claimed to have turned over a sketch of the bomb to Julius tells only of "a hand-written plan of the lay-out of Camp-2 and facts known to him about the work and the personnel." Ethel is revealed to have been aware of her husband's activities, but as of late November 1944 was not an agent nor active in his work.

On February 8, 1951, one month before the Rosenbergs' trial began, Justice Department representative Myles Lane met in secret session with the Congressional Committee on Atomic Energy. Lane informed them that Julius was the "keystone to a lot of other espionage agents" and that the Department believed the only thing that would break him was "the prospect of the death penalty." He added that it was important to give Ethel "a stiff sentence of twenty-five to thirty years" also as a means to

---

[8] Gold was sentenced to thirty years and served fifteen.
[9] Greenglass was sentenced to fifteen years and served ten.

break Julius, even though the case against her "was not too strong . . . . It is about the only thing you can use as a lever against these people." At that point, the case against Ethel was not only "not too strong," it was nonexistent. They knew Ethel was aware of Julius's work, but that was all. Eight days before the trial began, David Greenglass, under pressure from investigators, implicated Ethel in the single act that would take her life.[10]

Judge Kaufman, in pronouncing sentence, described the defendant's crime as "worse than murder." By "putting into the hands of the Russians the A-bomb years before our best scientists predicted . . . has caused in my opinion the Communist aggression in Korea, with the resultant casualties exceeding 50,000 and who knows but . . . millions more may pay the price of your treason." With this nonsense Kaufman sentenced Julius and Ethel to death in the electric chair. But their choice remained—confess or die, and the Justice Department fully expected them to confess.

On the night of the executions, FBI agents waited in make-shift offices on death row, armed with a stenographer and a month's worth of office supplies. The procedure was firmly defined. Both Julius and Ethel would be asked separately by a rabbi if they were willing to confess. If so, then their lives would be spared. Even if one was strapped into the chair, and indicated a willingness to talk, the execution would be halted. A system of signals was arranged for the benefit of the FBI agents waiting down the hall. When an execution had been completed, a guard would step into the corridor and wave his arm.

The executions began at eight P.M. By eight-sixteen, Ethel and Julius Rosenberg were dead.

---

[10]Greenglass and his wife Ruth claimed Ethel had typed up his notes on the atom bomb—the sole overt act that implicated Ethel in espionage. Until this point, however, in their pretrial interviews, the Greenglasses had consistently asserted that all the reports were handwritten. Thirty years later in a rare interview with Ronald Radosh, the Greenglasses were hopelessly vague in remembering the typing incident, although they clearly remembered other events. At one point, Ruth said, "It was almost as if we threw that in to involve her . . . ."

MORTON SOBELL

As a codefendant in the Rosenberg atom spy case, Morton Sobell was found guilty and sentenced to thirty years in prison. He served eighteen and a half, the first five in Alcatraz Federal Penitentiary. He is an impassioned man who has always asserted his innocence.

I knew Julius. He graduated from City College in the class after mine. We were both in a Young Communist League organization there called the Steinmetz Club. After New York, I moved to Washington, then to Michigan, but we kept in touch. When I came to New York I'd see him. So when they arrested him, they investigated *everybody* in the class before his and afterwards. Half of our electrical engineering class belonged to the Young Communist League. So they really went after everybody.

In fact, I had a FBI file even before that. I had gone down to Wrens, Georgia, with a letter of introduction to Erskine Caldwell's father.[1] Somebody down there didn't like this New Yorker and wrote a letter or something, and the mail that I sent was all copied and went to the local FBI. That's one thing. The other was when Paul Robeson sang at a concert in Washington and the FBI took down the license plates of all the cars parked around there. They had recorded my license plate.

In June of 1950 I went to Mexico.[2] I took a leave of absence from Reeves Instruments, where I was working, and went down there under my own name. While we were in Mexico, there was never any indication that the government wanted us back. They could have found us, because our apartment was registered in our own name—in Mexico when somebody rents an apartment they have to register. There was nothing secret about it.

My going there was a very ambivalent act. Things were heating up here—the Hollywood Ten and other things—and a lot of people were

[1] Erskine Caldwell, Southern novelist, first won fame with *Tobacco Road* and *God's Little Acre*. His father, Ira Sylvester Caldwell, was a minister for the Reformed Presbyterian Church and an outspoken civil rights advocate.

[2] At his trial and in the press, the trip Sobell and his family took to Mexico was portrayed as flight to avoid prosecution.

escaping the heat by going to Mexico. I had been looking around for a new job, and I couldn't find anything. I was going down there to sort of try to cut things loose and see what might come of it. But Julius was arrested while I was there, and boy, that really shook me up. At that time I tried to scurry around to find out if I could get out of Mexico. But then when I traveled around to Vera Cruz and all, I used pseudonyms.[3]

Then at one point we decided hell's bells, we'd better get back to the United States. We got our vaccinations[4] and we were ready to come back. That's when the Mexican security police kidnapped me.[5] They were not acting as agents of the Mexican government, but as agents of the FBI— they got a payoff. They dragged me down to the street, and I was yelling, "Police, police!" They hit me over the head and shoved me in the car. They took my wife and the children in another car.

They took us to their headquarters, where they made arrangements with the FBI. Then they drove us straight to the border, seventeen hours, where I was handed over to the Customs people. I guess it's like people going to the death chamber, I didn't stop yelling. At United States Customs I was directed to sign a card, searched, and then arrested. At the trial they produced the card with my signature, but it says "Deported from Mexico" on it. I was supposed to have signed it after they had written "Deported from Mexico." But they weren't very clever—the "Deported from Mexico" was in a different handwriting than everything else on the card. The government really lied all along the line on every occasion.

After about five days in jail down at the border, I was taken back to New

---

[3]During this period, Sobell inquired of his neighbor how one might leave Mexico without papers; he traveled to Vera Cruz and Tampico to inquire about passage for himself and family to Europe or South America. Marvin Salt and Morton Solt were two of the five names he used. Saypol, the prosecutor, portrayed these confused efforts as part of the elaborate escape plan allegedly laid out by Julius Rosenberg to both David Greenglass and Sobell. This plan entailed false travel documents, coded letters to the Soviet embassy, the receipt of forged passports, money, and instructions that take the fugitives to Sweden and then Czechoslovakia. Yet, two months after his arrival, Sobell was still in his Mexico City apartment, under his own name. Nor were any false passports or caches of money found in his possession. In a 1953 affidavit filed from Alcatraz, Sobell attributed his actions to panic. "Of course, I had no idea how it could be misinterpreted, and how dangerous it would turn out to be."

[4]Among Sobell's effects confiscated at the time of his arrest is a smallpox vaccination certificate issued on August 8, 1950, in his own name, with his correct U.S. address. While this cannot prove he intended to return to the States (many other countries required vaccinations as well), it does show that he did not expect to travel under an alias.

[5]On the evening of August 16, three Spanish-speaking men burst through the door of the Sobell apartment, waving pistols and accusing Sobell of being a bank robber named "Johnny Jones."

York and held on one hundred thousand dollars bail. My mother went around borrowing from relatives but could only come up with fifty thousand. My lawyer told me if I had come up with a hundred thousand they would have raised it, so I never got out.

Then they got onto this guy Max Elitcher, who was a very good friend of mine, my next-door neighbor, in fact. After the war he had signed a non-Communist affidavit when he was working for the Navy Department, but he had been a member of the YCL. So they had people who were willing to testify that he was a Communist. Elitcher was facing ten years. He was the one who fingered me and was the only witness who testified against me.[6]

He claimed that I'd been a member of the Party and that Julius had said I was giving him information. He testified that I got him to join the Communist Party in Washington, that I collected the dues. He testified to other things that involved me, which were not true.[7] For instance, that I had asked him about a Navy pamphlet for purposes of espionage. I *had* asked him about the pamphlet, because I was working on a project at GE; he was working for the Navy Department on the same project. But he turned it around to I asked him for espionage.[8] There is stuff in the files which shows how the FBI said to him, "Could it have been for purposes of espionage?" and he said, "Yes." But at the trial he just told it. This is a classic case of how the FBI operates. They presuppose the story and then they encourage a witness to put it into shape.

The Rosenbergs and I were all charged with one count, conspiracy to commit espionage. I was supposed to have committed naval espionage, and they supposedly atomic. The only thing they had on me was Elitcher, my trip to Mexico, and the fact that I was a friend of Julius. Here's the crucial

[6]By signing a federal loyalty oath in which he lied about his CP membership, Elitcher opened himself to charges of perjury. Although he could not testify to any overt acts of espionage committed by Sobell, the importance of his testimony was attested to when Judge Kaufman charged the jury: "If you do not believe the testimony of Max Elitcher as it pertains to Sobell, then you must acquit the defendant Sobell."

[7]Elitcher also testified that one night in the summer of 1948, he accompanied Sobell to a street near Rosenberg's apartment, where Sobell left him to deliver a 35mm film can to Julius. On cross-examination, Elitcher admitted he had no idea what was in the can. Sobell denied the incident ever happened.

[8]This occurred in 1946 when Elitcher was visiting Sobell while on a Navy business trip at General Electric, where Sobell also worked. As the men discussed their jobs, Elitcher mentioned that he was working on a gunnery control system. Sobell inquired if any reports were available on it.

thing. Before the trial, we tried to get a bill of particulars,[9] in which we would have learned exactly what acts I was accused of committing—which would have revealed that my case was not connected to the Rosenbergs' atom spy case. The presiding judge granted the petition for a bill of particulars and gave the government ten days to produce it. Thirteen days later, he says this is to be reargued. It was reargued—you know what happened? Nothing! Somebody got to him and told him, "You can't do this." I should never have been tried with alleged atom bomb spies, because it prejudiced my case.[10] All the publicity led me to believe that the atom bomb case was going to be the accusation. So how do you defend yourself?

The government tried to make the case that I was working as an agent for Julius, but not on the atom bomb. But they couldn't do it. This wasn't the only bad thing about it. During the trial, the judge and the prosecutor both kept yelling, "Treason! Traitors!" Now, treason is the only crime defined in the Constitution, and for one very good reason. Historically, anybody that wants to come down on dissenters redefines treason to suit that purpose. For treason you need two witnesses to the same overt act. Of course, there were no two witnesses. But the trial had all the overtones of a treason trial. Conspiracy is the darling of the prosecutors, because the rules of evidence are much less stringent. Traditionally, a conspiracy charge doesn't have the same penalties as a charge where you have an overt act. But in this case conspiracy called for the death penalty.

Until two weeks before the trial, they had nothing on Ethel Rosenberg. All of a sudden, after months of interrogation, David Greenglass, her brother, remembers that Ethel had typed up his notes on the structure of the atom bomb, thus implicating her by deed in the conspiracy.[11] So how did they

[9]Although Sobell was named as a codefendant in the Rosenberg case, none of the overt acts listed in the indictment mentioned or even alluded to him. When his attorneys petitioned for a bill of particulars specifying the acts of which he was accused, the only information they received was the date of June 15, 1944, as the approximate day Sobell "joined the alleged conspiracy."

[10]In 1952, Sobell's appeals attorney, Howard Meyer, argued that the rights of his client had been unfairly prejudiced by pretrial publicity, which included statements by J. Edgar Hoover, the Attorney General, and the U.S. attorney labeling him an atom spy, and as such, no evidence about him was presented at the trial. Nonetheless, Sobell's conviction was upheld by the court of appeals by a vote of two to one. The dissenter, Judge Jerome Frank, believed that Sobell should not have been tried jointly with the Rosenberg-Greenglass-Gold atom bomb conspiracy and declared that Sobell was entitled to a new trial.

[11]Ten days before the trial, the prosecution concluded that the case against Ethel needed additional evidence. Ruth Greenglass, David's wife, obliged, revealing that in September 1945 Ethel had typed up her husband's espionage notes. David Greenglass quickly confirmed her account, although six months earlier, when questioned about the same event, he swore his sister had not been present, nor had she ever discussed espionage with him.

justify giving her the death penalty and sentencing her? Judge Kaufman[12] said she wore the pants in the family. She was the she-devil. A lot of stuff has surfaced about the judge. For instance, he claimed that he didn't take any recommendations from anybody on the sentencing. It turns out he was in touch with everybody.[13]

When the judge sentenced me, he said, "I'm not doing the popular thing," as if people were telling him to sentence me to death.[14] The law is very funny, thirty years or death. Nothing longer than thirty years; otherwise, he would have given me more. The Rosenbergs got death for conspiracy.

But you know how Greenglass justified himself? I got it from people he knew in prison. How come you turned in your sister? "It was either my wife or my sister." Which was a lie, but that's how he justified it.

A book written recently by a lawyer in Washington pointed out that the Rosenbergs should have been tried under a different statute, the Atomic Energy Act. The Atomic Energy Act puts the question of death penalty on the jury. This lawyer, Fyke Farmer from North Carolina, together with another lawyer, Daniel Marshall from L.A., made a last-ditch effort to save their lives using this argument.[15] It's a crazy thing. As bad as my lawyers

[12]The Honorable Irving R. Kaufman, who had been assistant attorney general under Tom Clark, and who, according to a former FBI official, "worshipped J. Edgar Hoover."

[13]Roy Cohn, who as the assistant prosecuting attorney made his career on this case, claims in his autobiography to have persuaded Kaufman to give Ethel the death penalty, explaining, "The way I see it is she's worse than Julius. . . . She was the mastermind. . . . I don't see how you can justify sparing her." Cohn claims also that he and Kaufman were in secret communication throughout the proceedings and that "Kaufman told me before the trial started he was going to sentence Julius Rosenberg to death." (*The Autobiography of Roy Cohn* [Secaucus, N.J.: Lyle Stuart, 1988], pp. 76–77)

[14]Upon sentencing Sobell to thirty years, Judge Kaufman remarked: "I do not for a moment doubt that you were engaged in espionage activities; however the evidence in the case did not point to any activity on your part in connection with the atom bomb project." J. Edgar Hoover, however, had no such compunctions. In pressing for the death sentence for Sobell (in a report to the Attorney General), Hoover reasoned, "[Sobell] has not cooperated with the government and had undoubtedly furnished high classified material to the Russians although we cannot prove it."

[15]In a "next friend" petition to Justice Douglas presented at the start of the Court's summer recess, Farmer and Marshall argued that the case had been tried under the wrong law, that the 1946 Atomic Energy Act had superseded the 1917 Espionage Act. This last-ditch effort resulted in Douglas issuing a stay of execution and ordering the matter back to the district court. That same afternoon, under the prodding of Attorney General Brownell, Chief Justice Vinson reconvened the Court. Two days later, at noon, the Court announced that the Douglas stay had been overturned by a six-to-three vote. In Justice Black's dissent, he questioned the power of the full Court to overturn the stay, saying that the action was "unprecedented" in the Court's history and he had found no statute or rule permitting it. By eight-sixteen that same evening, the Rosenbergs were dead.

were, the Rosenbergs' lawyer was worse, Emanuel Bloch. They had been begging him to file this thing for months and he refused.[16]

As far as the Communist Party was concerned, it was hands off, because they thought we might implicate them to save our necks. Years later, I spoke to Max Gordon, who was the editor of the *Daily Worker* at that time, and he told us there were no clear-cut orders, but the Party just told people to stay out of it. So during the trial and almost for a year afterwards, the Party was hands-off because they didn't know what was going to happen. They finally got involved in it during the appeals process. And then all over the world the various Parties got involved. In France, there's a saying, "As the Dreyfus case divided France, the Rosenberg case united it."[17]

I don't think it would have made any difference if the Communist Party had gotten involved in the trial. The Party at that time was on the ropes, so how could they have done anything? Maybe they could have provided better attorneys, I don't know. The government got away with murder because our attorneys were that bad. Murder, literally.

The son-in-law of Kuntz, my lawyer, denounced me because I came down on my lawyers. But I do it with understanding. The Communist lawyers had all been socked with a lot of time for contempt of court,[18] and so my lawyers were frightened. The position of the son was, "Look, he took the case, you should appreciate that." But my point is, he shouldn't have taken it, because he wasn't willing to put himself on the line.

At the federal detention house, they kept threatening me with Alcatraz if I didn't cooperate. They started circulating rumors to this effect two months before the Supreme Court. Once I lose in the Supreme Court they could send me wherever they wanted to.

I lost in the court of appeals, I'm waiting for the Supreme Court, but we

[16]Many Bloch's enmity toward the Farmer and Marshall effort has never been adequately explained. While arguing before the full Court whether the Rosenbergs should have been tried under the far more favorable Atomic Energy Act (so much more favorable that the government openly conceded that a conviction most likely could not be had under it), Bloch appeared to be so undercutting the effort that Justice Black was prompted to inquire: "Mr. Bloch, you represent the Rosenbergs, do you not? And it's your duty to try to save them from the electric chair if possible, is that right?"

[17]Worldwide support for the Rosenbergs spanned the political spectrum. According to the *Washington Post*, in 1953, the White House received more than 200,000 messages on the case—most urging clemency. More than 20,000 were received in the week before their execution.

[18]By the time of the Rosenberg-Sobell trial, the rash of Smith Act prosecutions against the leadership of the Communist Party was already under way. Many of their defense attorneys found themselves the target of contempt citations and disbarment proceedings.

never got certiorari.[19] So I lose, and *bang*, they want to drag me out to Alcatraz. I had Howard Meyer at this point, so he goes into court and says, "Give me another week to confer with him on appeal." The week was up Thanksgiving Eve, and so they put me on a plane. The marshals were cursing because they wouldn't be able to have Thanksgiving. During a layover in Chicago, they set me up. They took me off the plane and onto the concourse without handcuffs or anything. There were FBI agents all around. This was a setup to make an escape attempt and then they'd be able to plug me.

The FBI planted an item in the *New York Mirror*, with one of the columnists, a FOB, Friend of the Bureau. This columnist was one of them. He wrote that when I hit the big-time prison I'd wish I had been executed like the Rosenbergs because the men are really going to come down hard. Of course, when I got there it was the other way around. On the Rock, the other prisoners treated me very nicely. A thirty-year sentence gets you respect right away. And then I was a high-profile case, so they knew the FBI had come down on me. The guards were quite nice also. At first they called me Mister. Yeah, the guards never really hassled me or anything like that—they'd been told hands off.

I was in Alcatraz from '52 to '58, five and a half years. But you know who got me transferred out to Atlanta? I found this out from the Freedom of Information Act. Eleanor Roosevelt. Of course, I didn't know it. My wife got to her, and Eleanor wrote a letter of inquiry to the priest on the Rock asking him to verify what my wife had told him—that there was no reason for me to be in such a place.[20] So instead of answering, he read the letter to the warden and the warden sent it to Washington, and Washington says, "Get him off!" A lot of people had written who knew better, like James V. Bennett,[21] and to no effect. But they were afraid of Eleanor Roosevelt, afraid she might start a public fuss. She was a remarkable woman. That's what got me off the Rock.

I've seen people in prison turn so bitter, and boy, it destroys them. I was a political person, so I knew there wasn't a prosecutor gunning after me as an individual. He was gunning after the Communist Party, and I happened to

[19]The writ by which a superior court calls up the records of an inferior court in order to review its proceedings.

[20]One reason may well have been J. Edgar Hoover. At that time Alcatraz was the depository for the federal government's most disliked prisoners, and Sobell had already earned Hoover's enmity by refusing to cooperate.

[21]Director of the Federal Bureau of Prisons.

be the fall guy. I fitted into the specifications—a friend of Julius, I had gone to Mexico, an engineer. So looking at a thing politically gives you a different orientation than if you take the thing personally.

The whole time I was in prison we were fighting back. We went back into court time after time because each time we came up with new evidence. For instance, Manny Bloch, during the trial, made the motion to impound Exhibit 8, Greenglass's sketch of the atom bomb. They claimed during the trial that Exhibit 8 was supposedly *the* most important secret of mankind.[22]

Well, my lawyer went in and got it unimpounded, and it was a real fight to do that. After it was uncovered, we got the physicists to look at it. They said it's a caricature of the bomb. So we got into court and we challenged them on it. Well, it didn't make any difference.[23]

I don't think that even with absolute evidence of innocence the government would ever back down. A lot of careers were made out of this case. Yes, the chief prosecutor, Saypol, they gave him a job on the state court. Of course, Roy Cohn became very well known. Judge Kaufman thought he was going to get an elevation right away, but they said you have to wait a decent period so it doesn't look too obvious.

Did Massachusetts back down with Sacco and Vanzetti?[24] Did California back down on Mooney and Billings?[25] The federal government has done some dirty things, and they've never backed down, not one iota.

[22]Bloch's strategy was to concede that espionage had taken place, but not by his clients. But when he declined to attack the value of Exhibit 8, and instead moved to impound it, he only underscored for the jury the importance of the information allegedly passed to Rosenberg. One year after the executions, General Leslie Groves, head of the Manhattan Project, told a secret meeting of the AEC: "I think that the data that went out in the case of the Rosenbergs was of minor value. I would never say that publicly. . . . I should think it should be kept very quiet, because . . . the Rosenbergs deserved to hang."

[23]In 1966, Marshall Perlin, Sobell's attorney, succeeded in winning the court-ordered release of Exhibit 8. Henry Linschitz, a Los Alamos scientist who worked in lens development and helped assemble the bomb, referred to it as "garbled" and "confused" before concluding: "It is not possible in any technologically useful way to condense the results of a two-billion-dollar development effort into a diagram drawn by a high-school graduate machinist on a single sheet of paper."

[24]The still hotly argued case of Nicola Sacco and Bartolomeo Vanzetti, two anarchists who were charged with murdering a pair of payroll guards in April 1920. Their arrest coincided with the first Red Scare of 1919–20, and the resultant political coloring of their case by the press and the authorities arguably prejudiced the case against them. They were executed in August 1927 amid worldwide clamor for clemency.

[25]The reference is to the most notorious labor frame-up in the first half of the twentieth century. Tom Mooney, a Socialist labor leader, and Warren Billings, his equally radical associate, spent twenty-three years (1916–39) in prison for the deaths of ten persons killed by a bomb explosion during the 1916 Preparedness Day parade in San Francisco. Mooney's sentence was commuted to time served. Billings was not pardoned until 1961.

HELEN SOBELL

Helen Sobell campaigned for twenty years in support of her husband's innocence.

My son was very young when we went down to Mexico, just a baby, and I had a ten-year-old daughter from a previous marriage. Morton had just finished a project that he was working on at Reeves Instruments, where I had worked previously too, but then I had this child and I stopped working for a while. We had been progressive people, not affiliated to any group. We were not members of the Communist Party. Morton had been, but he had drifted away by this time.

When Morton was kidnapped, I yelled at my daughter, Sidney, to call the embassy and then I went down the stairs after them, to see one of them hit Morton over the head and throw him into a car. We had a big pot of soup on the oven which was just about ready for dinner. I didn't know who the hell these people were. When Sidney called the embassy, she was told that there was only a custodian, nobody was there who could do anything about it.

They tried to push me into another car. There was a man who was trying to hold me and I bit his hand so hard that he swore at me and he pushed me into the car. I was taken by myself to some kind of a government building.

I saw Morton there, he was all slumped over and in very bad shape, absolutely. I called out to him, and the person who was taking me in said something, I don't remember exactly what, but I know I used language that I've never used before or since in my life! They took me into a room and tried to take my picture, and I was really so angry I would move every time they would get the camera set up. I just wasn't going to cooperate with any of that.

They took me to another room, and then Sidney came up with the baby. I asked them if I could have some milk for the baby and a cot for the children to lie down on. Finally, by and by, they brought one of these fold-up canvas beds, and so the children lay on that for a while. Then in the middle of the night or a little bit toward morning, they told us to get up and come along. They put us into a car with Morton in the front seat. Morton was in pretty bad shape. There was a Mexican in back with us, and we drove night and day without stopping. I tried to argue with them to get some milk for the baby, so finally they stopped at a store and got some canned milk. But it was very hot, and when I wanted another can for the baby—I wasn't nursing him—they gave me an argument about using this old leftover milk instead of a fresh can of milk.

It was an ordeal. They wouldn't even stop anyplace where you could use a toilet. They'd stop the car and you'd have to go around the back of the car. They drove night and day. We got to the border and the U.S. Customs man was waiting for us. It was about three o'clock in the morning. Of course, we hadn't packed anything, but they had packed up everything in the apartment. Some of it they should have left—it was a furnished apartment.

Morton couldn't remember what the combination to the safe was, and I remembered it. When Morton told me to, I told them what the combination was. They took everything we had in the safe. We had our passports there and some money. Finally, many months—maybe even years—later, we got it back from the FBI.

The children and I were taken to a hotel, and we went to bed. I don't know how much I slept, but quite early in the morning there was a knock at the door and the FBI agents were there. They wanted me to come down and have breakfast with them and they would have somebody take care of the children. I said, "No way I'm going to be separated from those children!" Then they said, "We'll take the children down too." At the breakfast table they were real cute, they asked Sydney whether she wanted pink ice cream. It was at that point they started explaining to me how if I were in Russia they would take me to Siberia, but that they were good guys and they weren't going to do that. It was really crazy, because they wanted information from me that I didn't have to give. They wanted me and Morton to become stool pigeons, or whatever the term is. They wanted us to give evidence that they didn't have about Ethel and Julius Rosenberg. They asked me right out front—I said no way. They made it very clear that all I had to do was to cooperate with them. I finally got the point that they wanted me to tell whatever story they had made up, but I just didn't respond. At any rate, they finally went away.

They told me I could visit Morton in prison. I found somebody from the hotel staff to take care of the children and I went down to see him. He had a big gash in his head. There hadn't been any kind of dressing or anything on it, but it had started healing. He told me to go back to New York and try to get a lawyer. So I took some of his clothes and got them pressed so that he would look nice before the magistrate or whoever it was. I got tickets for myself and for the children to stop off in Washington, D.C.—my mother and my brother were living in Arlington, Virginia, at that time. I figured I'd leave the children there and then go on to New York.

Morton was flown to New York City and put in the Tombs Prison. He was there for quite a while and I used to go and visit him. Very soon I learned to bring a box to stand on, because there's a little pane of glass there about eight inches by four inches so you can look at the person who is on the other side, and there are holes in the wall that you could talk through. They wouldn't allow me to be in the same room with him. And being short as I am, I couldn't even really see to talk to him. So I used to bring a box to stand on.

I developed all kinds of techniques to get by. My family helped me a great deal by taking care of the children. Then we had to find a lawyer, and we had no expertise at all. I just didn't know any lawyers. I think somebody probably mentioned Kuntz, who was a member of the American Labor Party, and then I went to see him and then afterwards he hired another lawyer. Morton had quite a temper and would have a fit over practically anything that I did or tried to do. But he was under strain, there's no question about that, and I was under strain, too!

We tried to get more information from the government as to what it was that Morton was supposed to have done. They weren't coming out with it, there were just the five counts.[1]

We went through this life for two or three years until finally there was the trial and then the conviction, and then the impending execution of the Rosenbergs. In the meanwhile, there was a writer who had written a series of articles on the case defending the Rosenbergs, and he wrote about Morton too.[2] He introduced me to a committee of people. They lived in Knickerbocker Village, neighbors of the Rosenbergs who were very distressed and who felt that this was all wrong. I started going to meetings and I got to know some of these people.

Initially, the organizing was to prepare some kind of a defense for Ethel and Julius Rosenberg and for Morton—although Morton at that time was a very minor character because the big scream headlines had been about the Rosenbergs. Although, with the FBI claiming we were trying to escape, the Mexico business was very inflammatory.

[1]When arrested at the border, Sobell was charged with "five overt acts" of "having conspired with Julius Rosenberg and others" to violate the espionage act.

[2]In August 1951, the *National Guardian* ran a seven-part series by William Reuben on the case, deeming it "a frame-up." Out of this came the creation of the Rosenberg defense committee. Only a handful of publications either supported the defense or cast doubt on the charges— *The Nation, The New Republic,* and *Scientific American* were among them.

At first, it was the Committee to Defend the Rosenbergs, Morton wasn't even a part, but then they tacked his name on later. The first meeting we had was at the Shriners Hall in New York City. There was a tremendous overflow of people. It was the first time I had ever spoken to a large audience like that. But I spoke and appealed for help, and a lot of people signed up to work and a lot of money was collected. I was so effective in my newness that they even sent me outside, where there had been a loud-speaker set up, to collect the money from the overflow crowd. I worked with the committee for a long time; before, during, and after the trial— something like twenty years.

There was a tremendous amount of effort and participation before the death of the Rosenbergs. Afterwards, everybody was just devastated, every-body had to be picked up and started all over again. But we went back to the same people. We had people who knew about the case, and we got new people. We had committees all over the country.[3] It became quite a large organization. We had a West Coast organizer—this was after the death of the Rosenbergs. We had committees in and around Chicago, and on the East Coast too. Then Morton's mother went to Europe and got support from many people there.

As you know, Morton was in Alcatraz before he was moved to Atlanta. Then he got very ill at one point and was transferred to a prison hospital in Missouri. Wherever he was I would visit him and form committees. Mean-while, of course, the FBI was very interested in what I was doing and tried to thwart my efforts. They followed me all over. Sometimes it was obvious. I even have documents okayed by J. Edgar Hoover that lay it all out. For instance, when I was on a radio program, they would get to the host of the show. Some would follow through and try to do what the FBI wanted them to do. In my FBI files, they have comments by the host where he says, "Don't you think I did a good job?" Or something like that, I'm para-phrasing. They did that all the time.

Dr. Urey, the famous atomic scientist, would come and speak at our meet-ings. And we had Malcolm Sharp, who was a professor of law at the University of Chicago, he wrote a book on the case. These were people

[3]Thirty-seven affiliates of the National Committee to Secure Justice in the Rosenberg Case were listed as "subversive organizations" by the House Un-American Activities Committee. Characteristically, HUAC dismissed their efforts as "a mammoth propaganda campaign . . . for the purposes of international communism."

who really were very active and very concerned about the case. We had a number of politicians, and some of them spoke at our meetings, congressmen and senators.

Jack Kennedy had promised me that he would free Morton. That was before he was President. And then later, after he became President, I met and spoke with him several times. We had people in Washington, and at one point I was very much in contact with his assistant. When Kennedy was elected, I was waiting and waiting because Morton was supposed to be released. There was a writer for the *Daily News,* I guess it was Murray Kempton, and he called me up. He said, "Well, Morton is only going to be transferred to Lewisburg." That's what it was, something far less than being released. And I said, "He promised me that he was going to free him." How could he do it, after he had promised me? What Kennedy did, actually, was free someone else, a Communist.[4] He figured he could only free one and this one was easier than that one. And this was after years.

I did a lot of traveling in those twenty years, and I dragged my poor little son around with me a lot of the time. My daughter got older, and she went to the University of Chicago. But when Jack Kennedy was down in Florida to give his famous speech after the Bay of Pigs, she and her then husband picketed him. We had a program of picketing him all over the place. We got a lot of publicity. In the *Washington Star* there's a front-page picture of me picketing. This was a time when I picketed by myself, it was on Yom Kippur, and I had a sign, "Bring my innocent husband home."

There was some harassment. My daughter was at the university when the FBI came to get her thrown out. But the people there were very supportive of her. I have a recollection of the teacher saying, "I don't want you bothering any of my students." The FBI was always there. On one occasion, a small group of us were picketing Robert Kennedy. He was dedicating a new law school near Lincoln Center. So we got our signs together. There were a couple of men there and I said, "Do you want to picket with us?" And they said, "No, we can't, we're the FBI." So I said, "Well, keep our signs from blowing away!" And they did, it was a very windy day. They were very gentlemanly.

When Robert Kennedy came out, we followed him and I tried to talk to him. He said, "Come see me at my office." I did, but he didn't see me. No, I never got anywhere with Bobby.

[4]This may have been Junius Scales (see under "The Fall of the Communist Party"), whose six-year sentence under the Smith Act was commuted by President Kennedy in December 1962.

We raised a million dollars over the years. I didn't do it all personally, but together with everybody. It was over a long period of time, too! On my European trip I was very well received, not only by the queen mother in Belgium, but I was taken to the Italian parliament in Rome, and I met with Bertrand Russell, who was one of our big supporters. I tried to see the Pope. Actually the Pope came out against the death penalty for the Rosenbergs.

The FBI followed me through Europe. I have documents that show they knew what flight I was on. They would look into bank accounts of the committees, and I have that in my files too. The purpose of all this surveillance and snooping was to discredit us, find something. Some of the FBI documents are really pretty straightforward. One of them says, "We've got to stop the efforts of this woman!" And that one is signed, "Okay, JEH." There's lots of material where Hoover was very much involved. They had a whole plan of what they'll do, what their program was. Gradually through the years I've managed to get more documents, the first were totally blacked, but then I got more, some of it is still blacked out.

There was one FBI informer that actually was the head of one of our committees in Los Angeles for a while. He happened to have been revealed by some mistakes that he made. His wife really was the one who hadn't known and who found out. I had even stayed at those people's houses. He was turning names over. Whatever the FBI wanted, he was doing. Wherever we went, the FBI was there to try and foul us up. At meetings where I spoke, and this was earlier on, there would be three of them just standing there. See, they have two roles, at least: one is for intimidation and the other is really to get information.

In the beginning, everybody was scared. If a friend who I had known before would see me, they would cross the other side of the street. But then there were some people who were courageous enough to come and to greet me, even early on. And then later, of course, I became welcome, once the fear had subsided, and once they realized their own susceptibility.

My family was wonderful, they stood by me. Morton's family did too. His mother fought for him. His father died early, and I think earlier than he would have, because of his grieving over what had happened to his son.

STEVE NELSON

Steve Nelson, an open Communist and a member of the Party's
National Committee, was alleged to be the go-between during World War
Two for "Scientist X" at the Berkeley Radiation Laboratory and the
Soviets. He was assailed by HUAC as "one of the leading espionage
agents and saboteurs of the Communist Party in the United States."

I was never officially charged with espionage, but it was continually being
brought up. It was all over the press, headlines that I was an inspector of
the Red Army and that I came to Pittsburgh to sabotage the mills, that I
knew J. Robert Oppenheimer, who stole the atomic bomb for me to give it
to the Russians. Headline stories that helped later to convict me of conspiring to overthrow the government.[1] I did know Oppenheimer for a while. I
knew him through his wife, Kitty. She had been married to my friend Joe
Dallet.

Joe was a radical, a graduate of Dartmouth College. We were friends
from 1928 on. A nice, handsome-looking guy. He was one of those guys
who turned against the capitalist system, although his father was in business. He became an organizer for the Steelworkers Union. He was organizing in Youngstown, and I was in the anthracite coalfields, near Wilkes-Barre
and Scranton.

We ended up on the same ship going to Spain to fight with the International Brigade.[2] On the ship, Joe tells me that his wife, Kitty, whom I had
never met, was going to be in Paris. He says, "I want you to meet her." We
spent a nice week in Paris, the three of us. They spoke French, I didn't, so I
hung around. I was like a fifth wheel, but we were friends.

To get across the Spanish border, we had to go sub rosa, over the

[1]See Steve Nelson under "The Fall of the Communist Party."

[2]During the Spanish Civil War (1936–39) about 35,000 foreign volunteers from fifty-two
countries took up arms to defend the Spanish Republic against a fascist uprising led by Franco
and aided by Hitler and Mussolini. Organized into five International Brigades, three thousand of
the volunteers were Americans, who named their units the Abraham Lincoln Battalion, the
George Washington Battalion, and the John Brown Battery. More than one thousand Americans died in the war. After the war was lost, they returned home only to be persecuted for
decades as "premature antifascists."

mountains, and be smuggled in. I went to the front immediately, and Joe remained in training for another battalion—the Mackenzie-Papineau Battalion.[3] We didn't see each other very much. Then I was wounded, and after I was wounded, I was sent to represent the International Brigade in the Soviet Union at their November 7 demonstration.[4]

It was an honorable thing for me, because the Soviet Union was helping Spain with ammunition and matériel, and I was a high official in the 15th Brigade, the English-speaking brigade—one of the three people in charge. So I was leaving for Paris to wait for my visa. Joe in the meantime wrote Kitty to meet me in Paris, because I'm on my way and I could tell her what's doing with him. Just before I left Spain, Joe was killed. So Kitty meets me in Paris. I'm shocked with the news, and I have to tell her.

She's shocked, she doesn't know what to do. I said, "Kitty, come and stay with us, Margaret and me. Join us in New York for a while." And that's what happened, she came to stay with us. In the meantime, she was distraught and nervous. Naturally, you would be, all of a sudden the bottom fell out of her life.

So there was an Englishman named Dr. Harris, who was campaigning in this country to aid Loyalist Spain. He was a good speaker, and the committee hired him to raise money. So Kitty met up with him. About three or four weeks later, she got attached to him and they got married. After a time, I heard she was going to the university out at Berkeley.

About seven or eight months later, there was a meeting in Berkeley for Loyalist Spain and I was invited to make a talk. I come out to Berkeley to this meeting, and who's on the platform but this guy called J. Robert Oppenheimer. First time I saw the man—first time I ever heard of him, in fact. He made a liberal, but good, talk on why the United States should have supported Loyalist Spain. The Second World War was going on at that point. He was friendly to the Left. His brother, Frank, was in the Party, actually, and Frank's wife was at one time also.

After I finished making my little speech, he said, "Steve, I'm going to marry a friend of yours. I'm going to marry Kitty." I had thought that she was married to Harris. He spotted my predicament immediately; he says, "Oh, that was a short-lived thing. They could not get along, and we're getting married." He didn't want to go into it, and I didn't want to ask him. That's how I met Oppenheimer.

---

[3]The Mac-Paps, as they were known, were a Canadian battalion formed in July 1937. At first they were led by American officers, Joe Dallet among them.

[4]The demonstration celebrated the twentieth anniversary of the 1917 revolution.

Now, the story is that I came to California because I knew that he was here and that he was an atomic scientist, which was a word I'd never even heard before. Here's a woman who attached to me, and later on to Margaret too; we just became good friends. And because of these circumstances they called me a master spy.

Several months later, it was rumored he was going to leave for somewhere. Oppenheimer called me up and said, "Steve, I want to see you." We had lunch somewhere on Telegraph Avenue. He said, "I'm leaving. I won't be around for a while. I just want to say goodbye. Don't ask me anything further." That was it. He was under obligation. I didn't know what he was going to do, so I had no reason to ask, even if I'd wanted to. Lawrence Laboratory,[5] that's all I ever heard. I'd never heard of cyclotron.[6] I'd never heard of those things, see.

I never saw Oppenheimer again, even after the war, or Kitty for that matter. Kitty became a botanist. And she went somewhere to the South Seas on a boat, and contracted some kind of disease and died before she returned. Poor woman, she went through hell. They paint her as a nasty woman and a drunk. I don't know whether she was nasty or not, but I know that she was not a drunk when I knew her. I felt sorry that I didn't connect back with them, but it would've just added more fuel to the fire.

Then there was a group of seven or eight young scientists[7]—some of them were radicals—who were students at the university in Berkeley. We were at some social events together, raising money for the *People's World,* or something. I think they were already—what do you call them?—graduate students. I didn't know that they were physicists. If they'd told me, I wouldn't have known what that was. They were involved with a group at the univer-

---

[5] Known during World War Two as the Radiation Laboratory, under the direction of Ernest Lawrence. The lab's importance in the development of the atom bomb centered around its efforts to produce quantities of the fissionable material uranium 235.

[6] The electromagnetic accelerator that separates out the 235 isotope. The device was developed at Lawrence's lab. In 1949, HUAC charged that Joseph Weinberg (dubbed by the committee "Scientist X") had passed some of this information to the Russians through Steve Nelson. Under oath, Weinberg denied knowing Nelson, and he was indicted on three counts of perjury. The government dropped one count, the judge dismissed the second, and the jury acquitted him on the third. Weinberg was blacklisted from academia for many years.

[7] David Fox, David Bohm, Max Friedman, Giovanni Rossi Lomanitz, Joseph Weinberg, and David Hawkins. Not only did these young scientists enrage the authorities by consorting with Steve Nelson, but they had the audacity to organize a union local at the Radiation Laboratory. To varying degrees over the next decade all were blacklisted in academia. Lomanitz, for one, was reduced to living in a shack outside Kansas City, working menial jobs for seventy-five cents an hour.

sity, mainly economists and historians, who had Marxist discussions. I didn't even attend one single class with them, you know.[8]

Then there was this guy Vassili Zubilin. He was one of the Soviet counsel men out here during the Second World War. Before the Second Front opened up, there was a campaign in the United States to aid Russia. There were barrels in front of movie houses, "Bring your old shoes here for Russia," that kind of thing.

I don't exactly remember when this happened now. However, there was this woman from Russia who was a sniper in the Red Army and supposed to have killed forty or fifty Nazis. I don't know how they keep records on that. Anyhow, she came out here to raise money for Russian war relief and she was to speak at Berkeley at the university. And the Russian counsel called me up—"I want to see you." So he came to Berkeley, where we had a little office. He says, "Well, I don't want to meet here. Let's meet in the bar or something." So we go to the bar, and he says, "This woman is coming. Will you do everything you can to get a good crowd out?"

That was the story. So I did talk to Zubilin, and whether he was discreet or indiscreet, I don't know. The FBI picked it up on a telephone which was tapped, no doubt. Now, of course, when you think about it, it's so easy to weave a story around this—because there was espionage going on.[9] But we in the Party were instructed to stay away from this. We're not going to do that—political stuff, *yes*. Whatever else the Party did, and if there was some idiots who might've done something, it was never officially condoned. And being that I was a member of the National Committee, I would be the last one to get mixed up with that.

Steve Nelson died on December 11, 1993, at the age of ninety.

[8]Nelson may have attended at least one. On August 14, 1949, in cloak-and-dagger overtones, a former security officer named James Murray testified before HUAC that six years previously he had peered from a neighboring rooftop into the second-story Berkeley apartment of Joseph Weinberg and spied Nelson meeting with the students: "I observed them sitting around the table . . . the conversation appeared to be very serious." He reported that the participants came and went openly; that "nine or ten" people were present and (aside from Nelson) met weekly; and that curtains, shades, and windows were all open to the summer heat. HUAC wanted spies; they got a study group.

[9]The story that HUAC and the FBI wove was that in 1942 and 1943, Nelson was in contact with Zubilin and Peter Ivanov, the Soviet vice-consul; that Nelson passed Ivanov "an envelope or package" while sitting in a park, and that a few days later Zubilin met Nelson in his home and paid him "ten bills of unknown denominations." However, with all the spy-hunters' dogged certainty that Nelson was a "master spy" in cahoots with Weinberg, and that the pair had betrayed secrets of the atom bomb to the Soviets, no espionage charges were ever brought against either of them.

The Fall of
the Communist
Party

The American Communist Party was founded in 1919 in the wake of the Bolshevik Revolution. A small squabbling sect through the 1920s, it emerged from the Depression era as America's strongest and most influential radical movement. Within a decade it would also be the most maligned and persecuted.

While attacked from without, the Party's internal politics managed to alienate much of its own following. American Communism's mechanical application of Marxism-Leninism and its internal reliance on "democratic centralism"[1] provoked a turnover in membership estimated at 30 percent per year. Its dogged following of Soviet direction presented its rank and file with a heart-wrenching series of policy reversals, exasperated its non-Communist allies, and lent evidence to the charge that the Party was the agent of the USSR. The best-known of these flip-flops occurred with the signing of the Hitler-Stalin Nonaggression Pact in 1939. Up to the very moment the news was released, the American CP had been energetically promoting a policy of collective security against Germany. With the pact, its policy changed overnight to one of extreme neutrality.[2] By 1958, the

---

[1]The principle that allowed Party members to participate in policy discussions and elections, but required that they ultimately follow decisions made at higher levels. As one ex-Party wit put it, "It meant all the democracy was centralized somewhere else." Although not drastically different from what was practiced within the autocratic machines of the Democratics and Republicans, the perceived gap between word and deed increased as the CP staked its claim as the defenders of democracy.

[2]The deleterious effects of this switch might have been lessened if the Party had defended the pact as a forced necessity. In the prewar years the Western nations had been all too willing to appease Hitler (witness England's own 1938 pact with Germany) and the Soviet Union had been repeatedly rebuffed in its efforts for a united front against the Nazis. Instead, American Communists attacked those who held to the anti-Nazi front, alienating the very groups they had labored so hard to create. In a further irony, this policy switch put the CP in bed with the decidedly pro-fascist America First, among whose adherents were Henry Ford (an early financier

strains of the Red Scare and internal dissatisfaction permanently reduced the Party to the tiny sect it had been in the 1920s.

Yet, 750,000 to 1,000,000 Americans passed through the CP ranks over its seventy-five-year history. During the Party's heyday (largely the Depression era through World War Two), Americans of all stripes flocked to the red banner. Beginning the 1930s with 7,500 members, the CP had 60,000 members seven years later. In those desperate years, the Party offered uncompromising antifascism and a coherent program for social and economic justice. It held out hope for a better world.

Despite its habitual myopia, the CP made vital contributions[3] to American life. The Party not only provided a departure from a traditionally narrow political dialogue, but as the engine of the Left it mobilized and sustained many a progressive cause. It was the first national party since Reconstruction to believe in and fight for civil rights.[4] The Party sent organizers to the Deep South as early as 1929, insisted on racial equality in labor unions, and supplied legal aid to African-Americans caught up in the lynch-law legal system of the South.

Communists agitated for such radical notions as the right to organize labor, the eight-hour workday, a minimum wage, unemployment insurance, and social security. Through the 1930s, Communist labor organizers formed the backbone of the Congress of Industrial Organizations (CIO) and were instrumental in organizing the auto, steel, and rubber industries, as well as maritime, mine, and migrant labor.

With the Nazi invasion of the USSR in 1941, the Communists switched back to a prowar line. Under the Democratic Front policy, the CP cooperated enthusiastically[5] with the war effort, insisting on a no-strike pledge for the duration. Fifteen thousand Party members marched off to fight. In 1944, under the direction of Earl Browder, the CP attempted to tailor itself to American conditions by abandoning its designation as "party" for Communist Political Association, indicating it would now function as a pressure group.

Though the Party carried an influence far greater than its numbers, it

---

of the German Nazi Party), Ambassador Joseph Kennedy, Sr., and lone eagle Charles Lindbergh.

[3]One of the many ironies of the CP lies in its internal discipline, which was key to its many positive accomplishments. Unfortunately, discipline also made it vulnerable to Stalinism and ideological rigidity, which contributed to its undoing.

[4]See "Fighting Jim Crow."

[5]As was its predilection, the Party was blindly enthusiastic, going so far as to support the wartime internment of Japanese-Americans.

never achieved mass acceptance. At the height of its popularity in 1944, Party membership did not exceed 100,000 out of a population of 140 million.[6] In 1945, the period of cooperation that had brought the Party its greatest success came to an abrupt end through criticism from abroad.[7] After some infighting, the Party took a sharp turn to the Left, expelled Earl Browder as an "enemy of the people," and reformed itself as the Communist Party U.S.A. under the leadership of Browder rival William Foster. Ironically, this change of policy later figured in keeping top Party leaders behind bars for years.

With the close of World War Two came the collapse of the U.S.-Soviet alliance, the beginning of the Cold War, and the ascendancy of the Right. The massive propaganda campaign that followed painted the CP in demonic shades as a criminal conspiracy to overthrow the government. The subversive label was pinned on the Communists only partly because they believed in international communism, but more because for decades they had fought effectively for causes considered anathema to the newly elected reactionaries in Congress.

In 1948, the twelve top leaders[8] of the Communist Party were indicted under the 1940 Smith Act—not for any overt illegal acts, but for the twice-removed speech crime of "conspiring to advocate the violent overthrow of the United States government."[9] The gist of the indictment was that in dissolving the Communist Political Association and resurrecting the CPUSA, the Party had entered into a revolutionary conspiracy dating from April 1, 1945. The notion of "conspiring to advocate" is crucial, for with this the Justice Department was able to conduct mass trials based on sympathetic association alone, obviating the need to prove the case against each individual. As will be seen in the following interviews, the Justice Department and the FBI were intent on

[6]The American CP was among the weakest in the Western nations. In comparison, the strongest was the Communist Party of Italy (PCI), which registered two million members out of a population of 45 million and won 25 percent of the seats in the 1946 parliamentary elections. The PCI followed the Socialist Party by eleven seats, making it Italy's third most powerful party.

[7]An article penned by French Communist leader Jacques Duclos criticized Browder's policy of cooperation with capitalism. Although the article's final intent was ambiguous, Party leadership, with its collective eye to the tea leaves, chose to interpret it as marching orders from Stalin to repudiate Browder.

[8]William Z. Foster, Eugene Dennis, Robert Thompson, John Williamson, Benjamin Davis, Henry Winston, John Gates, Irving Potash, Jacob Stachel, Gilbert Green, Carl Winter, and Gus Hall. Foster was later severed from the case because of poor health.

[9]Such are the exigencies of ideology that in 1940, when the Smith Act was first used to jail the leaders of the Socialist Workers Party, the CP loudly supported the persecution of their Trotskyist rivals. This, and the support for the wartime internment camps, raised serious doubts about the Party's commitment to civil liberties.

imprisoning Communists simply for being Communists.

So began the longest trial in American history. Nine months and four days later, the eleven were convicted and sentenced to five years[10] in prison. No sooner had the Supreme Court upheld the convictions than the government began a nationwide sweep, arresting the second ranks of leadership in fourteen states and Puerto Rico.[11] The Justice Department began a series of eight prosecutions based on the membership clause of the Smith Act, which paradoxically carried a heavier penalty—ten years—than did advocating the overthrow of the government.

In 1950–51, the Party initiated its "five minutes to midnight" policy. Anticipating a period of fascist repression in America, four[12] of the eleven top leaders jumped bail and disappeared underground. With them were several thousand others, organized into an operational structure designed to withstand the coming storm. They would live this shadow existence for five to six years before surfacing. (Veterans of that experience tell their story in the next section.) In 1956, the Bureau of Internal Revenue seized Party offices in New York, Chicago, San Francisco, and Philadelphia, as well as the Daily Worker offices in New York, Chicago, and Detroit.[13]

Federal anti-Communist legislation rapidly supplemented the Smith Act. In 1947, the Taft-Hartley Act[14] compelled all elected union officials to sign oaths that they were not Communists. In 1950, the Internal Security Act authorized concentration camps for emergency situations and demanded the registration of all organizations determined to be "Communist-dominated." The registration clause required the full disclosure of membership lists and finances and the self-labeling of the registered organization as "subversive" on all stationary and other printed matter. It also permitted the deportation of any alien (resident or otherwise) who was a member of an organization required to register. In 1952, the McCarran-Walter Act allowed aliens to be arrested without

[10]With the exception of Robert Thompson, who, in deference to his heroic war record, received a three-year prison sentence. For more on Thompson, see Sylvia Thompson under "The Arlington Case."

[11]In January 1951, the Justice Department announced to congress that it planned 12,000 to 15,000 more Smith Act prosecutions.

[12]Robert Thompson, Gilbert Green, Henry Winston, and Gus Hall. Hall was arrested in Mexico City four months later. Thompson was caught in the California mountains in 1953. Green and Winston surrendered on Party orders in 1956.

[13]During the years 1950 to 1953, Communist newspapers were banned from the newstands of New York, Los Angeles, and Detroit. In L.A., reporters from these papers were banned from attending city council meetings.

[14]For more on the Taft-Hartley Act and the stories of those who were prosecuted under it, see "Breaking the Working Class."

warrant, held without bail, and deported for actions that had been legal when committed. Aliens could now be deported who would have been inadmissible at the time of their entry if the act had been in force. This allowed the deportation of scores of ex-Communists who had long ceased being Party members. Many deportees had lived in the United States so long that they no longer spoke their native language and faced separation from wives and children. In 1954, the Communist Control Act was passed into law, stripping the Party of "all rights, privileges, and immunities attendant upon legal bodies."

By 1953, thirty-nine states had passed sedition laws aimed at the Communist Party. By 1955, the number was up to forty-four, sixteen of which denied the CP the status of a political party. By 1951, more than 150 cities and counties had passed anti-Communist legislation. Many municipalities required Communists to register at city hall. Los Angeles County required any "subversive" traveling through the jurisdiction to register with the sheriff. In Jacksonville, registration was extended to anyone who communicated with a present or former Communist. A few towns passed "get out or else" ordinances. Both Birmingham, Alabama, and Macon, Georgia, required Communists to leave town in forty-eight hours or face six months in prison.

Party numbers began an irreversible decline. By 1951, the toll taken by external persecution and internal dissatisfaction dropped the list by more than half from its 1944 peak. But it was the news events of 1956 that devastated Party ranks. At the Twentieth Party Congress in Moscow, Khrushchev publicly revealed the extent of Stalin's crimes. Then, within months, Soviet tanks rolled into Budapest to crush the Hungarian revolt. More than all the persecution, these two events dismantled the Party. For decades, American Communists had extolled the international leadership of Stalin and dismissed reports of his purges as reactionary propaganda. Now they were morally shattered, unable to deny the blood staining Stalin's regime. Membership stood at twenty thousand at the first of the year but dropped by half before the year was out. By 1958, less than three thousand members remained in the Party.

One hundred and forty-five Communist leaders were tried under the Smith Act; 108 were convicted and given sentences totaling more than four hundred years. At least twenty other Communists were imprisoned under state or local laws. Fifty-six thousand current or former Party members underwent deportation investigations. One thousand were eventually deported, with the majority first stripped of their citizenship. William Pennock, a Smith Act defendant, committed suicide. Robert

Thompson, imprisoned under the Smith Act, died after his release from injuries suffered in prison.

STEVE NELSON

A carpenter by trade, Nelson joined the Communist Party in 1925 and worked as an organizer in the Pennsylvania coalfields. During the Spanish Civil War, he was one of the leaders of the 15th International Brigade. By 1950, he was chairman of the Western Pennsylvania Communist Party. In August of that year he was indicted for "conspiring to overthrow the Commonwealth of Pennsylvania." In the middle of his trial, he was arrested by the FBI under the Smith Act to face identical federal charges. Convicted in both trials, he faced twenty-five years in prison.

Everything changed at the end of the Second World War. The ally Russia became the enemy. Anybody who had sympathy was suspect. Because I was local Party chairman, because I had studied in Moscow and fought in Spain, I was the devil himself.[1] I was the creature who came to destroy Pittsburgh.

What we had been doing, back in Pennsylvania in the thirties for example, was organizing the unemployed. It was the Party's idea to wage a campaign for unemployment insurance. We were the first to demand relief. We tried to get Congress to pass a bill that studied the unemployment question, to set up a system to get paid when you're out of work.

There was a group of local politicians interested in making use of this Red Scare. They organized a committee called ABC, Americans Battling Communism. Judge Musmanno was the main culprit. He had studied law in Mussolini's Italy, and after the war had been in the American military government in Italy. He thought he was watching the Communists come

---

[1] In 1931, Nelson attended the Lenin School in Moscow: "It was like a college where you would learn systematically, read books, hear lectures on organizing and political thought, all sorts of world topics. It was not at all like it was presented, that we were there to learn how to violently overthrow the American government. In fact, sabotage was rejected. It was considered an anarchist's weapon. Sabotage meant destruction of property and killing—that was absolutely taboo."

into power, and was frightened by the Italian partisans.[2] He started the committee.

In August 1950, Musmanno came after me. He became the private initiator of the arrests.[3] He arrested three of us: James Dolson, a reporter for the *Daily Worker,* then sixty-eight years old; Andy Onda, a Steelworker organizer; and myself. We were charged with sedition, conspiring to overthrow the government of Pennsylvania. They confiscated all the books at the office. Three thousand books and pamphlets, everything we had. When the trial opened, they had two dollies filled with books wheeled into the courtroom. These became the evidence against us.

About three months into the trial, I was driving to Philadelphia late one Friday night and crashed in a storm. I hit a tree and broke my knee and my leg in two places. I was separated from the trial. It was near the end—the judge was about to charge the jury. My two friends were convicted, but I would have to come back and have a separate trial, all over again.

I was staying at a friend's in Philadelphia after my release from the hospital. I required the doctors' constant care and wasn't allowed to go home. One afternoon, I was lying in this hot apartment by myself. My leg was in a splint with steel pins and I couldn't move, and who walked into the apartment but Musmanno! He was with two local detectives. I got so goddam mad, I yelled, "Who the hell let you in?" He just grinned. He had the nerve to ask, "How are you, Steve?" Even the detectives with him were embarrassed. "Get the hell out of the house, you dirty rat," I said, and I reached for my crutch. He beat it out of there. Apparently, he hurried back to Pittsburgh to impress on the politicians there that I was recovering quickly and the trial would have to start soon.

A couple of weeks later there was a knock on the door, and six men crowded into the apartment. One of them pulled a paper out of his pocket and announced, "Nelson, you are under arrest for violation of the Smith Act." Now I was held on federal charges with five others, including Onda and Dolson, who were arrested during the closing arguments of their sedition trial.

My "fair bail" was set at fifty thousand dollars. I couldn't meet it, so they put me in an old jailhouse in South Philly. It was a dirty place. They threw

[2]Like most of the European resistance groups, the Italian partisans were predominantly Communist. Since the end of World War Two, the CP has been a respected element of the Italian political scene. Before the collapse of the Soviet Union, the moderate wing of the Party split off to form the Democratic Party of the Left (PDS).

[3]Apparently, Judge Michael Angelo Musmanno also wore a sheriff's hat, for it was he that led the raid on Nelson's office at Party headquarters.

me in with a group of demented guys. I still had this cast on my leg with the steel pins, and I had to put solution on it every few hours. There were seven guys in a cell that was big enough for two. I remember one of them, this big husky guy with a couple of gashes on his face and a big one across his belly. He was a vet, just back from the Korean War, and he used to talk about the voices that called to him in his head. I'll tell you, it was an awful place to be in. Well, my wife raised hell, and finally they were able to get me out after about twelve days. I was brought back to Pittsburgh and ordered back to trial on the state sedition charges.

I came in on crutches. The presiding judge, Montgomery, was also a founding member of the ABC. He said, "Two weeks' time, the trial starts." I felt I couldn't do it; I still had the shakes, and my leg was inflamed—the pins weren't taken out yet. We argued about it, and finally he agreed to appoint two doctors to examine me, to decide whether I was fit to stand trial. One was a psychiatrist, the other the chief physician of the United States Steel Corporation.

These two doctors examined me, admitted me to the hospital, and ordered tests. They took a spinal tap, and after that you have to lay prone for twenty-four hours. You can't move. So I was in the hospital bed, and my wife and two kids were sitting in the corridor. Anybody who wanted to visit me had to be checked out first. And at some point this fellow comes right through the front doors of the hospital. He was mumbling something like "I'm gonna get that son of a bitch Steve Nelson." Before they could stop him he entered my room, and came up to me and said, "You're the son of a bitch who's responsible for my two brothers dying in Korea." And he shoved his hand in his jacket and pulled out a gun. Now there was this old man, a miner, still in pretty good shape, lying in the bed next to me. He saw what was going on. And when the gun came out, he jumped up and grabbed the guy. There were doctors and nurses all over the place, but this guy just walked out. Nobody bothered to get the police, nothing, and he was never caught. It was even reported in the newspapers.

Now the doctors had a difference of opinion. The psychiatrist wanted to postpone the trial, but the physician felt I was ready. We haggled over it in court, and finally the judge granted me two more weeks. I spent that time looking for a lawyer. There were two left-wing lawyers in Pittsburgh who were willing to take my case, Schlesinger and Steinberg,[4] but they had been

---

[4]In June 1950, the month the Korean War broke out, Hyman Schlesinger was arrested at a Pittsburgh bus station, handcuffed, taken to jail, denied an attorney, and assaulted by a guard in the presence of the state judge who supervised his arrest—Michael Angelo Musmanno.

put on trial by the Bar Association. I ended up writing letters to about thirteen hundred lawyers. Most claimed that they were busy, that they couldn't take that much time off, and so forth. Some were just out-and-out vicious, saying, "I wouldn't defend you for all the money you could get me." A couple were friendly, but I didn't get any takers.

I said to my friends in New York, "For Christ's sake, get me somebody." They sent one guy who'd just had his cataracts removed. In those days, see, you had to wait almost seven or eight months before you could read again. The man hadn't read a newspaper in a year. What good was he going to do me? He was in bad enough shape himself and he was already being smeared as a Red. So when Judge Montgomery asked me, "Are you ready?" I said, "No, I haven't got a lawyer." He said, "Monday morning, the trial starts at nine-thirty, with or without counsel."

I went in the courtroom that morning. Only my wife came in with me. Montgomery said, "Mr. Nelson, did you get a lawyer?" I told him I hadn't. "Well," he said, "you go in the corridor; there are a number of lawyers there, and you come back here into the courtroom with one of them." So I went out there and I asked questions, but there was no one to my liking. I came back and the judge asked, "What about Mr. so-and-so, didn't he agree to take your case?" I said, "He said that he would take it, but the man doesn't know a thing about this kind of case and I couldn't possibly take him." Montgomery said, "Well, I spoke to him."

"*You* spoke to him? In that case, I have good reason not to accept him. I'm not going to pay for the rope that's going to hang me." Then he said, "Call in the prospective jurors."

What's a man, who is not a lawyer, who is a workingman, going to do in that situation? Seventy people piled into the courtroom. Montgomery looked around and said to one of the lawyers, "You sit down with Mr. Nelson. Help him select a jury." This lawyer was a friendly guy, a local guy. He said, "What the hell's going on? I've got my own case coming up at two o'clock. I can't get tied up with this." "Put that on the record," I said, because I wanted it known what they were doing to me. When I said that, the lawyer backed down. "All right," he said, "I'll help you the best I can." And then he sat down with me while I wrote out questions. We knocked out fifty prospective jurists before we selected four. The ones that I accepted, the prosecutors rejected. Finally twelve-thirty came around, and this lawyer stood up. He said, "Your honor, I have to get to my own case." And that was it. Montgomery told me, "I'll appoint another man to help you finish the selection of the jury, but I'm going to limit the questions to five."

I knew how to ask the right questions because I had paid attention in that first trial. I learned how to find the shading. But I wasn't always right. Some people I thought were good turned out to be bad. They were clever enough to hide. But finally the jury was selected, and the next day the trial started.

Now mind you, the main witness was Musmanno. He and the presiding judge, Montgomery, were founding members of this Americans Battling Communism. And Musmanno's nephew, Cercone, was the assistant prosecutor. Also, Montgomery was running for state supreme court that year, and he was looking for a conviction to help him in the election. Lewis, the head prosecutor, was being advanced to county judge, and one afternoon during the trial a tailor came into the courtroom to measure him for robes. So you see it was all about making political gains in the election.

Musmanno was the expert on the literature from the point of view of the prosecution. I cross-examined him, grilled him for two days. I brought up his past, his Mussolini days, how he had once written a letter to the *Pittsburgh Press* referring to "the heroic work of the Fascisti." We wrangled over books and quotations and meanings. He sat there with a pile of stuff he had seized from my office and said, "I regard these books as more dangerous than any firearms."[5]

That was the evidence they used to prove I was seditious. They tried to set it up that I believed in whatever Lenin or Karl Marx or Engels said. It didn't matter that there were different historical periods, different situations and circumstances. They would say, "You fought in Spain. You went to Moscow. You were studying how to make bombs, how to destroy things."

Matt Cvetic was another one of the state's witnesses. He was the big hero. In April of that year, the film *I was a Communist for the FBI*, ostensibly written by Cvetic, had its world premiere in Pittsburgh.[6] It was a film made up of lies. There's a character in it, Steve Nelson, who commits a murder. Not me, supposedly, but the same name, and the guy who ghostwrote the screenplay for Cvetic also belonged to ABC, along with Musmanno and Judge Montgomery. The mayor even declared the opening "Matthew Cvetic Day." He sponsored a parade that marched right by the

---

[5]One bit of evidence entered against Nelson was a political cartoon from a leftist journal found in his home. The cartoon showed the devastation of Korea by United States forces. Nelson objected, protesting that he hadn't drawn the cartoon, and why didn't they read the accompanying article? His objection was overruled.

[6]"I was under the toughest orders a guy could get! I stood by and watched my brother slugged. . . . I started a riot that ran red with terror. . . . I learned every dirty rule in their book—and had to use them—because I was a Communist—but I was a Communist for the FBI!" Described by film critic Leslie Halliwell as a "crude and shoddy Red-baiting melodrama," Cvetic's 1951 film bio was nominated for an Academy Award as best documentary of the year.

courthouse where Onda and Dolson's trial was being held. The damned thing was playing while my case was going on.

There were headlines throughout the trial that I was an inspector for the Red Army, that I came to Pittsburgh to sabotage the mills. They said that I was a master spy, that I knew Oppenheimer, that he had stolen the atomic bomb for me to give to the Russians.[7]

The problem is that if you belong to the Party, it means that you're part of a conspiracy. How can you disprove conspiracy? It isn't possible. It took the jury twenty-three hours to convict me. Montgomery gave me the maximum sentence, twenty years in prison. There were fines too, but who cared about those? I wasn't going to pay them.[8] I had no money. So I was sent off to Allegheny County Prison, no bail allowed. Our friends in the courtroom proceeded to file papers to allow me bail, but that took seven months. I was in the slammer all that time. I don't need to tell you what it was like to meet my wife and kids coming in. I'd talk to them through the double screen, six feet apart, cops on both sides. Imagine my kids, nine and eleven years old, being brought in, and thinking, "What crime did my father commit?"

Everyone at the jail knew I was coming. They were waiting for me. I was a pretty notorious guy. You know, the officials there were awful. They never actually hit me, but they were nasty in every other way. Oh, there were so many things. They put me in isolation—they called it the hole—three times, nine days each on bread and water.

The hole was a crazy place, each cell completely empty except for a seatless toilet that flushed once every twenty-four hours, no bed, no chair, no running water. At night, they'd shove a plywood plank, sixteen inches wide, under the door, and they'd throw you in one blanket. The hole had about eighteen or twenty cells that faced a corridor about twice as wide as each cell was deep. There were washbowls against the other wall of the corridor, but you had to be let out of the cell to be able to use them, and this happened only once a day.

After a while, I became very popular. The prisoners were more and more with me. While I was still inside, a bunch of prison riots broke out all over the state. The officials feared that there would be one in our prison too. And goddamm it, the idea of starting a fire got into some of the men. The

[7]See Steve Nelson under "Atom Spies."

[8]In addition to the twenty years, Nelson was fined $10,000 and ordered to pay court costs of $13,291, which included the expenses of Cvetic and the other prosecution witnesses.

guys in the broom shop talked about sabotage, which I was against. When the men approached me, I said, "That's the worst thing you could do. It's not going to change a thing. All you'll do is hurt the men locked in here. I'm opposed to it."

I don't remember the details now, but for some reason I was put on the shelf—that's what they called solitary, because it was on the top floor. While I was there, I heard sirens blowing, lots of them. There was huge commotion going on. Later, I found out that fourteen fire engines turned up. Who did it, I don't know, but someone had started a fire in the broom shop and burned it down. They put kerosene in the buckets that were supposed to be filled with water. When the fire started, this so-called water was poured out, and it caused an explosion. The broom shop burned down. Forty thousand dollars' worth of damage.

The warden came onto the shelf, accompanied by the press, and said to me, "You're the one that was responsible for this thing." I said, "Oh, yeah? I had a long match, I was able to strike from here way down three blocks away." I couldn't believe what I was hearing. I told them, "I couldn't have possibly done it. I've been here for three days now." Finally they gave up and walked out. The newspapers reported that I was in solitary and couldn't have started the fire.

About a week before I was finally released on bail, I was in the prison barber shop. Now, the barber shop was arranged in a pit: three chairs, three barbers, and the guards above, watching everything. The barbers were more or less favored, short-term guys. One of the them was maneuvering to get me in his chair, letting other guys pass him by. When I sat down in his chair, he leaned down and said, "I knew one of the jurors who was in your case. He was for you." "Yeah?" I said. "How the hell was he for me? I was convicted." "Let me tell you," he said. "Let's get out in the yard." We moved out of the pit, actually went and played chess, and he told me, "Number six juror, a guy named Roman, hung out at Eagle's Bar in Etna. The night before your case went to the jury, he was there and some guys began to taunt him—'You're going to send that son of a bitch to prison.' He insisted, 'I ain't going to do anything like that. He ain't guilty.' When he went home, four guys waylaid him and knocked the shit out of him." Of course, the next day he voted to convict me.

That's all the barber knew. The case was still pending in the state supreme court; all of this was still of the utmost importance to me. As soon as I was released, I found out where this juror lived and went to his house. He didn't want to talk to me at first, didn't want to have anything to do with it anymore. He told me how he had so much trouble because of the case. He had lost two jobs. Finally I said, "The case is over. Please tell me what happened in the jury room. You owe it to me." "All right," he said. "I almost didn't make it to court that day because I had been so badly beaten the night before. On the first ballot, there were four of us that voted against conviction. One by one they caved in, until I was the last one holding out. We fought for hours. They yelled so much. They were all against me. They called me a Communist and told me I wasn't doing my patriotic duty. I finally just went berserk. They got the jail doctor to come up and give me a shot of something, and after that, I threw in the sponge."

That's all he told me. I never found any concrete evidence, but I've always suspected that the men who picked a fight with him weren't at the bar by accident that night.

Now I was out on bail, but I had to go through three months of another trial—the Smith Act case, along with five other people. Essentially the same case as the state one, just with different witnesses,[9] but you can always find people for sale who will testify to anything. The evidence was the same, although this time we managed to find a lawyer. Even Cercone was back, as an assistant to the U.S. Attorney General. I could go on about it, but the end result was we all were convicted and given five-year sentences. In the meantime, my lawyer successfully argued in front of the supreme court of the State of Pennsylvania that the state's sedition act had been superseded by the federal Smith Act. The opposition appealed to the U.S. Supreme Court, but they upheld the decision of the local court, and in 1956, my twenty-year sentence was reversed.

In that same year, the Smith Act case went to the circuit court in Philadelphia, and the judge ruled that there had been tainted evidence against us. One of the prosecution witnesses, Mazzei,[10] had perjured himself, and so the judge reversed the conviction and ordered a new trial. Now we were forced to go through that all over again, just because one of their goddamn witnesses happened to have been a liar. It put the burden on us.[11]

[9]In fact, Matt Cvetic was a prosecution witness at this trial as well. This time he arrived decorated with the American Legion's Americanism Award, which had been pinned to his chest by the governor of Pennsylvania and Miss America.

[10]Joseph Mazzei, a movie-theater manager who was arrested the following year for molesting a young boy in the theater he ran. Claiming that he had served as an FBI agent in the Pittsburgh CP from 1941 to March 26, 1953, Mazzei boasted that he had been trained to blow up bridges and poison water reservoirs, and "how to eliminate people." In 1956, the U.S. Solicitor General labeled him "a psychiatric case," and the Supreme Court agreed.

[11]Eleven months later, the case was dropped for good following the recantation of yet another another prosecution witness, seventy-three-year-old Alexander Wright.

You hear so much about the FBI in those days. I'll tell you, they came to me once after I had left the Party. I was working as a carpenter in New York, and I used to get up very early. One morning around six-thirty, I was shifting tools around in the back of my car when two guys accosted me. I knew exactly who they were and what they wanted. When they tried to talk to me, I turned around and said, "Get away, you bastards! You tried to frame me and now you want me to talk to you?" I grabbed for my hatchet, and they ran like rabbits. [Laughs.] I mean, I wouldn't have done anything, but I was so mad, and they were surprised. That was the last time I ever saw them.

But all along, that's what it was. All this fear just from people sticking up for themselves. All that over this little Communist movement that was in bread-and-butter kinds of issues. During the Depression, we fought against farmers losing their farms; men and women who couldn't pay their taxes. We said they should have set a moratorium on mortgages, stuff like that. We fought for better schools, and down the line. Now this was really what the movement that was called Communist was all about. We were not what they painted us to be. Even in the worst days of the Communist or Socialist parties, when they were sectarian and full of dreamers, we were never what they painted us out to be.

LORETTA STARVUS

In 1931, Loretta Starvus was a seventeen-year-old factory girl in a Rhode Island mill town. During a bitter strike she joined the Communist movement, and she stayed for twenty-seven years—primarily as a labor organizer, then briefly in the mid-forties as the district organizational secretary for California and a member of the state committee. On July 26, 1951, she was arrested, along with eleven other leaders of the California Party. Late in August, three more were arrested.[1] They were charged under the Smith Act with conspiring to advocate the violent overthrow of the government of the United States.

[1]The fifteen were William Schneiderman (West Coast leader), Al Richmond (executive editor of the *Daily People's World*), Carl Lambert, Albert Lima, Loretta Starvus Stack, Ernest Fox, Bernadette Doyle, Oleta O'Connor Yates, Philip Connelly, Dorothy Healey, Rose Chernin, Harry Steinberg, Ben Dobbs, Frank Carlson, and Frank Spector.

The national leaders of the Communist Party had already been arrested and convicted in New York City. Then, when their appeal was denied, a number of them skipped bail and went underground. I must confess when I heard that, I was quite shaken. I have never run away from anything. I felt it was wrong to go underground. It gave credence to the charge that we were a secret organization. I couldn't understand how they could do such a thing, because of the danger to the others who were going to be arrested. The government used this to justify arrests and deny bail. Then they started to arrest people in California.[2]

I'd been working as a waitress in a bakery and restaurant on Van Ness Avenue. I had been under surveillance for weeks. The cars were outside the restaurant, and big sleazy guys would come in and have coffee and then go back and sit in the car. So of course, you're not stupid, you figure they're watching you.

Early one morning in July of '51—about seven o'clock, I guess—the doorbell rang. That was very early for a doorbell to be ringing, and my husband had gone off to work. I went downstairs, and the kids—Joe was eight years old, and Mary was three—were looking down from the top of the stairs. I looked through the glass panel and there were five, six men there. They demanded I open up. I said, "Who are you?" They said, "FBI. We've got a warrant for your arrest." I said, "Well, where is the warrant?" And they said, "We don't need one."

I said, "I'm not letting you in," and I double-locked the door. I called a friend of mine who was in touch with pro-labor lawyers and I told her, "The FBI is downstairs and they want to arrest me. You'd better get in touch with the lawyers, because I'm not going to open the door for them. They didn't show me a warrant." Of course, I figure, the Constitution is protecting me. I was not going to show any fear. Anyway, they broke through the door. They threw their weight on it and they came up. I refused to get dressed. I thought, "These bastards!" I had a red bathrobe on, and I figured, "Let them take me in a red bathrobe!" The FBI were standing around and I was berating them. The children were hanging on to me, I was telling them, "Don't be afraid, look at these cowardly men. Five, six of them coming here, breaking into our house." And then I would turn and say, "Why don't you go down to Mississippi and arrest the lynchers there?" They just stood there. And of course, I realized later that they themselves were unsure how to handle this situation.

[2]On the day of the July arrests, U.S. Attorney Ernest Tolin announced in Los Angeles, "This is the first move in a program to destroy the Communist Party in the West."

They wouldn't let me get to a phone. They were going to send up a woman to take the children away. So I told them, "You're going to have to take me the way I am, goddammit, unless I have the opportunity to make my own arrangements for the children." So I called the woman next door. I said, "Will you take the children?" So anyway, she did. When the FBI sent this woman up, my children said, "Who's the lady, mama?" I said, "That's no lady, that's a goddam cop!" [Laughs.] And the woman flinched. She wanted to come in when I was putting my clothes on, and I said, "Come on, get off it!" The children and I went in the bathroom while I was getting dressed. So Helen came and she took the children. The FBI gang proceeded to lead me down the stairs. They were going to help me! [Laughs.] I said, "Don't you dare touch me!" Their hands were trembling, because I had held them off for forty-five minutes, an hour, and they were off schedule. They were planning to have all of us arraigned at once, most likely for the media.

The panel that indicted us was in Los Angeles—that was because it was a reactionary judiciary. San Francisco had some liberal judges. The judge set the bail at seventy-five thousand dollars each, except for two of us women. They allowed me out temporarily on two thousand dollars bail, to arrange for the children. They surrounded me everywhere I went for those two, three days. In fact, *Life* magazine had some reporters there. They wanted to get a story. I figured I couldn't get a sympathetic story, so I refused. I said, "I don't want my children to be subjected to this kind of stuff." They promised they would do a favorable piece, and they did. They took pictures for a column, "Women of the Week." They had Judy Garland, and Claire Boothe Luce, and I was the third one, with the two children. So that's how my family in New England learned about the arrest.

Now the Constitution states that it has to be reasonable bail. So how could seventy-five thousand dollars each for workers be reasonable bail, for Christ's sake? And Karesh,[3] he was a prosecutor, an arrogant guy who was out to make a name for himself. He said that we were traitors, worse than drug dealers. In those days, you know, we didn't even have drug dealers. But we were more dangerous than drug dealers. He was the prosecutor who asked for this big bail. It was outrageous. Eventually, he got to be a judge. It was just a way of spreading fear, and they kept us like that for more than six months. And then back in jail for another month while we

---

[3]Assistant U.S. Attorney Joseph Karesh, described by codefendant Al Richmond as "pumpkin-faced, a mobile jack-o'-lantern." (Al Richmond, *A Long View from the Left: Memoirs of an American Revolutionary* [Boston: Houghton Mifflin, 1973], p. 304)

were fighting again for reasonable bail. There were three women with children—Dorothy Healey had one child and so did Rose Chernin, and I had the two. The bail was moved up to, I think, one hundred thousand dollars for some of us.[4] And there we were.

Now, some of us could've gotten out, because there were people who were willing to put up money for us mothers. But if we had agreed, we would've set a precedent for high bail. None of us could do a thing like that. So we stayed. That was quite an experience. We were political prisoners, and on the main, we were looked to with respect in prison, no question about that. The other prisoners couldn't believe what we were in jail for, it frightened them. They'd say, "How can they tell you what to think?" They couldn't believe it. I remember Rose Chernin was sitting next to a very sweet-faced lady and the woman asked her, "What are you here for?" Rose was trying to explain, and the woman kept shaking her head about what a horrible thing it was. And then Rose asked, "What are you in for?" And the woman said, "Murder." [Laughs.] And Rose is sitting there with her mouth open.

The national leadership insisted that we defend Marxism and not stand on the First Amendment and the constitutional rights of freedom of speech and press. Why they did it, who the hell knows.[5] We in California decided we were going to stick to a constitutional defense. Otherwise we would be cutting the ground out from under us. Our defense was the right of free speech. The government was trying to convict us on ideas, not on acts. They were saying that just reading Marxism or believing it was an overt act. What they put on trial was writings out of context. They would read certain things that Lenin might have said, or Marx might have said. Really, that's what was on trial, was the books![6]

[4]In fact, bail was reduced to $50,000 each, or $750,000 for the group rate of fifteen. This represented a fortune to workers whose salaries ranged from $40 to $50 a week. Bail was further dropped to $5,000 to $10,000 each on appeal to the Supreme Court.

[5]The national leadership, which by this point was largely in hiding or in prison, was attempting to set down the "five minutes to midnight" line, which held that the United States was about to enter a period of fascism, not unlike that of Italy in the twenties and Germany in the thirties. With this in mind, they criticized the California defense as being too "legalistic" and not sufficiently "political." Al Richmond analyzed the national leaders' own trial tactics: "It appeared the defense was demanding the jury corroborate the correctness of the Communist Party's policies."

[6]Even though the books and therefore the theory were on trial, most prosecution witnesses readily admitted an unblemished ignorance of both. Such a witness was Butch Saunders, a mariner who had attended a Party school:

Q. Did you read some books on dialectical materialism?
A. I tried to read on it. It was over my head.

Oleta Yates was the only one who was going to take the stand. She also helped research the defense. A brilliant woman. When she was on the stand, she raised the question of constitutional rights and the marketplace of free ideas. The prosecutor demanded that she give names, and she refused. Then the judge took over the questioning, and then he sentenced her to five years for contempt of court—a year in prison for every person she refused to identify.[7] She began serving immediately, that very day. Some of us got out on ten to twenty thousand dollars bail. People like the Hallinans[8] put up the bail for me, and different people, not necessarily CP people, but people who were outraged at what was happening. When we got out on bail, Oleta stayed. During the trial, she was in several months. I used to bring her lunch and meet with her, because she was studying all the time, looking up references. She died a few years later, she developed lupus.

Years before, when I was on the East Coast, my husband had been a district organizational secretary for the Young Communist League. It was a very tough time in Philadelphia, we were starving half the time. There had been this black man there that I had known only because he talked with my husband. He appeared to testify against me in court. He said that I had gone to Moscow and learned how to shoot, that I was a crackerjack sharp-shooter, and that they taught me and others who were there how to over-turn streetcars. My children thought that was the funniest thing! [Laughs.] Mama overturning streetcars! It was a lie from beginning to end. It was like being denounced as a witch. How can you prove you're not a witch? Of course, this kind of nonsense hit the headlines.

So when the jury went out, they stayed out six days. Well, you figured at least it wasn't a hanging jury. For me, each day was important, and I gloried in that one day. No point in suffering ahead of time. But when they finally came out, the women on the jury were wiping tears from their eyes. Something happened in that jury room. Because you wouldn't have had that kind of reaction. So the judge asks what the verdict was, but of course he knew it already. Then he stopped the proceedings and he told the jury that what happened in there is secret, cannot be revealed, and if anyone reveals it they

[7]Yates ended up with eleven contempt citations, earning her a four-year prison term, plus an additional stipulation independent of the sentence that she was to remain in jail until she gave over the names.

[8]San Francisco's Vincent and Vivian Hallinan. Vincent was a brilliant and very tough left-wing lawyer who took on many such cases during this period. In 1952, he ran for President on the Progressive Party ticket, largely from a jail cell.

will be subjected to the full extent of the law, jail and fines.[9]

Before sentencing, each one of us had the opportunity to speak. I told the jury that I had always fought for what I considered to be justice, and whatever the judge says does not make this injustice right. My ideas came from my experience, I didn't know Lenin from a hole in the ground—that wasn't why I was organizing. It was because I was robbed of my childhood. I went to work at fourteen. I'd always done the best I could, and if there were any failings it was that I wasn't wise enough to do it better.

I received the full extent of the five years and the ten-thousand-dollar fine. It was appealed, but we had to go to prison, right then and there, for about five more weeks before we got out on bail. We had to fight for bail again. We had to take the stand and testify as to who put up the bail.

My family really suffered. I didn't know how fully until much later. My children, and all the children, paid a price—they were scarred by this experience. My younger brother, who was involved in the defense industry, had gotten himself a job as an estimator, a good position, and during the war he had been sent overseas to do construction for one of these big companies. I hadn't seen him since he was a kid. When I got arrested, his security clearance was taken away from him and he was no longer allowed to leave the country. They took his passport. Ten years later, during the Kennedy administration, he was cleared.

Then I found out that all kinds of cousins were approached, both on my father's side and my mother's. No matter where they were, what part of the country, they were visited and questioned because they were looking for those people who had jumped bail. My cousins didn't know me from a hole in the ground! It was a blot on the family name, you know. My parents were glad I had used my married name![10] [Laughs.]

The appeal for reasonable bail was going back and forth between the Ninth Circuit Court and the Supreme Court. Then the Supreme Court ruled in our favor. Of course, the question of bail was important for more people than us. It was important for all people arrested. And so the appeal for

---

[9]When asked about this event, Ben Margolis, one of the defense attorneys, responded, "When the jury was polled, there were three women who cried. I don't think their crying indicated anything other than that they didn't really want to do what they did. We were quite angry at the judge for refusing to allow the jury to be interviewed, not because we expected to find anything in particular, but because it was just another instance of depriving us of rights that we had."

[10]At that time, Stack was her name by marriage.

reasonable bail, it gets a name—*The United States v. Stack*. Mickey Cohen used my case in his appeal for reasonable bail. I don't know if you've heard of Mickey Cohen—he was an L.A. gangster. He was kept in jail with high bail. He took shelter under this law that was upheld by the Supreme Court. [Laughs.]

It took seven years from the day we were arrested to the day the Supreme Court heard our entire case. And then, based on the First Amendment, the Supreme Court ruled that it was an unfair trial. There were errors made in the constitutional interpretation, based on the cases of Al Richmond and Slim Connelly, who were from the labor press. The convictions were overturned for those two. That's how it went. So if they wanted to retry us, it would have to be retried without those two people, see. The conspiracy was broken.

After the trial, when I came back to San Francisco, it was difficult for me to get work. At that time, San Francisco was a union town. I had been a member of the waitress union. My husband tried to keep up my dues. But the union refused to take the dues, because in their eyes I was a criminal. I couldn't get back on waiting. I knew that whatever job I would get, the FBI would visit the employer and that would be the end of that job. I got work with a woman who gave me the cover of a catering job, so I was making a living that way. It was private catering.

Before I was arrested, we had lived on Green Street, and right across the street was a family with a boy Joe's age, whose name was Woody. The boys used to play together. Woody would come over to our house and Joe would go over to his house. Woody's father was the sports editor of the *Examiner*. Back then, I used to talk to the mother—she was pleasant. He was always a sourpuss. But the thing is this. It's after the trial and I'm catering a party at the Livingstons', they're big-money people here. I was working under a different name. And I met this Woody's mother there. I was presenting her with a tray of hors d'oeuvres when she said, "Why, Loretta! How are you?" and "How is Joey?" I said, "Fine," and I walked away. Well, she must've mentioned to her husband that Loretta was there, working under a different name. A week later there's an item in Herb Caen's column, who also worked for the *Examiner* then. He wrote that he saw me there and added some snide remark that although she's a Communist she was avidly interested in fashion. Now that was a lie from beginning to end. The son of a bitch. He also revealed where Oleta was working. Everything fell down on this poor woman who had given me the job. She was an excellent caterer, and when this showed up in the paper, the catering system lowered the boom on her. She lost a lot of work.

Some time after the Supreme Court decision, my one-hundred-dollar deposit for a place in the ILWU co-op apartments here in St. Francis Square was rejected by HUD in Washington, D.C. They claimed I was a security risk.[11]

[11]In 1952, Congress passed a rider, the Gwinn Amendment, to the Housing Administration Act, decreeing that no public housing shall be occupied by a current member of any organization on the Attorney General's list. Occupants were supplied the AG's list, along with a loyalty oath. Even though the government announced in 1956 that it would no longer attempt to enforce the amendment (after losing some twenty court cases), alleged Communists continued to be threatened with eviction from public housing.

DOROTHY HEALEY

A Party member from 1928 to 1973, Healey led the Southern California District for more than twenty years and served on the Party's national committee. She is now a vice chair of the Democratic Socialists of America. In 1951, she was arrested under the Smith Act. A warm, vibrant woman, she pulls her feet up under her as she leans into an overstuffed chair, takes a puff on a cigarette, and begins her story.

There was a significant difference between testifying before state or federal so-called investigating committees before 1947 and after. Before 1947, the committees inquired and concentrated solely on one's individual activities and/or membership in the Party. In '47, they discovered the little wrinkle that one way to trap witnesses was to try to force them to talk about other people. If you refused to talk about others' activities or membership in the Party, then you could be held in contempt. And the only way not to be held in contempt was to use the Fifth Amendment against self-incrimination. But once you had answered any questions before a committee that indicated you had a knowledge beyond that of the person on the street walking by, you had waived your right against self-incrimination. People were subpoenaed before federal grand juries to testify, never about oneself but about other people. When you refused to do that, you were held in contempt of court.

People who got called frequently, as I did, soon learned that in the post-'47 period, if you were asked a question by any of these committees, and you answered them with a very long speech on any one of a variety of subjects, they soon forgot what the question was and didn't notice whether or not you'd ever answered it. So I would make very, very long speeches and they would be exhausted by the time I was through [laughs] and go on to the next subject.

When I testified in front of the House Un-American Activities Committee, it was an executive session and the only person allowed in with me was my attorney, Ben Margolis. When they started trying to press on other people, I, of course, took the Fifth. But then I would walk outside of that hearing room and the press would be there, and I'd say, "Of course I'm a member of the Communist Party and all of you know it, and I have no objections to the world knowing it. There is nothing secret about it. But the fact is that this committee has no right to ask these questions because it cannot legislate on questions that come under the First Amendment." It was always so humorous; the secrecy inside, but the public admission on the outside.

Before 1947, I never had any objection at all to speaking quite freely on my activities as a Communist and what I was doing. Then it was mainly the California state committee, with Jack Tenney as the head. They were trying to establish this theory of a conspiracy that worked behind the scenes, that preyed on all these innocent people. Of course, people like me had no hesitation in answering all questions and in discussing in great detail what was happening.

As a matter of fact, I used to take particular delight when Jack Tenney would call me, because I had known him in the period when he was on the Left, when he used to meet with Communist Party officials and wanted our support. He had been the head of the Musicians Union, a very despotic head, but the Musicians Union was not famous for democracy anyway. He broke with the Party over two questions. First, within his own union a rank-and-file group started to challenge him, and he wanted the Party to denounce it. The Party, of course, refused to denounce it—it was a legitimate movement. He had also been one of the nominal leaders of the Labor's Nonpartisan League of California.[1] He wanted the support of Labor's Nonpartisan League for something that he was running for, and they refused to do it. He then became one of the most vitriolic of the Red-baiters and attackers.

When he questioned me, well, I'd sit back, smile, and say, "Now Jack,

[1]Founded by AFL and CIO unions in 1936 to work for Roosevelt's reelection. Its chief contribution probably came in the form of getting out the vote.

you know the answer to that. We discussed that in the meetings with the Party that you attended!" [Laughs.]

One time, the U.S. Senate subcommittee, the Dodd Committee, subpoenaed Pacifica Radio because, among other reasons, I was a publicly known Communist and had a program on KPFK.[2] They were threatening to take it to the FCC and revoke the license of Pacifica. So the entire board of Pacifica and the staff people were subpoenaed. And I, of course, was included in that.

The others just wouldn't testify. I testified [laughs] and had a great time exposing Dodd as a representative of the mining interests in the Congo. This was the old man Dodd, the father of Chris Dodd, who also served in the Senate. I made the usual soapbox speeches that I enjoyed so. Nothing came of it, because of course they couldn't legislate in regard to the radio and the FCC never got involved.

I have been arrested many times, but in 1951, I was arrested under the Smith Act. There were, in the beginning, fifteen of us—Bernadette Doyle was later severed for ill health—charged with conspiring to advocate the overthrow of the United States government by force and violence. The key word there, of course, is "conspire," because under conspiracy law you don't have to prove that the individual defendant ever actually did anything, but that other named people could do it. At this point, the Supreme Court had already upheld the first Smith Act case on the ground of a future danger. Not that there was any clear and imminent danger, but that at some unknown time, unknown and unnamed people could so conspire. We were in jail for four months before the trial actually proceeded, because the presiding Judge Mathes placed the bail at fifty thousand dollars. We appealed, the appellate court ordered him to lower it, and he wouldn't do it.[3]

Finally we took it to the Supreme Court and ultimately we were released on ten thousand dollars for some of us and five thousand dollars for the others. The trial lasted six months. The bulk of the testimony against us was actually the writings of Karl Marx and Frederick Engels and Lenin. It was

[2]An affiliate of the Pacifica Radio Network (founded by a group of pacifists who had been incarcerated during World War Two), KPFK began broadcasting out of Los Angeles in 1959. Healey hosted a fifteen-minute program called *Communist Commentary*, which later expanded to an hour. After she left the Party in 1973, she changed the name to *Marxist Commentary*.

[3]U.S. District Court Judge William C. Mathes, Texan, graduate of Harvard Law, and a devoted member of the American Legion, claimed to be so baffled when the Supreme Court ruled his bail decision to be unreasonable that he needed at least six days to think about it. Twenty-three days later, he ruled that indeed it was reasonable. It took the circuit court of appeals to overrule him and set the lower bail.

hysterical to watch these prosecutors stand up with passion in their voices and read from Karl Marx about "you have to shatter the bourgeois state." Of course, to Marx that simply meant that you had to find and install a new state administrative machinery. But to the prosecution and probably to the jury, it meant blood flowing in the streets. It was ridiculous to see books being used in this way. Another time, the prosecutor read from one of the speeches I'd made about how people had to continue to study and read all their lives, and he said, "Imagine, these people in their middle ages! They're talking like you still have to study!" Well, clearly to him, there could be no greater proof of conspiracy than if middle-aged people would continue to study.

There were about twenty-three witnesses for the prosecution. Some of them were very funny. One of the FBI informers, a man named John Lautner,[4] claimed that he'd given me a collapsible mimeograph machine to prepare for the days when we would really try to overthrow the government. He said that it was the kind of collapsible mimeograph machine that I could fold up and carry in my bra from New York to Los Angeles! [Laughs.] The image of this always staggered me. I kept trying to visualize such a contrivance. But that was really par for the course. There was some woman who claimed she used to bake cakes for *People's World* parties, and that part of the conspiracy was to trap unwary people into our coils by giving them dessert. It was hilarious.[5]

The jury was out four days. When they came back in, all the women had red eyes. It looked like they'd all been crying. We knew they'd come in with a verdict of guilty. Our bail was immediately revoked.

In order to get bail after conviction, the judge did something that was totally unheard of. Anyone who offered to provide bail for us had to take the witness stand and undergo questioning from the court on who they were, why they wanted to do this, and what were their connections with us. My brother offered to go bail for me. He was not anywhere near the

---

[4]Lautner was employed by the Justice Department at $125 per week (a pay scale that matched that of the middle 30 percent of American families at that time) and furnished with an office in Washington. He was paraded across the country as the chief prosecution witness in every Smith Act trial after 1950, as well as many congressional and SACB hearings. In the instance of several other Smith Act trials, it was revealed that the questions and Lautner's answers to them had been written out beforehand by the prosecuting attorney.

[5]Another FBI informer, Daisy Van Dorn, provided one of the prosecution's prized exhibits, a book, *History of the Civil War in the USSR*. She had identified it as the top-secret plans for the overthrow of the government, smuggled into the United States by Russian sailors. Testifying that she had won the book at a CP raffle, she claimed two of the defendants had warned her to keep its contents secret. Defense attorney Branton then produced three copies that he had checked out from the Los Angeles public library.

Communist Party, was extremely unhappy about his sister's involvement, but a very loyal brother. Of course, the newspapers published the fact that the judge questioned him. My brother had been slated to become head of the anesthesiology department at Cedars of Lebanon Hospital, and the appointment was promptly canceled.

This happened to other people as well. The punitive arm simply chilled the atmosphere for anyone who wanted to provide bail. Finally, we had to go to the Supreme Court to get the bail lowered, but we got out one month after the trial. We were sentenced to five years in prison and ten thousand dollars fine. Five years later, the Supreme Court reversed the convictions of Rose Chernin, Slim Connelly, Henry Steinberg, Al Richmond, and Frank Spector and ordered that a new trial be held for the rest of us because of insufficiency of evidence.[6] Some three or four months later, the government withdrew the indictments against us on the ground they could not get such evidence.

The harassment didn't end after the Smith Act case was dropped. In 1950 came the McCarran Act, which ordered the Party to register as a foreign agent of the Soviet Union. Of course, we refused to do it. KPFK, for a while, tried to carry out the provisions of the act. I was furious at them. Part of the McCarran regulation is that when a Communist spoke publicly on radio or television, there had to be a disclaimer before they were introduced, saying that so-and-so was an agent of a foreign power. KPFK was real scared about what was happening because of the congressional investigations and whatnot. They tried to figure out a way of complying with the law that wouldn't be too outrageous a violation of the First Amendment. I said, "If you use it, I'm just not going to appear; I'm going to blast you and say why I'm not appearing."

I was never sentenced under the McCarran Act, but the potential sentence was five years and ten thousand dollars for each day you refused to register. My mathematical son once figured out that I would have been in prison for at least twenty-seven thousand years and the fine would have amounted to fifty-five million dollars for the length of time that elapsed

---

[6]According to Al Richmond's *A Long View from the Left: Memoirs of an American Revolutionary* (Boston: Houghton Mifflin, 1973), the reversal of all the convictions rested largely on the meaning of "organize" as used in the Smith Act. The defense contended that it described the formative act of bringing into existence. The prosecution and the judge insisted the word also embraced ongoing administrative and organizational functions. The Supreme Court sided with the defense. As the CP was last "organized" in 1945, the statute of limitations had long since expired when the defendants were indicted in 1951. Subsequently, Smith Act charges were dropped against eighty-one other persons throughout the country.

between when the Department of Justice ordered me to register and when the Supreme Court overturned it.

When the FBI would have carloads of agents outside our home, before we were arrested in '51 under the Smith Act, my neighbors loved it, because they figured we were the safest neighborhood in the city. [Laughs.] Three carloads of agents, day and night, out there. When I would take my son to elementary school, a few blocks from the house, these three cars would swoop in and follow me. When I'd go shopping at the market, they'd get out of their cars and come traipsing into the market to follow me as I shopped! [Laughs.]

Once, I was sitting at a restaurant underneath the Communist Party headquarters, reading a paper, and one of the FBI agents, whom I of course knew by this time, came in. There was an empty seat beside me, and he said, "Do you mind if I sit here?" I looked at him and said, "It's a public place," and kept on reading. He said, "Now, look, Dorothy. I really want to talk seriously to you. With this decision of the Court, you know, we have great power now. But if you will cooperate with us, like Elizabeth Bentley[7] did, we will guarantee that neither your mother nor your son nor you will go to a concentration camp." He was referring to the fact that in 1940s, the FBI, whether or not it was legal, had designated certain individuals to be placed in concentration camps in the event of hostilities with an enemy nation; I was on that list. There was no federal legislation until the McCarran Act came along that allowed for that. But my file shows it as early as 1941.

I stood up, and I placed my hand over my breast and I said, "This man is attacking me! This man is attacking me!" Everybody in the restaurant knew me, and they all came flocking over to see what this terrible man was doing. In the meantime I got up and walked upstairs to my office. It felt wonderful to be able to put the FBI on the defensive for once.

They followed me everywhere I went. Most of the time I didn't give a damn. I never went anywhere that I cared whether they came. But sometimes just to have fun, to vary the routine, I'd drive real fast in front of a streetcar, then turn quickly to my left to get away from them and then circle around, or I'd drive through parking lots and then circle out. One night I got a phone call—"Dorothy, please, it's only a job we're doing! You don't have to endanger yourself or our lives because of it!" [Laughs.] It was so plaintive.

---

[7] A notorious professional witness and the source of many extravagant charges. See Joseph Rauh under "The Purge of the Civil Service" for more on Elizabeth Bentley.

In later years, when my son was in junior high and his friends would come over, he'd tell them what I'd tell people who'd come to my house: "Never say your name out loud." We had this experience where one of his friends came over and mentioned his name. His father was a lieutenant colonel and the next day the father got a phone call—"Do you know your son is consorting with Communists?" So we learned never say your name out loud, and it became a habit that when anybody was going to mention a name, you'd say, "Write it. Don't say it out loud."

The phones were tapped. My FBI files showed they started tapping the phones in '46. They also tapped my mother's phone. She lived in the front house, and I always thought that God had punished them, because they listened to all her phone calls, and my mother could go on for hours!

I don't know if the FBI ever stopped hanging around. Under the Freedom of Information Act, they had to send me a package of documents of their dirty tricks. The things they pulled were vile. For example, I'd testified before the Walters Committee, HUAC, in executive session. So the FBI printed up a leaflet, supposedly signed by black Communists, saying Dorothy betrayed the Party in these secret hearings and testified as an agent of the FBI about all our memberships. Then they circulated that leaflet around as if it ostensibly came from black Communists. It was the most childish nonsense.

I found an enormous difference between the FBI reports of the 1930s and 1940s and those of the early sixties. They became far more sophisticated. In the early days they were pretty stupid and clearly didn't know what they were doing. By the sixties they were very aware of how to stir up trouble, how to turn people against one another, how to get enmities aroused. They were very skillful, and very knowledgeable. I'll always be curious who in the FBI initiated this far more knowledgeable kind of investigation. I don't think it could've come from practice, because that presumes they had the brains to learn from experience. I don't think there was that capacity! [Laughs.]

You know what amazes me? Hundreds of Communists were arrested throughout the country under the suspicion of being traitors, of selling or giving secret information to the Soviet Union, yet no evidence was ever brought forth. If there was ever an opportunity for the government to have judicially substantiated their claim that we were traitors, the Smith Act trials would have been the time. But no one has remarked on the fact that not one Communist of the hundreds who were arrested during that period was ever so charged.

JUNIUS SCALES

A warm, voluble, man, Scales joined the Communist Party in 1939 while a student at the University of North Carolina at Chapel Hill and remained a member for eighteen years. After two years in the underground, he was arrested by the FBI. He is the only American ever imprisoned for mere membership in the Communist Party.

The Cold War began in '47, and you could see the lines being drawn. Anticommunism was growing to an enormous intensity. Things got so bad, in the press and all throughout North Carolina, in every walk of life, it just was insanity. So the head of the Party in the South and the new head of the Party in the state asked me on behalf of the national office if I would consider taking a stand as a public Communist, being a spokesman and so on. I thought about it, and I guess one of the big factors that made me do it was that I hated the duplicity of not being able to say "Yes, I'm a Communist" instead of saying "I'm a Communist sympathizer." So that appealed to me.

Finally, with many misgivings, we put out a leaflet on the high cost of living, but instead of signing it with the state organizer's name or just his postbox in Winston-Salem, we very unobtrusively put "Junius Scales, Chairman, Box 62, Chapel Hill." Well, the next day there were hysterical headlines all over the state—front page, eight columns, all the way across: "Prominent North Carolinian Says He's a Communist." From then on, I couldn't sneeze without being a public figure. That went on for the next twenty-two years.

It caused a lot of controversy and a lot of threats, especially later on. I had three crosses burned in my front yard, and slept through every one of them! I found the charred crosses in the yard the next morning, so it didn't have much effect. Things got very tough. I was watched by the FBI twenty-four hours a day for years. I remember in 1950 the FBI would follow me through Chapel Hill, two or three carloads of them. I'd walk across the campus and they'd go out like extended order drill in the Army. I'd have a dozen guys encircling me, moving as I moved, signaling to each other. It was a lot of malarkey, supposed to intimidate me. But it had a very practical effect. I couldn't go to a meeting and bring a traffic jam with me, or a crowd of FBI agents.

I lived in a mill house in Carrboro. The FBI had everybody on that street thinking they were doing the Lord's work and the government's work by reporting anything suspicious going on at the Scales house. They rented the upstairs of one house and kept constant surveillance on everybody that came and went. Around late 1950 I started taking precautions to throw them off. It wasn't as difficult as you might think, they were awfully stupid. [Laughs.] With all that surveillance, I could crawl out of my back door and by keeping in shadows and going in the ditch and so on, I could get out at night and they wouldn't know it. They had informers, and later they'd find out that I was a hundred miles away. It was a terror tactic. It didn't affect me, but it bothered other people. It was very disconcerting. Some of my lieutenants, for example, would find two cars parked in front of their house full of FBI agents. They'd be there all day, follow the kids to school. If the wife went shopping, they'd go along too. But when I married the second time, it was understood that I'd probably be going to jail.

The government didn't want to indict me until they knew they could arrest me, so they indicted me under the Smith Act on the afternoon and arrested me in the evening. That was in November 1954.[1] They put me in the backseat of a car. I was flown back to North Carolina handcuffed and in leg irons in a Navy plane and arraigned that night, about eleven o'clock. They'd gotten the indictment in North Carolina from a grand jury in North Wilkesboro, and they put me in the Shelby County jail, where I stayed for about five or six days. Altogether I was in jail about a month before the trial in Winston-Salem.

They set the bail at one hundred thousand dollars, and today that would be like setting the bail at one and a half million or something like that. It was just staggering. Of course, my mother was devastated by my arrest and all the publicity, which was national this time. And of course the state papers went crazy. An old high school chum who was a judge and later became a congressman tried to get me a lawyer, without success, because I was about as unpopular as anyone could get. I argued my bail down from one hundred thousand dollars to thirty-five thousand dollars, and that was just an opening wedge, I expected to get it down to about ten thousand dollars or so. But my mother went and put up some bonds she had as collateral, without my knowing it or wanting it. I thought that was much

---

[1]See Scales's account of life in the underground and his eventual arrest under "Five Minutes to Midnight."

too high a bail to get out on. Anyway, I was out, and my wife, Gladys, came down and we went to New York in time for Christmas.

I couldn't get a local lawyer, I tried every way, but I finally got a lawyer from Washington, D.C., whose name was David Rein. He was a wonderful guy. He would defend anybody before the Un-American Committee. His clothes were threadbare, he was on the verge of poverty himself! He and his partner, Joe Forer. He's dead now, but he handled the whole trial by himself. An incredible job.

At my first trial, in the spring of '55, they had two stool pigeons as witnesses, maybe three. It lasted about nine days, and a lot of it was reading from books. They used books that I'd read or given to other people or sold to other people. It was just a mishmash of books.

You can take Marxist literature and make a good case for advocacy of violent overthrow. Or you can take the same authors and make a very good case for a gradualist approach to socialism. It all depended on when they were writing. When there was armed uprising going on, they tended to be violent. When things were stable, they tended to be quite the opposite. But the jury didn't have the foggiest notion of what was going on. All they knew was that this guy was bad or had gotten into bad company. I think it took them an hour and a quarter to decide I was guilty. The judge had a weekend planned, so the next morning he sentenced me to six years in prison, which was the heaviest sentence ever given in the Smith Act cases.

John Lautner was a stool pigeon who was at both my trials. Previously, he had been a very unimpressive kind of Party hack, with a routine job. He had been unjustly accused of being an FBI agent. So in Cleveland he was confronted, and a guy who is still in the Party, appropriately enough, beat him up. He was ostracized, his wife divorced him, his whole life was ruined. He sat for six months, I don't know if he was becoming an alcoholic or what, he finally wrote J. Edgar Hoover, and of course they responded.

Ignorance got in his way frequently. He said he didn't know me, but he did. He had become a vicious person, he just lived on hate. His job was to characterize the Party, and his testimony didn't vary much. He spoke a good deal about force and violence, and it was absolute malarkey, because nobody I've ever talked to in the Party leadership can recall any advocacy of violence. In fact, nobody even thought about it until the first Smith Act trial. That shows what great theoreticians we were—nobody had even thought about the road to socialism, that was a never-never land, which is where it belonged, I guess.

They never tied the Party to any overt act, other than meetings and books. It was simply membership in my case. I wasn't tried on the basis of any conspiracy. And yet in the opinion of the Fourth Circuit Court of Appeals, of course, it was conspiracy. Dave Rein, who was still my lawyer then, said that was an interesting concept, since no one at the trial had known about a conspiracy. The jury hadn't been instructed about it, and it had never occurred to the prosecution or the defense that there was a conspiracy.

The McCarran Act and the Smith Act were both disabled because of my case. Years and years later, after I'd finished sitting in Lewisburg, the whole thing collapsed from the weight of its own contradictions.[2]

After the first trial, when the case was on appeal, I had to be more cautious than ever when traveling in the South, because I was more easily recognized. I didn't travel as much, and I did it differently. I'd try to get people to some neutral place like Philadelphia or New York and try to discuss Party work there. The key people were black, some of them, but because of the difficulty of meeting with blacks, I had to rely more on two white guys. So we would work out ways of getting together and I would meet them on the edge of the South. I went to the South several times, in fact, I made a trip throughout the South troubleshooting for the Party and trying to get some support against the Smith Act. I was supposed to meet with William Faulkner, but the old buzzard went on a real toot and they hauled him off to the hospital in Memphis the day I was there. We must have passed, me on a bus and him in an ambulance. I never got to see him. One of my old comrades there was a drinking buddy of Faulkner's and he said he really tied one on that time and they hauled him off. I don't think Faulkner had any idea this guy was an old Red.

I was in litigation for—let's see, I was arrested in '54, I finally got out of prison at the end of '62. So I was in constant litigation for seven or eight years. And always financial problems—nothing like a court case to keep you broke. The Party was supposed to supply money. The only reason I got

[2]One contradiction arose from the requirement of the McCarran Act (1950) compelling Communists to register as members of a subversive organization. When this piece of legislation was pending, Congress realized that since Party members were liable to prosecution under the membership clause of the Smith Act (1940), compelling them to register under the McCarran Act would be a violation of their Fifth Amendment right against self-incrimination. This encumbrance was supposedly resolved by section 4(f) of the McCarran Act, which provided that Party membership "shall not constitute per se a violation" of the McCarran Act "or of any other criminal statute," thus avowedly immunizing Party members from prosecution under the membership clause of the Smith Act and eliminating self-incrimination as a defense against compliance with the registration requirements of the McCarran Act.

Telford Taylor as a lawyer in the appeals stage from the first trial was that the Party insisted I get someone of national renown[3] and Telford said he would do it for ten thousand dollars. So the Party agreed and signed in blood that they would stand for the ten thousand dollars, and I had a committee that knocked itself out up here in New York. They raised money for printing and God knows what, it was endless.

I never could talk about my own case and make a pitch, it absolutely mortified me. Finally, I was at the end of my rope, and who should show up in the middle of a meeting I'm having but Paul Robeson. He interrupts me, gets up on the stage, puts his arm around me, and makes a speech.[4] It moved me to tears then, and it has ever since. He must have raised three or four times what I could possibly have gotten. I never asked him to come to any fund-raising things, but he had a radar, he would show up in somebody's apartment even, and he'd have an accompanist and he'd sing and make a pitch for money.

Paul Robeson had been my friend since '46. When he visited the Soviet Union in 1949, they fished out for him one of the Jewish poets[5] they'd had in a concentration camp. This poet knew the room was bugged, but he indicated to Paul that he knew he was going to be done in. And he was. Some of that got to me secondhand. Paul wouldn't talk about it with anybody. He did with his son, but he felt that it was so appalling and it would be a blow to the socialist movement. So much more was involved, terrible as it was, so he decided to keep his mouth shut, which I think was a mistake. But many years later I could understand what motivated him.

I left the Party at the end of '56, along with eighty-five percent of the membership, over the horrors of the Kruschchev reports—that was just staggering—followed by the Hungarian invasion. One of the first things they did when I left the Party was to stop my money-raising arrangements. And yet mine was a test case for the Smith Act, which could have put them

[3]Telford Taylor served as a brigadier general during World War Two and was chief Allied prosecutor at the Nuremberg war crimes trial.

[4]In part, Robeson said, "I must tell you something about this young man. . . . I have known him for many years. We are old friends. In all that time he has been fighting the good fight—our fight, his and mine—against racism and for democratic rights in the South. . . . His roots and my roots are in North Carolina—my ancestors, slaves; his, slave owners. We stand here tonight as two brothers in the struggle for human decency."

[5]Upon his arrival, Robeson was immediately alarmed by the anti-Semitic character of the state-orchestrated campaign against "Zionism," "Titoism," and "cosmopolitanism." Concerned about his many friends in the Jewish community, he pressured the Soviets for a visit with poet Itzik Fefer, a former Red Army colonel and head of the wartime Jewish Anti-Fascist Committee. Fefer reportedly assessed his likely fate by drawing his hand across his throat.

all in the poke. They were all vulnerable, but they were disrupting my efforts to raise money.

The Supreme Court reversed the conviction and sent it back to the trial court. And, of course, they started all over again. So in '58 I had a second trial, which lasted three weeks. Telford[6] was marvelous at cross-examining. One witness said that she had never known the Party advocated force and violence until after she had offered to inform on them.[7] I thought I would die. Things like that are so crazy. But it didn't make any difference. I was a Red, an admitted Red—although by this time I was an ex-Red—by the second trial, I'd been out of the Party for a year. When I went to jail, I'd been out of the Party almost five years.

The climate had changed a little by then, but my lawyers both knew that the odds of winning it in court were slim, it would have to be on appeal. In 1961, it ended up in the Supreme Court again, a five-to-four decision against.

It was argued before the Supreme Court three times. They ordered a reargument. So the third time, Telford still thought he was going to win, thought he was going to get a five-to-four the right way. Warren, Brennan, Douglas, and Black were my four. Funny, when I'd been sitting in jail three or four months, there was not a single Smith Act case on the books anywhere—they'd all been dropped. One of my lawyers said, "You know, if your case came up now, you'd win either five-to-four or six-to-three." [Laughs.] That was very comforting!

When I'd been in Lewisburg maybe five months, McNeil Smith, my Greensboro attorney, went up to Washington and had a meeting with Deputy Attorney General Katzenbach, who later became the Attorney General. He said, "He's got to name names." This is J. Edgar speaking through Katzenbach, of course. "It doesn't matter if they're people we already know or if they're dead even. He's got to name names, and he can be out in a matter of days." So Mac traveled all the way to Lewisburg to tell me this. I'd hardly greeted him when he gives me this proposition. I said,

---

[6]Telford Taylor was one of two lawyers representing Scales during his second trial and argued his case before the Supreme Court.

[7]This appearance marked Barbara Hartle's debut as a professional ex-Communist. Sentenced to five years in the Washington State Smith Act trial of 1953, she soon began singing her way to freedom. Ultimately, she named 470 people, including her former husband and her ex-lover. She was still naming names in 1963, although by then there was some suspicion that she was inventing them.

"I'll rot first."[8] And he gets a big smile on his face. We had a lovely visit. It was common knowledge among most of the inmates at Lewisburg that I was there because I wouldn't squeal on my "mob." [Laughs.]

I got along well in Lewisburg. There's no describing the horrors of prison, but . . . Oh God, I was a close confinement prisoner, which is the highest category. Close confinement means you're the highest priority of being watched, you're the most dangerous. I was in solitary for about six weeks, which was all right with me, because this was sort of a quarantine section. I read Proust and had a wonderful time. It's not like the hole. I'd go out for meals, but I was all by myself and there was no way of communicating to others except at mealtimes. Then I went into what they call "the Jungle," which is a dormitory with double-deck bunks, and down the middle of this long room were single-deck bunks, and on the far side more double-deck bunks. A huge, crowded room, the Jungle was deadly.

I never had any time to myself. I felt like I never could think about anything, I'd have to wait till lights out. I wrote a letter to my kid at Christmas by the reflection of the searchlights on the wall. You couldn't even do it in the john, because there were no partitions. The joke was they were so close together that you didn't know whose behind you were wiping.

My two prison buddies who saved my life[9] said, "Why don't you apply for honor quarters?" So I did and got a room about eight by thirteen. It had places to have your clothes, a foot locker, a bed, a sink, and a window. And they didn't lock the door. You could go to the john without any problem at night.

While I was in prison, our next-door neighbor, who was a loyal Party member, raised two hundred dollars in her Party club. The section organizer heard she was raising money for me. Here was this woman who'd been in the Party for twenty-five years and she's in a room full of people that had been in the Party as long as she had, and this jerk comes in and says

[8]McNeil Smith remembers this story somewhat differently. In conversation with the author, Smith recalled that the offer to name names came up during the second trial and was soundly turned down. He remembers speaking to an official at Justice, but not Katzenbach. Smith surmises that the possibility of cooperating arose during the visit to Lewisburg but was not, as he remembers, a direct offer from Justice. Telford Taylor, however, recounted to the author a conversation he held directly with Katzenbach, in which the deputy attorney general did indeed insist that Scales name names.

[9]In his memoirs, Scales tells of a fellow prisoner, an Italian underworld figure, who complained he couldn't get a square deal in court as it was assumed that because of his heritage he was Mafia. Scales suggested that he have his lawyer read a chapter of Daniel Bell's *The End of Ideology* entitled "The Myth of the Mafia." The gangster was so taken by the book that he had everyone in his mob read it as well. Later, the mob returned the favor, protecting Scales from a psychopath who was stalking him with murderous intent.

that it's against Party policy. She asked why, and he couldn't answer. So she and the whole roomful resigned from the Party on the spot. They went next door and turned over the money they'd raised to my wife.

Gladys was working. She had a job as a teacher and she lived off that. Occasionally people contributed so she could drive to Lewisburg. But otherwise, that was it. We didn't have a pot to piss in. But I was lucky in prison. It's a very dangerous occupation. In fact, if you have any insurance, they cancel it.

Just before I went to prison, a committee was formed that became very active in agitating for my release. Norman Thomas,[10] who was close to eighty then, was a ball of fire. I remember sitting in his office and him saying, "We need a committee. We need a group of four to be an anchor." He gets on the phone and calls Robert Goheen, who was president of Princeton at the time, and he agreed immediately. Then he called a Republican civil libertarian, whose name escapes me at the moment, he agreed immediately. And then he volunteered himself, and for the fourth he called a local number and said, "Hallo, Reiny?" This was Reinhold Niebuhr![11] He came along immediately. Not a squawk.

So then he starts thinking of others he can get to sign up with the committee. Jesus Christ, what a list we got up. Among the initial recruits were Martin Luther King, Jr.,[12] and W. H. Auden,[13] just to give you an idea.[14]

King got a number of other prominent blacks, like the president of the Pullman Porters—A. Philip Randolph.[15] This committee grew, and my

[10]Norman Thomas (1884–1968), anti-Communist leader of the American Socialist Party, ran for President of the United States six times on the Socialist ticket. Many of his early proposals became law under the New Deal.

[11]Reinhold Niebuhr (1892–1971), eminent Protestant theologian and philosopher of ethics, was a politically liberal anti-Communist. He was highly influential among members of the Democratic Party brain trust of the fifties and sixties.

[12]Martin Luther King, Jr. (1929–68), head of the Southern Christian Leadership Conference, was the principal leader of the civil rights movement in the fifties and sixties. He was awarded the Nobel Peace Prize in 1964.

[13]W. H. Auden (1907–73), was considered the foremost English poet of his generation; he was awarded the Pulitzer Prize in 1948.

[14]A partial list includes Roger Baldwin, Daniel Bell, Saul Bellow, John C. Bennett, Van Wyck Brooks, Theodore Draper, Robert Heilbroner, Sidney Hook, Irving Howe, I. F. Stone, Edmund Wilson, Pablo Casals, and C. Vann Woodward. Eleanor Roosevelt also wrote a "strong letter of support" to JFK.

[15]Asa Philip Randolph (1889–1979) was the founder and first president of the Brotherhood of Sleeping Car Porters and was elected vice president of the AFL-CIO in 1955. A militant Socialist early in his career, Randolph was a longtime presence in the fight for civil rights.

wife was the firebrand that kept it going. They kept getting more and more prominent names, and it got to be a real pain in the ass to the Kennedy administration. Bobby Kennedy really handled it—John didn't know beans about it. Finally he sent for Norman Thomas, and Thomas came down there with his usual cordiality and charm. Bobby Kennedy nods when he comes in and says, "Stop the pressure." So Norman says, "I beg your pardon?" He says, "Stop the pressure! I'm getting all this flak." And Norman says, "In exchange for what?" [Laughs.]

Kennedy said, "The whole department is against me on it. I want him out. I think the sentence was outrageous." Of course, what happened was that Katzenbach and the other assistant attorney generals, they all backed J. Edgar Hoover. It was Hoover versus Kennedy, really. Hoover had a definition of what an ex-Communist was. It's somebody that named names and said everything that was good before was bad now, otherwise the guy was still a Communist.

Kennedy says, "Okay, I will give his release serious consideration." But he wanted the pressure stopped. Gladys, my wife, said, "Absolutely not. It took months to get this pressure built up. I'm not about to take it off." Finally it got to the point where the *New York Times* had five editorials saying that I was a political prisoner and shouldn't be. The *New York Post* under Jimmy Wechsler[16] had—I lost count of those editorials, but he had six columns that he wrote on his own, just devastating. David Dubinsky[17] read one of them. It had a picture of Gladys and my daughter the day before I went to prison, and it got him and he called Wechsler and said, "What do you want me to do?" And he said, "Call your friend Bobby Kennedy." So not only did he call Bobby Kennedy, but he got George Meany[18] to write a letter. [Laughs.] Just a two-cents formal thing that he thought the sentence was too severe and so on. Just the name and the Dubinsky name—I think that really turned the tables. On Christmas Eve of 1962, to my utter amazement, I was on my way home. That was after a year and a half in prison.

[16]James Wechsler (1915–83) was editor and columnist for the *New York Post*. Although a member of the Young Communist League for a brief time in the thirties, Wechsler was well known as an anti-Communist liberal. One of the first journalists to criticize Joe McCarthy, he also became one of the first hauled before his committee. There, after a great deal of sparring, he submitted a list of names that he asked to be kept confidential. Joe, of course, released them almost immediately.

[17]David Dubinsky (1892–1982), president of the International Ladies Garment Workers Union, was an influential anti-Communist in labor and government.

[18]George Meany (1894–1980), dictatorial president of the AFL (1952–55) and the AFL-CIO (1955–79), devoted much of his time and influence to a vociferous war against communism.

These days, I'm not a Communist, even with a small "c." I don't think I'm even a Marxist. I do admire Marx, but I'm not very strong on Lenin at all. I think I would like Trotsky better, but I don't think I could get to the front door without fighting with either of them. I believe in socialism. I don't know how we'll survive without it.

Five Minutes to Midnight

By 1950, with the assault on the CP widening nationwide, near panic gripped the Party. Offices closed down, and activity diminished or ceased altogether in some areas. In a series of meetings, which may have begun as early as 1947, Party leadership reached the uneasy conclusion that war between the United States and the Soviet Union was inevitable. The Party would soon be declared illegal, and severe repression would follow. To survive this long night of fascism, the Party needed an underground organization, as successful as those developed by the Italian and Japanese parties during World War Two. With dramatic urgency, this became known as the "five minutes to midnight" policy. Much to the anger of Chairman Foster, the California Party (known as the "Yugoslavia" of the CP for its persistent iconoclasm) openly disagreed, arguing that it was premature to expect fascism and that the policy was destructive. Time would prove California correct, for the consequences of the underground policy were a major factor in the ultimate dissolution of the Party.

In the meantime, the Party pared itself down to a skeletal force of dedicated cadre. This was accomplished by a loyalty-security purge that would have made the State Department proud. By 1949, the Party had stopped issuing membership cards and destroyed its central membership list. Now the core membership were required to fill out a questionnaire that searched for questionable areas of ideology and personal behavior. Homosexuals and those in psychotherapy were purged as potential security risks.[1] This was followed by an ideological purge based on "white chauvinism." The Party, which had from its inception been the most race-conscious of all national parties, expelled members for such

---

[1]One of those purged was Harry Hay, who went on to form the Mattachine Society, the forerunner of the gay liberation movement of the 1960s.

extremes of political correctness as serving African-Americans tea in a chipped cup or watermelon for dessert. Early in July 1951, the Party purged all members who had not reregistered. Thousands of loyal though inactive members were expelled, considered unreliable because they had not reasserted their Party ties. From this skeletal crew, a dedicated cadre was selected to form the shadow leadership.

The underground to which they descended was organized into three levels. The first was known as the "deep freeze." These were members of the top leadership who had either jumped bail on the first Smith Act conviction or not shown up for their trials. This also included several hundred men and women who were not under indictment at all, but were chosen because of their knowledge, experience, and the expectation that they might be indicted. The second level was the "deep, deep freeze." These trusted members were viewed as a source of leadership in case all the other leaders had been arrested. Many were sent abroad to Canada, Mexico, and Europe and ordered to change their lives completely and not engage in any political activity. The last level was known as the "OBU"—operative but unavailable members who traveled about the country, often in disguise, as a liaison between the open Party and the leaders in the "deep freeze."

The move underground was triggered by the 1951 Supreme Court decision upholding the conviction of the first Smith Act defendants. As this also signaled the Justice Department's nationwide arrests of Communist leaders, the Communist plan appeared to have some justification. Aboveground, the CP went on much as before, with many of its spokesmen remaining at their posts. But who was in charge? With the Party command parceled out between the underground, the open Party, and prison, the reins of leadership were hopelessly tangled. Those in prison proffered advice through letters and family visits; those in the underground through couriers, pseudonymous articles in Party journals, and the rare meeting. The result was contradiction and chaos.

Life in the underground may not have been as chaotic, but it certainly was stressful. Even though the Party was not strictly illegal, nor was anyone engaged in sabotage or terrorism, and no arrest warrants had been issued (except for the aforementioned few), life in the shadow world took on the attributes of a B-movie thriller. The shadow Reds required false identities, forged papers, disguises, and safe houses, and they utilized a system of contacts based on such devices as a red rose or a copy of *Life* magazine.

Unfortunately, the FBI seemed to know all about it. Hoover sent out hundreds of his agents to play cat and mouse with the underground. As a countermeasure, the Party distributed lists that identified the cars used by federal agents by their license numbers. To throw off the agents, Communists ran yellow lights, pulled unexpected U-turns, and jumped on and off subways at the last moment. In many cases, the Communists were more than able to elude their pursuers, but the FBI had their successes as well, and occasionally revealed them to the Communists just to prove the point. As one cadre discovered when he sat down to a cup of coffee in a drugstore, only to be joined by a pair of agents who informed him, with corroborating details, that they had been following him for nearly five years.

The underground exacted a heavy political, financial, and personal toll. Several thousand men and women were separated from their families for as long as six years, in some cases. The rare visits husbands and wives did enjoy were managed in the most furtive ways. Many children knew only that Daddy was away on an "important mission." Those who followed their parents into the underground grew up with false identities, isolated from family, friends, and familiar surroundings. Marriages dissolved under the pressure. Millions of dollars that might have gone to organizing were spent on lodging, transportation, and the complex system of couriers. The underground membership, so carefully chosen for their experience and dedication, found themselves torn from their accustomed routines, thrown into unfamiliar occupations. In many cases, the strains of loneliness provoked mental and physical breakdowns. With so many of the key members "unavailable," political work and carefully nurtured contacts, representing years of effort, fell by the wayside. A political soul-searching ensued. Seasoned Communists realized the impossibility of carrying a political movement in this fashion. Profound doubts arose about the entire course of American Communism and chipped away at the most basic premises of the Party.

This degree of personal and political trauma goes far to explain why, with the upheaval of the 1956 crisis, nearly everyone who had been in the underground abandoned the Party within a year.

JUNIUS SCALES

At the time of his arrest by the FBI in November 1954, Scales was the Party chairman of the Southern District and district organizer for North and South Carolina, Virginia, Tennessee, and northern Mississippi.

During the last two years before I was arrested, I was in the so-called underground. The FBI business, the general McCarthyist spirit, made it so difficult for us to work that our influence had been cut sharply. But much activity still kept up. We were still a potent electoral factor, and there were all kinds of local issues. The same channels were still there, but of course we lost a lot of the membership.

I couldn't see my family more than once in two months, once in six weeks. Actually what it amounted to at first was just being unavailable, but later on I was pretty sure they were going to arrest me, so I tried to avoid them altogether. Which was very hard, because they had informants in the Party or near the Party that had a fair idea of where I was or where I would be. So what I did was just to radically change my way of living. I would not stay with Party people they knew, in the main. If I did I would do it very carefully. For instance, if I had to make a long bus trip, I would do it mostly by night. It would save room rent and I would have made careful prearrangements where only one person knew.

When I was finally arrested in Memphis, it was a young working-class couple that informed on me. They were good people, but they got to them some way. I think it might have been because they were having trouble with their mortgage, but they were the only two that knew I was coming to town. They were supposed to meet me at seven-thirty at a certain street corner, so the FBI broke their necks trying to intercept me before then, because that meant they'd give away two good informers, and they couldn't do that. I showed up at the street corner forty-five minutes early. I knew the FBI was there.

By that time I had my wife located in New York. She had an apartment in the Bronx. So I came from New York to make this trip, which I had set up very carefully. I caught a ride with somebody that I knew to somewhere in Pennsylvania. From there, I got a bus to Cincinnati, stayed overnight. Then I took another bus that I caught on the street to Memphis. Memphis had trolley lines that ran out in all directions, and you can see the overhead wires. When I got about fifteen miles from city limits I saw those and got off the bus. Then I caught the first bus I could and then caught a second one. When it got into Overton Park in Memphis—where the zoo is, there's a whole long area where you can't get from one avenue to another because of the park—I got off at the zoo, and ran to the next avenue. I hopped the bus going the other way into the heart of downtown Memphis, got off at a big intersection, caught a cab ten blocks the opposite direction, went through a store that covered a whole block, came out of the back of the store and into a movie. I sat in the movie theater working on my notes and plans for the meetings I was to have.

I was going to be in Memphis for the next five days—I was going to meet very carefully with different individuals. When it got close to time, I got on another trolley and went out and got three blocks from the rendezvous spot. A guy in a brown suit gets on the bus and I knew perfectly well that I had a tail, that he was FBI. Brown suit and loose lips. He rode the bus three blocks, one block past the rendezvous. And I got off two blocks past the rendezvous, and I walked around. There was a heavy thunderstorm coming up. I could see FBI cars parked along the road. When I would go by, they would lie down on the seats, I could see them. They had something like seven or eight cars, all over the place.

I lived out of a fifteen-pound briefcase, I had a shirt that I could launder and drip-dry overnight, I had a set of underwear that were nylon so they would drip-dry overnight, and I had all kinds of papers and even some phony identities, because I changed my name at every major city I was in. I had a different name which I used consistently in each city. I walked along and reached into my briefcase and tore up a lot of this stuff, anything I thought would be useful to them. A heavy rainstorm came up, and I swooshed it down the street sewer. So then I was approaching the rendezvous, I had five minutes to go, and I walked slowly along like I was enjoying the rain. I got there to the second and then all these car doors opened and the FBI jumped out with pistols leveled. "We got you, Scales! End of the road!"

ARCHIE BROWN

Hospitable, a good talker, Brown is a fireplug of a guy with labor battles reaching back to his teens. In '28, he went on strike with Oakland's newsboy union; in '35, as a waterfront organizer, he was framed on murder charges and acquitted; he survived the Spanish Civil War and the Battle of the Bulge to join the Communist underground; arrested in '61 under the Communist Control Act, his case was dismissed by the Supreme Court in '64. We drink beer in his living room in San Francisco as grandchildren run through the house. At one point, he pulls out an old encyclopedia and turns to "Communism." In a photograph, Attorney General Brownell stands before a diagram of the American Communist leadership. Amused, Brown points to his own portrait on the chart. (For more of Archie Brown's story, see under "The Fight Against HUAC.")

I was a trade union director for the California Party and a member of the Central Committee of the national Party from the time I came back from the war in '46 through about the middle of '51. When the verdict came down on the Communist Party leadership at Foley Square[1] it was decided I would be one of those who would go underground. I was gone from the middle of '51 to the middle of '55, four years or so.

We were inexperienced, and we had to feel our way, so to speak. It was a learning process, and we made a lot of errors. But we did have a network, and got it tuned up so that we kept contact with our folks who were still active on the front. It was pretty fierce for them, because there was a blacklist going on against those who were working and those in the professions.

I never went outside the United States. I was here in Northern California most of the time, sometimes I went to Southern California. I got myself a Social Security card, a driver's license, whatever I needed, but I actually never went to work. What I did is studying and then meet with people. You'd have to go through all kinds of maneuvers to do it.

[1]Site of the federal courthouse in New York City where the first Smith Act trial of Party leadership took place in 1949.

You'd have somebody who'd come along with an automobile, and you'd ride with them for a while. In the whole Bay Area I know more places, beautiful views and dead-ends, you'd go to one dead-end and walk over the bridge to another car on the other side and then you're gone in that car, you do it a couple of times if need be, and hopefully on their side they're doing it too. So sometimes the meeting would happen, sometimes it wouldn't.

I'd stay with people right here in San Francisco, or in Oakland. Nobody would ever see me except the people I was staying with, and people would come to the house. Either the person at the house or somebody would come with a car and pick me up and I'd go to meetings.

One time I went to New York. We had a whole house to ourselves. People who could show themselves to the neighbors, they did. The rest of us stayed in the house all the time. We were there for a week, to have our conferences and discussions.

What mainly brought the underground to an end was the California case of the thirteen, particularly the Oleta Yates appeal to the Supreme Court— that turned it around finally, so there was a question about the validity of the Smith Act. Our people were being released, the thirteen were being released. Things were changing, the atmosphere was changing.

About November 1955, I just showed up in the Bay Area. Nobody bothered me, so then I went down to Ontario, California, where my wife was staying with her family and made arrangements to come back to San Francisco. I came up by myself for a while, stayed with some friends, and went back to work on the waterfront. I had some problems there for a while, but the union, the ILWU, stuck by me.

The employers tried to use the fact that I had been away to keep me from going back to work, claimed that I had violated the contract. I lost my industry registration at the time—so did several other people for other reasons. Then the employers wanted to hire on some additional people. The union said, "If you want these additional people, you take these guys back first." So that was agreed and that's how I got back to work.

Living underground was hard, really a strain, particularly on my wife. The FBI chased her up and down this state while I was away, a really horrifying experience, and some really humorous experiences too. She really felt it, in many ways, more than I did. We always discussed when will it end, how to arrange things and so on. It was pretty fierce. But the get-togethers were good; oh, they were always good, we always had a lot of fun.

Archie Brown died at seventy-nine on November 23, 1990.

HON BROWN

Wife to Archie, a plain-spoken, neighborly woman. "I always worked in a law office as a so-called legal secretary. Once when I went looking for a new job this guy asks me who I had worked for. I tell him. He says, 'Well, you've worked for a lot of Red lawyers. Are you a Red?' I said, 'Well, I'm Redder than anything you ever saw.' That was the answer. I worked for him for twenty years. A criminal lawyer. Not a Red, but a very decent guy."

When Arch came home from the Army in '46, he didn't go back to work on the waterfront, he went to work full-time for the Party. In the summer of '51, he went underground.

I took my four kids and my dog and we went to my dad's farm in Ontario, near San Bernardino, where he grew roses. We came back in the fall to get the kids ready for school. When I started back, I'll bet I wasn't a mile off when I realized for the first time that I was being followed. Maybe it was in the back of my head, I don't remember. But I remember all of a sudden, "Hey, there they are!" Well, they followed me all the way back to San Francisco.

We lived on Potrero Hill at that time, I guess it was late August. Whatever I did, I felt like a circus parade. I mean, there was always one car ahead of me and two behind. Or if I walked they would be circling the block. Not only could I see it, but I figured everybody else could. The other thing is that your friends don't want to come around, because as soon as they come to visit then they're followed. So it got to be really ugly.

There was a Safeway on 24th and Potrero, and Betsy was just an infant. She was four or five months when Archie was gone. So I would take her in the stroller on a one-way street where they couldn't drive. They'd be at the corner waiting for me. I would go in the market and they would stand at the checkstand to watch me. I decided, hell, I can't stand this, it's too hard with just me and four little kids. I didn't want to stay up here by myself.

Some of the neighbors were good, but there was one woman across the street who was constantly watching me. I felt she had been employed by the FBI. She was always looking out the window. The funny thing, I didn't want to move back to that house when we came back. I never wanted to go back there and live.

Anyway, my dad said, "I'll get Mayflower-Hickey"—the moving van in Ontario—"to go in there and move you out—and don't worry about it." So they came and packed the dishes and everything.

I had a Studebaker Champion with one of those baskets that hung over the front seat into the back, and I had these four kids. Doug must've been eleven then, Susie was eight, Stephanie was four, and then the baby. I couldn't get anybody that would go with me, so I had to drive alone. I guess we had been going about an hour, maybe two hours, when Susie says, "Mommy, somebody's following us." Doug knew, of course, because he knew what was going on at home. I wasn't in any position to make any explanation, because I had to drive.

So I drove and they followed from the time I left in the morning until I got about a mile from Ontario and they took off, so by the time I got to my dad's they had disappeared. But they were there on the street the next day. The house was on the corner, and there would always be one car and then another car, and then another one. So whatever I did, one would follow me with two others behind. There were always three cars around the clock. Think of the taxpayers' money! Twenty-four hours a day, three cars with two guys in each. It went on for six solid weeks.

Douglas learned to drive at that time. One day we're driving and we got to a street that a lot of water ran down so it was kind of a wash. Doug stalled in the wash with the FBI car right behind him. He flooded it, as a kid will do. So I just sat there and let him figure out how to get out of it. And pretty soon the FBI guy came and wanted to know if he could help, and I said, "Hell no!" So that was that.

One of the other things that happened in that six weeks was that my brother-in-law suggested to my sister that we meet him in Nogales, Arizona, during the convention the Mine, Mill and Smelter Workers Union was having there. He was an organizer. So we decided to ditch these bastards and we would go. You know, the pressure of it is terrible! Every time you turn around—you don't want to go anywhere.

I have a big family, so I had a lot of help. At night, we turned the lights out in the yard and I went walking through the fields, maybe a mile, to where my cousin picked me up and took me to their place in town. In the morning, my sister walked down from ten acres away where she lived and took my dad's car. It already had my bag in it that we'd put in the night before in the dark so they couldn't see it. She got in my dad's car and she went for a drive to make sure that nobody was following her. She went uptown, she drove around, she did everything to make sure that nobody was following her. And when she was sure of that she went over to my cousin's and picked me up and we headed for Nogales.

It was a hot, hot day, and I remember we stopped in Indio, somewhere out in the desert. We were sitting there having a Coke or something and she says to me, she says, "You know, the tightness on your face is just starting to loosen up." So anyway, we went off to Arizona, "clean," as they say, nobody followed us.

We were gonna be gone a week. My dad made arrangements for a friend of the family to come and stay with him and the kids. You know, he's got rose fields way to hell and gone. Fifteen miles from home he's driving out on a private road through the field, and this damned FBI guy is right behind him, so he really got mad. He stopped the car and got out and he went over. The guy pulls up a map real quick and starts looking like he's lost. My dad says, "Hey, this is private property. You get the hell off!"

While we were in Nogales, Vincent Hallinan[1] spoke at the convention, so my sister and I asked him, "Is there something we can do? Have they got a right to do this?" He says, "Look, they're on public property, you can't do anything. But you know, you ought to harass them. Call the police and tell them you're afraid on account of your kids, get out there and take their picture, do everything you can to make their life miserable." So we decided that was a hell of a good idea.

I flew home from Arizona without calling, sending a telegram, or anything, because I figured it's just easier to do it that way. I got home on a Saturday. Sunday afternoon, the telephone rang and a voice says, "This is Western Union, I have a telegram for Mrs. Archie Brown. Is she there?" Now you know, in the country that's what they do. They phone you up and they read you the wire, and then they put it in the mail. So as soon as he said, "I have a telegram for Mrs. Archie Brown," I knew Arch would never send anything to Mrs. Archie Brown, I mean he wouldn't—I'm not Mrs. Archie Brown; I'm Esther Brown or Hon Brown or whatever, but I'm not Mrs. Somebody Else.

So I said, "This is Mrs. Brown." He read me some nonsense—"Wish you were here, love you very much." I said, "Fine, thank you, would you put it in the mail?" He says, "Sure." Of course, it never came. I knew it was a phony. They had missed me and they were trying to find out if I was back. And of course, then pretty soon they were there too, right back on the

[1]Radical lawyer from San Francisco, one of Harry Bridges's defense attorneys, and presidential candidate on the Progressive Party ticket in 1952.

street. So we got out the camera and we started taking the pictures. That's
the first thing we did. And about the second day, they're gone, no more. So
I thought, "Wow, this is a great system! I wish we'd have done it in the first
place."

But then I found out: I had a friend whose husband was also underground and she was staying with relatives in a place called Perris, which is
near Riverside, so we were kind of out in the same area and I used to visit
with her. She had three kids, and we used to compare notes. She had the
same problems. The FBI stopped following her at the exact same time. So
then it wasn't because we were harassing them, it was because they just
pulled off, I guess. I don't know if they figured that I was going to lead
them somewhere or they were just harassing, I don't know. Whatever it
was they were doing, they stopped doing it.

Now my friend Ethel, this woman who lived in Perris, she was staying
with her husband's brother and his wife. Her sister-in-law had family in
Philadelphia. So while Ethel and the kids were living with them, this sister-
in-law went to Philadelphia. She got on the train in Colton and went to
Philadelphia and, you know, those bastards followed her from her house, to
the train, and went all the way to Philadelphia with her. And here it wasn't
even the wife, it was the sister-in-law!

I stayed there on the farm for five years. My dad kept gas in the car and I
got enough from the Party to keep us in clothes and keep us going. I saw
Archie a few times in that period. It was very complicated and it took a lot
of planning. The first time, we spent a week on the beach with the four
kids. I forget the immediate detail for each one, but always I would leave
home in my own car and I would change cars. It was always this kind of
switching cars around and switching drivers and making sure that nobody
was following us. We had some weird tricks, like he would get off at a place
where there was an overpass and he could walk over to the other side and I
would be there. I think we did it three times in the five years. The last time
was in the summer of '55, and already the Party was changing policy and
people were coming up for air, so to speak. I think they had decided that
fascism wasn't as close as they had measured it.

SYLVIA THOMPSON

A radical out of San Antonio, Texas, Sylvia Thompson joined the People's Education and Press Association, a Communist Party affiliate, during World War Two. Not long after, she met and married Sam Hall, a Party organizer from Alabama (she tells their story under "Fighting Jim Crow"). Her second husband, Robert Thompson, was a highly decorated war hero and, at the time of his death, chairman of the New York State Communist Party. (For the fight to bury him in a national cemetery, see "The Arlington Case.")

Because of the atmosphere created by the Smith Act trials and what had happened in Birmingham and the fact that Sam had been arrested and tried for vagrancy,[1] we decided there was just no way we could live as open Communists in the South and be effective.

I was underground for six years, three and a half before Sam died, two and a half afterwards. We lived all over the South, constantly changing names. Sam did his writing, he had a weekly column for the *Southern Worker*.[2] I continued to work with Southern people, whatever union work was being done, whatever civil rights work was being done. We were trying to broaden a progressive population, to turn people's thinking around. It was a question of sitting down and discussing how to make people see the oppression of the Jim Crow system.

We got out a program specifically addressed to Southern people, and mailed out about one hundred and twenty-five thousand fliers. The mailing was done in every state by people who used Band-Aids on their fingertips so there'd be no fingerprints on the envelopes. I remember they were all

[1]Sam Hall was tried for vagrancy despite that fact that he was gainfully employed by the *Daily Worker*. But the head of the Birmingham Red Squad ruled that his means of support were "disreputable" and that the only work he ever saw Hall doing was "digging up his garden and hanging out clothes." Immediately after Hall's conviction, Birmingham passed an ordinance mandating that all Communists had forty-eight hours to leave town or face imprisonment.

[2]The Sunday regional edition of the *Daily Worker*. There was an earlier Party newspaper published out of Chattanooga called the *Southern Worker*, which ceased publication in 1937. Sam Hall also wrote for a short-lived publication called the *Southern News Almanac*, which survived from January 1940 to November 1941.

mailed from every state at the same moment, and when it came out in the newspapers, one writer said, "It's simple—somebody left New York with the trunk full of those pamphlets and went through every state and just mailed them out." And someone else answered that that couldn't be because they were all mailed out at the same time.

But in Birmingham the way we would sometimes put out fliers on important issues was that a couple of us, men and women, would go into the big department stores and at a certain time would open a window in the rest room and throw them out. The fliers would just scatter all over the main streets of Birmingham. That was an old method in the South of putting out leaflets, rather than standing on the corner and getting arrested.

When you said you wanted to see me, I started thinking, "What are the big events in my life?" It's almost a morbid topic, but I started thinking about the deaths of both of my husbands. Sam Hall died under another name. He had a brain tumor. We came up to New York to see doctors, and although we had the best neurosurgeon in the country, it didn't help.

The moment he died, I told the doctors at the hospital that his name was not William Brown, it was Sam Hall, and the next day the cops came to where I was staying to ask why he changed his name. I let them know that when he was ill, he didn't want his family in the South to find out about it. We didn't know it was going to end up that way. His illness went so quickly that there wasn't even time. Had the cancer been in another place, then I could have discussed with him what it was he wanted to do for the rest of his life. But there was not that kind of time. Neither one of us knew what was going to happen until about two months before he died.

When we were underground, the FBI was constantly trying to find out where we were. It's fascinating, because when I look through my FBI file now, I know when they knew where we were and when they didn't. The one time they did find out, Sam had been traveling and was staying in a motel overnight. When he checked out the next day, the head of the motel said to him, "Fellow, I don't know who you are, but you've got a couple of cars watching for you." So Sam came back to the city where we were living and we found another apartment, paid the rent, and started moving all of our things. We never got to that apartment. With the last load we had, a couple of suitcases, we kept driving for about seven or eight hours, three states away. They were so used to our making all these trips back and forth. [Laughs.] We just abandoned all that stuff.

I found out through my FBI file how wonderful my mother was at that time. She would go for months and never knew where I was. One of my reports said, "Agent blank approached the subject's mother and asked, 'What are you doing for the Christmas holidays?' Subject's mother replies, 'No plans.' Agent blank asks, 'Where are your children?' Subject's mother answers, 'My son's in Texas at law school and my daughter's in California.' And Agent blank says, 'Where's your other daughter?' Subject's mother says, 'I never know where she is. She has such a wonderful life, she's always traveling and vacationing, now I think she's in Havana.' " So the next few pages are from some fancy hotels in Havana: "Subject has not been seen at this hotel." And then there's one from a "reliable informant" saying, "Subject has not been seen at any meetings around here." We're talking about the early 1950s, when only very wealthy people went to Havana to gamble. And I began to giggle, mixed with anger. The time, the money, the effort, all of that. In the meantime, my mother with all of her middle-class Texas charm being able to say that, I loved it.

I got my FBI file in '78 or '79. My lawyer who was helping me said, "Mrs. Thompson, they say they have thirty-two hundred pages on you." And I said, "Sons of bitches, half my life and that's all they've got?" But it's very scary looking through those papers, they were clearly interested in arresting me: "Subject, Smith Act, 1940. Detention."[3]

[3]The "Detention" designation became familiar to many radicals as they acquired their FBI files through the Freedom of Information Act. It referred to Hoover's Custodial Detention list of persons to be rounded up and imprisoned in concentration camps should the need arise. Hoover ordered the preparation of the list in 1939, on his own initiative and without statutory authority. From 1950 to its repeal in 1971, Title II of the McCarran Act gave Hoover legal sanction for the list. Although it was supposedly discontinued in 1975 by congressional order, M. Wesley Swearingen, a former FBI agent (see under "Hounds"), contends that it still exists, albeit under another guise.

JOE PASSEN

Joe Passen joined the Young Communist League in 1938, then moved to the Communist Party in 1945. Before leaving the Party in 1956, he drove a cab and worked sub rosa to bring union democracy to Teamsters Local 265.

I was a courier for Archie Brown and some others. This was around '53, I was working as a Teamster then. Couriers were on call twenty-four hours a day. I would get a message from somebody. Wherever I had to go, I went; and if I had a job, I just phoned in sick.

I'd pick Archie up and he'd say, "We're going to go to L.A.—start driving, man." [Laughs.] I had my car. He'd pay for the gas. One time, he was going to stay with his father-in-law I guess, who lived outside of L.A. We were on a country road. They had one of those pea-soup fogs, real low, and around eight, nine o'clock at night, after driving eight hours or more, I'm really beat. I can't see shit. I said, "Arch, I don't know what the hell we're going to do but I can't even see the line on the road." So he had to walk in front of me, that's how slow we were going.

Other times, I would make deliveries to people I didn't know, messages in sealed envelopes. I never really knew what the hell it was. I wasn't the least bit interested, either. Those meetings were always set up by somebody else, nothing was ever set up by me. We'd meet at a certain place, at a certain time. And you had to be very exact, we're talking about two or three minutes within a designated time, otherwise I would leave. Normally, I could spot these people by where they were waiting—never in an area where we couldn't see what was going on around us. I'd spot them, say, "Hello, everything okay?" and hand them the envelope. They were always hungry for a little conversation.

Normally, I'd be delivering money. Until they found jobs, a lot of people underground had no money at all, so the Party had to see that they got money to live on, pay the rent and so on. I imagine that's what it was most about.

We had to take precautions. I don't know how sophisticated the FBI was in those days. I guess they were pretty good. When I went to meet Arch, I'd never just stop and wait for him. I'd always see what cars were there, drive around three or four blocks, see if there was anybody that I could recognize, a car or something. I was always on the lookout that I might be followed. At night, it was very difficult, all you could spot were headlights.

Going underground was a horrible mistake. It was the worst thing that the national level could've decided on. Whether that direction came from abroad or not, I don't know those answers. It just was horrible.

I know people who went underground who really suffered very badly. Guys went through an awful lot just to stay underground and survive. Things started getting fucked up, people getting disgusted, discouraged, families broken up. The husband would be in hiding, the wife would be someplace else.

I know people who had our top leaders, on the state level, hiding at their places. They fed them and took care of them—safe houses I guess you would call them. They must have thought that the government was really going to send them to jail, break up their families. They really overrated the thing terribly.

But I tell you, if I had been picked to go underground, I would have gone, so would my wife. When you are as dedicated as we were, even though we beefed about certain other things—but what we thought was very necessary at the time proved to be just a bunch of bullshit. Looking back, I'm so glad that I was never picked. Jesus Christ, I had enough trouble.

Joe Passen died at seventy-nine on June 6, 1992.

FAY BLAKE

Fay Blake joined the Young Communist League as a teenager. By 1942 she was a member of the Communist Party, active in organized labor and tenants' unions. She left the Party in 1956.

I was a courier from 1948 to about 1954. Two of the people I was a courier for I actually escorted into the underground. I have never given up regretting it. I never saw them again and I wish I could tell them how sorry I am that I was involved at all—it was such a bunch of nonsense. Not that I think it actually wrecked people's lives, but it certainly made them more uncomfortable and more unhappy than they needed to be.

This was a young couple I knew. I worked briefly in an insurance company doing this terrible office work. There was a young woman, a good deal younger than I, who worked in the same place, and we got quite friendly with each other. I began to do things with her and she was very open to what I was interested in. So gradually I began to talk to her about some of my political interests. She came from a middle-class family, had never had any experience before, but she came right along, she was really ready. In the course of going to various activities, I introduced her to a young man I knew who was in the Party, and the two of them hit it off like that [slaps hands], they were a couple from the first time they met.

Finally somebody from the national office came and spent a whole afternoon with me telling me about this brand-new brilliant idea they had to develop an underground. He told me what some of the problems were and that he needed people to go into it. And for some ungodly reason I'll never forgive myself for, I suggested this young couple. For one thing, because they didn't have families and they were kind of footloose—they could take off if they wanted to. He asked me to talk to them and I did and they said yes, just like that.

So then it was a matter of shepherding them through this. First of all, the three of us sat down together to decide what names they would take. I sent him off to get a new Social Security card—this should have been a hint to us how we were tripping ourselves up. We had decided on a name for him, I don't remember now, but say, Robert Johnson. His own name was, we'll say, James Jackson. He goes to get his new Social Security card, and he comes back so crestfallen. He said, "I started to fill out the application and before I knew what I had done I filled my own name!" So his new Social Security card had the same first name. [Laughs.] Then I sent her to get her Social Security card.

Oh, we had to get them married. They had been living together, and this was too risky. So we had to find somebody who would marry them quick. I remember, you had to wait three days for the venereal disease test, and they were supposed to go off right away. I had to plead with this big shot— "You've got to wait, I don't know how to get them married in less than three days." So they hung around for three more days. We had to work up a whole curriculum vitae for them, where they had been born and where they worked, all that kind of stuff. Then they took them underground. I remember driving them to some address and then I never saw them again.

But I did one additional thing that was strictly against everything I had been told. I knew that this young man's mother worked as a practical nurse in an old people's home in Los Angeles. Once you went underground, you weren't supposed to make contact with your families or tell them anything. She knew her boy was politically active, but didn't have a clue. I knew that for him to just disappear would be *devastating* for her.

So this kept eating at me, and finally one day I just couldn't resist it. I got on the streetcar and I trudged out to where his mother was working and I asked to see her. She came out and I said, "I just wanted to tell you that

James is fine and that even if he doesn't write, he's thinking of you." I turned around and walked out and the tears were coming down my cheeks and down her cheeks. I just wanted her to *know*. Otherwise, she'd be left never knowing what had happened. It could have been forever that she'd never see him again.

I never told my big shot that I had done this, because I knew he'd scream and rant and climb up the walls. But I just couldn't leave that woman without some word that her son was okay.

There's never been much attention paid in or out of the Party to the people who did a lot of the Jimmie Higgins[1] work that made it possible for this underground. Sometimes there'd be a knock on the door and somebody would say, "You have to find a safe hotel room." I would go to some sleazy hotel on Hollywood Boulevard or somewhere and rent a room for that night. Then I wouldn't turn up for the room, but somebody else would. They were hiding out, they wouldn't leave the room. They'd send me to deliver a message to somebody. I would provide books because they'd come with nothing to read.

I even got my poor mother involved. Some of the guys who had gone underground left very precipitously. They left without money, without anything. So one of the problems that they kept running into was how do you find a clean shirt for yourself when you haven't got any money, when you can't go to a laundry, and you've only got one shirt? At that time there wasn't any wash-and-wear.

So my mother, who was a very good seamstress and a very good person, went to the fabric store and bought a bolt of seersucker. They didn't make ready-made seersucker shirts. You could wash it in your hotel basin and hang it up and put it on. She ran up, I don't know, a dozen shirts, and I distributed them to these guys who were on the run. So I at least got them shirts that they could wash overnight and get into again.

The things I remember are such trivialities. I remember among the books that I brought once to one of these guys was *Hard Times* by Charles Dickens, because it has a strike in it and I thought he'd be interested in a nineteenth-century version of a very bitter strike. So I bring him the book and when he's ready to leave, I come back to send him on his way and he *throws* the book back at me saying, "What'd you bring me this piece of

---

[1]Jimmie Higgins is the prototype of the tireless and dedicated worker who performs without complaint the tasks of an organizing campaign. This mythical character was originally created by Ben Hanford, Eugene Debs's running mate in the 1904 presidential election. In 1917, Upton Sinclair published a pacifist novel titled *Jimmie Higgins*.

bourgeois crap for?" [Laughs.] Because, after all, Dickens wasn't a Marxist. It's not one of his best books, but it's a pretty good book! So I said, "Okay, I've learned a lesson, next time I'll just bring you *Party* literature—that's all you seem to be able to appreciate." Well, he didn't want Party literature— that was so deadly dull!

The Hollywood
Blacklist

To kick off its postwar campaign, HUAC needed a headline grabber, and what better than Filmland? Through the efforts of a titanic publicity machine and the production of more than six hundred films a year, Hollywood in its golden age was the focus of the nation's fantasies. Hollywood was news, and the purge of its Communists captured the public's attention.

Though few in number, the Hollywood Reds were among the Party's most favored offspring. In 1947, no more than three hundred out of thirty thousand industry workers were either past or present members of the Communist Party. About half of these were screenwriters, fifty or sixty were actors, fifteen or so were directors and producers, and the rest were scattered through the departments, back lots, and front offices. Yet their fund-raising efforts for Popular Front groups and the CP were staggeringly successful, dwarfing by far those of any other contributors in the United States. They were predominant in guild leadership, signed petitions with a prominent flourish, and left a wide trail as official sponsors of "suspect" organizations.

Eager to lend a hand in the HUAC purge were the committee's Hollywood allies. The most vociferous group was the militantly anti-Communist Motion Picture Alliance for the Preservation of American Ideals (MPAPAI), founded in 1944 by director Sam Wood.

The gulf between the Hollywood Left and Right dated to the 1930s and the founding of the guilds.[1] But with the fierce union battles of 1945 to

[1]For the most comprehensive treatment of Filmland politics between 1930 and 1960, see Larry Ceplair and Steven Englund, *The Inquisition in Hollywood: Politics in the Film Community, 1930–1960* (Berkeley and Los Angeles: Univ. of California Press, 1979).

1946, the distance became irretrievable. The dispute was a jurisdictional one between the conservative International Alliance of Theatrical Stage Employees (IATSE)[2] and the left-wing Conference of Studio Unions (CSU). The studios sided with the compliant IATSE and its zealously anti-Communist boss, Roy Brewer.[3] When CSU president Herbert Sorrell called a strike, one thousand of his pickets were tear-gassed by studio guards, while IATSE thugs and the LAPD clubbed them off the streets. Even the fire department turned its hoses onto the lines. Outgunned on all fronts, the CSU threw in the towel after two years. Smeared by HUAC and Brewer and hunted by a series of investigative committees, Sorrell's labor days were over.

While the studios were glad to Red-bait a pugnacious upstart like the CSU, they did not expect or welcome the arrival of HUAC in 1947. For their part, the studios would have employed all the Communists in Hollywood as long as their talents turned a profit. It was Brewer and the politicians who transformed the sympathies between the CSU and the left-wing film artists into a Red conspiracy. But once cornered by HUAC, the execs, always fearful of adverse publicity,[4] raced to disavow their suspect employees.

The MPAPAI openly invited HUAC to investigate Hollywood and supplied the committee with an extensive list of Reds and fellow travelers. In March 1947, Representative John Rankin of HUAC called for a cleansing of Hollywood. Two months later, the committee took direct aim at the New Deal with allegations that "flagrant Communist propaganda films"[5] had been produced during the war at the behest of Franklin Roosevelt, and that the National Labor Relations Board (NLRB) had "infiltrated" Communists in the film industry.

[2]From 1935 to 1941, IATSE was controlled by Frank Nitti's Chicago mobsters. President George Browne and Hollywood representative Willie Bioff extracted huge bribes from studio executives in exchange for limiting union demands. At the pair's trial for extortion, the execs testified they had saved $15 million through this arrangement. Bioff was succeeded by Roy Brewer, who took over in March 1945.

[3]See Roy Brewer's story under "Hounds."

[4]The most embarrassing example of this occurred in the 1930s. Fearful of losing the lucrative German market, the major studios appeased Nazi officials by suppressing offending projects and vetting films through prominent Nazis before release. Universal went so far as to confer with Josef Goebbels. In 1938, Fox, Paramount, and MGM complied with the ruling German sentiment by firing all their Jewish employees in Nazi-held Vienna. Needless to say, this particular alien intrusion into Hollywood was never investigated by HUAC.

[5]Produced in the wartime heat of the U.S.–Soviet embrace, such films as *Mission to Moscow, Song of Russia,* and *Action in the North Atlantic* were little different from the mass of other war films churned out for public consumption. See the stories of Howard Koch and Edward Dmytryk in this chapter for more on these films.

In September, forty-three witnesses were subpoenaed to appear for hearings in Washington. Nineteen were expected to be "unfriendly,"[6] the majority of whom were present or former members of the Party. The October hearings opened with all the glitz befitting a Hollywood event. Fans and autograph hounds, newsreel cameramen, and television and radio broadcasters all jammed the caucus room under the glare of blinding klieg lights. When romantic leads Robert Taylor and Gary Cooper testified as "friendly" witnesses, a thousand women packed the room.

In general, the "friendly" stars—among them Ronald Reagan,[7] George Murphy, Robert Montgomery, and Adolphe Menjou—donned the mantle of anti-Communist warriors and fell over each other praising the committee. Their drift was that Reds and fellow travelers bought the film rights to books by other Reds, then hired more Reds as writers, actors, and directors, thereby larding their films with un-American propaganda.[8] Anti-Communist witnesses were allowed to testify at length. Roy Brewer spoke for two hours. Walt Disney[9] revealed a plot by the left-wing Screen Cartoonists Guild to subvert Mickey Mouse into a Marxist rat. Jack Warner nervously blurted out the name of every liberal he could think of, labeling them "Reds" he had either fired or planned to fire (but hadn't gotten around to); several of them turned out to be anti-Communists.

This amiable climate changed drastically with the testimony of the "unfriendly" witnesses, who relied on the First Amendment in their refusal to cooperate. Chairman Parnell Thomas angrily pounded his gavel at every answer that did not directly (and immediately) answer his investigator's narrow questions. Each side attempted to shout the other down. At Thomas's direction, armed guards dragged offending witnesses from the hearing room. The resulting publicity ended the hearings abruptly, with only ten[10] of the nineteen testifying. In November the ten

[6]The Hollywood Nineteen. As in the Hollywood Party as a whole, most were writers. For a complete list of the Nineteen, see footnote 11 below.

[7]As head of the Screen Actors Guild, Reagan regularly informed on his members to the FBI. To date, he is the only President of the United States to have had a former career as a police stooge.

[8]In a study by Dorothy Jones (made at the height of the Red Scare) of 159 films released between 1929 and 1949, in which the Hollywood Ten (see footnote 11 below) had credits, she could find no trace of Communist propaganda—even by the hypersensitive standards of the times.

[9]This avuncular genius was also a bitter reactionary. As late as 1938, and only weeks after the horrific Nazi depredations of Kristallnacht, Disney entertained Leni Riefenstahl, Hitler's favorite propagandist, on a three-hour tour of his studio. In later years, Uncle Walt informed on his employees for the FBI.

[10]Actually, eleven—German refugee Bertolt Brecht also testified. Although never a Party

who had testified were cited for contempt by the House; in December they were indicted by a grand jury. Thus the Hollywood Nineteen became the Hollywood Ten.[11] By 1950, all ten were in prison.

The film bosses had faltered. At first they angrily opposed the HUAC probe as an unwarranted intrusion into private business, but on November 24, 1947, at New York's Waldorf-Astoria Hotel, they made a crucial turn. There some fifty studio executives, and their East Coast financiers, decided in closed conference that the only way to prevent further encroachments by HUAC was to sacrifice the Ten. Sam Goldwyn and Dore Schary opposed the plan, but gave in to the majority. A statement was issued that claimed "nothing subversive or un-American" had ever appeared on the screen, but the studios nonetheless intended to discharge without compensation those five of the Ten in their employ. None of the Ten would be allowed to work until he purged himself of contempt and declared under oath he was not a Communist. By giving birth to the blacklist, the producers attempted to draw the line of their debasement on the graves of the Ten—but HUAC had other ideas.

The four years following the 1947 hearings were uneasy ones for the Hollywood Left. The majority had been able to find work, but the fate of the Ten nagged at them all. In 1951, a newly determined committee returned to Hollywood, bolstered by the media frenzy surrounding the Alger Hiss case, the trial of the Rosenbergs, and the Korean War. This time they ignored film content and went after individuals. One hundred and ten witnesses were subpoenaed, and the committee demanded names, names, and more names. HUAC had already identified nearly every Communist and fellow traveler in Hollywood (either through the FBI, through the MPAPAI, or from executive session testimony). But a ritual of humiliation was required—only by informing on former colleagues and begging forgiveness for their past sins[12] could the penitent cleanse themselves before the Inquisition. Those who refused were blacklisted. In 1951, fifty-eight terrified ex-Communists duly recited 902 names—which, with duplications, amounted to more than three hundred Hollywood

---

member, the playwright took no chances and testified with his passport and plane ticket in his pocket. Brecht left for East Germany immediately after the hearings, where he felt much safer.

[11]John Howard Lawson, Dalton Trumbo, Albert Maltz, Alvah Bessie, Samuel Ornitz, Herbert Biberman, Edward Dmytryk, Adrian Scott, Ring Lardner, Jr., and Lester Cole. The other nine were Richard Collins, Howard Koch, Gordon Kahn, Robert Rossen, Waldo Salt, Lewis Milestone, Irving Pichel, Larry Parks, and Bertolt Brecht.

[12]Not untypical was writer-director Nicholas Bela, who toed the line after a few years on the blacklist: "I have to humbly apologize for the grave error which I have committed, and beg of you to forgive me."

Reds. The most obvious radicals were repeatedly named.[13] Among the repentant was Edward Dmytryk, one of the Hollywood Ten, who after serving his time elected to clear himself.

The defiant witnesses took a lesson from the Ten and cited the Fifth Amendment to avoid prison. But they faced the ruination of their careers. Actor Howard Da Silva, despite thirty-seven film credits, was blacklisted for twelve years. Actor Will Geer, with eighteen credits, was blacklisted for nineteen years. Neither screenwriter Robert Lees, with sixteen credits, nor actress Karen Morley, with forty-four credits, ever worked again.

Along with the blacklist came the graylist. This state of limbo was inhabited by liberals whose names were never publicized by HUAC, but who became unemployable through the signing of a long-forgotten petition, guilt by association, rumor, or mistaken identity. The graylists were the work of the American Legion magazines *Firing Line* and *Legion Magazine,* and the two gospels of the entertainment industry, *Counterattack* and *Red Channels,* all of which carried long lists of "subversives" and "fellow travelers." No studio was without a full set of these lists, and no studio failed to obey their dictates. But many of the graylisted never appeared on any lists; their names just "circulated." For them, the phone's mysterious silence was especially unsettling—no work was forthcoming and no reasons were given. With no radical history to speak of, many fought an invisible enemy and turned their doubts on their own talent.

For dozens on either list, the losses were more than long-nurtured careers: physical and mental health, wives and husbands, friends and family, and even lives fell by the wayside.

The film bosses panicked. Hollywood now avoided any topic that might be "controversial." Even a film on Hiawatha was shelved, as the Chieftain's message of peace could be construed as a plea to end the Cold War. To appease HUAC and the American Legion, Hollywood instead churned out a series of anti-Communist potboilers.[14] By 1951, fifty of these, along with many documentaries and shorts, were either in release or in production. The Reds of Hollywood fancy were little more than gangsters who called each other "comrade" and shot God-fearing Americans in the back.

[13]John Howard Lawson was named twenty-seven times, Herbert Biberman sixteen times, Lester Cole fifteen times, Paul Jarrico and Ring Lardner fourteen times each.

[14]Among these were *I Was a Communist for the FBI, Guilty of Treason, I Married a Communist, Conspirator, My Son John,* and *Red Planet Mars.* Most were commercial failures, tokens to fend off the gods.

HUAC had struck a rich vein in Hollywood and returned to mine the field in 1953, 1955, 1956, and 1958, by which time seventy-two friendlies had given over more than 325 names. Every studio now had a security man, the keeper of the lists by which all employment was checked, who arranged the public ritual of "clearance" for those willing to grovel for work. Keeping up the pace was a herd of reactionary columnists and self-styled print vigilantes. To occur their wrath meant instant inclusion on the blacklist. The most feared pressure group was the American Legion, with its 4.7 million members and auxiliaries. The *Legion Magazine* attacked as "Communist collaborators" such stars as Judy Holliday, Charlie Chaplin, John Garfield, and Burt Lancaster and urged readers to boycott their films. The film moguls courted Legion officials with studio tours, begged for the names of suspected employees, and asked the Legion for a procedure by which the "innocent" could clear themselves. With the Legion's blessing, three hundred employees were soon writing long pages of self-criticism explaining any past heresies and asking for the Legion's forgiveness.

With the best of the screenwriters on the blacklist, and producers always hungry for a deal, a black market sprang up in surreptitious scripts. The writers worked for a fraction of their former fees and were denied the screen credit, but it did put food on the table. The first break in the blacklist fell to one of the most prolific black marketeers, Dalton Trumbo, who in 1959 received his first screen credit in twelve years. Over the next decade, aging veterans of the blacklist began making their way in Hollywood once more. But these were the minority. For every one who found the way back, ten or twenty were irretrievably lost.

Including the Hollywood Ten, more than 350 screen artists and technicians were black- or graylisted. At least two of them committed suicide. Three others died as a direct result of the hounding.

RING LARDNER, JR.

One of the Hollywood Ten, Lardner was a member of the Communist Party, an Academy Award–winning screenwriter (*Woman of the Year*, 1942), and an activist in the Hollywood antifascist movements of the thirties and forties. From 1939 to 1948, he garnered ten screen credits. He was blacklisted for seventeen years, until *The Cincinnati Kid* in 1965. In 1970, he won another Academy Award for *Mash*.

The House Un-American Activities Committee announced an investigation in Hollywood, and held hearings in Los Angeles in May of 1947. They were private hearings, but we knew some of the people who had testified there, some of the heads of the studios and others. Then they announced they were going to have public hearings in the fall. In September I received a subpoena.

Nineteen of us who described ourselves in a statement as unfriendly witnesses, that is, unfriendly to the committee, met with lawyers to discuss what we should do. We agreed that we should challenge the committee's rights, that Congress had no right to investigate the screen because it was protected by extension of the freedom of the press clause in the First Amendment. If they had no right to legislate in that area, then they had no right to investigate it, or the political beliefs of individuals, for that matter.

We discussed various approaches and finally decided that the best way to challenge the committee's right was by just not answering the questions. We decided to go as a group to Washington. During that first week of hearings, Louis B. Mayer, Jack Warner, Adolphe Menjou, Robert Taylor, Robert Montgomery, Ronald Reagan, Gary Cooper, and Ayn Rand all testified about the Red Menace in Hollywood.

Rand said that the film *Song of Russia* gave a distorted picture of how things were in Russia. It showed Russian children smiling. She had been there until 1929, I think, and said children never smiled there. She testified after Louis B. Mayer did, and was attacking MGM for having made the picture.

The second week, they started calling the unfriendly witnesses. At that point a group from Hollywood, called the Committee for the First Amendment, sent a delegation as observers. It included Humphrey Bogart, Lauren Bacall, John Huston, Philip Dunne, Danny Kaye, June Havoc—a lot of people. They sat in the audience as the unfriendly witnesses, who were mostly writers, were called in turn.

I took the same position as the others. I didn't say anything at all. I had a prepared statement and was told I could read the statement after I testified. Parnell Thomas, the chairman of the committee, asked me the questions and got very indignant. He got particularly upset when he asked if I was a member of the Communist Party. I said, "I could answer that, but if I did I'd hate myself in the morning." He said, "You're dismissed. Take him away." I said, "You said I could read my statement." He said, "No, you can't." The uniformed guards were right there. They approached, ready to remove me by force if I didn't go myself.

We were cited for contempt by the House of Representatives for refusing to answer their questions. That led to our indictment and arraignment.

In November of 1947, the real heads of Hollywood, not the studio heads in California but the bankers in New York who ran the companies, held a meeting at the Waldorf Astoria Hotel in New York. They decided to institute a blacklist. They made a public announcement that they wouldn't hire any of us until we had purged ourselves of contempt. They would refuse to hire anybody else who took the same position or who refused to answer any questions before the committee. Five of the ten of us were not working at the time, and the five who were under contract were told that their contracts were abrogated. I was working for Twentieth Century–Fox at the time, and Darryl Zanuck, the head of the studio, first said that he wasn't going to fire anyone unless he was ordered to do so by his board of directors. His board of directors then met and ordered him to do so. It was only about five or six weeks after the hearings, and I had just started on a new assignment. They told me to leave the premises, and I did.

I later had a suit against them for breach of contract, which we finally settled out of court for very little. I had been getting two thousand dollars a week, and the settlement was for ten thousand dollars, a good part of which went to the lawyers.

During the two and a half years between the hearing and when we went to prison, we were all able to get some kind of under-the-table work. Not under our own names, of course, and for less money, about one-fifth of what we'd been getting before. I had several such jobs. I once worked under my own name when I went over to Switzerland and worked on a script for a Swiss company. They borrowed Cornell Wilde from Twentieth Century–Fox to star in this picture. Fox wanted to be sure the picture was going to be good enough for Cornell Wilde, and they were reassured by the producer, who told them he was hiring me. That persuaded Fox to lend Cornell Wilde. They figured they weren't releasing the picture so they weren't breaking the blacklist.

We decided that just two cases, John Howard Lawson's and Dalton Trumbo's, would go to trial. The rest of us would abide by the judicial decision in those cases, because it would cost too much money to fight through all separate trials. We hoped to win this case in the courts and thus immobilize the committee. On the basis of previous Supreme Court decisions, we thought we had a pretty good chance. But things were moving very fast to the Right in those days, starting with the end of the war in '45. By the time our case got to the Supreme Court in the spring of '49, it didn't look so good. The cases had been tried and appealed, with the judgment of the lower court being upheld by the appellate court. In May 1950, the Supreme Court refused to review the case. In other words, they wouldn't decide it one way or the other, and the decision of the appellate court was upheld.

As soon as the Supreme Court ruled, Lawson and Trumbo turned themselves in and proceeded to prison. Their sentences were a year in prison and a thousand-dollar fine. The rest of us had to go to Washington for perfunctory trials. The judges put off sentencing us for a week. While we were waiting for a decision, the Korean War broke out. That didn't help the situation. We had three different judges, one of whom decided it wasn't worth a full year's sentence, and sentenced two of the men, Edward Dmytryk and Herbert Biberman, to six months. The rest of us got a year. It all just took a matter of minutes. We went immediately to the Washington federal jail and then were sent to various places from there.

Lester Cole and I both ended up in Danbury, Connecticut. It's much better to be in federal prison than any of the state or local jails; they're on a higher level. They're cleaner and the food is better. Danbury had a farm and grew vegetables and raised chickens.

Parnell Thomas beat us to prison.[1] He was already at Danbury when we arrived. He was in charge of the chicken yard, and Lester Cole, who also had a job outside the prison walls, passed him one day and said, "I see you're still shoveling chicken shit."

It was just a little tougher than being in the Army. It's a sentence that you know is going to be only ten months. That is what a year sentence amounts to. You just sit it out. It's not like having to face several years where you have to change your whole life. For a shorter period you just wait it out and it's over with.

By the time we came out of prison in 1951, the whole situation had gotten worse. Senator McCarthy had come onto the scene in the meantime, and the Rosenberg case had been tried. The hysteria was much greater. Then it really clamped down in Hollywood. There was a lot of self-censorship on

---

[1]In 1949, the former HUAC chairman was convicted of padding his office payroll and sentenced to three years in prison.

the content of pictures. People just did not dare to come up with ideas that were progressive or might be frowned on. It was very difficult to get any sub rosa work for the first several years. So I left Hollywood after six months of that and transferred to Mexico and then to Connecticut. I have never lived in California since.

In '62, Otto Preminger hired me for a job and announced it publicly. He had already put Dalton Trumbo's name on the picture *Exodus*. He got indignant letters from the Americanism Committee and the American Legion saying there were plenty of loyal American writers he could have hired. Otto wrote them back that he respected their views about it and they could refuse to see the movie when it came out but he maintained his right to hire anybody he wanted to. That film never got made. The blacklist lasted seventeen years before I had a screen credit again: *The Cincinnati Kid* with Steve McQueen in '65.

I also wrote for television on the blacklist. It was my main source of income during the fifties. Ian McClellan Hunter and I wrote five different series. We wrote pilot films for American television shot in England. The first one we did was called *The Adventures of Robin Hood*. That survived on American television for three or four years, it was quite a popular show. We did several others. We got a whole bunch of other blacklisted writers involved in it, because it was much more work than we could handle.

I didn't have any problems selling these things under a different name. The producer, a woman named Hannah Weinstein, was an American who went to England and started producing films there. She knew when she hired us that we were blacklisted writers. That was actually part of her purpose in setting up the company, partly out of principle and partly because we were less expensive. We put fake names on the scripts, and we had to keep changing them, because if one name appeared on several shows then the networks would ask to see the writer.

At that time you could register an alias with the Social Security Administration. So you used your own Social Security number, just a different name. Technically, somebody in the Social Security Department knew we were using aliases. But I don't know whether anybody ever bothered with this. Apparently it was an existing rule that if a writer or actor used an alias for working purposes, he can have it registered with his Social Security number.

Even though I was working for someone in England, I never went there. We wrote the scripts in New York and sent them by mail to London. I applied to get a passport to go in '54. I was refused, on the grounds that my travel abroad would be inimical to the United States. I wasn't able to get a passport at all until 1958, when there was the Supreme Court decision in the case of Rockwell Kent, the artist.[2] The court ruled that everyone had a right to a passport.

I was never approached by the FBI to clear myself. In almost every case that I know of where someone was cleared, it was a question of the individual going to the FBI rather than the other way around. There was a whole clearance committee in Hollywood that people went to. Ronald Reagan was one of the members. So was Roy Brewer, and I believe Martin Berkeley, the witness who had named a hundred and sixty people before the Committee.

Dmytryk[3] and I weren't friends before all this. But we did get to know each other pretty well during those weeks of the hearings. Then we were in the Washington prison together for three weeks, and we'd see a little of each other in the exercise period each day before we were sent to separate federal correctional institutions. By that time I'd say I knew him fairly well. I didn't know he was going to change his mind and issue this statement from prison. He was only in for five months. I remember Eddie saying at one point, "It's amazing that I've held out, because you guys are all writers and can write under other names. I've never even directed on the stage. I only did film editing and direction in Hollywood, and there's nothing else I can do."

He was under a lot of pressure, but I think it was wrong of him to name names. He involved quite a few people and got them in trouble. Some people he mentioned erroneously. There was one director he named as having been in his Communist group. Eddie said he had left the Party in 1945 and been inactive since then, but this director, Michael Gordon, hadn't come to Hollywood until after the war, after the time Eddie said he'd left. When Gordon's agent ran into Dmytryk in Beverly Hills and confronted him with it, Eddie just said, "Hey, that's right. Is Mike sore?"

One man I had been good friends with was Budd Schulberg.[4] We had collaborated together. Once, after he named names, we had quite a public encounter in a restaurant in New York, an artists' and writers' hangout. Budd and I were there at the same time and we were standing at a bar and

[2]Rockwell Kent (1882–1971) was seventy years old in 1953 when he refused to sign a non-Communist affidavit for his passport application. The refusal was a principled one; Kent argued that only citizenship was relevant. The State Department replied that he would not be granted a passport "to travel anywhere for any purpose." The Supreme Court decision in *Kent v. Dulles* restored freedom of travel.

[3]Edward Dmytryk, whose story follows in this chapter.

[4]Well-known novelist and screenwriter. A onetime Communist, Schulberg rejected the Party after it attempted to interfere with the writing of his novel *What Makes Sammy Run?*

we got into what became quite a public discussion. All these newspapermen were hanging around, and they started listening. Budd was justifying what he did, and I told him he wasn't very consistent, because he had said he was doing this out of patriotism and because these people should be exposed, and yet he had deliberately not named several people who were very close to him, relatives. So he admitted that. We argued the whole thing for a couple of hours. I've seen him a couple of times since. On those occasions, we speak, but nothing warm.

I certainly don't regret what I did. You can't say what your life would have been if it had gone in a different direction, there's only the one direction it did go. In prison I started working on a novel, which I got published a couple of years after I got out. Although it didn't make a lot of money or sell well, it was something I was very proud of having written and it did get well received by critics and a lot of readers. I might not have written that particular book if I had stayed under contract with Twentieth Century. A lot of things might have turned out different.

Dalton Trumbo once said that there were no heroes, only victims. Maybe that was a little overboard, but in principle I agreed with him. Some of the people who did testify were under very strong pressures and just didn't have any other ways of making a living. I sympathize more with the couple of hundred people who never did get back to work in Hollywood because they hadn't been well enough established before they were blacklisted. They had to go into entirely different kinds of work.

Albert Maltz strongly disagreed. He insisted we were heroes. My position was that if it was a question of choosing to be a "hero" or a shit, you can't really say the decision not to be a shit is heroic.

FRANCES CHANEY

An actress, married to Ring Lardner, Jr. Although Frances Chaney was never publicly named, she found herself on the graylist.

The first thing you ought to know is that I had been married to Ring's brother, David Lardner. We were both very, very young. He was a writer.

I'd been a successful young actress in New York, I'd done a lot of radio and I'd also done theater. In radio I did everything under the sun. I had a morning program called *A House in the Country,* and in the afternoon I was on *Terry and the Pirates.* I did every important nighttime radio show there was, from *Mr. District Attorney* to *Gangbusters.*

In July 1944, David went overseas, got assigned to the Office of War Information, and by October 28th he was dead. He was riding in a jeep with Russell Hill, another newspaperman, when they hit a mine. I had two children with David. He was twenty-five when he was killed. We were very young and very successful and there we were. It was wonderful and great, then it was pretty terrible. I didn't know what had happened to me.

I married Ring two years later. I arrived in California with the two babies: one three and a half, one two and a half. I had always had political leanings toward the Left. I developed them in the late thirties along with everybody else who had any sense. When David died, I felt so strongly that his death must not be in vain, it made me become more Left. I did all sorts of things—I signed petitions, I worked hard for whatever there was. Naturally, Ring had already been involved in California. Jim Lardner, one of his other brothers, had been killed fighting in Spain.

I came to California with the idea of immediately starting work. My whole life had been acting. I had begun very early. I'd gotten a scholarship to the Neighborhood Playhouse. I got a play on Broadway the first season I was out, as well as getting into radio. So my whole "I am" depended upon being an actress.

When Ring and I came back from our honeymoon in 1946, there was word out that the committee was after him. I remember making a phone call to a friend of ours who told us not to come home. The warning was out. There had been an article in the *Hollywood Reporter* about the committee raking up anti-Red sentiment, and Ring had been named in the piece.

So we knew there was something in the offing, but I never gave it a second thought. As a matter of fact, I was cast almost immediately to play Lady Macbeth in a production directed by Richard Barr, who later became the New York producer of Edward Albee's plays. I started working and I did some radio. But the hearings happened a year later, in September '47.

The minute those hearings were over, I knew from word of mouth and reactions of friends that I was going to be in trouble. But somehow I managed to get work. The William Morris Agency sent me out on things. I became the voice of Fatima cigarettes [laughs], a ridiculous thing. I'd crashed this audition and they used me, they thought I had a sexy voice. I did odd radio shows, but we knew that it was going to be rough, and it really did get rough, and then it got rougher.

Life went on. It became a question of working for the cause, the Hollywood Ten. The process went on for three years: the hearings were in '47 and they went to jail in '50. We had to change our entire lifestyle. When Ring testified in 1947, we had just bought a big house in Santa Monica with a tennis court. By the time we came back from the hearings, we knew things were going to get tough. Of course, they really did get tough after the Waldorf producers' meeting. We knew that we were really out, and it was a matter of struggling and trying to get along with what we had, because I certainly wasn't going to be making enough money to support anybody at that point.

But we did manage. Ring put an ad in the *Hollywood Reporter* that said "House for Sale: Writer Going to Jail." God, that was marvelous. He really had a lot of dash. It was picked up by either *Newsweek* or *Time,* and that's how we sold the house, practically the day the thing came out. We sold it for much less than we paid, but we desperately needed the money. Then we arranged to move from this wonderful big house in Santa Monica to a little teensy house in Hollywood near what is now the Hollywood freeway.

I was very worried about the children. I wanted them to be as secure as they possibly could; I had just got them a father, and now they were about to lose him. They were still so little. I managed somehow, with the kindness of the people who ran it, to get them a scholarship at the Westland School. A lot of children we knew went there. I thought the one thing they did not need was to go to a public school in a neighborhood without moral support. Polly, who helped with the kids, was terrific; she stayed with us whether we could afford to pay her or not. Even Ring's ex-wife Silvia was terrific, not caring about how much money she was supposed to be getting, settling for less or waiting.

I was never harassed when Ring was in jail, which I think is remarkable and wonderful. We moved to this lower-middle-class neighborhood. The kids there played out in the street and were pretty rough. But everyone was very nice. My children were great. When kids in the neighborhood used to ask Joe, who was six at the time, where his daddy was, he said, "My daddy's in jail." They'd ask, "Why is your daddy in jail?" And he'd say, "Because some guy in Washington asked him something that was none of his business, and Daddy said it was none of his business and that's why he's in jail!"

The men went to jail at the outbreak of the Korean War. The terror in

Hollywood as a result of the hearings, the Cold War situation, and the Korean War was awful. There were rumors spreading that they were going to jail people and that the people who were thought of as Communists were in real trouble, that there were going to be break-ins to check on what books you had in the house. I remember calling a friend of ours and saying, "I don't know what to do, because we're loaded with political books!" [Laughs.] This dear man came over, looked through the bookcases, took some of the books, and put them down the basement. I don't know what good that was supposed to do. But at the time the fear was so great; it really was. You began to feel, I'm sure, the way people felt in Germany, although on a much lesser scale, because nobody was wearing Stars of David.

When Ring was in jail, I squeezed in little piddling jobs here, there, whatever I could. But it wasn't the way it had been in New York. There was no comparison. I was in a play at the Circle Theater. I also got a part in a movie, a small part, but it was a job. The Actors Lab was still around and I was doing what I could there, teaching and acting. I didn't get any money for that, but at least it made me feel good. My whole identity was wrapped up in being an actress. If I couldn't work, well, who was I? I wasn't anybody.

The wives of the Hollywood Ten had an organization and would meet regularly. There was a lot of work to do about the case. We were writing letters asking for parole, getting people to sign petitions, and trying to raise money to pay for the case. We held fund-raising events where we'd read letters from our husbands in jail.

Some close friends, people of importance whose involvement might have helped, didn't do it. Everybody was so scared, and justifiably so. On the other hand, there were people who came through. I know Katharine Hepburn wrote a parole letter for Ring, which was wonderful. But once the case fell apart, once the guys went to jail, the support really came from those people who understood the issues and were close friends. There were people that I could call on to help me do things if I needed them done. All the wives of the Ten were friends. It was wonderful that we had a support group of our own.

I must admit there was one funny aspect to it, and that is the one person we pushed politically to take a stand because she was cute and pretty was Jean Porter Dmytryk, who was married to Eddie Dmytryk. Jeannie, who was the least knowledgeable about anything in our little group, we thought would be a wonderful candidate for local politics in some way. She never said anything to us, but she hinted to her hairdresser that Eddie was going to name names and the word spread that her husband was going to prove what a good, loyal American he was when he got out. We began to suspect there was something not kosher about Eddie Dmytryk!

I remember stopping off in Chicago for a big meeting on the way to the hearings. I had dinner with Ring, Dalton Trumbo, and Larry Parks that night. The camaraderie and love among those men was just lovely. Larry said, "I don't know. You guys, you're writers. If anything happens you'll always be able to go on writing, but I'm an actor. I don't know what's going to happen with me." The three of them mixed blood as it were, the boys saying, "By God, if we ever work you'll work with us." It was very sweet and dear. When Larry finally broke down,[1] it was heartbreaking. The way in which he did it was sad and pitiful [voice breaking]. It was terrible, what can you say? It was so awful because the poor son of a bitch never did work again. Nothing good ever happened for him. He had this thing on his back for the rest of his life.

Ring got out of jail and decided we should go to Mexico. A lot of our friends had gone there. Dalton Trumbo was there with his wife and family. It seemed like a good idea. We couldn't work where we were, so we had to try to do something. We went to Mexico and stayed there for six months. It was rough. As I said before, we had sold the house at a big loss. One of the things that sustained us financially was that I had a ten-thousand-dollar policy of Davy's and John Lardner was instrumental in getting that cashed for us.

When we were back in New Milford, I said, "I don't care, blacklist or no blacklist, I can't stand this and I'm going to get a job." I found out that Jay Cantor, an agent who had tried to get me to sign with him in California, was now an important agent in New York. I went to see him and he decided to risk it. He knew all about who I was, but we didn't talk about that, just that I was back and I really wanted to work. You had to talk fast. He sent me about a part on *Philco Playhouse,* and I went and I read, and by God, I got the job. Apparently, they'd been trying to cast the part for

---

[1]"Don't present me with the choice of either being in contempt of this Committee and going to jail or forcing me to really crawl through the mud to be an informer. For what purpose? I don't think this is a choice at all. . . . I think to do that is more akin to what happened under Hitler, and what is happening in Russia today. I don't think this is American justice for an innocent mistake in judgment, if it was that, with the intention behind it only of making this country a better place in which to live." (Testimony of Larry Parks before HUAC, March 21, 1951) Parks later gave twelve names in executive session. In the twenty years prior to this testimony, Parks had appeared in forty-one films; after, until his death in 1975, he appeared in three.

a long time, so they decided they were going to take a chance with me. I did the show, a program called *Holiday Song,* written by Paddy Chayevsky, and that made me an official member of *The Philco Playhouse.* We got very good reviews and I was even singled out in the press.

But after that, nothing happened. No calls for anything. I kept trying. I got frantic about it—was I going to work or wasn't I? Finally, I got a job as an understudy to Maureen Stapleton in a play with Lee Cobb. It was wonderful to be involved in theater, even though I wasn't really doing anything except understudying. But it was very hard, because the children and Ring were in Connecticut, and so I commuted up there on Saturdays to see them. But I was glad for the job.

Then I got a call from Jay Cantor, saying that Paddy Chayevsky had written a television show with me in mind. All they wanted from me was script approval. I would have crawled on my hands and knees to have gotten the part, but all they needed was script approval. They told me they were going to send me the script, and then I should call them up and come in. You can imagine the excitement. God, it was so wonderful. Anyway, the very next day I was to call before I came over to the office. I started calling and was told to call in another hour. They said they had to get back to Fred Coe, the producer. This went on and on, I'd call in an hour and two hours and they would tell me to call back. Finally, in the late afternoon they said, "Oh God, this is a terrible mistake. We don't know how it could have happened, but Mr. Coe had cast the part and nobody told us." The script was *Marty,* and it became a very important motion picture and won an Academy Award for best picture.

I still wasn't sure whether it was the blacklist or what it was until the following September. They repeated *Holiday Song,* the first *Philco Playhouse* job I had gotten, and they didn't use me. I thought, "I just can't stand this anymore." I called Fred Coe and made an appointment to see him. He said, "Look, Frances, everybody on the show wanted to walk out when they knew that you weren't going to be on it. I had to point out that all that would do is make them lose their jobs." He said that he had made a pitch for Eli Wallach on another *Philco* program the week before and he just could not do it for me, he couldn't do the pitch twice. He was very nice, very sweet, but that was it. Then I really knew why I hadn't gotten *Marty.* That was clear-cut, I knew where I was. So I did everything I could to work in theater.

I ran into a very dear friend on the street one day who knew my work intimately. I had done the first radio show he had written that was a big smash hit. He said, "How are you, Frances, I'm so glad to see you," and blah, blah, blah. I said, "Well, how am I? I can't get work!" He looked at me and said, "Are you sure you're not blacklisting yourself?" It was sad. He was embarrassed. And I felt like a pariah. You can't help it. You begin to believe that the reason you're not working is that you don't know what you're doing anymore. You are also aware of the fact that your very presence makes certain people uncomfortable.

In '56, I got a little job on a daytime soap. They liked me because I was funny, so they kept writing the part in. I was on and off that show for nearly ten years. They kept it quiet, of course. It never became a contract part. It was just something they'd slip in. It wasn't until 1963 that I got a legitimate job on nighttime television, a program called *The Defenders.*

It's hard to say whether I was blacklisted because of my own political activities or Ring's. I think it's a mixture. I was never named and I never appeared in *Red Channels.* A friend and I used to laugh about how funny it was; she and I were the only people we knew who weren't in *Red Channels.* But they certainly could have listed me on my own. I had done all the things that you do, particularly after David died. I had collected money for Spanish refugees and all the other causes. All my friends were progressives, if not Communists. I don't know if it was entirely because of Ring or partly because of me, but what difference does it make?

Part of the trouble about this whole goddam blacklist is that you're of a different age in 1960 from what you were in 1948. Those years are very important in an actress's life. But I've had a wonderful marriage and wonderful children and I go on working and teaching and doing the best I can. I'm very grateful for what I've got, and I've had a great deal.

HOWARD KOCH

A tall man, soft-spoken. For Orson Welles, Koch adapted *War of the Worlds* into the radio play that panicked the country in 1938. In 1942, he shared an Academy Award for writing *Casablanca.* One of the Hollywood Nineteen, he was accused in 1947 by Jack Warner of insinuating Communist propaganda into his films. We meet in a modest home in the Catskills.

My chief sin was *Mission to Moscow,*"[1] which was made at the request of President Roosevelt for Warner Brothers. I had first turned down the assignment because I had done about four scripts in a row and I wanted to come East and see my father. I didn't want another assignment. Then Jack and Harry Warner called me up and said, "You can't turn us down." I said, "Why not?" And they told me they'd just had lunch with President Roosevelt and he had Davies's book on the table, and had said, "You want to do something important for the war effort, so we understand Russia better? Make a picture of this book," and he handed him the book.[2]

I don't know why they picked me. I guess because I'd had successful pictures, and they also knew I was politically inclined. So they put it to me that way, and in a way I couldn't refuse.

So I wrote the picture, but I made conditions: I could go East to visit Ambassador Davies, I wanted to get to know him since I was writing about him; all expenses paid; I could take a secretary, also all expenses paid—and I wanted a secretary who had some knowledge of politics and could be useful in other ways. And so, waiting for me at the Santa Fe train station— that's where we crossed the country then—was standing a very attractive young woman [points to his wife], and she said, "I'm Anne Green and I've been sent to help you." And she's been helping me ever since. [Laughs.]

Ayn Rand attacked the movie. She said on the stand that it was obviously Communist because it was the first favorable view of the Soviet Union. It wasn't all favorable, there were things in it that were against their form of government, but it was in the main favorable. And of course it created quite a splash when it came out. It got very good reviews, but of course it was attacked by the right-wingers even during the war. Yeah, well, they were never for that war. They were for a war on the Soviet Union.

Warners was glad to get all the credit for it, in the beginning, before the Inquisition set in. Then Jack Warner disavowed the film and me, saying that I'd put Communist propaganda in his films. He was up against the wall. He was scared because Warners had made the most progressive pictures in Hollywood in that period, and he didn't want them to come down on him.

[1] *Mission to Moscow* (1943), directed by Michael Curtiz and with Walter Huston, Ann Harding, and Oscar Homolka, was an adaptation from the memoirs of Joseph E. Davies, former U.S. ambassador to the Soviet Union. "Stodgy but fascinating wartime propaganda piece viewing the Russians as warm-hearted allies," according to *Halliwell's Film Guide.*

[2] Former White House officials later denied that any such meeting ever took place, and so did Ambassador Davies. But in the heat of the Red Scare, both Davies and the White House may have had good reason to disavow any encouragement they may have given Warner.

So I was one of those he was willing to sacrifice. He said what the committee wanted to hear about me.

In the parlance of the time, they would have called me a fellow traveler or a dupe. [Laughs.] You see, the committee was a little bit troubled about me not being a member of the Party. In fact, when they sent me a summons to appear, they canceled it because I would be free to defend all the other organizations that both the Communists and I were involved in. So they canceled that invitation, which I would have welcomed. I had a free channel; I couldn't name any names, because I wasn't a member.

The blacklist started for me in 1948. They didn't have to come and tell me, I just knew—the telephone stopped ringing. [Laughs.] I had been getting assignments pretty regular and now I was not. But I knew this was coming. They were afraid to hire any of us who were on that list. There was nothing my agent could do. He worked for me as long as I was acceptable.

And then through Martin Gang,[3] the committee got in touch with me, as they did with others of the Nineteen. They offered me the "Gang-plank." Taking his advice was called "walking the Gang-plank." Which consisted of saying "I've taken part in these activities and I'm sorry and I regret . . ." and so on. They couldn't say "Name names" because I wasn't a member of the Party. Our response to them was "No, no, and no."

See, I think we had an advantage. We had been so well trained politically, during that period in Hollywood, that I understood that they were not persecuting me in a personal sense. They didn't care about me at all. I wasn't their problem. But I had access to a medium, an important medium. And they wanted to shut down that access. I knew that I was caught in a historical situation and I understood that, it wasn't a personal thing and I didn't feel bitter about it. They had to start a Cold War, and they had to turn everything around that Roosevelt and the New Deal stood for, and that took a little doing. I was simply one of the ones they had to get rid of. It was as simple as that. I was unhappy about the whole Inquisition period. But I knew why it had to be.

After that, Anne and I came here to Woodstock to get our bearings. It was quite a change—on my last assignment I had been making three thousand dollars a week, that's about ten thousand dollars today, you know. I had always been on assignment, chiefly with Warners, although later Metro and Columbia.

[3]Attorney Martin Gang, a symbol of collaboration by 1951, represented more cooperative witnesses than any other lawyer in Hollywood. His talkative clients included Lee J. Cobb, Lloyd Bridges, Sterling Hayden, Richard Collins, and Meta Rosenberg.

Around 1951, a promoter by the name of John Nash came to me and said, "I read a story of yours called 'An Ordinary Spring.' " And he said, "I'd like to do it in three languages. I will take you and your wife to Europe, pay all your expenses, and you work in Italy and then Germany, France, and then England. 'Cause we're going to make this film in several languages." We were very glad to have the job, and he was paying us right away. He wouldn't pay us in checks, he would hand us hunks of money. "This is your fare to Rome; this is your fare to Berlin; this is your fare to Paris." And there is where he deserted us, in Paris. Not a bad place to be deserted. [Laughs.]

His money had failed, but he didn't come and tell us, he just left us drift. So we said, "Well, what we'd better do now is get to England, where we speak the language. And get a job, writing for them." Well, as soon as we got to England, J. Arthur Rank[4] gave me an assignment, they were the big people there. It was to be an international picture, American money. They called me in one day and said, "Look, you have to let us out of this, because we need American support and they saw your name on it and they said, 'Nothing doing.' " They weren't at fault, so I let them out of the contract.

Then Anne and I both changed our names. I used Howard for my last name and Anne did the same thing with hers. And then we worked with Joe Losey on a film which finally came out called *Finger of Guilt*, which is a crazy title. *The Intimate Stranger* was our title, which fit the material. After that, well, we lived very happily in England and saw a lot of Europe. We were there for five years. Anne was working on the original *Robin Hood* series, with Richard Greene. So I can't give you a sob story on the blacklist, 'cause it didn't work out that way.

Five years later, when we came back from England, we understood that the blacklist was over for us.[5] For instance, Columbia wanted me right away for a film, and they said, "It's okay." And then the head of Columbia, Harry Cohn, called me in and said, "Look. We still have a problem. You're off the other list, but you're still listed by the Americanization Committee of the American Legion. You're still on that, and we've got to get you off. There's a lawyer in Washington by the name of Edward Bennett Williams, a very prominent lawyer. We think he'll take your case and he'll probably be able to do the job."

[4]By the mid-1940s, Lord Joseph Arthur Rank (1888–1972), heir to a flour and milling fortune, owned more than half of the British studios and more than a thousand theaters.

[5]Koch asserts his stay on the blacklist lasted about five years. Other sources have him on the list for closer to ten: see Ephraim Katz, *The Film Encyclopedia* (New York: Harper & Row, 1990).

Well, I met him in New York, and I told Cohn, "I can't pay what he charges." They said, "Well, don't worry about that." Williams asked me a lot of questions and said, "Well, look, I'll do a little investigating and I'll call you back." He called me back and said, "I've investigated you and I find you very clean and no problem." I said, "Well, I'm still on this list." He said, "Well, come down and let's see what we can do." When I got there, he picked up the phone and called the Americanization Committee. "I've just talked to Howard Koch, he's here with me. We want him off the list tomorrow, or it's going to cost you two million dollars, 'cause we're going to sue you." I was off the next day. [Laughs.] Money talks.

It's funny, not too many years ago, the *New Yorker* film critic, Pauline Kael, was here for lunch. And to my amazement, she said, "Aren't you embarrassed now, that you once wrote *Mission to Moscow?*" I said, "Look. It's the thing I value most in my life—that I was able to stand for something that needed to be said." And she shut up and didn't say anything more! [Laughs.]

PAUL JARRICO

Jarrico earned twelve screenwriting credits from 1937 to 1949, then none until 1968. During that period he wrote under various pseudonyms for the black market. In 1953, he produced the award-winning *Salt of the Earth,* America's only blacklisted film, written and directed by blacklisted talent. A member of the Communist Party from 1937, Jarrico remained so until shortly after the Khrushchev report in 1956.

It was a watershed event in Hollywood—the hearings and the blacklisting and the informing. The memories die hard, though the people involved are dying. We're talking about forty years ago. Close to forty years ago for the people who were called in '51, and more for the Ten who were called in '47. There are only two of them left. One of them is Ring Lardner, who's a good friend. The other is Eddie Dmytryk, who became an informer after going to prison in order to be able to continue working, who was a friend but no longer is.

I was named by Martin Berkeley and Richard Collins, among others. I was named fourteen times. I didn't know all the people who named me! [Laughs.] But I did have a fairly high profile and I was fairly well known as a radical in Hollywood, so it was not too surprising.

Richard Collins was more than a friend; he was a collaborator. We collaborated on a couple of pictures together. When he became an informer he seemed to go out of his way to name people who had befriended him, people who'd helped him, and people who'd loaned him money. And in my case, he not only said I was a member of the Party, which was true, he implied I was a foreign agent, which was not true: he said that I would refuse to defend the United States in a conflict with the Soviet Union and was just a real unpatriotic type, and—I mean the whole formulation of "would you fight for your country" and so on. I already had. He hadn't! [Laughs.]

You know, he really went out of his way in his betrayal. It was very well known that in our collaboration I had more or less carried him, and somebody once said that his going out of his way to nail me was a kind of declaration of independence. And I said, "Yes, he wanted to stand on his own two knees!"

My attitude towards informers has more or less moderated over the decades. I understand some of the pressures they were put under and that some of them were reluctant informers, and some of them were eager informers. They weren't all the same, any more than the people that they named were all the same really. And I've—forgiven is not quite the word—but I've moderated my animosity in a number of cases, but not in the case of Richard Collins. [Laughs.] He was a real son of a bitch, and has flourished economically, so he got his reward.

The committee really hit Hollywood for the second time and in a much broader way in the spring of '51, which, as it happened, was when the Ten were coming out of jail, most of the Ten. A couple of them had come out a little earlier. Back in 1950, I produced a film about the Hollywood Ten, on the eve of their going to jail, in which they looked directly into the camera and explained why they thought they were going to jail. It was designed as a fund-raiser and was part of a campaign to get them out of jail. I'd been active in the campaign for the Ten from the very beginning.

I got subpoenaed late in March of '51. There was a list of people they wanted to subpoena, and they had trouble finding people they had named. So by the time they cornered me, there were a number of newspaper people with them, with the marshal, you see. I made a statement saying I've been here all the time and I've been working at the studio, and I don't know why there should've been any problem locating me. But aside from that, which was mostly played for humor, I said, "If I have to go to jail like my courageous friends of the Hollywood Ten or crawl through the mud with Larry Park, you may be sure I'll choose the former." Well, this was in the evening. The statement appeared in the papers in the morning, including pictures of me. And when I arrived at the studio that morning, I was employed at RKO, which was owned by Howard Hughes [laughs]—I was barred from the lot. This was before I'd appeared, too. Well, my politics were fairly well known, but it was that statement which made it clear where I stood. I said I've got personal papers up there, I've got whiskey up there! They wouldn't let me onto the lot. So you might say the blacklist for me began the morning after I was subpoenaed.

At the time, I was working on *The Las Vegas Story*. It wasn't much of a film, but I had just about completed the script and it was already scheduled to go into production fairly soon thereafter. Howard Hughes hit the ceiling and said he wanted the script rewritten so that I could not possibly have any credit on it. They tried very hard to rewrite it in the time available. New writers were assigned and a real effort was made to write me off the script. But they didn't have enough time for a totally new script, and by the time it went into production the Writers Guild, which had control of credits, awarded me the first of two credits, I believe, or three. And Hughes then issued a statement saying—by that time I had appeared before the committee—he was certainly not going to put my name on any movie made by him and his studio, and if the guild didn't like it, they could go on strike.

So I sued him, he sued me, the guild sued him, he sued the guild. There were a whole bunch of suits. And because anything connected with Howard Hughes got a lot of publicity, this was all front-page stuff for quite a while. I sued him for breaking my contract, for depriving me of credit. And he countersued, saying that by refusing to cooperate with the committee, I had placed myself in public obloquy and thus violated the morals clause of my contract with the studio. Of course, I said that standing on one's constitutional rights couldn't possibly be construed as immoral, and I attacked him. I said he had broken all ten of the Ten Commandments and who was he to talk about morality? [Laughs.] And so on. It was quite a brouhaha. But the upshot is that I lost and he won.

It was the last time that Hughes, who testified in the trial, ever appeared in public. He was already well known as a recluse, but he came out of hiding to testify in this case and was never seen in public again. I had a good lawyer, Ed Mosk, who died not too long ago. We gave them a fight for their money, but we lost. It was the temper of the times, really. One of the ironies was that the judge shook my hand and said, "Pleasure to have been associated with you," and this was five minutes after saying, "I hereby declare that you have placed yourself in public obloquy!"

When I appeared in front of HUAC, I took the Fifth, which kept me out of jail, but I also took the First and in general attacked the committee. Ben Margolis was one of my lawyers. He sat at my right. And Robert Kenny, who'd been a judge and who'd been attorney general of California and who really sacrificed his political career to defend people like me because he really believed in the Bill of Rights, sat on my left. And I was getting a little heated in my answers, and Kenny was tugging at my left sleeve and whispering into my left ear, "Take it easy, take it easy." Margolis was whispering into my right ear, "Give it to 'em! Give it to 'em!" [laughs] I'm afraid I took Margolis's advice, rather than Kenny's.

I had some savings that I was able to live on for a little while. Then I worked on the black market, under phony names or through fronts. One of the ironies of the blacklist was that they took our passports away at the very time that they blacklisted us. I had been abroad several times before. I had contacts there, I felt that if I could get to Europe I could get employment. But I couldn't get out of the country. But by the time the Supreme Court ruled in the fall of '58 that the State Department did not have the right to withhold passports on political grounds, there was less need to get abroad. That is to say, the black market had improved, if one may use that phrase. Work on the black market was more plentiful, and it was less difficult because it went through several stages. In the very earliest stages, if the producers discovered that they were using the work of a blacklisted guy, there was hell to pay. The project was abandoned, people were fired. I mean, one really had to be underground. After a while the producers who hired blacklisted—or who hired fronts for blacklisted people or bought material that had phony names on it—were sort of looking the other way and not really enforcing the blacklist, except that your name certainly couldn't be on the screen. And then it got easier. Sometimes toward the end, they were looking for blacklisted writers. They were cheaper and they did good work.

So by '58 when I got my passport back, there was less reason to go abroad. But I'd worked up such a head of steam on wanting to get out of here that I took off, and in fact I stayed in Europe for close to twenty years, with occasional daring forays back into the States. In Europe, I continued to work under other names, though certainly the people who hired me knew who I was. And the reason for the lack of credit during the earlier period, or at least the first ten years I was in Europe, was that they were very often international films. That is to say, made in Europe but backed by American or German companies, or some combination of coproduction money. Some of them thought they might jeopardize the market for the film in the United States if they gave blacklisted people credit. It was mixed. Some people got credit earlier than others.

Dalton Trumbo broke through as early as 1960, when he got two big credits in *Spartacus* and *Exodus* in one year. At that point we all thought it was over, but it wasn't over. It really went on for some time. But for varying lengths of time for varying individuals. I didn't get my first screen credit until 1968—seventeen years after I was blacklisted. But as I say, it varied. At any rate, I was able to make a living on the black market. It went up and down, but employment goes up and down on the market in general, black or any other color.

A number of us who were blacklisted formed a company to try to make films with content. It was a counterattack on the blacklist. We had this pool of talent, and more than that, we had a desire to make films that would have some real content. We had several scripts in preparation. Dalton Trumbo wrote a script about a woman whose children were taken away from her in a divorce action because she was accused of being a Red, based on a true story. We had a black writer named Mason Roberson working on a script about the Scottsboro Boys. We were hoping to make a picture starring Paul Robeson in something or other; we were looking for the right vehicle for that.

I devoted myself to producing *Salt of the Earth*, working with Herbert Biberman, who directed it, with Michael Wilson, who wrote it. And I received no recompense for that—none of us did. I mean, not the writer, not the director, not the producer. I happened more or less by accident to meet an international representative of the International Union of Mine, Mill and Smelter Workers, Clint Jencks.[1] Jencks was assigned to the Silver City area, where there was a strike of zinc miners. He and his wife, Virginia, told me and my then wife how the company they were striking against had gotten an injunction. The strike seemed lost until the wives of the strikers said, "The injunction says striking miners may not picket. It doesn't say anything about their wives. We'll take over the picket line."

The men were reluctant to, as they put it, "hide behind a woman's skirts," but there was really no alternative. The women did take over. They held the line against all kinds of police attacks. They were jailed in droves.

[1]See Clinton Jencks under "Breaking the Working Class."

The men found themselves at home, taking care of the kids and washing diapers and so on. Mike Wilson's[2] script dealt with the change in the relationship between a miner and his wife, in the course of this fight. It was a drama, not a documentary. But it was based on a real situation. And we shot it where it had happened, using people to whom it had happened as actors for the most part. We had a few professional actors who had been blacklisted in Hollywood. The wife was played by Rosaura Revueltas, a professional actress who came up from Mexico City to New Mexico to star in the film.

We were shooting and the picture was going along fine when the stuff hit the fan. Walter Pidgeon, the head of the Actors Guild at that time, said he'd gotten a letter from a schoolteacher in New Mexico that Reds were busy making a film there. He notified the FBI and a whole bunch of other Congress and government people and so on—though actually they were watching us before. But this became the public attack. And when the publicity started, there really was an enormous attack on us. First on the floor of Congress by Congressman Jackson, who'd been a member of the House Un-American Activities Committee, who denounced us, and without having the script or knowing anything about it, said we had imported carloads of blacks and our intention was to whip up racial conflict. The picture had to be stopped. It was subversive by its nature.

Some of the reactionary columnists pointed out that we were shooting not far from Los Alamos, where the atom bomb had been tested. We had all of this crap going on. And then the congressman's speech was repeated on a local radio station, over and over, and vigilante action was whipped up to try to stop the picture. Real vigilante action. They tried to set fire to our sets; they fired bullets through Clint Jencks's car. They told us to get out of town or be carried out in black boxes. They knocked over our camera when we would try to shoot in the street, and so on.

We managed to get the state police in New Mexico to come down and protect us. But meanwhile they arrested our star, Rosaura Revueltas, on trumped-up charges that had to do with her passport—that her passport had not been properly stamped when she came across the border. We put up a legal fight to keep her in the country. Ben Margolis flew from Los Angeles to El Paso to fight this thing. But we lost, and we were fighting against time, because all these other pressures as well as our original schedule required that we either get her out of hock quickly or try to solve the problems created by her arrest in some other way. So she was deported. We

[2]Screenwriter Mike Wilson was blacklisted for ten years. Among his uncredited films during this period were *The Bridge on the River Kwai* (1957) and *Lawrence of Arabia* (1962).

finished what shooting we could using a double. And then we departed the area. But meanwhile the attacks continued. The union hall in a neighboring town was burnt down. Meanwhile, the people who had loaned or leased us equipment and the laboratory that was developing our film, they all ran for cover. The laboratory said they would develop no more of our film.

This was 1953. This is the year in which the Rosenbergs were executed. The atmosphere was such that if a laboratory is accused of helping Reds to make a film, that laboratory issues a statement immediately saying, "We didn't know they were Reds and we will never do another thing for them. And furthermore, we're donating a thousand dollars to a good patriotic cause." This is all public relations and fear. But it left us in just a terrible fix. We got two-fifths of our film developed; three-fifths undeveloped, and no laboratory in the country will touch us.

I trotted around the country with cans of film under my arms, putting *Salt of the Earth* through under phony names like *Vaya con Dios* [laughs] and other things. Our biggest problem was to try to get the shots that we absolutely had to have of Rosaura Revueltas, to try to pick up those shots in Mexico, and though the Mexican newspapers and professedly the government were outraged by the treatment of their star and the fact that she'd been deported, and we were treated like heroes, we couldn't get permission to do what we had to get done, because the American pressure on the Mexican government was so great. They wouldn't say no; they'd say yes, but then they wouldn't do it! [Laughs.] We went crazy trying to get those shots, though we did get them, and smuggled them across the border. And we were able to finish the picture, though it took us a year of postproduction work undercover.

We couldn't get editing equipment. Aside from possibly some pornographic films, it was the only film ever made underground in the United States or at least completed underground. We had great difficulty getting any theaters in New York for our premier run. Certainly not on Broadway or in the Times Square area, where we wanted to open. We finally got a third-rate theater on 86th Street. We opened, and to our delight, we got good reviews in the *New York Times, Time* Magazine, and a lot of other places. Turnaway crowds for ten weeks, and we thought, "Well, we're in! We licked them!"

A bunch of exhibitors signed contracts with us to play the picture, and then the pressure of the major studios began. "You play this picture, you'll never get another Paramount picture." "You play this picture, you'll never get another MGM picture." One by one, the exhibitors dropped out. And we were left with a picture that nobody would play. We managed to play in thirteen theaters out of what at that time I think were thirteen thousand theaters in the United States.

Roy Brewer[3] was one of the leaders of the efforts to stop us from completing the film. It was his instructions to the IATSE guys which appeared in their bulletin—that being the International Association of Theatrical Stage Employees, which was the monopoly union in Hollywood then and to a certain extent is now as well, though the nature of the union has changed. He succeeded as head of the IATSE two gangsters who'd been sent to jail.[4] Brewer made it a personal vendetta to stop the film.

We couldn't at that point get out of the country, though we eventually did. It won some international prizes and a big reputation abroad, but we had trouble getting the money that was owed us, because we couldn't get out of the country. So, what money did come in we plowed into a suit against the industry, under the antitrust laws, which dragged through the courts for ten years and which we finally lost. The studios and labs and so on, all said, "Yes, we refused to help this picture. We even took steps against the picture. But we didn't do it in collusion with other companies." In other words, they denied conspiracy, and under the antitrust laws, we had to prove conspiracy. And under the instructions of the judge to the jury, which was very sympathetic, the jury found that we had not proved conspiracy.

However, we then began to get sixteen-millimeter distribution, and the picture became a cult film during the sixties and early seventies on campuses. And the reputation of the picture grew abroad. We're talking now in terms of decades. It became respectable. It was safe controversy. And the picture's now played on public broadcasting stations and it's out in cassette and doing fairly well. But to this day it has never been distributed theatrically in the United States.

It's a dramatic story, and I'm very proud of the picture. Basically because it represents real issues—labor's rights, women's rights, minority rights—that are still alive today. But what it represented for us was a counterattack, a fight-back so that we were not simply accepting the role of victims. If I had any advice to you in dealing with this period, I think you have to be careful not to picture the casualties of that war simply as victims. It's true

[3]For Roy Brewer's story, see under "Hounds."

[4]IATSE president George E. Browne and Hollywood representative Willie Bioff were controlled by Frank Nitti, Al Capone's heir to the Chicago crime syndicate. Both were jailed in 1941 for extortion. Brewer succeeded Bioff as Hollywood representative.

that there were casualties, but they were casualties in a fight, and the people who took the casualties more or less knew that there was a price to pay for dissent in this country. There is a history of struggle in this country. The abolitionists paid a price for fighting against slavery. The trade unions were organized at great cost in the lives and fortunes of the people who did the organizing. And the Left, or at least that part of the Left that I knew well and was a part of, we weren't absolutely amazed because the obverse side of the coin of the Cold War was blacklisting and McCarthyism and an attack on civil liberties in the United States. It didn't come as a total surprise.

JEFF COREY

A soft-spoken man with a dry wit, Corey began his stage career in the mid-1930s, then went on to play a wide range of character roles in Hollywood. From 1941 to 1951 he garnered thirty-six screen credits, then none until 1963. During his blacklisted years, Corey won recognition as an outstanding acting teacher.

I remember hearing the 1947 hearings, the Hollywood Ten. I knew those guys and I trembled, I had the shakes. I knew it was going to be bad. And coincident with that, I had the best period of my career. I did *Abe Lincoln in Illinois* at the Actors Lab and got wonderful reviews and a lot of attention. I did *Home of the Brave* and did one film after another. But I knew that it would catch up with us. And it did in 1951. I was blacklisted twelve years. I think I was the first one to go back to work.

I was first named by Marc Lawrence, who said I'd been at meetings at a time when I was actually a combat photographer on the U.S.S. *Yorktown*, but that's irrelevant. You took the Fifth Amendment or you didn't. If you took the Fifth Amendment, you had to do it consistently. You couldn't be selective. Then Paul Marion, who's now an agent—he was a radio actor, principally—he mentioned me. Through the years I go to see screenings at the Motion Picture Academy. I don't know why, but both those guys always seem to be there for me to snub them. Maybe they go out of their way to be snubbed.

Then Lee Cobb named me. I respected him and we were friends and we were fond of each other. It's a pity Lee did what he did. Judging from the work he did the last ten years of his life, I think it affected him. He once played Lear, who has this line "I am a man more sinned against than sinning," and I just doubt he could've said it with conviction.

One afternoon in the mid to late seventies, I was doing a pilot at the Columbia Ranch and the Irish actor Dan O'Herlihy and I were both bad-mouthing Lee because of the rotten work this onetime great actor did. And I got in my car to leave the ranch and I heard that Lee was declared dead on arrival at an emergency hospital. And like a crazy man, I addressed the radio and said, "I forgive you, Lee." [Tears in his eyes, he falls silent for a moment to recover himself.]

It was funny. Years later, I worked with his daughter Julie and I told her that story and was surprised at her reaction. She threw her arms around me and thanked me and began to cry. I spent the next hour comforting her.

Cobb once told her that he was very hurt when he said hello to me one day at the Universal back lot and I walked past him. She said he rarely talked about the blacklist, but one time he said, "Julie, you have no idea how anxiety-making it is to have every arm of the government zero in on you," and I told her, "Julie, you have no idea how exhilarating it is to tell every arm of the government they're behaving poorly and to go fuck themselves." And she looked at me as though, Jesus, she never thought of that.

I have immense compassion for the children of people who caved in. One time two carloads of kids came to our house. They were going to the country with friends of my daughter Evie, and they all said, "Let's drop by the Corey house," and there was one kid there who said, "When you introduce me, don't mention my last name." When he left the house he had told some of the kids, "God, they're such nice people, wonderful people." That was Marc Lawrence's son. What a burden to put on kids.

One night I had a dream and in the dream I was in the back lot at the Roach Studios in Culver City and a fellow who was then my very best friend came to visit me during the lunch hour and he looked very disturbed. And I said, "What's the matter?" And he said, "I'm thinking of informing," and I was so upset in the dream. I said, "How can you do that?" and I tried to dissuade him. I told the dream to a psychoanalyst friend, who looked at me very seriously and said, "Jeff, you know, there's an old saying, you're your own best friend." In other words, I projected onto my friend my self, so that's how close I think everyone thought, "What if I informed, and only mentioned the people that had been mentioned," and so forth. So it crossed everyone's mind. Oh, I thought it. I thought of it not as a plan but just "What if" sort of thing. And I rejected the notion because I wouldn't be able to live with myself.

I tried to avoid the subpoena for a long time, but they caught up with me. I remember rendezvousing with my wife, who was taking care of the three children. Coming to my house laying on the bottom of the floor of the station wagon, covered with blankets, thinking a marshal might come—oh, it was a very trying time. When I did get subpoenaed I spat on the damned thing.

Fortunately a friend of ours suggested, "Why don't you see if you can still get in on the G.I. Bill of Rights? Because I get one hundred and twenty bucks a month." So opportunistically, I enrolled that summer. I was before the House committee in September, but during that summer before the appearance, I took some French. And then the day I was supposed to appear before the House committee, I had to enroll as a freshman at UCLA. And then I drove out to the Santa Monica pier to look out forlornly at the ocean—"Oh, what am I getting into?" Then I went to the House committee hearing on the fifth floor of the Federal Building, and they didn't see me that day, but they saw me the next day.

What a bad lot. I didn't like the way they dressed. White-on-white shirts. Black shoes, brown suits. A terrible bunch of people! Congressman Wood practically said he'd be pleased personally if I was blacklisted, suggesting that way I could no longer contaminate the youth of this country. I had a good record as a father. I went on to teach thousands of people. I got a citation—the right kind of citation—from the grand jury of Los Angeles County for starting creative dramatic workshops for kids who are in juvenile hall.

Robert Kenny, who was Earl Warren's Attorney General, he always helped us guys. He said, "Somebody has to throw himself in front of the juggernaut," and a lot of very decent men and women, friends of mine, threw themselves in front of the juggernaut. We can be very proud that we did the right thing, the American thing.

I'm not a very brave person. Even those citations I got in the Navy were just freaky. The adrenaline took care of a bad moment where sensibility would say, "Duck." I don't look for trouble and I don't like trouble. I was in front of the committee very briefly. Congressman Jackson, that twerp, he said, "We don't need your soapbox oratory." And I got kind of grandiloquent about "You have no right to do this. You cannot buy the key to my brain." Actually, I heard Bob Kenny use that phrase, and I loved it. He had a great flair for English.

I took the Fifth Amendment. I not only took the Fifth, I quoted certain amendments in the United Nations Charter about the right to profess or not to profess your beliefs in public. And they said, "This is not the United Nations," and Congressman Wood expressed his disdain for the United Nations. So I was one up on him, I thought the UN was a pretty good idea. I had speeches about the genesis of the Fifth Amendment through the Star Chamber hearings in England under the Puritans, and forcing people to testify by using thumb screws; about how the Fifth Amendment was incorporated in the Articles of the Confederation, the Mayflower Compact. But I got very little of it out. They didn't like me! [Laughs.] I could've told them that Jefferson said the tree of liberty has to be nurtured by the blood of tyrants every ten years! Oh, boy, what a time.

Back in 1951, my then agent told me, "Jeff, you want to work, you got to play ball." He didn't encourage me to play ball, he just told me that this was the score. And I knew it. I was so hot. I wanted to direct, and I think I would have had a damned good crack at it. I was set for a William Cagney movie. I'd done a very good part in a Bill Cagney production with Gregory Peck. It was *Only the Valiant,* and I was up for other things. And at least as my agent told me, I was up for *High Noon.* So I went to work on construction. I got fourteen dollars a day and the foreman would constantly yell, "We're not building pianos. Keep those hammers ringing!"

Bill Anderson, a very nice guy, was working at CBS, and he sent me a script to play Leon Trotsky, and he thought too it would be a nice idea to show the people that you're not a zealot Stalinist the way you play Trotsky. I said, "Bill, it won't go. They won't let me work." He said, "Yes, they will," and he arranged an appointment for me to see a lawyer for CBS, who I have a feeling was a very important lawyer. When I went to his office, he says, "Jeff, it appears you are still unregenerate." I said, "Oh? What have I done?" He said, "When John Howard Lawson was released from jail, you spoke at a luncheon welcoming him back." I didn't remember it, but I figured it must be so. And I appeared on the same platform with Linus Pauling,[1] the double Nobel laureate winner. I appeared on the same platform with him at the First Unitarian Church and I read from the writings of Thomas Paine! That was in my dossier. "This is the winter of our discontent," that's what I read. Garish, isn't it? He had my file right in his hand.

One time the FBI came to visit me. They had nothing on me, because I didn't have much of a political past, really. Normal affiliations, I guess. My wife was very upset when they came, and they apologized for upsetting her.

[1] For Linus Pauling's story, see under "Red-ucators" and "The Peace Movement."

I never asked them to sit down. They wanted to know how I felt about the Soviet invasion of Hungary. I said, "I think it stinks." They said, "Maybe you'll make some statement about your political past." I didn't kick them out of the house or anything like that. I just told them, "Jesus, I don't particularly love Khrushchev. But just because he's an oaf doesn't mean I got to make a statement to clear myself. It's just gone too damned far."

In 1960 I got a job on *The Untouchables*, two years before the blacklist was over for me. I knew absolutely that the newspapers would make a thing about it. The *Hollywood Reporter* had a front-page story about my going back to work. Bob Thomas of the UP and Murray Schumach of the *New York Times* called me, and I knew if I made a statement, they would print it and I would not work again. But I said, "To hell with it. I don't want to work on this tenuous level."

I described what the committee did. That they said, "Just mention the names of people that have been mentioned and give us two more names to show that you're a good guy." That was the deal. And if you didn't, you didn't work. If you just mentioned the people who had been mentioned or were dead, it was not enough. You had to keep the committee going. It was a wonderful article, syndicated all over the world. And I didn't work for another two years because I'd been such a big mouth! [Laughs.]

If there's any value to this kind of colloquy you're having, I hope it lets people know we're really quite human. [Laughs.] And we weren't knuckle-headed people with rigid mental sets. We just wanted things to be better, and we didn't always make judicious choices, nor could we foresee monsters like McCarthy and the House committee.

I'm glad to say, now that I'm seventy-five years old, I don't take a bilious view of my past. I've had a pretty damned good career, even though I've been unemployed for most of it. Most people in the industry will understand what that means. So I get a pretty fair pension from the Screen Actors Guild, but it's probably about half of what I would have got had I worked those twelve years. And that also applies to my AFTRA pension and the Actors' Equity pension. Because I didn't work during the golden age of television, I missed a lot of stuff. I helped a lot of actors and directors prepare for those things. Sometimes people told me that during the blacklist period the studios would say, "We're looking for a Jeff Corey type."

JOHN SANFORD

Sanford speaks of the past with great emotion, especially in regard to his
wife; his love and regard for her is unadorned and deep. He is the
author of more than twenty works of fiction, history, and autobiography.
In 1938, he married Marguerite Roberts, a top screenwriter for Metro-
Goldwyn-Mayer with twenty screen credits over the previous fifteen
years. In 1951, they became unfriendly witnesses. Marguerite was
blacklisted until 1962.

Martin Berkley[1] named me, for one. That I know definitely, 'cause it was in
the newspaper. And he named Maggie. But there were others who named
Maggie. And there may have been others who named me, because they
generally cross-checked.

We were Communists. That is, I was a Communist, Marge was a screenwriter. I was at home writing books. She used to go with me to an occasional meeting. Finally some official said to her that she couldn't come
anymore unless she was a member; she was getting to meet too many
people. She decided that it was about time to join, and I didn't say anything. A matter of great regret to me, because I didn't feel that she was
becoming a member out of profound conviction. Nevertheless, in order to
be with me, she joined. She went to maybe four meetings in her life, I mean
real meetings. And finally, I came home with a story one day about something that had happened within the Party. Something very disgraceful.
[Laughs.]

Two lovely members of the CP writing fraternity in Hollywood decided
that a very good idea would be to take de Maupassant's *Boule de Suif*,
modernize it, change the names, and submit it as a screenplay, an original
screenplay. And they did that, with no credit to de Maupassant. They had
no success in selling the story. So finally one guy said, "To hell with it.
Forget it." But the other guy persisted. He took the second fella's name off
it, hawked it around, and by golly, he sold it for eight grand—and pocketed

---

[1]Screenwriter Martin Berkeley was undoubtedly Hollywood's number-one friendly witness.
While five sources give as many differing figures, the number of names he turned over to HUAC
ranges from 150 to 162.

the eight grand. Well, guy number two found out about it and demanded a share, and this other guy wouldn't give it to him. So he called for a conference of CP officials and it was decided that the money must be split and he had to cough up four thousand dollars to his associate. I came home and told that story to my wife. She was horrified. "They made one thief give the other thief half the money? Why not to the French Academy? Why not to de Maupassant's heirs? I'm out from now on." And she was.

That was about 1944. She no longer went to meetings, I did. We signed a few petitions and made a few contributions here and there. And lo, when the House committee came here in 1951, we got subpoenaed. We appeared in the fall, and I took a straight Fifth Amendment. I told them nothing. But Marguerite, who was a contract writer for Metro and had been for thirteen years, couldn't do that. For her to take that position would be tantamount to admitting that she was—not *had been,* but *was*—a Communist. And she could not say, "I haven't been a Communist for years." Because they would say, "Who did you know as a Communist when you were a member?" And that was becoming an infomer. That she would not do, and of course I would not ask her to do.

So I, as an ex-lawyer, fiddled around and talked it over with her and finally came up with something that I devised. It was called, later on, because a lot of people adopted it, a "diminished Fifth Amendment position." You ever heard of that? I doped it out. I said, "This is what you're going to do. When they ask you the question 'Are you now or have you ever been a Communist?' your answer will be 'I am not a Communist.' They won't let you stop there. They'll say, 'Were you ever?' Then you take the Fifth Amendment. But you are not a Communist."

She said, "What's the value of that?" I said, "You're telling the studio that you're not a Communist." I said, "You have that advantage. That's the only one you'll get. You're not lying and you're not committing perjury. You cannot be put in jail for it. You're telling the absolute truth. You're not a member, but you can't say you were not a member yesterday. They'll bring it right up to this morning. You tell them you're not a Communist now."

The result was that while she didn't go to jail, she was discharged from Metro. They bought out a five-year straight contract that she had with them which was due to stop.

We went through ten weeks of meetings with the studio. Dore Schary was the chief of production at MGM. He was not a leftist, but he was a very liberal guy. He taught at one of the labor schools where I taught—the

Progressive Educational Center, on Vine Street.[2] I was in one room; he was in the other room. I used to meet him in the hall. I don't know what he taught or what he said in the class. But he certainly was liberal, or he wouldn't have been there. He was present at one of the conferences where they tried to persuade Maggie to change her testimony. She persisted, she wouldn't do it. And Dore went at her. "Mention a few names. What does it hurt? Mention the names of people who've been named already."

So I popped up and I said, "Would you like her to say that you were in the next room to me, when I was teaching the modern novel?" He said, "When I need your help, Sanford, I'll ask for it!" [Laughs.] He was one of the biggest pricks in the business.

I have the whole thing in a diary that my wife and I kept in the fall of 1951. Every day's meeting was reported. And what's reported is what was said to us by these executives. They were more scared than we were. This is conference number three, October 31, 1951 [reads]:

One forty-five: We reported to Eddie Mannix's office and were admitted after a few moments' delay. Ben Thau was also present. . . . Mr. Mannix and Mr. Thau asked Marguerite if she would not go before the Un-American Committee again, and either deny ever having been a Communist or admit to having been one and leaving the Party and name names of people that she knew or suspected of being Party members.

Nothing short of this, they said, would satisfy the committee or the American Legion. We repeated what we had said before about the risks of either the risk of perjury or of naming people. Both Mannix and Thau scoffed at this and said no risk could be run and there could be no stigma for naming names. We differed again, saying both causes were bad, and that Marguerite had taken an outstanding oath of allegiance and loyalty and had denied being a member of the Party at the moment.

They said this was not enough. She had gone ninety percent of the way, but she should go the other ten percent of the way. Neither Thau nor Mannix seemed to seriously believe that Marguerite was a member or had been one. Thau seemed to think it would be advisable to deny everything and take chances on perjury.

Mr. Mannix leaned toward admitting attendance at meetings, naming a few names. Mannix stated that it was not Berkeley who originally put me on the spot, but that we had been "on the list" for some time. And that Marguerite was there because of me.

[2] By itself, association with a labor school was usually enough to garner a subpoena or stint on the blacklist. Funded by labor unions, the Communist Party, and private donors, the labor schools provided a free college accredited education for working people. Pilloried as "schools of subversion," by the end of the fifties the dozen or so schools across the country were driven out of existence.

"On the list"—he's talking about the shit list.

> Mannix said Berkeley was a yellow son of a bitch.
>
> Marguerite asked Mannix and Thau what would the studio do if she found it impossible to do either of the things suggested. Mannix indicated that they would have to talk settlement of the contract. Thau emphasized, however, that this was a friendly talk at the moment and had nothing to do with settling of the contract.
>
> Both Mannix and Thau were extremely friendly and the interview lasted from one forty-five to approximately three-fifteen. It was left like this: we were to go home and talk it over and inform Mannix and Thau of decision. I made it very plain that the decision was one that must be made by us according to our own likes and left the impression that Marguerite would stand pat on opposition.

My big trouble in those years was with my wife sitting there twiddling her thumbs and her typewriter covered over. I couldn't write. Her disability became my disability. I felt guilt, and I couldn't sit there and dash off words with the same élan that I had before, not when she was sitting in a chair staring at a wall. And not until she got back into pictures in 1960 did I take off again. And I took off with the novel Norton published.

The lawyers took her five-year contract and they stretched it out over seven to benefit Maggie. Otherwise, they could have paid her off in one lump sum and automatically she would have lost forty or fifty percent of it to taxes. So they were good to her, but they never again contacted her to work for Metro.

There was a group that funneled black-market scripts out. But they never contacted Maggie to write one. And she felt bad about that. Not that she wanted to take one. They gave them to needy writers in the main, and we were not needy. But she felt bad that she wasn't offered. She wanted the pleasure of refusing. It was not good for her ego not to be offered.

Her writing stopped the day she was kicked out of the studio. We walked out, her career was over—she thought. She began to make some stabs at writing about halfway through that exile. She dramatized a novel of mine, and we actually succeeded at getting a Broadway producer to take an option on it. The play was not ultimately produced. And she did a dramatization of *The Life of Stephen Crane*, wrote an original story—a beauty— which we hawked around, and tried to sell. But at least she had something on paper. It was good for her to do it, and we had a little measure of success. And she felt in some way she was back in the swing. But nothing counted until the day she actually got back at Columbia.

In '52, a guy from the State Department came around and wanted our passports back. I told him to fuck himself. I says, "Nothing doing. They belong to me." He said, "Well, that's true that the piece of cardboard belongs to you. But don't ever try to use it, because we'll stop you." And of course, they expired after a while, and we made repeated efforts to get the passports renewed. Nothing doing, unless we made a statement before the committee again. You have no idea what it is to be in a jail that's three thousand miles wide. You could walk your ass off, but you were still in jail.

The Academy Awards came up, and a picture that won the best screenplay was *The Defiant Ones,* written by a couple of lefties. So we sought out their agent and he represented her in the sale, or the attempted sale, of this Stephen Crane thing, and that fiddled around till about 1960. But there was action there, we never stopped trying. We applied to agents and to producers with the screenplay, oh geez, we must have had that script at a hundred different producers. Some of them liked it very much. In fact, I knew Joan Crawford personally. So sometime during that period I decided that I'd ask her if she'd want to play a role in this picture. I sent her the script and she liked it. She called me on the phone. She said, "What do you want for it? What's your price?" So I said, "Well, before we talk price, Joan, I want to tell you that Maggie and I are still in that bind with the State Department and the House committee." She said, "I thought you cleared that up, John." I said, "No, we're still Fifth Amendment unfriendly witnesses." She said, "I'm sorry." She couldn't go through with the deal.

Would you like to know how our friends treated us? Like shit. All our other screenwriting pals? Oh, boy! They wouldn't have anything to do with us, wouldn't be seen with you. Not only that, we had relatives who wouldn't talk to us. My former comrades? Never had anything to do with them again. They were loaded with finks. You didn't know who the hell you were dealing with. The Party members were the ones who squealed on you.

The FBI had the neighbors working for them. You know, Maggie and I applied for our FBI file through the Freedom of Information Act, and it came back all blacked out and hers too. But I gleaned one little bit of information from it, that they couldn't possibly know about. We were in the habit of talking about making trips to Europe with a certain neighbor up the street. She knew we went away in '52, and she knew we went away in this year, or that year, I forget when the hell it was. So one of the things in the report was "Informant says the Sanfords have no plans to travel this year." [Laughs.] So automatically I knew it was this bitch up the street. She used to ask me every once in a while, she'd pass me in the car, "Well, you going to Europe again, John?" "No. Not this year." That was the dame.

My wife used to tell me, "Johnny," she says, "I love you because you're an idealist, that's something that warms my heart. But don't ever get the idea that you're living in a revolutionary country. I'm a realist; you're a romantic. Sure you're the vanguard, but there's nobody backing it!" [Laughs.] She was a wonderful, wonderful woman.

She died almost two years ago. [Chokes up; tears come to his eyes.] And I can't rid myself of a thought. The fear that the stress of those ten years of deprivation, mainly on account of me, contributed to her death. I think it took something off.

EDWARD DMYTRYK

A man of medium stature, fit and energetic. Dmytryk began in Hollywood at fourteen as a messenger boy for Paramount and became a director at thirty. His career was flourishing in 1947 when he became one of the Hollywood Ten. After serving a prison sentence for contempt of Congress, he elected in 1951 to reappear before HUAC, where he gave twenty-six names. His fifty-two films include *The Caine Mutiny, Broken Lance, Raintree County,* and *The Young Lions* and have garnered eleven Academy Award nominations.

There was always the extreme Right that believed every Communist was a son of a bitch out to kill everybody. During the war, particularly after we became Russia's ally, they had to cool down a bit on that. But the minute the war was over—*wham!* [claps hands]—it took off, more than ever. Because they realized that the Russians would be in a powerful position—and they were scared to death. I've forgotten who it was that said that nothing is as frightened as a million dollars. Well, the million-dollar people were scared to death that somebody was going to take it away from them.

And I don't wonder. I recall walking along Sunset Boulevard with a guy who was an avowed Communist. Sunset Towers at that time was very high-class, perhaps the best in Hollywood, George Raft lived there when he was a star, and this guy looked up at that tower and said, "Someday, I'm going to be up there and they're going to be down here!" [Laughs.] So, to some extent, the extreme Right were entitled to be frightened. Yet when I look back at it, they really never were, because it's impossible for anybody to come along and upset the whole damn country that way. There's no question that these people were absolutely scared of bogeymen.

I was a Party member for about a year, and I attended very few meetings. I joined them in about . . . [long pause] well, I have the card someplace, late '44 or something, and got out in '45. I figured out the other day, I paid altogether about three and a half, four dollars in dues is all.

I didn't do anything when I was in the Party, I mean that. I didn't get that far. Nothing really happened at Party meetings. Mainly, we discussed what was going on in the world. We certainly weren't conspiring. Oh Christ . . . conspiring. Conspiring against what? Nineteen out of twenty of these people were successful. We talked about the political situation and what was going on. They were all good things, what could we do to improve housing, or to improve the racial attitudes of the people.

But there was no question that their aim was to get people into the guilds and unions. I imagine they had a long-term program to eventually take over the unions and run them. And if they could run the unions, they could eventually control motion pictures more or less.

You never knew someone was a Communist unless you saw him at a Party meeting. I didn't know that most of the Ten were Communists. Nobody came up to you and said, "Hello, I'm a Communist." I didn't know Adrian Scott was a Communist until we went to this one meeting together. I could never believe Dalton Trumbo was a Communist—actually I didn't find out until the hearings. Trumbo was a man with a great sense of humor, a true liberal. He was the one guy that said that there were no villains, no heroes, there were only victims.[1]

These guys were still hanging on to their dreams. They believed if they could make them come true, this would be a far better world. There's no question about it. The only way they were not far-seeing was that there was no question that the Communist Party of the United States was being run out of Moscow. Most of the people didn't know that, because it came only through the few who were the wheels in this country. If they had eventually taken over, we would have been living under a Stalinist regime. They didn't realize that. They were still looking back to pre-Lenin days, to the wonderful ideals of the Communist Party that wanted the best for everybody in the world. They let that blind them completely.

So even though the ideals and ideas of Dalton Trumbo or Albert Maltz

---

[1] "It will do no good to search for villains or heroes or saints or devils because there were none; there were only victims." This was a portion of Trumbo's speech accepting the Laurel Award from the Writers Guild of America in 1970.

were one hundred percent good, nevertheless they were members of an organization that wasn't, whose basic aim was to take over. As a result, they were helping them, and they shouldn't be helping them, which is why I got out and why I talked.

I left the Party in '45 after I directed *Cornered*. I've talked about this in my biography,[2] and I mentioned it in my second hearing to the committee: Adrian Scott and I worked together on four pictures. We had big success with *Murder My Sweet* and made a second one with Dick Powell, an even greater success, called *Cornered*. It wasn't one of my favorite films, but the picture did very well. It was originally written by John Wexley. He was a Communist, and he wrote a script that was full of propaganda. You could have taken some of those pages and put them up as Communist proclamations. He had replaced a good whodunnit writer who was a right-winger. I wondered at that time why Scott did it, I didn't really know.

We read it and said, "We can't do this." We couldn't, it was too goddam obvious. At the drop of a hat, the guy would get up and make these speeches. So we got Johnny Paxton in and threw out most of that crap and wrote a story that everybody could accept and made the picture.

Then a committee from the Communist Party got me and Scott on the carpet afterwards for having wanted to replace it all. John Howard Lawson[3] was one of them, of course. Wexley had asked for the hearing. At the first hearing we didn't know quite what the hell it was all about, then we found out that Wexley wanted us to put it all back. The picture was practically ready to be released, the negatives had been cut, prints had been made. We'd have to go to the head of the studio and explain why we wanted to remake all this stuff. How the hell could we?

They were the most illogical of all people when they had this kind of a thing on their minds. We couldn't do it, so Wexley said, "Well, we'll have another meeting." So we had another meeting, and this time Adrian called Albert Maltz and had him come in on our side.

Lawson was against us. As a matter of fact, after the last meeting, we stepped outside. I said, "Jesus, if this is the way it's going to go, I don't think I want to be in the Party anymore." And Lawson said to both Scott and me, "I think that'll be better. You can get out, and maybe later on,

---

[2] *It's a Hell of a Life, but Not a Bad Living* (New York: Times Books, 1978).

[3] John Howard Lawson (1894–1977), screenwriter and playwright and a cofounder of the Screen Writers Guild, was a leading member of the Hollywood Ten. He never recovered his career from the blacklist.

when you have thought about things, you will have changed your mind."

Those hearings are what got Maltz so mad that a short time later he wrote an article for *The New Masses*. Boy, did he get hell for that. He had to recant.[4] Poor Maltz had to recant several times. Yet he never realized this was against all those things he believed in. Never realized the stupidity. I was bright enough to get the hell out of there. Anyway, we eventually said to hell with them. Scott reacted the same way at the time. Later, I understand, he rejoined the Party.

We used to call Lawson the Gauleiter. [Chuckles.] That's a German word—the gauleiters were Nazi leaders of groups. We called him the Gauleiter because he was the leader of the Hollywood Communist Party. He was ideal casting. Never a sense of humor, always a little smile on his face. It's almost as though he's smiling at you stupid people who think what you're thinking, and this isn't the way it's going to go. We found that out time and again when we were having our meetings planning our defense before going to trial. He was the law in Hollywood, as far as the Party went.

Now this is a funny thing—none of this would've have happened if it weren't for Hedda Hopper, and Sam Wood, and John Wayne, and a few of the extreme rightists in Hollywood.[5] They *begged* the committee to come out here and investigate. The committee, I think it was in May of 1947, before they'd had the regular hearings, came out here and had preliminary hearings, talking to people like Menjou and those other people. Actually, the chairman made it clear two or three times—I think they were trying to sweep it off their shoulders—that it was the people of *Hollywood* who had asked for the hearings.

I was subpoenaed because I was the most important member of the Directors Guild who had been a Communist. Nobody named me at that time. They had a facsimile of my card. Look, they used to say that in any Communist meeting we had here in Hollywood, there were more people

---

[4]Maltz's "What Shall We Ask of Writers?" was published in February 1946. In it he decried "the vulgarization of the theory of art that lies behind left-wing thinking, namely 'art is a weapon.' " He believed too much emphasis had been placed on the weapon and not enough on the art. The furies descended, and two months later he recanted with "Moving Forward," again published in *The New Masses:* "I consider now that my article [could not] contribute to the development of left-wing criticism and creative writing."

[5]Dmytryk refers here to the Motion Picture Alliance for the Preservation of American Ideals, a zealous anti-Communist group pledged "to fight with every means at our organized command, any effort of any group or individual, to divert the loyalty of the screen from the free America that gave it birth." Other officers of the alliance included Walt Disney, Robert Taylor, Adolphe Menjou, Gary Cooper, Ward Bond, Charles Coburn, and Roy Brewer.

there working for the FBI than Communists.[6] This I believe. If they had been smart they would have known I left the Communist Party at a certain time.

After the '47 hearings, I was blacklisted for about four years. I went to England to work for J. Arthur Rank. They couldn't give me a salary. It was not long after the war, and all the countries had currency control. I worked purely for expenses, which weren't very much. I got fifty pounds a week expenses when I was working, and that's we lived on. Yeah, it was quite a change. [Chuckles sadly.] But it was work, and I got to meet wonderful people, with none of that stupid prejudice.

I don't feel sorry for the blacklisted ones. I knew why I was blacklisted. I knew how to get off the blacklist, and I did eventually. So did others, including those who testified without the public ever knowing about it. The ones that never got off are the graylisted ones.

I remember the first picture I made at Columbia after I got back in late 1951. I asked to have a certain man who I didn't know as a dialogue director, a kind of creative assistant. The studio said, "Okay, we'll check on him." They checked and the word came back I couldn't have him. I said, "Why not?" And they said, "Well, it's better not to." I said, "Well, I'd like to have him." Then I found out when they said "It's better not to," that was it—period. We had security people in every studio. If they said no, it was no.

There were hundreds of people in that category. You know what they did? They probably donated a few bucks to the Spanish War Relief or something, or they signed some petition. They were liberals, most of them were never members of the Party. And there were hundreds of those. Their lives were ruined. Some of them may have gotten back ten, twenty years later, but I don't know what the hell they were doing in the meantime.

I served my full sentence. Thank God, I had less of a sentence than eight of them. Biberman and I both had the six-month sentences. I served, and he did the same I think, four months and eighteen days.

I served eighteen days in maximum security in Washington and then the rest at Millpoint Prison Camp in West Virginia, in the midst of the mountains. Like all prison camps, the guards didn't carry guns. As matter of fact, we had no walls. I said to one of the guards, "What keeps anybody from

[6]This included the dues secretary for the Hollywood subsection of the Los Angeles County Party, most likely the source for the facsimile of Dmytryk's card.

walking out? There are no fences." "Well," he said, "you can walk out, but where are you going to go?" [Chuckles.]

I couldn't pick up a telephone and call my wife the way they do now. I could only write two letters a week and only get letters from my wife and one other person. But the food wasn't impossible, nobody mistreated anybody. We all did our work. Most of the guards were very decent. There were a couple that weren't, but they couldn't do anything. One of the captains said to me, "God, we're not allowed to beat anybody. I wish to hell . . ." [Chuckles.] He was very unhappy about that.

The thing that's indescribable—it's hard for me to even imagine it now, but I can remember—is the feeling that you are not free. It's a dreadful feeling which dominates every moment that you are there. Oh Christ, you get angry at nothing. I used to get angry every time Fast[7] made a stupid move, and he made a lot of them. Thank God we weren't in prison together for very long. As a matter of fact, I had a job, I was the garage clerk. That's the other thing which Fast said which was so funny, he said the only time that anything happened to him in jail—he also said that nobody bothered him or anything like that—the garage clerk threatened to kill him as a Communist. I happened to be the only garage clerk around when he was there.[8] [Laughs.] So this was certainly a stupid thing that he said. I called him a "fictioneer," and that's what he is. He makes up these things that sound right for the situation.

He also said on the first day he met me there, I threatened to turn in some guys who weren't mowing lawns with us. Which was the stupidest thing in the world. You know, I had already been in maximum security prison for eighteen days. Anybody who would even think of turning in anybody, you'd know goddam well you'd get your throat cut the next day. He makes these things up. I think he wanted to set reasons up why I later talked to Congress.

I got out of jail just before Thanksgiving in 1950 and testified again in April of 1951. I would never have made a second appearance before the committee if I didn't have to. Two things there. First, the Right wanted their

[7]Howard Fast, best-selling author and former Party member, who also served time for contempt of Congress. His memoirs, *Being Red* (Boston: Houghton Mifflin, 1990), contain uncomplimentary assertions about Dmytryk, which Dmytryk here refutes.

[8]"The only man in the prison who hated us as Communists was the prisoner in charge of the garage, a huge, surly brute who snarled at us every time we passed him. . . ." (Fast, *Being Red*, p. 255) Fast also states he arrived at Mill Point two weeks before Dmytryk and Maltz. Could Fast be referring to another clerk? But in an unpublished memoir, Dmytryk points out that the garage clerk he replaced was a "quiet, elderly man finishing a two-year sentence for embezzlement."

revenge. We had done everything we could to call the committee idiots and undemocratic. Those are little men in Congress, they wanted to get theirs back, and they had a right to get it, I suppose—but I was the one who was coming back to talk to them again. I always looked at this as kind of a war—you win or you lose, and if you lose, you don't go around crying about it.

Second, I had issued a statement just before I left prison saying, "I'm not a Communist. I haven't been a Communist for all these years, I don't believe in Communism." I thought it would get me off the hook. It didn't—that wasn't what they were looking for.

Sure, I went to the slammer first. I wasn't planning at that time to appear at another hearing. I went to the slammer strictly because I had made up my mind to separate myself from the Party. I *had been* separated from them, but the Hollywood hearings brought me back again. Now, there's no question that everybody in the country was sure we were all Communists. We weren't commenting on whether we were or not. We went through every goddam fake thing in the world to convince people that we weren't, except we wouldn't say we weren't. So, I was damned as much as everybody else.

If I had separated myself before the slammer they would have said, "He's doing it because he doesn't want to go to jail." Isn't that so? Absolutely, that would have been my only reason as far as they were concerned. If I had said, "I'm doing this because I think it's an evil thing," they would have said, "Oh, Christ, you're doing it because you're afraid of going to jail." I decided to do the second hearing after I got back, when I no longer had any other way out.

There was a committee[9] that had been organized to review people that wanted to talk, to get off the blacklist which Reagan said never existed. Our lawyer, Bartley Crum, a Republican, incidentally, and a wonderful guy who lost a great deal by this whole damn thing, he went to the committee and they laid down the regulations.[10] One was that somebody write an article about the thing and have it published in *The Saturday Evening Post*. It was written by Richard English. We spent several weeks together in town here and then finally went down to a hotel in San Diego. He wrote a very good

[9]The Motion Picture Industry Council, originally founded by Dore Schary to fight the blacklist, was now facilitating it. Roy Brewer was the man on the council to see for clearance.

[10]Bartley Crum was a Republican supporter of FDR and Harry Bridges and president of the National Lawyers Guild. Blacklisted, haunted by financial ruin, alcoholism, and the suicide of his son, Crum gave in to FBI demands and informed on Guild members. He killed himself in 1959.

article, and very complete.[11] The other thing was to appear before the committee a second time. That was an absolute [thumps table] qualification.

I find that when you write biography you've got to look very carefully and say, "Did I really feel this way then or do I feel this way now?" I think my strongest feeling at that time . . . [long pause] was that I had to break with the Party. I knew as far as people's concept was concerned, I was still a Communist. And the only way I could really break was to do it officially [thumps table three times] in—that—way.

I got to D.C. the night before, went to a hotel, didn't see anybody. The next day, I was told where the committee was holding its hearings. There were a number of people in the audience—it wasn't like the earlier one, where it was huge. There were probably fifty people there. This was public. I didn't appear *in camera*,[12] that's just the point. They didn't want me to do that. No, since I had been one of those who'd caused them trouble three years before, I had to take it.

I didn't crawl. I didn't put myself in that position like poor Larry Parks had to. Larry tried to defend the thing at the same time he was trying to deny it. We knew Larry very well. Betty still says that's what killed him finally.[13] I know it was. It was with him as long as he lived. He took it very hard. But he did it the wrong way. I didn't defend the Party. I told them I had joined it for what I thought were very good reasons, but that it was window dressing—that's what they had it for, to attract people.

When the committee asked me, "Did any propaganda ever get into a picture?"[14] I said, "How is it possible for me to get propaganda into a picture that the workingman will understand, but that the executive in the studio will completely miss, particularly if he's a pretty bright man?" I said it is absolutely impossible, unless we had Communists running the studio.

They asked general questions about my experiences: why I was a Communist, why I got out of the Party, how I felt about it, who I knew. That

[11]"What Makes a Hollywood Communist?" *Saturday Evening Post,* May 17, 1951.

[12]In private, secretly; used to indicate a committee hearing not open to the public.

[13]Betty Garrett, actress, was married to Larry Parks from 1944 until his death in 1975. Garrett's own movie career stalled after her husband's confession of past Party membership. See Frances Chaney earlier in this chapter for more on Larry Parks.

[14]The notion of what might constitute "propaganda" was never too taxing. In 1947, Ginger Rogers's mother, Lela, testified that her daughter had courageously refused to speak a line typical of Red indoctrination: "We'll run this like a democracy, we'll share and share alike." The film was Dmytryk's *Tender Comrades,* written by Dalton Trumbo, in which a group of wartime working women band together to share expenses on an apartment. The tainted line, Lela Rogers notwithstanding, remains intact.

was the main thing, they asked for names. I gave them nineteen or something, I've forgotten, that was all I knew. Of all the people I named, I think
there was one person they didn't already know.[15] They were very strict with
me on this kind of thing. I did talk to one of their investigators before, but
all he said was "We don't want you to mention any name that you didn't
see there. Don't mention someone because you heard that he was a Communist or because somebody told you." They were very strict about that.

The purpose of naming names was that they wanted to make sure that I
really meant it when I said I was getting out of the Party. If you don't name
names, you're still protecting them, whether you're actually a Communist
or not.

The idea that it would be a matter of conscience *not* to name names
never entered my mind. I could live with it. I can see how someone else
would feel that way, but in a sense, it all comes from fear—you don't want
to be called a renegade. In other words, I think I was more courageous than
they were.

Sure, there's room for the stand that says, "Look, I can't name names
because my conscience won't let me do it, and I don't give a damn what
I'm called." There's room for that, and you know where the room is? It
depends on how you can support your family. Arthur Miller had no danger
of going broke, he had Broadway. Lillian Hellman had no danger of going
broke, she had Broadway and the novel. But for Lee Cobb, acting was his
only work. For Bud Bridges, acting was his only work.[16] There were a
whole lot of people like that.

I was the only one of the Ten that was a director. The rest could try to
work under the counter selling scripts—even at low prices. All it meant was
that they had to get back down to where they used to be. I'm sure that
Trumbo got one-tenth of what he would've have gotten if he hadn't been
in that trouble. But even with one-tenth of what he got—as long as he
didn't keep his ranch up in the valley, which he didn't, he sold it and lived
simply—he could live. I couldn't. I couldn't direct a film quietly. I couldn't
go out on a set where there were reporters and all these people and say,
"My name is Joe Brown, I'm directing this picture." It was my only work.
The only work I had done my whole life. My only out would have been to
go to England and work, which I could have done, but I would have

---

[15]To be accurate, Dmytryk gave twenty-six names, four of which had not been named before:
Bernard Vorhaus, Michael Gordon, Maurice Clark, and George Cory.

[16]Better known as Lloyd Bridges, well-known film and television actor, father of Beau and
Jeff Bridges. Both Cobb and Bridges named names.

considered that a defeat. And for a while there was the definite danger of being denied a passport.[17]

In another way, naming names mattered tremendously, because in this country we have what I call the "Mafia Syndrome." All the immigrants over a period of time have left their mark. The English left their Puritanism and a few other things, the Italians left the Mafia, the *omertà;*[18] even if your friend kills somebody, you're not supposed to say anything. I don't think that's necessarily a very good attitude.

This country has adopted it to a very large extent. I remember I said at the time that if you were a member of a Boy Scout troop, you wouldn't mind naming your Boy Scout buddies. In this organization, the very fact that it is so secret makes it a bad organization to begin with. If they are an honest organization working for honest purposes they should be out in the open. The Communists said they were secret because they were being persecuted, but I think if they had been open they wouldn't have been persecuted. Which comes first, that's the point.

The Jews have been persecuted for how many thousand years? I can understand their wanting to hide themselves, because it's open persecution. But in this case, I don't grant them that right. I was not in the position to ever tell anybody I was a Communist. I used to wonder why the hell you had to be so quiet about it all. To me it was funny. Then I found out that I couldn't read a book by Koestler because he was an ex-Communist. I remember saying to Adrian, "I've been reading a very good book." He said, "What?" I said, "Koestler's *Darkness at Noon.*"[19] He said, "Oh my God! Don't tell anybody that!" I said, "What do you mean?" He said [assumes conspiratorial whisper], "He's an ex-Communist—you're not supposed to read him!" This was the very first time that I realized it wasn't quite what I thought it was.

----

[17]After 1947, the right to hold a passport was customarily denied to Communists, unrepentant former Communists, fellow travelers, and critics of American foreign policy—or anyone suspected of being one of the above. Among the untold numbers of Americans denied this basic right: Paul Robeson, Arthur Miller, W.E.B. Du Bois, Owen Lattimore, and Supreme Court Justice William O. Douglas.

[18]Italian for silence; the underworld code of a self-imposed gag concerning knowledge of wrongdoing, most aptly expressed in the perhaps apocryphal Italian saying "I saw nothing, I heard nothing, and even if I was there, I was asleep."

[19]Influential novel first published in 1940 that drew much attention to the cruel and arbitrary nature of Stalin's regime. Koestler was also a contributor to *The God That Failed,* edited by Richard Grossman (New York: Harper & Row, 1950), a collection of essays by six intellectuals describing their initial attraction to and ultimate rejection of communism.

I'm very sorry in some ways, because this has followed me through the rest of my life. It has ruined it, but the thing that gets me very angry sometimes is that some people in writing about this say—and this is a Communist line, not a normal line—anybody who has gone back on them, who has betrayed them, who has become a "rat," loses all his talent. He has no integrity anymore. He has nothing.

But the thing is, I made some of my best films after I got back into Hollywood. As a matter of fact, *Young Lions* was the best picture I ever made in Hollywood, along with *Raintree County* and *Broken Lance*. After I got back, I made more films than I ever made before.

Actually, to be kind, I think that it becomes more than just political. Although the minute they say that, I don't know that they are Communists but I know their political leanings are. What I had specialized in before was sort of whodunnits. I'm given credit for being one of the innovators of film noir, which is a lot of nonsense. I had done *Cornered, Murder My Sweet,* and the last one was *Crossfire,* but that's what they were, whodunnits, except for *Crossfire,* the only one that had real body to it. Afterwards I did films with real serious content.

This thing still follows me because . . . oh Christ, as you know, the liberals are in control of the business. That's one of the reasons I retired. After the sixties this thing has gone both ways. There were a couple of times when I was still working and still doing good films, when I was turned down. I won't mention the people, but they said, "Over my dead body." One of them was Jack Warner, I don't mind mentioning him. Thank God, I had people like Darryl Zanuck at Fox and others who didn't feel that way and let me make some very good pictures.

But eventually it got worse. The older I got, the worse the animosity got. I still meet it a little bit here and there, and I know damn well that when they do an obit on me in the paper they won't talk about the films I made. When Monty Cliff's death is written about, several pictures he made are mentioned, but they will not mention *Raintree County* and they will not mention *Young Lions*. I keep noticing it. Anything that I had to do with, they won't talk about. *Young Lions* and *Raintree County* are two of the best films he ever made. The only film that can compare to it is *Place in the Sun*. The newspapers have taken that kind of attitude too. It's better not to mention my name than to mention my name. [Long pause.] I can live with it.

What would have happened in Hollywood if the Red Scare had never come about? Nothing, it would have gone on. I don't think the Communists would have gone anywhere. They'd be dead now anyway. This is the thing—the Communists had the seeds of their own destruction within them. I don't think things would be terribly different today if there never had been the hearings.

No, it would be better today, because without question the Red Scare did affect Hollywood for at least two decades until the end of the sixties. No question about it. People were scared to death. Why the hell do you think we're doing all this shit on TV and on pictures? Why don't we put out a decent film that has something to say? There are still people who are afraid to say anything for fear someone will get on their backs. The executives are afraid of it. They don't want to lose a nickel. Without question this is the hangover from the Red Scare. If nobody else remembers the Hollywood Ten [chuckles], these people still do.

Looking back, I don't think I'd do anything differently. I think about it, of course. The only alternative I had was to go to England. As a matter of fact, they don't give a damn about those kinds of politics over there. When I still was blacklisted and first went over there in 1948, I had to see Rank, he said, "I don't care about your politics." He was one of the richest men in the country, and it didn't bother him. I made *Give Us This Day* for him, one of my best films. One that wasn't seen in this country by anybody but the reviewers, because the American Legion boycotted it.

I could have gone back there, but I would have had to take my wife back there and raise my family back there, and as much as I love England, it isn't Southern California. This is where I wanted to be. Do I want to leave this? Where do I want to be buried? I want to be buried in this country.

DAVID RAKSIN

Raksin first came to Hollywood in 1935 to arrange Charlie Chaplin's music for *Modern Times*. Throughout a long career he has scored more than one hundred films (including *Laura* in 1944), Broadway shows, and television programs. He joined the Communist Party in August 1938 and left in early 1940. Reading his testimony before the committee, one is struck by his careful distinctions, his unwillingness to be pushed into sentiments he did not hold. He gave eleven names.

Hollywood . . . remember, Hollywood let everybody down. They realized that the stakes were tremendous, and they betrayed everybody. I'm talking about the bosses, who never stuck up for their people.

I was in the Party for a year. I once said to somebody that if they really wanted to expose the extent of our nefariousness and make us crawl with humiliation, they would reveal that for almost a year a group of us tried to read *Das Kapital.* [Laughs.] It was a kind of study group that met at somebody's apartment in Westwood. I don't think everybody there was a member of the Party, but it made us feel like hot stuff. We punished ourselves one night a week. What kind of a schmuck do you have to be to keep doing that to yourself? But anyhow, when I was later asked, I said, "I am convinced I never saw any nefarious act done or proposed." I said this many times, including when the dear gentlemen of the committee were questioning me.

But we did idiotic things. For instance, I remember I went out willingly, several times, to watch elections. For Christ sakes, they could've stolen a goddam ballot box in front of my nose, I wouldn't have known what was happening. I went there with a young woman; I don't know if she was actually a Party member, but I guess she was. And the two of us stood there like schmucks, embarrassed as we could be, watching people vote. What was that all about? I finally said to them, "Listen, I'm not going to do this anymore." I said, "I figure that if I learn to become somebody as a com-poser, I can do more good to our cause"—or whatever the hell word I used at the time—"than I can do by watching ballot boxes."

I left the Party after a year, if my memory serves me correctly. I was invited to leave. It was not the first time I was invited to leave. There were things I didn't like, and I expressed opinions contrary to the Party line. I got called in several times by a very nice, very intelligent woman who was apparently one of the general heads of the organization here. She said to me, "David, do you realize that not everyone is capable of maintaining a straight-ahead attitude on these things? You're a very disruptive influence." I said, "I realize that, but I can't help it. I am telling the truth as I see it." It was not a case of rigid discipline. This idea of rigid Party discipline is a crock. It was more like bringing a bad boy into line, or something like that.[1]

[1]Before the committee, Raksin testified to three instances where he had spoken contrary to Party direction: his position against the censure in the Soviet Union of the composers Shos-takovich and Prokofiev; his assertion that when ignoble means debase the one who performs them, then "it is time to examine not only the substance of the means but the end itself"; and his assertion that writers who deliberately imposed a social consciousness into their work, at the

I'm sure there were instances of rigid discipline, but what could they do to me? Take away the C-major scale or something? [Laughs.] There's nothing they could do to me. Eventually, the request for me to leave got sufficiently strong so I left. But I have never been an apostate Communist, I don't like apostasy.

It wasn't till later that the dear committee caught up with me, in the spring of '51. My first wife and I were living in Northridge on a farm, and we had invited two of our friends to come out and have dinner. I got a call from a guy named Russell, an investigator for HUAC, saying he was coming out to see me. So the first thing I did was to call my friends, because I didn't want to tar them with that little brush, and I told them, "Please delay by an hour." So Russell came out and gave me a subpoena and informed me that I was not to talk about this to anybody. I said to him, "I find it very reassuring that you guys know all this stuff about me, because if you know that much, you know that I have never done anything even remotely wrong." Strangely enough, it sort of stopped him in his tracks. I could see it made him think a little bit.

I was working at MGM at the time, and as the time grew nearer for my appearance, I was being asked by them to sign a new contract. I couldn't do that, because I couldn't tell them that I was under subpoena. There was no way I could tell them, because I'd given my word that I would not tell. I couldn't see signing a contract without telling the truth. My agent kept saying, "They want to know what the hell you're stalling about." So I pulled a trick that they might've understood. I just said, "Listen, Phil, tell them that I'm up to my ears in the picture." In other words, I was shaking my shaggy mane and being an artist. I said, "Tell them I'm really so busy I haven't got time to read the contract. It's their picture; they want me to finish the score . . . tell them we're on good terms and everything'll work out."

I had to get a lawyer. I needed advice about what my rights were. The only lawyer I could think of was Martin Gang. So I went to Martin and told him about it. He had experience with this, because other people had gone to him too. He was the only guy I really had any contact with. He advised me

---

expense of that work, "were making a great mistake." He identified the Party functionary mentioned here as Madeleine Ruthven, "a very mild woman . . . very reasonable." She thought he should be "more prudent."

to spill it all. Meanwhile, I'd had several calls and even a visit from Martin Berkeley, who'd named around two hundred and fifty people.[2] He named everybody, everybody. How he knew about guys like me, I don't know. He said, "Now, listen, don't attempt to deny it, because I named you." I wasn't mad at him, I knew somebody would have to name me. I'd been just too obvious after I got out, telling people, "Yes, I used to be a member of the Party."

Anyhow, I went to Martin Gang and he said, "Don't attempt to be devious or hold anything back, because they know everything about you." And I thought and thought and thought, and I was really in hell. I mean, *in hell.* I couldn't talk to anybody about it. I had a wife and a little kid. I saw my career and my life going down the drain. I didn't know what to do. I thought the only honorable thing to do was what some of my friends had done. Not all of them, I think, did it for reasons I would find entirely honorable and selfless. Some of them didn't have the guts to come out and talk about whether they were disaffected or not. They were afraid of the opprobrium that would come from the Left. But I was convinced that there was no other way to handle it than to get up there and defy the committee.

I went to the two people I thought had the most integrity of anybody I knew. One guy was a psychoanalyst. He was pragmatic in an honorable way. The other guy was an impeccable moralist, who has since died, I'm sorry to say. I talked to both of them. I can't remember which one of them it was who said the "Magic Woid"—you know, Groucho's word. He said something about a *ritual.* And I suddenly realized that in this there was something of the Spanish Inquisition. Before that, it hadn't really occurred to me that they had no right to do this to us. I knew that, but what would have been the point of talking about it, when they have the power to do it? But suddenly I realized that maybe there was a way to handle this that I could live with. And that was to do the following: if I could pretend to observe all the moves of the ritual, as they saw it, I might not have to do some of the things which I couldn't stomach.

So what I decided was that I would keep up with the newspapers and see who was named, and that I would not name anybody who had not already been named, and when they asked me about other people who had not been named, I would deny that I knew them or that I was in the branch with them.

When I told this to Martin Gang, he had a hemorrhage. He said, "Don't you realize that they know all about you? Don't you realize what they'll do? They'll ask you questions about people you were in a branch with, and

[2]The most loquacious of all informers, Berkeley actually gave no more than 162 names.

every time you tell them a lie, they'll expose you, and you're going to get one year in prison for every one of those." I said, "That, Martin, is a risk I'm willing to take. I'm just not going to get out there and spill everything."

It interests me that there are people who profess to see no difference in this strategy and the behavior of others who named names. What I'm telling you here is verifiable by reading the transcript.

Before I made my public appearance I went through stuff with Tavenner, and Russell, and a couple of other people. It's what people later called the Star Chamber procedure,[3] which I think has colored my perception of it in that I see it as being sort of dark with a light on me. It never happened that way. I was in an office, but it really was intimidating as hell. I'm not sure whether they were playing good cop/bad cop on me, but if so, there was no good cop. They grilled me: "Were you a member of this?" "Yes, I was a member of the China Aid Council, and the Musicians Committee to Aid Spanish Democracy," and all the rest of that. And they asked me some names, and I said yes to those I was prepared to say yes to and no to those I was not prepared to say yes to. I later became convinced that they knew I was lying about some people.

So then came the big appearance, which everybody in town watched— you'd be amazed, everybody. Everything stopped at the studios while they watched the hearings on television. I'll never forget the courtroom, which had these cameras, motion picture cameras and television cameras, and lights. It was hot as a son of a bitch. Everybody was in a state of stress and agitation. The committee was incredible, to my mind. I'll tell you what I mean by that. This was before I testified, I went into the gents' room and a guy came and stood beside me. It was Whitey Hendry, the chief of police at MGM, and he said, "Now, listen, David, did you know so-and-so?" I said, "Sure, I know him." He said, "No, no, I mean, did you know him? Was he a member of the Party?" Well, of course he was a member of the Party. But I said, "Not to my knowledge." You see, now I wonder if Whitey really knew, because I know the committee must've known. Anyhow, the funny part of it is, they did not pursue me in this matter.

I refused to have my lawyer on the stand with me. I said to him, "I know you're a lawyer and you have a relationship which keeps you clear of your client, but I don't want you being on the stand with a guy who's not going

---

[3]The Star Chamber was an English court, existing from the fifteenth century until 1641, that was characterized by secrecy and was often irresponsibly capricious and oppressive. Raksin first met privately with Frank S. Tavenner, chief investigator for the committee, and the others to ascertain his testimony before his public appearance.

to do what you think he should." I was still going against Martin's advice. I denied knowing people that I knew perfectly well, right there under oath. And the people I named were people who'd not only been named, but one or two of them were dead and several of them were out of the business completely. I think they knew I was not naming everybody I knew, I really do believe that. Why they chose not to hammer me is beyond me.

There was a guy there, I think his name was Doyle, one of the committee.[4] He had lost a son in the war. From the way he would glare at me, I couldn't help thinking, "This guy probably thinks I'm the fella who killed his son." There was another guy there named Donald Jackson, a miserable son of a bitch of the worst kind,[5] who, I am convinced, was bought by the studios. Because later, after my appearance was over with, I was watching the hearings on television when a Hollywood big shot was called and Donald Jackson walked out so there wouldn't be a quorum. I think somebody got to him, maybe Harry Cohn. I'm convinced that is absolutely true.[6]

At the beginning of my testimony, I said, "Look, I'm not going to make any pious statements. I was a member of the Party." Jackson got after me hammer and tongs. I defended my point of view, I said I never saw anybody do anything wrong. At the end they asked me, "Have you got any suggestions to make?" This is where you're supposed to grovel and suggest that it would be a wonderful idea if they brought in the fire hoses and "extinguished" the Party and everything. I said to them, and this you can look at in the testimony, I said, "Look, it strikes me that this is the wrong way to go about it." I said, "If you suppress this, it will lie there and fester. But if you let it out in the open air," or whatever word I used, "people will discuss it, they will contest it, and it has a chance to make its point—if it doesn't have a point, it doesn't have a point." I tried to say to "let it be heard." It was so absurd to say "Let an opinion be heard," but that was what was at stake there.

Jackson suddenly realized I was almost wriggling out of their grasp, and

---

[4]Clyde Doyle (D–Calif.).

[5]Donald L. Jackson (R–Calif.), described by David Caute as a "primitive bigot." (*The Great Fear: The Anti-Communist Purge Under Truman and Eisenhower* [New York: Simon and Schuster, 1978], p. 92) Upon reading much testimony, one would be hard put to argue with this assertion.

[6]On September 25, 1951, Sidney Buchman, a screenwriter and producer who had been an executive assistant to Harry Cohn, head of Columbia, testified that he had been a member of the Party but refused to name names. Jackson departed the hearing before Buchman refused to answer, thus leaving the committee without a quorum and unable to issue a contempt citation. Buchman was again subpoenaed in January of 1952; upon failing to appear he was cited for contempt and subsequently convicted.

boy, what a torrent of talk. He says, "It's not as simple as you make it, and we're in danger. . . ." I can't remember what the hell else he said. He went on and on and on, and suddenly I realized, this guy is not going to ask me a question, he was making a speech. I was actually very cool throughout the whole thing, to my surprise. And the reason was, I'd already gone through it so many times in my mind. I would lie awake all night, unable to sleep: "What'll I do? What'll I do?" I went through these scenes, having conversations with myself, arguments and stuff like that. So when I actually got in there, strangely enough, it was as though I was prepared. So, as he was saying this, I felt very calm. And the more he ranted, the calmer I got. Eventually he ran out of gas and there were no more questions, so I just sat there. And they sat there. And I sat there. And they sat there. And somebody said, "Well, all right, Mr. Raksin, we want to thank you very much for your testimony." They wanted to thank me very much for my testimony!

I later used that line with some schmuck who was attacking me as unpatriotic. I said, "Have you been thanked by the House Un-American Activities Committee?" That's no laurel to my mind, but of course, it meant something to him. Not to me.

After my appearance, I got a call from Eddie Mannix to come see him. He was one of the second in command at MGM, a powerful executive and very affable. I don't think I'd ever met him before. On the way there, I was stopped by some right-wing son of a bitch who said to me, "Well, you didn't come clean." Well, he was perfectly right, I didn't.

When I met with Mannix, he said, "We want you to know that we understand what you did when you refused to discuss the contract with us, because you knew you couldn't talk. We would like you to know that we appreciate that." I said, "Mr. Mannix, I thank you. It's nice to know that had the situation been reversed, you would've done the same thing." And I left.

I made a point of coming to the studio the next day. I wanted to show that I was not afraid to be seen. They used to have a huge employee dining room—it's not quite as big now. Mr. Mayer took great pride in it, they had chicken soup there, and it was very good, by the way. Well, there was a music table where my colleagues and I sat, and I decided that I would not embarrass them, or me, and make it necessary for some guys to get up and ostentatiously walk away. I would go and sit by myself—which was really kind of unusual, because I usually sat there. I'm sure some of them felt very friendly toward me, maybe most of them. Anyhow, so I'm sitting there by myself, and after a while, a guy arises from across the room and starts to walk toward me—I knew instantly who it was, of course—and he ostentatiously walks all the way over to be seen coming to sit with me. And he sat with me, and that was John Houseman,[7] who was my friend and a guy I'd worked with. I've done several film scores for him. It was a wonderful thing for him to do. Because, you know, there were people on the Left who thought I was a fink and who were never going to think any other way. One of my friends—he died tragically of a heart attack some years ago—I heard him say once at a party when he was talking to his wife, "But he was an informer, wasn't he?"

But one of the most amazing of all those guys, by the way, and this was very important to me, was a man named John Howard Lawson, who was a great man. I mean a really great man.[8] I think he may have been the head of the Party here. As the boss of that, he had to exercise a certain amount of discipline, but the funny part was he was a good friend and a client of my friend Inez Melson. She was my business manager—she was also Marilyn Monroe's business manager, and she was also John Houseman's business manager. In other words, she took care of my insurance and stuff—a witty, wonderful woman who's now gone. She told me several times, "You know, I've talked to Jack Lawson about you." I never called him Jack. "I talked to Jack about you and he says he understands perfectly and he bears you no ill will." I'm sure she never said it this way, but it was clear—and she told me that several times, because she knew that I was like a wounded schmuck and that it was good to know there was somebody who was in a position to know all this without needing a scapegoat. It meant a lot to me to hear that. It also meant a lot to me when Houseman, who is a man of integrity, came over and spoke to me.

This thing has a long memory. I once went to a party in New York with my wife, who was working in a show, and I could see people whispering and withdrawing. It's quite an experience, if you think you've led a relatively decent life, and I'm convinced I have.

I was at a concert one time. It was late and I was backstage and this guy brushed past me, a bass player in the L.A. Philharmonic. He said, "Don't worry, you'll get yours." I knew he was a left-wing type and I didn't like him, because I thought he was a person of no consequence. But that was his big moment, and you can't take those away from people. I don't think the Communist Party had it in for me, but I received calls at night, threats, stuff like that.

---

[7]John Houseman (1902–88), producer, actor, director, and stage and screen writer, co-founder with Orson Welles of the Mercury Theatre.

[8]For another view of Lawson, see Edward Dmytryk earlier in this chapter.

Jesus, I'll never forget one day. I was out in Malibu, at the house of a director, and there was a very beautiful young woman there, a very well-known person in films, and he of course was a hell of a fine director. They were just having a little conversation as if I wasn't listening, because I was with a couple of other people. And I'll never forget him whispering to her while I sat there, "Do you realize what this guy *did?*"

However, in the intervening years, there are some people who seem to have—I don't know that the expression suits me—"come around" in a very interesting way, and have decided—I don't know whether they've decided on the actual issue of whether I did right or did wrong—but somehow they've become convinced that I am just a person and not just some son of a bitch they can pin a label on.

I was, as you know, written about, and there are people who, to this day, consider me to be a person of moral turpitude. As I told Victor Navasky[9] myself—I remember what I said to him, I would never say this to myself now, but I feel it—I said, "Isn't it funny, I've forgiven everybody else, but I have not forgiven myself." And I just had to turn away, you know.

I may've encountered a few of the people I named, but none of them vilified me. One of the guys who called me up to tell me he'd named me was as bewildered as I was in a way, except he seemed very self-possessed. After I testified, I saw him and it was business as usual, except strangely enough, I was a little annoyed with him. Not so much for naming me, but because I think he abased himself. But remember, that committee was incredibly cruel. I mean, the way in which they humiliated Larry Parks. Was that necessary? It was *not* necessary.

You understand what they were doing? They were in the business of intimidating people. They were in the business of saying, "Mine is bigger than yours. We're the patriots and you guys are the subversives." And I was trying to say, "Show me where we were subversive. Show me something we did. Tell me."

I don't like being given the opportunity to "exculpate" myself, because people are going to make up their own minds and I don't give a fuck what they think. It's too far gone, and I have, in a way, made my peace with it—and I'm sure that you can see that I *haven't*. But it's still a very strange thing, and I am not sure that it would've done humanity any good if I had destroyed myself, if I'd just gone and said "Screw you" and gone to jail like

---

[9]Victor Navasky interviewed Raksin for his book on the ethics of informing, *Naming Names* (New York: Viking, 1980).

Adrian Scott, and those guys who hated me bitterly. I see one of them frequently and he does not appear to hate me—he went to jail. I still run into people who were active then. And there are a couple, I'm sure, who would walk on the other side of the street to avoid me. And I'm very happy about that, because they get a little extra exercise that they wouldn't get any other way. If you can't make any other contribution to society, what is life? It's pretty wild; it's pretty wild.

I'll tell you what I would do differently. I would try to be a bit more eloquent and defiant—but I was defiant enough for anybody. I think I was as eloquent as you could get. I found out that Dalton Trumbo—I hardly knew Trumbo, but he was one of Inez's clients—he also told her that he understood my situation and was able to make a differentiation. That was why John Houseman came to me, because he did not see this as being the same as all those other abject belly-scrapings. I was amazed that Trumbo would do this, because he was a man of fabulous integrity and he also was a man of very great bravery. He just let 'em have it.

Arts and Entertainment

From Hollywood the Red Scare hit radio and television, attempted an ill-fated run on Broadway, then turned to the print media.

In radio and television, the premier blacklister was *Red Channels: The Report of Communist Influence in Radio and Television,* a regular publication of American Business Consultants,[1] a Red-baiting concern founded by three former FBI agents. Behind its garish cover (depicting a red hand reaching for a broadcaster's microphone) was a list of 151 persons who, the editors claimed, were linked with a variety of "Communist causes." The "links," cited in each case, were organizations deemed subversive by the Attorney General, HUAC, California's little HUAC, and other sources, including the authors of *Red Channels* themselves.

Despite its claims, *Red Channels* rarely revealed anything more sinister than volunteerism.[2] But its first appearance in June 1950 marked the onset of the most vicious blacklisting in the entertainment industry. Known as "the Bible of Madison Avenue," the little anti-Red book was huddled over by network executives, advertising agencies, radio-TV packagers, and sponsors. Its belief that Communists were "infiltrating" the airwaves and must be removed became dogma. Accepting *Red Channels* also meant accepting *Counterattack*'s political doctrine. As John Cogley observed, "The standards of employability were *Counterattack*'s; the measure of patriotism was *Counterattack*'s; 'pro-Communist' and 'anti-Communist' opinions, acts, and associations, in the last analysis, were judged as *Counterattack* judges them."[3]

---

[1] Also the publishers of *Counterattack: The Newsletter of Facts to Combat Communism.*

[2] In 1945, actress Ireene Wicker lent her house for a benefit for Spanish refugee children. For this, she garnered a mention in *Red Channels* and was banned from television.

[3] John Cogley, *Report on Blacklisting* (Fund for the Republic, 1956), Vol. 2, p. 2.

The great threat was that unless the listers had their way, a massive consumer boycott of television sponsors would ensue. No such effort ever materialized, but faced with sporadic letter-writing campaigns and criticism from such reactionary columnists as Ed Sullivan and Victor Riesel, the industry buckled to a chimeric fear of lost revenue.

The first to fall was Jean Muir, a film actress contracted to play a lead role on CBS's *The Aldrich Family.* Muir was listed in *Red Channels.* In August 1950, *Counterattack* organized a protest aimed at Jell-O, the General Foods sponsor of the show, and Young & Rubicam, its advertising agency. At the first sign of adverse publicity, the sponsor replaced the actress.

Security officers soon reigned over network hiring; loyalty oaths and security checks were required for even the lowliest of employees. By 1952, blacklisting was embedded in the industry—and went far beyond the names in *Red Channels.* Blacklisting rags sprang up like stinkweed, touting an aura of vigilance: *Aware, Inc., File 13,* and *Firing Line.* Given the capacity to wound and to heal, the editors of these journals (known as "clearance men") would work their restorative powers on the listed for a hefty fee.

The rapid breeding exacerbated the already complex industry. In Hollywood, hiring was largely controlled by a handful of studios, but in radio-TV, advertising agencies, networks, program packagers, and sponsors all had a voice in the process. The result was a multiplicity of lists and procedures, with different policies for different agencies. Political screening became a secret maze which required the most arcane knowledge to navigate. An actor might be acceptable for one agency or network, but not to certain sponsors, or to none at all.

In order to work, a blacklistee needed to be "cleared." Hollywood had its open ritual of humiliation, but the way home in radio-TV was an obscure trail with few markings. Anyone who was "cleared" had to satisfy those who had blacklisted him or her in the first place. Potential employers had to be assured of no difficulties if the blacklistee was employed. Sponsors had to be certain that those who demanded the original blacklisting were placated. To travel this passage one needed a guide, a sort of political Sherpa, who knew the "right people."

Traveling under the guise of "public-relations experts," these envoys would first arrange an FBI interview, where the blacklistee was to declare his patriotism and answer all questions. The next step for this "expert" was to discover where his client was blacklisted, who in the industry was blocking employment, and who outside the industry was keeping up the controversy. Each one of these "clearance men" must then be courted and convinced of the client's repentance and Americanism. This process required multiple "confessions" and tearful private audiences. If all went smoothly, a well-placed phone call allowed the performer to appear on a CBS show, the toughest of the networks, as a general signal that the artist was usable.

In August 1955, HUAC held hearings on "Communist infiltration" in the Broadway theater. Twenty-three witnesses were called, twenty-two of which were decidedly "unfriendly," invoking not only the First and Fifth Amendments to the Constitution, but the Fourth, Sixth, Eighth, Ninth, Tenth, and Fourteenth Amendments as well. In Hollywood or on Madison Avenue, such a response would have led to professional oblivion, but not so on Broadway. In the main, it was ability and not political conformity that counted in the theater. A number of Broadway performers did have trouble finding work, but there was no organized blacklisting, no "security officers," no "clearance" system.[4] The independent traditions of New York's legitimate theater militated against political blacklisting.

The most crucial tradition was the freewheeling entrepreneurial nature of theater. The complex financing of Hollywood and radio-TV did not exist on Broadway. Individual backers had to be convinced the show had possibilities, and this was arranged by personal contacts between a producer and his "angels." Playwright Arthur Miller, banned in Hollywood and television, had no trouble mounting a production on Broadway. Given Miller's reputation, any investment in his work was considered wise—including his 1953 production of *The Crucible*, an open attack on political witch-hunting. The audience also played a role. Dedicated New York theatergoers were the last to stay away from a play because of an actor's politics. Tourists, who might feel differently at home, were on holiday in New York and unlikely to discriminate in so gala a mood.

Outside of the Big Apple, however, offending actors were regularly picketed by the American Legion, and a number of road shows were closed. Provincial theaters were attacked. Seattle's Repertory Playhouse collapsed under the combined weight of Washington's little HUAC and the trial of its director for contempt of Congress. But theater resisted here as well. In 1956, Gale Sondergaard was billed to star in *Anastasia* at Philadelphia's Playhouse in the Park. Blacklisted in Hollywood since 1951

[4]One unforeseen result of blacklisting was the rapid growth of off-Broadway theater. With the glut of blacklisted artists from Hollywood and television, top talent filled small theaters with productions of Ibsen, Shaw, and Chekhov. Of course, there was an equal reaction to this as well. Now talent wishing to make it in Hollywood and TV found themselves blacklisted for appearing in off-Broadway productions.

for pleading the Fifth, Sondergaard was a red flag to the bulls of the American Legion and the VFW; even HUAC arrived in town to subpoena the actress (she took the Fifth again). Yet, in spite of all the publicity, the show went on to become the highest grosser of the Philadelphia season.

Without the enthusiasm of the right-wing press and the timidity of its liberal counterpart, the Red Scare would have made far less headway. The Hearst chain, with its eighteen newspapers, nine magazines, and three radio stations, led the pack. Hearst papers from coast to coast composed their pages into one long Red-bashing howl. Though none could compete with Hearst columnists[5] for venom and vindictiveness, the columnists of the Patterson-McCormick chain (with papers in New York, Chicago, and Washington, D.C.) were a close second. Hundreds of local papers sustained the panic,[6] corning their readers with ever larger portions of hatred, while hunting for secret Reds among the rosters of their rival papers.

On the other hand, the avowedly liberal New York Times offered only token resistance. While sensitive to the civil liberties of anti-Communist liberals, it remained largely numb to the civil liberties of the Left. After March 1947, the Times refused to carry ads from organizations deemed subversive by the Attorney General. Increasingly its headlines reflected the assumptions of the Right: COMMUNIST INFLUX SEEN IN ALL FIELDS. The respectable New York Herald Tribune abandoned its calm mien: THE THREAT OF RED SABOTAGE: SARDINE CANS USED TO IMPORT COMMUNIST MANUALS OF DESTRUCTION.[7] The Tribune also ran regular installments of "The Red Underground," purple tales of Red intrigue penned by FBI informer Herbert Philbrick.

When it came to firing left-wing journalists, the liberal press was no less trigger-happy than its reactionary brethren. Scores were fired from major newspapers and small-town dailies, magazines, and wire services. The American Newspaper Guild offered little support, especially after 1948,

[5]George Sokolsky, Howard Rushmore, Westbrook Pegler, Victor Riesel, and J. B. Matthews were among the leading Red-baiting journalists of the era, active not only in destroying careers but also in reviving them in their equally lucrative careers as "clearance men."

[6]The Miami Daily News discovered Red Army plans to make Miami its first port of call. One Cincinnati Enquirer headline read: COMMUNISTS MARK 12 CITY PLANTS FOR SABOTAGE!

[7]In 1949, a sailor clearing spoiled goods from the hold of a ship in Philadelphia harbor opened a sardine can in which he found thirty-three tiny pamphlets published in Spanish in 1946 and 1947. Purported to be sports handbooks, they contained instructions on how to sabotage public utilities. The cargo was intended for Spain, where resistance groups still battled the forces of fascist dictator Generalissimo Franco.

when fourteen years of effective Communist leadership went down to defeat in guild elections.

In 1955, the Senate Internal Security Subcommittee (James Eastland presiding) opened hearings on subversion in the press. Eastland's star witness was CBS correspondent Winston Burdett, who had once worked on the defunct *Brooklyn Eagle.* Burdett admitted his past Party membership (1937 to 1940), named thirteen former colleagues and ten others as Reds, then confessed to an astoundingly inept career as a Soviet spy in Europe and Asia.[8] On the second round of hearings, Eastland specifically targeted the *New York Times,* which had long been a bone in the senator's throat for its strong criticism of his segregationist policies. The subcommittee passed out thirty-eight subpoenas, all but eight of which were directed at the *New York Times.*

Eastland and SISS claimed that reports of investigative hearings held by Senators Pat McCarran and Joe McCarthy had been twisted in the press. In New York, only the doggedly independent *Post* sounded the alarm.[9] Calling the sub-committee's tactics "crude political blackmail," the *Post* announced that "if the United States press is prepared to have its news columns policed by Senator Eastland, it is headed for total servitude. It is time for publishers and editors to stand up." Unfortunately, very few chose to rise. One poll reported that out of 190 daily papers in the nation's largest cities, 112 remained silent on the SISS investigation, thirty-three strongly supported it, and only thirty-five criticized it.

While Angus Cameron, who was forced out of Little, Brown, was perhaps the sole editor to be blacklisted in the publishing industry, works by "controversial" writers were rejected for any number of noncontroversial reasons. Author Howard Fast found his best-selling novels no longer to the industry's liking. The venerable *New Yorker* closed its pages to longtime contributor Kay Boyle. Similarly, Nelson Algren, John Sanford, Josephine Herbst, Meridel Le Sueur, Tom McGrath, and numerous others

[8]For more on this story, see Melvin Barnet in this chapter.

[9]Not until January 5, 1956, the last day of the hearings, did the *New York Times* respond editorially to its predicament. Entitled "The Voice of a Free Press," the editorial accepted the propriety of an investigation of the press by a government agency, unless it was "motivated by ulterior purpose." Further, the *Times* would not "knowingly employ" a Communist in its news or editorial departments. All such employees would be summarily dismissed. The editorial asserted, "It is our business to decide whom we shall employ and not employ. We do not propose to hand over that function to the Eastland Committee." Regrettably, the *Times* had already fired three editorial employees who had refused to inform before the sub-committee. For the story of one of them, see Melvin Barnet in this chapter.

found major publishing houses closed to them. Literary grants were not awarded to radical writers, book clubs rarely selected their works, and radical critics were dropped from the review media. The small presses that took up the slack labored in obscurity, isolated from the media and ducking occasional blows from Red-hunters.[10]

More than fifteen hundred radio and TV employees were blacklisted, at least nine of whom were pushed to suicide. Three other deaths were a direct result of the blacklist. Thirty-five hit the blacklist in the print media.

[10]For the trials of one small press, see Angus Cameron's tale in this chapter of publishing Harvey Matusow's *False Witness.*

MARK GOODSON

A highly successful television producer whose game shows have included *What's My Line, To Tell the Truth, I've Got a Secret, Password,* and *Family Feud.* He is cordial, cool, and direct. We meet in a posh office on Wilshire Boulevard.

I'm not sure when it began, but I believe it was early 1950. At that point, I had no connection with the blacklisting that was going on, although I had heard about it in the motion picture business and heard rumors about things that had happened on other shows, like *The Aldrich Family.* My first experience really was when we settled into a fairly regular panel on *What's My Line?* in mid-1950. The panel consisted of the poet Louis Untermeyer, Dorothy Kilgallen, Arlene Francis, and Hal Block, a comedy writer. Our sponsor was Stopette, a deodorant.

A few months into the show, I began getting mail on Louis Untermeyer. He had been listed in *Red Channels.* He was one of those folks who had supported the left-wing forces against Franco in Spain. I know that he also had allowed his name to be affiliated with the Joint Anti-Fascist Refugee Committee and had been a sponsor of the 1948 May Day parade. Back in the early 1920s,[1] he had written articles for *The Masses.* But he was certainly

[1]Louis Untermeyer (1885–1977) began publishing his poetry in *The Masses* in 1913. During World War One, the magazine's antiwar position ran afoul of the Postmaster General, who

not an active political person, at least as far as I knew.

CBS and Stopette also began receiving letters of protest. First, it was just a few postcards. Then it grew. Members of the Catholic War Veterans put stickers on drugstore windows, red, white, and blue stickers, warning, "Stop Stopette Until Stopette stops Untermeyer."

We didn't pay too much attention until we got the call from CBS. Untermeyer and I were summoned to Ralph Colin's office, who was the general counsel for CBS at the time. Louis and Colin knew each other. Ralph asked him why he lent his name to the group. "I thought it was a good cause," Untermeyer said. "Louis, you're being very naive. These are very difficult times and you've put us in a bad spot. We're going to have to drop you." Untermeyer was very apologetic, but the decision had been made. He was let go.

I remember leaving that office feeling embarrassed. Untermeyer was in his sixties, a man of considerable dignity. He was a good American poet and I liked him; he was funny and articulate on the show. What's more, I had no political ax to grind.

That was the last of that kind of meeting. Soon afterwards, CBS installed a clearance division. There wasn't any discussion. We would just get the word—"Drop that person"—and that was supposed to be it. Whenever we booked a guest or a panelist on *What's My Line?* or *I've Got a Secret,* one of our assistants would phone up and say, "We're going to use so-and-so." We'd either get the okay, or they'd call back and say, "Not clear," or "Sorry, can't use them." Even advertising agencies—big ones, like Young & Rubicam and BBD&O—had their own clearance departments. They would never come out and say it. They would just write off somebody by saying, "He's a bad actor." You were never supposed to tell the person what it was about; you'd just unbook them. They never admitted there was a blacklist. It just wasn't done.

Some fairly substantial names were off-limits—big stars like Leonard Bernstein, Harry Belafonte, Abe Burrows, Gypsy Rose Lee, Judy Holliday, Jack Gilford, Uta Hagen, and Hazel Scott. Everyone, from the stars to the bit-part actors, was checked. We once did a show in California called *The Rebel,* and we used wranglers to take care of the horses—we had to clear all of their names. CBS, in particular, asked for loyalty oaths to be signed by

---

revoked its mailing license under the Espionage Act of 1917. *The Masses'* editors were vindicated in court, but lost access to the mails through a legal technicality. The magazine was succeeded by the *Liberator,* which ran until 1924.

everybody, making sure that you were not un-American. So far as I know, no one ever refused.

In 1952, *I've Got a Secret* got a new sponsor, R. J. Reynolds Tobacco Company, with its advertising agency, William Este. When they came aboard, someone from the agency called me and said, "Please get rid of Henry Morgan," one of the regular panelists on the show. Morgan had been named in *Red Channels*. I had known Henry for a long time; he was one of those young curmudgeons who was acidic at times, but he was by no means a Communist. His wife was involved with radical politics, but they were getting a divorce, and to some extent his name was just smeared.

I went to the agency and told them that they were crazy to try and get rid of Henry Morgan. They agreed that the charge in *Red Channels* was absurd, but they said they couldn't take the risk. That was the main thing— mail accusing them of being pro-Communist was not going to sell cigarettes. They gave me an ultimatum: dump Morgan or face the show's cancellation.

So I went to Garry Moore, the MC of the show and an established comedian. He was a conservative, a Republican from Maryland. I knew that he liked Morgan. I said that if he'd be willing to back me up, I'd tell the agency I'd do the show without a sponsor. He agreed without hesitation. I phoned up William Este and said, "We're not going to do the show without Henry." The people at the agency were flabbergasted. It was virtually unheard-of to have this kind of confrontation. They told me they'd think about it, and in the end, they actually backed down. The show was not canceled, and some weeks later Morgan's name simply vanished from *Red Channels*.

Morgan never even knew. When I wrote the article about my experience,[2] Henry called me. "I did not know that I was about to be dropped," he said. "I knew I was in *Red Channels* and I was outraged about that, but I didn't know I was about to be dropped." It was a revelation for him.

The Morgan episode was my first act of resistance. It was not something my lawyers ever encouraged. The watchword in the business is "Don't make waves."

The studios and the advertising agencies didn't have to subscribe to *Red Channels*. It was one of about a dozen publications. There were several private lists, and the major agencies and networks exchanged lists, most of which had several names each. I'd help you out by giving you my list and you'd help me out by giving me your list. There was a big interchange of

[2] *New York Times Magazine,* January 13, 1991.

listings. A fellow called Danny O'Shea was in charge of the listings at CBS, an ex–FBI man. *Red Channels* would maybe have a couple of hundred names, but there might be on the other list at CBS several hundred more. Anybody could show up on a list, stars, technicians, cowboys.

Faye Emerson was a regular panelist on *I've Got a Secret* around the same time. Faye was a liberal, very attractive actress who was also hostessing a show called *Author Meets the Critics*. It was a show like *Meet the Press*, with a series of critics dealing with a book. On one episode, they discussed a book that advocated the United States' possible recognition of Red China. For the most part, the critics agreed with the author. The show went on the air live. The very next day I got a call from the William Este Agency, the same people who had protested Morgan. They told me to drop Faye Emerson, that, because of what she had said, she was a Red China sympathizer. I said, "It doesn't make any sense. We have no control over what Faye Emerson says on a different show." We stood up and said, "No, we won't drop her." And for some reason, they ended up listening to us. But she could very easily have been cut.

Anna Lee was an English actress on a later show of ours called *It's News to Me*. The sponsor was Sanka Coffee, a product of General Foods. The advertising agency was Young & Rubicam. One day, I received a call telling me we had to drop one of our panelists, Anna Lee, immediately. They said she was a radical, that she wrote a column for the *Daily Worker*. They couldn't allow that kind of stuff on the air. They claimed they were getting all kinds of mail. It seemed incongruous to me that this little English girl, someone who seemed very conservative, would be writing for a Communist newspaper. It just didn't sound right.

I took her out to lunch. After a little social conversation, I asked her about her politics. She told me that she wasn't political, except she voted Conservative in England. Her husband was a Republican from Texas.

I went back to the agency and said, "You guys are really off your rocker. Anna Lee is nothing close to a liberal." They told me, "Oh, you're right. We checked on that. It's a different Anna Lee who writes for the *Daily Worker*." I remember being relieved and saying, "Well, that's good. You just made a mistake. Now we can forget this." But that wasn't the case. They told me, "We've still got to get rid of her, because the illusion is just as good as the reality. If our client continues to get the mail, no one is going to believe him when he says there's a second Anna Lee." At that point I lost it. I told them their demand was outrageous. They could cancel the show if they wanted to, but I would not drop somebody whose only crime was sharing a name. When I got back to my office, there was a phone call waiting for me. It was from a friend of mine at the agency. He said, "If I were you, I would not lose my temper like that. If you want to argue, do it quietly. After you left, somebody said, 'Is Goodson a pinko?' You could get yourself a very bad label around town." That would have caused me a lot of trouble. All I had to be was in *Red Channels* myself.

Abe Burrows was a regular panelist on *The Name's the Same,* a show we had on ABC in 1952. The sponsor was the Swanson Foods Company. Burrows was a brilliant comedy writer, a nice round-faced fellow whose big hit was a radio show called *Duffy's Tavern.* During the war years Burrows had apparently taken part in cultural activities sponsored by Communists in California. To clear his name, he appeared twice before the House Un-American Activities Committee. They released him from further questioning, apparently cleared. But when he went down to testify, it made headlines, and if you made headlines, you got in *Red Channels.* It wasn't long after we booked him on the show that the protest mail began to roll in.

ABC was a brand-new network at the time and didn't have a clearance department. So I would just take the mail and quietly throw it away. One day I got a call from one of the Swanson brothers. He asked if we were getting mail on Burrows. I said we were. He said they were getting a lot of mail. I said we were getting some. He asked if Burrows was a Communist. I said, "I don't think so." "Then why is he in *Red Channels?* Why is he getting this mail?" I said, "I think that a long time ago, during the war, he wrote some stuff that was pro-Russian and once belonged to some very liberal groups." Swanson sounded relieved. "If he's not a Communist now, then forget it," he said.

Six months later, he called me back. He said, "Are you familiar with the Johnson Supermarkets up in Syracuse, New York?" I had heard about them. Although Mr. Johnson only owned three markets, he was famous for influencing policy throughout the country in the grocery business.[3] Whenever a "controversial" performer appeared on television, he hung signs over the sponsoring company's goods, warning the public that they employed

---

[3]By the early 1950s no one worked in radio or television without the consent of Laurence A. Johnson. He and his family monitored all network programming and took down the names of those actors, writers, and directors whose politics were considered offensive. Working in concert with a local American Legion post, Johnson threatened the sponsors of the programs with a consumer boycott of their products unless the artists he named were fired. It was the implied support of the American Legion (and its millions of members) that made him such a powerful figure. Johnson died in 1962 at the age of seventy-three, a few days before the courts awarded radio personality John Henry Faulk $3.5 million in a suit against him and Aware, Inc.

subversives. Swanson told me that Johnson had put out ballots in the store that said, "Do you want any part of your purchase price of Swanson Foods to be used to hire Communist fronters? Vote yes or no." Of course, nobody said yes. They took the ballot and marked no. Then Johnson gathered all these ballots together and sent copies of them to stores all over the country. They began getting rid of all Swanson Foods products.

Swanson said, "Look, we love you, we love Burrows. We would like to be liberal, but we're not going to let our business go down the drain for one man." I said, "I understand." That was the end of Abe Burrows, at least on television. Abe understood completely. Luckily for him, he had a major Broadway hit at the time called *Guys and Dolls,* so he did not suffer. The people who suffered the most were the ones who had little or no names. Every once in a while, they'd get a part in a theater on Broadway, but basically they just vanished.

It was difficult to get people to stand up against this. The people who did stand up were your conservative friends, like Garry Moore and in the beginning, the Swanson brothers. I can understand that. The more liberal the network, the more frightened they were. CBS, after all, was concerned because in Congress, CBS was being called the Communist Broadcasting System. All three networks were run by Jewish Americans. They were concerned with being thought of as un-American. The first major company to break the blacklist was Ford Motors, with a broadcast of a Leonard Bernstein concert. They were strong enough and conservative enough that nobody could accuse them of anything.

I think it's very important to note that I was not really dealing with Communists. I was dealing with people who were being tarred with the brush at a time when it was dangerous to be liberal. That was basically it. Whether I would actually have gone to bat for someone like Paul Robeson, an avowed Communist at the time, I don't know.[4]

My life had been apolitical, I had never been involved. I was just operating out of a sense of not wanting to see people pushed around. I did not do it from any ideological point of view, except out of a fairly liberal, centrist position. My lawyers, nice liberal guys, certainly did not advise me to stand up and get involved. Most people looked at the names in *Red Channels* and said, "Somebody says they're left-wing and that's that. We don't want to get into trouble."

You can't know what it was like. Nobody today has any feeling of what the atmosphere was like then, to know that one remark in Jack O'Brien's

[4]Robeson, although very close to the Party and to the Soviet Union, denied under oath in 1946 that he was a member.

television column in the *Journal-American* could hurt somebody badly. We were all scared.

Mark Goodson died on September 18, 1992, at the age of seventy-seven.

FRANK TARLOFF

An articulate, considered man, with traces of Brooklyn still in his voice. "I do talks on the blacklist at various colleges. The kids are fascinated by it, they sit there spellbound. The blacklist is now more than forty years ago. So to them it's an academic thing, and suddenly somebody says, 'I was part of it. I lived through this.' Well, it's a revelation."

I came out here cold in '42. Luckily I got a job at MGM. At the commissary, I found myself at what was known as the Red Table, sitting with Dalton Trumbo, with Paul Jarrico, all the lefties. It was a marvelous experience for me, these people were much more established than me, I was just a beginner. But because of the political affiliations I was their peer. I must tell you, with everything that's happened and horror of the blacklist, I don't regret one minute of it. I got to know people I'd never gotten to know otherwise, people that I admired and respected a great deal. I got my money's worth out of it, I certainly did, despite the fact that the shit hit the fan.

I joined the Party in the mid-forties. I was never that actively involved. I went to meetings. I had my reservations about what was going on at the meetings, but like many of us it was, "Okay, there are things we're not too happy about, but overall it is very important, very good, and well-intentioned," and so you overlook a couple of things, including some very boring sessions—*very boring!*

I was blacklisted for about twelve years. I wrote with fronts and phony names for twelve years. David Lang and Pauline Townsend named me.[1]

---

[1]Pauline Townsend, screenwriter, gave eighty-three names on March 12, 1953. David A. Lang, screenwriter, listed seventy-five names for HUAC on March 24, 1953.

The breach between the friendly and the unfriendly witnesses was like a wall coming down—to this day. We don't talk to each other, we don't acknowledge them as people. They are pariahs. They destroyed lives. It's as sharp a division as can be. They don't exist.

I was subpoenaed in the late fifties, maybe in the last batch, but I had left the Party long before. It was not fear that did it, I just stopped going. Around '51 or '52, I just lost interest. When I appeared, I took the Fifth Amendment. I was totally uncooperative. I never doubted what I would do. There was never any question that I was going to be other than an unfriendly witness.

The practice of the committee was not to reveal a name until they had served a subpoena. So you were not blacklisted until you were named. Now if you had a clue—and most of us suspected sooner or later they were going to get to us—what you tried to do was work as long as possible and avoid the subpoena—evade it really. I knew they were looking for me, and when I was working on a job, I knew what I earned might be what I was going to live on for I didn't know how long. So it became essential not to get served.

When my wife and I would come back from an evening out, we would stop the car about a block or two away from where we lived. I would get out and she would drive on to the house to see whether anybody was lurking there. And if it was clear, she would wave me on and I would come running into the house. I had done nothing, but I was living like a fugitive.

I never answered the doorbell. Never. We had a housekeeper at the time and she answered the door one day and there were the two guys with the hats. She was smart enough to say I was not home, then she came and said, "There were those two men there, and I think you should know that they're looking for you." I knew they were out with a subpoena for me, so I began to really avoid the thing very actively. It became very important not to get that subpoena, or to hold out as long as possible.

They finally caught up with me. I was at a studio writing a television show called *I Married Joan,* with Joan Davis. Getting onto a studio lot was impossible if you didn't work there, but the investigator for the committee had no trouble getting on the lot. He served me in my office. I was immediately fired, not only by the studio but by my agent, the William Morris office. In ten or fifteen minutes, there was a wire—"We no longer represent you." It was that clear-cut.

You've heard about the clearance process. If a show was going to hire any writer, actor, director, or anybody, the names went somewhere—somewhere at the networks, somewhere in the studios—to someone. And the list would come back with names crossed out and names not crossed out and the crossed-out ones simply were not hired. Nobody was in a position to hire without submitting these names. It was a marvelously well organized operation, and they were hitting people in their most vulnerable area, which was their livelihood. Dreadful things happened to people—you just couldn't work.

Now for a writer, for me, it was not as devastating. For actors and directors who had to appear on stage, obviously, they were in terrible trouble. A writer could work at home and manage to get somebody to front for him, which I did a great deal of, but I was very lucky.

In television, there were only a handful of us doing comedy. We all knew each other very well. So I had no trouble getting fronts. I never paid for a front, but a lot of people did. There was a going business on it, in New York especially.

I was working through a front within six months. I knew a writer who knew Sheldon Leonard,[2] and he recommended me to Sheldon. He said "Okay, do me a script for *The Danny Thomas Show.*" Which I did, and apparently he liked it well enough to continue doing it. He hired me despite the blacklist, taking a big big chance.

At that time he and Danny Thomas owned *The Danny Thomas Show, The Dick Van Dyke Show, The Andy Griffith Show.* They were kings of television. Now Danny was not political at all, and if anything his friends were sort of on the Right. So I asked Sheldon at one point, "Does Danny know?" And Sheldon said, "I would never have done this without telling Danny." So Danny knew, and it got to the point where I used to go to rehearsals and Danny would see me and let me know that he knew I was there.

There's a very funny story on that. The problem with working with fronts was that the front's name was officially the writer, which meant the withheld tax was in his name, the withheld Social Security was in his name, and there was no way to get it back. So one day Sheldon said, "Look, let's establish a pseudonym for you and we'll avoid the front situation. For the first one I'll have to give you a couple dollars less as a new writer, and then the second one, you're right back on top of the scale." I said, "That's a marvelous idea."

So I had to go find a name, and it's not easy to pick a name. But my son's name was Eric Shepherd Tarloff. So I figured I'm Eric Shepherd. Sheldon had to submit the name to the William Morris office. So he says, "I'm

[2]A former stage actor who played character parts in dozens of films, usually the gangster. He later became a successful television producer and director.

going to hire Eric Shepherd." The William Morris office gets in touch with Sheldon, he was a very big client then, and says, "Sheldon, don't do it, there's too much at stake here. This is such a phony name. It's obviously a phony name. There is no Eric Shepherd as a writer. You are jeopardizing major television shows."

So Sheldon said to me, "Pick a name that sounds like every other comedy writer." Now at that time, I would say ninety-nine percent of the comedy writers were Jewish. If there was a non-Jew, he was like a freak in this thing. We were all Jewish. So I picked a name, David Adler. And he submitted it. I knew it was the right name when a very funny thing happened.

I was having lunch at Schwab's, the old Schwab's, with a fellow named Henry that I was working with as David Adler. Two writers came in who knew me very well, 'cause they were also writing *The Danny Thomas Show*. They say, "Hi, Frank. Hi, Henry." Then they turned to him and say, "Who are you writing with these days?" And he says, "David Adler." They say, "He's wonderful." [Laughs.] It sounded like a comedy writer, you see—so I knew it was the right name.

At first there were fronts and then there was the David Adler pseudonym. But apart from whatever psychological trauma there was, and my wife being frightened and uneasy, I suffered probably less than almost anybody else out of this thing. After six months, I was in there earning as much as I could, as much as was earnable. I simply couldn't have wanted more—except it was not under my name.

If the studios had said no to the committee, what could they do? Nothing, it would've been over. But they buckled, and it was fear that did that whole thing. And to me, one of the major villains of the piece was Dore Schary. The major liberal in town at that time. A major screenwriter-producer, very liberal man. I think they bought him because he went to the Waldorf meeting in Washington and when they said, "Give us the Ten and that will be it," he bought it. He came back and became head of MGM.

When we were going up before the committee, we went with lawyers, of course, and we had to raise money for the legal fees. People would give me twenty-five dollars or something like that.

Now some marvelous things happened and some terrible things. I said to a guy I knew very slightly, we had just met, "We're raising money, and I hope you'll give me something." He said, "Meet me here on such-and-such date." He came in with two hundred dollars, and I said, "Jesus Christ! This is too much." He said, "Take it." He became a friend of mine for a long, long time.

On the other hand, a very close friend of mine refused to give me any money. Even though it was just between me and him. He didn't have to say why. He was scared. What if it got out? That's the thing that is hard to grasp—the fear. Because one wrong move, and you're in my position. It was not a happy moment, I'll tell you that. But on a very small other hand, I could understand it, because everybody was scared shitless. Important people in the country wouldn't say anything, until later on.

A lot of people, friends, wouldn't come to our house when we invited them. Nor would they invite us to their house. And the reason why? It was strongly believed that investigators for the committee, if they knew there was a party, went taking down license-plate numbers of cars that were parked in front of my house. Or if I would go to somebody else's house, my license number. Now, whether that was a fact or not, I don't know. But that's what kept people from doing it. They were afraid that someone's going to take down the license number of their car in front of the house of a suspect and thereby become suspect themself. It got that crazy.

In the late fifties, I went to England, and began to write pictures there. I wrote one for an American producer who was living in England, a picture that has become a kind of a minor classic, *School for Scoundrels*, with Alastair Sim and Ian Carmichael. The prick producer put his name on it. One of the shits of the Western world. I sued him and won a huge judgment, but I'll never see a penny of it.

Once Trumbo was hired publicly on *Spartacus*, the blacklist began to open. If they could hire Trumbo, then Mike Wilson and Albert Maltz could get hired. In effect it trickled down to those of us who were less well known. So that, in 1964, I did *Father Goose* for the same producer I did *School for Scoundrels*. I got an Academy Award for that. It was the first time my name was used.

Students I talk to sometimes ask, why did I become an unfriendly witness? Why did I risk this thing? I tell them I knew that someday it would be over for me. It was longer than I would have hoped, but I knew it would be over. For those who talked, it's never over. Their whole lives they carry that pain of having informed, and not out of principle. Not one person, I guarantee you, cooperated with that committee and named names out of principle—not one. They did it out of self-preservation, and if in the process it meant destroying other people who were close friends, they did it.

Taking the moral position, while maybe painful and unfortunate, is in the long run the preferable one. Even the kids carry the taint of the fathers that did this thing. You have a father whom you are supposed to respect and admire, and you get to be sixteen, seventeen, and you read a book and it's says your father finked. That does not give you a lot of stature with your children.

KAY BOYLE

A charming and eloquent woman and the author of more than forty-five works of fiction, essays, and poetry. For seven years she was a foreign correspondent for *The New Yorker*. Her husband, Baron Joseph von Franckenstein, was an OSS officer during World War Two serving behind German lines. A military government officer during the occupation, he was second in command of public affairs in Frankfurt and Bad Godesberg. After 1952, when he was denounced as a security risk, they were both blacklisted. We meet in a retirement community in Mill Valley, California.

Just toward the end of the war, my husband was captured by the Gestapo and tortured. He never revealed that he was an American officer, which was extraordinary. They talked to him in English; they refused to speak German to him. They said, "We know where you were trained," and they gave him the place in Virginia outside Washington. They knew all these things. He spoke German with a heavy Austrian accent. He kept saying, "I'm just a poor Austrian peasant. I don't know what you're talking about." So he was put in prison and sentenced to be executed the next day.

That night, he escaped with another man who'd been sentenced to death. The other man was shot in the forest where they were hiding, and my husband got to Innsbruck, which was his hometown, and the Americans were coming in on tanks. He jumped up on every tank, hugged and kissed the soldiers. And he was at the mess that evening in a tattered German uniform! [Laughs.] He said he was absolutely unconscious of it, he was so deliriously happy to see the Americans, you know. And these GIs didn't seem to notice it, until an officer came over and said, "You know, we like you a lot. We think you're great, but [laughs] could you get another uniform?"

He could've come home almost immediately, that was something like two or three weeks before the end of the war, but he was so interested in getting a democratic government in Innsbruck, and he worked on that.

There was a man in Germany who I really think caused all the trouble about my husband. He was an elderly man, and he'd been head of the Communist Comintern[1] in Central Europe years before. He was through with Communism by the time the Americans hired him. I think he was hired probably because he spoke English. He had published several political books with Faber & Faber, and took for granted that when I joined my husband there, he would be able to meet me, because I also was published by Faber & Faber. But I was working very hard and I wasn't encouraging any kind of social activities at all. Apparently a bitterness built up in him.

He was my husband's assistant in Marburg. Marburg was a lovely little university town where all sorts of hideous things were going on underneath. In the university gymnasium the students were doing military things, which they weren't supposed to do, of course, as it was during the American occupation. They were slashing each other's faces in the old Teutonic tradition of having scars.

But this man complained to everyone—especially to higher-up people—that my husband was not trying to work on the Communist question at all, that he was working on which men had been Nazis and in power. This man worked up a lot of people. My husband told him, "My directions from Washington are de-nazification. That's what I have to do." And at that time, of course, the Soviet Union was still our ally. But all that worked very much against him, obviously. If I had known I probably would've been a little bit more social, because there was another man who was very jealous of my husband, envious of all his gifts, and they, he and his wife, asked me to dinner several times, and I was writing a book, and I just said I couldn't do it. So he became very annoyed and he took on the battle too, of saying that my husband really should go after Communists.

One day, when we were on home leave in New York, I was having lunch with Roger Baldwin,[2] and on the front page of the *Herald Tribune* there was a list of names, including mine. A list of people who had been friendly with fellow travelers, or something. And Roger, who of course was a terrifically intelligent lawyer, said, "Kay, you have to write a letter to the *Herald Tribune*." And I said, "But Roger, why should I bother? It's ridiculous." And he said, "It's very important," and I didn't do it. It might've made a slight difference if I had. Who knows? The whole thing seemed to be so

---

[1]Communist International, established in 1919 and dissolved in 1943.

[2]Roger Nash Baldwin (1884–1981), founder and director (1920–50) of the American Civil Liberties Union.

absurd. I was accused of having given ten dollars to the Committee of One Thousand,[3] and about the same amount to a Bill of Rights rally in Central Park, sponsored by Paul Robeson.

Then Louis Budenz testified that I had attended Communist Party meetings with him every Saturday night in New York City, while my husband was in the Army during the war. And I never attended a political meeting anywhere, either Democratic or Republican or anything at all. But apparently—I don't know where I learned this, but I think it's accurate—he was paid one hundred and fifty dollars for every name he turned in. You know, he was working with the FBI, and when he got to me he was sort of scraping the bottom of the barrel. He'd run out of names.

In 1952, we were in Bad Godesberg. My husband got a letter from the State Department saying that charges were going to be brought against him.[4] And he could either stand trial for them or he could resign and nothing would happen. And so both of us said, "Well, of course, we'll fight it," you know. And that's what we did.

So then our lawyer suggested we should go see John McCloy, the high commissioner. Benny Ferencz was our attorney. He was the head of the Jewish Restitution Committee in Germany, one of the great people I met in my life, absolutely wonderful. He said, "We should go together, the three of us." And so we did. We went up the stairs for our appointment, and the secretary said, "I'm terribly sorry, but Mr. McCloy had to cancel all his engagements; he's not here." So then we went down the stairs and from the stairs we could see into a little hallway, partly blocked with a screen, and we looked down and there was Mr. McCloy hiding behind the screen.

The strange thing was, my husband had to read all the newspapers that were in German or French, and he would start at six o'clock every morning and he would have to have a complete résumé of them on McCloy's desk by nine o'clock. And even when he was under suspicion of being a Communist! If he wanted to, he could've, you know . . . It was absurd.

The questions at the hearing were so extraordinary. They knew every-

---

[3]An organization created to raise defense funds for the Hollywood Nineteen, declared in 1948 to be a "Communist front" by the California Fact-Finding Committee on Un-American Activities.

[4]The charges were (1) that he had been a swimming instructor at a youth camp in New Jersey which was Communist-sponsored; (2) that Kay Boyle had been a friend of Alexander Trachtenberg, a leading Communist official (Boyle had never met him); (3) that Kay Boyle had sponsored several organizations which appeared on the Attorney General's list; and (4) that Franckenstein and Boyle had been guilty of "immoral conduct" before their marriage.

thing about you. They knew when I lived in the French Alps and that it was very near Geneva, Switzerland. The prosecutor knew that the Spanish Loyalists had toured famous Spanish paintings all over Europe, and I think they were going to go on to America too, to raise money for their cause. So this prosecutor asks me, "When you were living in the French Alps, did you ever go to the shows of the Spanish painters in Geneva?" And I said, "Yes, I went several times, and took my children." And he said, "Had you been aware that those exhibitions were sponsored by the Spanish Loyalists, would you have?" But how they find out these things about one is amazing.

Well, our character witnesses were incredibly wonderful. Janet Flanner came down from Paris.[5] She'd known me for twenty-five years. And she was so wonderful, because Janet always has to speak absolutely truthfully and wittily. She was absolutely marvelous. And the prosecutor asked her if when we would have dinner together in Paris, sit in cafés talking, were there many Communist writers with us? And she said, "Well, you know, Kay and I never thought too much about that, because one doesn't in France. A very good young writer may be a member of the Communist Party, but you know, it doesn't make much difference. You don't talk about it, you're not interested in it. We haven't got the same approach to this that you people have in America."

And one of my husband's immediate superiors was there, in the Intelligence Service, and he was really terrific. He said that he was chief of the Intelligence Service, and he said, "Sometimes I wonder why we call it that, when we are questioning Joseph Franckenstein." And who else was there? Oh yes, then Bill Clark, he was the head of all the American courts in Germany, was also a character witness for my husband. And his wife, she was an American journalist. She testified for me. So we had many terrific people speaking out for us. The members of the Consular Board were weeping, because they were men we knew, who'd been to the house for cocktail parties and that sort of thing.

My husband was completely cleared in the loyalty-security hearing.[6] And

[5]Janet Flanner (1892–1978), *New Yorker* correspondent in Paris, contributed to the magazine from its founding in 1925 until her death. She wrote under the name Genet.

[6]One week after Franckenstein was cleared, State Department security officers were already preparing the ground for the charges to be reinstated. In a letter to John Sipes, legal counsel to the loyalty-security board, from Huston Lay of the general counsel's office in Bad Godesberg: "Quite apart from the questions before the Board, Franckenstein is not Americanized. . . . We did not delve into the relations between the two in respect to the child born before their marriage, although we probably should have." Seven days later, again to Sipes: "Unquestionably, [Kay Boyle] was a 'parlor pink' with a possibility that she was a member of the Communist

then Cohn and Schine came on the scene.[7] And it was really shocking. The first night they were there, they had a woman in a very nice hotel, in Bonn I guess, and apparently they got very drunk and they swung from the chandelier in their hotel room and the chandelier came down. Then the next day they went to see the high commissioner. They had an appointment with him at something like nine-thirty or ten o'clock. They had terrible hangovers apparently, and of course all this is hearsay, but I think it's a lot of truth. They had such hangovers that they had one jacket that belonged to another suit, and the pants the other man was wearing! And they really looked like derelicts.

But another thing was very interesting—in the American enclave where we lived in Bad Godesberg, people would come up to us, State Department people that we didn't know at all, and say, "I'd like to shake your hand for fighting this out." Yes, it was really extraordinary. People we didn't know at all. We had terrific support, it was really very wonderful.

Long before the hearing started, I wrote to the Whites [E. B. and Katherine]. I didn't know them terribly well, but I knew them well enough to write to them. And of course Harold Ross was dead then.[8] Now he would've just raised hell; he was such an extraordinary person. And he was always so badly treated by the other people on *The New Yorker*. We had lunch at least once a week all the time I was living in New York. I just found him fantastic. I'd pick him up at the office sometimes—and the way William Shawn[9] and the other people would be treating him. Then when I had dinner with the Whites, they would always make derogatory remarks—"Oh, poor Harold," as though he were a country bumpkin and didn't know what he was doing. It was really very sad.

So I wrote to Katherine White. I said that we were going to have a hearing and that I would appreciate it very much if I had a letter from them.

Party. . . . Franckenstein appeared to be to be almost wholly European in his outlook." Lay closed with the observation that should the board's decision be reversed, he would "certainly feel that there has been no injustice done."

[7]One month after Joseph Franckenstein was unanimously cleared by the loyalty-security board, two of Joe McCarthy's aides, Roy Cohn and David Schine, passed through on their infamous junket ferreting out Communists from the ranks of American officials abroad. Franckenstein, along with every other Foreign Service officer who had been tried, was declared "surplus" and suspended pending further inquiries in Washington.

[8]Harold Wallace Ross (1892–1951) was founder and editor (1925–51) of *The New Yorker*.

[9]William Shawn (1907–92) became the second editor of *The New Yorker* upon the death of Ross and served until 1987.

And she wrote back and said, "Kay, darling, you couldn't possibly be a Communist. Why don't you just forget about the whole thing?" Just slithering out.

Then William Shawn withdrew my accreditation.[10] I'd been seven years a foreign correspondent for *The New Yorker*. Harold Ross had been very anxious for me to write stories for him, which I did. And everything I wrote, they published. And then Harold died, of course.

I called my agent in New York and I said, "Tell William Shawn that never in my entire life do I want to have a word of mine published in *The New Yorker.*" So what does William Shawn do, when people go and talk to him about that? "Well, what could I do?" he says. "Out of the blue she said that she would never have another word . . ." He twisted it around.

Janet Flanner almost lost her mind when William Shawn withdrew my accreditation. She was just irate about this thing. When she testified for me, Shawn wrote her a very nice letter—she showed me the letter—and said that he was very sorry she had done this and that she had put *The New Yorker* in a very strange position and all that. She was enraged. She said to me, "Kay, I think you know what I want to do. I want to resign from *The New Yorker* and never write anything for them. But I can't do it. It's my one source of income." And I said, "Well, it's not necessary to do it, don't." But she really felt terribly that she didn't do it. She was a great person.

When we came back to States[11] my husband was teaching at a girls' school in Connecticut. I had an agent, and she didn't have the same requests for my work that we'd had before. And then one day she called me up in great excitement—some television company wanted my story. And she said, "It's wonderful! You're going to get six thousand dollars." I said, "Oh, marvelous." And then the next day she called me and said, "Apparently the man who was preparing the contract for it, another editor spoke to him and said no."

We fought for nine years to clear my husband's name. Our lawyer in New York was retired General Greenbaum. He was very active and very

---

[10]Shortly after her firing by Shawn, the American Civilian Occupation Forces in Germany posted a ruling that no wife of a Foreign Service officer could be accredited as a journalist. The *Stars and Stripes* noted that this ruling would affect only two people: Sonia Tomara (Mrs. William Clark), correspondent for the *Herald Tribune*, who had testified for the defense in the Franckenstein hearing, and Kay Boyle.

[11]Upon his return, Franckenstein applied to the State Department for clearance. The department then refiled the same charges of which he had just been cleared. A request for a hearing was denied, and Franckenstein was then declared a threat to the security of the United States under Executive Order 10450.

wonderful. He got out a booklet of letters from people who believed in us and all that. And with the help of William Shirer and also Ed Murrow, they wrote all sorts of letters to the State Department. So after nine years my husband was reinstated with apologies. He was sent as the cultural attaché to the embassy in Tehran. Well, I was so happy about it, it never occurred to me till I read Bill's memoirs the other day, he said it was just about the most insulting place that they could send him—even then, after all those years!

My husband went to Tehran in 1962. My son and I were going to join him in August, I think it was, or June, 1963. And when we got over there, he was dying. No one had realized it, because they said that he insisted on always coming to his desk, although they thought he didn't look very well. He was a heavy smoker, cancer of the lungs. He died at the Presidio in San Francisco.

I remember when we were having our hearing, which lasted three days, we'd come back at night to our apartment in the American enclave and I would open the windows—it was summer—I'd open the windows and I'd put on Paul Robeson singing "That's America to Me." You remember? It's a beautiful song, really beautiful.[12]

Kay Boyle died in January 1993 at age ninety.

---

[12]"The House I Live In" (Arr.: L. Allan–E. Robinson)

What is America to me?
A name, a map, or a flag I see
A certain word, Democracy
What is America to me?
　　　　* * *
The place I work in, the workers at my side
The little town or city where my people lived and died
The howdy and the handshake, the air of feeling free
The right to speak my mind out
That's America to me

JOSEPH RAUH

A prominent Washington lawyer and civil libertarian, Joseph Rauh was also a founder of Americans for Democratic Action. One of his many clients was the radical playwright Lillian Hellman. (For more on Rauh, see under "The Purge of the Civil Service.")

In 1952, Lillian Hellman[1] came to see me. She handed me her subpoena from the House Un-American Activities Committee, and I explained to her all her options. She said, "I'm not the kind of person that can go to jail. On the other hand, I don't want to plead the Fifth Amendment."

I said, "Madam, that makes you a very difficult person." She wouldn't tell about others, she wouldn't plead the Fifth Amendment, and she wouldn't go to jail. It would be a rather complicated performance.

If you tell about yourself, you have waived the privilege as to others. That's what was wrong with the whole idea. If Lillian Hellman had gone in and said, "Sure, I'll tell you about myself—I was a Commie," then when asked, "Who else was in your cell?" had answered, "I'm not going to tell you that. I plead the Fifth Amendment," the plea is no good. She has waived it by having told about herself.

I tried to explain to her why she wouldn't get away with it. Finally, we decided that she would plead the Fifth and then hold a press conference saying she only pleaded it because of the waiver: "I was ready to tell them all about myself, but I couldn't because I would have waived my privilege." So she and I are working on drafts of what we're going to say when suddenly I had this idea: "Why don't we have this out with the committee? We'll write them a letter saying, "I'm perfectly willing to tell you everything about myself. All I want is your assurance you won't ask me about other people." She agreed, and I wrote the letter. It is very famous for one sentence, "I cannot cut my conscience to fit this year's fashions," which I didn't write; Lillian did.

We delivered the letter to the committee. Three hours later we got a

---

[1]Lillian Hellman (1905–84) was a well-known playwright and screenwriter; her works include *The Children's Hour* (1934), *The Little Foxes* (1939), and *Watch on the Rhine* (1941). She also wrote *Scoundrel Time* (1976), an account of her experiences during the Red Scare. Hellman was the longtime companion of novelist Dashiell Hammett, see page 453, footnote 3.

snotty reply: "We do not make deals with witnesses." So we decided as follows: when they ask her if she's now a Communist Party member, she's going to answer no. When they say "Were you last year?" as was their practice, she'd say no. "The year before?" No. "The year before that?" "I plead the Fifth Amendment." It's a technique referred to as the "diminished Fifth."[2] The theory behind it is that there's enough period within the statute of limitations that she can plead the Fifth Amendment after two denials of the present. It is not a waiver. She's going to answer some questions, but she's not going to answer any more questions about her Communist relationship.

On the way to the committee, we agree that the proof of whether we've won or lost is going to be the headline in the *New York Times*. Does it say, "Lillian Hellman Pleads the Fifth Amendment," or does it say, "Lillian Hellman Refuses to Name Others"?

As the committee began their questioning, my associate handed out to the press the letter explaining what we're doing. The committee gets mad as hops about that. Their lawyer's screaming at me that I'm in contempt, she's in contempt, everyone's in contempt. Yet all we were doing was passing out a letter. It's pretty hard to be in contempt when you're passing out a letter.

Finally, they dismiss her. I told my associate to take Lillian to a bar and I'd meet them in a few minutes. I didn't want her to talk to the press. So he ran out with her, and I went and explained this whole thing to the press in even more detail. I was trying to be careful, giving them lots of facts, the names of cases where you'd waive your Fifth Amendment rights.

The next day, the *New York Times* headline said, "Lillian Hellman Refuses to Name Names." We had won.[3]

Joseph Rauh died on September 3, 1992, at the age of eighty-one.

---

[2]For how this technique was arrived at, see John Sanford under "The Hollywood Blacklist."
[3]While Hellman did not go to jail, she remained on the Hollywood blacklist until 1961.

ARTHUR MILLER

Miller takes time from the household chore of laying tile to spend an hour on the phone. One of the twentieth century's most influential playwrights, Miller is the author of more than a dozen plays, as well as numerous works of reportage, essays, fiction, screenplays, and autobiography. He was awarded the Pulitzer Prize in 1949 for *Death of a Salesman* and again in 1955 for *A View from the Bridge*. In 1953, he wrote *The Crucible*, a courageous treatment of the Salem witch trials of 1692 as a parable for America during the Red Scare. His most recent work, *Broken Glass*, opened on Broadway in 1994. Blacklisted for years from film, television, and radio, Miller was convicted in 1957 of contempt of Congress for refusing to name names before HUAC.

I drew some attention when I became involved with the Conference for Peace at the Waldorf in 1949.[1] That was a kind of crossroads, I guess, at the time: when the Russians were—in fact, up to that moment almost—our allies and then suddenly they were turned into our enemy, and that conference was very important from that point of view.

At the time I was not working in films, or for any broadcasting companies, or advertisers, so the effect on me was more obscure. It was simply that I would be attacked in the press from time to time. But I had no job to lose, so it was quite a bit different than it was for a lot of other writers who had either actual jobs that they would be thrown out of, or contracts with publishers that would have been affected. I didn't have anything like that, and obviously the Broadway situation was quite different, because we didn't have any big corporations investing in Broadway, there were just a lot of small investors who threw in their money to put a play on. So they were not so easily tampered with as the big companies were in Hollywood or the broadcasting industry. They could maintain more independence.

[1]Sponsored by the left-liberal National Council of Arts, Sciences, and Professions, the Cultural and Scientific Conference for World Peace was held in March 1949 at the Waldorf-Astoria Hotel in New York City. The conference was heavily picketed by right-wing groups and harassed by police and government agents. Many of the international delegates were unable to attend because the State Department refused them visas. Eighteen thousand people attended the closing peace rally at Madison Square Garden.

They had blacklists of writers, and as it later turned out, practically every American writer was on it. But not all of them were out front the way I found myself, because they weren't putting plays on, especially not in the Middle West. So the impact was greater on me than it would have been on, let's say, Steinbeck or somebody else.

We had a road company of *Death of a Salesman* in the Middle West that we finally had to close down. The American Legion especially, and I think the Catholic War Veterans, picketed it so heavily everywhere that people were intimidated and they didn't come. So there wasn't much business. They were attacking the play and me as being an anti-American.[2]

Death of a Salesman questioned the ethos of the business civilization, which the play intimates has no real respect for individual human beings, whereas the going mythology was quite the opposite: in that nobody of any competence ever fails and that everything was pretty sound and terrific for everybody. So to put a play on where somebody who believes in the system, as Willy Loman does to his dying minute, ends up a suicide, it was rather a shock.

In fact, when they made the film they made Willy appear crazy. That was the whole drift of the film; that's why it was such a bad film in my opinion. They made him into a lunatic, and consequently you could observe him with the same distance you observe any crazy person, you don't really identify with him. In my opinion that was to make the play politically more palatable, but there were other artistic problems with that production which I disagreed with, but certainly this was the major one.

Columbia Studios actually made a short, cost them a couple of hundred thousand dollars, which they wanted to run before each showing of the film in the movie theaters. The short was shot at City College in New York City and was basically a very boring set of lectures by business administration professors who made it clear that Willy Loman represented nobody and that the play was really quite absurd and that the system was altogether different than as it was portrayed in the play and that the salesman's job was one of the best imaginable careers that a person could have and indeed that the system was based on salesmanship. When they got finished with this kind of analysis you wondered why they had produced the play at all as a film. I managed to make an empty threat that I would sue them if they did this, but in fact I think they themselves saw that the absurdity of the whole thing was even too much for them. They may have shown it, somebody

---

[2]Vincent Hartnett (a founder of Aware, Inc., a major blacklisting concern), while addressing a Conference to Combat Communism held in Peoria, declared the work to be "a Communist-dominated play."

told me that he had seen it once in some theater, but I don't think it was very widespread.

A few years later, I wrote *The Hook,* a screenplay about the corruption in the waterfront union in New York, Brooklyn actually. Elia Kazan[3] and I went to Hollywood to try to get a producer for it, and Columbia Pictures definitely wanted to do it. But they submitted it to the FBI, which promptly declared that it was a dangerous film because it would tend to alienate the dockworkers, upon whom shipments to Korea were dependent. Then, of course, the main union guy in those days was a man named Brewer[4] who controlled all the Hollywood unions and was a very good friend of the head of the New York waterfront union, a man named Joe Ryan who was a big shot in the AF of L. Anyway, this Brewer pronounced the script unreal and dangerous and fake because there was no corruption in the Brooklyn waterfront. And they wanted me to change the gangsters to Communists, in which case they would then proceed to produce the movie. Within about a year and a half from that point, Ryan went to prison for racketeering. But that didn't change anybody's mind. The film never did get made.[5]

Later, I was approached by a young guy who wanted to make a film about what was then called juvenile delinquency, namely, gang warfare, which was very widespread in Brooklyn. So I wrote a script for that with the cooperation of the City of New York, because the city was interested, of course, in curbing that kind of crime. To make a long story short, I began being attacked by the *World-Telegram,*[6] which was a Scripps-Howard newspaper in New York, to the point where Mayor Wagner got cold feet and they had a meeting of all the heads of departments of the City of New York and they voted, I think it was twenty-two to twenty-one, to cut off any relation with this film.[7] So that film got destroyed, because you needed to have the

---

[3]Stage and screen director who in April 1952 reversed his unfriendly stand before HUAC and gave eleven names. Perhaps his best-known film is *On the Waterfront,* written by Budd Schulberg, who gave fifteen names. Marlon Brando played Terry Malloy, a longshoreman and potential informer, who is torn between his loyalty to his friends and the moral imperative to squeal on the mob. There are those who say the film is an attempt by Kazan and Schulberg to justify their HUAC testimony.

[4]For Roy Brewer's take on this story, see under "Hounds."

[5]After Miller declined to bowdlerize his script, Harry Cohn, president of Columbia, cabled him: "It's interesting how the minute we try to make the script pro-American you pull out."

[6]Along with the *Journal-American,* Aware, Inc., the American Legion, and the Catholic War Veterans.

[7]One city commissioner who voted against Miller explained, "I'm not calling Miller a Communist, my objection is that he refuses to repent."

cooperation of the police department to make it, since the early agreement that this producer had with the city was that they could enter city facilities like the police department in order to shoot the picture.

Oh, yes, they didn't like *The Crucible* either. [Laughs.] As soon as they smelled what that play was about, they froze like water in January. A play about the seventeenth-century witch hunts, which in my opinion the same basic process was taking place.

I wasn't there, but I was told about an incident at some performance where at the point when John Proctor is executed the audience all stood and observed a couple of minutes of silence. It was the same day the Rosenbergs were executed.

However, I have to say that the original production was faulty. The director was trying to make what he called a Dutch painting out of it. But even so, it was pretty strong anyway. But for the times, it was just too tough; the times were against it. But it's my most-produced play in the last twenty-five years, certainly. And it goes on all around the world all the time. But that time, when it opened, I was really out in the cold.

You know, I don't even remember anymore which of my plays got picketed and when. But they were being picketed very often. Not in New York, I would say; New York is a different thing. At least, I don't recall any picketing in New York, but certainly out of town in the rest of the country. The attacks were terrible. Of course, within a year after we opened *The Crucible* here, it opened in Brussels, for the first time in Europe. And the State Department wouldn't give me a renewal of my passport. They said it was not in the best interests of the United States. So I couldn't attend the performance at the invitation of the Belgo-American Association, which is an association of Belgian and American businessmen. When the time came to take a bow, the American ambassador stood up and bowed, and a lot of people thought he was me. It wasn't until the next day that they were aware that I'd been prohibited from traveling. It took five years to get my passport back. I applied many times. But it was only after the Un-American Activities hearing that I managed to get one.

I was called before the committee because about five years before, I'd attended a couple of meetings,[8] and they wanted to know who was in the room, and whether certain particular people were in the room. They named

[8] In 1947, Miller attended "four or five" meetings of Communist writers in order to "locate my ideas in relation to Marxism. . . . I went there to discover where I stood finally and completely. I listened and said very little." (Testimony before HUAC, June 21, 1956).

the people and I was supposed to corroborate what they had. I told them I wasn't going to talk about anybody but myself. I was cited for contempt and convicted in a federal court after a trial of a week. I don't think they would have come after me excepting that I was about to marry Marilyn Monroe.[9] They thought they'd get some quick publicity on it.

Then the whole thing was thrown out by the court of appeals on the grounds that the committee had overstepped its charter or legitimate right to demand certain answers from me. There had been a case called the Watkins case just before this, and my lawyer, Joe Rauh, had argued that case, and the point was that Congress couldn't ask questions at random on these matters unless they were directly connected with proposed legislation, and of course there was no such thing. So on the basis of the Watkins case they threw the whole thing out.

I think the roots of all this lie in that the Right had been out of power since 1934, and the prospects were bleak that they'd ever get back into power on the presidential level. They were defeated time and again, and this was a terrific way of reversing the whole liberal trend in the United States, which they succeeded in doing. They managed to create this atmosphere, which was basically a ploy by the right wing of the Republican Party from the outset, and also some of the Democrats, to turn the country to the right. They managed to turn back everything that had happened since Roosevelt started the New Deal. It was basically a domestic political struggle, which they won for a long time.

We still suffer from the effects. We're still wasting our time arguing stuff that the rest of the world disposed of thirty, forty, fifty years ago—the whole place of trade unions in the society. After all, they broke the union movement here. The women's movement now is the only bold sign of a resistance to this rightism.

The ostensible reason and part of the emotional background was the victory of communism in China, which took place in '49. Before China went Communist, China was generally referred to as ours. This is like a mouse owning an elephant, but that was generally the conception among even very intelligent intellectuals who thought that we could and should and would always call the shots in China. So when that went, it created a kind of a pathos in the country toward those who would tell us that we had to act at once lest the entire world turn to communism. And the best

---

[9]Committee chairman Francis Walter offered to call the hearing off if Miller would permit a photograph of Walter standing with Miller and his soon-to-be bride, Marilyn Monroe.

evidence imaginable was that the largest population in the world was now Communist. That gave it a real shot of steam.

The cultural effects are all over the place. They're obvious in the theater, for example. For the longest time until even now, the idea of a theater which is engaged with the society gradually withered away until theater became just mere entertainment and lost its audience, by and large. It no longer was engaging the great moral issues that the society throws up, that O'Neill tried to deal with, that a number of other people tried to deal with. O'Neill went out of style along with—for the most part—the very idea of reaching into the gut of the audience in order to reach into its mind. Instead, there has been far too much aping of abstractions-for-their-own-sake. But it will change again. It always does. And something genuinely felt and perceived with artistic clarity will surely survive.

JOHN RANDOLPH

A tall man with a wide, ready smile, Randolph doesn't *tell* stories so much as they burst forth from him. A much-respected actor on Broadway, in television, and in films, Randolph was blacklisted for ten years. We meet in a borrowed apartment in New York City.

This was 1955, I was in *Much Ado About Nothing* up in Cambridge when I got my subpoena. I was also up for a part in a play called *Wooden Dish*. Now the same day I got the subpoena, my name appeared in the paper in the theatrical section: "Amongst those actors subpoenaed by the House Un-American Activities Committee were . . ." and then my name. The column next to it, by a drama editor of the time, said that *Wooden Dish* was going to be done on Broadway, starring Louis Calhern,[1] and the producer was a guy that I knew in Hollywood, a son of a bitch.

[1] Louis Calhern (1895–1956) was a romantic lead in early silents and later became a powerful character actor for MGM.

After I saw the newspaper, I came in to New York to see the executive secretary of Actors' Equity to tell him that I was going to fight this thing. He was so scared—"Well, you got to do whatever the committee says. We have nothing to do with it." I said, "Well, I think we do. And I expect you to object to it, and I certainly will."

While I was in New York, my wife came to me with the contract that they wanted for *Wooden Dish*. I would be playing opposite Louis Calhern, I would get four hundred bucks a week.

I know that this producer's gonna see *that* item in the paper and then he's gonna to see *this other* item. And as soon as I get that telegram from the committee, I'm going to get another telegram from the producer and it's going to say, "We're giving you your five-day notice and canceling your contract." I knew I was in trouble.

Then I got the telegram from the committee. It was by a guy named Don Appell[2] for the committee to appear on such-and-such a date. I had to go back to do the show that night. And all the way out on the train, I'm thinking, "I've got to write a statement that will be printed and I'll send it to four thousand people. I have a right to believe in what I want to, I've never done anything harmful."

I'm writing all the way from New York to Boston. And all the time I know I'm screwed. I know that I'm going to get a telegram at the theater, and I got a wife and a kid. Then I come to the theater, and there's the stage manager with a telegram [laughs], and my fucking heart began to beat faster. The reality was more terrifying than I thought. Let's face it—it means you may not work for a long, long time. And I opened the telegram and it said, "Just want you to know, very happy to have you in the show. Know we'll have a splendid engagement together. Signed, Louis Calhern."

He had to know what was happening, just like I did. It was the most wonderful telegram. I still have it in my scrapbook.

I was feeling good when I went in front of the committee. I knew I was finished, it didn't make any difference. At least I said what I had to say. My wife was called too, and she was wonderful. They asked all the same questions. A lot of nonsense about the money that was spilling from the coffers of Broadway actors to the Soviet Union. With eighty-five percent unemployed at any given moment? Out of a salary of forty dollars a week? If you were lucky to be working. It was that kind of idiocy.

I wasn't allowed to read a statement, but my wife managed to make one.

[2]Investigator for HUAC, legman for Nixon in the Chambers-Hiss case.

She said, "Now look, I'll answer all your questions, but my ancestors who were Presidents of the United States and signers of the Declaration of Independence [laughs] would not look with favor on this committee." They got her off so quick it was incredible.

One of my best friends is James Whitmore. He and I were in *Command Decision,* a big hit play right after World War Two, and we roomed on the road together. Whitmore went to Hollywood right away and became a big star. After the hearings, he called my mother he was so worried. He said, "This is Jimmy. How's John doing? I know he was in front of the committee." And she said, "Oh, he got the first laugh!" Because when the committee asked me, "What are you doing now?" I answered, "Without any reflection on this committee, I'm in a play called *Much Ado About Nothing.*" [Laughs.]

There were many different aspects of the Red Scare. I'm talking about things that happened to people who were very progressive. One of them was this kid who was more radical than I was. We all had come out from the war together, and he became very successful in voice-overs.

By now, my name and my wife Sarah's is smeared across the headlines of the newspapers as defying the House Committee on Un-American Activities. One night we were in the kitchen and there was a knock at the door at midnight, and we'd had that before. The last knock at the door around that time was by a HUAC investigator who wanted me to fink. [Laughs.] You know what I mean? You never know what the knock is. Anyway, it was this kid and he said, "Listen, I just walked from my house, 55th Street, all the way up here to 163rd. I feel terrible and I want to help out." He said, "Your name appeared in the *New York Times,* pictures of you and Sarah. I was at the studio, and one of the guys said, 'You know these jokers?' and I said, 'No, no, I don't know them.' I felt like a shit. I felt sick. How could I do that? Yes, I'm making twenty-five thousand dollars a year. I never made that kind of money in my life. I was afraid that this guy was one of those people on the Right who'd finger you if you said you knew John Randolph or Sarah Cunningham." He says, "I just kept saying 'I don't know them.' So I'd like to give you a hundred dollars"—a hundred dollars in those days was a lot of money—"to help towards the lawyers. And I just want to tell you that I don't feel good about it." You talk of the Red Scare, now that was an idea of what was going on with your friends.

The other thing was the disavowing that you're a Communist, every time you got up to speak about anything. You want to talk about an issue, you say, "Look, I'm not a Communist, but . . ." And always disavow the most incredible things that were labeled as Communist. Medical care for poor people, housing, all Communist, right? Every good thing that ever came was labeled Communist. After a while, if you're smart, you say "Listen, I'd better find out who these Communists are, because they're saying a lot of things that I believe in."

Once, my mother came to sit and talk with me. Very worried, as a mother. She sits in the kitchen and says, "Listen, I know you're a nice boy. You really believe in the violent overthrow of the government? You can tell me, I'm your mother."

"Ma!" I said. "Everybody in the service got a medal for sharpshooting, I almost killed myself! I can't handle a gun. I'm so busy rehearsing all day and fighting the committee. At night, I don't have time to overthrow the government!" She said, "I know. I just wanted to ask 'cause I knew you'd tell me the truth."

When I was in *The Wooden Dish*, I was picketed by the Brooklyn Un-American Activities Committee, set up by Godfrey Schmidt and Roy Cohn. When that happened, I found myself really unemployable in every way. I mean, I couldn't work on radio; I couldn't work on television; I couldn't work in movies; I couldn't work in anything you could make any money on. And the stage was the last resort, and here I am, picketed in the flesh. And I was not famous. Well, I figured I'll never work again. The show closed in two weeks. I had Christmas coming up. I had thirty-eight dollars in my pocket and I was trying to get a job. I have a three-and-a-half-year-old kid. I have Sarah, not working—she's blacklisted too. So it was a very rough time.

Now when I got into *Inherit the Wind*, I then saw something new. This was 1955; it still took me ten years after that to really get back to work. The guy who hired me is a guy by the name of Herman Schumlun. Herman Schumlun was in jail a year because he refused to give names of those who contributed to the Joint Anti-Fascist Refugee Committee. And this guy was a big producer. When I spoke to him, he said, "Listen, John, you know, I've lost a couple of actors who didn't want to work when they heard that you were in the show. They said you were a Communist or a radical. But I insisted on hiring you. You're the best person for this job. But do me a favor, don't make waves." [Laughs.]

Here a guy himself that had been put in jail was scared. And in a way he wanted to protect me. We were threatened with a picket line by Ed Clamage, the head of the American Legion group in Chicago.[3] Because of Schumlun and me and Melvin Douglas, all Commies.

Luckily for us, a guy by the name of Goldberg, who was our company manager, knew all of the gangsters all over the world, wherever it was. He said, "Let me handle this." And got ahold of a friend of his in Detroit who was the head of the Teamsters Union and says, "I'm in a theater group here, a nice group of people, and they threaten to picket." The Teamster said, "Well, what's the name of the guy?" He says, "A guy by the name of Clamage. He's a florist." He said, "Leave it to me, Harold."

Now I don't see no picket lines. They never showed up. I said to Goldberg, "What happened?"

"Well," he says, "my friend just called 'em up: 'Listen, Clamage, you give trouble to my friend Harold Goldberg who's handling *Inherit the Wind*, and the trucks won't roll, and you ain't gonna get any delivery of flowers or anything.' " [Laughs.] So Harold said, "I told him thanks very much. He says, 'Nah, they're gangsters.' He says, 'They only know one kind of language.' "

We toured across country. We played every town. Right up from Chicago; we played Detroit, we played Cleveland. We played right to the West Coast. I had not realized how the shades of McCarthyism had darkened the land. I had a whole list of names of people, from the *National Guardian,* at that time a progressive paper. I thought, I'll contact these people, we'll talk. It was a time for change. And boy, I mean I hit towns—big towns where what had been done under the banner of anticommunism and witch hunts; doctors, lawyers, farmers, businessmen, deadly afraid, even then, when already we were beginning to fight back.

Whenever I could, I'd call people on that list. I have never heard such fear. Farmers, lawyers—"Who are you?" "Just let me tell you; I know you're scared. I just defied the House committee just before I took this show on," I said. "I think there's a fresh wind blowing across this land. I'd like to meet you and tell you what went on." Some people were glad. Some people were just careful. Probably the most wonderful experience was in Cincinnati, where I met a bunch of coal miners and I ended up talking to them. But it was hard to get anybody to organize—they were afraid. Hollywood was the only place where at least they got people together.

---

[3]Edward Clamage, a member of many a Legion antisubversive committee, was the leading spokesman for his point of view in the Chicago area. He once declared stripper Gypsy Rose Lee to be a Communist. By 1956, he was stale copy in the Windy City.

When we hit Hollywood I insisted on talking to the people who've been blacklisted, to tell them how we fought in New York and to give them encouragement, because they weren't reading it in their papers. I went to a house, they were actors that I knew in the old left-wing days. They went to Hollywood, made a fortune in radio and voice-overs and acting. And there were a lot of people, including a guy named Frank Wilkinson who had also gotten the shaft.

I went to this house, and I'm talking a beautiful home, swimming pool, more Mercedes-Benzes than I've ever seen in my life. And the room—I swear, all the shades were drawn—it was like the entrance to Death itself. I got more nervous there than I did when in front of HUAC because I look at all these glum people. But the more I talked about what was going on, the eyes began to sparkle. 'Cause they hadn't given up the hope to fight back; they were just terrified. The devastation in Hollywood made New York look like kids' stuff. Writers giving four hundred names. Actors finking, writers finking, directors finking. I mean, it was incredible. And the list spread—there was the guy who was head of the committee to defend Ethel and Julius Rosenberg, a stoolie. He gave the names of everybody in that movement. I don't blame them for being scared.

For me, the blacklist showed itself very simply. There was a guy named Sidney Lumet,[4] who was directing me in a live television show with Anthony Quinn. You rehearsed, and then you're put on live. We'd been rehearsing all week. In the middle of the rehearsal, the day before we were to go on the air, the vice president called up and wanted to talk to Sidney and the producer. I didn't know why we had a half-hour break. They came back very subdued. Sidney Lumet is a very fine person, and I didn't know what happened. At the time, we never knew quite how the blacklisting worked. But the producer was a nice man and he took me aside and he said, "John, we just came back from the vice president. And he said he'd gotten a call from Young & Rubicam"—which was the advertising agency of the show—"to get rid of you." They'd gotten a call from a guy name of Johnson in Syracuse, had three supermarkets, head of the Legion branch there, and then I think Amm-i-dent toothpaste was one of the sponsors of the show. And Johnson was putting a sign up in front of every toothpaste display that Amm-i-dent toothpaste hires Communists and that television shows had to blacklist.

I mean, to not buy Amm-i-dent toothpaste in three supermarkets in

[4]Film and television director who started out as a child actor on radio and Broadway. His films include 12 Angry Men, The Pawnbroker, Serpico, Dog Day Afternoon, and Network.

Syracuse? Well, that was enough to send Young & Rubicam, and they didn't even know who the hell I was. But they got in touch with the CBS vice president and he called Sidney and said, "Get rid of him."

Sidney said, "We can't. We're paying John five hundred bucks for the show, and it's live television. He's got a big part. We got to go on the air tomorrow." And the vice president said, "Well, you hire John Randolph again and you're finished."

Matter of fact, I didn't work again for him for twenty-seven years, until I did *Serpico* with Al Pacino. I don't think it was because he was afraid. I just think that you're out of their mind as an actor. You just disappear.

Phil Loeb was a wonderful trade unionist. He was one of the few people, along with Sam Jaffe,[5] who had won a lot of things in our union—rehearsal pay, for instance. We had a resolution against blacklisting then and against loyalty oaths. At CBS, you had to sign a loyalty oath. There were one hundred and sixty subversive organizations you couldn't belong to.

We were going to make a big fight around Loeb being kicked off *The Goldbergs*. He played Papa Goldberg. He was going to stand up in front of what we called a TVA meeting. TVA was then the temporary union that was formed of all three unions in the field to cover the area of television. And Loeb was supposed to speak at this union meeting.

Loeb came in front of a packed meeting to introduce a resolution with George Heller, the executive secretary, and proceeded to say that he had made a settlement which we didn't know about. He couldn't do anything else because of circumstances, and he started to cry.

We introduced a resolution anyway, setting up the Committee to Investigate Blacklisting in TVA. Every one of us on it ended up being blacklisted. Later on I spoke to Phil Loeb. He said that his son was a schizophrenic, was being treated and doing well, but that he ran out of money because he was blacklisted. He needed several thousands of dollars, otherwise they were going to send his son to the mental institution that we have up in Rockland. A terrible, terrible place. He couldn't do that to his son. That was why he did it. He was a good union man. Not long after, he committed suicide.[6]

What's the residual of it? Fear. It stopped the thinking, it stopped the

---

[5]Sam Jaffe (1891–1984) made his stage debut in 1915. He went on to make twenty-one films, including *Gunga Din, Lost Horizon,* and *The Asphalt Jungle.* He also portrayed Dr. Zorba in the *Ben Casey* TV series.

[6]A working actor for forty years, Loeb was cited in *Red Channels* seventeen times. He was fired and blacklisted in 1951 after CBS and his sponsor, General Foods, received a total of four letters protesting his appearance. In 1955, broke and despondent, he checked into New York's Hotel Taft and took an overdose of sleeping pills.

fighting. Took the heart out of a lot of progressive people, and a lot of other people were frightened and just didn't want to get involved. Now it's the other way around. Now you're honored. Now you get tributes. That's gratifying in some ways, but I'm sorry for those people who didn't live to see it, who committed suicide or who died out in the middle of this thing, whose heart was taken out of them. These are the casualties that we don't talk about anymore. They've been dead a long time. So many good people paid a terrible price.

ANGUS CAMERON

Forced out of Little, Brown in 1951 and blacklisted from the industry, Cameron joined with Albert Kahn to form Cameron & Kahn, Publishers. Their first project was Harvey Matusow's *False Witness*. In 1955, they were charged by the Justice Department and the Senate Internal Security Subcommittee with participating in an "international conspiracy" to discredit the FBI's professional witness program.

We read Matusow had gone to Bishop Oxnam, the Methodist bishop—and a kind of progressive bishop he was, too, although he didn't act very well in front of one of the committees.[1] Anyway, Matusow went to him and to Drew Pearson, a famous *Herald Tribune* columnist in Washington, and admitted that he had lied. Matusow had testified not only for the Department of Justice, but for McCarthy too. So we decided, hell, we'll get that book, we can make these bastards eat crow. Have you looked at *False Witness?* Well, it's not a bad book, had a tremendous influence.

We knew the FBI was watching the Chelsea Hotel, where Matusow stayed while he was working on the book. We didn't make any effort to hide it. We knew that they would know about it. When the book was in galleys, they

[1]Bishop Oxnam appeared at his own request before HUAC on July 21, 1953. A liberal anti-Communist, Oxnam wished to refute HUAC charges that he "served God on Sunday and the Communist front for the balance of the week." At the close of the hearing, in an amiable mood, he and the chairman posed for the press shaking hands.

decided to stop it. They did get our suppliers to give up. When the binder and the printer and the distributor all backed out of the agreement to publish the book, we pressed them and they said they'd been visited by the FBI. But finally we got hold of one printer—he was a wonderful character! [Laughs.] When the FBI came to visit him he said, "You interfering with an American's freedom of business? What the hell, I'm allowed to publish anything I want—you guys must be a bunch of Communists!" He was wonderful! Anyway, he went ahead with the book.

So the Justice Department began to investigate this, and they called a grand jury to discover whether this was part of a Communist conspiracy to discredit the FBI system of informers. But *really* what they were doing was trying to stop the book. They subpoenaed all materials and us, the two publishers. It backfired on them, of course, because the press was fairly sympathetic to us.

When they got us in front of the grand jury, they had it rigged so they would have one of us in front of the grand jury and then in front of the Senate Internal Security Subcommittee, by that time under that senator from Arkansas, McClellan. We would appear before the grand jury and two days later we'd get subpoenaed by the Senate Internal Security Subcommittee. We figured out very quickly that the grand jury was breaking the law by letting the Senate committee have testimony.

When we went in to the grand jury the first day, we were met on the steps of the courthouse by the press. We elected to really take them on. We said, "This is purely a freedom-of-the-press issue, because they have subpoenaed every piece of paper having to do with this book, including all copies of the manuscript, page proofs, galley proofs, and in effect they've stopped the publication of the book." And this is the line we took with the grand jury.

The grand jury had on it the husband of a former publisher of the *New York Post*. Also a broker in the back row, who was a real ignorant, redneck reactionary. The chairman was a kind of an innocent, but the vice chairman was a middle-class black woman. She was real reactionary, just incredible. Anyway, we had decided we would open by asking if we could make a statement, or if I could make a statement, 'cause they had us in separately. I asked the foreman if he had ever operated before with a grand jury. He said no, and I said, "Well, this grand jury should be investigating the U.S. attorney sitting there." There's a precedent for it, because after World War One the grand jury did investigate the U.S. Department of Justice because of its illegal activity in the Palmer Raids.[2] I said we're not the ones who used this paid liar; the U.S. attorney is the one who used him, and Senator McCarthy. Well, this threw a little confusion into them. Finally Attorney General Brownell came up to replace this young U.S. attorney whom we had handled like a child.

At one stage I said to Brownell, "Since you people don't let people who testify here have counsel with them, I can only count on you. You tell me, should I answer that question or should I take the First and the Fifth Amendment?" And he answered, "Well, you should take those amendments." Oh, yeah! So that freed me with the grand jury—everybody figures if you take the Fifth Amendment you're guilty as sin of everything, but this made it a little different.

I can't remember now how many times I was shuttled back and forth—three, I think—between the grand jury and the Senate committee. It's real tricky—you've got to remember exactly what you've said. Not that I lied, but you can never tell when you can be trapped in a compromising situation, because you have to remember exactly what you said. It's hard to do. In the end, they found no bill against us. The Justice Department would love to have had the grand jury find that we had conspired to get Matusow to lie, that's what they were trying to show.

They were also investigating Matusow, of course. Matusow testified that Roy Cohn had instructed him as to what to say on the Trachtenberg case.[3] Cohn, of course, denied it, and they got Matusow for perjury and sent him up for five years.

When they sentenced him, I went in with Albert Kahn and I said, "I'm going to be on tenterhooks here, because they're going to give him a chance to deny this." So when they asked him if he would have anything to say, I wouldn't have been too surprised if Matusow had retracted the whole thing. But no, he stuck by his guns and he went to jail for it, because naturally they took Roy Cohn's word instead of Matusow's.

Anyway, the book came out, sold fifty thousand copies. *The Saturday*

[2]The centerpiece of the post–World War One Red Scare, the Palmer Raids were a nationwide roundup of nearly ten thousand citizens and immigrants on the night of January 2, 1920. Sponsored by Attorney General A. Mitchell Palmer and orchestrated by his young subaltern J. Edgar Hoover, the raids were noted for their conspicuous brutality and a virtual absence of due process. In the ensuing backlash, Palmer and Hoover partly justified their actions against the aliens in purely racist terms, saying that "from their lopsided faces, sloping brows, and misshapen features may be recognized the unmistakable criminal type."

[3]Matusow testified that Cohn had suborned perjury in the 1952 Smith Act trial of thirteen Communist leaders. See Harvey Matusow under "Hounds."

Review of Literature ran a major review by John Steinbeck. The headline on his review was "The Death of a Racket." Later, about a third of the press services and the news stories and editorials considered that the book was a Communist conspiracy, but two-thirds of them were wonderful. You could tell that the people that wrote them had been censoring themselves for years and hadn't said any of the things they knew were the case, and now they had a chance to speak out, just in reporting it, and some of them spoke with enthusiasm!

The general view was the same as Steinbeck's; the book at that time had a real impact. The Justice Department never recovered from it—they never were able to use these informers again. Matusow's recanting did get Jencks off, you see. But Trachtenberg and Elizabeth Gurley Flynn,[4] that grand old woman, it didn't get them off.

At the time we were subpoenaed, along with all of our stuff, I wrote a letter to eight publishers, to Bennett Cerf, Alfred Knopf, Arthur Black of Doubleday, the head of Viking, and four others, saying that the government was overthrowing the First Amendment, and I thought that no matter what they thought about us, they should take a position against this. Never heard from one of them. Not one. [Laughs.] And it was never mentioned between Alfred and me—I never mentioned it and he didn't either—when he finally hired me five years later.

[4]Elizabeth Gurley Flynn (1890–1964) joined the Industrial Workers of the World at sixteen and became its most illustrious orator and organizer. Christened "the Rebel Girl" by IWW bard Joe Hill, Flynn was instrumental in founding the ACLU, only to be expelled in 1940 for her Party membership. In spite of Matusow's recantation, she served three years in Alderson Federal Penitentiary.

MELVIN BARNET

Short, somewhat rumpled, Barnet carries the distracted air of a man fighting a long-standing injustice. In July 1955, Barnet was fired by the *New York Times* for pleading the Fifth before the Senate Internal Security Subcommittee. We meet in a Federal-style residence just across the Brooklyn Bridge from Manhattan.

In 1955, Winston Burdett came forward to testify about his previous associations. He wanted to clear his skirts so that he could keep his job as a CBS correspondent. Burdett and I had worked together as writers on the *Brooklyn Eagle*. He was a good man, a Harvard man too, about a year ahead of me. We lived together for about a year before I got married. He was the best man at my wedding.

Burdett went to Europe around 1939. I didn't know it at the time, but he had some notion about being useful to world Communism. He was going to snoop around abroad, look for an assignment from Russia and tell them what he saw, I think especially in Finland, what the mood in the population was, stuff like that. He thought that as a reporter he might be helpful to the movement. From the point of view of the Comintern, it was well-intentioned. But he never did succeed in finding out anything about anything. It was a farce.[1] He succeeded in painting himself Red, especially in the eyes of the FBI. Ultimately they caught him; he confessed everything.

Burdett didn't warn any of us before giving our names. He was not going to keep correspondence with his old Red acquaintances. In his testimony, he spoke well of us. We were the cream of the earth, doing the best we could. He didn't exaggerate our involvement. He was as honest as he could be, considering he was peaching on everybody he knew.

Now, before Burdett's testimony, a friend of mine on the *Times* by the name of Charles Grutzner told me that he was going to be named by Burdett, and probably other people too. What he had decided to do is to plead the Fifth Amendment not against self-incrimination, but against self-degradation. He had a wild notion that you didn't have to testify in a way that would incriminate or degrade you. I told him that if it ever came to my turn, I would plead the Fifth Amendment, I couldn't see any other way to do it.

When Charlie found out he couldn't plead non-self-degradation, he spoke to Louis Loeb.[2] Later, Charlie told me, "We're not going to have any dinners together anymore," because he was going to cooperate. I say this now, Charlie being dead. He didn't want to lose that house that he just

---

[1]Burdett testified to considerable time spent waiting in hotel rooms and on street corners for contacts who rarely showed up. He said his mission to Finland at the close of the Finnish-Soviet War was to discover how the Finns felt about the war—apparently they did not feel good about it. He went also to Ankara, where his mission was to find out if the Turkish government was really neutral. It was, he determined. At this point, the Russians should have asked for a refund, since it was plain beyond a doubt that the Turks were pro-German.

[2]Counsel for the *New York Times*.

had bought in Palisades, it was very important to him, as was his *Times* job. He was an old newspaperman, and this was his crowning achievement. He wouldn't hurt anybody, but he was going to cooperate, and he advised me to do the same.

Actually, when it came to naming names, he remembered about three. Two of them were dead, and one or two others were well-known Communists in New York. So he really wasn't hurting anybody, but of course it might have hurt somebody. Some of these people did lose jobs, actually. I knew one guy that worked for the Polish Cultural Bureau[3] in Washington who lost his job. Not that they didn't know that he had earlier on been a Communist, but nobody likes to have people in their employment accused of being a Red, even if they hired them because he was a radical. So that was Charlie's position, and it was the end of a beautiful friendship. I told him I wasn't going to name anybody. We were both naive, for starters. He was naive about self-degradation. I was naive about freedom of speech and the *New York Times*.[4]

I was working at the copydesk when I was called to the committee.[5] I had a meeting with Ted Bernstein, the managing editor, Frank Adams, the city editor, and Louis Loeb, the *Times* attorney. They said, "You've been named by Burdett—what are you going to do? We don't want you to defy any congressional committee. We won't stand for that." Meantime, they had never fired anybody for this particular offense. I started out very adamant—"If I am or ever was a Communist, I won't tell you. It is legal, for God's sake! I do my job and you pay me for it. My politics are my own business"—from which I beat a fairly hasty retreat. My lawyer, Lenny Boudin, said, "That's very principled, but you're only going to get fired, not for pleading the Fifth Amendment, but for lack of candor."

I said, "I don't want to be fired for lack of candor. If they fire me for pleading the Fifth, they should take the rap." He said, "They're not going to admit that. Tell them enough about yourself to satisfy Louis Loeb."

So I did. I told Loeb that I had joined the Communist Party in 1937. I

[3]Cultural representatives of the Polish People's Republic.

[4]Two years previously, Arthur Hays Sulzberger, publisher of the *Times,* delivered a speech at John Carroll University in which he suggested that anyone who had parted company with the CP or its fronts no later than the Berlin airlift (1948–49) should benefit from a moratorium. Sulzberger asserted, "Nor is it the super-zealots who bother me so much in all of this—it is the lack of plain old-fashioned guts on the part of those who capitulate to them." He added that he was determined to allow no witch hunt at the *Times*.

[5]Barnet and twenty-nine other *Times* staff members were subpoenaed by SISS in 1955.

went to meetings, I left the *Daily Worker* on subway seats. I advanced to the best of my ability the Communist line. But I have not been a member of the Communist Party since 1940. He said, "Yes, this is what I want. This is candid enough for us."

In further meetings, management pressured me to not defy the committee. They said, "Don't rack your brains. You don't have to remember everybody you ever went to a meeting with. But you must satisfy the committee that you are cooperating. They will not brook defiance, and neither will we." I said, "I'm not going to give one bloody name. You're satisfied with my candor. The rest is my own business." They repeated themselves. "Do not defy this committee. Louis Loeb will tell you how much you have to remember."

I did not know when I went down to Washington whether I would get fired or not. I didn't think they would dare. I would pin Fifth Amendment firing on them, and they had repeatedly expressed sympathy with Fifth Amendment pleas in editorials. But still, I couldn't be sure. During my testimony, the committee even asked, "Are you going to get fired for this?" And I said, "I don't know. I hope not."

I had a brief session. They called us the *Brooklyn Eagle* cell, the fifteen of us that Burdett had named. Burdett had not racked his brains. I could have done better than he did in dredging up names from the remote reaches. The testimony is uninspiring. I pleaded Fifth Amendment, Fifth Amendment, Fifth Amendment.

Toward the end of the testimony, they asked me to tell about myself. I had gone through almost the whole testimony without my Party membership getting on record. I finally slipped it in. I told the committee that the *Times* knew about it. When I got down off the stand, an office boy came up and said, "They want to see you at the office." I hotfooted it over there and was handed a letter from Sulzberger, prewritten no doubt. "Ever since your name was first mentioned in connection with Communist membership and the *Brooklyn Eagle,* you have pursued a course of conduct that has caused the *Times* management to lose confidence in you. As a result, please collect your pay and beat it."

Jimmy Wechsler at the *New York Post* was sufficiently sympathetic to write an editorial, "The Silent Copy-Reader." He knew well enough that I'd been fired for pleading the Fifth Amendment, but he didn't want to tangle with the *Times.* He did, however, want to maintain a liberal position. So he wrote a weasel-worded piece saying, "It certainly looks as if the *Times* has fired Barnett for pleading the Fifth Amendment. If they did so, that was a naughty thing for the *Times* to do. On the other hand, if in fact Barnett had pursued a course of conduct etc., it's understandable why the *Times* did that.'"[6] He went back and forth, but he essentially got my point of view across. When I saw him, Wechsler told me, "You know, you caused a lot of trouble there amongst the higher-ups. They didn't know what the hell to do with you." Apparently there was some controversy on the *Times* board. They must have wished to hell they had just kept me on. It would have simplified everything.

I took the case immediately to the grievance committee of the *New York Times*. It was their job to help people who'd been fired unjustly. They put on an appearance of being very friendly. In fact, the grievance committee and most of the employees of the *New York Times* were strongly against me from the start. Most *Times* people think that the *Times* can do no wrong. When the *Times* says someone was fired for misbehavior, nine out of ten will believe them. The grievance committee behaved in a friendly fashion. They got me to make what they thought were damaging statements. But I would have made them without cross-examination.

For example, one of the *Times*'s charges was that I kept the fact that I had been a Party member a secret. I said, "Telling people you're a Communist when you're looking for a job is not a smart idea. I don't think they would have hired me if I'd told them I had been a Communist." They said, "Then you lied to the *Times* from the very beginning. You didn't tell them about yourself."

This was one of the reasons the *Times* unit of the guild refused to handle the case. Meanwhile, the New York guild had issued a statement critical of the *Times*. On several occasions they said it should go to arbitration. But when I pushed them for it, I was told, "We've taken four similar cases to arbitration already. We can't get to first base with them. Do you really want us to try again?" I wanted them to because this case was different. I worked for an ethical publisher not the *Enquirer* but the *New York Times*.

The *Times* grievance committee and the *Times* unit refused to make a grievance out of the case. For the next two years the *Times* unit of the guild and the New York Newspaper Guild were at odds. They argued over who had the authority to determine whether a case goes to arbitration: was it the *Times* unit, or the New York Newspaper Guild? The case went as high as the State Supreme Court and ended up being a compromise. The *Times* unit said, "Okay, we agree that the New York Newspaper Guild has the authority." In return for which the New York Newspaper Guild said,

---

[6]Describing himself as a "responsive but not a friendly witness," Wechsler had already appeared before Joe McCarthy's committee on April 24, 1953, and again on May 5. On his first appearance, when he was asked for the names of fellow members of the Young Communist League, he responded, "Do you want a long list? A short list? How do you want this?" On his second visit, he supplied the long list.

"Okay, concede us that authority and we'll drop the Barnet case. Now that we can take it to arbitration, we won't!" [Laughs.]

When I was first fired, the ACLU issued a statement deploring what seemed to be a firing for the plea of Fifth Amendment. The *Times* replied that it did not fire me for pleading the Fifth Amendment. It ran in the *Times:* the ACLU's complaint, the *Times* response, and then an ACLU statement: "We are happy to learn that the *Times,* despite appearances, does not fire anybody for the Fifth Amendment." When I saw that, I was furious. They never questioned me. I complained to the ACLU, "Why didn't you ask me something?" They told me, "Send us your stuff and we'll see." I sent them the letter that I had given Loeb about my Communist membership and anything else that justified my case. The head of the New York ACLU, Patrick Malin, said, "You have good reason to believe you were fired for pleading the Fifth Amendment. We'll get back in touch with Sulzberger and try to renew this debate."

Later he told me, "Sulzberger doesn't want to continue the argument. He says your case probably will get into the courts via arbitration and now is not the time to try it on the pages of the *New York Times.*" I said, "But it's never going to go any further. They have to try it on the pages of the *Times.*" He said, "You've made a prima facia case, but we can't do anything further. In your case, you pursued a course of conduct, not the Fifth Amendment." I said, "You are making me a scapegoat for this achievement of getting the *Times* on record." They said, "It is an achievement and we *did* get the *Times* on record. Maybe you are a scapegoat, but there's nothing further we can do. We have achieved our purpose. You're just one guy—here's a whole fucking principle that has been laid down. Nobody gets fired for pleading the Fifth Amendment on the *Times* anymore! That's something that you've accomplished." Of course, the very next time they had a chance to fire anybody for pleading the Fifth Amendment, they did.

I went to work for William Douglas McAdams, a medical advertising agency. They put out medical newspapers and magazines. The president of McAdams was Arthur M. Sackler, a big philanthropist, and he let his people hire some guys who were desperate for jobs. Now most of these were experienced newspaper editors looking for jobs at cut rate, happy to take anything.

Jack Schafer worked for McAdams also. He got the ax from the *Times* not for the Fifth, but for being unable to make up his mind whether he wanted to be a Communist or not. He joined and dropped out, and then joined and dropped out again. The *Times* said, "We hired him and what assurance do we have that he's not going to rejoin?" What an offense that would be to the world at large if he joined the Communist Party while reading cable copy for the *New York Times*.[7]

There had been a number of firings—Bill Price on the *News*, Danny Mahoney on the *Mirror*, Willie Goldman on the *Mirror*. Some of the cases had gone to arbitration. The guild units wouldn't fight for most of them. If they got named, they got fired.

It's been thirty-six years since the *Times* fired me for pleading the Fifth Amendment. They have never issued an apology, never made any kind of restitution or offered compensation. They never said they were wrong in any respect. I'm sure if you asked the *Times* why they fired Barnet for pleading the Fifth Amendment, they would tell you, "No, he was fired for following a course of conduct that caused us to lose faith in him." A couple of years ago, New York revived the old teachers union cases and they sent out checks to victims' families. The attorney general of the state decided that they were fired wrongly and there should be some kind of restitution, even if only nominal. I wrote a letter to the *Times* and said, "The attorney general of the state is able to confess error and do his best to make up for it. How about the *Times* saying that they made a mistake in the Barnet case and they're sorry?" I never heard from them. Nothing. They never even printed the letter.

[7]Schafer, who pleaded the Fifth before SISS, told an arbitrator he had been a Party member in the years 1940–41 and 1946–49.

Troubadours
of the Left

The Weavers were straight-ahead folksingers with a genius for simplicity.
Founded in 1948 by Pete Seeger, Lee Hays, Ronnie Gilbert, and Fred
Hellerman, the group recorded their first release for Decca Records in
May 1950. The 45 had "Tzena Tzena" (an Israeli soldiers' tune) on one
side, backed by "Goodnight Irene," a ballad written by a black ex-convict
named Leadbelly. Within weeks they were stars. By June, Decca couldn't
press the vinyl fast enough to supply the demand. The Weavers had their
choice of the country's nightclubs and were offered a weekly television
spot on NBC.

Within two years, the Weavers were banned from the air and
blacklisted from nightclubs and county fairs. Haunted by the FBI, they
were eventually hauled before the musical critics of HUAC. The
folksingers were obvious heretics—Pete Seeger's banjo had been an
antifascist weapon since the 1930s, and after all, they had played at
Peekskill with Paul Robeson. Individually, they had also been associated
with leftist labor unions and a variety of progressive causes. Now their
tunes were considered seditious. Congressional inquisitors gravely
analyzed the lyrics of "The Rock Island Line" to determine if it wasn't
really the Communist Party line. "If I Had a Hammer" was blasted as Red
propaganda for celebrating such subversive notions as "justice" and
"freedom," to say nothing of "love between all of my brothers, all over
this land."

The Weavers never did beat the blacklist, although Seeger broke
though to a television appearance on *The Smothers Brothers Show* in
1968. Still they continued singing, inspiring along the way the folk revival
of the 1960s and a new generation of activists.

PETE SEEGER

As an uncooperative witness, Pete Seeger made a command performance before the House Committee on Un-American Activities in 1955. The witness offered to sing—but only folk songs—and was quickly charged with ten counts of contempt of Congress. His sentence of two concurrent five-year prison terms was finally overturned in 1962.

When Lee Hays and I and Mill Lampell formed the Almanac Singers, we got a lot of publicity in the Communist *Daily Worker* and were singing all around New York and then across the country. Woody Guthrie soon joined us. As Communists we were singing for trade unions and singing for peace in early 1941. But in the fall of '41 we were singing to support the war effort. In January of '42, the Almanacs were on a coast-to-coast network show directed by Norman Corwin called *This Is War*. The next day a headline in the *New York World-Telegram* said, "Commie Singers Try to Infiltrate Radio," and that was the last radio job that Woody Guthrie and I got in 1942. In '43 he went in the Merchant Marine. In July '42 I went in the Army. People who participate in radical politics assume that you're going to lose jobs—it is nothing unusual. What happened in the 1950s, though, was a more extreme form of it: if you *knew* somebody who *knew* somebody, you got blacklisted.

For example, my older brother is politically rather conservative, but he was a scientist, a radar astronomer. He kept getting offered good jobs around the year 1951 and then the job would suddenly be canceled on him. Finally he decided the only way he could get a job was to leave the country. He went to Sweden and Holland and worked there for ten years until things cooled down here and he came back.

If he had been willing to condemn me in public or something like that, he probably could have kept a job, but he didn't feel like doing that, so he had to take the punishment. It was a lot harder on him than me. I just kept doing what I'd always done, but he had his career come to a dead stop in the United States.

People who were concerned about our influence must have been rather thunderstruck when in 1950 all of a sudden the Weavers had a best-selling record. They thought that we were just reaching a few hundred people here and a few hundred people there. All of a sudden we were reaching millions with "Goodnight Irene" and then "So Long, It's Been Good to Know You" and "Wimoweh." They probably said, "How did we let those Commie so-and-sos slip through our fingers?" There were a whole batch of people who wanted to blacklist us. Some were in it just for the money. Some believed sincerely that it was a showdown between the Soviet Union and the United States of America and as patriots they must expose anybody who had friendly feelings towards the Soviet Union, whether they were Communists or not. They started chopping the Weavers down and succeeded in doing it in a couple of years.

Anything's "subversive" if you want it to be. That's the silliness of these situations. I was in Italy recently and learned that five hundred years ago some Pope declared that a diminished chord was the "devil's chord" and wouldn't allow anybody to play it in church.

"If I Had a Hammer" was considered subversive 'cause it talked about freedom and hammers. I sang it at the Peekskill concert in September '49, where Robeson had asked me to sing some songs at the beginning of his concert. In 1950 the song was published in *Sing Out*. A man wrote in, "Cancel my subscription, all you left out of that song was the sickle."

The Weavers had made a little record of the song in '49, before we were well known. It's a collector's item. No one but collectors ever got it. However, seven years later, three young people,[1] as you know, changed my melody, and the words had been slightly changed by the women radicals, "all of my brothers" became "my brothers and my sisters," and with these slight changes it became a worldwide hit in the late fifties.

The Senate Internal Security Subcommittee became concerned about a song called "The Midnight Special," because I had once introduced it saying we are all in a sense waiting for that midnight special's light to shine on us, all of us in the world are in a prison of our ignorance, and one day if the light shines on us maybe we will go free. It was a millennial way of thinking, I confess, but it was still a good song.

Up here in the country we knew our neighbors and we knew the people in town. Occasionally there was a few problems. When I was called up for questioning, the neighbors got scared, and I quit having a little singing group. I used to go down to the one-room schoolhouse my children went to and led singing with ten or fifteen kids. Then at Christmastime we'd go

---

[1]The group Peter, Paul, and Mary (Peter Yarrow, Paul Stookey, and Mary Travers).

sing Christmas carols around the community. And the parents got scared in '55, and said I'd better not try and do that anymore. However, a year later the principal of the local school sent a letter to all the teachers saying, "If anybody makes it hard on the Seeger children because of this publicity about their father, please let me know." It was a very decent thing for her to do.[2]

She was the wife of a local plumber and a working person and she just didn't figure that was fair. Curiously enough, the most hellish time I had in my hometown was years later in 1967 when a headline in the local paper said, "Seeger Sings Anti-American Song in Moscow." Well, it wasn't true, I sang a rather sad lament for a soldier killed in Vietnam. But as the editor agreed when I wrote him, this was not necessarily anti-American. I said if somebody in Germany had written a letter about a German soldier killed when Germany took over Austria in 1938, would he have been anti-German or anti-Hitler?

Anyway, Toshi and I were almost run out of town. But we hung on. This led me to be more active in my hometown. I had treated my hometown like a hotel. I went down, got my groceries and my mail, and went back to my home on the mountain. But the Clearwater campaign[3] forced me to change my ways. I got a nice brass plate from the town for good citizenship a few years ago.

During that blacklist era I did what I'd done all my life, I sang for schools and summer camps and little left-wing fund-raising parties. My income had never been high. Right now I'm making a better income than I ever did in my life, because songs I wrote forty years ago are still selling and royalties keep coming in. But in those days we raised a family on beans and potatoes and we drove cheap cars and made 'em last as long as we could. I did do something my father advised me to when I was quite young. He said, "Keep in mind a rich man can live cheaper than a poor man." I said, "What do you mean?" He said, "Well, take rent, for example. The average poor person pays more out in rent every year than somebody who's rich enough to own their own land and house." So I scraped up enough money back in 1949 to buy a few acres of land, one hundred dollars an acre, that was cheap

---

[2]Once, while shopping in town during the worst of his political troubles, Seeger encountered the local hardware man, who looked him in the eye and said, "I don't know what your politics are, young man, but this is America—you got a right to your opinion."

[3]The Clearwater campaign was an effort to clean up the Hudson river, long polluted by industrial waste and public water usage. The campaign was kicked off in 1969 with the launching of the *Clearwater*, a 106-foot sloop, that was to be used for fund-raising and environmental education.

even then, way up on the side of a mountain, and built a log cabin for all of nine hundred dollars. We raised a family in it. So I kept my expenses down. My wife and I have always pinched pennies. She was used to doing it as a child. As a matter of fact, my parents were pinching pennies in the Depression too.

Things fade into history, and my guess is the average young person doesn't even know this Red Scare period existed. It's worth having these stories written down, because the establishment, needless to say, would like to forget about it. For some people still believe in America *über alles*.

To a certain extent, people's organizations have to start from the bottom again. Exactly how, no one's quite sure. People are charging off in this direction and that direction. There was a strong, viable socialist movement in the U.S. at the beginning part of this century. It's mostly gone now. My guess is that, sooner or later, there's going to be people pulling together a coalition of working people again.

I urge people, take the long view of it. For thousands of years, people from time to time have spoken up, said, "This is wrong, it's unjust." All around the world this happens. From ancient times around the Mediterranean right through the Middle Ages up to modern times, people striving for a more just society would organize and they'd win a few gains sometimes and then they'd get burnt at the stake or slapped down in some way. But along comes another generation learning from them.

During the civil war in England between Cromwell and King Charles there was chaos. Some dozens of people that were starving went into the lords' lands and started gardens and built little cottages, probably out of stone or thatch or sod, and were doing very well for themselves. But finally the establishment took over again. The troopers were sent and they burnt the cottages down and destroyed the gardens and kicked all the people off because it was not their property. But their leaders put down some beautiful words, and Leon Rosselson in England put them into this song, called "The World Turned Upside Down" [sings]:

> *You poor take courage*
> *You rich take care*
> *This earth was made a common treasury*
> *For everyone to share.*

My guess is that there will be people who perhaps right now are in diapers who twenty years from now will be doing some extraordinary things. I won't be around to see it. But the American soil gives rise to all sorts of different movements. Long live the First Amendment to the U.S. constitution.

FRED HELLERMAN

A tall, rangy man, energetic and passionate. A music publisher now, he writes scores for film and theater.

Why the Weavers? I'm the wrong one to ask about that. You have to ask the sons of bitches on the other side! We didn't do anything. We just sang some songs. Songs we cared about. I don't think the issue was what we were singing—nobody gave a damn about that. I don't think they were attacking the teachers because of what they were teaching, or the plumbers for the way they were doing their plumbing. The aim of the exercise was to shut people up. And the Weavers no more than [sighs], than anyone else who was speaking up.

The first time we were attacked was in June of 1950 when the very first copy of *Red Channels* came out. And actually it was Pete that was singled out there. We were just finishing up a long run of our first big job, which was at the Village Vanguard. We were about to get a TV summer replacement show for Van Camp's Beans, and we were all buddy-buddy with them and chummy-chummy and they were sending us all cases of their goddam Van Camp Beans! And then the day after *Red Channels* came out, the whole thing was off and a whole lifetime supply of beans went down the drain! So that was the end of that. So we were among the early victims of Van Camp Beans. [Laughs.]

I think it was Harvey Matusow[1] who actually named us a group. He claimed to be friends of ours. And, in point of fact, we did know him. I knew Harvey. I guess Pete knew him. I'm not sure whether Ronnie knew him or not.

---

[1] A onetime aide to Joe McCarthy, notorious informer, and paid government witness, Matusow recanted in 1955, confessing that his anti-Communist career had been based on lies. He served five years in prison for perjury—not for his previous testimony, but for his disavowal of it. See his story under "Hounds."

From there on out, it was just part of our existence, whatever work we did was attacked with American Legion pickets or threats of pickets. At first, the record companies and club owners didn't pay much attention to it. But very quickly, the club owners got an education from it, oh yeah. A lot of very decent guys. They'd start out very indignant. [His voice rises as he mimics an angry club owner.] "I've got a list from these people. What the hell? Where do these people get off telling me how to run my business and who I can have in my club?" A few weeks later, they'd come by very sheepishly and say, "Hey, you know, they're threatening to cut off my beer supply and the papers won't take my ads. And you know . . ." They got a lesson in the way things work. [Laughs.]

At one point, we happened to have been in Ohio at the precise time that Harvey Matusow testified before the House Un-American Activities Committee. Harvey was a big-time local boy there because he graduated to the House committee after working for the Ohio State Un-American Activities Committee. The papers were whipping up hysteria, and the atmosphere was really thick and heavy. We left the next day. I had the feeling that we left an hour ahead of the posse. We were receiving threats. I guess the closest thing I can liken it to was being at Peekskill,[2] where the violence actually erupted. That was a very frightening experience. So I don't have great memories of Ohio! [Laughs.] Not one of my favorite places.

The blacklist followed us around. Almost every job we ever got was in spite of the blacklist. It was a cumulative effect. At first the stations wouldn't play our records, and then as a result of that Decca dropped us. If you have no record, you have no play, no one will hire you. By the end of 1952, it was clear that we really couldn't go on anymore. At least in the venues that we were in, which were nightclubs.

It was at the end of 1955 that Harold Leventhal, our manager and friend, got us back together to do a concert at Carnegie Hall. Back then, a concert was a longhair affair. Period. And when Harold went to Carnegie Hall to book us, they said, "You mean the recital hall?" He said, "No, I mean the main hall." They'd never heard of such a thing. And Harold was not very sure whether anybody would show up. And of course, it was a big thing. And then at the end of the year someone said, "Hey, can you do it in Chicago?" Well, sure, okay. "Hey, can you do it in Boston?" Yeah. And before we knew it, we were back doing concerts. But not through the channels of the ordinary concert people, but by local friends. These people had never run a concert before. And Harold would say, "Okay, you get the

[2]For more on this story, see "The Peekskill Riot."

hall and these are the kinds of ads you place . . ." And so they were all being done by amateurs.

We were doing concerts in San Francisco, Chicago, L.A., and so on. And people were coming. There may have been bomb threats but people were coming. And after a while, the commercial promoters said, "Hey, this is worthwhile." So they began taking it over.

We weren't recording for Decca anymore. When we did the Carnegie Hall concert, we recorded it ourselves. And we ended up making a deal with Vanguard for the tapes. But no record company would've recorded us at the time. I'm not trying to detract from Vanguard, because they went out on a limb at that particular time.

But in a sense what happened was that we created our own concert world. It's funny, it only dawned on me recently, and it sounds like such a big statement to make that I can't believe that it's accurate. But someone had asked me recently, "Well, who else was doing concerts at that time?" and I couldn't think of anybody. We may have been one of the very first of the popular performers to do concerts.

The FBI would come around periodically. The first few times I was a little curious, but after that I really got very annoyed with them. I said, "Look, I really don't want to talk to you. If I've broken the law, then arrest me. If I haven't, then get the hell away from me."

The fact is, neither I nor most people who were charged with some terrible thing ever did anything wrong. We never did anything illegal. We cared, we went out on picket lines. But what the hell was wrong about that? What do I have to apologize for? That I made mistakes that I wouldn't make now? Jesus Christ! Everybody makes mistakes. The American people elected Richard Nixon, for Christ's sake—twice! They elected George Bush and Dan Quayle. I mean, everybody's entitled to their mistakes.

I'm not real sure that the blacklist ever did end for the Weavers. I think even at the time that we disbanded in '60—whenever it was—the blacklist was still going. Because a few years after that, for example, ABC had their *Hootenanny* show, on which just about anyone who played a guitar appeared—with the exception of Pete Seeger. A lot of people raised a fuss about it, but Pete was still never on the show. So for the Weavers the blacklist never really ended.

Politically, it didn't inspire me to raise the ante. At the same time, it didn't cause me to shut up either. You know, the architecture of a church is fantastic—in terms of function. It does what is meant: you walk into a church and you automatically speak in hushed tones. Nobody speaks in a normal voice in a church. It's meant to overawe you and to make you humble. Church architecture is wonderful in terms of cause and effect and what it aims to do.

In the same way, you walk into a U.S. courthouse and that architecture also humbles you. You feel the whole force of the government of the United States of America arrayed against you! You saw how some people behaved up there, and you had to question yourself. When push comes to shove, how am I going to react? Better people than me have cracked. But the fact is that when that moment of truth came, you looked at all these sleazebags sitting in front of you and you say, "Am I going to align my life with *them?*" And so it was a very easy decision. Surprisingly easy.

One of the things that puzzles me is, we hear a lot of liberal talk, about all the innocent people who were hurt, and so on, without making any reference to so-called "guilty" people. "Isn't it terrible that a person was accused of being a Communist and they weren't!" I mean, that's really terrible. But now how about the people who were Communists? What the hell were they guilty of?

Nowadays having been blacklisted is a badge of honor. I was talking to Ring Lardner, Jr., recently. He told me how the Hollywood Ten has somehow become the Hollywood Ten Thousand. [Laughs.] Everybody thought he was blacklisted.

There was a guy—he didn't quite name names or anything, but I remember at the time he was really trying to cover his tracks. He was writing letters saying, yeah, he used to hang out with a lot of left-wing people, but he had big arguments with them—trying to distance himself as much as possible. And over the last few years I see him, and I overhear him talking about how he was blacklisted. You know, you just have to shake your head and laugh at it a little bit.

RONNIE GILBERT

We talk across the dining-room table in a modest home in the Berkeley hills above the San Francisco Bay. An ebullient, charming woman; her laughter is contagious and warm.

My interest in the Weavers was political as well as musical. We sang for unions. We sang for the Henry Wallace campaign.[1] I was all of eighteen or nineteen at the time. My background was political. My mother was a rank-and-file unionist, belonged to the International Ladies Garment Workers Union, and she was a singer. She taught me all the songs. So I come from a very proud, political union background. That was part of my nature and my life, you know. I still sing political songs. There's a different style and shape, I'm not so much a "folksinger" as I was then. I sing a wide variety of musical styles. But the lyrics that attract me are lyrics about something.

We incubated most of our material at the Village Vanguard. We were there for six months. It was a small club in New York that did all kinds of stuff, radical stuff, nonradical stuff, jazz. Betty Comden, Adolph Green, Judy Holliday, and Al Hammer performed there as an act called "The Revuers." They were full of political material.

We sang everything that we sang later on. But we were very aware that we were entertainers. We would never even think of singing a song that wasn't good fun to do. Sure, we sang Spanish Civil War songs, one or two of them, 'cause they were musically exciting. And we would refer to them and say that this was a song that was written during the Spanish Civil War, and that perhaps if Hitler had been turned back during that war, we would never have had World War Two. We said really "subversive" things like that. And every now and then we'd sing something that related to a union. Very subversive, you know. You bet, that's the kind of thing we did. But when we appeared on television, we knew that we were singing for a very broad audience that wouldn't sit still for the explanation of a song. The song had to be directly of interest to them, and we sang what we thought was best in American folk music, and that was what we represented.

The Weavers were headline-makers. We were the hottest thing to come along in a long time in the music industry. I've often thought about this. I don't think it occurred to any of us that we would be making commercial records. We sang because that was what we did. Had we not made "Goodnight Irene," had we not become hot performing artists, it's very possible that we would never have been caught up in the blacklist, because we wouldn't have been worth anything to anybody.

I mean, why are entertainers picked up in a blacklist like that? 'Cause they made headlines for the committee. The headlines you see in these old

[1] Former Vice President under Franklin Roosevelt, Wallace ran for President in 1948 on the Progressive Party ticket.

movies from the thirties—the Criminal or the Hunted Person comes into a hotel lobby, and everybody's reading the papers: "So-and-So Wanted," you know? Well, that actually happened to us. We were playing a nightclub engagement in Springfield, Illinois. And we came into the hotel lobby, and there were people reading the newspaper, and it said "Weavers Named Reds!" [Laughs.] And there we were!

It all started with a guy by the name of Harvey Matusow. He claimed we were all friends. He claimed a lot of things! [Laughs.] But I did not count myself a friend of Harvey Matusow at any time. The last I had seen of Harvey Matt, as he called himself, he was making a nuisance of himself selling the *Daily Worker* in the cafeteria, going from table to table, getting subscriptions and interrupting everybody's conversations and generally making an ass of himself. That was what I knew about Harvey Matusow. Evidently he knew something about me, 'cause he told the committee that he had seen me at Communist Party meetings—which of course was a total lie, and he later recanted that. But it didn't make any difference, we were out anyway.

We were being followed all the time. I remember walking down the street in some place in Ohio, it might have been Akron, with these two guys following us behind. I was terrified. By that time it was very scary, because it involved groups like the American Legion, the Catholic War Veterans, and a very patriotic kind of macho. I was present at Peekskill, at the Paul Robeson concert, where people were badly injured by rock-throwing goons, with the police standing by doing absolutely nothing. So I knew that kind of thing could happen very easily. These guys followed us a long ways. I stopped and turned around and confronted them. One of them seemed very surprised, and he said, "Well, do you want your subpoena here, or in the club, while you're performing?" I said, "I'll take it now!" [Laughs.]

That first subpoena was for the House committee. This was early on and we never went. Because at that time the committee was not sure of its legal grounds. If they forced you to break a commitment they might be in some kind of trouble, so they let us go and said they would pick up on us at another time.

I never did get subpoenaed again. Very quickly our work came down to nothing, there was no work to be had. We stuck together as long as we possibly could, and then it was pointless. Decca was not going to do any more recording. Decca was in the red when we recorded for them and we pulled them right out. It didn't help. It didn't make them loyal to us.

[Laughs.] The music industry is the music industry. The Weavers were merchandise. Our songs were merchandise, just the way people are now.

My then husband and I had been planning to go and live on the West Coast. And it looked like there was no reason why not. So we went off. We made an automobile trip through Mexico. I got pregnant, which was another thing I wanted to do, and had a baby in California. And then we came back after two years, for the concert at Carnegie Hall, which was what brought the Weavers back together again during the blacklist time.

A few months later we did a follow-up concert to that. I traveled again from California to New York. There was a phone call from a woman who worked for the committee, and she said, "Oh, Miss Gilbert! I want you to know that you girls can't hide from us!" [Laughs.] *You girls!* She used that phrase. She said, "Now we understand that sometimes girls don't like their husbands to know what they've been up to. We can promise you total secrecy." So I had to decide whether I was going to talk to the committee, and I decided I would not. But I did call them and I said, "By the way, I'm not hiding. My name is in the phone book. I live in Los Angeles. You can find me there anytime you want." And I went home. They never did call, and so I never appeared before the committee. Of course, for a long time I was very glad of that, but now I wish I had. In hindsight, one imagines one would have been heroic. [Laughs.]

My husband was a dentist, and the FBI annoyed him with visits to his office. I have read that people had friends who deserted them and betrayed them, but it wasn't true among my friends. But what did happen was that some of the people that I had known well, wondered. There was a period before the Weavers got tagged, when our records were still up there—it was only a matter of time, of course. But there were people from the old People's Songs[2] who wondered why we were still up there. Some of them suspected that we had come to some kind of terms with the committee.

I was incensed by that idea. It made me very angry and very bitter. I felt like we couldn't have made it easier for the enemy, turning on each other that way. And as a result, I've had very little to do with those folks after that. Years ago, I met one of them, a woman that I had admired very much.

[2]Founded by Pete Seeger in 1946 with a loan of $155, People's Songs, Inc., aimed to provide the labor movement with a muscular musical arm—providing singers for picket lines, publicity, and building attendance at meetings. Out of this grew People's Artists, a booking agency, and *Sing Out!* magazine, which became the bible of the folk movement. In May 1947, the U.S. Army's *Weekly Domestic Intelligence Summary* cited People's Songs as a Communist front.

She had cancer and she was dying. And I was really very glad to see her again—I didn't know she was sick—it just felt like it was time to let go of all that junk. The minute I saw her, she threw herself into my arms and cried. And how many years was that? More than thirty years. She said that she never forgave herself for being part of that.

"Wasn't That a Time" was a song that Lee Hays wrote with Walter Lowenfels, who was a poet. A terrific song about freedom and freedom of expression. And it started out [begins to sing in a beautiful, clear voice]:

> *Our fathers bled at Valley Forge*
> *The snow was red with blood*
> *Our faith cried out at Valley Forge*
> *Our faith was brotherhood*
> *Wasn't that a time?*
> *Wasn't that a time?*
> *A time to try the soul of man*
> *Wasn't that a terrible time?*

We won't talk about the patriarchal "man" and "our fathers," but for the time it was a wonderful song. It was a poetic song, a really good tune. It was what we felt about this blacklisting and the witch-hunting that was going on. It was cited during Lee and Pete's testimony before the committee as "this subversive song," but they would not let Pete sing it. After his testimony he sang it to a bunch of reporters, and it went out over television. But that song figured prominently in the HUAC hearings.

The silence that was imposed on this country by those times. That infiltrated everything in our lives. People simply don't know how things lead to other things. It's like you start all over again, as if nothing ever happened. It's incredible to think that there are young people today who don't know about Vietnam. I'm not very articulate about these things, but it seems to me that is the price we've paid for what's now called the McCarthy Era, when everybody went silent and left the field to the boys to play in.

Not everybody did. There were people who stood up and said, "You have no right to inquire into my political beliefs." Pete tried to do it on the basis of the First Amendment. It didn't work, but at least he has the satisfaction that he did it.

Breaking
the Working Class

The founding of the Congress of Industrial Organizations (CIO) in 1936, at the height of the New Deal, signaled a new militancy and strength for American labor. The CIO swelled the ranks of labor by organizing the unorganized in steel, auto, rubber, electrical, maritime, and meat-packing industries, among others—workers long shunned by the exclusionary craft unions of the American Federation of Labor (AFL). By 1945, union labor had reached a previously unknown strength, representing 35 percent of the total work force.

The CIO played a major role in Roosevelt's fourth-term election. Labor leaders encouraged cultural programs in union locals, promoted attendance at labor schools,[1] established libraries on union ships, and nurtured ties with dozens of progressive organizations seeking to move the country forward.

At the center of this flowering was the Communist Party. Far from "infiltrating" the CIO, as their foes would have it, the Communists were a major force[2] in building it. The CP had cut its teeth on the labor struggles of the twenties and early thirties; its organizers were the most experienced and dedicated. The dozen unions they led or were close to[3]

[1]For more on labor schools, see "Red-ucators."

[2]The main impetus to form the CIO and to pass much of FDR's New Deal labor protections came from the Unemployment Councils, which were formed in nearly every major city during the early years of the Depression. Organized by Communists as self-help and mutual-support groups, the councils opposed FDR's original option of "official company unionism," modeled after labor relations in Mussolini's Italy. Challenged by the councils at every turn, FDR soon realized that the conservative AFL was not in command of the situation. By 1935, the Wagner Act was passed, allowing the enormous growth of organized labor.

[3]While many Communists and sympathizers were among union leadership, there was only one union boss who was an admitted Party member, Ben Gold of the Fur and Leather Workers Union. Gold joined the Party in 1919 and publicly resigned in 1950 to comply with the

operated as models of rank-and-file control and honesty. And the rank and file rewarded their efforts by returning Communists and progressives to leadership in election after election.

To the reactionaries in Congress and their business allies, the growth of the CIO was a Red nightmare. The National Association of Manufacturers (NAM), representing some seventeen thousand companies, spent several million dollars annually decrying the New Deal's labor protections as a conspiracy directed from the Kremlin. The like-minded U.S. Chamber of Commerce spent vast treasure and energy warning of "the menace of socialism." In 1946 and 1947, the Chamber of Commerce distributed nearly one million companies of two pamphlets, *Communist Infiltration of the United States* and *Communists Within the Labor Movement.* The following year its Permanent Committee on Socialism and Communism published a *Program for Community Anti-Communist Action,* which instructed the loyal on how to keep watch on the suspected disloyal.

This collective paranoia was aimed less at oncoming totalitarianism than fears of restrictions on freewheeling capitalism. Those fears were revived with the resurgence of labor militancy in 1945. During the war, labor had held to a no-strike pledge. But while wages were stabilized, prices rose, despite controls. Business profits soared to their highest point in history. After Truman dismantled price controls in 1946, consumer prices rose at a rate seven times higher than in the preceding three years. American workers, many of whom had forgone a raise for the duration, were now in dire straits. Corporate America dug in its collective heels.

In 1945 and 1946, eight million workers walked out for higher wages, the largest strikes in American history. What they wanted was an additional twenty-five cents an hour; they settled for eighteen and a half cents, but not before Truman asked Congress for the power to draft striking workers into the military. When Charles Wilson, president of General Electric, joined the Truman administration in 1946, he summarized the prevailing corporate attitude: "The problems of the U.S. can be summed up in two words: Russia abroad, labor at home." Although his arithmetic was poor, his message was clear. The massive strikes must not be repeated.

The purge that followed was carried out by various arms of the government and, ironically, by the trade unions themselves. Sensing the

---

Taft-Hartley Act (see below). Four years later, he was indicted and convicted on perjury charges for filing a false non-Communist affidavit. His conviction was overturned by the Supreme Court in 1957.

changing tide, conservative elements in labor abandoned union solidarity for divisive Red-baiting. The pretext was the support of the leftist unions for Henry Wallace's 1948 run on the Progressive ticket and their opposition to Truman's foreign policy. Walter Reuther of the United Auto Workers, Joe Curran of the National Maritime Union, and Mike Quill of the Transport Workers wrested control of their unions from elements friendly to the CP. Failing to overcome rank-and-file loyalties to the Left, James Carey of the United Electrical Workers set up a rival union, with CIO support. At the same time, the CIO, under the leadership of anti-Communist Philip Murray, imposed a strict political orthodoxy on its member unions—all must now support the Truman Doctrine and the Marshall Plan. Maurice Travis of the Mine, Mill and Smelter Workers objected justly, "I'd like to know where in the CIO constitution it says we have to support the foreign policy of the Democratic administration."

In 1946, the CIO executive board empowered Murray to confiscate the funds and property of any labor council that refused to conform. The pro-Communist unions resisted, pledging their support for Henry Wallace and maintaining their opposition to Truman's foreign policy. The bitterness deepened. Murray removed left-winger Harry Bridges as regional director of the Northern California CIO and removed the charters of several local CIO councils. A number of pro-Communists within CIO national headquarters were also forced out by Murray, including general counsel Lee Pressman and *CIO-News* editor Len De Caux. The overwhelming defeat suffered by Wallace strengthened the resolve of the anti-Communists. In March 1949, the CIO board banned Communists from holding office in CIO unions and demanded the resignation of officers who did not agree with its decisions. At the eleventh CIO convention that same year, Murray fumed against the "skulking [Red] cowards . . . lying out of the pits of their dirty bellies." The convention resolved that it would "longer tolerate within the family of CIO the Communist Party masquerading as a labor union." In 1949 and 1950, ten unions representing nearly one million workers were expelled.[4] The CIO set up rival unions to raid their membership. Pockets of progressive influence were also purged from the AFL unions.

By 1954, fifty-nine out of one hundred unions banned Communists

---

[4]The list of expelled unions included the American Communications Association, the Farm Equipment Workers, the Food, Tobacco, and Agricultural Workers, the International Fishermen and Allied Workers, the International Fur and Leather Workers, the International Longshoremen's and Warehousemen's Union, Marine Cooks and Stewards, International Mine, Mill and Smelter Workers, the United Electrical, Radio and Machine Workers, and the United Public Workers.

from holding office. Forty-one also discriminated against Party sympathizers. Forty banned Reds not only from office but from membership. Across the country, dedicated trade unionists were expelled from the very unions they had sweated to create. Without a union, they were also without a job.

Additional pressure came from government legislation and investigating committees. During the first two months of 1947, the 80th Congress introduced more than sixty bills and amendments to curb the powers of organized labor. Out of these emerged the Taft-Hartley Act. Written largely to the specifications of the National Association of Manufacturers, which spent more than $3 million to ensure its passing, Taft-Hartley supplanted many New Deal labor protections and emasculated American labor. Among other restrictions, the Act placed exacting constraints on union organizing, plant elections, strikes, and political action. With the support of both the AFL and CIO, President Truman vetoed the bill,[5] as it would "reverse the basic direction of our national labor policy . . . and conflict with important principles of our democratic society." Congress promptly overrode his veto.

The harshest mandate of Taft-Hartley was Section 9(h), which required every union officer to annually file a sworn affidavit disclaiming Communist membership or affiliation. Any union whose officials did not file would be decertified by the National Labor Relations Board (NLRB) and cease to function as a union. Awaiting those accused of filing false affidavits were perjury charges punishable by a $10,000 fine and ten years imprisonment.

Within the first three months of Taft-Hartley, employees filed 224 petitions with the NLRB to remove union bargaining rights. With Truman safely in the White House after the 1948 elections, the Justice Department began a rash of perjury trials aimed at the renegades who had supported Henry Wallace. Radical, non-Communist officials who had complied with Section 9(h) were confronted by FBI informers who swore they were secret Communists. Communist labor leaders who complied by publicly breaking with the Party and cutting all left-wing ties encountered the same. Scores of radical unionists pitted their word against that of a paid informer. And in the midst of Cold War hysteria, there was little question whose word would be trusted in the federal courts.

Corporate security officers kept a watchful eye on the plant floor, alert

---

[5]Truman had proposed more drastic anti-union measures himself, but with the 1948 elections in view he needed to retain labor's support. The flood of nearly 450,000 letters calling for a veto was certainly a reminder of this.

to employees active in plant organizations. Workers were encouraged to report the "suspicious activity" of fellow workers. Working closely with the security officer was HUAC, among other committees. The investigators leapfrogged across the nation, scouring industry for "secret Reds." Their arrival usually coincided with an impending strike, or a stalemate in negotiations. Traveling with them was a stable of professional informers whose job was to testify that the offending union officials were in violation of Section 9(h). With perjury charges laid against their leaders, the turn fell to progressive elements of the rank and file. "Are you now or have you ever been . . ." was the usual question, directed at membership in hundreds of progressive organizations. Once past or present membership was admitted, the next demand was for names.

Workers who resisted by taking the Fifth could count on losing their jobs; so could workers merely mentioned unfavorably. These were considered "security risks," no matter how long their tenure or how innocuous the job. Republic Aviation reported in 1954 that it had fired 250 workers as "security risks." Two Westinghouse workers with sixty-five years of service between them were fired after taking the Fifth. Both were admitted to be excellent workers. A teenage pot washer in a Seattle hospital was fired because her husband and father were mentioned.

Shop-floor tensions, particularly in the auto industry, grew to a violent pitch. Patriotic workers physically ejected colleagues named by HUAC. In one Chrysler plant a posse of veterans systematically hunted down their left-wing coworkers. *Fortune* magazine captured the events with a photo of a blood-soaked autoworker on the verge of collapse as he attempted to escape the plant. The press had been notified in advance by the vigilantes; the police were also there, but did not interfere. When Congressman Kit Clardy took his HUAC subcommittee on a spree through Michigan, the subsequent violence at the Flint auto plants included stonings. Clardy commented, "This is the best kind of reaction there could have been to our hearings."

In 1954, Congress replaced Section 9(h) with the Communist Control Act, which simply made it illegal to be a Communist and an elected union official at the same time.[6] It also imposed drastic liabilities on any union found to be "Communist-infiltrated"—denial of access to the NLRB elections and, inability to complain of unfair labor practices or to sue in federal court to enforce collective bargaining agreements. With commendable tidiness, the act also created the Subversive Activities

---

[6]It was also illegal to have been a member of the Party within five years of running for office.

Control Board (SACB), the sole body to determine "Communist infiltration."

The impact of this widespread purge was aimed not just at the Left, nor was it intended to be. Workers quickly took note and with few exceptions withdrew to political orthodoxy or disinterest. By 1955, when the newly purified CIO merged with the American Federation of Labor, the American labor movement had become the weakest and most compliant among the Western democracies.

Approximately 1.5 million union members were subjected to security checks as a requirement of employment, union membership, or both. Of these, 232,000 were obligated under Taft-Hartley Section 9(h) to file yearly non-Communist affidavits. At least twenty-four were indicted for perjury and convicted. While the majority of these convictions were eventually overturned by the Supreme Court, seven union leaders were imprisoned *after* conviction. At least one union member was murdered for his radical beliefs, and more than seventeen hundred others were blacklisted.

CLINTON JENCKS

A representative of the International Mine, Mill and Smelter Workers Union, Jencks was sentenced in 1952 to five years in prison under Section 9(h) of the Taft-Hartley Act. After his conviction was overturned, he was hounded by the FBI for ten years, forced from job after job.

The basic crime of Mine, Mill was that we really believed in rank-and-file democracy. You couldn't buy off a Mine, Mill leader and get him to see it your way. Mine, Mill always had a referendum on key issues, on any changes in the union constitution, direct election of union officers. This was the kind of democracy that grew out of the West when there wasn't a government out here.[1]

---

[1]Mine, Mill grew out of the Western Federation of Miners, a legendary radical labor movement founded in 1893, influenced by the socialism of Eugene Debs, and affiliated with the Industrial Workers of the World (IWW). The WFM's militant resolve was forged by Army

Of course, miners all over the world are an independent lot. They have to be or else they can't survive underground. A lot of people wondered, "Why are they so collective?" And I always answered, "Their survival depended on it." They also had a clear concept of their own worth, because they could see the wealth they brought out of the earth, the gold, the silver, the coal. They weren't just turning a bolt on an assembly line, they knew how many millions of dollars they were producing and how few of those dollars they got. [Laughs.] You didn't have to have big political theories, because you saw it every day! You knew you were being ripped off, but doing something about it is another story.

Right after the war, I was a shop steward for Local 557, working at Globe Smelter in Denver, Colorado. I was there a year or so when the local union president called me off the job to meet a fellow from the international. They were looking for someone to move down to the Silver City mining district in New Mexico. They had five local unions down there that were under attack from the mining companies. These locals had formed secretly in the mountains, because the companies would fire anybody immediately if they learned they had joined the union. The locals had said they were willing to chip in to hire their own representative as a go-between for the union and the companies, because the international couldn't afford it.

I didn't know how big a job I was taking on, but I said, "Sure, I'll go." It was kind of a natural for me, because my grandparents were farmers in northern New Mexico, right across from the Colorado line. Around Easter 1947, I bought a used cattle trailer, loaded up all my worldly possessions, and headed down to New Mexico. By that time I had a wife and two children. We were a sight right out of *The Grapes of Wrath*.

When I got down there, I found the work force was ninety-nine percent Mexican-American. Meetings were conducted totally in Spanish. I knew a little street Spanish, mostly how to cuss. I didn't know how to communicate, but I learned fast. We had a little log cabin for a union hall—it would hold all of a dozen people. When we wanted to have a big union meeting, we'd have to hire out one of the dance halls.

Down there, discrimination against Spanish-speaking workers was at least as bad as in the Deep South for the black workers. Which is even stranger in a way, because the Spanish-speaking people were the original

---

bayonets, prison camps, and violent repression. In 1916, the WFM formally became the International Mine, Mill and Smelter Workers Union.

inhabitants, going clear back to the Indian roots. Nevertheless, the companies' attitude was this belongs to us and even those people who had been there for generations were regarded as foreigners.

The towns were generally company towns.[2] There was strict segregation on the job and in housing. There was the Anglo town and the Mexican town—usually a railroad divided them. There was a dual payroll; the Anglo payroll, of course, was much higher than the Mexican payroll. There were different churches. Kids were punished for speaking Spanish on the playground even though that was the language they spoke in the home. Unbelievable stuff. Spanish-speaking workers could only rise to about the level of helper, even if they'd been working there thirty, forty years. They would bring in Anglos, whom these guys would have to train, and then the Anglos would go on up the scale and become journeymen. They even tried to bring in the craft system.[3] They couldn't do it underground, but in the mills and smelters they'd have the boilermakers and the painters and the ironworkers. Then they would segregate those according to race.

I saw we had a big job—the discrimination and the prejudice was so strong that the people had lost confidence in themselves. They thought they had to have an Anglo speak for them. I had a hard time convincing them otherwise. I said the companies would listen to them. I knew the only strength a union had was the strength of the rank and file. So I set about trying to build that confidence, trying to get people involved in doing something about their own conditions.[4]

I was knocking my guts out, working every day, every night. But I'm fighting two, three hundred years of prejudice and exploitation. I remem-

[2]Before union-led reforms ended the practice, the company town worked to keep American industrial workers in a state of peonage, particularly in mining. There, as a condition of employment, the worker and his family rented company-owned housing, much of it substandard, and bought their goods in the company-owned store, usually on credit or with company-issued scrip. Union troublemakers could quickly be evicted, while low wages and high prices maintained a continual cycle of debt. Many towns were armed camps, ringed with barbed wire and guarded by company thugs on the alert for a midnight departure by a debt-laden miner, or the nighttime visit of a union organizer.

[3]Through the last decades of the nineteenth century and up to the passage of the Wagner Act in 1935, attempts to organize the mass of unskilled labor were usually met with violent repression. Samuel Gompers and the AFL relied on craft unionism, the organization of skilled workers vital to production. Craft unionism became a vested interest with the AFL, which the companies exploited to their benefit by pitting the crafts against unskilled labor. Throughout much of its history, the AFL was openly hostile toward the mass organization of labor.

[4]During the seven years of Jencks's leadership, the five local unions amalgamated into one, Local 890, with a new union hall, a bilingual union newspaper, a radio show, and a highly effective shop steward program. Jencks brought Mexican-Americans into leadership and pushed the daily wage up from $3 to $12 to $18.

ber one guy who was working one of the mines, he'd gotten drunk and he was feeling sorry for himself. We had a grievance involving him, and I was trying to talk to him, but he was too drunk. Something he said just roared through me, right in my heart. He looked at me, and you could tell there was a real hurt there, and he said, "I hate you—all of you with blue eyes."

It was like I was all of the people who had kicked his ass for I don't know how long. Something was telling him that this was different, but he didn't dare believe it. God, I cried over that one. He came around, but it took a long time. He was a strong guy, but he'd had his whole human-being-hood kicked around, let alone his manhood. So he had to see this white-skinned, blue-eyed privileged guy do a little test of fire. He wasn't wrong. He was right.

One of the things I'm proudest about—it's funny, what's it got to do with anything?—the people gave me a nickname. If you know the Chicano heritage and the Mexican people, you know that when they give you a nickname they love you. People handed me the nickname of El Palomino because I was white with blond hair. In the Indian-Mexican culture, there's nothing more beautiful than a wild palomino horse.

I signed my first Taft-Hartley affidavit in 1949, and it was a truthful affidavit. It was so ridiculous—of all the representatives in the country, here I'm isolated out in this place—there's no Communist Party, Socialist Party, or any other.[5] There's the old Democrat and Republican Party, that's it. But that didn't matter. The companies weren't convinced just by McCarthy. They were convinced our rank-and-file brand of unionism leads to revolution. And *I* was partly responsible. I would go into negotiations, and the companies would push us so hard. I knew a little bit of the history, because I was born and raised there. So I'd tell the company, "Look, we were here before you ever saw this country. Our grandparents were here—they owned this land before you bought it." And I said, "We're producing the wealth that you send back East. You'd better share a little bit of it or we might not let you stay here."

Well, of course, that's provocative. It was done laughingly, but these guys take it very seriously. They said, "This guy, he's talking communism, right?" That's the way they saw it. They were scared.

The local paper was strictly on the mine owner's side, the *Silver City Daily Press*. I was the tow-haired Communist polecat in the woodpile. It was

[5]New Mexico was hardly a hotbed of Red activity, even by the typically inflated reports of the FBI. In 1951, J. Edgar Hoover reported a grand total of twenty-two Communists in the Sunshine State.

easier than dealing with the issues, you could just pass it off that way. I was named a troublemaker, a double traitor, a traitor to the whole English-speaking community. Here I was aligning myself with the Mexicans, giving them ideas. I was getting the ideas from the people, not them from me!

Well, less than a year after I signed the affidavit I started having problems. There were a couple of attempts to get me. I was summoned to appear before a grand jury in Albuquerque, a secret grand jury. They asked me a whole bunch of questions as to whether I was a Communist, what my associations were. I answered the questions, and nothing happened. The FBI was running around like crazy—I don't know how many agents they had assigned to that one little district.

They would knock on the doors of union members and intimidate them, they would say, "We're from the FBI, and don't tell anybody we came. We're just trying to get some information." Mainly it would be directed against me. At first a lot of people got very scared, because these were agents from Washington—the big power.

Clearly it was part of a coordinated effort to get the union. This union historically had been known as a socialist-minded union—it's a natural target. They were going to weed out that kind of influence, 'cause it's dangerous, it's un-American. The truth is, it was rooted deep in the conditions of the people there. Nobody had to come in and tell those workers what to do.

Oh, it became such a laughing matter, even the FBI that formerly scared everybody. They'd come in and say, *"Don't tell anybody."* So the guys would say, "Ah, we tell everybody!"

They didn't succeed in their first attempt in Albuquerque with the grand jury, and they gave that up. But in the meantime the Cold War has heated up and the whole McCarthy period has been going full blast. Then this little company, Empire Zinc, fully owned by New Jersey Zinc, took us on—it was their turn to take us on.[6] They refused to make a contract, they refused to meet the district-wide standards, and had all sorts of reasons. We had this strike that went on for eighteen months, really bitter, with full use of injunctions and evictions and Red-baiting and the whole bit, all stops.[7]

Salt of the Earth[8] made it a national issue. They could have bottled this

[6]Every year one of the companies would take Local 890 on by forcing a protracted strike, probing for weaknesses that could be used for the benefit of all the companies. Jencks suspected a concerted effort by the mine owners' association, with guaranteed profits for the striking company.

[7]Including tear-gassings, beatings, and the mass arrests of women and children.

[8]For the story behind *Salt of the Earth,* see Paul Jarrico under "The Hollywood Blacklist."

up, kept it secret down in New Mexico, that's what they'd rather do. But when we made a film about the Empire Zinc strike that not only lefties would want to see but that was so dramatically powerful that it was going to be in every movie house in the country, they pulled all the stops. Jackson went on the floor of Congress and accused it of being a propaganda film for Russia![9] [Laughs.] I didn't know nothin' about Russia, nothin' about any of that, it was just about ordinary working people and a family. We started getting threatening phone calls. "Get out or you'll be carried out in black boxes." Vigilantes shot up my car, filled it full of holes. I got plenty of direct messages.[10] But that's what these guys were all about. They take something that is constructive and good and people will understand, and they make it something conspiratorial.

In 1953, Empire Zinc sent their big Eastern head of personnel relations all the way to Congress. He appeared before the House Committee on Education and Labor. He used the Red Scare, said that it isn't possible for us to have this kind of a dispute just over wages, there's got to be something deeper. He demanded that they do something about it. Nobody can say that there's not a direct connection between his appearing before the House Committee on Education and Labor and the fact that thirty days later Harvey Matusow[11] showed up. This guy Matusow, according to his story, had been in the Party and he'd gotten out. At the time he was working for McCarthy as one of his professional witnesses. By the way, give the man credit, he's a wonderful storyteller—makes it out of whole cloth, but he's wonderful.

Thirty days after this personnel guy appears before the House Committee on Education and Labor, Matusow tells the story that he was idly walking through the Department of Justice and he stops in to see this guy he knew and this guy's tearing his hair out. He says, "I don't know what I'm going to do—I've only got a few weeks before the statute of limitations runs out on Jencks and I haven't got a thing." And Matusow says, "Hell, I can take care of that. Give me a plane ticket." They put him on a plane

[9]Donald Jackson (R–Calif.), a HUAC regular, took the floor of the House on February 24, 1953, to denounce the yet unfinished film as a "new weapon for Russia. . . . It will do incalculable harm, not only to the United States, but to free people everywhere." Over the next two weeks, Jackson's charges were frequently replayed over Silver City's local radio station, and the regional press made a habit of reprinting his speech.

[10]In general, the messages included more beatings, gunplay, and the firebombing of the union hall and the home of Floyd Bostick, the only other Anglo officer of the union besides Jencks.

[11]For more on this story, see Harvey Matusow under "Hounds."

down to El Paso. He tells a story to the grand jury, secretly. They didn't call me to the El Paso grand jury, I never knew the grand jury was even meeting. They just had Matusow, that was all they needed.

He made up a story that he had met me at San Cristobal Ranch and I had told him I was a member of the Party and was planning to use strikes to stop production of copper in order to sabotage the Korean War effort.

I had friends who ran this ranch. I'd take a vacation sometimes and go there with my family. I didn't know Matusow, but my friends said that he was there at the time that I was there. See, that's where the guy was smart. I met him briefly, but I never really talked to him. I certainly wouldn't have talked to him about the kind of things he claimed. I thought he was an absolute nut. Everybody there did, because he was crazy, it seemed to us. He wasn't a natural person.

They sent FBI officers up to Silver City, arrested me, threw me in jail. I was living in a little government housing project and was playing with my son in front of the house. They wouldn't even let me go in the house to put on my shoes. They said, "We can't let you out of our sight." I called my wife, she brought me my shoes, and they took me and put me in jail. The union put up the bond, so I was in overnight, that's all. That started the whole thing.

I was charged with two counts of filing a false anti-Communist affidavit— membership in, and affiliation with, the Party. Matusow was the main witness against me.[12] It took about twenty minutes for the jury to return, convicted me on both counts. A jury, by the way, devoid of blacks, Chicanos, women, or union members. They got very clear instructions from the judge. He was the justice west of the Pecos. No bullshit with him. He gave me five years and ten thousand dollars on each count, to run concurrently, so effectively it was five years and ten thousand dollars.

Immediately, the judge is trying to get me the hell in jail. My lawyer's saying, "But he's under bond and we're appealing. What is this?" He's got ahold of me with one arm, the marshal's got me with the other. When my lawyer would be talking the marshal would relax, then as soon as the judge would say "Take him away," the marshal would start pulling, and my lawyer would hold me.

The judge ended up giving us something like twelve hours to perfect our appeal or else I'm going to be in jail. Regardless of the fact we're filing a

---

[12]The prosecution had no documentary evidence that Jencks had ever been a Communist, before or after he signed the affidavit, but they did have Matusow. Out of the handful of witnesses that claimed Jencks had Communist connections, it was Matusow who swore Jencks—after the date of his affidavit—had revealed his continued membership to him.

brief in one of the really important cases to both the government and the union. So then the appeal process started and went on for five years.

First, it went up to the Fifth Circuit Court of Appeals. They rejected our appeal the first time around. Then Matusow recanted, he got so disillusioned with all this stuff that he'd been doing, he sincerely wanted to right some of the wrongs. And of course the Red Scare tried to make a whole conspiracy out of that, that he was paid before and he was paid now.[13] Eventually it went to the Supreme Court, and they ruled seven to one in my favor.

Matusow's recantation was key. He was the only witness. Of course, it was an ancient principle of common law, against the Star Chamber and the fact that the government's got to come with clean hands, that they're supposed to search for justice, not to conceal information that would aid the defendant.[14] So it was very clear, and it was wonderful at this period of time when there were very few victories. It just was a celebration, it was very, very important.

In the meantime the union was fighting a battle on a dozen fronts at once. Fighting off some of the unions that for greed wanted to get a piece of the membership for the dues, fighting the Subversive Activities Control Board, which is one of the witch-hunting agencies the government set up, the Senate Internal Security Subcommittee, the House Un-American Activities, and charges of conspiracy under the Smith Act. They used all of these things to try to label the union as a Communist-front organization.

At the time, the executive board was carrying on national bargaining, and these guys would have to rush back to be in court to defend themselves against all these attacks. It was a transparent effort to make the union's job impossible. The effect was that the union was spending enormous amounts of time and energy that should have been devoted to bargaining and protecting workers' rights to defending the union in the courtroom. It was a very difficult struggle.

I wasn't aware of it, but what was happening in the leadership of the

---

[13]In 1955, fourteen Mine, Mill officers, representatives, and employees were subpoenaed before a secret federal grand jury in Denver. The issue: whether Mine, Mill had bribed Matusow to recant his testimony. Also see Angus Cameron under "Arts and Entertainment" on publishing Matusow's *False Witness*.

[14]During the trial the defense asked the judge to subpoena the original reports made to the FBI by Matusow and one other informer in order to test their credibility if the reports varied from their testimony. The judge refused. The appeals court refused the same request after Matusow's recantation, in which he testified that his original reports would reveal that the FBI knew he was lying. The Supreme Cort ordered a new trial at which these reports were to be made available to the defense. The government thereupon dropped the case.

various progressive unions was they were reluctantly coming to the conclusion that they weren't going to be able to make it. They just had to make the best deal they could, merge with one of the mainstream unions in order to maintain the rights of the people they represented. The international union executive board of Mine, Mill reached that conclusion and called me in, together with the secretary-treasurer, Maurice Travis, also charged under Taft-Hartley.[15]

They said, "Clint, for the good and welfare of the union we want you to resign your post as international representative." Travis was also asked to resign. For me at this time there's a lot of history under the bridge. I had stopped being local union president, because we finally achieved what we'd been working for so long and elected a guy right out of the local area as president and I became international representative to aid in the transitional period. I said, "Well, what the hell has got into you guys? Since when do you think that's going to satisfy anybody? The only thing they're going to do is say, 'See, we told you there was a fire there, now let's get 'em.' "

But they had made up their minds that they had to make the best deal they could. So I had a choice—I could go back to New Mexico and conduct a fight within the union. Well, the union's already facing so much stuff that trying to win that kind of a battle was more disruptive than it was constructive. My second option was pushed very hard by the people in New Mexico—they were ready to hire me back as local union representative. The local was a big local, but it's only fifteen hundred or two thousand members; it couldn't support two full-time representatives, and it was only a couple of years that we had actually gotten a Mexican-American in the job. I was not willing to reverse the tide and have that be another victory of the Red Scare, so I resigned.

Then I began hunting for a job. To make a long story short, I found I was thoroughly blacklisted everywhere in the Southwest. I was just too well known. I ended up working in a horrible open-shop steelyard, working out in the open sun in Tucson and handling I-beams that were bent into making underground supports. They all knew who I was, too, they had ways of making it hard on you.

There wasn't enough union strength in the Southwest for me to survive. The only place I knew where there was that kind of union strength was in California, so I picked up my family and moved out to San Francisco. Why

---

[15]Travis was indicted in 1954 for filing a false Taft-Hartley oath, convicted, and sentenced to eight years in prison. After his conviction was overturned on appeal, he was retried and reconvicted. The Supreme Court overturned his conviction in 1961.

San Francisco? Because of the 1934 General Strike.[16] That was such a high point of inter-union cooperation that it was known throughout the labor movement. There was something deep in the rank and file that that period of cooperation has still left an imprint sixty years later. Guys that were targeted and marked could go into San Francisco and they could get a job and be protected by their union. Which isn't to say the protection was perfect.

I began to hunt jobs wherever I could. Got a job in a roofing plant as a machinist. Hard, dirty work, but it was a job, and I had a family, was doing a very good job and joined the Machinists Union. Six, eight months go by. One day the shop steward came to me half scared out of his wits, said, "What the hell did *you* do?" I said, "What do you mean?" He says, "Well, a couple of guys came in here and threatened to close this place down if we don't have you out of here." I said, "Who's that?" "I don't know," he says, "but there's an awful lot of steam behind this. The best thing you could do is pack up your tools and find a job somewhere else."

And that's exactly what I did. As soon as I satisfied myself that they didn't feel like they could make a battle out of it, I packed up my tools.

That became the pattern. I'd go in and get another job as a machinist, mechanic, a millwright, and I'd work a period of time and I'd be doing a very good job, then a short time later I'd be out. I was just trying to feed my family, but they wouldn't let me. There's no question in my mind that it was the FBI. For five years I went job to job. They did it wherever they could. It's still hard for me to understand why.

The unemployment representative down at the state office put it beautifully, finally, after I was in there for the umpteenth time. "I've just become aware of the fact that there's a new classification," he said. "You're politically unemployable!"

When the Supreme Court decision came down in 1957 I was working for American Can Company, installing about forty million dollars of new high-speed can-cutting lines. So when my picture came out with the whole story in *Time* magazine, I got a call. Into the office I go. He sits me down and says, "What's this we have here? I see you made *Time* magazine." I hadn't even seen it. Turned out the guy was fairly decent. I told him a little bit

[16]The General Strike grew out of a long and bitter fight to win union recognition for the longshoremen. The actual event was sparked by "Bloody Thursday," a long morning of running battles between strikers and police, capped by a military-style assault by police on union headquarters. In the hail of gunfire, two strikers were killed and more than one hundred other persons were wounded, including numerous bystanders. To this day, an annual wreath-laying ceremony commemorates the date.

about it. He says, "You're doing a damn good job here, I don't want to lose you. You're safe as long as we're putting in this line." But he said, "I checked around, and I just have to tell you, as one human being to another, that I wouldn't count too much on continuing here after this job's finished, because the management's going to have to let you go."

Actually where the engineer was wrong is that as soon as that job was done, I took a big cut in pay. If I wanted to stay on I had to go work on the production line. By that time, I could see I was just not going to be able to make a living. I was just going to be running from one job to another.

They were getting all computer-linked anyway. A student at the University of California came to me and said that he was working for one of the big credit firms and they had a huge file on me. You see, the companies were using the credit firm as a front for screening employees. They just had me cross-referenced till hell wouldn't have it. I figured that my chances of surviving in the ordinary marketplace are not very good. And I wasn't ready to throw in the towel.[17]

[17]Jencks eventually escaped the blacklist in the groves of academe. In 1959, he applied for a Woodrow Wilson Fellowship—and was called before HUAC for accepting it. In 1964, despite subsequent Red-baiting, he joined the department of economics at San Diego State University, where he retired in 1988 as professor emeritus.

JOE SACHS

In 1947, Sachs was sent to the Panama Canal Zone as an organizer for the left-wing United Public Workers of America (UPWA-CIO), a union of federal, state, county, and municipal workers.

Starting in 1904, when the canal was built,[1] employees were paid either in silver or gold. U.S. employees were paid in gold; the native employees were paid in silver. So the canal developed two classes of employees: U.S. citizens, the Gold employees; and West Indians and Panamanians, the Silver employees. And this hung on. All facilities were completely segregated—living communities, schools, health care, transportation, recreation, shopping centers—all segregated. All drinking fountains and rest rooms were

[1]Construction on the canal began in 1904; it was opened to traffic on August 15, 1914.

designated either Gold employees or Silver employees—so God help the Silver employee that drank at a Gold employee fountain.

The United States built all the housing on the Canal Zone, and the difference in housing between the U.S. citizens and the Panamanians and West Indians who lived in housing for the Silver employees was incredible. They really built slum housing, these great structures where each family was given two little rooms and a porch. The toilets and bathrooms and water supplies were all in the middle of the building, and they had to carry it down. Now it may have been very similar to the slum housing in Panama City, but this is what the United States built!

Generally the less-skilled jobs were relegated to the native employees, the Silver, and the higher-paid positions to the Gold. However, in some cases they both did very similar or closely related work, but the Silver were paid according to a Caribbean wage scale, which was generally one-third of the American level. If an American got three dollars per hour for the job back in those days, he got one dollar.[2]

Looking back now, it seems incredible. But it was an accepted pattern of life at the time. The U.S. government was firmly committed to a policy which they said would not upset Caribbean wage standards, which fit of course conveniently in with the situation. The Gold employees were represented by the American Federation of Labor in their craft unions, and they were firmly hostile to the Silver employees.

The Silver employees finally called on the CIO for help—"Come down and organize us, we're ready. We'd like to have a union." So the United Public Workers did that. Sent an organizer down in 1946, and with the help of some local people, organized them into a very large union, about eighteen thousand in one local.

I went down as an international representative the following year, to teach trade unionism, so the local people could develop their own local leadership, and to negotiate with the Canal Zone on wage scales and working conditions, to help with handling grievances, and all the other things connected with trade unionism. Of course, the AFL was immediately hostile, because they saw us as a threat. They literally had a paradise down there. They not only got good pay scales but they got a differential based upon employment in the tropical zone. They were free of income taxes. They were able to shop in government commissaries which are subsidized, the same way that military personnel did. They got extra-long vacations to

[2]According to a report issued by the UPWA in 1952, the Silver pay scale was 25 percent of what a Gold worker would be paid for the same work.

give them surcease from the tropical heat, although the climate down there is delightful. They got low travel fares on government-subsidized steamers to travel back and forth to the States; subsidized housing; schooling was good. They truly lived in a tropical paradise. and they saw this as being threatened by the new organizing efforts.

There were numerous grievances on the job, because the white employees, the foremen and supervisors and so forth, just lorded it over the native employees as if they were in some sort of a colony. But the union produced a tremendous amount of improvements—in pay scales, working conditions, and equalizing conditions in general.[3] The union got rid of the hated Gold and Silver signs, all Gold and Silver nomenclature—that disappeared completely. But there was still a great amount to do.[4]

The AFL used all of the weapons at their command to destroy this union. So they got the AFL in the United States active on the job too. And they found that the best way to get rid of it was the point of greatest vulnerability—the Red Scare. They got a number of writers in the United States to write scare stories in the press. One of the most well-known was Victor Riesel, a columnist and a so-called labor writer for the McCormick press in Chicago, the *Tribune*. He was syndicated all over the country, a so-called anti-Red writer. He wrote a famous series called "Stalin's Hand in Panama," which was an "exposé" of the union. He claimed this was the most serious strategic threat to the canal that was on the scene—a Communist-dominated union with its American agents in the Canal Zone, indoctrinating the native employees of the canal with their pro-Russian philosophy. And when the Soviet Union chose to strike—only a question of time, of course—they would find one of the most strategic arteries of the United States firmly undermined.

So the next thing we know, the House Un-American Activities Committee decides to schedule hearings on the Canal Zone. During this period, our union leaders, union functionaries, and staff people were being harassed by the local U.S. district attorney. His name was McGrath, a close friend, we later found out, of J. Edgar Hoover. And the reason I know this is that I was able to get my FBI record under the Freedom of Information Act. I've got all of these letters from McGrath to J. Edgar Hoover, J. Edgar Hoover back to McGrath, and so forth. This guy's screaming to J. Edgar

[3]Before unionization, the minimum hourly wage for Silver workers was twelve cents; after unionization, thirty-one cents.

[4]When the Gold and Silver signs went down, company foremen maintained the color line by painting water fountains and rest rooms either white or brown.

Hoover, "We've got these Reds in the Canal Zone and you're not doing anything about it!"

So McGrath's putting people in jail locally. He arrested several of our people and convicted one of larceny—a very important organizer—a local former employee of the union, Panamanian, and a very able guy. They were able to convict him of larceny, which I'm still convinced was trumped-up charges. But the thing is that the juries on the Canal Zone were made up of white male U.S. citizens—the Gold employees. So anybody arrested from our union found themselves prosecuted by a district attorney who was a vicious enemy of the union in front of a jury of AFL employees—foremen, supervisors, straw bosses—who were their sworn enemies. There wasn't a chance that they could get an acquittal, let alone a divided jury.

Meanwhile, when our regional representative down there was sent back to the States for a conference, the government lifted his passport. He wasn't able to travel anymore. So I'm there by myself, I'm the only one. Usually we had a staff of two people from the States, plus a number of local organizers. The union tried to replace him with others, but the State Department, who was in on this too, wouldn't issue any passports. At this point, McGrath issued a statement to the press that I was embezzling the local union's funds. Can you imagine that? A U.S. district attorney issuing a statement like that to the press—huge headlines.

So he prints this big story. Well, even though the union knew that the newspapers were lying, it's still going to create a certain amount of unrest and consternation. I had to answer these charges. So on the Panamanian radio a day later, I made a speech in which I challenged the district attorney to put up or shut up. "What kind of evidence did you have to make these charges? And if you don't have any evidence, shut up." And I accused him of harassing the Union.

Two weeks later I was arrested for criminal libel. Criminal libel, yeah. Only in Panama! The libel was "I challenge you to put up or shut up about the embezzling charges," and the accusation of harassing the union. The jurisdictional grounds were that even though the speech was delivered in Panama, I had given my speech to a secretary of the union to type in the union office, which was in the Canal Zone, so the actual giving of the speech to the secretary to type constituted the grounds for libel in the U.S. jurisdiction.

I was arraigned and put on fifteen or twenty thousand dollars bail, then let out. The trial came up about a year later. The union sent two attorneys down from New York from Pressman, Whit, and Kammer. Lee Pressman was at one time the general counsel for the CIO. A well-known labor lawyer. And Whit and Kammer were his law partners.

They defended me at the trial, but they'd never seen anything like this. They knew that coming in front of this Canal Zone jury was hopeless. Well, in the first place—they brought the jury back in fifteen minutes! Yeah! You thought they would at least have the decency to give the semblance of weighing this thing, or having a cup of coffee or something. But they brought it back in fifteen minutes—guilty. They had a sentencing procedure in which they brought up all kinds of FBI information about us, about supposed Red-tinged organizations we were involved with back in the States. The penalties were either a fine or jail term. The jail term was up to a year, maximum, and up to ten thousand dollars fine. So they settled for a jail term of nine months. First conviction on record for criminal libel—nine months.

We appealed it, but the Supreme Court refused to hear it. So I began serving sentence in the Canal Zone in the fall of '49. We had to go out with machetes in the jungle and cut underbrush. But they were supposed to only make you do it the first month; then they put you on some other kind of detail, because it's terrible work. You can't imagine what it was like. But they made me do it much longer, and the district attorney used to come out and watch in the afternoon while I was there. He would stand in front of me, so I would be sure and see him. [Laughs.] Then I got ill, and after I was in the hospital for a while they decided to put me in the library.

I was due to come out, and word got around in Panama. A big demonstration was planned for that day. Of course, the Canal Zone authorities got wind of it. So a couple weeks before I was due, they woke me up about four A.M. and said, "Come on, you're leaving." Drove me out to the airport and put me on a plane for Washington. They didn't want any demonstrations.

By this time the atmosphere had become so hysterical, it's almost impossible to realize unless you were there. The union in the Canal Zone fell apart. The United Public Workers were expelled from the CIO under Phil Murray's campaign to purge all left-wing unionism. It became impossible for the United Public Workers to function—they disintegrated. People were so afraid for their jobs, they wouldn't come near a UPW organizer with a hundred-foot pole.

Coming out of the UPW with a prison background—I came under surveillance by FBI agents. They came around to my place of work, asked me if I was ready to cooperate. And there were sly attempts at intimidation and warnings. This was the period at which the McCarran Act was being considered in Congress—it authorized the establishment of concentration camps in this country to incarcerate pro-Red sympathizers. The FBI would mention that steps were being taken and so forth—"Are you ready to talk yet?"

CLAIRE HARTFORD

We meet over coffee in the kitchen of her friend's house in Berkeley. She speaks hesitantly of the past, troubled by the memories. She was once the Midwest regional director of the American Communications Association, CIO.

I came from a very wealthy Jewish family who lost all their money in the Depression. We had an eighteen-room house, a chauffeur, a maid, everything. It was all lost in '29, and it was tough. My father couldn't handle it and abandoned the family. We moved into a tenement slum.

What the Communists were saying made sense to me. The capitalist system spawned depressions, didn't care about people. There were evictions and breadlines and no help from the government. How could this system be good? And there was the Soviet Union, this wonderful new country where workers allegedly ran things, owned everything, and everyone had a job. It was very easy to become Communist. You would think that any intelligent person would find it a viable option. That's what we thought. Of course, we were very disillusioned.

I couldn't afford to go to college and got a job working in a doctor's office. I began to identify with the working class and joined the Office Workers Union, where I was assigned to organize the telegraph messengers. Eventually, I got a job organizing for the American Radio-Telegraphers Association, later called the ACA, the American Communications Association, a CIO union. I was sent from New York to Chicago to organize there.

Because the FBI knew that there were some Communists in the union, they kept tabs on us all the time. But of course, we didn't know that. Actually, we weren't at all concerned with revolution. All we were interested in was bona fide union organizing. The Communist leaders were most devoted in doing that. They made sacrifices. Union leaders today wouldn't even understand the kind of idealistic, honest unions that we were. No official could earn more than the highest-paid worker. There were none of these hundred-thousand-dollar salaries. Half of the salary we got was turned back to the union to pay the rent for the local office. When I think of the way we worked and lived, we were really idealists. [Laughs.]

So I worked in Chicago and my husband, Ken, also worked for the union. He was a real mountain type from Kentucky, never finished high school. We met at a union convention in New York. He was a very bright man, self-educated. Somehow or other, he found books on Karl Marx in Kentucky, and decided that socialism had merit. He came to believe in communism on his own.

The union sent him to organize the telegraph workers in the South, where he used to travel around in a homemade trailer. He had a loud-speaker system and would play Paul Robeson's records in the trailer parks! I thought it was a good invitation to get lynched. But since he was one of the old boys himself, they accepted him—he wasn't a Red agitator, wasn't one of those Jews from New York! [Laughs.] He was a great asset to the union.

So he was in the South and I was in Chicago. Then I became pregnant and Ken was brought back up to take my place as the regional director of the Midwest.

Right after the war, the union sent Ken to California to organize telephone workers. So we moved west. When our baby was old enough for day care, I got a job as an organizer for the ILGWU, Dubinsky's outfit,[1] to organize the unorganized needle-trades workers in the dress shops of L.A. Because the leadership was real progressive, they hired me, knowing that I came from the ACA, which was regarded as a Red union. I worked for the ILGWU until the Taft-Hartley Law was passed. That was the beginning of the repression. Elected union officials had to sign an affidavit saying that they were not nor had ever been a Communist. It was a serious encroachment on personal liberties and on unions.

Since Taft-Hartley only applied to elected union officials and I was a hired organizer, the law didn't require me to sign. However, Mr. Dubinsky insisted that I sign, because he knew that I was from the ACA and therefore assumed I was a Communist. He was determined to oust the leadership of the ILGWU of Los Angeles, which he thought was too left-wing. So even though Dubinsky had loudly opposed Taft-Hartley, he used it for his own purposes. The L.A. union people tried to reclassify me as a janitor, but Dubinsky said if I wasn't fired he would take over the local. So I was fired.

[1]International Ladies Garment Workers Union, headed by David Dubinsky.

By this time, the Red Scare had kicked in. But it developed so gradually that we weren't that alarmed at first. I don't think anybody was aware as to how it would snowball. You went to meetings; you protested what was going on in the country. But you carried on as usual. Although Ken and I were at that time no longer union organizers, we were still Party members.

The Un-American Committee was interrogating lots of people, and things were beginning to get heated. Pretty soon, the FBI was coming around and questioning neighbors about people they had on their list. Two of them came to the house one day. They looked like the cartoon figures of FBI agents—they really wore fedora hats and belted trench coats. Of course, I wouldn't talk to them.

My son Bruce was about four years old at the time and very friendly with the neighbor's little girl. One day she was playing at our house and her mother came and said, "I want to take Sylvia home. I would rather she didn't play with Bruce anymore." I said, "Why?" "Well, some people from the government came and said that you and Ken were Communists. I can't let my little girl play with your son anymore."

Not too long after, a bill was passed in L.A. County, where we lived at the time. It said that if parents were considered dangerous subversives, then they were unfit to be parents and the children could be taken away from them. The ordinance scared the hell out of us. We didn't have any relatives in L.A., so we depended on our progressive friends and other Communists. "If you're arrested, I'll take your kids. If I'm taken, you'll take mine." We tried to protect the children, to have a visible sign of support. We were absolutely petrified. As a result, we sold our house and moved into the city itself, as not to be in the county where the ordinance was in effect. We had to sell quickly, and we lost money. During that time, we also got rid of all of our books: Lenin, Marx, and all the radical ones. We were afraid that they might raid the house and use them as evidence against us. It was very painful. I know we didn't burn them, but we got them out of the house.

By this time the Un-American Committee was after people who'd worked in unions. Of course, our names were mentioned. But we weren't called directly by the committee, because we were no longer working for the union. Ken was working as the director of a community medical center. It had been started by the Furniture Workers Union as an interracial pre-paid medical plan offering low-cost health care for union members. Ken was suddenly subpoenaed by the California State Un-American Committee, which was attacking the medical center as a Communist health organization! [Laughs.]

The hearings were held, and he took the Fifth. They wanted the names of the doctors, wanted him to point out the Communists, to say the center was run by Communists. He refused to answer the questions. In his Kentucky mountain talk, Ken said to Senator Burns, the one in charge of the committee, "I feel like Alice in Wonderland." Burns answered, "You don't look like Alice in Wonderland." So Ken said in his drawl, "You don't look like the Queen either, but you act like her: 'Off with their heads!' " [Laughs.] Everybody was howling with laughter, and it was in the newspapers, but it was damned serious. Many of the doctors were scared off, there was a lot of publicity, and the center folded. Ken was out of a job. We suffered a hell of a lot economically.

I got a job at a health-food store. I did the bookkeeping. The owner thought I was wonderful and one of his best workers. My office was on the balcony and I could see who was coming into the store. One day, I saw two men with their trench coats. I knew exactly who they were, our "caseworkers," as Ken called them. They spoke to my boss, and within a half hour, he was upstairs in my office. "Claire, I have to cut my staff, and since you're such a good worker, you can find a job anyplace. So you have to leave right now. I'll give you two weeks' pay." He was red in the face and fidgeting, because he'd liked me so much and I had liked him. I said, "I guess you were told to fire me." He hemmed and hawed and finally said, "I guess so." That was it.

I was active with the PTA. Once, I was supposed to speak at one of their meetings. The day before, I got a call from the program chair, who was very embarrassed. She said, "Claire, it won't be necessary for you to address us." I said, "Why? I have my talk all ready." "Well," she said, "I don't think it would be politic, you know, your names have been in the papers."

It was all the little things. People who you thought respected you and that you respected, people you called friends, became aloof and cold. You knew what was behind it. That's the way the Red Scare developed, by ripples, widening and widening, until it was everywhere.

After Ken was subpoenaed, several of the doctors from the center stayed at our house. They felt it was safe because the process service had already been there. I remember the kids being so puzzled as to why doctors were sleeping over. They were avoiding the subpoena.

I was very active in fighting what was happening and circulating petitions for the Hollywood Ten, especially since John Howard Lawson[2] was a very close friend. I was also active in the Progressive Party. But we weren't that effective, because the American people literally were scared to death. The

[2]John Howard Lawson was a Party leader in the film industry. See Ring Lardner, Jr., and Edward Dmytryk under "The Hollywood Blacklist."

government had frightened them into imagining that the Communist Revolution was at their doorstep. Nothing could have been further from the truth.

Ken and I were hardly active in the Communist Party. We were simply trade unionists who happened to be Party members. And by this time, I was very critical of a lot of things in the Party. I really hated the dictatorial inflexibility of the leadership. When we were union leaders, the Party always wanted us to take positions on issues, usually political ones, that we felt had no place in the union. We were always running into trouble with the Party for being independent.

My first disillusionment was when Russia signed the Nonaggression Pact with Germany. We were hard put to understand that, because it negated everything we believed in. But we were finally convinced that they had to do it, to give them time to prepare to fight the war. That left a bitter taste, as a Jew particularly. But we were prepared to defend it nevertheless.

We became disillusioned and unhappy with being Communists. But we didn't feel like deserting either. We had a sense of loyalty, a belief in the ultimate goal, even though we didn't like the way it was being done. We didn't want to abandon the Communist Party, especially when they were being persecuted. And we were being persecuted along with them. It would be like leaving your family; you couldn't do it, or didn't want to.

But my loyalties were wearing thin. Bruce was having difficulties at school, partially because of the publicity in the newspapers. He was being taunted. I felt that he was suffering emotionally because of our involvement. I decided I should talk to a child psychologist, to try to help him. This was '56 or '57. I went to a Party psychologist, but the Party had passed a rule that no member should go to a psychiatrist or a psychologist because they might say things that might later get to the FBI. So you weren't supposed to go. I was called in and told, "We understand you are seeing a psychologist."

"Yes, my oldest child is having some problems."

"Well, you can't do it."

I said, "I'm going to a Party person."

"That's besides the point, it's a rule."

"Well," I said, "the hell with you—I resign." That's how I got out. I'll be damned if they're going to tell me what to do about my child. So I can't say that I left the Party because of a blazing idealistic disagreement. [Laughs.]

Ken left at the same time and for the same reasons. Still, we continued to sign petitions and we went to public meetings, but we were no longer members. If there was an issue that we believed in, we went and fought for it.

One day at work—I had just started a new job—in walks the two men, my "caseworkers"! [Laughs.] They went to speak to my boss. A half hour later I was called in and he said, "Two gentlemen were here who say you are a Communist and I should fire you." I said, "That's nothing new—I've lost other jobs for the same reason. Have I been dangerous in your organization?" "No," he said, "you've been wonderful. I don't like what's going on. I'm not going to do a damned thing about it."

So I stayed on the job. A couple of months later, the two men came back, and this time they wanted to speak to me. They said that the former president of our union had told them that I might give them information about Harry Bridges,[3] who was on trial at that time for his citizenship. This guy had turned stool pigeon and gave the FBI the names of all the organizers. Frankly, I didn't know Harry Bridges from a hole in the wall.

I told the FBI, "I wouldn't tell you anything even if I knew something. I'm not even going to talk to you." They said, "You know, your job is at stake." I said, "Go fly a kite." Then they left me alone. I never saw them after that.

I think if we didn't have the children, we would've been less fearful. If you starve it's one thing, but if you have kids, you constantly feel that responsibility. But it didn't stop us from doing what we believed in. We lost jobs, we were hounded from pillar to post. We watched friends of ours in the most awful situations—a lot of them went to jail. I think we survived pretty well emotionally. But we felt this terrible rage at what was happening, that we couldn't stop it, that it was going to be a long time before people woke up. It was sickening, it destroyed you in so many ways. But you had to live. You picked yourself up and went looking for jobs again.

I don't think that history can ever document the personal suffering that went on: marriages were destroyed; people became really ill, some committed suicide; careers ended; neighbor mistrusted neighbor. Somehow the fabric of the society was torn, and torn in such a way that I don't know whether it could ever be the same again.

I know that my trust in the government vanished. I always feel that it can happen again, and that we're never very far from it. I don't think [sighs]

[3]The much-persecuted leader of the International Longshoremen's and Warehousemen's Union (ILWU). Australian-born, Bridges was the only person in American history to be specifically named in a deportation bill passed by Congress. Never a member of the Party, he was tried four times, over a twenty-year period, for being a secret Communist.

that our elected officials really believe in the democracy that we're supposed to be. I feel that corruption has taken over, that morals and principles can be abandoned. A demagogue like McCarthy could come into power again; we're not immune to a Hitler. It's being proved every day. Violence is rising; hatreds and ethnic divisiveness are escalating.

The kind of country we are known to be is in jeopardy. It has always been true; even more so today. But then there are a lot of people who'd fight. The same way we fought it then, we'd fight it now.

On the
Waterfront

At the forefront of radical labor stood the maritime workers. In no other industry was the spirit of class consciousness and internationalism so high. Throughout the 1930s, merchant seamen and longshoremen fought as ardently for political issues as they did for better working conditions. They refused to load scrap iron for imperial Japan or cargo intended for Mussolini's war against Ethiopia; they boarded German ships to tear down the hated swastika. While the Communist Party was a major force along the waterfront, the maritime workers didn't need the CP to tell them about the class struggle. Their radicalism was the outgrowth of a brutal legacy that had informed a half century of unionism.

For centuries the seaman was regarded by law and custom as something less than human, more a chattel slave or pack animal. As late as 1897, the Supreme Court denied seamen the protection of the Thirteenth Amendment, banning involuntary servitude; the Court ruled that they were "deficient in that full and intelligent responsibility for their acts which is accredited to ordinary adults."

"I'd rather be in hell without claws than on a Yankee clipper with the mates down on me" ran the old sailing adage, and it held a hard and bitter truth. Workers at sea suffered under a killing discipline. Flogging was routine for the most minor of infractions, with sentences of six or seven hundred lashes not uncommon. Seamen died with alarming regularity at the hands of their officers, many under conditions that elsewhere would have warranted a murder charge. But the archaic traditions of the sea, backed by the law ashore, allowed sadistic officers to vent their demons without hesitation. One mate's fury left a seaman with "a piece bitten from his left palm, a mouthful of flesh bitten from his left arm, and his nostril torn away as far as the bridge of his nose."

While flogging was outlawed in 1850, the practice continued for decades. Only the solidarity of determined unionism halted the cruelties that plagued sailors well into this century. Living conditions were primitive beyond belief. Sailors' quarters, described by one reformer as "too large for a coffin, too small for a grave," were typically airless, vermin-ridden holes, overcrowded, badly lit, and suffocating. Rations were considered "stuff seagulls wouldn't eat," and "more fit for pigs than humans." Safety conditions remained deplorable, and many a crew was lost for the want of them. But safety cost money and cut into the owner's profit.

Conditions for longshoremen were hardly better. Selected like cattle off the streets in "shape-ups," workers by the thousands waited around the clock to beg the gang boss for a job. The lucky few kicked back 10 percent of their wages for the opportunity. The work was dangerous and the pace deadly. Shifts ran without rest for twenty-four to thirty-six hours. Those who dropped from exhaustion or were injured or killed on the job could easily be replaced. The pay was $10.45 a week.

Out of these deplorable circumstances grew the most militantly democratic and volatile forces in the labor struggles of the 1930s, and the reaction against them was equally volatile. No other group of workers faced a more murderous opposition. In the bitter East Coast strikes of 1936 and 1937, it was not uncommon to find a picket on some lonely pier with his skull crushed by a baseball bat. Twenty-seven insurgent sailors were murdered. Strikers retaliated. Joe Stack, a charter member of the National Maritime Union, recalled their desperation: "We used to take these scabs down to the railroad tracks, put their legs across the track and jump on them. That way, they couldn't go on the ships for two or three months. We did things that the average person would think was crazy. Well, we were crazy. We were starving to death. We were fighting for our lives. It was guerrilla war." The turmoil swept both coasts and the Gulf states, but the unions that resulted put an end to centuries of abuse and degradation.

Out of this struggle emerged one of America's great labor leaders, the admirable Harry Bridges.[1] A native Australian, Bridges left home at fifteen for a life at sea. In 1920, he came ashore for good in San Francisco. By 1934, he was at the reins of an insurgent labor movement that would become the International Longshoremen's and Warehousemen's Union (ILWU), a proud union that transformed the lives of Pacific workers from San Pedro to Ketchikan and Hawaii. Undaunted by adversity (and he faced plenty, including a number of assassination attempts), Bridges was rigorously honest and dedicated to the welfare of the working class.

[1] For more on Harry Bridges, see Robbie Bridges under "Red Diapers."

Although he always denied membership in the Party, Bridges was an outspoken Marxist who at times worked closely with the CP. Many in the ILWU were Communists, but for Harry the interests of his beloved union came before politics.

It was this unapologetic radicalism that marked Bridges and the ILWU for destruction. Bridges himself was hounded for more than twenty years by the FBI and the Justice Department. In 1936 and again in 1939 he was tried as a secret Red; both times the charges were dismissed. In 1940, Congress passed a bill specifically marking him for deportation (it failed in the Senate). That same year, and once more in 1945, he was again arrested as a Red. The Supreme Court attempted to call the campaign to a halt in 1945: "The record in this case will stand forever as a monument to man's intolerance to man," wrote Justice Frank Murphy. "Seldom if ever in the history of this nation has there been such a concentrated and relentless crusade to deport an individual because he dared to exercise the freedom . . . guaranteed to him by the Constitution." But in 1951, Bridges was jailed again for criticizing the Korean War, and in 1955 he was tried in a civil suit calling for his deportation.

Other radical mariners were imprisoned and their unions destroyed. Hugh Bryson served three years under Taft-Hartley, with his interracial Marine Cooks and Stewards harried out of existence. Ferdinand Smith, a black leader of the National Maritime Union, was expelled to his native Jamaica, as his once-proud union took a hard turn to the right under the Red-baiting Joe Curran. The Masters, Mates and Pilots and the Marine Engineers Union were both decimated. The Marine Firemen, Oilers and Watertenders Union joined the NMU in actively purging Communists and their supporters. Only the ILWU, under the inspired leadership of Bridges, survived the onslaught with its membership and values intact.

The bureaucratic machinery that ensured the destruction of the radicals was installed in July 1950, when the Secretary of Labor and Secretary of Commerce met in Washington with maritime employers and right-wing waterfront unions. The subject under discussion was a plan to break Communist influence on the waterfront and demolish the ILWU and the Marine Cooks and Stewards, both previously expelled from the CIO for heresy. It was decided that the Coast Guard should manage the purge, served by the files of the FBI and Naval Intelligence, with the anti-Communist unions supplying the muscle to run the Reds off the docks and ships. A month later, Congress passed the Magnuson Act, which provided for the political screening of all seamen and waterfront men.

In December, the Coast Guard began the Port Security Program. Those suspected of "being under the influence of a foreign government" were denied clearance. They were entitled to appeal the ruling before a review board, many members of which were the very same employers the unionists had battled through the 1930s. Before this kangaroo court, the accused were not entitled to know the evidence against them. Instead, they were interrogated extensively on every aspect of their political and private lives. For these veterans of union battles and thirty-six-hour workdays, of shipwrecks and German U-boat attacks, to be taxed with "the wife's" lack of church attendance must have seemed utterly insane. But the narrow bigots of the screening boards were intent on enforcing a rigid social and political conformity.

Marine workers were quizzed on the newspapers they read, the meetings they had attended, the politics of their siblings and cousins. One steward was blacklisted for having twice rented his basement for a fund-raising function by the Progressive Party, even though he did not attend himself. Another sailor was denied clearance because he had signed a petition supporting Henry Wallace (although he finally voted for Truman). Worst of all, it was discovered that he had donated money on behalf of blacklisted seamen.

For years, the blacklisted were pursued from job to job by the FBI and other security agencies. In most cases it took only a word to the boss before the now unveiled "subversive" would be fired. In self-defense, the hunted changed their names and moved to more remote areas, only to repeat the process once the agents tracked them down again. This policy of harassment continued as late as 1964.

Roughly 800,000 maritime workers were screened under the Magnuson Act. Nearly four thousand of these were denied clearance and blacklisted.

BILL BAILEY

Bailey first went to sea in 1929. By 1931, he was a leading activist in the fight to organize the Marine Workers Industrial Union (MWIU). In 1935, during an anti-Nazi protest, he and five other seamen stormed the German liner *Bremen,* flagship of the German merchant fleet, as it lay docked in New York Harbor. Urged on by fifteen hundred wildly cheering demonstrators, Bailey and fellow seaman Adrian Duffy ran a gauntlet of German sailors to tear the Nazi flag from its mast. Known as the *Bremen Six*, the left-wing seamen touched off an international incident. Bailey later fought with the Abraham Lincoln Battalion in the Spanish Civil War and sailed aboard Liberty ships during World War Two. In 1951, he was screened out of the Marine Firemen, Oilers and Watertenders Union (MFOW) as a security risk and blacklisted on the waterfront. In 1955, he found safe harbor with the International Longshoremen's and Warehousemen's Union (ILWU).

My problems started when the Magnuson Act became law and the Coast Guard carried it out—it became known as the Screening Act. The shipowners and the Coast Guard and the McCarthyites was putting heat on the Left and on the unions. A deal was made that the Coast Guard would issue a new set of passes if the right-wing Unions would name all the lefties they had in the Union. See, the union says, "We can't expel this guy, the membership would go overboard, they'd throw us the hell out. He's a popular guy. He's been twenty years in this union. You're crazy! We couldn't get away with it."

So the Coast Guard said, "All right, we'll set up our commission and we'll take it out of your hands, so all you got to say is, 'Look, we can't help it. It's the Coast Guard. We can't buck 'em. It's the whole government.'" And they guaranteed that these lefties wouldn't get any passes to keep going to sea. Of course, it was ideal at that time, because of the Korean War and all the sabotage scare talk.

Well, in our Firemen's Union it was made for them, because all the officials there were right-wingers, and the Left in the union, through a number of mistakes through the years, most had made themselves known—"You're goddam right I'm a Communist! Put my name on the rolls that I'm a Communist; I'm proud of it!" Left and right, guys were getting up who were Communists and who the officials didn't even know were Communists—they were surprised at some of them. And here the secretary is writing them all down, fast as a son of a bitch. And of course I knew right away, I said, "Boy, somewhere along the line an awful mistake was made, and it came from the top." I'm sure some FBI agents was in the right spot in the CP who was promulgating this type of program. We didn't think right—like we didn't think about Joe Stalin, we worshiped the bastard instead of thinking—and this is what we got. But be as it may, when the Korean War took place and the Coast Guard set in, that was where the

Left started going downhill, and their influence on any of the maritime unions was completely negated. That's when myself and maybe forty to fifty other guys in the Firemen's Union was completely wiped out.

They set up a clearance board, which was actually a trial, and they said, "We want to know the following. . . ." Well, there's no way you can go before such a trial without sitting down and naming everybody, where you been, what you did, how long were you a member of that, and so on. Maybe one or two did, but on that score, I would say that ninety-eight percent of them just went down with the ship.

First of all, every one of the board was a right-winger. One represented the Firemen's Union, there's some guy in it from the MEBA,[1] there's another guy in it from some other outfit. But all staunch right-wingers— that guaranteed you're not going to get back in, see? So anyhow, the Coast Guard set the hearing, and I decided it was a waste of time, that I was not going to go up there, have them say, "Show us good faith, name all the Communists in the union." I'd tell them to go screw themselves, and they'd say, "Well, you haven't got good faith, get out! You only proved to us that you're a Red."

After that, they put changes in the union constitution saying that any man screened by the Coast Guard, which was the same as being identified as a leftie or Communist, will not be allowed to become a member of the union. Then the union says, "Well, if you don't have a pass, you can't even come in the union hall."

It was a wipeout. Our influence was completely destroyed. The unions came out clean, but they were the culprits. It was a simple case of the FBI saying, "Okay, let's get rid of all them bastards. You supply the list and we'll do the dirty work." So it was perfect for the right-wing union officials, they'd say, "Now's the chance to clean up our union, so we'll have no opposition when we run for office. And in the meantime, all the rest of the guys who may become liberal will be so goddamn intimidated aboard ship, they'll shut up." And that's what was happening. Guys on ships—some guys—"I don't want to be the delegate, let somebody else be the delegate." Because being delegate meant that they would have to stick their neck out a little bit to support the rank and file. And once they stuck their neck out, how far do you go before the line of demarcation is a leftie?

The saddest part was talking to the rank-and-filers who knew us, sailed with us for twenty years. Talking to some of them guys, you could see they felt

[1]Marine Engineers Beneficial Association.

bad. But they couldn't do nothing, because they got told, "If you keep your mouth shut, you'll get by. But if you're going to start jumping up and yapping to save these known lefties, then we're going after you too." And that's what happened. Some guys said, "Screw it! It's a matter of principle." And they got up and started talking—"Where is Bailey and all these other guys? Where are they? Why don't the union defend them?" Then the next thing was "Sit down, Commie!" That was the beginning of them getting the business so everybody said, "Well, shit, we got a living to make. We got a home, we got wives, we got this and that. After all, them Commies can take it, they know how." So this is what happened.

We maintained contact with rank-and-filers, and I know I've told many of them, "Take it easy, don't get excited, don't go bananas exposing yourself. Just let us know what's happening in the union. Our day will come." In the meantime, we go to the ACLU. They took a wishy-washy position on it. We went to some of our lawyers who deal with unions, who make their living from unions. They took wishy-washy positions too, figured if they got too out-front that they would start losing some of their clientele.

We were greatly discriminated against in that period. But just being out of the Firemen's Union was not the thing. I had to survive. When I went for a job, I said, "Okay, I'm going to stick to the waterfront. They're not going to get rid of me," 'cause they know that if I went, say, to Idaho and picked potatoes, there'd be no problem, see? But I said, "Them sons of bitches ain't driving me off the waterfront." And so I got a job as a machinist. Instead of the name William J. Bailey, I put W. J. Bailey, or W. James Bailey. Okay, I show up for work, and so on—down working on some ship, doing something. Three or four days later, I was supposed to become a full-fledged member of the union. And I'll be a son of a bitch, some fireman or some conservative saw me, and passed the word on to the machinists. So when I went up to get my full-membership book, which would now give me a little status, the committee was waiting for me. They says, "Well, before we give you a book, we want to see your Coast Guard pass." I said, "I haven't got one." They say, "Well, no Coast Guard pass, no membership."

I said, "But half your members don't have it!" They said, "Yeah, but we want *you* to have one." So, I lost that job. I said, "I'll work—I'll get a job someplace." So I work for Pacific Gas and Electric in the engine room. I've always been a sober son of a bitch. They say, "Be there at eight o'clock," I'm always there five or ten minutes to eight, that type of stuff. I'm working three, four months and doing all right, and it's a job I like. One day I get a call from the head engineer—"Come on upstairs, I want to talk to you." It's always over the loudspeakers, you know.

So everybody figured, "Jesus Christ! Bailey, they're calling you upstairs. You must be going to get a big job. They never do that." So I go upstairs. There are four people standing there. They were really embarrassed, when I think about it. I walk in, and nobody wants to talk to me. I thought, "Jesus Christ! What's happening?" The three of them turned their back and left it to this other guy, and he's fumbling some papers and dropping them. And I said, "Yes, sir, what can I do? Here I am." He says, "Well, I'm glad the FBI told us that we have a number-one Communist working here, and we found out in time before you blew up the plant!"

I said, "Excuse me, what was that again?" [Laughs.] And the other guys are trying to tell him to shut up, put his temper down, because he's letting the cat out of the bag by saying the FBI told them. He said, "Well, we don't want this plant blown up and we have a guard to escort you to your locker. You're going to be out of this plant within five minutes." I said, "Look, I don't know what's going on, but will you put that down on paper?" "No, we won't put nothing on paper!" All the other guys are jumping, "No, nothing on paper! Nothing!" And so you're stuck. What the hell is there to do? So you're steaming. But I did remember he said the FBI told him. Now the only way the FBI would know that I was working in a PG&E plant was that some of the conservatives in the union heard it. There may be one hundred firemen, oilers there; and there's always one of them, while waiting for a ship, that goes to work for PG&E, or someplace else. And he probably brushed alongside of me, the son of a bitch, and he ran back to the union hall and says, "I just seen Bill Bailey working at a PG&E plant." "Oh yeah? Call up the FBI!" This is the way the conservatives were working to get you completely out of their hair. They didn't give a goddam. All they wanted was to make sure you'll never take over their position in the union or influence the union one way or the other.

So anyway, when I walked down it was just tough. Everybody's saying, "What the hell's going on? Where are you going?" I went to the locker, never said anything, took out one or two things—"Hey, wait a minute"—I left the plant just humiliated.

Another job I got with the CIO machinists in Oakland. They say, "We don't give a goddam about it, come on over here. You can organize for this union." So I went over, and where do you think they put me? On a destroyer, fixing a valve way down—all by myself. When I come to think of it, Jesus Christ, way down in the bow of the ship where only one man can shimmy his way down. There was a little goddam intake valve or something down there and I had to work on that for three or four hours, then shimmy myself back up, pull all the tools up—not a soul around. If I was a bomb-throwing son of a bitch, I could've done all sorts of things!

Anyway, I worked about three, four days, maybe—no, a whole week. And all of a sudden, "Mr. Bailey, you come back here Monday, you got to have a Coast Guard pass." Just like that. I had talked to a bunch of other guys working the Oakland Yards. "Do you have passes?" They say, "Nah, we don't need a Coast Guard pass. Nobody needs one around here." But when it came time, that's the way they got to me.

So this went on and on, a job here, a job there, and finding myself losing them all. Four, five years, one job after another, just blown left and right. So I said, "Ah, to hell with this!" I talked to some guy I knew in the ILWU International. And he said, "Bill, maybe there's a place for you in longshor-ing, but you'll have to go north. Either Alaska or Eureka." I say, "Well, let's try Eureka, it's closer."

"All right," he says. So I hopped in a car and I head off for Eureka, and done it secretly—at three o'clock in the morning, shut everything down, got out of the house, just in case some son of a bitch was standing around, and took off. Well, I'm up in Eureka the next day, got a little room, and went down to the union hall. Sure enough, I got a longshore job and got settled. And I'll be a son of a bitch, after six months, the dispatcher up there, he got ahold of me and said, "Hey, Bill, I don't know what the hell is going on. Some FBI guy was up here and making all sorts of inquiries about you." I say, "Yeah, what'd he want?" "Well, he wanted to know how long you been working here, where you're from, did you come from San Fran-cisco, this and that."

So apparently, for some reason, it took them six months to find out where the hell I was working. But this guy, being a good dispatcher, told them, "That's as far as we go. We don't give out any more information. He's working for us. We'll defend him." They put a good front on, and the guy backed off.

I lasted the whole year up at Eureka, then I got my book and transferred down here to San Francisco. I longshored on most piers and I'd see these bastard officials coming aboard and I could see them eating their cud when they saw me—they didn't know how to accomplish further their dis-criminatory business, because the longshoremen wouldn't go for it. You see, Harry Bridges wouldn't allow his membership to be screened out. The ILWU worked a deal with the Coast Guard, they said, "All right, on commercial ships you could put anybody you want on them, but on Navy and Army ships they have to have special passes." So there's where Bridges goes, "Okay, we'll go for that." So I was able to go aboard commercial ships, and most of the ships that I went on were West Coast ships with MFOW guys—old-timers. "Hey, Bill, what are you doing here?" I say, "Well, I'm a longshoreman." "Oh, sit down! Have a beer! Come on in and have a meal with us." And the officials, these bastards who did the job on me, would see this and there was nothing they could do about it.

So anyhow, that period was pretty tough, some lean, miserable goddam times, yeah. You had to be careful, you'd look around if anybody was watching you. Trying to get a job, running your unemployment insurance out. Mostly, it was sad—not that you didn't miss a meal, or sometimes you didn't know where the hell you were going to sleep or get a job, but to run into some of the guys you sailed with and hear them rationalize what had happened—"Well, Bill, I want to do something. Can I give you a couple bucks?" I says, "Aw, I don't want a couple of bucks, just keep the faith some way." But to hear them talk about how sorry they was, they couldn't do nothing. So naturally, to be a good guy, you'd say, "Hey, you did okay. Now don't get involved, don't lose your job. You got a family." As if I didn't. But to make it easy for them, you know.

The FBI did come to the house a few times. A very peculiar thing happened right after the Hungarian revolt when I decided to drop from the Party.[2] You now, my theory was that if the people hit the streets fighting for things, there's got to be something wrong. After all, we go into the streets when we think something's wrong and demonstrate. Nobody has the right to come down with a goddam battleship and blow them away just because they're squawking. So I said, "That's it."

The minute I quit the party—the next day!—the FBI was at the door. I was down at a girlfriend's house at the time, on Grant Avenue, and the FBI came and knocked and she answered the door and said, "Yeah? What's ya want?" Two guys: "We're looking for Bill Bailey. We're from the FBI." I'm sitting there eating at the time, taking all this in, see. She says, "Well, what is it about? Has he done something?" And they say, "No, we want to talk to Bill Bailey, we don't want to talk to you." Anyhow, to save her embarrassment, I got up and said, "Okay, what's all the bullshit about?" The guy says, "Well, first of all, we wanted to congratulate you for leaving the Party!" And that was like an anchor dragging. "Yeah, a great thing to do, Bill, great thing. And the second thing is, do you want to sit down and

---

[2]A mass exodus of American Communists out of the Party took place after the Soviets put down the Hungarian Revolution of 1956. Khrushchev's revelation of Stalin's crimes at the Twentieth Party Congress was another instigating factor.

talk with us now?" I said, "Sit down and talk with you guys? Get out of here!" I slammed the door in their face! All I could think about was how fast the machinery was they had in their apparatus, that they knew immediately that I had quit the Party. Now it had to been somebody working within the organization. We always did say that you couldn't call a quorum unless the FBI attended! [Laughs.]

Then on the job, of course, I'd run into a couple of FBI guys; they'd come in every now and then. "Hello, Bill. Look like you're working hard." "Yeah, working hard. Who the hell are you?" "Oh, hi, I thought you knew me, I'm FBI." "Well, just by accident that you're here on the waterfront?" "Well, I thought maybe you'd like to sit down and talk with us." "I got nothing to say to you! Come off it!" "All right, all right, don't get mad!" I'd walk off, and a month, two months later, I'd be sitting in a restaurant having coffee and I'd turn around, the same guy's standing there. "You feel like talking, Bill?" "Get away!"

So this would go on, and pretty soon, we got to know each other in the sense of calling each other by the first name! [Laughs.] And laughing at each other, you know. He'd say, "Oh, no sense in talking to you. I guess you don't want to talk, right?" I say, "Yeah, I don't want to talk!" "Okay."

You know, all them sons of bitches in the Firemen's Union who did that to me. All them characters are long gone dead—heart attacks; one guy, his wife ran over him in the car accidentally; another guy dropped this way, another guy that. And I can say I lived long enough to piss on their graves! So that's the only satisfaction you get.

Recently, I went down to see one of the new officials in the union. A younger guy, broader outlook on life, who remembered me. I said, "You know, I don't want nothing from the union. I don't intend to sue the union. But it would be nice if the membership were told that people within their union were allowed to be ostracized and humiliated, their union books taken away from them without a trial, their livelihood and everything else destroyed." All I wanted is my book back to show that a mistake was made and that it should never happen again to anybody. That was all I wanted.

So he said, "Well, at that time, there was about six passages in the old constitution dealing with if you're a left-winger you can't be a member of the union; if you're caught reading left-wing newspapers, they could throw you out of the union." He put those rules to a vote and all that Red-baiting was taken out. So we're back to the way it was in the old days: as long as you're a working stiff and you believe in the struggle and stay together—

that was the gospel in those days. I don't know, I tried to convince him that he should do something, but on the other hand it takes a hell of a lot of courage to stand up and say, "Hey, fellas, during the McCarthy period, we screwed some guys, and now we want to give them their books back."

On July 5, 1989, Bill Bailey was reinstated with honorary membership in the Marine Firemen, Oilers and Watertenders Union "in recognition of over fifty years of devotion . . . to the principles of unionism."

JACK O'DELL

Jack O'Dell first began as an activist as a member of the National Maritime Union, the first international maritime union to break the color line. The coming of the Cold War saw the NMU riven by a bitter internecine struggle between progressive and reactionary factions. O'Dell was expelled from the union in 1950, and subsequently blacklisted off the waterfront. (For more on O'Dell, see "Fighting Jim Crow.")

I was an active member of the National Maritime Union and sailed for some five years. I got my union papers in '43, during World War Two, and sailed until '46. I took a year off to work in the South with Operation Dixie[1] and then came back and sailed from '47 to '50.

NMU was considered a very progressive union,[2] and one of the reasons was that it had the highest-ranking black in the trade union movement. The general secretary of the National Maritime Union was Ferdinand Smith.[3] The union was very strong on the unity of black and white workers and

[1] Initiated in 1946, Operation Dixie was the CIO's drive to organize Southern workers into integrated unions. The AFL opened its rival organizing campaign by blasting the CIO as "Communist-dominated" and urged Southern industrialists to cooperate or "fight for your lives against Communist forces."

[2] From its beginning in 1937 until its purge of its left wing in 1948, the NMU was one of the most radical labor unions in the United States. Founder Robert McElroy described it in its prime as a "militant, class-conscious, racially integrated, rank-and-file-controlled, revolutionary union of seaman and waterfront workers."

[3] Ferdinand Conrad Smith (1892–1958), Jamaican immigrant and seaman, was also executive secretary of the Harlem Trade Union Council and a member of the National Committee of the Communist Party.

against any divisiveness and had generally set a good record. I was privileged to get in a union like that. The AFL maritime unions followed the pattern that prevailed in the South, with segregated union halls and segregated jobs. But NMU was a CIO union and believed that "an injury to one is an injury to all," and therefore they organized on different principles. You could throw in for any job in NMU regardless of race or color.[4]

But with the McCarthy period that union, like many others in the CIO, came under attack on the issue of foreign policy. Those unions had a different attitude toward the Marshall Plan. They were for the post-war reconstruction of Europe, but they were in favor of doing it through the United Nations. There was already a United Nations Relief and Rehabilitation Program being run by the UN, headed by the former mayor of New York, Fiorello La Guardia. We felt that the reconstruction of Europe ought to be done through this international agency and not unilaterally by the United States. We knew that while it was being sold to the American people as an altruistic program to rebuild Europe, it was really an economic lever for getting American corporations into the European economy. The Marshall Plan *did* help to rebuild Europe, but that wasn't its only purpose.

So being a union whose membership traveled a lot, we became a target in the government effort to whip the trade union movement into line. And the Curran[5] machine inside the union carried out this work for them. I was in New York at the NMU convention in 1947 when Joe Stack[6] was expelled by one or two votes, that's how divided the union was. That's also the convention that affirmed that Paul Robeson would have an honorary membership in our union. So you could see how the currents were going back and forth.

The critical point was the 1948 elections, in which Ferdinand Smith and Blackie Meyers and some others[7] represented an attempt to maintain the traditions of the union against Curran and his machine that was using

[4]Prior to the advent of the NMU, black seamen had been restricted to jobs in the stewards' department.

[5]Joseph Edwin Curran (1906–81), president of the NMU from 1937 to 1973, was described by one observer as having "a head like a block of granite, a loud, angry voice, and the attitude of someone struggling against an impulse toward mayhem." (Bruce Nelson, *Workers on the Waterfront: Seamen, Longshoremen, and Unionism in the 1930s* [Urbana and Chicago: Univ. of Illinois Press, 1988], p. 229) Allied with the left in his early years, Curran moved far to the right with the coming of the Cold War.

[6]Joe Stack (b. 1916) was NMU founding vice president and a member of the Communist Party.

[7]Surrounding Curran in the NMU leadership was a constellation of veteran seamen—along with Smith, Myers, and Stack were Jack Lawrenson, Al Lannon, and Tommy Ray—all of them gifted mass leaders and members of the Communist Party.

anticommunism to consolidate its position in the union. The progressive forces lost in 1948. The Curran machine began a purge of those who voted for the other group.[8]

In '48, I was down in New Orleans, very active in a group called Seamen for Wallace. In fact, maritime workers across the country had organized for Henry Wallace in the Presidential campaign of the Progressive Party. But that automatically tagged you as being "Communist." So once the election's over, I grabbed a ship and went to Japan. When I got back to New Orleans, it was 1949. All the guys I knew had been expelled. But I was able to go in the union hall, because I had recognized that the membership was on the ships and had shipped out and it really protected my union book.

Well, the NMU continued to deteriorate in terms of maintaining working conditions on the ships, and the Red-baiting continued to be Curran's chief weapon. Of course, working out of the South, we saw this in its very naked form. In Houston, for example, the Curran forces lined up with the Klan and the police to eliminate all of the people that were identified as having voted for Ferdinand Smith in the '48 elections.[9] The port agent in Charleston—a native-born South Carolinian, an outstanding union representative who had stood up for equality for all the seamen—was killed by an assassin, he was stabbed to death in his office.[10]

When Ferdinand Smith fulfilled his obligation as general secretary to inform the other ports that a port agent in South Carolina had been murdered, he was brought up on charges of "malfeasance in office" by the Curran machine. They argued that this was not the responsibility of the general secretary, that he had acted inappropriately. Smith had telegrammed the NMU port agents, and Curran called appropriating the money to send the telegrams malfeasance.[11]

---

[8]Joe Curran's purge was backed by squads of New York City policemen, volunteer muscle from the newly cleansed Transport Workers Union, and hired goons paid for by Phil Murray, president of the CIO.

[9]In both Houston and Galveston, NMU anti-Communists and their allies relied on brass knuckles, clubs, and guns to drive the militant seamen, many of them black, off the waterfront. In Galveston a pitched gun battle erupted between the two factions. Whether the Klan was involved in Houston is difficult to establish. Histories of the period are silent on the matter. Several NMU veterans of the Gulf turmoil have no such recollection, except for one who recalled "hearing the story" and that it was generally believed at the time, but could not vouch for it.

[10]The murderer was not hard to find. Rudolfo Serreo, an anti-Communist member of the NMU, had telephoned police of his intentions to kill the port agent, twenty-eight-year-old Robert Now, chairman of the local Wallace for President committee. Serreo was charged with manslaughter only and sentenced to three years. Apparently, the victim was known around town as a "nigger-lover."

[11]The broader charges brought against Smith and two other left-wing officers, Howard

In any case, Ferdinand Smith was removed from office, and then the immigration authorities came right behind that a few years later and had him deported to Jamaica.[12] That was a big loss for the whole progressive movement. I had come to know Ferdinand Smith in New York, he was a very fine man, we all felt that very personally. We felt that as long as the union stood by Ferdinand Smith, that was at least symbolically representative of a commitment to a nonsegregated union, a union that regarded all of its members with the same respect.

I continued to sail and remained very active in the union. In 1950 I came off a trip to Beirut where some of Curran's people had been part of the crew. When we came into dry dock in Galveston, Curran's people went to the port agent there, named Tex George, and told him I was a Communist. So he brought me up on charges! Never saw me before in his life. All he had was some stamps in my union book. The campaign for the NMU Progressive slate had sold stamps to finance its activities. You might put your stamps in your union book, so they saw a couple of those stamps with Ferdinand Smith on them in my union book and automatically concluded, "Well, we got one here."

So they brought me up on charges of "bringing the union into disrepute." That meant you supported a different policy from the government, not from the union. For example, we didn't agree with the Marshall Plan—Curran did. Remember, a union is an economic organization, it is not a political organization. You may have many political opinions in a union, but certainly foreign policy is not the decisive thing that determines the union. So being identified with a different trend in the union meant that according to them you were bringing the union into disrepute. That's the kind of thing that was being imposed by the Cold War.

Many guys in '48 and '49 never had a trial. They just identified people, and when you turned in your union book trying to get a job they would

---

McKenzie and Paul Palazzi, included violation of the union's constitution and participation in a conspiracy

to disrupt the labor organization. One specific accusation was that they had spent $1,000 of unauthorized union funds to send investigators to the Gulf of Mexico to discover whether union officials were being denied access to union-contract ships in Gulf ports.

[12]Smith was declared an "undesirable alien" by the Truman administration and deported in 1951. Upon his departure he told reporters: "I helped build a union which enabled sailors to marry and have children and a home just like other workers, instead of being kicked around like bums. For this I earned the enmity of the shipowners and their agents in and out of the government."

snatch it and that was the end of it. But in 1950, I did have a trial. I didn't know anybody in Galveston, it was the first time in my life I'd ever been there. I was there about four or five days from the time we went on dry dock until the time I was brought on trial, so I really didn't have much time to organize an opposition. And as it turned out, the Korean War broke out on the 25th of June and on the 26th we had the union meeting. The port agent, Tex George, brought me up on charges and I was expelled. I lost by about twenty votes, out of more than two hundred cast.

So that ended my seagoing days. Then right after that the Coast Guard began to implement its screening program. So even if I was going to appeal the actions taken in Galveston, I and many others still faced being screened. Of course, this had as one of its by-products consolidating the Curran machine inside the union. All they had to do was pass your name on to the Coast Guard and—boom!—you ended up losing the papers required to sail, even though the papers you had been using allowed you to sail during World War Two, when the struggle was against fascism. But in the Cold War you couldn't sail, because suddenly you had become subversive.

After that, I took odd jobs in construction and waiting tables, that sort of thing. I stayed in the South, because I had shipped out of New Orleans, I had gone to school there and knew my way around. But I was blacklisted as far as working on the docks was concerned. I tried to get work in longshore, and got a little bit, but then when they found out my name, I wouldn't get any more. The same was true with standby work. The Marine Cooks and Stewards had a port agent down in New Orleans, a good guy, and he used to give guys who'd been screened preference on relief work while the ship's in port. I got some of that. But then pretty soon the shipowners got onto it and said no, anybody whose name was on that blacklist couldn't do port work either. The idea was not only can't you sail because you might sabotage the ship, but you might sabotage the port. It was that kind of hysteria that was carefully cultivated.

But one must keep in mind that was not the actions of Joe McCarthy or any local official, that was the official government policy. The tone and atmosphere was set by the Truman administration, by the President himself, by the Attorney General that he appointed, and by a Democratic Party Senate that had confirmed his cabinet—that's who set the tone for McCarthyism. Joe McCarthy just saw the opportunity to take that and run 'cause he wanted to be President someday.

It would be a big mistake for Americans to regard this period as merely an unfortunate episode from a fading past. The Cold War lasted forty-five years and represents a tragic chapter in the American experience—as well as a major setback for millions of people all over the world struggling to improve their quality of life. Without doubt, the whole thing was avoidable. The question today is whether we as a nation are able to achieve the moral and spiritual maturity and strength required to recover from its influence.

Red-ucators

Of all the professors and teachers purged or investigated during the Red
Scare, not one was ever accused of incompetence in the classroom, nor
was any credible evidence presented that they propagandized their
students. The majority of the purged were highly honored instructors, and
invariably it was acknowledged that they left their politics at the campus
gates. The sad fact is that American educators have always been targeted
by suspicion during a national fit of patriotism—not for their classroom
conduct, but for their beliefs and associations.

During World War One, more than twenty professors suspected of
pacifism or pro-German sentiment were fired. Between 1917 and 1923,
thirteen states leveled charges of disloyalty against teachers. By 1940,
twenty-one states required teachers to swear their loyalty annually; by
1952, the number was up to thirty-three. But the intrusions of the postwar
Red Scare quickly went beyond loyalty oaths. Nearly twenty states
banned teachers from membership in a vast catalog of progressive
organizations. State and federal investigators and private vigilantes
competed to expose the "Red-ucators." In 1949, HUAC demanded from
eighty-one colleges and high schools lists of textbooks used in literature,
economics, government, history, political science, social science, and
geography. The Department of Defense clamored to investigate the entire
curricula of two hundred universities engaged in military research.
Administrators on all levels of education carried out independent purges.
Colleagues informed on colleagues, students on their teachers.
Abandoned by their institutions, professional associations, and nearly all
unions, targeted teachers faced years on the blacklist, exile, sporadic
violence, and prison.

UNIVERSITIES

The first assault against higher education was aimed not at the faculty but at the students. During the Popular Front years of the late 1930s, the nation's campuses had been a ferment of radical activity. With the end of World War Two, many left-wing veterans returned to academia and picked up where they had left off. The brief flowering that ensued was nothing like that of the prewar era, but it was significant. Nearly all major public and private universities and colleges had some form of student Left.

From the start, campus administrators were hostile toward their youthful activists, but the advent of Truman's loyalty program in 1947 encouraged a wide purge. Pressured by investigating committees and their own trustees, universities and colleges revoked the charters of the American Youth for Democracy (AYD), the American Veterans Committee (the Left's answer to the American Legion), the Young Progressives, and the Labor Youth League, as well as a flurry of local Marxist study groups. An alternative expedient, and far more popular, was to demand of the suspect organizations a full membership list that would be available to government investigators. This method came recomme..ded by HUAC and in many cases prompted a quick disbanding. At the same time, restrictions on outside speakers intensified. All Communists were barred, including novelist Howard Fast and singer Paul Robeson, along with almost anyone left of center. In banning the appearance of a Communist philosophy professor, the president of Wayne University explained, "It is now clear that the Communist is to be regarded . . . as an enemy of our national welfare." By 1950, student radicalism was all but extinct on American campuses, and would not be revived for another decade.

Faculty radicals kept a lower profile. Even in the 1930s they had been much less in evidence than their student counterparts. After World War Two, they simply did not exist in any organized form. Many had disengaged from the CP and, with the exception of the Wallace campaign, had given up much of their political activities, especially on campus. Those who were still in the Party affiliated with community groups rather than academic ones. This, however, did not make them immune. With the catalyst of the Truman program transforming the CP into a national threat, pressure mounted to rid the nation of politically undesirable teachers.

The first shot of the campaign was fired in Seattle. In July 1948, the Canwell Committee, Washington's little HUAC, announced an investigation into the Communist infiltration of the University of Washington:

"There isn't a student who has attended this university who has not been taught subversive activities." The University's board of regents welcomed the intrusion and promised to cooperate fully. President Raymond Allen had warned the faculty the previous December that any Communists should get out "before they [are] smoked out." Eleven professors, all tenured, were subpoenaed. The ensuing circus became the model for the national purge that followed.

Professional ex-Communists testified at length on CP plans to over-throw the government by force, violence, and subterfuge. Local informers provided the same service for the Seattle Left and linked the academics to its nefarious activities. Of the eleven, two denied they had ever been in the Party; one talked of his short period of membership and named names; another couldn't remember any names; four admitted past member-ship but declined to inform; the remaining three refused to answer any questions about their politics or associates and were promptly cited for contempt.

Now came the university's turn. Six of the eleven were put on trial by the academic tenure committee. Even though the committee finally recom-mended that all six be retained, three were fired at the insistence of Presi-dent Allen. Allen then set himself up as an anti-Communist expert and spread the gospel of the new logic: the Communists themselves endan-gered academic freedom by submitting to the mind control of the Kremlin. The well-respected teachers were now "incompetent, intellectually dis-honest, and derelict in their duty to find and teach the truth."

Cornell, the universities of Michigan and Minnesota, Harvard, and Yale rushed to follow suit, depicting CP members as "fanatics" who habitually resorted to "deceit and treachery." Wallace Sterling of Stanford doubted Communists were capable of being "free agents" and held that they were "by definition precluded from being an educator." Also precluded was anyone who resorted to the Fifth Amendment before an investigating com-mittee. Rutgers ruled that reliance on this particular constitutional protec-tion was "incompatible with the standards required" of the academic com-munity.

The most damaging encounter began in 1949 when the regents of the University of California voted to impose a private oath on its faculty. Those who had not signed by the last day of April 1950 would be summarily fired. With the principled refusal of some three hundred senior faculty, the controversy achieved national prominence. Moral support and money poured in from sympathetic faculty at Stanford, the University of Chicago, and Princeton. Albert Einstein and J. Robert Oppenheimer publicly urged resistance to the oath. Sixty-two recalcitrant members of the academic senate were tried by the committee on privilege and tenure. Six were immediately fired, and the remainder were released upon termination of their contracts. By 1951, the UC system had lost 110 scholars—twenty-six fired, thirty-seven who resigned in protest, and forty-seven others who had refused appointments. In that one year, fifty-five regular courses had to be dropped.

By this time, the FBI had permeated American campuses. Whenever a student applied for federal employment, an agent interrogated his professors and checked for his name on the membership lists of liberal campus organizations. The dean of the Columbia School of Journalism complained that agents from the FBI, CIA, and civil service were "following up leads like prosecuting attorneys." At Princeton, government agents demanded to read student term papers. A national organization of former FBI agents established campus chapters that reported suspicious activities back to headquarters. In June 1952, twenty-eight California colleges and universities, including Stanford and the UC system, agreed to collaborate with the state's Un-American Activities Committee and to install an ex-agent responsible only to the committee on each campus.

The end result was widespread intimidation and fear. The academics who had not been fired fretted over when and how they might be. The University of Wyoming undertook a complete search of its textbooks for subversive or un-American material. Controversial topics were avoided in classrooms, syllabi were pruned, scholars now celebrated the status quo. A poll conducted in 1955 of 2,451 teachers in 165 colleges revealed that 84 percent were worried not of being accused of Party membership or of having to take the Fifth, but of being tagged as "subversive" or "un-American." The fear of recommending radical reading material was as high as the fear of student informers.

The purge not only blighted lives but took them. Harvard's beleaguered literary critic F. O. Matthiessen jumped from a hotel window in 1950. Stanford biochemist William Sherwood took poison and killed himself before his HUAC appearance in 1957. Another academic suicide was a professor tortured over his decision to inform. In 1961, an anti-Communist fanatic burst into the Berkeley offices of Thomas Parkinson, a Yeats scholar and alleged Communist, shot him point-blank in the face, then killed his teaching assistant, Stephen Thomas.

LABOR SCHOOLS

An alternative system of higher education also came under attack. These were the labor schools, a dozen or so fully accredited institutions[1] that provided a free education in a wide variety of disciplines for anyone who cared to partake. They offered technical job-related courses and a chance at college life that many Americans missed because of the Depression and the war. Returning veterans flocked to the labor schools on the GI Bill. In music, art, literature, and drama classes, longshoremen and ship scalers, fresh from the dirtiest work on the docks, sat next to office clerks and women in furs.

The majority of teachers worked without salary, and volunteered from industry, labor, and neighboring universities. Among the many guest lecturers were architect Frank Lloyd Wright, poet Muriel Rukeyser, journalist Eric Severeid, and actor Orson Welles. Utilizing the talents of the Hollywood Left, the People's Educational Center of Los Angeles was the first school to offer a comprehensive course in film studies and technology. By 1946 the attendance of the California Labor School had risen to 2,600 students a semester, spread through seventy different course offerings. In the same year, the Jefferson School serviced nearly ten thousand students a year.

From the beginning of the movement in the mid-1930s, the Communist Party played a major role in the organization and funding of the schools, along with AFL and CIO unions, private foundations, wealthy businessmen, and philanthropists. But from the start of Truman's Red Scare the schools fell under constant attack. The Justice Department listed them as "subversive organizations." HUAC pronounced them "schools of Communist indoctrination." The attack was joined by the Senate Internal Security Subcommittee, the Subversive Activities Control Board, and the IRS, which revoked the schools' nonprofit standing and demanded large sums in back taxes. Teachers and administrators were grilled before the committees and hit with contempt citations. Funding dropped off—non-Communist unions were scared away and the pro-Communist unions had their own defense campaigns to fund; foundations and private donors disappeared.

[1]These included the Jefferson School of Social Science (New York), the Tom Paine School of Social Science (Philadelphia), the Sam Adams School (Boston), the Abraham Lincoln School (Chicago), the Michigan School of Social Science (Detroit), the Joseph Wedmeyer School of Social Science (St. Louis), the Seattle Labor School and the Pacific Northwest Labor School (Seattle), John Reed Labor Studies (Portland), the Ohio School of Social Science (Cleveland), the California Labor School (San Francisco), and the People's Educational Center (Los Angeles).

More than one labor school was padlocked by court order. By the late 1950s, virtually every labor school had been destroyed.

PUBLIC SCHOOLS

The attacks against public school teachers were nationwide, but the hardest-hit locations were metropolitan California, Philadelphia, and New York City, the three largest pockets of radicalism in the teaching profession.

The Los Angeles board of education followed the same rule as its New York counterpart: automatic dismissal for any teacher invoking the Fifth Amendment. To cover any loopholes, the Dilworth Act of 1953 mandated instant dismissal of any public employee who refused to testify about CP membership during the period since September 1948. With the passage of the Luckel Act in the same year, the state board of education and every local school board were conferred investigatory powers. The state Un-American Activities Committee and the state senate's Investigating Committee on Education, aided by the Sons of the American Revolution, centered their attentions on the Los Angeles area.

Alarmed, the superintendent of schools announced that every teacher would be required to read a pamphlet on Americanism and sign a loyalty oath. He also encouraged all citizens and parents to report any instances of subversive teaching. The board of education then turned over the entire roster of thirty thousand employees to the chief counsel of the Burns Committee, with the result that more two hundred teachers were either fired or refused appointment.

From 1946 to 1960, California schoolteachers faced at least nine major investigations by state or federal inquisitors, hundreds of teachers were named as subversives, and scores were fired.

Teachers in Philadelphia were harassed by school superintendent Louis Hoyer, who put thirty-two teachers on trial before the board of education for taking the Fifth or refusing to answer his questions. Twenty-six were fired for "incompetence." HUAC visited the City of Brotherly Love three times between 1952 and 1954 and raked forty-one teachers over the coals, thirty-six of whom took the Fifth.

In New York the 1949 Feinberg Law placed a security officer in each school district, whose job it was to file an annual report on the politics of every employee. Membership in subversive organizations automatically disqualified teachers for employment. Past Party membership was considered conclusive of present membership, unless proved otherwise. The burden of proof, of course, rested with the teacher. This was rapidly augmented in 1950 by a state supreme court ruling that allowed the board of education to fire teachers who refused to answer questions posed by congressional committees.

The main target was Local 55 of the Teachers Union of New York. Not only was the TU affiliated with the United Public Workers of America, CIO, but it supported the Wallace campaign and tirelessly criticized the board of education for its failure to integrate the city's school and for its tolerance of prejudiced teachers and textbooks. Beginning in 1946, the TU was under attack from the board of education, the Catholic Church, and the House Committee on Education and Labor.

That same year, the superintendent of schools sent a trio of investigators on a surprise visit to a school on Staten Island, where they interrogated TU activist Minnie Gutride about political meetings she allegedly attended in 1940 and 1941. When the startled woman asked to consult a lawyer, they threatened her with a charge of conduct unbecoming a teacher. That afternoon she dropped by the TU office for advice; that night she committed suicide. She had lived alone since the death of her husband in the Spanish Civil War. In 1950, the president and secretary of the TU, along with five other teachers, were summarily suspended without pay. When the SISS came to town in 1952, the entire union leadership was subpoenaed; all took the Fifth, and all were fired from their teaching positions.

In early 1952, the notorious informer Harvey Matusow was hired by the board of education as a consultant in the arduous task of ferreting out the heretics. He was given a tour of the superintendent's interrogation room, complete with a two-way mirror, where suspected teachers were grilled on their reading habits, their acquaintances, their feelings about Spain, their voting patterns, and what petitions they had ever signed. With Harvey's help, fourteen more teachers were put on the streets.

New avenues of dismissal came in 1955, when the board of education ruled that teachers must inform on their colleagues when ordered to do so by the superintendent. Forty teachers who had previously refused were pressed again to execute the ignoble service: thirty-five submitted, the remaining five were fired. The board also took pains to publish the names and addresses of all suspended teachers—not only would they be unemployed (and unemployable), they would also suffer round-the-clock harassment and threats.

Not until 1961 was this vicious board thrown out by the state legislature. Three years later, the TU, with its treasury defunct and its membership depleted, voted to disband. In November 1973, after a long court battle, thirty-one teachers, waiving any claim to back pay, had their pension rights restored—but only on the basis of the much lower salaries prevailing twenty years previously.

More than twelve hundred college and university professors were investigated, with more than 330 forced to resign or fired, many of them blacklisted. At least seven were indicted for contempt of Congress, and at least four served time in prison. Three professors committed suicide. One graduate student was murdered.

In the public schools, at least sixty thousand teachers fell under some form of investigative scrutiny. More than five hundred were forced to resign or were fired and blacklisted. At least one committed suicide.

Universities

LINUS PAULING

The recipient of the Nobel Prize for Chemistry, the Nobel Peace Prize, and the International Lenin Peace Prize, Linus Pauling came under fire for his stand against the arms race and circulating a peace petition to the scientists of fifty nations. The work that brought him international acclaim also earned him the enmity of his government and of the board of trustees at Caltech. We meet at his research institute near Stanford University. Gimlet-eyed in his early nineties, he sports a beret atop a halo of white hair. (For more on Linus Pauling, see under *"The Peace Movement."*)

I was never a part of the University of California system, so I didn't have to deal with the loyalty oath. But I sent a letter to the governor protesting it, and I was hauled before the California State Committee on Education in Los Angeles. They asked me, "Are you a Communist? Did you send a protest letter to the governor?" "Yes, surely I did. I don't think an oath is a

proper criterion. I don't think people should be required to sign them."
Then, again, "Are you a Communist?" "I refuse to answer."

I was asked—probably subpoened, I'm not sure—to return in front of
the committee the following week in Pasadena. Some people at the Institute said, "President Du Bridge[1] might be put on the hot spot about this
matter. You've refused to answer the question as to whether you're a
Communist or not." I said, "Everybody knows I'm not a Communist, but
I don't like these people in authority asking me questions of that sort."
Someone suggested, "Why don't you write a letter to President Du Bridge
explaining your situation; that you object to being forced to answer questions about your beliefs, but you don't mind telling him or any other
person that you feel like telling that you're not a Communist and never
have been; you're not even a theoretical Marxist and actually not much
interested in these questions?" So I did.

Then I had to reappear before this committee. The chairman said, "Now
I ask you again the question: are you a Communist?"

"I refuse to answer the question—not on the grounds of the Fifth
Amendment or the First Amendment—I'm just not willing to answer the
question about my beliefs."

So he said, "Do you recognize this document?"

"No. What is it?"

"It's a letter that you sent to President Du Bridge. Are the statements in
this letter true?"

"Yes, of course. I wouldn't write statements that aren't true." [Laughs.]

He and the members of his committee fiddled around awhile and then
he said, "Well, you're dismissed. That's all." And I left. When I was going
out, I heard one of the members of the committee say, "All that I know is
that he's made a monkey out of this committee." [Laughs.]

I was one of the earliest Guggenheim Fellows, and I'd been a member of
their committee of selection for about ten years. When the foundations
were attacked, they dropped me from the list of members.

I was also denied grant money by HEW.[2] I phoned someone at NIH
that I had contact with and said, "I don't understand. I received this
telegram saying, 'Despite the letter that you received two months ago

---

[1]Lee Alvin Du Bridge, president (1946–69) of the California Institute of Technology (Caltech), where Pauling taught for more than twenty years.

[2]In 1954, it was revealed that a number of scholars had research grants either withheld or
canceled, without charges or hearings, on instructions of Mrs. Oveta Culp Hobby, the Secretary
of the Department of Health, Education, and Welfare. As late as 1969, HEW was still maintaining a blacklist, barring many distinguished scholars from advisory panels.

assuring you of a grant, it has been canceled.' " I asked why. He didn't really answer. Finally he said, "Well, here's a suggestion. This grant was supposed to cover several different fields of work under your general direction. Why don't you divide it up—you apply for a grant to support some of the work and have your different colleagues apply for separate grants under their names?" So we did. Mine was never accepted, but the other two were, and I eventually got all the monies that I had originally asked for. I was fortunate in that way. I met a man from Columbia whose grant had been canceled. He was just despondent. The university wasn't going to give him money for this work, and he couldn't do what I had done, couldn't use somebody else's name. Some were badly hit.

I found out that the board of trustees at Caltech had set up a committee to look into the possibility of firing me. The committee reported that they couldn't fire me, that I hadn't been guilty of moral turpitude. In 1957, I was asked in to see the president. He told me, "We're losing millions of dollars from donors because the Institute hasn't fired you, and one of the members of the board of trustees has resigned. I'm sorry that we can't fire you, but I can remove you as chairman of the board of trustees of the Division of Chemistry and Chemical Engineering." I had held the position for twenty-two years.

I said, "Fine. You know, I said to you a couple of years ago that I thought I'd been chairman of that division long enough. So why don't I just resign, with a decrease in salary?" And I did.

Then they told me that I would have to give up my main research projects. That they needed the space for younger members. I was still some years away from retirement age. I decided then that the time had come for me to leave the Institute, and I began looking around for another job. Then I received the word that I'd been given the Nobel Peace Prize. I was at our home at Salmon Creek. A couple of days later we went down to Pasadena. I saw the *Los Angeles Times,* there was an article about my getting the Nobel Peace Prize. And the president of the Institute said, "It's very remarkable that a person should get a second Nobel Prize, but there's much difference of opinion about the value of the work that Professor Pauling has been doing." Two weeks later, I announced that I was resigning from Caltech.

Linus Pauling died on August 20, 1994, at the age of ninety-three.

OSCAR SHAFTEL

Oscar Shaftel was fired from Queens College in 1954 for refusing to
testify before the Senate Internal Security Subcommittee. After a decade
on the blacklist, he returned to teaching in 1964; he is a professor
emeritus at both Pratt Institute and Queens College. We meet in an upper
gallery of the New York City Public Library. He speaks easily, well
prepared to tell the tale.

In the late forties, the Cold War began; early fifties, the investigations
began. You get a crazy dogfight between McCarthy's committee, the Un-
American Activities Committee, and the Senate Internal Security Subcommittee, all trying to get their investigative show on the road first. In October 1952, the Senate Internal Security Committee sent two senators and
staff people to New York.

I'd taught at Queens College since the college opened in '37. I had
tenure. I had served in the military from '42 to '46, came back, and was
promoted to assistant professor. I was also active in the College Teachers
Union, an affiliate of the American Federation of Teachers, and served as
chairman of the Queens chapter for several years.

When the Senate Internal Security Subcommittee came to New York,
they got lists of names of union people and leftists who would probably
refuse to answer the direct question. They checked the letterhead of the
College Teachers Union. It listed the vice president for each branch of City
College—Hunter, Queens, Brooklyn—and committee heads. They simply
subpoenaed everybody on the list. I had stepped down as the chairman of
the Queens College chapter, but the current chairman was a dear friend of
mine, Vera Shlakman, a professor of economics.

Vera was subpoenaed on a Monday. On Tuesday, the students called a
protest meeting. I spoke there and got a subpoena on Thursday. Simple as
that. A bunch of us were called and were ordered to show up at the Judicial
Building downtown on Columbus Day. There were people from schools all
over New York. It was amazing, all of these people who had turned up to
be fired on Columbus Day.

They ran out of time before I had to testify. So I continued teaching into
the next semester with this ax hanging over my head.

Of course, they wanted only one thing. No questions about education theory or practice—all they asked was "Are you or have you ever been . . . ?" If you say no, they had lists of perjuring accusers and you could go to jail for perjury. If you say yes, then the next question is "Name everybody you know you ever attended a meeting with." Some tried to say, "I was, but I'm not any longer." Then it's a question of naming all the people you knew back then. You were stuck with the Fifth Amendment, and that's what they were trying to get in the first place. The Fifth Amendment always smells bad in public press. Then you get fired, because most of the colleges, either by fiat of the president or the board of trustees' rules, said anybody who pleads the Fifth Amendment is not worthy of teaching.

In New York City, there was a resolution dating back to the Tin Box graft days and the Seabury investigation[1] in the thirties. This was when public officials had cash boxes in their desks full of one-hundred-dollar bills and would refuse to say where it came from. The college trustees passed a resolution—Section 903—saying you had to cooperate with any duly constituted committee investigating the business of New York City. The federal people knew that this was enforced, and they used this gimmick to their full advantage. If you pleaded the Fifth Amendment, they could get you on Section 903 for refusing the cooperate. That's what hit my group.

A couple months later, early February 1953, I got a telegram from the committee which said, "Report in Washington on Monday, February 9, for a hearing." About a half-dozen of us went down at that time. We were what they called unfriendly witnesses. This was the first headlines they'd had since October. On Tuesday, February 10, they had the great big show with TV in the caucus room of the Senate, jamful.

They called me first. I was on the stand for an hour. There are about thirty pages of testimony, with me arguing and answering questions on why I wouldn't give an answer. First I tried to explain what the principles of a free education were. But the five senators were naive. Instead of simply shutting me up immediately, they argued back. They were trying to get publicity for themselves. Finally, they pinned me into a corner and said, "Answer the question. Are you or have you ever been . . . ?" I said, "I plead the First, the Seventh, the Fourteenth, and the Fifth." One of them was dumb enough to say, "We don't recognize the First Amendment in this committee." [Laughs.] There were some low-grade individuals in the U.S. Senate, a couple of drunks and characters with no dignity. They had no

---

[1]The Seabury Committee (1930–31), headed by Judge Samuel Seabury, investigated municipal corruption in New York City. Its findings sparked a powerful reform movement and brought about the fall of Mayor Jimmy Walker.

objective except to keep it going. Doing their dirty job with a perfectly straight face.

I had to wait a week for the transcript to come down from Washington. Then I was called into the president's office and suspended. I wrote a letter of protest to the president of Queens[2] at the time, a rather low-grade character. I won't ask you to censor that, he *was* low-grade. My case then went on the agenda of the board of higher education to be changed from a suspension into a discharge. I was fired within two months of the hearing.

They didn't discharge me for cause. They simply left the line blank and said there was no more job. You have to understand that very few people were fired for being Communists. You were fired for Section 903, not cooperating with a duly constituted investigating committee. This, despite the protest that education is a state affair. What does the U.S. Senate have to do with education? But they got around that somehow.

Some of my colleagues remained friendly, but most of them had the normal reaction you'd find in a case like that—they crawled. If they said hello, they looked around to see who was reporting. It was not nice. I was already known as one of the leaders of the Left. I spoke all the time at student meetings—it was not as if they had suddenly discovered a carrier of a disease. But after being fired, there was really no movement of support. Even the AAUP[3] didn't want to handle it. We appealed to them and they turned us down. They said they simply didn't have the forces. A couple of us from New York made a presentation at the next meeting of the AAUP and tried to get some help from the leadership, but nothing happened. There was no guts.

I didn't bother trying to find another academic job. The blacklist was just too strong. That would have been absurd. But I had to find something, I was supporting a family at this time, a wife and two and two-thirds children. I was fired in February and my third child was born in May.

I had worked as a stringer at the *New York Times* after college. At Queens, I had been the adviser to the student newspaper. So journalism was in my background. A neighbor of mine, a decent guy, was vice president for advertising of a small trade publication outfit. He introduced me to the editors of two of the trade journals they published, a roofing magazine and an aluminum window magazine. They let me go out and do articles for

[2]The president of Queens at that time was John J. Theobald. For more on Theobald, see Harvey Job Matusow under "Hounds."

[3]American Association of University Professors.

them. They were very brave; it sounds cynical when I say this, but at that time they had no notion where this madness would go. I took an assumed name and went around writing articles about successful roofers and window salesmen for about twenty-five dollars apiece. It was a tough way to make a living.

Of course, I got some foul phone calls and dirty mail, and there was a certain amount of coolness from some of the neighbors. But on the other hand, there were some families, Catholic working-class people, firemen, who were very supportive. I remember with eternal gratitude one person who was concerned with only one thing: Oscar lost his job. She was very sweet and kind and gracious, even though you could assume she disagreed with me politically. This was after the Father Coughlin[4] days, but the church was still known to be anti-Red. To many of my neighbors, it was a personal issue and simply a matter of we're friends, its a terrible thing.

The FBI came around to my neighborhood. Years later, when I sent for my FBI and Air Force intelligence dossier, I saw that they had written letters to my former administrators, to chairman of the department and colleagues. They contacted military people, fellow officers in the outfit I was with before I went overseas. I could tell who the letters were from, even though the names are blanked out. Out of all of this tremendous batch of papers, they had only one basis for their investigation: I was a member of a local college teachers union which was thrown out by the AFL. They kept repeating each other, giving as authority a letter from so-and-so in the FBI who used somebody else in the FBI.

I worked as a freelancer for two years. Then an old friend of mine who ran an architectural rendering service asked me if I would be interested in working for *American Builder Magazine.* Their office was moving from Chicago to New York, and they needed New York bodies. I got the job.

I worked there for two years, almost happily. I became their expert on prefabricated housing. I'd go to the prefab conventions, chat with the people there about the latest, and write a big story. In the spring of '57, I went to one of the editors to make plans to attend the convention, as usual. He said, "Er, let's have lunch." The two editors and I went upstairs to the lunchroom, and one of them said, "I'm sorry, it's this Queens College stuff. We have to fire you, the publisher says." That was that. Immediately

---

[4]Father Charles Edward Coughlin (1891–1979), the pro-fascist, anti-Semitic, anti-Communist, anti–New Deal "radio priest," gained an audience of millions during the thirties. He was silenced by the Roman Catholic Church in 1942.

after lunch, I went to talk to the publisher. He said, "You're controversial. I have to concern myself with the welfare of all the employees of the magazine." So I looked at him and said, "Did the FBI come around?" He didn't deny it. He simply looked down. Because, you know, this was their common practice. A year or two later, he killed the magazine. Not enough profit.

After that, I went and worked on other trade magazines. I had no trouble finding work. Encyclopedias, that sort of thing. In '63, I met some people who knew the chairman of English at Pratt, a man named Sherwood Weber. I told them that I'd like to go back into teaching. I didn't know how strong the blacklist was anymore. They mentioned me to Sherwood, and he said, "I know Oscar. Good scholar, honorable man. Let's try it out."

I give him credit. It was a courageous thing to do. He had to face the trustees. Then again, he was trying to build up the humanities department, and my Harvard Ph.D. would not do him any harm. I taught one evening class in the fall of '63, two classes the term after, and then he slipped me into the day session with a full program. I had tenure in two years. According to several people whom Sherwood spoke to, I came to Pratt as a hero. I made sure to tell every class who they were dealing with.

In '73, some friends of mine in the Queens philosophy department were putting together a religious studies program. I had just finished a book on Buddhism, and they took me on as an adjunct professor. It was strange. Here I was working at Queens and they still hadn't apologized for firing me.

For years, the teachers from the elementary and high schools who had been fired in the fifties had been receiving pensions. That meant they had been reinstated, fault recognized by the board of education. But the board of higher education, now called board of trustees of CUNY, simply ignored the precedent of the public high schools. I wrote a letter saying, "Get on it, brother. The board of ed has done what's right. It's about time the board of higher ed faced the problem." No answer. I sent a second letter—"Time is getting on and people are beginning to die off." Nothing. In a third letter, I offered a solution: I would teach for no pay if they agreed to make an adjustment first, and pay us some kind of pension or settlement in reference to the board of education. No answer. Finally, in 1980, about a year later, they passed a resolution of recognition of impropriety and guilt. With the words "We hope money will be found to make a financial settlement." [Laughs.] I got up at a trustees' meeting at which this was stated and said, "Thanks, but no thanks."

It took them another two years to arrange a financial settlement. It was forced by a court case. Another teacher and I began to demand reinstatement in the classroom with full back pay whenever they ignored us. Legally it was what we were entitled to. Finally, we reached an agreement. No back pay, no reinstatement in the classroom, but an annuity based on a sum we would have earned within a certain period.

I told the faculty on student scholarships that I would devote the money to paying scholarships. When I went to City College, the class of '31, there was no tuition. You paid fifty cents for a library card or something, that was the extent of it—in some classes we were even given books. So I figured that is a good way of marking the distinction between the good days of the Depression and the present bad days. So my money goes to pay tuition for promising freshmen and upperclassmen, preferably minorities, and it's been working well. One Talmudic agreement: I don't know who the students are and the students don't know where the money comes from.

CHANDLER DAVIS

While a young professor of mathematics at the University of Michigan, Chandler Davis signed a check that paid for the printing of a pamphlet attacking the House Un-American Activities Committee. From this signature, a chain of events ensued that eventually led Davis to the blacklist and a prison cell.

We went to the University of Michigan in the summer of 1950. My wife enrolled in graduate school, and I was an instructor. I was immediately active in politics. The principal work was organizing speakers to come to campus. There was interest in the civil rights movement; we had action against some of the legal lynchings and frame-up convictions of blacks in the South. And meetings for world peace, the Stockholm Peace Petition,[1] and international control of atomic energy.

[1] A worldwide peace petition launched out of Stockholm, Sweden, in March 1950 by the World Peace Congress. After an American organization, the Peace Information Center, printed and distributed 485,000 such petitions, the Justice Department indicted five of the PIC's leaders for failing to register as agents of a foreign power. Among those led off in handcuffs was the eighty-three-year-old scholar W.E.B. Du Bois.

I remained in the Party longer than many of my friends, until the summer of '53, not too long before I was subpoenaed. But the Party was less and less important to my political activity, because I was organizing on campus with a group of people most of whom were not in the Party. One of the things we did was turn out an anti-HUAC pamphlet titled *Operation Mind*. The pamphlet was prepared in January of 1952 and issued in February. We duplicated the thing at Edward Letterprint. I guess they saved the check and took it to the FBI or the Un-American Activities Committee. They must have, because the only thing that the committee appeared to know about the genesis of the pamphlet was that my signature was on the check.

HUAC arrived in the spring of 1952. We assumed there were to be hearings at the University of Michigan, but we hadn't yet heard of any subpoenas at the university. In the summer of 1952, the State Department said, "It is alleged that both you and your wife are members of the Communist Party." They came around, knocked on our door, asked us to give them our passports, which we did. I suppose we could have refused.

The passport denial lasted six years, until 1958. It would have lasted longer as far as the Red-hunters were concerned, but Paul Robeson won his case against passport denial. So as soon as Robeson won his case I went right down to the courthouse and applied for my passport, and when I came to the loyalty-oath phrase, I left it blank. And they said, "Oh, you have to fill that in." I said, "No, I don't," and I showed them the story in the morning's *New York Times*. They said, "We don't know anything about that, we're just following our instructions from Washington." I said, "Okay, you take this application the way I've filled it out and you see what your instructions from Washington are." Sure enough, I got my passport.

I was subpoenaed by HUAC in the fall of 1953. After some postponements, the hearings were held in May of 1954. The university knew I was going to be subpoenaed, but they didn't admit it until sometime in 1954. They told me that the committee investigator had come to them with fifteen names and that they, the administration, had talked them down to four,[2] not including students. The eventual list ended up with two students who were called. We know now, although they did not tell me at the time, that among the eleven whose names were dropped, some of them were called to testify in executive session. One of those was Lawrence Klein, who

---

[2]The remaining three were Clement Markert, zoology; Mark Nickerson, pharmacology; and Nathaniel Coburn, mathematics.

later became a well-known economist.[3] Some of the others must have been persuaded to be friendly witnesses in secret and I never discovered anything about that.

My decision to use the First Amendment instead of the Fifth was *real* easy. By the time I made it in the fall of 1953, I had been through a whole bunch of experiences of friends and relatives, including my father.[4] My wife and my friends and so forth had discussed all this with me, and we'd looked at all the things you could do in the legal and political context of the time. We hadn't said, "Gee, if they subpoena any of us tomorrow we're going to take the First." But when it happened it was just obvious. The effect of taking the First was that you let yourself in for an uphill fight to make a court test of the legitimacy of the hearings. I had told the university administration I was going to do this.

It's hard to really put together why this seemed like the thing to do. My wife and I didn't have a realistic idea of how much of a strain it would be to fight the thing through the courts. One thing we were unrealistic about was how long it might take. One person I talked to had been a First Amendment defendant earlier, Leon Josephson.[5] He told me it took him less than a year from getting the first subpoena until exhausting all appeals. For me I got my first subpoena in the fall of '53 and I exhausted all appeals in the fall of '59—it took six years.

At the hearing, almost the only thing HUAC brought up was this pamphlet: "Come on now, you can't fool us. Admit it, you wrote it." They didn't seem to know much else about me. That was sort of insulting. I couldn't imagine with all my political activity that they weren't aware of me!

I only gave them my name, rank, and serial number. As soon as they began asking did I know so-and-so, was I a member of such-and-such, I just told them I was going to refuse to answer all questions of this sort, and I told them why, which was that I regarded the whole proceeding as illegal. I was then indicted for contempt of Congress.

I was immediately suspended from the university. The executive com-

[3]After cooperating with HUAC in 1954, the future Nobel laureate was denied a promotion in 1955 on political grounds. Klein resigned, concerned, he said, with "a serious deficiency of academic freedom" at Michigan.

[4]Chandler's father, Horace Bancroft Davis, had been a conscientious objector during World War One and a member of the Party from 1931 to 1950. He was fired for his politics from the University of Kansas City in 1952, and subsequently from Benedict College and Shaw University.

[5]Cited for contempt of Congress in 1947, Josephson, a legal adviser to the Party, challenged HUAC's right to exist by refusing to be sworn in.

mittee of my department met at once and called unanimously for me to be reinstated without prejudice. The executive committee of the College of Literature, Science, and the Arts unanimously made the same recommendation.

But then came the hearings that really counted—the two faculty senate hearings. These committees, although each included at least one liberal, clearly felt mandated to smoke out Reds. Many people who took the position I did before the HUAC nevertheless answered questions before the university on the basis that the university inquisition was somehow different—it was your friends asking. It was different, all right, but I felt that the university, by holding this political inquisition immediately following the congressional hearing, was making itself part of the operation. It's too bad that some of my colleagues whom I otherwise respected made themselves part of this, but nevertheless they did.

If I were to cooperate with the university committee, then I'd either say yes or no to Party membership. Really, the problem with cooperating with that committee was that there was no way I could tell the truth. If I said yes it would be a lie, and if I said no it would be a lie. If I said yes, then the image that would spring into their mind of what I was and what I was up to would have been false and there would have been no way that I could correct it. And if I said no, the image would also be false, because the image would be of somebody who had seen the error of his ways and was a good anti-Communist liberal the same as everybody was supposed to be, unless they were conservative, of course, which was okay. Neither of those was true.

I was pretty angry that people were saying that I was doing something devious in refusing to answer. The image of me as devious, which of course was regarded as preposterous by my friends, was presumably based on the theory that I was refusing to answer to pretend to be a non-Communist refusing out of principle, whereas I was really a Communist insidiously maintaining my position in the community. I could understand that image, but I couldn't recognize myself in it! It didn't have any resemblance to the way I felt about things.

The reason they could have this comic-book image is because of the way Communists in general had been caricatured, and that's an important ingredient in the thing. The caricature affected every reader of the newspapers, and it affected my liberal colleagues along with everybody else.

This is now June or July of 1954. A second university committee had been set up in advance by agreement between the president and the faculty senate. After the first committee had brought in its reports, I only had a couple of days to look at it before they were scheduling the meetings of the second committee.

The questions the first committee asked were essentially "Are you a nasty Red?" The second committee was again essentially saying, "Well, are you going to exonerate yourself of the charge of being a nasty Red?" The second of those two committees had much shorter hearings—it was really just rubber-stamping what the previous committee had decided.

Before the first of the two committees, they called in my colleagues to try to get the dirt on me without my even knowing that such a session was taking place. In the second one they called me in at the same time as the department executive committee. That consisted of the head of the department, who was a kindly old conservative, and three professors. Two of the three professors said that if they were in my position, they would do just what I was doing. In principle, that ought to have been very embarrassing for the committee, because they were not saying they had discovered that I was a subversive felon, they had said that I was not welcome as a professor because of the stand I was taking toward their committee. So here are these colleagues saying that they would do the same thing. But they refused to allow themselves to be embarrassed.

Right after this I was fired without severance pay. I had savings enough to last for a few months. My wife went to work as an unskilled clerical employee for a few months. I job-hunted like crazy. Quite a lot of places simply weren't interested, and some places the mathematicians tried to get me in and the administrations turned me down. Many of my friends said it's because you have the court case hanging over your head. But I made another job hunt in 1961, when the court case was not hanging over my head because I'd served my time, and the same thing happened. I've been blacklisted ever since.

We used up our savings, and eventually I got a job. I worked for an ad agency from April 1955 to September 1956. My friend Lloyd Barenblatt, a professor of psychology at Vassar, was subpoenaed a few months later than me and indicted very soon after me. He was a defendant most of the same time I was, but we were in New York at the same time working for ad agencies. A small item about his case happened to be spotted in the *New York Times* by some higher-up in his agency, and he was fired the same day. The same thing would have happened to me.

Lloyd's case went through the courts quicker than mine. In 1959 the Supreme Court ruled against him in a five-to-four decision.[6] My case was

---

[6]Barenblatt had invoked the First Amendment before HUAC a few weeks after Davis had. In the Barenblatt decision, the court ruled that because of the Cold War, Congress could ask

simply denied a hearing by the Supreme Court because it was covered by his case. I then had to serve out my sentence in the contempt case.

I was no longer living in Michigan, and the sentencing judge refused to allow me to go into custody in New England—he did that because he knew it would be inconvenient for me. I had to fly out to Michigan, was taken into custody in Grand Rapids, transported in handcuffs to Milan Correctional Institution in Michigan. Then I was transferred from Milan to Danbury. That took a month, because one is transferred under armed guard with other convicts by special Greyhound buses that are made over with wire mesh. So I had a week in Milan and then the bus took us down to Terre Haute Reformatory, then another bus took us to Chillicothe Reformatory, then another bus took us to Lewisburg Federal Penitentiary, and so forth, on to Danbury.

There, Barenblatt was one of my fellow prisoners, and another guy, a personal friend, with a court case just like mine, was also there. And there were several conscientious objectors. There was another guy who was really a political prisoner, Alfred Slack. He was sentenced for passing military information to the Russians, but it was really a political case, because this was at a time when the Soviet Union was an ally of the United States.[7] The guy was a saint, a wonderful human being. He had been helpful to everybody. He was appreciated for all the correct reasons. All the time he was in the penitentiary, he got no time off for good behavior. There's something ironic about that.

I always told the other prisoners what I was in for, and I got a few amusing responses, like "Tell Khrushchev to parachute us some machine guns, we're with him." Which of course was a joke and was known to be a joke. Then I got a different kind of joking response from a con man—he was in for running an abortion mill. He was a friend of mine, and at one point some months after I had told him what I was in for, he casually said to

---

questions about political affiliations that "in a different context would certainly have raised constitutional issues of the gravest character."

[7] Caught up in the Klaus Fuchs–Harry Gold atom spy hysteria that eventually swept away the lives of Julius and Ethel Rosenberg, Alfred Dean Slack, at the time of his arrest in 1950, was a $75-a-week assistant superintendent at a Syracuse paint factory. He was never a member of the Party, nor accused of atomic espionage; his arrest was immediately connected with what *Time* magazine termed "the plot and counterplot by which Russia had stolen U.S. atomic secrets." What Slack had done, by his own admission, was pass ordnance data to Gold in 1943–44. The information concerned RDX, an explosive developed prior to World War One. Even though the report he gave Gold was composed from public information, he was sentenced to fifteen years in prison.

me, "Six months of this for a principle?" But, of course, there again there's something ironic about that too, because although he was simply a professional criminal, the crime that he was in for was a moral crime. He was insistent on the fact that his outfit did good abortions, he was performing a public service.

I got out in the spring of 1960, and at this point I was a hero in many people's eyes. But that didn't help me with employers. In the fall of 1961, I began job-hunting again. I tried dozens of places and was turned down at all of them. But there were several, including Western Reserve University, University of California Santa Barbara, and the University of Colorado, where the mathematicians really were trying to get me a job. Probably, no matter how long I encouraged them to stick to it, they would have failed. When I got the job offer from the University of Toronto, I just told them, "I give up, I'm accepting this job. Don't bother continuing to fight." And they were relieved.

ROBERT COLODNY

Robert Colodny fought in Spain with the Abraham Lincoln Battalion from 1937 to 1938, and was badly wounded. After serving with distinction in World War Two, he became the vice chairman of the Joint Anti-Fascist Refugee Committee in San Francisco. It was then that he began his academic career as a historian.

In 1950, the University of California suddenly sprang the demand for a loyalty oath. The fight against it involved people quite apart from the Left, people who were ultraconservative, as this went against the constitution of the university. A majority of the faculty simply refused to sign it. The Korean War began that summer, and that's what broke the thing open. All the foreigners on the faculty, who included some of the eminent people, had to sign or be deported.

A dozen of us who were Ph.D. candidates in the history department, and hence teaching assistants and graduate assistants, got together and agreed that either all would sign it or none would sign it. We agreed none would sign it.

The university set up a kind of hearing board. And you could come before the board and give your reasons for not signing. They simply didn't renew my contract, which is tantamount to firing. I was blacklisted for six years within the university system. You see, the office of teacher placement at the University of California sends out all of the credentials of its graduates. In my case, this included the raw data from the files of the FBI. Every time I applied for a job somewhere, that garbage went with it.

I finally found out about it when a dean at one of the colleges in California was so enraged by this that he phoned me and told me about it. They stopped doing that when it was brought to the attention of the high officials.

I finally got a job in '56 at San Francisco State College. Soon after, the FBI visited the president of the college and told him what a terrible person he had on the faculty. Secretly, I received word that my contract would not be renewed. So when I got an offer from the University of Kansas in Lawrence, I went there.

Kansas, in fact, was one of the most liberal schools I was ever at—as long as you didn't get divorced, seduce freshmen girls, or get drunk on Sunday. But in terms of what liberals usually think of as liberal, in terms of freedom of ideas, of speech, and opinion, they were way ahead of Princeton, Columbia, Yale, and Harvard. That job lasted for two years, then Pittsburgh came looking for me.

Things in Pittsburgh went along fine—until 1961, then it all came pouring out. What seems to have been the trigger was when I—along with Jean-Paul Sartre, Simone de Beauvoir, and others like that—signed an ad for "Fair Play for Cuba" that ran in the *New York Times*. The FBI started tracking down everybody on that list. This led them to Pittsburgh.

They got one of their patsies in the press to interview me. I gave a fairly accurate biographical account in defense of this and that. The article appeared on the front page of the Sunday edition of the *Pittsburgh Press*, with sidebars detailing everything I had done, well-known Communist front, and what-have-you.

Meanwhile, the Senate Internal Security Subcommittee, under Eastland, had convinced itself that Spanish Republican exiles were primarily responsible for the rise of Castro. So one thing led to another and I found myself subpoenaed.

The Senate asked me why I had applied for a fellowship that had been advertised in *Science and Society*.[1] Apparently they had an informer in there, too. *Science and Society* had a social history fund and they were offering small grants. I had applied for one of them.

I told them what I had proposed to invstigate, which was the disjunction between Marxian ontology and Marxian epistemology, but neither Senator Eastland nor the stenotypist could understand what the hell I was talking about. So I said, "Give me a pad, Senator, and I'll write this down with definitions." And the committee sat there while I explained what epistemology was, what ontology was, and why there should be a neat fit in a monistic theory. They took all this down, then they got tired of talking to me. [Laughs.]

When this newspaper article was published, the university was compelled by state law to certify that I was not subversive within the framework of the constitution of Pennsylvania. So they hired one of the most eminent law firms in the city to act as a gatherer of information. One hundred thousand dollars later they had compiled about twenty volumes of testimony from all over the world, including a great deal of testimony from police informers. They tracked me all over the globe, always coming back to Spain and the Joint Anti-Fascist Refugee Committee. Some things I was accused of I would have been very glad to have done. For instance, one informer said that Robert Colodny was the commander of the Chicago post of the Veterans of the Abraham Lincoln Brigade. I'd have been very honored to have been, but simply wasn't. So then I knew that the son of a bitch was a paid liar who would say anything he was told to.

The university hearings went on for days. They put me under oath, and the lawyer for the big legal corporation that was supposed to be gathering evidence and neutral turned himself into a prosecuting attorney. He used all the tricks of a criminal trial to try to trip me up. He tried to demonstrate that I held an unbroken sympathy for Communist causes, for the Soviet Union, and for revolutionary movements.

The FBI actually tried to subpoena the notebooks of my students, and the students wouldn't give them. Furthermore, the FBI forged letters from my students directly to the board of regents. There was even correspondence about it between the FBI in Pittsburgh and J. Edgar, who gave them permission to go ahead.

I found out about that almost purely by accident. I got the files after

---

[1] An independent journal of Marxist scholarship established in 1936 and listed as a subversive publication by HUAC in 1944.

Congress demanded that they be made available to the victims of the COINTEL program.[2] They drove up to my little house one day in a big government Cadillac and presented me with this stuff from the Department of Justice.

The whole case went on uninterruptedly for about six months. The Senate came first, then HUAC. The HUAC and university hearings overlapped. I would fly to Washington and back. I never missed a class during the whole damned business.

The Senate was interested in more geopolitical stuff, but HUAC wanted to know everybody I knew that they had the name of: "Did you know so-and-so as a member of the Communist conspiracy?" Including the chief Episcopal bishop of California, Bishop Oxnam [laughs], because he was a cosponsor of the San Francisco chapter of the Joint Anti-Fascist Refugee Committee. So they asked me if I knew him as a member of the Communist conspiracy, and my answer was "No sir, I knew him as a toiler in the vineyard of the Lord." Then they dropped that kind of questioning.

Eventually the chancellor of the university issued a report clearing me of all charges, which was submitted to the governor, and that was the end of the Colodny case. But the support was quite unusual for a city like this, in that the famous labor priest Charles Owen Rice, who had done in quite a number of radicals in the unions, came to my defense. Ninety-eight percent of my colleagues were in my favor, not only at the University of Pittsburgh but all the universities around this part of the country. Later on, the industrial financial elite, who had great hopes of a renaissance at the University of Pittsburgh, came to my defense too. I think because they were able to find out through their connections in the intelligence community that a lot of the charges against me were unfounded. And they were able to find concrete evidence of what would be called "considerable service to the state," particularly during World War Two. I think they didn't want to see the university name blackened and didn't believe that I was such a dangerous type after all. They simply told the tinhorn politicians and the yellow press to lay off, and they laid off. So that is probably why the case ended in that peculiar acquittal of all charges.

After that incident, nothing else ever came up, because I was a full professor. Nobody was willing to take on professors anymore, because the inquisitors lost. They gave the game up, and that was the end of it.

[2]For more about the FBI Counterintelligence Program, see M. Wesley Swearingen under "Hounds."

M. BREWSTER SMITH

In March 1953, Smith was called before the Senate Internal Security Subcommittee to testify about his student membership in the Young Communist League some fifteen years previously. There, to his regret, he named names. He is a professor emeritus at the University of California at Santa Cruz.

I started at Reed College in Portland, Oregon, in the fall of 1935. Even at that time, Reed had a reputation for being radical and bohemian. I began to have my eyes opened politically. I joined the American Student Union, a coalition of socialist organized groups, and discovered that the leadership of the ASU was held by a small unit of the Young Communists League. Since they were the decision-makers, I joined that group. It didn't involve making the kind of life commitment that Party membership would have required, but you did have to stick your neck out a bit. One's membership was supposedly secret.

When I transferred to Stanford, I rejoined the American Student Union there, but I did not establish any footing in the Young Communists group. I was getting nervous about it. The Hitler-Stalin pact was absolutely decisive to me. I decided at that point I was just not going to have any more truck with Stalinism. Then the war began, and I got drafted. The Soviet Union was our ally, and Uncle Joe was portrayed as a benign figure. The conflicts aroused by his deal with Hitler were in abeyance, and so I viewed the Soviet Union with rosier overtones.

I had completed two and a half years of graduate work before I got drafted. After the war, I went back to Harvard and got my Ph.D. I was invited to stay on as an assistant professor there, which I did. I was not heavily politically active, but I received a good deal of solicitation in the mail to sign this or that. I signed some of it, but my participation in radical politics was minimal.

I went from Harvard to being chair of the psychology department at Vassar College. After a couple years there, I moved into New York to work for the Social Science Research Council, a private organization dependent on foundation resources that supported graduate training in the social sciences and encouraged research.

I was still at the SSRC when I was subpoenaed on March 2, 1953. I was called up to appear before the Senate Internal Security Subcommittee. The terror was in my heart. At Vassar, I had encountered a right-wing mimeographed publication that published an article on so-called Red-ucators in women's colleges. I was listed in it. The Senate Internal Security Committee focused on the same items listed in "Red-ucators," so they'd obviously read it.[1]

Since I was at the Social Science Research Council, which had good foundation connections, the director suggested I talk with one of these really high-class foundation lawyers in New York and get advice as to how I should handle myself before the committee. I thought a good deal about it and decided that I did not want to be a hero. On the other hand, I did not want to be a fink. And you know, I had family, I was not really ready to make an heroic stand. But I thought that I could do a decent thing by trying to stand on principle but being ready to name only the names of the open Party members who had recruited us and forget about anybody else who was involved. I was in a good position, because we had no formal relationships with faculty. Although I knew informally of some faculty members presumably being Party members, we had no official dealings with them. So that memory was not at all at risk.

I was encouraged by the lawyer. He said, "That's a good strategy. If you have to give names, give the known names, and let your memory stop at that point."

I remember coming into the hearing and being interrogated by the chief counsel, a Mr. Morris, with Senator Jenner,[2] the chair of the committee, in the background. There were a couple of senators in the hearing room and stenographers. I tried to be self-respecting and explained my scruples about naming names. They said, "That's too bad, but we need those names. If people are no longer involved, that will enable us to establish that fact."

Having tried to maintain my honorable position, I was led into naming one or two additional names of people I had no intention of naming. One of them was the woman I had been married to, but I knew that she was no longer involved with the Party.

I was not able to maintain the posture that I had originally intended. I

[1] Allen Zoll, a professional anti-Communist and prewar fascist, published a series of reports on "Red-ucators" in schools. Despite the inaccuracy of his charges, at least one major university consulted this work, as did apparently the SISS.

[2] William R. Jenner was the ultraconservative Republican from Indiana who greeted General MacArthur's dismissal with the charge that "this country today is in the hands of a secret inner coterie . . . which is directed by agents of the Soviet Union. . . . Our only choice is to impeach President Truman to find out who is the secret invisible government."

went away feeling absolutely sick. I remember going up to my room in the old Willard Hotel and retching, as though I was the lowest form of life. It was a miserable feeling.

I felt so badly about having named names that I shoved it out of my memory. Many years later, a progressive psychological organization that I belonged to, the Society for the Psychological Study of Social Issues, was planning a fiftieth anniversary of its founding. They asked if I would be willing to comment about McCarthyism. I said, "Yes, yes, I would. I had experience with it." In order to do that, I requested documentation under the Freedom of Information Act. When I got the stuff, I realized that I had repressed the fact that I gave names I never intended to give. I received these transcripts and I couldn't look at them. When I finally mustered up the courage, I saw why I didn't want to: I saw the very unheroic role that I played.

When I spoke at the anniversary meeting of the psychological group, a lot of people came up to me and said, "Thank you for saying what you did." It was like a public confession, and people seemed to need to hear it. One of the people who had been fired in New York City, Bernard Riess,[3] came up to me and seemed to be very grateful that I had made a clean breast of the whole experience. Others said, "A lot of us had that same experience and have been hesitant to talk about it. The only ones you hear about are the people who were heroic, went to jail or lost their jobs. But a lot of other people tried to compromise and were hurt. They've just laid low because they felt so badly."

While I think the committee had the overt and partly legitimate case of trying to smoke out former Stalinists in the universities, I'm sure they were trying to introduce a chill factor. They wanted to make people on the Left lie low and give freer reign to the expression of right-wing ideas. People become more hesitant to speak out. The professoriate is more individualistic and less coerceable than other professions, so the long-term effects in academia were probably less than on the entertainment industry or the government. But I believe it had to have affected the way people taught, the types of subjects they taught. People tend to pull in their horns in that way.

My appearance before the Jenner Committee was in executive session. It was not in any way publicized at the time. My colleagues, acquaintances,

---

[3]Riess was fired from his tenured job at Hunter College after taking the Fifth before the McCarran Committee in 1952.

the people I named, didn't know about it. Had I been heroic, it would've probably come out. But I was unheroic, so it didn't.

Labor Schools

DAVE JENKINS

A large man, plain-spoken and humorous. "I joined the Party about 1930, I was sixteen or seventeen. My mother was a Party member too. She was originally a milliner, one of the six women who established the Millinery Workers Union in 1913. She was passionately on the side of working people." We meet in a well-kept Edwardian below the Haight-Ashbury district of San Francisco.

The California Labor School was started in 1942. It was founded as the Tom Mooney[1] Labor School, and its first president and vice president were the sister and brother of Tom Mooney. We found the name an obstacle to recruiting and broadening the school. I think they both resigned. We were determined to, quote, not live necessarily in the past. But other than that, we didn't get away from what they represented. We kept the name of the library as the Tom Mooney Library.

I had been the educational director of the National Maritime Union, where I set up classes in the national headquarters in New York—classes on the history of the labor movement, public speaking, labor journalism (a lot of guys that went to sea wanted to write), *Robert's Rules of Order,* the history of American politics, political economy, pretty orthodox stuff. We

---

[1]Almost forgotten now, the Tom Mooney case was an international *cause célèbre* for radicals, trade unionists, and defenders of civil liberties through the 1920s and 1930s. A radical Socialist and secretary of the International Workers Defense League, Mooney was framed with perjured testimony for a fatal bomb attack on the San Francisco Preparedness Day parade on July 22, 1916. After his death sentence was commuted, he languished in San Quentin for twenty-one years until he was pardoned by Governor Olson in 1939. He died in 1942, having spent his last two years bedridden with illnesses that developed in prison.

didn't teach them how to tie knots—although it would've been a good idea. [Laughs.] If we'd been less doctrinaire, we could've used the skills of the old sailors, but we pulled in a lot of the young guys. I also invented a program called Books at Sea. We put chests of books on every ship—titles identified with the labor movement and the Left—and got rid of the crap that the missions and the well-intentioned do-gooders put aboard. We just threw them away. Those sea chests went on every ship in the Atlantic and the Gulf.

I had just landed in San Francisco, off the ship the *President Coolidge,* where we had collected a lot of money for the idea of the school. The idea didn't originate on the *Coolidge.* We just were asked to help, and we made such a big contribution—we had eight hundred crew members—mostly through the fact that I was aboard the ship. People felt there was a need to facilitate the integration of new workers, who because of the war were coming into the Bay Area by the thousands. Most of the workers were from the Southwest or the Deep South. On this side of the bay the black community had about four thousand people, and suddenly it went up to as high as eighty or ninety thousand. The East Bay always had a larger black community, and that doubled and tripled. Unions which had a hundred members like Shipyard Joiners and the Boilermakers suddenly expanded to ten, fifteen, twenty thousand members. There was a tremendous blossoming of the unions.

The idea of the school was a general, popular one. The people that, in the main, organized and put it together were the Communist Party and other sections of the community close to the Left, most notably a guy named Frank Carlson, who was really the first director. When I came off the ship I was asked to take it on, which I did.

Most of the time my salary was thirty-five dollars a week. We had a big staff and more students than any other labor school in the country, mostly because we had a trade union base. The Abraham Lincoln School in Chicago, the Jefferson School in New York, the Tom Paine School in Philadelphia, and some others, these were really schools of academics and intellectuals, some working trade unionists. In San Francisco every single union with few exceptions officially supported the school and gave it money. It was true in the East Bay and it was true in Santa Clara and Contra Costa too. Five college presidents—Stanford, UC Berkeley, San Francisco State, a couple of others—were advisers to the school. As a matter of fact, the associate director of the school was a guy named Holland Roberts, who'd been a professor of education at Stanford and resigned to come on as my associate—which was a little peculiar inasmuch as I'd only gone to the eighth grade. We also got foundation grants. When Sinatra made that film

The House I Live In," [2] we were given seven thousand dollars from the proceeds. After World War Two we were accredited under the GI Bill of Rights.

Before the Red-baiting started in '47, we had the support of all the local papers, the *News*, the *Call-Bulletin*, the *Chronicle*, the *Examiner* . . . oh, the *Examiner?* Never the *Examiner!* [3] But all the others. They wrote long articles about the school, its programs, and about me. The mayor even put me on the Council of Civic Unity during the war years. I got a lot of support from business. Crocker Bank gave us five hundred dollars a month. Bank of America and Shell also gave us money; they were all over the concept of unity to win the war.

One woman, whose father was one of the Big Five [4] in Hawaii, gave a lot of money. She and her uncle owned most of the real estate in the city. Louise Bransten, whose family were Rosenberg Rice and Dried Fruit—they sold their business to Consolidated Groceries for twenty million dollars— she not only gave me interest but she gave part of her capital for the school. Dan Kochler—head of Levi Strauss—was a heavy supporter. At the same time he was fighting a dollar minimum wage for operators up in Sacramento. I remember saying, "You're worth millions of bucks. How the fuck can you oppose somebody getting a dollar an hour?" He's say, "Dave, it'd drive us out of California if we have to pay that."

A woman named Durham, whose family established Goodyear Rubber, gave me a lot of money. One day, she told me she had a small account in Ohio that had been irritating her, so she'd like to give it to me! [Laughs.] So I had this funny relationship with a lot of people who were very generous to me and to the school.

Then the baiting began. I was called up in front of the Tenney Committee [5] as director of the labor school. They accused the school of being Communist, of putting out a "pro-Soviet line," whatever that was. To some extent they were not inaccurate about the fact there were Communists in the leadership, including myself. But by that time, the school had many other

[2] An Oscar-winning short made in 1945 dealing with themes of racial discrimination.

[3] Never the *Examiner* indeed. The *San Francisco Examiner* was the flagship of the archconservative Hearst newspaper chain and a bitter enemy of anything tinged with pink. Radicals on protest marches would steer themselves past the *Examiner* offices just to thumb their noses at the building.

[4] The five corporations of the Hawaii sugar cartel—Castle & Cook, Alexander & Baldwin, Theo. H. Davies, C. Brewer, and Amfac (which began as the German firm H. Hackfeld). The Big Five completely controlled Hawaii's economic and political life until World War Two. The multiracial organizing efforts of the ILWU finally broke their stranglehold on the islands.

[5] California's Fact-Finding Committee on Un-American Activities, steered by Jack B. Tenney.

influences. Stan Isaacs, who was big in the labor movement, was president of the board. Another guy from the railway unions was a major factor in the school. The school was a genuine coalition. What we were teaching, what we were doing, included Communists. We wouldn't have taught an anti-Soviet policy, but we wouldn't have been antiunion either.

Our class in comparative philosophy was taught by an Episcopalian bishop, Parsons, who was a leader in the civil liberties movement. We had a tremendous art department, which was taught by a great variety of famous artists, a bigger art school than the San Francisco Art Institute. Then we had huge classes in psychology and psychiatry and psychoanalysis; those were unbelievably popular. So we had a big debate going on about the question of Freud and Marx and Adler and Jung. Our teachers were drawn from a variety of specialities in that field, and they were the biggest classes in the school. Now it's true that our classes in labor and philosophy *per se* hedged closely to a Marxist position, but there was a lot more going on at the school.

When Tenney asked me if I was a Communist, I didn't refuse to answer. I said, "I want you to redefine what you mean." We wrangled about it, and I told him he was full of shit. They threw me out. Same thing happened in the federal committee.[6] I brought a lawyer, they threw the lawyer out, so I got another one. They eventually threw four lawyers out. One time, I said, "I'm sorry, I can't answer that question. Mostly because I got to take a piss." So the chairman said, "Marshal Fink"—they had a marshal named Fink—"Marshal Fink, escort him to the john." It was hilarious. My intention was to fuck it up. But it was an absurd hearing anyway. How could you identify the origins of what we were teaching? There were some Communists among the teachers, but we had such a broad curriculum they were actually a minority. I was functioning in a labor movement which by and large did not have a Left ideology, except the longshoremen and a few other unions. I understood that you couldn't have a school leadership that ignored those realities.

The school lasted until '54. I left in '49.[7] First of all, I got tired of raising

[6]The federal harassment of the California Labor School began in 1948 with Attorney General Clark's announcement to the press that he was placing the school on his list of subversive organizations. The Treasury Department then rescinded the school's tax exemption, demanded back taxes from 1942 to 1948, and seized the school's bank account. In 1954, Attorney General Brownell ordered the school to register as a Communist front under the McCarran Act of 1950; the school refused. By March 1956, when the Subversive Activities Control Board ruled that the school was "dominated by Communists," there was little money left to appeal the ruling.

[7]The California Labor School closed its doors for the last time on May 5, 1957, aided by the padlocks installed by the IRS, whose stated purpose was to forestall an announced May Day celebration and fund-raising book sale.

money. I wasn't teaching, which I liked to do. And then I started to disagree with the Party, who were putting a lot of pressure on me to drop classes in psychology. And I started to disagree with them—not too openly—on the issue of the amount of emphasis put on language in relation to the black issue. Not that it wasn't important, but not as important as some. Even if you used the word "black" in studies—we had one case where a guy was teaching the history of primitive economics and he used the word "black," indicating negative. He was attacked savagely for perpetuating "black" as a negative. So I started to disagree with them on some of this. There was a series of black films put out by Hollywood which the Party negatively characterized as just a more profound form of white chauvinism, and I didn't agree with that either. By that time I had become very good and warm friends with Paul Robeson, who had some influence out here in this discussion.

The school grew enormously. At one point we had one hundred and sixteen teachers between here and Oakland and Los Angeles, plus extension classes. I was raising close to a quarter of a million dollars a year. The school staggered on for five more years without me, and became more driven in part because of the attacks. It was forced into isolation, it became more and more a Party school, which I was fighting and was opposed to.

I stayed in the Party until about '56. I would've gotten out earlier except McCarthyism came along. I felt, "Fuck it, this is not the time to leave. It would be tantamount to running away." So I stayed and took on the fight on labor defense and the Smith Act fight and the McCarran Act fight, deportations and all that shit. But my heart was not in the Highlands. When the Khrushchev report came out, I left the Party, which is now thirty-three years ago, I guess.

Dave Jenkins died on June 18, 1993, at the age of seventy-nine.

HERBERT APTHEKER

An independent and prolific Marxist historian, Aptheker was a defense witness for many of the Communist Party leaders prosecuted under the Smith Act. He was also a prominent figure in the Jefferson School.

I began teaching American history around 1936. I was a teacher at the Workers School before I was in the Party. Then the Workers School became the School for Democracy and I taught there. Then the Jefferson School was created during the war, '43 or '44, by which time I was in the Army. When I came home from overseas, I became associated with that.

The Left at that time was very strong. First, in terms of the New Deal in the thirties and the tremendous growth of the labor movement, which was a fundamental source of support, especially in California. And with the struggle against fascism, the whole Spanish War business—several of our teachers were Spanish vets—the school attracted thousands. Whenever I came to the California Labor School, it was always jammed. I spoke once or twice at their annual dinner, that kind of thing. It was part of the euphoria with the defeat of fascism and the Wallace movement, in which the Left was very strong.

The Jefferson School had its own building on Sixth Avenue at about 15th or 16th Street. There were several people who were very influential in it. One was Alexander Trachtenberg, who was the owner of International Publishers and whose history went way back into prerevolutionary Russia.[1] He had a Ph.D. from Yale, and was associated with the old Rand School. Trachtenberg was important in the creation and sustaining of the Jefferson School. Howard Selsam, who had been a professor of philosophy at Brooklyn College and had been summarily fired in the thirties in a witch hunt, was a leader in the school and taught there.[2] And an African-American chap, Doxey Wilkerson, who had been a professor at Howard, quite distinguished in social sciences, especially education, and had published important studies for the federal government. Doxey was also one of the leading figures at the Jefferson School. And I was. I taught classes there in what we called Negro history and American history from then on until the persecution by the government in the McCarthy period.

The school was open to everybody and it was attended by everybody. By about 1946, we had thousands of students and we had to put in another elevator, it was a seven- or nine-story building. We had a very large bookstore on the ground floor, which was very busy. We had a considerable

[1]A left-wing Socialist and native Russian from Odessa, Trachtenberg took part in the revolution of 1905 as a young man of twenty. Emigrating to the United States the following year, he was naturalized in 1914. An early member of the Communist Party, he was convicted in 1952 under the Smith Act and sentenced to three years in prison.

[2]Contrary to the prevailing logic of the witch-hunt era, Selsam, in the early thirties, was recruited into the Party by one of his students.

faculty, including Dashiell Hammett,[3] who taught short-story writing and detective writing; Sidney Finkelstein, one of the few geniuses I've known in my life, who taught art and music. W.E.B. Du Bois taught a course on Africa for a while. Very distinguished people not only taught but visited. Alice Childress, the well-known black author, was a student there. All sorts of people were students. Mostly young, men and women, black and white. Lorraine Hansberry was one of my students,[4] for instance, and her gorgeous friend Yvonne Gregory, who was a poet and couldn't take Jim Crow anymore and left for France and married there. They were two such beautiful women that when they entered the room, everything stopped and people looked at them, fresh and gorgeous, full of life. And then Susan Brownmiller, who later wrote some best-seller,[5] she mentions that she studied with me—in fact, she boasts about it.

It was a very busy place. Most of the classes were in the evening. We had thousands of students, and everyone paid tuition. Faculty wasn't paid, except in special cases where someone needed ten dollars or something to get food. Sidney Finkelstein, for instance, had been fired from various jobs and finally he was employed by the Post Office as some sort of clerk. He tried to organize a union and was fired. He had very great difficulty getting jobs. He published numerous books, of course, but the royalties were very slim. I was one of the people that insisted that Sidney be paid five or ten dollars when he lectured.

All kinds of classes were taught: languages, writing, music, dance, history, economics, sociology, political science, labor organizing, philosophy, and dialectical materialism. There were straight courses in philosophy in which Marxism, of course, was one of the subjects studied. It was simply a left-leaning university, that's the way I would describe it. What students could find at the Jefferson School that they couldn't find at CCNY was reality. For instance, I was perhaps the first outside of black universities to teach anything remotely resembling the truth about American history, and particularly African-American history.

[3]Author of *The Maltese Falcon, The Thin Man,* and other influential crime novels, Hammett was imprisoned for six months for refusing to divulge a list of contributors to the bail fund of the Civil Rights Congress. In fact, Hammett hadn't a clue as to who was on the list or where it was, but refused on principle to say so.

[4]Two of the leading black women writers of the period, Alice Childress and Lorraine Hansberry both wrote for *Freedom,* Paul Robeson's Harlem newspaper, and were firm supporters of W.E.B. Du Bois. In 1959, Hansberry became the first black woman to have a play produced on Broadway with *A Raisin in the Sun.*

[5]*Against Our Will: Men, Women, and Rape* (New York: Simon & Schuster, 1975).

There are any number of professors now who took my courses in history, and some are quite distinguished. Most of them will acknowledge this. I inspired studies of the Negro in agriculture, the Negro in the trade union movement, the Negro opposition to imperialism, and so on. I couldn't get a job in a university, but I have been the adviser of many dissertations. My book *American Negro Slave Revolts,* published by Columbia in a moment of madness in 1943, was the first significant attack upon the racist nonsense on docility and passivity and so on. It's now a classic. It had to fight its way through the incredible racism of the history profession and anti-Semitism, but it's made its way. You have to read Aptheker now.

I lectured quite often at all the other schools, the Sam Adams School, the Abraham Lincoln School—William L. Patterson[6] for a while was director of that school—and then the labor school in San Francisco. There was also something in L.A., and I lectured there. There was no formal organizational connection between the labor schools. They were all Left schools and sympathetic to the Party, though they weren't Party schools. The Party had its own schools, which were held at specific instances and were directed by and had comrades who were students. They trained cadre and let them know something of the history of the Party and what the program was.

The school was closed in the McCarthy period, probably around '55. We fought to keep it going, but we couldn't. It was on the Attorney General's list, there were hearings before various boards, and there was also physical violence. The windows of the bookstore were repeatedly broken, the students were attacked, epithets and so on. We finally had to brick the bookstore windows, and you then had to enter the bookstore through the entrance to the building, which of course was impossible in terms of sales. I later learned that some of the terrorism came from students at the Xavier School, a nearby Catholic school. It was an organized campaign. One of the students who finally came to his senses told me about it. This violence would not have closed the school—the government persecution and the legal fees and the whole goddamn business did.

The government charged that the school was a subversive institution. It had to register under the McCarran Act, which of course the school refused to do, so there were hearings.[7] I didn't participate in those hearings, I was

[6]National executive secretary of the Civil Rights Congress, general manager of the *Daily Worker,* and trustee of the Jefferson School. In 1954, Patterson was jailed for contempt for failing to provide a grand jury with CRC records he claimed he did not possess.

[7]The McCarran Internal Security Act (1950) created an administrative nightmare for hereti-

so busy doing other things. The government declared the school illegal, subversive, and seditious. Above all what they wanted was the names of students and the names of contributors—because we had annual dinners—and of course we wouldn't give them names.

My publishers were attacked. Columbia took my book, *American Negro Slave Revolts,* off its list in '47, although it was in its third printing. I finally persuaded International Publishers to buy it, and they brought it out in '51 and sold many copies.

When the school had to close, it simply was closed—and then people demanded a school. By that I mean, they stopped me on the street and said, "Why don't you start a school?" Well, I spoke to Sidney about it, I spoke to Victor Perlo, a very distinguished economist, and we started a school. I rented rooms on Broadway near what was Klein's department store. We began to get dozens of students, pretty soon hundreds of students. We rented more rooms and there we were. That lasted several years.

The collapse of the labor schools is simply one example of what was lost. Over the course of years, tens of thousands of Americans wanted the schools and paid to go to them. There were pressures against them, psychological and otherwise, but they went.

---

cal organizations. Justice Hugo Black described it bluntly: "The plan of the Act is to make it impossible for an organization to continue to function once a registration order is issued against it. To this end, the Act first provides crushing penalties to insure complete compliance with the disclosure requirements of registration. . . ." The act then established penalties for not registering as a "Communist-action" or "Communist-front" organization—$10,000 and/or five years in prison for each day of failure to register.

Public Schools

RUTH GOLDBERG

Short and grandmotherly, forthright. We meet in Berkeley, at her son's home; there are children everywhere. In 1947, back in New York City, she ran as a Progressive for president of her local PTA.

My children went to a public school in Queens. It was Sunnyside—a section of Queens that had been developed by Henry Wright. He'd built these small attached houses in an attempt to do an ideal community. Mrs. Roosevelt was interested in it. They attracted a rather interesting group of people—artists, writers, a lot of progressive people. We all knew each other and it was very pleasant. But outside of Sunnyside Gardens, it was a whole other story—that was where the conflict began. There was a good deal of anti-Semitism. My nephew went to junior high; he was older, and he was chased home by kids. The kids had their lunch money taken from them. It was a combination of a rather tough neighborhood and the protected enclave where we lived.

I was on the PTA board. Because I have literary interests, another woman and I ran the PTA newspaper. And I must say it was pretty good. But looking back at it, we did a number of rather foolish things. We'd invited outside speakers at PTA meetings who were political, and that riled up a lot of people, and I can see why—it was ridiculous, but at the time we were caught up in that kind of thing. Anyway, there was a big struggle over who was going to run for presidency of the PTA. There was somebody who was much more radical than I was and then there was a very reactionary candidate. I was supposed to be the unity candidate of the whole thing. I didn't want to do it. I had three small children, and it's a lot of work. But I thought, if it's going to mean peace in the neighborhood, I would do it.

The politics of this thing is just ridiculous. A group that considered themselves Trotskyites, I believe, decided that I was representing the Stalinist Communists. And so they decided to run another candidate, with the result that we had a microcosm of the Cold War. It really was. Nearby, there was also a very strong Catholic church, whose priest was really very conservative and very scared about anything progressive. He denounced me from the pulpit of the Catholic church during a Sunday sermon, and all the children went home from Sunday school with fliers telling their parents to go vote. The children went to parochial schools, but they were told to vote in the public school election, because I was the devil incarnate.

Some neighborhood woman that I had been quite friendly with—our kids played together—said to my oldest son, "You know, your mother's a Red. She should be put up against a wall and shot." A little kid who was eight years old! And David came home crying. Looking at it now, after forty years or so, I think, "My God! How ridiculous this whole thing was." But it was very real. I got threatening phone calls; the bushes were pulled up on our front lawn. Finally, the board of the PTA decided that we should have the Honest Ballot Association monitor this election because these people whose children were not even in the public schools were going to come and vote. And they did. They came out in masses. It even got into the *New York Times*.

With the Honest Ballot Association, you had to prove your child was in the public school. So we had this awful election and I won overwhelmingly. When they inducted me as president of this PTA, the superintendent of the district said, "I don't know why Ruth would want this job!" And I was standing there thinking, *"I don't know why I want it!"*

Aside from that, that spring I had bought myself a nice red coat and I wore a black dress and my red coat, and some of the people in the audience cackled, "Oh, now she's showing her true colors!" I must say I can laugh at it now, but it was a madness that went on, that stirred people up against one another: Jews against Catholics. It was a small thing, but it was an indication of what had happened with the Cold War, with this Red specter—that somebody like me could be a danger to a community.

Well, my husband was so upset, he couldn't stand it. He had envisioned our having a nice, peaceful life, and so he decided—I was very much opposed to it—that we should move to the suburbs. Well, I stayed there about a year and a half as PTA president, and then I left.

After we moved to Westchester in 1949, I said to Sam, "I'm not going to get into the PTA. I'm just going to tend my garden and take care of my children and do my writing and forget all this nonsense." Unfortunately, what happened was, again, we had a very bad school system and a very poor PTA. Someone came to me with some other women and said, "Look, we've just got to do something about getting rid of a member of the board of education." So I got involved again. And the FBI started following me around.

They had been turned on to me through the activities in the Sunnyside PTA. We later learned that a woman on the board of the Westchester PTA was reporting to the FBI, and she had us all tagged as Reds!

We were all so careful and so suspicious of one another. I remember these women that I was working with going out to lunch together one day, and we finally broke through when one of the women said, "Well, who didn't give to support the Loyalists in Spain?" And that loosened things up a bit. So we were able to talk, but basically we didn't talk.

There was a presidential election, Truman against Dewey; Henry Wallace was running on the Progressive ticket. And we'd been talking in the house, the kids always listened. We didn't know whether we were going to vote for Truman or Wallace. By this time the atmosphere of fear was so great, the kids knew enough to shut up—except for the youngest, who was not inhibited the way the older two were. And when the kids across the street, who were strong Republicans, said, "Who are you going to vote for?"—you know how kids talk—he said, "Wallace!" Our middle daughter almost killed him! She said, "Lenny, shut up!" Came back and told us, "That kid is nuts."

You didn't say these things. You didn't tell anybody you were going to vote for Wallace. And of course all these women that I knew so well at that time, we didn't discuss the election at all. It was as if there were no election going on.

The FBI were following me around. Later I sent for my file. I figured I had to have a file, and I did. They call you a "subject"—subject's car was parked outside a house where there was presumably a meeting going on. Subject's license plate was noted at this home. Subject was seen going into New York on the train. In fact, the day I went into New York on the train, why they followed me I don't know—it was my birthday and I was going to have lunch with somebody. But going to New York is a subversive act, if you live in the suburbs, right?

One thing was that they were aware of what I had written. I had a story published in the *California Quarterly,* and in *Partisan Review,* and in some women's magazine which obviously is not Left. But the FBI knew every story I had published. And they said that the *California Quarterly* was obviously a Left magazine. I guess it was a little bit.

They visited all my neighbors, and I found that out because next door to us there was a family of refugees from Germany. They were German Jews who had escaped from Hitler. The FBI asked them if I had meetings in my house or if they saw strange cars coming out. She said, "Look, this is a community-minded woman. She collects for the Community Chest." Then they said, "Please don't tell her that we were here." She said she saw them go across the street to good neighbors of ours, whose children played with our children, all up and down and around. Nobody told me except this woman; she would have no truck with it. She invited Sam and me over there and said, "I'm telling you because this was the way it started in Germany."

FRANCES EISENBERG

A gentle woman. In 1946, Eisenberg was attacked by the California State Committee on Un-American Activities as a "skilled propagandist for Communist totalitarianism." She was called before state committees three times (once for writing a letter of support for a friend's husband) before being blacklisted in 1954. She never again taught in public schools.

I was the child of immigrant parents who treasured public education. They had none in old Russia, from which they came. I tried so hard in school. My mother couldn't read or write, and here I was getting A's on every paper I ever wrote. The family always said, "This one has got to go to college and become a teacher." And this one did.

In 1936, I got assigned as substitute teacher to Canoga Park High School. It was run by an arch-Republican reactionary. I had always been extremely active in demonstrations, especially during the Depression. So was everyone else I knew: my husband, my family, my friends. We were trying to bring about some sort of relief—employment, welfare, or just support to the thousands of people out of work.

At the time, the Los Angeles school system was treating their substitute teachers very badly. They were paying us extremely low wages, significantly less than the permanent teachers got for the same work. So a number of us from Canoga Park got together and formed the Probationary and Substitute Teachers Organization. We went to Sacramento and got a law passed regulating the L.A. board's practices. Shortly afterwards I was made a probationary teacher, the first step in becoming tenured.

Jack Tenney[1] was running for state senator, and one day, he made a campaign stop in Canoga Park. The people that initiated the political meeting were diehard Republicans. They called Roosevelt a Communist. To them, he was the worst kind of President that you could have. At the school, we were supporting Roosevelt in every way in his war effort. We had paper drives and bond drives, and were so successful that Bob Hope

---

[1]Once strongly associated with the Left, Tenney turned Right with a vengeance as head of California's little HUAC—the Tenney Committee. See Dorothy Healey under "The Fall of the Communist Party" for more on Jack Tenney.

came out to praise us at an assembly. The people in town hated the liberal trends at the school. Mr. Robinson, the editor of the *Canoga Park Herald,* the local paper, and one family in particular, the Nofzigers, supported the Jack Tenney campaign. They said to him, "You have got to get into that nest of Communists up at the high school. They are endangering our country, poisoning the minds of our youth. We want them out! Especially that Jew," meaning me.

Adding fuel to the fire, Lyn Nofziger[2] was in my journalism class. He was in his mid-senior term when he came to me and asked if he could write a gossip column. I didn't like the idea, and the student staff voted one hundred percent not to permit it. Lyn went home very sullen. For the rest of the semester, he did not write anything. I gave him a courtesy B, because he had fulfilled his assignments up until midterm, and I suspected there was home influence working at this.

On the last day of school, I was getting ready for summer vacation, sorting my papers and getting rid of junk. School had been dismissed at noon, and so the place was empty. I remember that I had my door propped open because it was such a hot day. Then I heard a click, click, click of heels in the empty hallway. It stopped at my door. A voice said, "Are you Mrs. Eisenberg?" I said, "Yes, come in."

"I don't want to come in. I'm Lyn's mother. I have his report card in my hand. How dare you give my son a B? That's a disgrace in my family. You dirty Jew, I'll get even with you!"

Jean Wilkinson, the teacher in the room next door, heard this. So did the janitor. I was so shocked, I just sat there in utter disbelief.

In October of 1946, I received a summons to appear before the Jack Tenney California Un-American Activities Committee. I believe Mrs. Nofziger used her personal influence with Jack Tenney to get me summoned.

I had been advised by the teachers' union[3] lawyer not to answer any questions beyond giving my name—if I answered one, I would have to answer all—and that's what I tried to do. They asked about my work as a representative of my teachers' union at the labor school in Los Angeles, the People's Educational Center. Apparently, it was organized by Communists. I didn't know they were Communists. I only volunteered to be a delegate because I was interested in adult education. In the end, I only attended two sessions at the center because my workload at school was so heavy. Then they asked about meetings I had attended. I had once gone to

---

[2]Later press secretary under President Nixon.
[3]The American Federation of Teachers (AFT).

hear Paul Robeson sing. All the people there must have been Communists, because he was one. Of course, they asked me if I was a member of the Party. They always asked you that. I refused to answer.

The Nofzigers and Mr. Robinson of the *Canoga Park Herald* testified against me. One of them, I don't remember which, told the committee, "Mrs. Eisenberg had copies of the *Wall Street Journal* in her room!" [Laughs.] And Lyn Nofziger's sister Rosemary manufactured an item to suit them: "She had *People's World* tacked on the door! She had the *Daily World* in her room." Absolutely ludicrous! It would have been bona fide journalistic instruction to show it as a contemporary newspaper, but I found that it had no place in a high school instructional room. I put up the best—the *Christian Science Monitor,* and yes, the *Wall Street Journal,* because I was teaching journalism. [Laughs.]

They went after my methods of teaching. According to the committee, some of the editorials that I approved in the school paper were "Communistic," because they advocated that we should participate in the United Nations and that we should teach young people to practice their inherited rights at school. They said, "You are accused of teaching them Communistic doctrine." I answered that I faithfully taught the course of study that the board of education has approved. I had never gone beyond that. They didn't believe me. They asked me the same question over and over and over again. I referred to the course of study, which I held in my hand, time and time again. I said, "Gentlemen, please read this. This is what I followed in all my classes."

I was the first of the public high school teachers in California to be so investigated. During those four days of hearings, the local and Los Angeles papers ran headlines—"Red Teacher Investigated by Un-American Activities Committee."

After I appeared, the Los Angeles teachers' union demanded that the board of education appoint four principals to hold a public session to hear any parent, teacher, or concerned alumnus testify about the accusations made against myself and the other teachers. The union, parents, and alumni all came to my defense in great numbers. There were more than three hundred graduates who left their work to come and testify. The students talked about what they'd learned, and the parents about how happy their kids were at school. After the principals' hearings, I was cleared of all accusations.

The teacher investigations were an educational tragedy. But it went along with what President Truman was saying when he initiated the Cold War:

we must be sure that teachers and educators are on the side of our government. The start of the Cold War meant tragedy in many lives. One teacher in New York burnt herself. An elementary teacher committed suicide; she couldn't stand the publicity. [Begins to cry.] In California, a Stanford professor with four children killed himself when he received a summons. I know of one Ph.D. who became a truck driver. The vice president of our teachers' union, a brilliant teacher, became a salesman of washing machines. Isn't that disgraceful?

The teaching profession as a whole was frightened into submissiveness. At one point, a bunch of us had written to Albert Einstein and said, "What shall we do?" He wrote back, "Become plumbers, become anything, but do not sign the loyalty oath." To us, it was the beginning of American fascism.

After I was exonerated, I stayed on at Canoga Park. But one of my students came from a very prominent, very wealthy Republican family. The mother was a member of the National Republican Women's Committee. Her son was incredibly infantile. After about six weeks of table-pounding, the way a baby does on a high chair to get attention, I went down to the local furniture store and borrowed a high chair for a couple of days. I brought it into school and told my students, "Class, I hope you will understand that I am not trying to ridicule a member of this class. But I must cure him of this childish behavior." I called the young man forward and I said, "During this class today, you must sit in this chair." He laughed and the class laughed, and he sat in the chair. Well, the mother, as I said a very prominent Republican, heard of this and was outraged by my audacity, as she put it. She went to the principal and said [pounds on table for emphasis], "This teacher has to go."

Within a very short time, I was summoned to the superintendent's office in downtown L.A. He told me, "Mrs. Eisenberg, you've got to leave that school." I asked why. He said, "For various reasons, but I want you to make the request for a transfer." I consulted my union and they told me to do it. I agreed, under the condition that I could choose my school. I wanted to teach at Fairfax High School [located in a predominantly Jewish neighborhood]. During this period, Jewish actors and Jews in general, above everyone else, were being summoned by the committees. Although my family never went to synagogue—we were too poor to pay the dues and too proud to admit it—we held our heritage sacred. After everything that had happened, I just wanted to be with my people. So I was assigned, at my choice, to Fairfax High.

That wasn't the end of it, though. Once, as I stood on a corner in downtown L.A. and distributed leaflets, the FBI drove by every fifteen minutes photographing me. For years, they came to my house, attempting to interview me. I always said no and slammed the door in their faces.

I wasn't conscious of being followed, but I know it must have happened. Once, while testifying in front of one of the committees, the license plate of a car, purportedly my own, was cited. It couldn't have been mine, because at the time I didn't know how to drive. The agents made lots of mistakes, dozens of errors with names and places. They weren't the best trained.

I had three and a half marvelous years of teaching at Fairfax High. Freely, I talked about everything that was going on: the hearings and my own beliefs. Then in 1952 I was summoned again before a state committee— the Burns Committee, this time.

Rabbi Cohen, a close friend of mine whose children were in one of my classes, organized a public meeting. Some of my students wrote a pamphlet called *Why Are They Attacking My Teacher?* Others distributed leaflets announcing the meeting. They wrapped them in newspaper, standing on the four corners of campus to pass them out, because the principal would not allow any distribution of leaflets on school grounds. I still have one of them, which I will treasure to my dying day [voice breaking]. The meeting was held in a theater, and it was packed. It was decided that Frances Eisenberg was not a menace to this community, or to any community. They did all that they could. But I was dismissed in February 1954 for "unprofessional conduct."

The school administration knuckled under to the investigating committees and the board of education. They knew in advance that I was going to be fired. But I never was called in and asked "What are you teaching?" by anybody.

I was dismissed at a public meeting that the board held, crowded by my supporters. Police and plainclothesmen by the dozens in the hallway. When I exited from that room, a plainclothesman grabbed me by the shoulder and a policeman in uniform threw him aside and stood there beside me.

There were some loud voices of opposition there. As I sat there, I couldn't believe that after all those years of such devotion to my students and to my profession, I was being fired. I could no longer teach in the Los Angeles Unified School District. It was a shock.

Afterwards, I went out to educate the community about what was going on in the schools. The teachers' union didn't have enough to pay our lawyers' fees, and we had to get the money somewhere. I was chairman of the Teachers' Defense Committee for four years, from 1954 to 1958. I talked to more than ten thousand people. I kept a notebook of every organization, every house meeting, and the numbers of people that I addressed in the course of raising funds for our union lawyers. I talked at union halls and homes. These weren't rich people—Beverly Hills and Bel Air never called me for a meeting—they were working-class, many of them very sympathetic to my political views.

My children did not understand why their father would not let them go to any of the public meetings that were held on my behalf. My husband said, "They don't understand enough of the political implications. I don't want them photographed. I don't want them identified. I want to keep them as safe as possible." I concurred.

I became a tutor and taught hundreds of children by personal recommendation. I became quite famous. [Laughs.] People who had not supported me as a public school teacher sent me their children to be educated. They paid me so well that I am able to be comfortable in my old age. So in a way, the committee did me a favor! [Laughs delightedly.]

I'm proud that I'm an American. Look how I flourished in this country, despite all of its wars and depressions. I've had a good life, and I want that life for every person in this country, especially the youth.

Thirty years later, in 1986, five of us decided to initiate a legal action. We went before a Republican judge of the superior court, and we won. The judge ruled that the Los Angeles board of education had acted unconstitutionally in dismissing us. As a group, we were awarded two hundred and fifty thousand dollars, forty percent of which went to the lawyer. I promptly had a big party. [Laughs.] We celebrated not the financial victory, although the money was welcome, but the moral and educational victory. That will always remain sweet to my heart.

JEAN WILKINSON

Jean Wilkinson's journey began in 1952 when her husband, Frank, was called before California's little HUAC for refusing to reveal his political associations. Jean was blacklisted until 1965 for her own refusal to reveal her political beliefs. (For more on Jean and Frank Wilkinson, see under "The Fight Against HUAC.")

When Frank and I were first married and undergraduates at UCLA in '39 or '40, the Red Squad raided the campus and took away some people I knew, the student body president and two or three others. Their crime was that they wanted a debating organization, one that would be open to all ideas.

The provost suspended them. I knew the students but I didn't even know what the word "Communist" meant. There was one woman named Celeste Strack,[1] who was an avowed Communist, but I didn't know her, just her name.

Then I came up here to Cal Berkeley, got my teaching credential, taught a year up in Winters, and then back to Canoga Park to teach. My principal at the time, a really wonderful person, a Republican from Kansas, called me in one day and said, "You know, the local chapter of Associated Farmers[2] have been complaining that you were involved in that Red riot at UCLA." I said I wasn't, I told him what had happened. He said, "Well, why don't you just go and explain it to this Protestant minister who's a member of this club, he's very decent."

So Frank and I drove out, and he was very decent and very nice. He said, "These fellows are the kind that hit you over the head with a baseball bat and ask questions later." Frank told him about his background, the Methodist Church and his father's activities in cleaning up vice in Los Angeles, and I told him that my mother and father were both schoolteachers and raised in the Presbyterian Church. We were just getting along fine, then he said, "Do you mind telling me, are you Communists?" I remember Frank leaning forward and saying, "I don't mind telling you, I'm not." I didn't know beans, I couldn't have defined the word "communism" for you. But I said, "Well, I do mind telling you, because I think that's my right of privacy as an American citizen. When I go to vote, nobody has to know how I vote, so I'm not going to tell you."

Then in 1952 Frank was called before the state Un-American Activities Committee because at a housing authority hearing he had refused to say

[1] Later a national leader of the Young Communist League, Strack resigned from the Party in 1958, along with twenty-five other leading Communists, in protest against the CP's growing isolation and rigidity.

[2] While the Associated Farmers of California began in May 1934 as a harsh countermeasure to the growing unionization of agricultural workers, its presence quickly became characteristic of all strikes throughout the state. It was financed by Pacific Gas and Electric, Safeway Stores, and a large number of banks, railroads, oil companies, realty firms, farm implement manufacturers, and food packers; its methods included large-scale surveillance, strikebreaking, and vigilante violence.

whether he was a Communist or not. In the press reports, the committee is quoted as saying that they discovered that Frank Wilkinson's wife is a schoolteacher so why not subpoena her. It was on that kind of basis that I was called to testify in front of the Tenney Committee. They actually held the hearings out there in the school. I was on leave at the time, because I was pregnant and got polio while I was pregnant.

These committees look for every little tie. They took the fact that I was a UCLA graduate and tied me into this ridiculous Red Scare thing on campus, which I had no part in. They make these great leaps, because you were in the vicinity at the time then you must have been part of it. So it's almost like the making of a radical. I began to feel that if that's what a radical or a Communist was, maybe I was one—because all the good things that I wanted and believed in, these people were attacking. They were calling me a Communist, whether or not I knew what the word meant or what the organization was like.

But the hearings had *nothing* to do with education. And in fact, Frances Eisenberg was dragged in when she wrote a letter of protest about that hearing. Then I tried to help Frances by recalling that incident where she was called a dirty Jew by the Nofzigers.[3] So Frances and I were implicated early, before the Dilworth cases,[4] and were fired before the other teachers were.

At the hearing, I refused to answer their questions on the grounds that they were investigating Frank and I was not going to talk about my politics. I was fired immediately, but the school board had to follow the tenure laws, which allowed us a year and a half or two years to defend ourselves and to go through the courts.

We challenged the case, which went to the California Superior Court. I remember this white-haired judge named Thomas White, a good Catholic soul, who said that I had been sowing the dragon seeds of treason in the classroom. Isn't that lovely? And of course that really made me mad, because it had nothing to do with teaching or what kind of a teacher I was, it was not the point. I have a clipping from the *Examiner* quoting William Hearst on these great judges that have been so brave to damn these terrible people in the classroom. Again, saying that we were bad teachers, ruining the kids, when the question of our teaching, of course, never came up.

[3]Refers to the family of Lyn Nofziger, later press secretary to Richard Nixon. See Frances Eisenberg earlier in this chapter for more on this story.

[4]Named after legislation sponsored by California State Senator Nelson S. Dilworth. The Dilworth Act of 1953 stipulated that all teachers must take a non-Communist oath and that any who refused to testify would be dismissed.

At the time, I belonged to a very prestigious academic sorority, Delta Kappa Gamma. Although I was a lot younger than most of them—many of them had their doctorates and taught in colleges—I was supposedly being groomed to be president. They sent me out to speak for the group, fighting the attacks on education. So they were quite progressive. I remember having a discussion with them a few months before I was called, in which I explained that if I were ever subpoenaed I would take the Fifth Amendment and refuse to answer. When the hearings came about, they began getting cold feet very fast and wrote me saying I should resign. I replied that I hadn't done anything to make me want to resign—"If you want me out then you have to expel me."

So they sent a letter to all the members, calling for a vote on whether I should be in or out, and I was put out of the organization. I'm sure the vote was overwhelmingly against me—in those days, everybody was terrified of losing their jobs. But I have one letter from a member who was very prominent in statewide education. She wrote them back and said, "I am not familiar with Jean, I don't think I would know her if I met her on the street, but obviously she had qualities that made you want her to join and stay in the organization, and I don't see that she's done anything to nullify this situation, so I refuse to vote for this."

To be expelled, that hurt the most to me personally. I admired these women and felt they had the guts to fight the good fight in terms of education. For them to be so frightened and to run at the first encounter was pretty hard to take.

I remember when my principal was down at the board of education for a meeting, other principals would come to her and ask, "What's it like having a Communist on your staff? What does she look like?" As though I had a tail and horns. My principal was a very loyal and good friend and a believer in civil liberties. In the last stages, when they had decided they were going to fire me but they had to wait so many months to let it take effect, they said I should work in the files to keep me away from the children. The funny part was that I was teaching in a school for delinquent girls on the east side of Los Angeles. It was a great job and I loved it, but not many people wanted to deal with these tough customers. So my principal said, "No, Jean's my best teacher, and I'm not going to give her up until I have to, so I'll keep her in the classroom."

I found some letters from the girls at that school. These were mostly Mexican-American kids, and there's a certain style in their writing. They don't know how to spell, but express themselves they did. One of them offered to go down and beat the shit out of the board of education, which I thought was the best offer I'd had.

They called me Wilkey, when they weren't calling me Wilkey-Balls. "Hi, Wilkey-Balls." This was their tough talk; these are not ladies, these are women. But in this letter one just said, "How are we going to pass our test? You're not here, it's like you've failed us, how come?" But she said, "You really did the right thing, Wilkey, to stand by your husband." The loyal-wife syndrome was strong in their culture and they thought that was a beautiful thing I had done. [Laughs.]

So I stayed on until Christmas Eve, when some lackey in the board of education called and said, "This is to notify you that you won't be going back to school." After that, I had to find another job. I went to work in private schools. A lot of people who own private schools are interested in different approaches to education. They also don't have much money and therefore don't pay their teachers very much. So the salaries were pretty pitiful, and of course I'm a trained secondary school teacher, I didn't know how to teach little kids. And I had kids that were emotionally disturbed, so I had to learn to deal with that. Then I would go to homes and tutor kids who were having problems in school.

I was thinking just this last day or two, what has been the effect of McCarthyism on my life? Financial, for God's sake. Because when I finally did break out of the blacklist in 1965 and got a job teaching in Berkeley, they would only credit me for five years of teaching, which put me way down in the salary schedule.

I'd had at least fifteen years' experience, but that didn't count, because I was teaching in private schools. If I had continued in public schools and accrued automatic raises, I would have gotten a much better salary. My retirement is based on what I made in public schools, so I have a very low pension, and that means that I'm broke. I realize more and more as I get older that my colleagues have security and their children have security, and they're able to do things for their children.

The lawsuit that Frances Eisenberg took part in didn't include me. I was already teaching in the Berkeley public schools, and the point of their suit was to get back into the public schools. They won and also got some money. So I didn't participate, I would be glad to, though. I'd like to sue them now for back pay. I could use it.

Fighting Jim Crow

> Slavery was the greatest blessing the Negro people ever had.
> —Rep. JOHN RANKIN,
> Mississippi (HUAC, 1945–48)

> If someone insists there is discrimination against Negroes in this country, there is every reason to believe that person is a Communist.
> —ALBERT CANWELL, chairman,
> Washington Fact-Finding Committee
> on Un-American Activities

As the first national party to call for complete social and economic equality, the Communist Party traveled south to join the fight for civil rights in 1929. They chose Birmingham, Alabama, as headquarters for their new Southern District, and labor as their vehicle. Over the next several decades, the Party organized interracial unions in steel, mining, agriculture, and maritime. Southern blacks embraced the opportunity, seeing the Communists through old eyes: the Yankees had returned to give deliverance one more try.

At mass rallies that drew hundreds of blacks and poor whites, Party speakers excoriated Southern racism as the stumbling block to improving the lives of all workers, advocated social and economic equality, and called for the integration of cafeterias and public transportation. They led successful strikes for better conditions for sharecroppers and other workers.

The reaction was swift and violent. "Criminal anarchy" laws were passed which made it illegal to advocate racial equality by print or word of mouth, or to join any such organization. Communists, black and white, were gunned down, lynched, bullwhipped, tarred and feathered, their homes firebombed. Pitched gun battles erupted between sheriff's posses and armed unionists. Hunted, with bounties on their heads, white organizers were forced into hiding, able to emerge only in the dark of night. From their black counterparts they learned many a survival lesson handed down from the days of slavery and abolitionists. It was courage and fortitude that allowed the Party to exist as an active force in the Deep South until the early 1950s.

By 1955, when Rosa Parks sat down in that bus in Montgomery, the Party was largely moribund in the South and the North.[1] Red Scare repression had taken its toll, and most of its leaders were either in hiding or fighting in the courts. In 1956, Southern Party leader Junius Scales, in search of a defense attorney, happened by Montgomery and chanced to observe the bus boycott. "It was a marvelous sight to see. Of course, I realized that the handle we'd been looking for these past decades had been found by circumstances. This movement was going to go, and it was in good hands. I never felt more irrelevant. I didn't feel deserted, I just felt we'd done our stint." But whether or not any Red had ever stepped foot south of the Mason-Dixon Line, the new movement was immediately denounced as Moscow-inspired subversion.

From the start, reactionaries had been quick to see Red in supporters of civil rights. But by 1955 and with the growing strength of the modern civil rights movement, the witch-hunters formed the bulwark of segregation. The racists of HUAC and SISS tied their kites to the national storm and defended American apartheid under the guise of national security and patriotism. What they were safeguarding was a social and economic system that channeled the prerogatives of wealth and power into the hands of a few. The disenfranchisement of blacks was central to their system.

The longtime chairman of SISS was James Eastland of Mississippi, a state where violence and law combined to keep all but 5 percent of its black population from voting. Eastland was the personification of segregation and the owner of a huge plantation in the Mississippi Delta. He claimed the entire desegregation effort was "a plot of a few agitators."

Another Mississippian was John Rankin, who pushed through the 1945 resolution transforming HUAC into a permanent committee. Rankin was elected with 10,400 votes in a district with a population of more than

[1]There were moments, though, when the old radicalism still breathed. In 1965, Stokely Carmichael and a handful of SNCC organizers opened a voter-registration drive in Lowndes County, Alabama, the site of a bloody cotton pickers' strike thirty years before. The nonviolent activists were startled when poor farmers of all ages, especially the older folks, arrived at the meetings fully armed. One old sharecropper told Carmichael, "You turn the other cheek, and you'll get handed half of what you're sitting on."

200,000. He contended that segregated blacks had been happy until stirred up by "Communist agitators." He was quite friendly toward the Ku Klux Klan, which he endorsed as "an old American tradition, like illegal whiskey selling."

Edwin Willis of Louisiana, another two-term chairman and thirteen-year member of HUAC, was elected with a total balloting of 8,962 votes.

Their Northern counterparts were active as well. Francis Walter of Pennsylvania, a fourteen-year member and five-term chairman, was discovered in 1960 to be intimately involved with the funding of the Draper Project, a crackpot scheme to prove that blacks were genetically inferior. HUAC chief counsel Richard Arens was a salaried consultant on the project.

Among the frequent visitors to the file rooms of HUAC and SISS were the state investigating committees which sprang up throughout the South in 1954, the year of the Supreme Court decision on school desegregation. Masquerading under such grave misnomers as the Legal Education Advisory Committee or the Committee on Offenses Against the Administration of Justice, state investigators rampaged for a decade against "Red" integrationists. In 1961, the Texas committee issued a much-publicized report that determined the state's racial "agitation" to be the result of "orders from Moscow."

Borrowing a page from their federal mentors, the state committees hired a pair of thoroughly discredited professional witnesses. By 1957, Manning Johnson, a black ex-Communist, had been investigated for perjury by the Justice Department, but Louisiana legislators accepted his word as gospel. He targeted Martin Luther King as a "dastardly misleader" taking blacks "down the road to bloodshed and murder." Johnson pinned the Communist label on a number of civil rights organizations, including the NAACP, where he claimed the "Communist Trojan horse is stabled today." The following year, J. B. Matthews appeared. Joe McCarthy had dropped him from his stable of informants in the early 1950s, after Matthews had claimed seven thousand Protestant ministers to be supporters of the Communist cause. But in Dixie he was a star witness. He swore before the Florida committee that "Communists or Communist influence" had inspired every racial incident since the 1954 Supreme Court decision, and that 145 national leaders of the NAACP were Communists. Such misinformation was sent to HUAC and SISS, which in turn channeled it to back to the state committees marked with a federal seal of approval. It was then hailed in the Southern press as proof of the Communist menace behind desegregation, and used as the basis for legal action against integrationists. The Ku Klux Klan, White Citizens' Councils, and the American Nazi Party reprinted much of this HUAC "documentation."

With the movement under national attack as Communist-inspired, white sympathizers became fearful of being tagged as traitors. Many who had been involved dropped out; others on the verge of joining shied away. Some of the whites who remained found their motives questioned by their black allies. Anxious to avoid the Red taint, some national and regional civil rights groups made massive efforts to disprove the charges, publishing rebuttals and purging all those tagged as Communists. Some groups refused to cooperate with others who declined to take such steps. To convince the public that *they* were not Communists, others even joined in the Red-baiting. Even Martin Luther King purged two key figures—Stanley Levison and Jack O'Dell—from the Southern Christian Leadership Conference under pressure from the White House.

ANNE BRADEN

Anne Braden is a longtime civil rights activist. "I always say Joe McCarthy and I got active about the same time, but I really was active before that." She and her husband, Carl, ran the Southern Conference Educational Fund (SCEF), a spin-off of the Southern Conference for Human Welfare, one of Eleanor Roosevelt's interracial civil rights groups. In 1954, the Bradens were indicted for sedition and faced fifteen years in prison. In 1967, they were again indicted on the same charges.

I always say my husband and I were some of the luckiest victims of the witch hunt because there were so many people who quietly lost their jobs, or even quietly went to jail. The thing about the case here in Louisville was that it gave a lot of people a way to fight back. Eventually we got a tremendous amount of support around the country. But not in Louisville—everybody in Louisville was scared to death.

It started in the spring of '54 when this African-American man named Andrew Wade came and asked if we would buy a house and transfer it to him, if he gave us the money for the down payment. It was right after World War Two and he and his wife wanted to move out to the suburbs, like everybody wanted to do in those days.

The housing shortage for blacks in Louisville was appalling. He had tried to buy in a number of places, and as soon as they found out he was black the deal was off. There was an unwritten law that wasn't just in Louisville, and it wasn't just in the South either, and it still exists in some places, but there were neighborhoods he just couldn't buy in, and one of them was the suburbs. We didn't even think too much about it, we said sure. It just never occurred to us to say no.

Later that became a standard procedure for people in open housing movements—dummy purchases. But there was no open housing movement in Louisville at that time. We didn't buy the house to start a movement. We had no idea that it was going to cause all the stir it did. Wade was kind of a crusader, but he just wanted a house. Once he was under attack he was determined to stay, and it became a movement. But as he said later, there'd been an earlier incident where a Filipino woman had moved into a white neighborhood and there'd been a lot of protests and rocks thrown at the house, but some neighbors got together and brought her flowers and fruit and everything settled down. So he thought if there was any trouble it would blow over pretty quick.

There were a couple of coincidences that I think made it different. One was the neighborhood he picked. It probably couldn't have been more inopportune, because it was an area where a lot of white people had moved to get away from another part of town where more blacks were moving. So you had not the most receptive people, and then he moved into the house the weekend before May 17, 1954, which was the Supreme Court decision against school segregation.[1] This made the Supreme Court decision come home to them. We became a lightning rod. People couldn't get at the Supreme Court, but they could get at us. So that contributed to the hysteria.

Almost immediately there was a cross burned and rocks were thrown through his window and shots fired into the house. That was in May, and then people formed the Wade Defense Committee to support him. It was interracial. We didn't have that many whites, but there were a few. People would take turns going out to guard the house. He and his then wife—she changed her mind later—were determined to stay. The police were supposed to be guarding the place. They kept getting threats, but gradually things quieted down, and we began to think that everything would be all right, although we also were getting a lot of threats.

We had a mob come to our home one night. That was right after they

[1] *Brown v. Board of Education.*

found out that we had sold the house. By the time I got home, Carl had chased them off. But they came to find out if this was true. They couldn't believe it. They were very angry. They said, "Have you sold that house to a nigger?" Carl said, "Get out of here and quit stompin' on my grass."

There was a newspaper out there called the *Shively Newsweek,* a little suburban newspaper that saw a way of building circulation. So every week they would run something inflammatory, and that was the first place the Red Scare was raised. This little paper said it looked like Communists were trying to stir up trouble. We didn't take that too seriously, because you always were called Communist in those days if you did anything. Meantime, a few white people came forth to support the Wades, including a small branch of the Women's International League of Peace and Freedom, the women's peace group that Jane Addams[2] started. They were very much concerned with the issue of racial equality. They sent out a letter to everybody in the neighborhood urging them to welcome this family. Then we tried to get the churches to do somethin' and they were all scared to death. It was a strong Catholic area, and each priest thought where this happened was in the next parish—it wasn't in his parish.

This went on all of June. But things quieted down, and we thought it was going to be over soon when one Saturday night the house blew up.

It was just by the grace of God somebody wasn't killed. The Wades had this little girl, and she was spending the night in town with her grandparents to go to Sunday school the next morning. She did that every Saturday night. We don't know whether the people that blew it up knew that or not, they may have. The bomb went off right under her bedroom, so if she'd been there she'd have been killed. The Wades had just come home and were out on the side porch on the other side with a couple of people. Nobody was hurt, but all one side of the house was pretty much destroyed. So they moved into town with his family. Then this Wade Defense Committee began camping on the doorsteps of the police and the prosecutor, pushing them to arrest the people who blew up the house.

The house had to be rebuilt. It was insured, but it was tied up in court a long time over questions of ownership. After the first incidents at the house when the shots were fired into it, the original insurance had been canceled. We got in touch with an insurance man that somebody told us cared about

---

[2]Jane Addams (1860–1935) was the leading figure in the social settlement movement. From 1919 to 1935 she served as president of the Woman's International League for Peace and Freedom. A founder of the American Civil Liberties Union in 1920, she received the Nobel Peace Prize in 1931.

justice, and he got Lloyd's of London to insure the house. He told me years later that he happened to be in London the day after the house was blown up [laughs], and he went into Lloyd's of London to tell them, "You remember that house you insured for me in Louisville? Well, it got blown up last night." And the guy said to him, "If you got any more like that, let us know—we'll take 'em."

So anyway, it was insured, but it was just sittin' there in ruins all that summer. In the meantime, there was this effort to get the authorities to arrest somebody.

The police chief called Carl one day and said, "I really want you to come down here and talk to me, because it may be the most important thing you ever do in your life." So Carl went down. The chief said, "We've gotten word that they've gotten a confession from the man who set the dynamite at the Wade's house and there'll be an arrest in a few days." But in the meantime they had heard some of these people were planning to blow up our house, and he says they're going to put guards at our house. We were right across the street from what was then the fairgrounds. And he told him things to do, install lights in the backyard and check under the hood before we got into the car. So we did.

Then time just worried on, a week went by, ten days, and nobody was arrested. They finally took the police away from our house and put them over in the fairgrounds. I remember Carl called this police chief and said, "What's happening?" He said, "Well, I just couldn't leave the police there anymore, they're all getting bit by chiggers." Carl said, "But you said they had a confession." He said, "Yes, they do, but they're trying to get some more corroborating evidence." This was in early July. Nobody was ever arrested, haven't been yet, except us. It became kind of an open secret who that confession was probably from. But in the meantime the summer worried on and we kept going down to the courthouse worrying them about what they were going to do about this.

In September, the guy who was then Commonwealth's attorney, that's what we call our prosecutors in Kentucky, his name was Scott Hamilton, announced that he was going to have a grand jury investigation. So in the middle of September, the grand jury opened and we were the first witnesses called, which didn't seem unusual. I believe I was the very first witness. The minute I sat down I could see what was going on, because immediately they began asking about me and not the house and not the bombing.

They wanted to know what groups I belonged to. Was I a member of this? Was I a member of that? Everything you can think of, including the

Communist Party, but also was I Progressive Party? What did the Wade Defense Committee do, and what sort of books did I read, what books did I have in my house? Well, I knew what was going on in the country, so that was a familiar line of questioning. I was just horrified. I said that has nothing to do with who blew up Andrew Wade's house. So I just refused to answer any of those questions and I left and came on home.

So this all got in the paper, and Scott Hamilton subpoenaed all these people from the Wade Defense Committee, and the head of the Women's International League that had sent the letter. So then he says in the paper the next day that the grand jury's investigatin' the bombing and there are two theories. One is the neighbors blew up the house to chase the Wades out of the neighborhood. The other theory was that the purchase and the resale and the bombing of the house had been a Communist plot to stir up trouble between the races and bring about the overthrow of the government of Kentucky and the United States.

Things got more and more hysterical as they subpoenaed more and more people. If you haven't been in a community where there's a hysteria, it's really hard to describe and it's hard to believe. One of the guys who had been helping guard the house was Vernon Brown. He shared an apartment with an older man. Vernon was fairly young then, but this older man was a riverboat captain who had retired here. He'd been a radical all of his life, had run for mayor somewhere as a Communist years before. So they raided the house where this Brown lived and took all their books, which were a lot of Communist books. Pictures of these books were all over the front page of the paper. People were talking about how we ought to be lynched, they were talking that on the streets—I mean, we heard this.

What came together here was a combination of the anti-Red and the anti-black hysteria, and when you put that together it was overwhelming. My husband and I became the symbols of all of this. To a certain extent also the other white people who were involved, but mainly us. We became the devil. It was a peculiar position to be in.

The climax was on October the 1st. The grand jury indicted Carl, me, and five other white people, including the head of the Women's International League and Vernon Brown, who had gone out there to guard the house, and this old man he lived with, even though he hadn't really been involved. They indicted seven of us, but none of the blacks, because the theory of this prosecutor was that we had stirred this up. It became a familiar theme all through the South as the civil rights movement developed that the blacks were perfectly happy until these white radicals came along and stirred 'em up.

blown up the house but he couldn't prove it so therefore he was asking that that be dismissed too. So legally that was the end of the case.

I guess I've learned that the things that happen to you that seem the worst at the time may be the best. That seemed like an awful thing at the time. We had two little children, and we figured we were going to be in prison for at least fifteen years. Looking back on it, it's the best thing that ever happened to me, because it opened up this possibility of mounting a fight against the repression of the fifties. It gave us the opportunity to meet the cream of America all over the country, the people who were fighting back, and hurled us into full-time civil rights work.

It was not so good for Andrew Wade. He never was able to move back to that house, and they never arrested the people who blew it up. There was a couple in Chicago that inherited some money and they gave Andrew Wade the money to pay off the mortgage. So he sold the house and then bought another in an old part of Louisville, which is what they had not wanted to do three years before.

But for him, the dream of having a nice house out in the suburbs was destroyed. And I guess that got lost in the shuffle for a lot of people. When this thing first started, it was the Wade case, that was in the summer of '54. Then when we got indicted in September, it was the Wade-Braden case. Imperceptibly over the next year, it became the Braden case, that was the way people knew it around the country. And I've often wondered, could we have done more to have kept that from happening? I say this not to criticize anybody, 'cause people were wonderful to us, but I think it's an indication of the depths of the racism in this country. Here was this white man facing fifteen years in prison, and here was this black man who couldn't even have a house to live in. We just never could mount the fight that we wanted to. Then part of it was Andrew—he got to the point where he didn't see much use in fighting anymore. But I still think there was just a terrible contradiction that is related to a lot of the unsolved problems in our country.

While our case was still going on, the world changed on December the 1st, 1955, when Rosa Parks sat down on the bus. That was the beginning of the end of the 1950s, it really was. You had this new movement developing. We got involved in SCEF[4] and went to work full-time for very little pay. SCEF was interracial—our job was reaching out to white people to get them

[4]Southern Conference Educational Fund.

involved. We knew we weren't reaching masses of people, the fears and the hysteria was too great, but we reached some. SCEF provided a beacon light for the whites who did want to give moral support to those who would have had a pretty lonely struggle without it. That's what we were doing all through that period into the sixties. Then the student movement came along and there was a lot more people willing to be active.

But the witch hunt was not over at all. We had these little state committees in the South. You had the Louisiana Un-American Activities Committee, LUAC we called it, 'cause we called the other one HUAC. FUAC in Florida. Georgia called it something else, but they all had 'em in one form or another. Kentucky set one up late and we kinda laughed it out of existence 'cause we called it KUAC [laughs as she pronounces it "quack"]. We put out a pamphlet: *KUAC KUAC.*

As I say, the witch hunts were doomed the moment Rosa Parks sat down. By the time you have a mass movement in the streets, things are a little different—and I'll tell you how it came home to me. You see, we were indicted for sedition a second time.

SCEF had different projects, and one was organizing in eastern Kentucky and some over in West Virginia. We called it the Southern Mountain Project. About '63, the civil rights movement had really begun to look at economic issues. People began talking about it's no good to sit at the lunch counter if you can't afford to buy the hamburger. Out of that, with SCLC and some other groups, we were working to build coalitions between working-class poor white people and blacks, as had been talked about in the thirties and had been silenced in the fifties.

So we had this project in Pike County fighting strip mining, where they tear the top off the mountains to get the coal out and ruin people's land. People were standing in front of the bulldozers. Coal operators didn't like that a bit. So one fine day, the guy who's the prosecutor in Pike County, who turns out to be a major coal operator[5] down there, arrested Al and Margaret McSurely who were then working down there, and another guy and charged them with sedition. Well, we were a little surprised, because we really thought the sedition law was dead. So Carl went down to see about

---

[5]Thomas Ratliff was the prosecuting attorney. A report leaked to the *New York Times* from the Office of Economic Opportunity (the sponsor of the Appalachian Volunteers, for which one defendant worked) charged that the reasons behind Ratliff's actions were "economic and political: [Ratliff] made a fortune out of the coal industry and still has coal interests. He is running for Lieutenant Governor on the Republican ticket and thinks it is a good campaign issue." Ratliff denied that he still owned coal property. Strip-mine operators, however, were quick to grab the credit. Robert Holcomb, president of the Chamber of Commerce and of the Independent Coal Operators' Association, boasted to a reporter, "You might say we spearheaded the investigation."

getting them out on bond. He calls me up and says, "Well, how would you like to be indicted for sedition?"

Now this was August of '67, thirteen years after the other case. I thought he was kidding. He says, "No, they're getting ready to indict us too." So sure enough they did. We went down to surrender and be arraigned. We stayed in jail about a week in Pike County.

I brought this up because the difference between the 1950s and the 1960s was dramatized to me in the courtroom. We got in touch with Bill Kuntsler and Arthur Kinoy,[6] and they went into federal court and asked to convene a three-judge court to rule on the constitutionality of the Kentucky sedition law.

See, the Supreme Court in the Nelson case, which was used to reverse Carl's fifties conviction, had ruled that the Smith Act had preempted states from prosecuting for sedition against the federal government. But that didn't keep them from prosecuting for sedition against the state itself or a local government. So this prosecutor in Pike County said he wasn't prosecuting us for sedition against the federal government, he was prosecuting us for sedition against Kentucky and Pike County! That was kind of interesting, because once we got into the Pike County jail everybody thought it'd be a great idea. [Laughs.]

Kuntsler had warned me, "He's going to ask you whether you're a Communist," and I said, "Well, I ain't gonna answer that, I never have and I'm not fixin' to now."

The courtroom was packed, not like in the 1950s with people wanting to lynch us, these were mostly students. There was quite a student movement in Lexington at that time. So I got on the stand and Kuntsler questions me first about what our program was in Pike County, and what we were trying to do in the mountains, what SCEF was all about, and I answered all those questions. Then this prosecutor Ratliff gets up and pretty soon he kind of swells up like a toad and he says, "Mrs. Braden, are you now or have you ever been . . ." At which point that whole courtroom burst into laughter! One of the young women who was there said to me later, "I always heard people quote that but I didn't know anybody ever really said it!"

As soon as the laugh died down, he finished the sentence, ". . . a Communist. By which I mean, do you subscribe to the teachings of Lenin, Marx, Trotsky, Mao Tse-tung," and he named two or three other people.

Then I said, "Mr. Ratliff, in that question you have covered a wide range of political and economic thought and I really don't see how anybody could

---

[6]Two radical lawyers prominent in political defense work through the sixties and seventies.

give an intelligent answer." One of the federal judges said, "I don't either, Mr. Ratliff, ask her somethin' else."

Then he said, "Mrs. Braden, is it true, that in your basement in Louisville"—here I am charged with sedition, like I'm going to overthrow the government, and he didn't ask me if I had any guns or bombs in the basement—"is it true that in your basement you have a printing press?"

"Yes, as a matter of fact we have two of 'em."

That was it. In a little while, Carl testified, then the judges retired, stayed out an hour, came back, and declared the Kentucky sedition law unconstitutional. To me that whole thing dramatized one of the things the civil rights movement had done for the country. Because in the fifties it took us three years to win. In 1967, it took us a week. And the question that scared people to death in the early fifties was now a joke.

SYLVIA THOMPSON

A native Texan from an upper-middle-class family, Thompson speaks with a soft inflection. During the late forties, she and her husband belonged to the Communist Party and worked for civil rights in the Deep South. We meet in her apartment in a Manhattan project.

After the war, in '46, I worked as an executive secretary for the Civil Rights Congress[1] in Houston, Texas. Then I went to Winston-Salem, North Carolina, to work in a factory. I worked for a year and a half trying to recruit workers into the United Electrical Workers, part of CIO Dixie.[2] Then I fell in love with and married the district organizer of the Communist Party. His name was Samuel Joseph Hall.

Sam was from Alabama, and shortly after we were married we moved down to Birmingham. Once we bought a house, maybe two months after

[1]Post–World War Two Communist Party organization formed to defend the civil rights of African-Americans. In 1947, the CRC was declared to be a subversive organization by Attorney General Tom Clark.

[2]Phil Murray, president of the CIO, decided to purge all communists from Operation Dixie, the CIO's Southern organizing drive, even though the Reds were Murray's most potent organizing tool. Apparently, he missed at least one.

we arrived, he put ads in the Birmingham paper saying he was there as the Communist Party organizer, and that the Communist Party was a legal party and we stood for certain things. That's what the Party people in Alabama wanted, someone who was Alabama-born to be a spokesman for the Party. We might have had a few hundred members scattered all over the state. A lot of them solid members. People in the black belt who'd been part of the sharecroppers' struggles in the thirties.

Most of the work was based on the question of Jim Crow. Sam wrote a pamphlet called *The Case of the Ten Dollar a Week Robbery* which we distributed by the thousands, only to white people, telling them how Jim Crow worked to keep wages down, and what it cost them—ten twenty-two a week—in terms of what people up North doing the same work were getting.

The history of the Party in the South goes back to the thirties with the sharecroppers' struggles. People openly trying to defy the Klan. I knew a gentleman who once killed four Klansmen when they tried to get into his house. He had bored a hole in the floor and put in a great big wooden pole to block the door, almost like the trunk of a tree, and as they tried to come in, he used his ax on them, then he buried them. The Klan never made it known because people wouldn't stay with them.

Life was pretty rough. I thought that North Carolina was South, but I didn't know anything could be like Birmingham, Alabama. Once we were there three or four months, I thought of North Carolina as North! Birmingham was really pretty awful. You could feel the oppression of TCI— Tennessee Coal and Iron, a subsidiary of U.S. Steel. Sam and I lived in Birmingham for about three and a half years until it actually became impossible to function there.

Bull Connor[3] was active then. My God, he had interviews constantly where he would say things like if he were in charge, he would take all the Communists in the country, put them on boats, send them off to Russia, but see that the boats sank in the Atlantic.

I remember the first time I went out looking for a job, I went to a paper factory and talked to the personnel person and it all went pretty well. He told me to fill out the application. I filled it all out, but, in little print down at the bottom of the page, was written, "I am not now, never was, and

---

[3]Eugene T. "Bull" Connor, Birmingham's pugnacious police commissioner, later achieved national notoriety for turning police dogs and firehoses on civil rights marchers in 1963.

never will be a member of the Communist Party." So I took the application back and handed it to him. He said, "You know, Mrs. Hall, you didn't sign this."

I said, "I can't," and he asked why.

I said, "I happen to be a member of the Communist Party." I almost felt sorry for the man. He looked like he was just going to keel over.

He said, "I never met a Communist before." So I said, "You meet them all the time—they're just not in a position to say so." Of course, I was lying through my teeth. "My husband happens to be the chairman of the Communist Party in Alabama, so I'm able to tell you."

He said, "Listen, what's your phone number? I'll call you. No, you call me tomorrow." So the next day I called him and he said, "Mrs. Hall, you're so lucky, it's such a beautiful day and you're so lucky not to be in an office and not to be working. It's such a beautiful day to be outside."

After that, I'd get a job and have it for one or two days and then be fired. Sam and I decided it wasn't worth it.

I registered to vote for the first time in my life in Birmingham. I guess I was about twenty-two then. They asked me questions. Me being a white person, the old gentleman just said, "You don't believe everybody should vote, do you?" And I said, "Yes, I think everybody should vote." So he said, "Don't you think anybody should be limited from voting?" And I said, "Well, I guess people in prison or insane asylums." That told him what my thinking was, and he sat there and thought for a while, and finally he said, "Okay, I'm going to let you vote." When I walked out of there I really felt I was voting because he would let me, not because it was my right.

In between meetings, if an emergency came up, someone would have to see Sam. It was usually a black woman. She would come to the house, don an apron, take a broom, go to the front porch, and sweep, so that any neighbors looking out of the window would assume that person was a servant. We used to laugh about that, because who the hell had the money for a cleaning person? [Laughs.] Then the person would come back in the house. We'd sit and write down what we had to communicate, because we knew the place was bugged.

But the main thing was the anti-Communist hysteria. There was a radio program, I forget the preacher's name. For weeks he would go on every day about the dangers of Communists, the threat of Communism, and how we've got this Communist living right here in Birmingham, Alabama—Sam Hall and his wife. And he'd give out our address, 4609 Tenth Avenue

North, I think it was. This was every single day, hate stuff, which was continuing to whip up hysteria.

We lived with bomb threats and constant surveillance. We were followed everyplace. Sometimes if I decided I wanted to do some shopping, I would have an FBI man right next to me. We looked as if we were a couple who were angry with each other and weren't speaking. Sometimes I would even go into a department store and walk into the lingerie department, thinking maybe the guy wouldn't have the guts to walk in there, and he usually would wait outside until I was leaving. [Laughs.]

If we ever went away for a few days, we'd come back and there'd be a bedroom window screen just leaning against the house, with a big old muddy footprint right inside. I lost things like art books—what the hell they wanted with art books, I don't know. But they would constantly come in and take things. Once our poker chips were gone. We figured maybe they wanted to get us for gambling. Every time they'd come, they'd find a suitcase to put the loot in and take it away. We were constantly buying luggage because they would always take it.

It was just plain old harassment. This is what they were spending the time and the taxpayers' money on. We were no threat to them. There was going to be no revolution in Birmingham, Alabama. But the object was to run you out of town and make life difficult. To stir up people with a phony kind of patriotism.

It was unpleasant just taking out the garbage. Sam got to the point where he put the garbage out at night, because every time we'd go in the backyard, our neighbors would sing "My Country 'Tis of Thee." They were frightened.

Sam Hall came from that kind of people. He had tremendous confidence that someday when the white people learned what Jim Crow cost them—not just in dollars and cents but in terms of being total people—they would change. And when he learned how he'd been lied to, he turned around with anger; he was such a fighter for the rights of blacks.

Victories in Birmingham? Those are things you can't count. The only victories that you can count are in terms of the people that you affect and the people you give strength to by speaking of their rights, and the people who listen and think that it makes some sense. A black child was shot in the back for having stolen a case of soda pop—then it was ten cents a bottle, so you figure for a dollar and twenty cents this kid was shot in the back. How do you live with that? So you put out leaflets, you go out late at night and throw them on people's porches. We never passed out literature openly. It just wasn't the kind of place where you could do that. Someone would have beaten you up or else the cops would have shown up to arrest you.

Alabama has a history of this—there's a Southern Room in the Birmingham library where they have file folders of stories about all these people getting beaten up. It's filled with violence against anyone who would speak out for black people. There was an old librarian who was so proud of the fact that she kept things that she didn't sometimes distinguish what she kept. Wonderful file folders of who got beat up when, the sharecropper fights in the late thirties.

Once a big sign was put out front of our house—"There is no room in this country for wild dogs, snakes, or Communists. Get out." The Klan threatened us constantly with bombings. We had a loaded shotgun by our bed. Everyone who was in any danger had a shotgun. We kept firecrackers on our windowsills—that's in case the Klan ever tried to put the house on fire when we were sleeping, we'd wake up. Every time it rained or was very damp, we'd check the firecrackers and if they were damp we'd throw them away and put fresh ones down.

After a couple of bombs had gone off in the black community, we decided the bomb threats were coming too often and maybe it would be a good idea if we didn't sleep in the house. The back bedroom and the front bedroom were so close together that sleeping in the back wouldn't really protect us if a bomb were thrown. So we decided we should leave at night after our neighbors went to sleep and come back early in the morning, so the car would always be seen there. For maybe as long as a month we used to leave at night, go out of the county, sleep over in a motel, wake up very early, and try to be home by five-thirty or six o'clock so that if our neighbors looked out, the car would be there and we would be there. But at least we could have a night's sleep and not worry about hearing a car slow down, which used to be a problem. Every time we heard a car pass the house—it was a quiet street in a working-class community—and we heard it slow down, we'd immediately look out of the blinds to see if there was anything going on in front of the house.

After the Korean War began, we started circulating the Stockholm peace petition.[4] With that, Sam was arrested for vagrancy, and they put him in jail. At his trial, the head of the Red Squad said the only work he ever saw this boy doing was working in his garden and hanging out clothes. At which

[4]Also known as the World Peace Appeal. In March 1950, the World Peace Congress met in Stockholm in an effort to ease Cold War tensions by circulating a worldwide peace petition. In 1951, HUAC denounced the effort as "the most extensive piece of psychological warfare ever conducted on a world scale. . . . a smoke screen for [Communist] aggression."

time the Klansmen in the audience all laughed, because they thought it was funny as hell, a man hanging up clothes. The head of the Red Squad finally said, "This boy has a job but his means of support is disreputable." Actually Sam's salary came from the *Daily Worker* rather than the Party organization. Sam got a suspended sentence. After the trial, we left Birmingham. By the time we got up to New York about two days later, we learned that a city ordinance had been passed in Birmingham that every Communist had forty-eight hours to get out or they'd be imprisoned. We never went back. Sam died three and a half years later.

That's the way it was. We lived openly as Communists for three years in very rough times. I look back on it now and I think to myself, did that really happen? It's funny, because sometimes people say, "If this would happen to me" or "If I could be that frightened, I couldn't go through it." I think people go through what they have to go through and what they choose to endure. I wouldn't have done it differently. I wouldn't have run away or said this is too much for me. But when I look back on it, I wonder how I ever endured it.

VIRGINIA DURR

Clifford and Virginia Durr were old-family Southerners who came North to join Roosevelt's New Deal Brain Trust. They eventually returned to Alabama and continued their work in civil rights. "My husband was a lawyer and he won the Parks case, you know, Rosa Parks about the buses. Yes, he was the lawyer in that case, with another lawyer named Fred Gray."

I came up from the South to Washington, D.C., in '33. My husband was in the Roosevelt administration. He was one of the three heads of the Federal Communications Commission. I got interested in the struggle for the vote, getting rid of the poll tax.[1] So through that I came in contact with all the

---

[1]A capital tax levied equally on every adult as a prerequisite to voting. Enacted widely through the South between 1889 and 1910, the poll tax effectively disenfranchised many blacks and poor whites. In 1966, the Supreme Court ruled that the poll tax violated the "equal protection" clause of the Fourteenth Amendment to the Constitution.

legal people and left-wing people. I belonged to an organization called the Southern Conference for Human Welfare. It was started by the Roosevelts along with some labor leaders. That was back in '38.

But I was never called up or had any trouble really, though, of course, all the Southerners said all the people who were against the poll tax were Reds. It was only when Eastland got after us—he was the biggest Red-baiter in the Senate—that was '54, just before the *Brown* decision. If you supported any rights for blacks, he said you were a Red.

My brother-in-law was Justice Hugo Black, and he was on the Supreme Court, as you know. He took quite a lead in the *Brown* decision. The first thing my husband and I knew was that Eastland had said if the Supreme Court passed the *Brown* decision it would show that it was dominated by Communists. And of course he said if the *Brown* decision was passed that would mean interracial sex mixing, and he just went off on that score. He was trying to do everything in his power to smear the Supreme Court and also the idea of schools being integrated.

Then he said that Justice Hugo Black had a sister-in-law, which was me, and that I had been a member of an organization, the Southern Conference for Human Welfare, that had Red connections. Eastland called us down to New Orleans to appear in front of the Senate Internal Security Subcommittee. He also called Aubrey Williams, who was in Southern Conference, and Jim Dombrowski, who was executive secretary, and Myles Horton of the Highlander Folk School, and he accused us all of being tied in to the Communists. Especially me. They didn't have any of the blacks in the Southern Conference testify, just the white people. He wanted to paint us as manipulators.

They had a paid informer named Paul Crouch, and he just told a string of lies. He said he'd seen my husband and J. Robert Oppenheimer together at Communist meetings, all of which was totally a lie. He said I had close connections with my brother-in-law, Hugo Black, and he intimated, he didn't actually say it, but he intimated I had influenced the Supreme Court. He accused me of subverting the White House and being a friend of Mrs. Roosevelt's—well, I really was a friend of hers but not an intimate, personal friend, but I was in meetings with her a lot. When he accused me of subverting the White House, my husband got furious and tried to hit him, and the marshals rushed in and separated them.

It was just the most fantastic, mad sort of absurdity you can imagine, but he was paid by the United States government to inform. It was just the most ridiculous thing you've ever seen, and the purpose of it was to try to implicate my brother-in-law Hugo Black as tinged with Red.

The whole thing was such a lie, I just refused to testify. My husband refused as well, and Jim Eastland said he was going to send us all to jail for contempt of the committee, and I certainly was in contempt of it. But we never went to jail. Lyndon Johnson was one of the main friends we had in the Senate. And Lyndon I think struck a deal with him.

Down in Montgomery it was just awful. It made people suspicious of us, and at that time the Red Scare was everywhere. My husband's family's been in Montgomery for generations, and that really saved us. The great disagreement was that we believed that blacks had the right to vote and we believed in integrated schools. They didn't agree with us but they stuck by us.

There were cross-burnings and threats, and when they did pass the *Brown* decision and integrate the schools, I had to take my children out of school and send them off. The teachers would say things like "You tell your uncle Hugo Black that I'm not gonna teach those black children. I don't care how many laws he passes!" That was hard on the children.

Eastland trying us for being Red was one of the dirtiest things that happened that I know of in the whole long struggle. Because he did it to influence people's opinion about the *Brown* decision. He didn't think he could scare Hugo, but he thought he could make other people think there was something wrong about the decision. He was a very nasty man, no doubt about that.

That whole Cold War period was one of the worst things that's ever happened to the United States. For forty years this country believed all that junk—that Russia was about to bomb us and the whole country was full of Russian spies. We spent all that money and look at what happened. We ruined Russia, and Russia ruined us. What's so sad is the American people actually believed it. All that stuff was so wickedly wrong and lying.

LEE LORCH

In 1946, Lee Lorch joined in the struggle for integrated housing and public schools. During the next thirteen years, he was driven from four university positions, denounced on the floor of Congress, hauled before investigatory committees, and pilloried in the press. Finally, unable to find employment, he and his wife, Grace, left the United States for Canada, where he retired from York University in 1985.

Housing was in very short supply after the war, and for the first year I lived in New York, I shared a room with my father and visited my wife and daughter in Boston on weekends. Then we got a half a Quonset hut over a garbage dump in Jamaica Bay in a temporary housing project for veterans. Finally we found accommodations in a huge housing project called Stuyvesant Town, which was built by the Metropolitan Life Insurance Company in New York's Lower East Side, built by them but with enormous financial assistance from the City of New York. This project was large enough for twenty-five to thirty-five thousand people, a small town in itself.

Now Metropolitan had agreed that preference would be given to war veterans. However, they extended that preference only to white war veterans. They refused to accept applications from nonwhites. The NAACP, the American Civil Liberties Union, American Jewish Congress, and some other organizations brought suit. This case went all the way up to the U.S. Supreme Court. Metropolitan Life Insurance Company did not contest the facts. No, they stipulated to the Court that they would not accept applications from any other than whites. They insisted that a landlord had the right to choose tenants on any basis decided by the landlord. And the Supreme Court of the United States accepted this argument, in a vote of seven to two, Black and Douglas dissenting.

Well, this started a big struggle. After all, we had just been through a war which had shown where racism led. The smell of the gas chambers, the horrors of the concentration camps, were still vivid in the memories of the war veterans, perhaps even more than the rest of the population. The tenants set up a committee to fight this discriminatory policy. I became vice chair of that committee.

We were very surprised to learn that about two-thirds of the tenants surveyed were opposed to Metropolitan's exclusionary policy. It was hard to believe, because previous struggles to open up housing to African-Americans usually led to the opposition of the bulk of the whites in affected areas. But this turned out to be an accurate measure, and in fact the level of support kept increasing as the militancy of the activity developed.

At that time, I was teaching at the City College of New York. This committee became public after I was recommended for promotion. The appointments committee of the department decided not to reappoint me and refused to give any reasons. Delegations that went to see them also received no reasons. The college president admitted that I had done my work well and that there were no charges against me. I was dropped without explanation.

I soon got another job at Penn State. My wife and I decided we would keep the apartment in Stuyvesant Town, as the lease had not yet expired. We invited an African-American family to occupy this apartment as our guests. This was very widely publicized in the papers. The *New York Times* reported on it extensively. When I got to Penn State, the acting president told me that he'd been receiving a lot of calls from wealthy alumni wanting to know why the hell I'd been hired and how quickly I could be fired. This was before I'd got my first class—in fact, it was before I spent my first night there. However, that discussion ended more or less amicably and there were no threats made. The year went on. Incidentally, Penn State did not have on its payroll a single nonwhite. I'm not talking just about the teaching staff—there was no secretary, no janitor, no yardman. Meanwhile, in the Metropolitan Life Insurance Project, the support was growing for this family that was living there. They were made to feel very welcome.

Then in late March I was suddenly summoned by the acting president and told that the board of trustees had given him a list of questions to ask me. He had already reported to the board that I'd been recommended for reappointment, and that there had been no criticisms of my work nor of my relations with my colleagues. However, the board had instructed him to ask me the following questions. Would I be willing to give up my apartment and get out of that issue? No. Would I be willing to do it when the lease expires? No. Well, when would I be willing to do it? I told him I was in that fight for the duration. Then he wanted to know, "Are you a Communist?" I said, "Well, I cannot take upon myself the responsibility for legitimizing this type of question. Therefore, without refusing to answer, I'm asking you to withdraw the question."

Well, he sort of huffed and puffed and said that he was going to report to the board and the board would take action, one way or the other. The next week I got a one-sentence letter: "Your appointment will not be renewed." That was it. No statement of reasons. No criticisms, no nothing. It's true there were some highly placed insurance executives on the board. It's also true that the board consisted primarily of big-time money men. In fact, when the American Association of University Professors intervened,[1] the

---

[1]The AAUP never did conduct a formal investigation of Penn State. In fact, it did little or nothing on most of the cases involving major universities.

chairman of the board expressed genuine amazement. He said, "Why should a big association take an interest in the dismissal of one young assistant professor?"

On April 10th, 1950, the *New York Times* had a front-page news story about my dismissal, and the next day ran an editorial calling on Penn State to reinstate me. There was some support among professors and among students, and very strong support in the weekly newspapers addressed to the African-American community. The *Pittsburgh Courier* editor referred to me as a minor legend for these struggles. The editor in chief of the Afro-American chain of newspapers personally came to Penn State to investigate the situation. Also the Pennsylvania Federation of Labor at its convention in June of 1950 voted overwhelmingly to demand my reinstatement.

After Penn State, thanks largely to the intervention of Judge Hubert T. Delany, who was, I think, the first black judge in New York City, I was appointed to Fisk University in Nashville, Tennessee. That's a private university founded after the Civil War by the Freedmen's Bureau of the government and the Congregational Church for the education of the newly freed slaves. I taught there from 1950 to 1955. And in that period I served as state vice president of the NAACP as well as on the board of the Nashville NAACP. I was chair of the defense committee that was set up for a thirteen-year-old African-American boy who had been charged with raping a forty-year-old white divorcée in her own bedroom while her ten-year-old son and twenty-year-old daughter were asleep in the house and didn't wake up while all this was supposedly going on. The whole thing was a complete frame-up.

The case was too ridiculous to even have an indictment, although he was kept in prison the entire time. The judge refused bail for him on the ground that the guilt was evident. But then the grand jury didn't indict. Anyway, I was constantly active in the community. But I was also very active in the educational front, not only in regard to my own students but in regard to the atmosphere into which they would go.

May 17th, 1954, is a watershed date in that period. On that Monday the U.S. Supreme Court handed down its unanimous ruling[2] that segregation in public education is unconstitutional. Terror began in the South to invalidate that decision. It was not a self-enforcing decision. In fact, there was no

[2] *Brown v. Board of Education.*

enforcement provision of any sort until a year later, and even then in a very limited way. There was no order issued to desegregate the schools. In order to set an atmosphere of peaceful compliance with this decision and to show there was white support in the South for it, my wife and I endeavored to enroll our daughter in the public school nearest our home. We were living on the Fisk campus, and therefore the nearest school was a school that was, up until then, reserved for African-American children.

I went to see the principal of the school and asked him his opinion, and he said he would welcome her. In fact, he already knew her. You see, all her playmates went to that school. She was ten at the time. We then made application at the school board headquarters and they refused her admission.

At that time the *Nashville Tennessean* was a very prominent newspaper, and it was busy backing Gordon Browning for governor. Browning was running on a platform of preservation of segregation. He said that one hundred percent of the whites and ninety-nine percent of the blacks wanted things to stay as they were. He would see that they did. This was his program. And of course our action showed that the one hundred percent wasn't quite one hundred percent. The *Nashville Tennessean* then began to make inquiries about me, and I was immediately subpoenaed by the House Un-American Activities Committee.[3]

The subpoena was served September 7th, 1954, for me to appear in Dayton, Ohio, September 15th. A week in which to prepare. So anyway, I went to the committee hearing. It was a pretty raucous affair. "Were you ever a member of the Communist Party?" and so on.

I was an unfriendly witness. I refused to answer the bulk of the questions, and eventually I was cited for contempt of Congress. Meanwhile, panic had started at Fisk University. The *Nashville Tennessean* hammered away at this, day after day, and I was summoned before the board of trustees. I learned later that the board had initially voted seventeen to two against taking any action; but then one of the white members of the board, a local manufacturer, got up and had said that if that decision stands, he will resign from the board and spread his resignation in the press, and that the other dissenting member would do the same.

The board then voted to withdraw that motion and refer it to its executive committee for final action. The executive committee voted ten to one to dismiss me. The ten whites versus the one black on the committee.

---

[3]Purportedly, the hearing was held to investigate Communist infiltration in Dayton, Ohio. Lorch, who had never before set foot in Dayton, was not made aware of this until he arrived.

It must be understood what a black institution is. It's not an institution controlled by African-Americans; it's one attended by them. The control still rests in the hands of those who control the rest of society. With some of the historically black institutions of the South, in those days, every single member of the board was white. This was normally the case with the state-owned institutions. And in most others, the majority was white. The then president of Fisk was the first nonwhite president in its history.

Well, at any event, this issue at Fisk kept going. My case was then put before the full board. All the whites present voted for my dismissal. Most of the African-Americans present voted against my dismissal. I was then dismissed.

I applied far and wide for jobs. Of all the twenty-one hundred degree-granting institutions in the United States, Philander Smith College was the sole institution that had nerve enough to offer me a job. It was a small, historically black institution in Little Rock, Arkansas, operated by the Methodist Church. I started teaching there in September 1955, immediately after my term at Fisk ended.

I was still under indictment for contempt of Congress when we got to Little Rock. I should have been tried by then, but the government kept postponing. Before the 1956 elections, the government requested a further postponement of the trial. We refused to agree. They were anxious to avoid having the trial prior to the election, because the weekly press would be very interested in why the federal government could attempt to imprison somebody who'd been consistently active against racism, and successful in education in historically black institutions, especially since in those days the government was doing nothing to stop the killings that were going on in the South—killings of people who were committing the crime of trying to register to vote while of African ancestry.

Now, Little Rock was soon to become notorious throughout the world when Governor Orval Faubus called out the Arkansas National Guard in full battle dress to surround Central High School and keep out the nine African-American children who had been authorized by court order to attend that school. To my mind, it was unfortunate that the school board had elected to send only nine African-American children to one formerly all-white school, and not to send any white kids to formerly all-black schools. If they had issued a massive desegregation order, the segregationists could not have been able to focus their strength on this single school and against nine children.

There were cars with license plates from all over the Southeast parked in the area around that school. The drivers and passengers were part of the mob which gathered. Now, just by mischance, one of the nine became separated from the other eight. It was a big school covering a whole city block. Eight were together at one corner. And the ninth, a young woman, fifteen years of age, had taken the bus and the bus stop was on the other corner. She didn't know that the National Guard was there to keep her out, so she started to walk to the school. The Guard closed ranks and wouldn't let her through, and she went back, confused, shocked, and sat down at the bench at the bus stop. This made the local mob realize that the Guard was there for them—not for the Constitution, not for the children. And they began to heckle this young woman. But one white woman stepped out, succeeded in shaming the mob, got the young woman safely onto a bus, and took her home. That was my wife.

She just happened to be passing by. Our daughter was still in junior high, and Grace had taken her to school. And then had to take the bus back home. The bus went past Central High School, so Grace got off to see what was going on. It was just happenstance.

Before that bus came, Grace had wanted to call a taxi to get the girl out of there and herself as well. There was a drugstore on the corner, and Grace went toward the store to use the phone. The owner slammed the door in her face and locked it. Grace went back and sat with the girl until the bus came.

She didn't abuse the mob. She didn't say what would have been easy to say—"You're a bunch of ignorant hoodlums; go on with you." What she said to them was, and this was reported in the late edition of the *New York Times,* "This is a child you're menacing. What will you think of yourselves six months from now?" A number of the people in that mob—in fact, most of them—were women. Women from the ragged edge of life themselves. Grace recognized in them other human beings, capable of revising their positions. This recognition so startled them that they were no longer equipped to go forth to battle. They were not being challenged as enemies; they were being challenged as human beings.

The result was that they made no effort to stop Grace from taking this young woman away when the bus came. When the bus driver opened the door, a young hoodlum who should've been in school but who was playing hooky attempted to follow onto the bus. The driver, a white guy, chased him off and protected Grace and her companion.

So you see, there were all sorts there. But Grace's remarks had prevented this from developing into physical abuse. Grace wrote about it later. She said, and I think she was quite correct, that those who really benefited from segregation weren't there. The ones who were there were people who were themselves victims of poverty and ignorance and who saw in releasing blacks from some of their bonds threats to what little status they had. So the struggle had to be for the liberation of all, and for the growth of democratic rights for all. I think that's an important lesson.

Well, one of the reporters present recognized her. So her name was in the press—not only in Little Rock, but nationally. The *New York Times* even had a reference to her editorially, praising her by name for this act. Within a few days, Grace was subpoenaed by Senator James Eastland of Mississippi, to appear before the Senate Internal Security Subcommittee in Memphis, where he was sure of a solid segregationist clique. She was given only two days in which to make the trip to Memphis, get a lawyer, which she didn't get. Neither of us had been able to get counsel to appear before the committees.

When she appeared before the committee, she attempted to make a statement. They kept shouting at her so that she couldn't. Eventually they threw her out, said they were going to prosecute her for contempt of Congress, which they didn't do. The next day the *Washington Post* had a beautiful editorial, condemning Eastland and praising Grace.

Grace is no longer living. She died October 28th, 1974. And oddly enough, I think that was exactly the anniversary of her appearance before the committee.

After that, a cross was burned on our lawn and dynamite was put in our garage. The dynamite was not fused, it turned out. I was not using the garage except for storage, and they knew that. They phoned anonymously to the FBI to claim I was storing dynamite. [Chuckles.] That's how I discovered the dynamite, when the FBI showed up at my house. The cross-burning was not very effective either. It wasn't even completely consumed. They sort of dumped it and ran. I never saw who did it.

The worst of the situation was that our daughter was still in an all-white school. She was beaten, pushed downstairs, had food dumped over her by a number of kids. It was very tough for her, but she stood up. She went regularly to school, and it mustn't be thought that her persecution was at the hands of every teacher or every pupil. It takes only a few to pull stunts of this kind. She had some support. In fact, Alice was elected to the student council while all this was going on. But vicious things were done. On one occasion some man pretending to be me called the principal of her school, saying her mother had just died and she should be notified of this. The principal fortunately had sense enough to phone me to verify it.

We had to keep changing our phone number because of round-the-clock phone calls. They'd call one o'clock, two o'clock in the morning to prevent you from sleeping. Even an unlisted number would soon get out. We were living across the street from Mr. and Mrs. Bates; Daisy Bates was the president of the state NAACP and was the leading figure in this struggle. What they went through was hell. Gangs would drive by and throw Molotov cocktails through their windows, trying to set their house on fire. Fortunately, they were in a brick house and hard to do. But they had to replace windows very frequently.

And these nine kids were persecuted viciously. Again, the white kids in that school were not uniformly in favor of preserving segregation, and even those who wanted to preserve segregation were not always interested in persecuting the particular kids involved.

But the names of these kids would be taken by the segregationist kids surreptitiously, and the parents of white kids who were friendly to the black kids would get late-night phone calls: "If you don't want to fish your kid out of the river, tell him to stop being friendly to those niggers." Warfare on every front, however cruel.

It was terribly hard on my wife's nerves. I had a job to do. I had a heavy teaching load at this small, badly financed college. But my wife had to sit all day and think about our daughter in school. That was a much greater strain, 'cause we never knew in what straits she'd come home. We couldn't let her go to school on a bus. I drove her to school and picked her up all the time. Of course, the governor of the state and the segregationist press was busy denouncing us all the time. In fact, a congressman from Little Rock even made a speech in Congress against us.

I mentioned that in 1956 the federal government had requested postponement of the trial, to which we didn't agree. They thereupon dropped the indictment, which meant I was under no charges of any sort. This way they avoided facing the issue before the 1956 presidential elections. Immediately after the elections, they reinstated the indictment. [Chuckles.] The trial was eventually held later in 1956, in the federal district court at Dayton, Ohio, Justice Lester Cecil presiding. It was held without jury. My defense attorney was Judge Hubert T. Delany, who had recently retired as a judge in New York City Courts.

When I was before the committee, I had put into the record—and I didn't have a chance to put a hell of a lot into the record—that I'd never been in Dayton before in my life. That I didn't understand how they could call me when they claimed to be investigating communism in the Dayton area. I'd even left the state of Ohio thirteen years previously and had never been back.

This testimony showed the judge that the committee had subpoenaed me for other than legislative purposes. A few months later he came down with an acquittal. He said that he had been unable to find that there'd been any reason for calling me.

But the witch hunters had gotten what they wanted. They called me in order to cast a shadow over the effort to desegregate the schools peacefully, and to get me dismissed from Fisk. In this they had succeeded.

In Arkansas, the situation was more complicated. I don't think they would have dared to have cited my wife for contempt, because her bravery and her humaneness in silencing a mob and getting this child out of danger had attracted national and international notice. For them to have persecuted her further, especially when they had already been condemned for this much persecution, would not have served their purposes.

The president of Philander Smith College, M. Lafayette Harris, later a bishop of the Methodist Episcopal Church, was actually rather supportive. He vacillated, it's true; but it was out of concern toward what would happen to the school. Great pressure was brought. The school was financed by collections from the Methodist Church, primarily white Methodists. And segregationists were getting Methodist constituencies to write in and say that they would no longer take up a collection for this school.

There were threats to dynamite the school. In Little Rock, a prominent reporter for one of the best-known of the weekly newspapers was stoned. A photographer for *Life* magazine was actually arrested, as he put it, for hitting a segregationist in the fist with his face. Anything could've happened, especially as the political situation continued to deteriorate.

Governor Faubus kept up the pressure, plus constant statements from other state officials, including the attorney general, all of which had to be reported in the media, both print and air. I was being denounced all the time, especially in the weekly newspapers put out by segregationist circles. So it was there all the time, even though the two daily newspapers were not engaged in any particular crusade against us, in fact, the *Arkansas Gazette* not at all.

Then the following happened. As I've mentioned, this was a Methodist school. The leading Methodist school in the U.S. is Wesleyan University in Middletown, Connecticut. And just by chance, the head of their math department was going on leave and they asked me whether I would replace him for that one year. So I agreed with the president of Philander Smith that I would take leave to accept this visiting position for a year at Wesleyan University.[4]

It was under these circumstances that I left Little Rock that year. This was 1957–58, the year of the big struggle; the year of the National Guard; the year that the President of the United States finally had to put the National Guard under federal control, and send in troops to enforce the orders of the federal court. Without, by the way, ever saying that he supported those orders.[5]

The court order provided that the schools had to be run in a certain way. It didn't provide that they had to be run. So the state closed down all the high schools in Little Rock for the next year. The kids who came from well-to-do families, of course, could go to private schools; but the poor, white and black alike, were being kept out of school for a year, in order to promote segregation. Well, you can imagine this reflected a worsening of the situation in the area. The growing tension, and the pressures on Philander Smith didn't let up. And the president wrote me rather sorrowfully that he didn't see that it was practical for me to come back. I was compelled to agree with him, because I didn't want to give the segregationists the satisfaction of having them say that they'd been able to drive me out of town and force this institution to bow. This institution resisted the segregationists by inviting me there in the first place, and by supporting me during that year, and by praising my contributions to the school.

I then accepted one of several offers made to me by Canadian universities and have been in Canada ever since.

[4]For hiring Lorch, Wesleyan came under attack from the *News Leader,* a reactionary newspaper published out of Manchester, New Hampshire.

[5]Eisenhower never said a public word in support of school integration, even though he believed American racism was being exploited by the Soviet Union in the race for world leadership. Chief Justice Earl Warren recounts a White House dinner held just before the Supreme Court decision on *Brown v. Board of Education* during which Eisenhower took him aside and said, "These [segregationists] are not bad people. All they are concerned about is to see that their sweet little girls are not required to sit in school alongside some big overgrown Negroes." After the decision, Eisenhower never spoke to Warren again.

JACK O'DELL

An outgoing, erudite man, O'Dell started his civil rights activism during World War Two sailing in the National Maritime Union.[1] After being blacklisted off the ships, he carried the struggle ashore to the South. In the early sixties, his talents led him to a key position in Martin Luther King's Southern Christian Leadership Conference (SCLC). There he became the target of a Red-baiting campaign by J. Edgar Hoover and the Kennedy administration.

When you're living behind the Iron Curtain down South, who was Communist by definition was anybody who was fightin' for civil rights. So here's James Eastland, senator by virtue of the disenfranchisement of the black population of Mississippi, and he was the chairman of the Senate Internal Security Subcommittee.

In 1956, he comes down with his committee, allegedly lookin' for "communism in the South." I had moved from an address on Louisiana Avenue in New Orleans to another address. The landlady was keeping some of my library when they tried to issue a subpoena to me.

One of the guys I had sailed with was a white brother named Grady—they subpoenaed him too. He was from Tupelo, Mississippi. Grady had poor health as a child and he had periodic relapses of tuberculosis. He was having one of those relapses at the time and he was in a hospital run by a Catholic religious order. The police officials that came to serve his subpoena had him chained to the bed so he couldn't escape the hearings they were holding at the New Orleans Custom House.

Now they didn't know where I was, because I had changed addresses, but they seized my library as evidence that I was a Communist. There were some books in there by Marx and Engels and some others—those weren't the only books in my library, but I certainly did have some Communist literature. So they made an issue that this proves he must be Communist because he's readin' these books. And that was the headline of the *New Orleans Tribune*. "Local Communist Library Seized!" And then the article opened with "Books by the leading Reds of the world . . ." [Laughs.] Boy,

[1]See Jack O'Dell under "On the Waterfront."

I read that, I said, "These people are going crazy!" During the hearings a lawyer for one of the defendants was thrown down the steps of the Custom House and his arm was broken. It was that kind of an atmosphere.

I had a good lawyer named Milton Friedman. It wasn't Milton Friedman of this economic foolishness! [Laughs.] This was a Madison Avenue lawyer. I said, "I want to make it clear, I don't mind going to jail for contempt. I am not going to be friendly to this Eastland Committee. I'm going to speak my mind, and if it's gonna result in a contempt charge, then I'm ready to go to jail."

He said, "You can state your position and not go to jail, and the Fifth Amendment against self-incrimination is your protection." With the insistence that at no time would I address Eastland as "Senator" we prepared for the hearing.

They asked the same old thing—"Are you or have ever you been a Communist?" I said, "That is none of your business, you don't have the right to ask that."

I told Eastland, "You wouldn't even be sittin' there if blacks could vote in Mississippi, and you're callin' everybody subversive?" I gave him a fit, man. The net result is that they turned me loose after a very brief session. He never bothered me anymore, didn't ever call me back. I was just getting warmed up! 'Cause you know, with all the cameras in there and those marble halls, it looks so imposing. It takes a while for a country boy to get used to that. But I got used to it in about an hour, so, man, if he'd come back for a second session, he'd a been in serious trouble.

But their point was to create an atmosphere in the South that "exposed" any progressive people in the civil rights effort as Communists. So white Southerners who were for civil rights had been called nigger-lovers for years, but now you could call them Communists, and the segregationists hid behind that—they weren't opposed to civil rights, they were just against Communists.

Eastland and Strom Thurmond,[2] people like that, they used their position of power to try to stop the civil rights movement. Because if we won the right to vote then some of them would not be in office any longer.

So anyway, that was the 1956 hearings in New Orleans. Then I got a job in Alabama through a friend of mine with a small black insurance company, the Protective Industrial Insurance Company, and I worked in Birming-

[2]J. Strom Thurmond, staunch segregationist and former Democrat from South Carolina, joined the Republican Party in 1964.

ham. Then I was promoted to manager of the Montgomery district in 1958, and it was in that period that I got involved in the Montgomery civil rights movement and in the Alabama Christian Movement for Human Rights. In Alabama, the NAACP had been outlawed under this atmosphere of anti-Communism. So we formed the Alabama Christian Movement for Human Rights with the Reverend Fred Shuttlesworth as its president. We carried on under that banner.

Then in 1958 the House Un-American Activities Committee came South on the same errand that the Senate Internal Security Subcommittee had done two years earlier, that is, trying to expose the extent of "communism's" spread in the South. So they passed the names around again and I got subpoenaed.[3] Well, that cost me my job, because the FBI told the insurance company that they were going to audit their books if they didn't fire me. Well, I told my boss, "Hey, man, you don't need to go through all that, that's all right, I can get another job."

From '58 to '60, I worked with the Harlem Tenants Movement in New York, organizing tenants. In 1959, I volunteered to be the Southern organizer for the March on Washington for Integrated Schools.[4] Part of that march was a petition to Congress to pass legislation immediately to implement the letter and spirit of the 1954 Supreme Court decision and prevent another Little Rock School crisis. The white supremacy resistance had begun to develop through the White Citizens' Councils and various other Ku Klux–like organizations in the South and there was a need for a federal initiative. We brought twenty-five thousand people to Washington.

So we had this march on Washington, and then in 1960 I was called back to the House Un-American Activities Committee. They were investigating the same thing, communism in the civil rights movement. That's all they did. They never investigated the Klan, but they investigated anybody progressive. If they said you were Communist, then it was up to you to prove you weren't. And the very fact that you were subpoenaed, in many people's mind, you must be Communist. So that was the weapon and that's the way it was used.

[3]HUAC Counsel: "Do you honestly feel, and are you trying to make this committee and the people of this country believe, that you, a member of the Communist conspiracy, responsive to the will of the Kremlin, are in truth and in fact, concerned with the welfare of the Negro people of this country?" O'Dell: "I wouldn't try to make you believe anything." (HUAC hearings, July 30, 1958)

[4]The second Youth March for integrated schools in April 1959, organized by A. Philip Randolph and led by Harry Belafonte and Bayard Rustin.

After that I became head of the New York office of SCLC. I had two jobs, I was director of voter registration after 1962 for SCLC, and the director of the direct-mail fund-raising efforts, in which we raised about half the budget of SCLC.

Those are key positions, and the point is, if you want to slow down an organization, you would certainly find some way of going after a key position. Because if our adversaries could cripple an organization by eliminating people in those type positions, that would be to their advantage. And SCLC was gaining a lot of prestige and a lot of momentum, so that's one way they went at it.

They started chipping away at my position with the King organization. President Kennedy told Martin Luther King I was the number-four Communist in the United States.

King said, "Well, I don't know how he would have time to do that, 'cause he has two jobs with me!" [Laughs.] He just took it down to its most pragmatic level, he says, "I don't understand, where would he find the time?"

So then Martin asked to see my file. They went to Burke Marshall, who was head of the Civil Rights Division, who agreed to produce a file when we got down to New Orleans. Martin sent Andy Young down there. And Burke Marshall said he couldn't get the file from J. Edgar Hoover. It was a bluff.

They started pressuring King right after Albany, Georgia, and continued to pressure him for about a year and a half. And of course Kennedy himself played a role in that. They had a meeting at the White House again, June the 25th, 1963. Kennedy said that Strom Thurmond was going to make an issue of King having Communists on his staff and therefore if he did, then he, Kennedy, would have to back off his civil rights bill. In other words, Kennedy said he wouldn't even try to defend his own civil rights bill if the Dixiecrats[5] like Strom Thurmond made an issue of Communists in the civil rights movement.

Kennedy was saying O'Dell was a Communist because Burke Marshall had said that the FBI had said that the House Un-American Activities Committee had said—you know what I mean! I guess that is a measure of the extent to which intimidation can be developed and crystallized. So that if

[5]A states' rights party organized for the 1948 presidential campaign by Southern conservatives opposed to Truman's civil rights program. Strom Thurmond, then governor of South Carolina, headed the ticket. The segregationist bloc persisted as a potent force in Congress for as long as Southern blacks remained effectively disenfranchised.

it's institutionalized into a political outlook, then everybody has to duck around it if they want their political future not to be tarnished.

When Kennedy met with Martin he was on his way to Britain to meet with the prime minister at that time, who had been involved in the Profumo scandal.[6] He said, "There's a man over there in London whose career is being ruined, and I'm not going to have mine ruined by being associated with the civil rights movement if it's got Communists in it." that's what he implied. And he was using the Profumo affair as an example of how careful you had to be.

Well, we had a meeting and King thought that I ought to resign, and I did. They went on as long as they could. It went all the way up to the President. And so King says, "Well, you know, when the President of the United States says you gotta do something, you have to do it." The larger question was not to give them an excuse to back out of supporting the civil rights legislation, and they were prepared to use that as an excuse, no matter how frivolous it was. That's how deep their commitment was. They were looking to the next election, and they didn't feel they could win in such a battle against the Dixiecrats. If Strom Thurmond and Eastland said somebody's a Communist, they would just back away from it. They were willing to abide by the scapegoating and keep on steppin'.

So I left SCLC and I remained on good terms with Martin and the whole staff. They understood what was goin' on—we all did. The harassment of King continued after I was gone. In fact, it stepped up![7] He said, "Hey, what is this?" Of course, he'd realized it at first. It was what we thought it was in the first place, an attack upon the movement.

But we also knew from the practical politics of it that the Kennedy administration was not committed in principle to civil rights. They were committed as a matter of expediency. There was pressure on them by the civil rights movement to act, and Kennedy's tendency was not to act. So pressure had to be consistently pushed.

We were having demonstrations all across the south when he went to

[6]Notorious affair involving British politician John Profumo, who in 1960 was made secretary of war under Prime Minister Harold Macmillan. He resigned in 1963 after lying to the House of Commons concerning his entanglement with Christine Keeler, a teenage showgirl, who was also involved with a Soviet naval attaché.

[7]For a decade, J. Edgar Hoover pursued a policy of vicious harassment against Martin Luther King, Jr.—attempted blackmail, relentless surveillance, electronic eavesdropping, an army of paid informants, and a carefully orchestrated campaign of character assassination.

meet with Khrushchev, and they sent the word down from the Justice Department that we should call off the demonstration because it would embarrass the President! We said, "Well, man, get rid of the problem if you don't want to be embarrassed!" But you see, this is the way they were operating. They were always weighing the political cost of a given situation and what was the political cost of not doing it. That's how you got those people killed when James Meredith went to the University of Mississippi—the delay in federalizing the Mississippi National Guard got people killed! It was clear that's what they should have done in the first place. The same was true of Albany, Georgia, in the summer of '62. The fact is, we lost the campaign in Albany, Georgia, to desegregate that city because the local official violated our First Amendment right to freedom of assembly and locked up everybody who got in the demonstration. And the Kennedy administration sat there and did nothing. Yet it is the President who is sworn to uphold the Constitution of the United States, not the sheriff of Albany, Georgia.

After I left SCLC I went to work for a magazine called *Freedomways,* a quarterly of the movement that became very authoritative.[8] Every now and then the FBI would show up and ask what I thought about the Communist Party. I'd just refuse to talk with them. I never accepted the anti-Communist thing. The Communist Party is a party just like every other party, people come in and out of it. But they were establishing that it was an international conspiracy of some sort. You couldn't yield to that, because they could do that to any group.

It's important to stress the special problem that this McCarthy period posed for people in the South struggling for rights that were already in the Constitution but never implemented. The black community in the South had segregation imposed on it from the time of Reconstruction, and so for seventy-five years we had been living under an American variety of apartheid.

I think the assessment of Truman must take into account the role of that administration. It comes through in history as being pro–civil rights. Well, he desegregated the armed forces, that's true. But he also created the atmosphere which slowed enormously the momentum for civil rights in this

[8]Published from 1961 to 1985, *Freedomways* was perhaps the most distinguished African-American political-cultural journal of the period. Contributors included Paul Robeson, W.E.B. Du Bois, Ruby Dese, Angela Davis, Alice Walker, Harry Belafonte, Shirley Chisholm, Ron Dellums, Jesse Jackson, Derek Walcott, and host of other intellectuals and activists.

country. He gave the segregationists a major weapon when he developed this Cold War anti-Communist hysteria. And McCarthyism grew out of that.

It was the Truman administration that implemented the Smith Act. It was the Truman administration that originated the Attorney General's subversive list. You can't separate that out in making an assessment of what the Truman civil rights record was. He had a record of desegregating the armed forces and giving lip service to civil rights, while at the same time he gave real weapons and power to the effort to maintain segregation. And while he didn't like the Dixiecrats because they destabilized the Democratic Party in terms of his own reelection, the fact is that his administration's policy with respect to foreign policy was very much in alliance with the Dixiecrats.

They used anticommunism and the McCarthy hysteria to their own purposes, and it became increasingly difficult to carry out civil rights activity in that atmosphere. In South Carolina, for example, schoolteachers were fired who were known to be NAACP members. And in Texas, the legislature passed a law that made it punishable by death to be a Communist.

Yes indeed, this thing went far and wide. They were frightened by organized efforts among these so-called simple black people. They didn't believe that foolishness—they knew blacks were intelligent. These racists don't always believe their own racism, they understand the role it plays—that's for propaganda, that's for the mass of people to swallow.

Then the other part is, whether they called you anything or not, they created an atmosphere. Look at Mr. and Mrs. Harry T. Moore, who were murdered on Christmas Eve in 1951 down in Florida. They were leaders of the right-to-vote movement and their home was bombed and both of them were killed. They never found who did it.[9] This was the green light for all these Ku Klux elements. Whether they ever called you a Communist or not, if they thought you were subversive they had an excuse. They'd just say, "Well, we're just gettin' rid of some Communists anyway." *Boom.*

[9]An Orlando journal commented, "Communists, bent on destroying tranquil relations between the white and colored people of Florida, could well have plotted it."

The Peace Movement

There was something about the word "peace" that raised the collective hackles of the Inquisition. For them it conjured not the absence of war but the face of the enemy. It signified capitulation, defeat, the global victory of the hated Kremlin.

Thus HUAC in 1956 explained the objectives "of all these misnamed 'peace' groups: the dissemination of Communist propaganda aimed at discrediting the United States and promoting a dangerous relaxation in the ideological and military strength of our country."

In fact, the American peace movement long predated the existence of the Communist Party and has drawn its support from a wide variety of philosophies. Activities first began in the early nineteenth century among religious and utopian groups. Within the social movements of the 1840s and 1850s, issues of peace figured highly, along with women's rights, abolitionism, and temperance. As the United States took on the "white man's burden" with the invasion of the Philippines in 1898, anti-imperialist movements drew upon a wide circle of intellectuals and writers, among them Mark Twain. Opposition to the American entry into World War One was carried by religious pacifists and radical socialists, among them labor leader Eugene V. Debs, who in 1920 campaigned for the White House from his prison cell and received 900,000 votes.

In the 1920s and up to the mid-1930s, the Communist Party worked the anti-imperialist front largely in isolation. But the sectarian barriers were flexible enough to allow a coalition of Communists, Socialists, and religious activists to protest the American invasion of Nicaragua in 1926.

In the late 1940s the most visible peace campaigning was found in Henry Wallace's Progressive Party. A significant bloc of New Dealers rejected the Cold War confrontationism of the Truman administration and its equation of "freedom" with the international freedom of American business. Wallace's 1948 presidential campaign took aim at the Cold War, but quickly became one of the main targets of Red Scare reaction. In 1949, what remained of the Left carried the banner of peace against the unpopular Korean War, but was almost entirely isolated by pro–Cold War sentiment.

Into this relative vacuum came the pacifists. Imprisoned by the hundreds as conscientious objectors during World War Two, they forged new links in subsequent years and exerted considerable influence on the East and West Coasts. Pacifica Radio, in the San Francisco Bay Area, brought anarcho-pacifists together with progressives. Beat poet and bookstore owner Lawrence Ferlinghetti played an important role as an impresario of peace, along with another bookman, Roy Kepler. Both City Lights Books of San Francisco and Kepler's Books of Menlo Park were at the center of West Coast activism for decades; the latter was firebombed a number of times during the Vietnam War. Intertwined with this milieu was the folk music revival, which was strongly attacked as Red-tinged for its antiwar sentiments. Sparked by Pete Seeger and the Weavers in the 1950s, it was carried on by Peter, Paul, and Mary, Bob Dylan, and Joan Baez. Baez, an early and outspoken critic of America's efforts in Vietnam, founded the Institute for the Study of Nonviolence under the direction of her Gandhian mentor Ira Sandperl. In turn the institute played a significant role in the civil rights movement, training many of Martin Luther King's activists in the techniques of nonviolent resistance.

Concomitant with this activity was the growing opposition to nuclear testing and the arms race. The pacifist Fellowship of Reconciliation widely circulated a petition calling for an end to testing. Albert Einstein and Bertrand Russell united prominent scientists worldwide with their appeal of 1955. (Similar efforts by Nobel laureate Linus Pauling earned him years of harassment from the federal government.) A flowering of peace institutes and research organizations ensued, many with radical pacifist connections. Direct action was involved as well, such as the 1960 resistance of two thousand New Yorkers to the annual Civil Defense Drill. This matched the rebirth of student activism, which was inspired by the successes of the civil rights movement. The Student Peace Union, founded in 1959, circulated petitions and organized marches and rallies.

It is no surprise, then, that nearly every group calling for "peace" or "friendship" or an end to nuclear weaponry found itself harassed by the FBI and listed by HUAC as a subversive organization. The Justice Department ran guard for the State Department, marking for suppression such organizations as the Council for a Democratic Far Eastern Policy and the Council for Pan-American Democracy. (Both opposed the Truman

Doctrine.) The Peace Information Center, the American Peace Crusade, and many similar groups were ordered to register as foreign agents with the Subversive Activities Control Board. The Peace Information Center, for one, decided a court battle was a luxury it could not afford and voted to dissolve itself.[1]

The Vietnam War sparked off the largest resurgence of radical activity since the 1930s and the most massive campaign of anti-Left suppression since the early 1950s. The FBI, CIA, Military Intelligence, and local law enforcement Red Squads collected information on student and community dissidents through informers, wiretaps, mail checks, and surveillance. Files on one and a half million Americans were collected by the government during this period. Agents operated virtually unchecked to infiltrate and disrupt organizations. As early as 1962, HUAC was busy investigating all stripes of the new radicals, from the progressive Women Strike for Peace to later Maoists and Yippies. But this was a different country from a decade earlier, and a new generation. The widespread youth culture disdained the establishment watchdogs and were buoyed by an alternative economy largely immune to HUAC's bullying. Who could be blacklisted from an underground newspaper or a commune? New Left radicals hauled before the Inquisition were delighted to affirm their ideological allegiances and used the opportunity as a forum for their own beliefs and attitudes.

The Yippies, who were of a more playful bend, transformed their hearings into guerrilla theater. Jerry Rubin testified dressed as a soldier in the Revolutionary War and once attempted to attend Dave Dellinger's hearing clad in a Santa Claus suit. For his appearance, Abbie Hoffman equipped himself with a shirt made from an American flag.

LINUS PAULING

For his work against nuclear proliferation and for world peace, Pauling was denied a passport and called before the Senate Internal Security Subcommittee. A two-time Nobel Prize winner (Chemistry in 1954, Peace

---

[1]This did not deter the Attorney General, who responded that it must register even if it did not exist.

in 1962), Pauling was awarded the International Lenin Peace Prize in 1972. For more on Linus Pauling, see under "Red-ucators."

Not long after the war, I was asked to speak at the Rotary Club in Hollywood. I was known as a popular speaker on scientific subjects. So I gave a talk about what the atom is and what the nucleus of the atom is, and what nuclear fission is; how it's possible for one pound of substance to undergo fission and produce twenty million times as much explosive energy as you would get from a pound of TNT or dynamite. So far as I remember, I didn't say much beyond just the aspect of atomic physics.

I was asked to give more talks, and pretty soon I was saying: "It seems to me that with the tremendous explosive and destructive capability of these weapons, we'd better be sensible and stop going to war between great nations." So that was how I got started talking about nuclear weapons and later about world peace.

Then I was asked to join the board of trustees of the Emergency Committee of Atomic Scientists, usually called the Einstein Committee—Einstein was the chairman. The whole committee consisted of seven or eight atomic scientists. The committee collected about five hundred thousand dollars and used it for making a film about atomic bombs and for various educational activities. The committee ceased to function when the McCarthy period came along, but I kept working. My estimate is that I spent half my time doing research and half my time working in this field of social, political, and economic questions and giving hundreds of lectures over the years. I don't really know how many. At one time I think I estimated fifty lectures on world peace a year.

In 1951, I was on my way to Israel, at invitation of their research laboratory there, and I had several hours' layover in Paris. I decided to go over to the Sorbonne and see people that I knew. I was talking with a professor there who said, "You ought to go talk to Madame Joliot-Curie, the daughter of Marie Curie. She has something interesting to show you."

So I went over. She gave me a letter. She was a Fellow of the American Physical Society and had applied for membership in the American Chemical Society, of which I had been president a couple of years before. So the letter she got back informed her that she was being rejected on grounds of moral turpitude. The charge was that she was married to a Communist. I wrote a letter that was published in *Chemical & Engineering News* saying, "Here we have Madame Joliot-Curie, who's applied for membership. She is a Nobel laureate; her mother was a Nobel laureate; her father was a Nobel laureate; her husband is a Nobel laureate. She tells me that she is not a

Communist." Madame Joliot-Curie never became a member of the American Chemical Society. I think it's rather embarrassing.

In 1952, I wanted to go to a meeting, a symposium arranged by the Royal Society of London to discuss my discoveries on the structure of proteins. I was to be the first speaker, and people from various countries working on protein structure were the other speakers. My passport had expired, so I had to apply again. I didn't get the passport. We got as far as New York and Washington, my wife and I, led on by the Passport Office, who kept saying things like "When you get to New York, you can get the passport," and then I went down to Washington and at the last minute they said, "No, we're not issuing the passport." So we went back to Pasadena. I missed the symposium. Some say that if I'd been there, I would have discovered the double helix in place of Watson and Crick. I won't go into it, but if I'd gone to that meeting in London and seen Franklin's X-ray photographs, which Watson and Crick saw . . . well, who knows?

I asked on my various stays in Washington why I had been denied, talking to the authorities and the officials in the Passport Department. The first answer I got was "Not in the best interests of the United States." This wasn't very illuminating. Then they said, "Your anti-Communist statements haven't been strong enough." They couldn't say, "You haven't made any anti-Communist statements." I was having a fight with the Communists at the same time. The Soviets had come out in 1949 with an attack on me, saying that my ideas about chemistry were incompatible with dialectical materialism, that no patriotic Soviet scientist should use them. The professor who had translated my book *The Nature of the Chemical Bond* into Russian was fired and never got his professorship back. One of the young professors who attacked me got his professorship. So I was persona non grata in the early 1950s in both the Soviet Union and the United States.

The following year, I was invited by Nehru[1] to visit universities and scientific laboratories in India and to help dedicate a new scientific institute, and I accepted. I also accepted the invitations to give a set of lectures in Greece and then a set in Jerusalem. So, we went to the Passport Office in New York, and they said, "Come back tomorrow, we don't have word." And then they said, "You have to go to Washington and see the authorities in the Passport Division." So I sent a cable to Athens canceling my lectures. We went to Washington about the 18th of December, and for several days

[1]Jawaharlal Nehru (1889–1964), chief political heir to Mahatma Gandhi and first prime minister of independent India; a principal architect of the politics of nonalignment.

I went to the Passport Office. And then they said, "Come back after Christmas." So I sent a cable to Israel, canceling. Then I went back after Christmas and they said, "Come back after New Year's." So I sent a cable to Nehru, canceling. By this time my wife and I were so unhappy and discouraged, being in Washington, D.C., on Christmas, with this hanging over our heads, we just gave up and went back to Pasadena.

Senator Morse of Oregon introduced legislation that required the State Department to set up a system whereby anyone whose passport was denied could appeal. The State Department went ahead and set up an appeal board. But I couldn't appeal, because Mrs. Shipley, the director of the Passport Division, never refused to issue the passport.[2] She was too smart for me. She never officially denied me a passport; she just wouldn't issue me one. So I had nothing to appeal! [Laughs.]

The next year, 1954, I was reinvited back to India, and I applied again for the passport. I had had one issued a couple of times in between, limited usually to two months. In each case, I had participated in important scientific meetings. So I sent in an application to go to India again, and it was just denied. I thought, "Well, the heck with it. I'll notify Nehru that I can't come." But then it was announced, in late October of 1954, that I was to be given the Nobel Prize in Chemistry. The *New York Times* carried an article—"Is Professor Pauling going to be allowed to go to Stockholm to get his Nobel Prize?" The State Department didn't have the guts to stick to their policy, so I received the passport through the mail. That was the last time I've had passport problems.

In 1957, I issued a press release that two thousand American scientists had signed a petition to stop testing nuclear weapons in the atmosphere. Two days later, I received a subpoena from the Senate Internal Security Subcommittee ordering me to appear in Washington. They were investigating possible Communist influences in the bomb test petition. I sent them a letter saying that I was scheduled to make a trip to Europe to give some scientific talks and asking that they postpone the hearing for a month or two. I got back word that they had canceled the hearing for that date. It was two or three years later—'60, I think—that they again subpoenaed me to testify.

Senator Dodd, the chairman of the committee, had written an article

[2]Ruth Shipley and her successor Frances Knight, crusading anti-Communists both, worked assiduously to ensure that any heretic who criticized American foreign policy would be denied the right to travel. Those temerarious enough to associate with or show sympathy to heretics could also be denied a passport. This policy continued unabated until 1958, when the Supreme Court, in the face of ardent opposition from the Eisenhower administration, ruled that the right of travel can be removed only with due process.

called "Eight Fallacies of Nuclear Test Ban," and presented it so it appeared in the official proceedings of the Senate. He said that I should bring with me all of the letters and documents by means of which signed copies of the petition had been communicated to me.

I was questioned for several hours about which organizations I'd been with, whether I had sent a telegram to President Eisenhower asking that the Rosenbergs not be executed. All sorts of stuff—sometimes about things I couldn't remember having done. Finally, the senator said, "You were ordered to bring with you the names of all the people who had signed your petition." I said, "Well, I did bring the names of all of the people who signed the petition. I've given them to you. You have them. I have three big bound volumes of signatures." He turned to his aide and discussed the matter with him a moment, and then he said, "You were ordered to bring with you all of the letters or other documents by means of which these signed copies of the petition were communicated to you. Are you prepared to comply with this order?" I said, "No, I'm not willing to obey this order. I'm not willing to give you the names of these idealistic young people who are working for world peace, in order for them to be subjected to the sort of harassment that you're subjecting me to. I am not obeying."

So then there came the moment when we had to wait. My wife told me later that during noon break, a young man had rushed up to her and said, "Is your husband going to give the committee the names of those people?" And she said, "I don't know, we'll just have to wait and see." finally Senator Dodd just said, "Very well," and went on to some other matter. So I was off the hook, instead of a year in jail for contempt of Congress, which I hadn't been looking forward to with much pleasure. Of course, even if the committee had recommended that I be found guilty of contempt, the whole Congress might have rejected it. I had published an advertisement in the *Washington Post* explaining why I was not going to give the committee these names, and many newspaper editors published editorials supporting me rather than the committee. So the committee decided they'd better back off.

Initially, we wrote this petition as an appeal by American scientists to the governments of the world to stop testing nuclear weapons in the atmosphere. But after word of it got out, I began getting copies of the petition with "American" crossed out and signatures of scientists all over the world. So I had a lot of these appeals mimeographed with "American" left out, and I got a book, *Universities of the World,* and went through it and picked out the names of one person, usually a biologist or a biochemist, in almost every country in the world, and sent copies of this petition around. So by the next summer or spring, I had nine thousand signatures from all over the world. And my wife and I presented copies of them to Dag Hammarskjöld of the United Nations. Ultimately, when they stopped coming in, we had thirteen thousand signatures from scientists in forty-nine countries. Later, I found a letter in the kitchen of our home that had fallen down behind a desk in the corner. It was from a scientist in the fiftieth country, that had just happened to have got lost.

Up to McCarthy's time, there had been quite a lot of scientists who had been saying the same thing that I'd been saying: that nuclear war was really too terrible to look forward to in the future. Nearly all of them stopped being active when McCarthy began operating. For one reason, that's easy to understand. A scientist could say, "Here I am, a chemist or a physicist or a biologist, and my job is to teach and carry on research in this science. It's not my job to get involved in politics, and so why should I continue doing it, putting myself in jeopardy?" Of course, some of these people lost their jobs. I was fortunate.

So I'm asked, "Why did you continue?" And one answer that I've given sometimes is that I'm just stubborn. I said, "I don't allow anybody to tell me what to think, except Mrs. Pauling!" [Laughs.] And another answer that I've given is that my wife knew me better than I knew myself probably. She always knew not only what I did but why I did it. So I had to keep the respect of my wife.

For a short time I was a member of the national board of directors of SANE.[3] Then when McCarthy attacked SANE, Norman Cousins, I guess it was he, replied that there was no need for the government to investigate the people associated with SANE, that they would carry out their own investigations and question members of the board of directors about their beliefs. So I resigned and sent a note saying I didn't give the chairman of the board of SANE or anybody else the right to question me about my beliefs.

My wife and I argued with two matters in these organizations that we were affiliated with. One, the right of organizations to question individuals; and the other, a policy of not keeping left-wingers out of an organization. We said, "We support any organization working for world peace." Well, we went to a peace conference in Oxford, England, as representatives of ourselves. We didn't go as representatives of any organization. And there were representatives of various peace groups that were going to participate in this organization. The Americans objected to the fact that there were going to be some people from behind the Iron Curtain attending the peace

[3]Otherwise known as the National Committee for a Sane Nuclear Policy, founded in 1957.

conference. And the peace conference was not held. It broke up after the first meeting or two, when there was a fight as to whether the American policy of throwing out the people from behind the Iron Curtain would be followed or not. So my wife and I wrote an article about the Oxford Peace Conference that was published in the journal *The Minority of One,* in which we said this hardly seems a sensible policy, to be working for world peace but not to be talking with people in the other countries that are working for world peace too. [Laughs.]

I always hesitate to classify myself in respect to political matters, but I'm probably closer to being a socialist than anything else. Of course, the powerful people in the United States are really worried about socialism, not communism. No one has ever thought that the United States suddenly will go Communist, so far as I'm aware. But the Communist scare was a good ploy, a way of stopping the Roosevelt New Deal idea of doing justice to all people; Social Security and a graduated income tax. They're still fighting, of course, they're still engaged in dismantling the New Deal.

You know, when I was awarded the Nobel Peace Prize in 1963, *Life* magazine came out with a half-page editorial, "A Weird Insult from Norway." An insult to the United States of America, to give me the Nobel Peace Prize, yes. [Laughs.]

EDITH JENKINS

A memoirist, poet, and teacher, Edith Jenkins is a longtime activist in the peace movement. "I got into the student Left at UC because I found the world was not as I had thought it was. First into the National Student League, then later the Young Communist League. I got involved in the peace movement in 1933, but it was the San Francisco strike of '34 that thoroughly radicalized me."

During the war, I ran a mass meeting for Paul Robeson and Walter Huston on Fair Employment Practices, that was in 1945, towards the end of the war. I know the time because I was very pregnant, and every time Paul Robeson saw me after that, he said, "Edith, you've gotten so thin," and I'd say, "You've never seen me when I'm not pregnant."

The whole time I was raising children I was active in the peace movement and active in the PTA, trying to get the PTA to have a more active peace program. I also initiated programs on what was then called Negro History Week and Women's History. I got interested in the PTA's history and doing women's programs for PTA. And then I was active in antiwar organizations of various kinds during that period.

In 1950 there was going to be a World Peace Congress in Sheffield, England.[1] My husband, Dave, and I were talking about who should go, and I said, "Why don't they send some ordinary women, mothers who are interested in peace, instead of just big shots?" And Dave said, "Why don't you go?"

We were pretty poor then, but Dave had just gotten a settlement over an accident. So in a week's time we decided that I would go. I represented the Independent Progressive Party there, just because I had to have some organizational designation.

There were about twenty-eight delegates. We went off in a chartered flight, a very old plane. All the water froze on the way over and there was nothing hot to eat. Paul Robeson was supposed to go, but he couldn't leave the country then, his passport had been taken away. So we took messages from him.

We got to the airport in London, and Scotland Yard came and interviewed us. They said we couldn't enter England,[2] and they wouldn't let us talk to counsel. We were kept incommunicado overnight. Scotland Yard interviewed us one by one. They asked the woman before me to let them look through her purse. When she demurred, they said, "Well, if you don't do it, we'll search you forcibly." So I went into the bathroom and tore up addresses I had of British friends and flushed them down the toilet.

It had been only the week before that I had decided to go, but what was amazing was when they interviewed me they had a whole dossier on me. They asked me all sorts of questions. They must have had State Department cooperation. I was very frightened. I had left four children behind and didn't know what was going to happen.

[1]The first congress was held in Paris, April 20–23, 1949. Both were represented by HUAC and SISS as part of an international "Communist 'peace' offensive" against the North Atlantic Defense Pact.

[2]The second World Peace Congress was originally scheduled to be held in Sheffield, England, November 13–19, 1950, but the British government denied visas to many of the delegates and it was moved to Warsaw, Poland, and held on November 16–22.

Then we got word that Warsaw would have the congress there. So we flew to Paris and took a train to Eastern Europe. We stopped in Prague for a couple of days, and then we went to Warsaw. In Warsaw, unbelievably, they had worked day and night for forty-eight hours and finished a sort of Peace Palace with huge statues of a woman holding the Picasso dove.

It was a terribly moving congress, and I have to do a double take on it really, because I was so totally uncritical of the Soviet Union at that time. When I look back, I realize that the picture that I received was one that in many ways I would be very skeptical of now, in terms of the . . . Well, there was no question that the peace message was an absolutely sincere and strong one. But the fact that I did not know what was going on in the Soviet Union at the time makes me look back and reevaluate how much I was taken in by what I thought was the totally unrelieved goodwill of the Soviet Union and the Iron Curtain countries.

But this was shortly after the war, and the women we met in Prague told us of the liberation of Czechoslovakia by the Soviet Union and how they didn't know whether to laugh or to cry or to dance in the streets. It was very moving, when we were in Poland we saw the remains of the Warsaw ghetto and the statue to the heroes of the uprising. And we went to Jewish theater in Poland, which was amazing; this was before the anti-Semitism in Poland reasserted itself. We met with the Korean women,[3] and that was terribly moving as well. They asked us to bring back their message here, and I felt it was a real injunction that we had that role to play.

Joliot-Curie was at the meeting. And I think Shostakovich was there, and J. D. Bernal, the British physicist. He was head of the World Peace Congress for a while, and he was a leading molecular physicist who also wrote an extraordinary book called *Science and History*. He addressed the American delegation with words of wisdom in which he said, "It's always very tempting at a delegation like this to take very far-left positions that will subsequently be quoted in your own country. Don't say anything here that isn't something that you will stand by when you get home."

There is a kind of dizziness or excitement in delegations and a feeling of peace and extraordinary camaraderie when you're with people from all over the world. When we got back to this country, I spoke at one mass meeting. I had never really done any public speaking before, and to my amazement I got a big ovation. And so I did a tremendous amount of speaking against the Korean War, mainly in San Francisco. I spoke sixty-five times the first

[3]The Korean War was on at the time. Presumably these women were from North Korea, which was taking a terrible pounding from American airpower.

year at house meetings where people would invite their neighbors. Although they were organized mostly by left-wingers, the people who came wouldn't necessarily be Left at all.

Then in 1951, I believe, there was a subpoena out for me by the Burns Committee, which was the California House Un-American Committee. As you know, it was perfectly legal to dodge subpoenas, but once you got them you had to appear. As somebody at that time said, it was a question of prestige, and people who didn't get them suffered from "subpoena envy"!

I was dodging the subpoena, and my children were told to say I was not home. At that time, they ranged in age from I guess fourteen down to three. The process servers hadn't been able to find me, so they had the police try to present me with a subpoena, which I don't think was legal at all.

One day, Becky, my oldest daughter, answered the door and said I wasn't home. The other children were playing in front. Becky called them to come in for dinner, but they didn't pay any attention to her. Then I heard her shout, "Momma says come in for dinner!" And the process servers were right across the street. [Laughs.] Well, they didn't catch me at that moment, but then the police stopped my son on the street when he was riding his tricycle and said, "Your mother's just won a police auction. Can you tell us where we can find her?" Finally they caught up with me, and I appeared before the committee.

We were told not to say anything, just to take the Fifth Amendment. But on the stand I became very angry and I said I want to protest the use of the San Francisco police in serving me a subpoena and harassing my children on the streets. There was a stirring in the whole courtroom, and my lawyer said, "You'd better be prepared to back that up," so I did. And then I said, "I feel it's ironic that a woman who's spent her entire adult life working for peace is being called before this committee for advocating force and violence." And then there was a great stir, I guess there was applause. Burns said he would clear the courtroom if it didn't stop.

Our neighbors circulated a petition not to prosecute me for taking the Fifth. All the storekeepers in the neighborhood and a lot of the neighbors signed it. The local butcher said to Dave, "They ought to be investigating the price of meat, not your wife." That was very moving, very touching.

Then a curious thing happened, a few months after I came back from Warsaw. I don't remember which side of the Burns Committee hearings this was on. I got two letters in rather rapid succession addressed to "Jean Jenkins, 456 Belve Street." Both had the wrong address: Belve Street, not

Belvedere Street; and the name on my passport said "Jean." That was the name my family had given me, which I didn't realize until I got my passport. They had wanted to name me Jean, and my grandfather, who had a German accent, said, "You can't name her Jean because everybody will call her Sheenie Arnstein." So they called Edith. But Jean was the only name on my passport.

One letter was from the West Indies, and it said, "Dear Jean, As you know we claim the Congress in Defense of Children was not organized by the Communists, but it was." And it went on about that. It was signed by someone from the Congress in Defense of Children, which was a group formed shortly after the Warsaw congress, and the signature read, "Yours for the overthrow of the bourgeoisie by any means necessary." Well, we knew this was an attempt to frame me, and I was rather frightened by that. A few weeks later I received another letter from somewhere in Eastern Europe, saying, "Enclosed you will find maps of Shell installations in South America which ought to be blown up, and you are to give these maps to somebody else"—and it specified to whom—"and if you do not, something dreadful will happen to you." The letter was on the stationery of the CGT, the French trade union organization, signed by Louis Saillant, who was the head of the CGT.

We got this letter to Harry Bridges, who wrote to Saillant, and Saillant said his stationery had been stolen and his signature forged. These letters had been sent all over the world. A man in the Philippines was doing a life sentence because of receiving the same communication. We gave both letters to the postmaster. Handing things over to officials was the last thing we'd do at that time, but we felt we needed to be covered.

I think it must've been the CIA. It wasn't one person who was sending it out, because it came from two different sections of the globe, with the same name and the same mistake in the address. They were doing this because I'd gone to the Warsaw congress and I was speaking against the Korean War.

What was harder for me personally than appearing before the Burns Committee—because you know your adrenaline helps on something like that—was the first PTA meeting I had to go to afterwards. I remember I circled the block three times before I could walk in, because I knew some people would speak to me and some wouldn't. And some parents wouldn't let their children play with ours.

When I was in Warsaw, my second daughter, who was seven, was in the Brownie Scouts and I guess she was kind of disturbed about her mother being away. She went to the Brownie meeting to celebrate the birthday of the Brownies, and they were all supposed to make a wish. She said, "I wish I didn't have to belong to the Brownies!" [Laughs.] And then she said "damn" about something, and they tried to kick her out of the Brownies for saying "damn." We fought that one through, but it was very very hard on the kids.

Our oldest daughter, who was pretty political by that time even though she was only fourteen, spoke against the Korean War in school, and the teacher put her on the spot, made fun of her in front of the whole class. She was a tough kid, but she ran home from school crying and was terribly upset. Dave and I went to the school to protest. Dave went in ahead of me, and as I was waiting to go in, I heard some teachers saying, "Well, if I were the dean, I just would've gotten the FBI down here."

Then years later we found that when my son was just starting Polytechnic, the same high school where this event had happened with my daughter, the teachers had singled him out to be in the fast-moving class. He was a kid who never tested well, but they also singled kids out that they knew were capable. The other teachers objected. They said no, his parents were Reds and they wouldn't have him in the accelerated class.

The thing that was really hard in those years was when the doorbell rang and when we wouldn't know if we were going to be either subpoenaed or taken off to jail. They had taken some people—mothers—off to jail in the middle of the night. It was terribly hard on our kids. They were very brave at the time, but I think they paid for it.

But funny things happened too. I remember when Becky, the oldest one, was in grade school, the Bridges had a big Irish setter that ran into the schoolyard and was jumping on kids, taking their lunches. You know, they're friendly, dumb dogs. And Becky said, "Oh, I know whose dog that is, that's Harry Bridges's dog!" And the principal said, "That's all I need on the first day of school, to have Harry Bridges's dog knocking down children!" [Laughs.]

The Fight
Against HUAC

By the end of the Eisenhower administration, the reactionary grip had loosened. A number of Supreme Court decisions had begun to breathe life back into the Bill of Rights; the civil rights movement was in the process of reviving student activism; and the American public, at last, was starting to tire of the stale vitriol of the reactionary Right.

For once HUAC found itself on the defensive. Richard Criley and Frank Wilkinson, founders of the National Committee to Abolish HUAC, had organized against the Red-hunters for a decade; now their efforts were paying off in increased congressional support.

In May 1960, a critical victory from another quarter occurred when spontaneous demonstrations by a coalition of students and old-time progressives drove HUAC out of San Francisco. By 1965, the momentum was clearly with the opponents of HUAC.

RICHARD CRILEY

Criley is a descendant on his mother's side from William Whipple, a signer of the Declaration of Independence, and on his father's side from Giles Cory, who was pressed to death during the Salem witch trials of 1692. He and Frank Wilkinson were leaders in the fight to abolish the House Committee on Un-American Activities. "My FBI file is ten thousand pages.

It starts in the thirties and goes up to about '77. We were effective, so they hated our guts and we became targets."

I left the Communist Party in 1960. I had been having some real policy differences, particularly around the First Amendment. I was supportive of free speech, but the Communist Party was utterly ambivalent, for reasons that are pretty obvious. They were totally supportive of Stalin. Although, to some degree, most of us were truly ignorant of what Stalin had actually done until Khrushchev made his famous speech. The Party was justifying the dictatorship of the proletariat and building on various theories that you can't defend fascist free speech, racist free speech.

Look, I argued, the minute you put forward the concept that we only defend free speech that we agree with, since not too many people agree with the Communist Party, you're putting yourself in a very little box with nobody to defend you. You have to be committed toward defending everybody's free speech.

I had taken part in a discussion before the Illinois state committee at the time of the Khrushchev statements in 1956. Khrushchev really shook the Communist Party up. Even the way the material got to us was interesting. The *Daily Worker* didn't print it, the *New York Times* did, then after the *New York Times* did, the *Daily Worker* had to. So I talked to the people in this committee meeting and said, "It's time a lot of us did some rethinking for ourselves. I joined the Young Communist League because I was a nonconformist, a rebel against a status quo that was unjust and repressive. But in a strange kind of a way I've become a conformist. I assumed that because I wasn't born with a red diaper I didn't know as much Marxism as somebody else and contented myself with being an implementer of policy and not really taking responsibility for policy decisions. I'm not going to do this anymore. I made a lot of mistakes, other people's mistakes, but I accepted them uncritically. Any mistakes I make in the future are going to be my own. I'm not taking anybody else's positions without critically examining them first."

It went over like a lead balloon. That was the beginning of the end. I found increasingly sharp relationships. I stayed nominally a member for a number of years, but worked more and more on my own.

When I was no longer a member, the FBI knew it and went after me harder than before. They were devoting more effort to screw me up, because my work was actually more effective. I was doing *very good work* to abolish the House Un-American Activities Committee.

HUAC was the right arm of J. Edgar Hoover and the FBI. The main way they would neutralize you would be to get you subpoenaed by either the Senate Internal Security Subcommittee or HUAC. It wasn't an accident that I was subpoenaed five times—three times with SISS and twice with HUAC.

I made myself obnoxious. I said, "This whole committee is illegal, because the chairman is a man named James Eastland, elected in Mississippi, and in Mississippi the Fourteenth Amendment[1] has been a dead letter since Reconstruction, and Eastland has no more right to sit on this committee than I have."

Senator Hrushka banged the gavel and said, "I'm not going to let you blaspheme my coworkers! Those remarks are expunged from the record."

"You can't expunge them, I said them."

"They are expunged!" [Laughs.] They printed the verbatim testimony from that hearing, and they were in fact expunged from the record.

The FBI went to the extreme of writing a poison-pen letter about me to the board of the Chicago Committee to Defend the Bill of Rights. They were aware that I was probably more radical than most of the board members were. This would have been around 1963.

The board included Victor Obenhouse, who was probably the leading Protestant theologian in the Midwest and professor of Christian ethics at the Chicago Theological Seminary; Robert Havighurst, who was the primary professor in the field of education in the United States; and leading ministers of the major Protestant nominations, some prominent Catholics. This letter was supposedly from a guy that had known me when I was a member of the Communist Party. He claimed that he knew that I was still a secret Stalinist and I didn't believe in civil liberties for anybody but Communists and I was really there to defend Communists, period.

The letter said the board should demand a meeting and fire me. I called up Obenhouse and said, "What do you think we should do—should I call a special board meeting?" And he said, "There's only one thing to do with an anonymous letter, that's put it in the wastepaper basket." This was the reaction of just about everybody on the board, except, strangely enough, one guy who was the representative of the Friends Service Committee.[2] I

[1] Passed on June 13, 1866, and sent to the states for ratification, the Fourteenth Amendment defined U.S. citizenship and forbade the states to deny the rights of citizens. If any state denied qualified people the right to vote, its representation in Congress would be reduced proportionally.

[2] American Friends Service Committee, founded in 1917 by the Quakers to provide relief and reconstruction aid to war-torn Europe. In 1947, the committee shared the Nobel Peace Prize with its British counterpart, the Friends Service Council.

think he was scared it would hurt his fund-raising abilities, guilt by association, so he quietly withdrew.

There was another person on our board who earlier had been visited by the FBI and had dropped out and not explained why. Then they visited a woman board member whose husband was a doctor in a veterans' hospital. They threatened her husband's job unless she withdrew from the committee.

The FBI went to my family. This was in the sixties. My brother had two sons, one of whom was a doctor doing some government-funded research on heart problems, the other was a brilliant mathematician who was doing government work. So every year I used to come out to California for Christmas with my wife, and I'd visit my mother in Carmel and then I'd visit my in-laws and then go to Los Angeles to visit my brother.

This particular year I got a tearful phone call from my brother Ted saying, "Don't come—the FBI has been talking to us, and they've said that if we see you they're going to withdraw the security clearances from my sons, and I have to protect my kids."

They went to my sister-in-law in San Francisco. Her husband was a Norwegian who made his living selling haberdashery, called slop chests, for seamen. He was Norwegian, so he was covering all the Norwegian boats, quite a few of which came to San Francisco. He needed a Coast Guard clearance.[3] They went to Martha and said, "If you see your sister or brother-in-law, we're going to have to take Arnie's clearance away." So we got this tearful letter from Martha saying I love you both, but we won't be able to earn a living without that certificate.

These were the standard operating procedures of FBI neutralization. I got threatening phone calls. I would get letters, including some that enclosed human shit. All of a sudden I'd get a whole bunch of phony life insurance policies along with a death threat, a note that had rifle sights on it.

The FBI was very concerned with protecting and saving HUAC. At some point they gave up and decided it was hopeless. The committee had gotten itself into too much hot water and there was too much opposition to it. Their intensive operation against us stopped about '67. But it was clear that Hoover didn't care whether you were a member of the Communist Party or not, but were you effectively doing things which the FBI disapproved of.

---

[3]The Magnuson Act of 1950 required all seamen and waterfront workers (including those on the Great Lakes and Western rivers) to receive a security clearance from the Coast Guard.

If HUAC came to town, we would help organize a local operation dealing with the media. The last hearing that was ever held outside of Washington was in Chicago in '65, and we organized the resistance to that. We had a picket line that went up to a thousand people and every day was led by a different person. Reverend Obenhouse led it one day, a very prominent rabbi led it the next, so if the newspapers came around, here was the person in charge. By '65 we were getting an equal shake in the press. In contrast to earlier years, when, whether you were on the witness stand or anything else, they would just fill their pages with the HUAC stuff, but nothing that we had to say.

HUAC sent out letters to a bunch of people, invitations to become informers, saying, "We happen to have you on the list, but if you want to come in confidentially and cooperate with us, we'll arrange that." Somebody brought me a copy of this letter. So I called a press conference and said, "Here's the kind of stuff these people are doing to suborn people into becoming stool pigeons for HUAC." At the end of that hearing, they had taken such a beating politically that every member of the Chicago delegation in Congress took the floor to protest their misdeeds in the Chicago area. We started the Committee to Abolish HUAC in 1960, and the committee was abolished in '75. But after the '65 hearing they never left Washington again.

When HUAC was abolished we had to give ourselves a broader focus and another name, so we took the name of National Committee Against Repressive Legislation. In the later years of HUAC we had become involved in a number of other things—repeal of Title II of the Internal Security Act of 1950,[4] which we did together with the Japanese-American Citizens League. We had a campaign against the no-knock law and had been successful with that. We fairly had the Internal Security Act nullified.

HUAC had reached the point where they decided it was counterproductive to call in hostile witnesses. They ceased being a show, ceased going around to your hometown, they lost all of their umph and they weren't getting the press anymore. They were fairly much limited to calling in some prominent anti-Communist so-called expert to be a consultant, and that had no juice in it.

[4]Title II provided concentration camps to be used in times of national emergency, invasion, or insurrection. Anyone who was a member of the Communist Party since January 1, 1949, was to be detained without trial. The camps held in readiness were those previously occupied by Japanese-Americans during World War Two. Title II remained on the books until the fall of 1971.

Then Un-American Activities Committee became a bad word, so they became the National Security Committee instead.[5] The more they cleaned up their act, the less reason they had to exist, because to have a constitutionally observing committee doing witch-hunting is a contradiction—you can't observe the Constitution and conduct witch hunts at the same time.

In our Chicago suit, we were able to interrogate the associate director of the FBI under Webster, and we asked him for the number of informers in Chicago in the years '66 to '76. The number was five thousand, one hundred and forty-five paid political informers. These aren't the ones working on the Mafia and criminal cases, these are political. And not one arrest or prosecution ever resulted from that number of informers, not one case flowed from it. So this is enormous big business.

Now the Cold War was something bigger than the FBI by far, but the FBI implemented it. Its hundreds and thousands of press contacts were manipulated, were fed materials. The FBI made a major imprint on the ideology of America.

One interesting part of my FBI file covered a trip that I planned to make to Cleveland, where Frank Wilkinson and I were going to be on the Mike Douglas show, a nationwide phone-in television broadcast. My file revealed that the producer of the show was one of the guys that cooperated with the FBI, and so he arranged to have the script for that interview written by the FBI offices of Chicago and Los Angeles. The Los Angeles office wrote the questions to be asked to Frank Wilkinson and the Chicago office the questions to be asked me.

It was interesting that the FBI was writing the script of a television broadcast. Their entry into the American mind was so profound that it implanted a blind kind of anticommunism, which still exists.

When we started out to abolish the House Un-American Activities Committee in 1960, people thought we were crazy, "Nobody's ever going to abolish that committee—you guys are nuts." I don't think it would have happened without us. Obviously changes happened that made it possible. But no member of Congress would take them on until we got Jimmy Roosevelt to do it, and he was spurred to do it by a petition of thirty thousand names from his district asking him to do it. Then we gradually built it up so we had six people that dared speak out, then it was twelve. We had found out early on that there were at least a hundred members of the House who really disliked the House Un-American Activities Committee,

[5]In 1969, HUAC renamed itself the House Internal Security Committee.

but were afraid to deal with it because they thought if you take them on, you'll be branded soft on communism and you'll be destroyed. They had destroyed congressmen who did that. We changed that. We forced them into retreat.

First of all, we took ten districts and worked like hell to get a base there so we could get the representative to do it. Then we moved out to fifty districts and worked on the fifty districts, and kept moving it up and moving it up. Then we began to get test votes on things like cutting their appropriations. The man who implemented the first cut was a guy named Frank Annunzio, who was the Mafia guy from Chicago [laughs], but he was in a district where I had a lot of friends, so I met with him. He agreed to do it.

I was called in front of the Senate committee first in '54, then in '59 I was called before HUAC. Then I was called in '61 again before HUAC. Then in '63 I was called twice before SISS.

The first time they subpoenaed me, I got to Washington and they said, "Oh, didn't you know we called the hearing off?" I said, "Wait a minute, I had to spend airfare to get here and take off a day from work. You guys have got to pay my expenses."

They said, "Okay, as long as we're paying expenses we'll have a hearing." So they had a closed hearing. Then they subpoenaed me a second time to ask the same questions—the record was exactly the same as the closed hearing—so that I would receive adverse publicity and lose my job.

The '61 hearing had to do with a conference that was called after the Supreme Court came down with a decision which upheld the basic constitutionality of the Internal Security Act. There was a national conference called to focus on that. Now that conference was initiated pretty much by the Communist Party, but the majority of the people in it were not Communists. But it was one of these stupidly organized things where the guy that rented the auditorium where we met had a month before been an official representative of the Communist Party somewhere else. It gave the FBI a marvelous opportunity to attack this thing through HUAC. The Chicago committee had voted to officially send delegates, and I went. So I was subpoenaed again to show the Red threat. [Laughs.]

I started out by saying, "The first reason why I'm not answering your questions is that I'm descended from a man named Giles Cory who was executed in 1692 during the Salem witch hunt. You can understand that my family has a long tradition of opposing witch hunts. I oppose this one and that's why I'm not answering your questions." And he went bang, bang, bang on the gavel.

The interesting thing was by '61, the role of the news media had changed enough so that the lead of every story on that hearing read, "Descendant of Giles Cory called before HUAC. . . ."[6]

[6]Old Giles Cory had stood mute before the court, refusing with his silence to place himself on trial. The placing of rocks upon his chest was a time-honored method of inducing testimony; few in the history of English law had had the fortitude to endure it. Tradition records that before his chest was crushed, Cory's only utterance was to gasp, "More weight."

FRANK WILKINSON

Along with Richard Criley, Wilkinson was a prime mover in the formation of the National Committee to Abolish HUAC. For his work for integrated housing and civil liberties, he was hounded by the FBI for thirty-eight years. In 1964, the FBI learned of a plot to murder Wilkinson. They knew the place, the time, the date, and even the name of the assassin—and they stood by that night to watch. We met in the compact offices of the First Amendment Foundation in Los Angeles.

I did not learn about the FBI's surveillance of me until 1980, when I was sixty-five years of age. It began in 1942, and they followed me for thirty-eight years. What they did, and how they did it, is all something that's come to me from the settlement of our lawsuit.[1] Under Civil Discovery (not FOIA) we got amazingly valuable data from them showing what conversations were wiretapped, which of them were with informants, the names of informants, in case after case, and details that were never available to us under the FOIA. That gave us the information we needed.

The settlement provided that the FBI had to remove every page that they had on me in all fifty-nine offices. They offered to burn them. I insisted that they be placed in the National Archives under seal so that historians later on can look at these things and understand what we call the McCarthy Era, which in my opinion was really the J. Edgar Hoover Era.

There is not one line in the entire one hundred and thirty-two thousand

[1]Brought on Wilkinson's behalf in 1980 by the ACLU of Southern California, settled in 1987.

pages that indicates any criminal activity or thought of crime on my part. Nowhere in that file can you say it began *because* . . . I can tell you what I was doing at the time it began, but not why, because no one knows.

I come out of a very Methodist, Republican background. In Beverly Hills High School, I was head of Youth for Herbert Hoover. At UCLA, I was the conservative fraternity man, who ran for student body president against those we referred to as radicals. I'm not very proud of that, but that's part of the background.

I planned on the Methodist ministry all my life. As a graduation present from UCLA, even though it was the seventh year of the Depression, my family gave me a trip to the Holy Land. I left filled with Christmas carols, and when I arrived in Bethlehem on Christmas Eve, 1936, there were so many beggars in front of the Church of the Nativity that I was unable to get in. I was shocked by the contradiction of two thousand years of Christianity and still beggars at the birthplace of Christ. You can say the same thing about five thousand years of Judaism, or twelve hundred years of Islam. All three Western religions were there.

I felt the church was hypocritical, and I decided not to become a Methodist minister. But I was determined either to practice the religious ethics that I had or admit I didn't give a damn.

I did not come home at that point. A fraternity brother and I bought bicycles and spent that whole year, just before the outbreak of World War Two, bicycling from Jerusalem through every country in Europe. Never going to hotels, sleeping in the streets, unbelievable trip. I lived under Mussolini for three months, I was a guest of Franco in Spain for a few days, and I lived under Hitler for three months. I went into Poland and lived in the ghetto of Warsaw.

I came back to Los Angeles more shocked than ever about the hypocrisy of religion. Many of those countries were Christian countries. I came back a great disappointment to my family and my bishop.

At that point the archdiocesan director of Catholic Charities came to my home, a Monsignor Thomas J. O'Dwyer. He was starting a campaign of slum clearance in L.A. I remember seeing that Roman collar come in my house, and my anger at him, I remember almost shouting at him that you can't blame the Methodist Church for the ghetto of Warsaw—that's a Catholic country.

After I did all the talking, he very calmly said, "My son, you did not need to go so far to get so excited." He drove me eight miles from my home in Beverly Hills and showed me housing conditions in Watts and the barrio equal to what I'd seen in Bethlehem. I couldn't believe that we had the problem right where I'd grown up. He then offered me a job at fifteen dollars a week as his secretary, and I grabbed it.

I worked with him for the next three years. We got the housing authority administrative laws through the state. We got the first three housing projects built, and by 1942 they were ready for occupancy. But '42 is five years before restrictive covenants were outlawed and twelve years before *Brown v. Board of Education.* Los Angeles was rigidly segregated.

The only place in Los Angeles that was naturally integrated was Watts, which, at that time, was one-third white, one-third African-American, one-third Hispanic. The housing authority, still operating under the old 1896 law of the land, *Plessy v. Ferguson,* separate but equal, decided to build three projects and separate the Hispanics, whites, and blacks. They were segregating people that were already integrated. So Monsignor O'Dwyer, myself, and a committee we had of the YWCA, the Catholic Women's Club, League of Women Voters, groups like that, set up a picket line to demand open occupancy. The press paid attention to the fact that a leading Catholic prelate was there.

The housing authority gave in. "Okay, Father, we're going to mix 'em—who do you want to run it?" O'Dwyer said, "Let's try Frank." So from a picket line, I'm taken inside to become the manager of the first integrated housing project in Watts in 1942. When we got the FBI files, we found it was that month that the FBI first named me as a national security risk and began following me. Over the next thirty-eight years, upwards of seventeen million dollars was spent on this effort. Everything that I considered to be McCarthyism was found to be orchestrated directly by J. Edgar Hoover and the FBI.

Chavez Ravine lost me my job. I started out in '42 as manager of the project in Watts. By '52 I had been manager of half a dozen projects and was then assistant to the director at the housing authority, charged with site selection for a one-hundred-and-ten-million-dollar slum clearance program for the City of Los Angeles.

I was in an eminent-domain proceeding on the necessity of taking Chavez Ravine for a housing site which I had selected and the city council and mayor had approved when the FBI came in with a dossier on me developed by Chief of Police Parker and turned it over to the owners of the slums whose lawyers were fighting us in court. So in the middle of my testimony on the correlation between disease and delinquency and bad housing, rat infestation, stuff like that, the opposing attorney suddenly stops his cross-examination and asks, "Now Mr. Wilkinson, what organizations, political or otherwise, have you belonged to since 1929?"

Up to that point, my civil liberties record was lousy. I had signed every loyalty oath California and the federal government ever had—anything to save slum clearance programs. Beginning in '42, I took a loyalty oath, swore that I was not a Communist. Every year in the housing authority as I advanced, and as the domestic Cold War set in, I took a loyalty oath. I was liaison with the American Legion and the VFW, all the veterans' groups. Every time the loyalty oath came up, we called a press conference, invited all of the veterans' groups in their uniforms, and the mayor, and the housing commission, and with the flags and all we proudly said we were loyal.

I had reached the point a couple of months before of feeling sick and tired of trying to prove I'm loyal. My lawyer had been a liberal at UCLA when I was the conservative—now he was working for a large Republican law firm. He knew me in terms of my Youth for Herbert Hoover business and my fraternity/sorority leadership. But it was the second year of the Korean War, the Rosenbergs were due to die within a year, the Hollywood Ten were in and out of jail, the first Communists were on trial. He remained quiet, and I refused to answer the question and I was fired.[2]

By '56, I had developed a civil liberties consciousness. I came under the influence of a great philosopher, Alexander Meiklejohn, who later received the Presidential Medal of Freedom under President Kennedy. It was from him I learned the absolute concept of the First Amendment: it ain't no difference who Congress might be targeting, whether it be Communists or Nazis, as long as it was speech, it had to be protected.[3]

For three years I'd been assigned by the local ACLU to try to get somebody who was subpoenaed before the committee *not* to use the Fifth Amendment but the First Amendment, and if need be go to jail. The ACLU felt that some of the dicta in one of Earl Warren's decisions showed that the Supreme Court was ready to take on the First Amendment violations of the Un-American Activities Committee. But everyone was afraid to

[2]Wilkinson's refusal made headlines in the next day's *Los Angeles Times.* The court disqualified him as an expert and struck his testimony from the record. The city council passed a resolution calling upon HUAC to investigate the housing authority. The Los Angeles housing program collapsed, and Chavez Ravine became the home of the Dodgers. Wilkinson was reduced to janitorial work in a department store at $1 an hour, on the condition he tell no one where he worked.

[3]Eventually, Wilkinson was hired as the secretary of the Citizens Committee to Preserve American Freedom, an enterprise dedicated to organized resistance against HUAC.

do it, because it was a year in jail. The Hollywood Ten had already been in, and that had had a terrifying impact upon people. The Fifth Amendment was the way you kept yourself safe.

By that time, I'd seen teachers and musicians and lawyers and doctors and trade unionists, every kind of person, wiped out, their jobs taken away from them, by the Un-American Activities Committee—all people I knew were doing nothing illegal or wrong, but whose ideas were enough for that committee.

I had already made up my mind that if I ever did get a subpoena from the House committee that I'd go to jail. Then I got a subpoena. I went to ACLU and said, "We don't have to look anymore—I'll be your guinea pig."

We tried it, and the committee was so dumbfounded that I wasn't using the Fifth that they backed off. They never cited me for contempt—I walked away from it. They couldn't believe it. At one point the chair asked, "Did you use the Fifth Amendment?"

I kept saying they violated the First Amendment, I'll answer nothing, not even my address. Then they asked again, "Are you using the Fifth?" and I'd say, "My answer is my answer."

Finally the chair, Clyde Doyle, came clear down from the podium where the committee is sitting and looks in both my ears and says, "The committee notices that you're wearing a hearing aid, you're deaf. When we asked you if you're using the Fifth Amendment, did you hear us?"

Our efforts in organizing protection of the subpoenaed people in Southern California and San Francisco had proven so successful that I was brought to New York to work nationally. I went to Gary, Indiana, to Boston, Philadelphia, finally to Georgia. We had skills, we knew how to get people together to fight back and develop rallies and get good lawyers and public relations to save jobs.

In '58, I was brought down to Atlanta to work with Martin Luther King's father and the Southern Christian Leadership Conference and the Southern Conference Educational Fund. The FBI were waiting for me. They had me under twenty-four-hour surveillance. Within a minute after I arrived at my hotel I was subpoenaed by HUAC. So again I called the ACLU and said we got another subpoena here, let's go. The national ACLU took it all the way to the Supreme Court. We would have been happy to get just Warren and Douglas or Warren and Black on our side, anything to get the dialogue going in the court. The vote was five to four; we had Chief Justice Warren, and Black and Douglas and Brennan. One more vote and we would have won.

Carl Braden[4] and I went to jail together. It was a one-year maximum sentence, and we served it in Georgia, South Carolina, Virginia, and Lewisburg Penitentiary. We were moved around all the time, due to the FBI's in-prison surveillance of us. Everything we did was attacked. I just got a stack of documents with every letter that was written to me or that I wrote while I was in prison. The FBI copied everything.

We were treated very poorly in prison. Our bunks were searched for contraband, I'd say, three nights a week. We'd catch 'em at it. When everybody else went to church services we'd come back early and find five guys going through my foot locker trying to find something illegal.

The inmates in the South were illiterate. Four hundred moonshiners and bootleggers with a third-grade education. Forty of them signed their names with an X. But when I came in, the warden said, "I know all about you—we don't want any teaching here." So for six months I was not allowed to help these guys so much as learn their alphabet. Then we went to the warden and pointed out to him that the only time these guys get any recreation is Sundays. Their primary recreation is comic books, which most of them couldn't read, but they loved the pictures, and the library, a very lousy library, did have comic books. So we said to the warden, "If you will open up the library Sunday, we'll take charge and we'll issue comic books and we'll get every one collected two hours later." He agreed. So the guards came that first Sunday and opened it up at two o'clock, came back at four to close it up, glaring at us, hating us. We became the heroes of the prison because we got the library open on Sunday.

That was on a Sunday afternoon at four o'clock. The following Tuesday morning our names are called out to go to Control, and we went in. We were jumped, slammed, handcuffed, stripped of everything, even my hearing-aid batteries, put on a bus, and shipped north without telling us anything. Two days later we arrived at Lewisburg Penitentiary and put into solitary for seven days.

At that time Aubrey Williams, who had founded the Committee to Abolish HUAC and had been a New Dealer under Franklin Roosevelt and Harry Hopkins, was writing to me two or three times a week. He wrote to South Carolina and his letters came back "Address Unknown." So he called up James Bennett, a friend of his who was the director of the Bureau of Prisons, and asked him where we were. Bennett said, "They're still in South Carolina," and Aubrey said, "That's not true—mail isn't going

[4]Carl Braden was also called before HUAC at this time. Both he and Wilkinson stood on the protections of the First Amendment and refused to answer any questions. They were both convicted of contempt of Congress. For more on Carl, see Anne Braden under "Fighting Jim Crow."

through there." So Bennett checked it out and told Aubrey, "Your boys got caught spying for Russia and they're now in solitary up at Lewisburg Penitentiary."

Aubrey said, "How can you spy for Russia from inside a prison?" It was checked out again by Bennett, and he found out that these two guards who had to give up their good Baptist Sunday services to come open that library up had gone four miles away to a military airbase and reported they had seen Carl and me looking out of the windows of our prison at that airport and were reporting the military planes taking off to Russia. On that basis we were picked up and sent north. We were accused of everything, everything.

Up on a prison farm outside of Lewisburg we were accused of teaching communism. We got into trouble up there because . . . Well, I'll tell you. In South Carolina, the only place that was integrated was the federal prison! We had a joke, if you could just get Strom Thurmond in there for one weekend, we could clean up his act. They were all moonshiners and boot-leggers who have only one enemy, the revenue agents. Blacks and whites hit it off perfectly. So sitting together, fraternizing, was no problem. When we went north, the Lewisburg Penitentiary and the prison farms outside of there were sharply segregated. There's an invisible color line. All the white inmates sat together, and the blacks sat there. So, of course, Carl and I went and sat deliberately at black tables and struck up friendships.

While we're eating at one of these places, an inmate came up to me but was overheard by an inmate who was three feet away. This guy said they used to have a public forum, and if they could get a forum started did I know anyone who would come and speak? I laughed at him, I said, "A forum at this place?" He said, "Yeah, we used to have one." I said, "Well, okay, if you can get one, I'll get you some speakers." I offered him Rein-hold Niebuhr, Martin Luther King, and a couple of other very prominent names. This other guy goes to the warden and reports that he heard me arranging classes on communism. So the warden calls me in and says, "Pack your gear—you're going back to solitary."

"What in the world are you talking about?"

"You know I told you don't do any teaching here. You're teaching communism."

"I have not."

By that time, my morale was so low that instead of saying "Well, fuck you" or something like that, I said, "I did not." I began to cry, because I couldn't stand going back to solitary without my hearing aid. They would take it away in solitary. The only time that concrete wall opens up is when they make a call in the hallway outside. A big lever opens up all the solitary cells and if you push your door you can get out, and you go lockstep to the toilet or lockstep to eat. I couldn't hear, so I never got that chance. I was always unable to get out. So I really broke down and said, "I have not been doing anything wrong, I assure you."

"Well," the warden said, "you go back to your bunk and you think about it." I went back to my bunk, and that afternoon went by. I was scared stiff. The next morning I went into the bathroom and a guy came up to the urinal next to me and whispered, real softly and quickly, "Your problem is you've been sitting with the blacks. Secondly, don't try to organize any forums."

Oh my God . . . I turned around—where is this guy? By that time he'd disappeared. I hardly saw him, I just heard his voice. So I hurried to the warden, came in beaming into the warden's office. "Hey, I finally figured it out. Thank God I've got a friend here." I didn't talk about eating with blacks, I said, "This guy came up to me and said you used to have a forum here, and I gave him the names of Martin Luther King and these others who would come if you ever had a forum here." The warden just glared at me.

I said, "Thank God, I've got friends here who told me what happened. That's what your problem is." He said, "Look, Wilkinson, for every friend you've got here, I've got six. You keep your nose clean or you're going to solitary." I spent my last six weeks under that pressure.

The guy in the bunk next to me turned out to be the guy who informed—he hated me. So I slept with one eye open. Every motion of the bed next to me, I'd jump, thinking somebody was going to kill me. And no inmate would ever snitch. If you snitched, you'd get killed. I just went on that way. Life in prison was very rough.

When we were finally due to get out, Pete Seeger and others planned a welcome-home rally at a big auditorium in downtown New York, and that was wonderful. But the FBI got wind of it, came to the prison, and told them not let me out at eight A.M., which I was entitled to, but hold me until five P.M. so I could not get into New York in time for this rally. They said buy him a ticket to California, put him on a Greyhound bus.

But the inmates were always wonderful, other than the real snitches. So they came to us and told us. We had twenty-four hours to find some inmate that was leaving to get the word out. One inmate only was getting out the next day, and he was the most unlikely guy you can imagine. He was totally isolated from the rest of the prison population. He wore a yarmulke and a prayer shawl, read the Torah all day long. He was a black Jew from Brooklyn. I'd never known of black Jews until I met them in prison. We sat down with him and explained what our problem was, and he memorized Pete's phone number. He got out the next morning, got to a telephone, and told them the problem. We said, "Tell people we can't get there until ten-thirty. Have a car behind the Greyhound bus at Lewisburg at five o'clock."

They held us right to the last minute and put us on the bus. They thought they had fixed us good. The doors close and we jumped right back out in front of the prison authorities. Five carloads of people were waiting there. We hop in a car, turn around, and get into New York at ten-thirty at night. Right until the end they were screwing us.

From then on, they tried to disrupt every speech I made, every speech Carl made. Forty-one separate talks I was scheduled to make, the FBI attempted, and did in some cases, disrupt. That was documented in just the first four thousand pages we got. We got ten times the audience we would have if they'd just let us alone.

In 1983, we received a document under FOIA dated March 4th of '64 that reads: "From Agent in Charge, FBI, to J. Edgar Hoover. Subject: Frank Wilkinson. 'Name blacked out' to assist in assassination attempt on Frank Wilkinson when he speaks tonight at eight o'clock P.M. at 13130 Bloomfield Avenue, Sherman Oaks, California. Then, 'name blanked out' will stake out the residence to witness the assassination."

When I'm not killed that night, there's another document dated the next day, March 5th of '64: "Agent in Charge, to J. Edgar Hoover: No attempt was made on the life of Wilkinson last night, we'll watch for further developments."

That was what we got under FOIA nineteen years after I would have been killed. In 1989 we got the same document free of redactions. They still don't tell us who is going to kill me, but the person who was staked out to witness my assassination is now identified as "Confidential Source: LA3184, Head, Anti-Subversive Detail LAPD." So working with the FBI is the commander of the Red Squad of L.A., waiting for me to be killed that night.[5]

I called up the guy whose house this was—I didn't even remember having been there. He said he remembered very well, because people were worried about two men outside in a car. So he went out and took down the license number. He called the police and said there's two men in a car

---

[5]The identity of the Red Squad commander staked out to witness the assassination has long been a puzzle, though Daryl Gates's autobiography, *Chief: My Life in the LAPD* (New York: Bantam, 1993), offers a possible answer. Gates was transferred from the captaincy of the Highland Park station to head of intelligence in June 1963. One of the units he oversaw in his new function was "deep within Intelligence . . . unknown to most. This unit dealt with Communism, Communists, and other subversives." It was headed by one Lieutenant Carl Abbott.

outside that's worrying my guest. The car drove off in five minutes. He went the next day to the department of motor vehicles and asked who drives such-and-such a Plymouth, license number so-and-so. The department of motor vehicles said there's no such license plate existing.

JEAN WILKINSON

While husband Frank fought HUAC, Jean took on the arduous task of guarding the home front. For more on Jean Wilkinson, see under "Red-ucators."

Since Frank was gone most of the time traveling, we had a big dog. I used to walk him at night to check the cars parked out front, where the two FBI guys were sitting. They were almost always there. The arson squad were the only friendly authorities that we ever encountered. They really seemed sincere—I guess there's something about protecting people from fire that overrides political considerations.

I don't remember how many times they were out to our house because of threats. Once when Frank was away, I went to have dinner with some friends in the Hollywood hills. My son Tony called to say, "Mom, we're all right, but somebody tried to bomb our house." By the time I tore down the hill and got to the house, the fire department was already there.

We lived in the upper unit of a duplex. The owners, a lovely couple, lived down below. My two kids—the older boy wasn't living at home by then—had been downstairs playing games with the other kids. Then my daughter, Jo, went upstairs to where our dog was—supposedly the big protector, he didn't care. On her way, she saw this bottle with a fuse in it. She thought it a little strange but didn't do anything about it. She went on upstairs and a few minutes later the bomb went off.

It damaged the downstairs porch, windows, front door, and some other stuff. It didn't damage our place. But it scared the landlady and landlord out of their wits. He had just come home from the hospital after having his voice box removed because of cancer, and he did not need anything like this. They were very apologetic, but they were too scared to let us stay there. So I had to look for another place to live. That was hard. I don't look dangerous—I look like a schoolteacher or a librarian, so people trust me. There was no problem about getting a house, but then I would think, "Oh God, am I going to tell them that we may get bombed? What am I going to do?" I went through such agony. I never told them, but I died about it.

Some of our wealthy friends, in encouraging Frank's proclivity for taking on causes, had told us, "If ever you need money, just come to us." So I thought, "Why don't I borrow some money and put it down on a house?" I floated that idea around—nobody wanted to be involved. But the next thing I knew they had raised ten thousand dollars to put down on a house to buy for us. It was a duplex—we could live upstairs. Frank had already been found guilty and had to go to jail, so we fixed this place up and it was wonderful.

Earlier on after Frank was fired from the housing authority, our two boys were denied attendance at the YMCA summer camp. They were all set to go, but when all this came out the Y had second thoughts—they didn't think our kids should go to camp. They were seven and nine, real threats to the community. This hurt Frank particularly because the church and the camp was part of his upbringing, and these people knew him personally. Frank's old Sunday school teacher was an official of the summer camp. The Y finally decided that if Frank and I did not visit them on parents' day, the two little boys could go.

Most of the neighbors were quite good. I remember the milkman arriving one morning, laughing about how funny it was that the newspapers were saying that Mr. Wilkinson was a "Commonist" and that was just the funniest thing he had heard. But there were people around all the time that I had to watch out for. I'm not very courageous physically. I had to get over that. In the worst times we had people come and guard the house.

One time, Frank was on the television debating somebody, I don't remember whom, some creep, and the debate was hot and heavy. My kids and I and a few friends were watching it when the phone rang. A voice said, "When this thing is over, we're going to kill him." I called the police. Well, they sent two policemen out to the house. I let them in and told them what it was about. Then I took a few steps to the den, where they saw the television, and one of them said, "Oh! It's him!" and just left.

The second one hung back and said to me very quietly, "If anybody comes around, call again." The first one was not going to have any part of us. So we always felt that the police were our enemies, and certainly the FBI, and the FBI records show it.

Frank's office was bombed at least once. In fact, recently I found a list of items that were taken in burglaries. No money or anything like that, it was always the files, the political stuff, that they wanted.

One of the scariest times was a big rally in New York with about five thousand people just before Frank and Carl Braden went to prison. That was just after the Hungarian Revolution,[1] and all these crazy Hungarians were out chanting in their broken English, "Ve vant Vilkinson!

They were paid to show up and agitate. They were told, "This is the price of your Americanism. This is what America is, free speech. You go and yell at Wilkinson, who's a dirty Communist." And of course they hated communism, so they were happy to do that. They didn't have the faintest idea who Frank was, but they were yelling. We came out of the building, and it was scary. They were physically threatening, and the police, who were on horseback, were very aloof and not too interested. We never had the feeling that the police were interested in protecting us, never.

The big thing that McCarthyism did to me was to make me poor all my life. There are lots worse things. I'm not saying that I haven't had one great life, 'cause I have. On the positive side, I *know* we were rich in the friends we had, marvelous people who have made a mark on this country. That was exciting, to participate in big movements and feel that you're a part of it.

The children even said this to me, that they felt rich because they got to know so many great people, Pete Seeger being tops because of his singing. The Meiklejohns were very dear, Alexander and his wife, who remained my friends until they died here in Berkeley. Across the country we had the greatest support. So the kids felt, "Wow, we aren't nobodies, and we aren't forgotten."

Once when the kids and I drove back East to see Frank in prison, we went up to see the Seegers, Pete and Toshi and the kids. I'd written to them and told them we just wanted to come by and say hello, but they insisted we stay the night. They put us up in the barn, which they had fixed up with beds. My daughter, who plays the guitar and is just crazy about Pete Seeger, kept saying to me, "Don't you dare tell him that I play!" After dinner Pete just took it for granted, he got out all the guitars and the banjos and they all had a jam session.

Then in the morning we were wakened by Pete Seeger and his son Danny coming up the hill picking at the banjos, singing "Wake Up, Darlin' Corey." Now what more can you ask out of life? Do you blame my kids for

[1]October 23 to November 4, 1956, when the fledgling government of Imre Nagy was crushed by Soviet troops.

thinking, "This is a good life we're leading, it's just great." So I don't want to mislead you, it was not all tragedy.

ARCHIE BROWN

A long-standing member of the Communist Party, Brown found himself at the center of the first major demonstration against HUAC. For Brown's story of life in the Communist underground, see under "Five Minutes to Midnight."

In 1961 the Committee on Un-American Activities came out here to San Francisco. That was when these big demonstrations started. This was a subcommittee of the main committee headed by this guy Willis from Louisiana. We called them the Un-Americans—they didn't like that.

This particular hearing was focused on education, mainly teachers and professors who got caught in, quote, "the Communist conspiracy," or who were Communists. The committee was going to expose them, that's what they were here for. They subpoenaed some of us who weren't in the educational system to prove the connection with them. Anyway, they subpoenaed me too. And that was when the great Friday the 13th happened, Black Friday. Which was when [chuckles] the police washed the kids down the stairs at City Hall.

We had a little fracas inside the hearing room before that day. Here I am subpoenaed, I've got to appear, chambers are crowded. I got a telegram that says the cops gotta leave me in the chambers, but they don't leave anybody else in unless they'd been subpoenaed or supported the committee. Except here comes some woman. She walks in and she's got what we called the white card, which only right-wingers got. Willis's header-upper, I forget his name, he was the chief attorney for the committee, he had arranged with the American Legion for these cards which would allow five people in with each card. This woman came in on a card. The place was jammed and they let her in, wouldn't leave anybody else in.

I had a suit on. I was being subpoenaed, so I better come in a suit. This woman comes to me thinking because of the suit that I work for the committee. She says, "Where can I sit?" She showed me this card. I said, "Oh, come here with me." So I went to the press box and I said, "Hey, you see what's happening, this woman's got this card, but they won't let anybody else in." [Laughs.] Well, she got wise to me then and snatched the card back.

About eleven o'clock that morning they were going to have a recess. I'm looking around and the only black person in there was—she's dead now, I forget her name—she was one of our comrades and she had also been subpoenaed. She's the only black person in there, the others were on the outside. So when Willis said he wanted to call a recess, I says, "Your honor, I wish to get a redress of grievance from my country."

He didn't know what the fuck I was talking about. He looked at me, and so I says, "Here you got all these people on the outside and you have one black person here and that person's subpoenaed—how come there aren't any black people in here?" He starts banging the gavel. Pretty soon he ordered the cops to throw me out, which he did, but I got a subpoena so I gotta come back in. So that noon hour when they adjourned for lunch, we got together all the defendants and we decided we're gonna have a protest in chambers, so we started singing "The Star-Spangled Banner" and holding speeches and using their microphones and all that kind of stuff. Then they come back in at one o'clock and he bangs the gavel and we all want our redress of grievance. They had to clear us out, so they brought in a squad of motorcycle cops. They came in and grabbed us, arrested us, mishandled us. Pretty brutal with some of us, particularly myself, tore my suit.

All the kids thought we were wonderful! You've got to understand, the students came to protest that their teachers and professors were being subpoenaed—what the hell was all this about, see? Then it broke into the papers, so more students came and they began to picket, and then they got to where they wouldn't leave the students in, they says there's no room for them. The students began to chant, "Open the doors! Open the doors! Open the doors!" So this hearing's being held in City Hall and the judges in other courtrooms began complaining about the noise. Pretty soon they issued an order to stop it and all that kind of crap and the kids didn't give a goddam about it.

Every day the crowds grew bigger. They'd throw us out and that got in the paper, so more kids came. I never saw so many people come to protest what was going on here. One day there was five thousand people outside City Hall protesting and the committee walked out on the top balcony to look down over the crowd. Somebody gave a "Heil Hitler," then everybody did. It was something else, it was really something else, five thousand people giving them the "Heil Hitler."

So that Friday I come in, it was Friday the 13th, and the sheriff had arranged with the student delegation that he would see that a certain number of seats was reserved for them so they could hear. He never kept the promise. Geez, that asshole. The sheriff went off someplace, he's supposed to have a speaking engagement. The mayor was out of town. It's all a frame-up. Nobody was there, nobody was in charge, except the sergeant of police who ordered the hosing. They got the fire hoses to wash the students down the stairs. The only thing was that [laughs] if there had really been a fire that system was horrible, because there was no pressure—all that came out was just enough to give them a bath across the marble steps. The marble steps were slippery and the kids all joined arms and sat down. They wouldn't budge. Finally they had a really brutal assault. The cops got 'em from behind and pulled them down all these marble stairs. Some people hurt their backs. Anyway, that was the Battle of City Hall.

Did you ever see the *Chronicle?* The whole front page was nothing but a picture of the cops washing people down the stairs. [Laughs.]

Oh yeah, I testified, you're damn right. We had looked up the details on Willis. That year ten thousand black people had registered in his parish. They disqualified nine thousand of those ten thousand. I says, "You know the honorable chairperson of this committee, Edwin Willis, he was elected to Congress with nine thousand votes. I got thirty-five thousand votes here in San Francisco[1] and I couldn't be elected dog catcher. How did you get to be elected?"

Oh, that did it, see. Threw me out. The cops would come where I was testifying and take me out of the door and throw me out. I had to testify three times and Willis threw me out three times.

When it first started, they asked me about my education. I said I was only able to go to grade school and one year of high school. But I says I hold a Ph.D. in the school of hard knocks—see, I'd just gotten beaten in the head. This attorney for the committee, he never paid any attention. He was always reading his stuff. So he looked up at me. He looked me in the eye. I told him I graduated from the school of hard knocks.

It was a great demonstration. San Francisco and the whole Bay Area was in an uproar. Mayor Christopher came back from out of town and he says,

[1]Brown ran for the San Francisco board of supervisors three times from 1939 to 1959.

"Well, that's it. The next time any of these committees want to hold a hearing in San Francisco, they can go to the armory."

The people of San Francisco ran that damn committee out of town. We chased the bastards out of town. They had to leave through the back door.

HON BROWN

The wife of Archie Brown. For Hon Brown's story on the Communist underground, see under "Five Minutes to Midnight."

I'll tell you another thing. The House Un-American Activities Committee made a movie about the City Hall demonstrations called *Operation Abolition*. They took all the film clips and they mixed things up. They got Harry Bridges coming early and he came on the last afternoon, and they maneuvered all this stuff to suit themselves. It's a hilarious movie—we saw it a couple years ago. But it was really scary in those days.

It has the head of the committee sitting in his office in Congress with the American flag flying talking about the danger and all this kind of stuff. And then they have clips of Archie on the stand. He gives his name. "My name is Archie Brown. I live at 1027 Brussels Street, San Francisco. I have a statement I want to read." Then it begins. They shout him down. They won't let him speak. He yells at them that he wants to speak, and so it goes.

They showed this movie in every American Legion hall throughout the country and to schools.[1] We would get reams of letters from classes. You could tell they were all from a class because they'd be from some small town in Timbuktu and all addressed to Archie Brown at 1027 Brussels Street, San Francisco. He's got them someplace. "Why don't you go back where you came from?" "How can you be a traitor?" And on and on, and every once in a while, somebody would write, "I'm very interested in knowing more about communism, please send me more information."

[1]Rendered with all the melodrama of a grade-B gangster flick, *Operation Abolition* proved to be a camp favorite on college campuses. Civil liberties activists followed it on the circuit with their own film, *Operation Correction,* which straightened out the scrambled footage and twisted facts. For instance, one reason why so many "known Communists" had been present at the demonstration was that HUAC had subpoenaed them.

The Arlington Case

As far as we know, no known Communists are buried at
Arlington.

—Lt. Col. DOUGLAS C. JONES,
Defense Department,
January 28, 1966

SYLVIA THOMPSON

In 1949, Sylvia Thompson's second husband, Robert Thompson, a highly
decorated veteran of World War Two, was among ten other top leaders
of the American Communist Party charged under the Smith Act with
"conspiracy to advocate the overthrow of the government with force and
violence." He served a total of five years in prison. Upon his death in
1965, Sylvia wished to bury him at Arlington National Cemetery.

I thought a lot about Bob even before I met him, because when Sam Hall
was having his brain surgery in September '53,[1] it was just about the time
that Bob Thompson was hit over the head in prison. The cosh he got on
the head almost killed him, and certainly the results of which he suffered the
rest of his life. And I was thinking that here were two men, both with head
problems, one was getting the best neurosurgeon in this country and the
other had a prison doctor. Bob was hit on the head by a Yugoslav fascist
who was supposed to be deported the next day. Bob always wondered who
within the government could have been responsible for that incident. A
prisoner in a cafeteria line does not come across a big piece of lead pipe—it
just doesn't happen.

Bob came out of prison after three and a half years, which was his
sentence, but he was still under indictment. There was an administrative

---

[1]For more on Sam Hall and Sylvia Thompson, see her stories under "Five Minutes to
Midnight" and "Fighting Jim Crow."

thing that anyone jumping bail would be given extra time. There was an appeal as to whether he would have to serve an extra year and a half for jumping bail. When he came out of prison, he and his wife separated, and I met him shortly thereafter. Later, he did have to go back to jail for that year and a half. Actually, he was given less than some of the other Smith Act victims because of his war record.

He was never a well person all the time I knew him. He had a very large metal plate in his skull, and one doctor told me he had as much plate in his head as was possible for a person to have and still have his faculties.

Bob died on a Saturday morning in the middle of October 1965. He was to appear later that day as a leader of the first big anti–Vietnam War parade to take place in New York. Someone got word to the leaders of the parade that he had died that morning, and I remember being told by so many that when it was announced there was a hush through the whole crowd because it was so unexpected. He was fifty years old at the time of his death.

It just made sense to me that he should be buried in Arlington Cemetery. The man was a soldier—he led a battalion in Spain and he won the Distinguished Service Cross[2] in World War Two. And there were those who said that had he not been a Communist he would have won the Congressional Medal of Honor. As a matter of fact, Bob used to tell me how MacArthur would talk to him, and I wondered why a general would speak with a sergeant.

This was a man who had no formal education. Bob went to work with his father in logging camps when he was twelve years old. Anyway, he was proud of his record in Spain and of what he accomplished in the South Pacific, and he knew the thousands of American lives he was responsible for having saved because of that bridgehead he established on the enemy side of the river.

I'd received a letter from the Army, the superintendent of the cemetery, saying the interment was approved and I should let them know what day I wanted and how many people would be coming with me. The ashes were sent to Arlington, and there were a few articles in the *New York Times* about it. About a week before the interment was to take place, I had a call at my job from a general in the Army, saying the government had changed its mind and I should let them know where I wanted the ashes to be returned.

I called friends to let them know what happened, and a close friend called

[2]A U.S. Army decoration, second only to the Congressional Medal of Honor, awarded for extraordinary heroism in combat.

back saying that CBS wanted it on the news that evening. There was an interview, and then an attorney for the ACLU in Washington was interviewed. The next day I met with an ACLU attorney who agreed that the ACLU would take up what then became known as the Arlington case. It's probably one of the pettiest things that I can think of that the government could do.[3] The reason they cooked up was that anyone who was guilty of a felony who served as long as five years in jail could be denied burial in Arlington. It's pretty well known that there's one Nazi, a prisoner of World War Two, who is buried there.

Bob had received the Distinguished Service Cross, he'd been injured during World War Two, he was recognized as a hero. It was a pretty brutal thing. It took three years for the case to be resolved. There were all kinds of briefs on the part of the ACLU, the government kept appealing. It was a long battle. Much came out of it in those years.

Bob was a very modest person—he rarely talked about himself. He was very self-effacing. I learned more about him during the three years of the Arlington struggle than I learned when I lived with him. I'm not talking about ordinary details, but about the regard people had for his courage and abilities.

Apparently, Bob's lieutenant and captain thought so highly of him that they went to him for advice. That's in letters that appeared in newspapers in the Midwest, that he was really in charge. I understand that his name was submitted several times for officership but was always turned down because of his politics. Bob told me that they would talk to him about how it was a shame about his politics, he should have been a full-time military person. [Laughs.] This is a man who never went through junior high school.

There's a place in Haymarket Square where William Z. Foster and the Haymarket Seven are buried, and it's seen as a very hallowed ground for the Left.[4] There's only a handful buried there. But I just felt that Arlington was

[3]While still in prison and recovering from his head wound, Thompson learned from the Veterans Administration that under a clause excluding persons guilty of "mutiny, treason, or sabotage," his war-casualty pension had been stopped.

[4]On May 1, 1886, 350,000 workers nationwide struck for the eight-hour day. During a rally held three days later in Chicago's Haymarket Square, a bomb was thrown, killing several policemen. Firing into the crowd, the police killed or wounded at least two hundred protesters. Eight labor leaders were later arrested and charged with murder. Only one, the main speaker, had actually attended the rally. One received fifteen years, three were sentenced to life imprisonment, and on November 11, 1887, the remaining four were hung. Years later, it was concluded that Rudolph Schnaubelt, a sometime anarchist and police agent, actually threw the bomb. Out of Haymarket Square grew the significance of May Day as an international labor day.

proper. A lot of people didn't understand that. It's what Bob would have wanted. What he did in World War Two was something that he was very proud of, and he knew his worth as a soldier. He thought of himself partly in terms of the two wars in which he'd fought. Soldiering had been part of his life, and to me it was only fitting that he be buried in Arlington.

Bobby Kennedy submitted two editorials from the Washington papers to the Senate floor. He also was quoted by Arthur Schlesinger, Jr., in *Bitter Heritage*. He's talking about phony patriotism and things that could happen as a result of that. Schlesinger says, "Thus an American Communist, who had won our country's second-highest decoration, the Distinguished Service Cross, for extraordinary heroism in the Second World War, has been forbidden burial in Arlington Cemetery." Then he goes on to quote Bobby. "So Robert Kennedy read aloud on the floor of the Senate an editorial from the *Washington Daily News* condemning the decision not to bury the Communist war hero in Arlington. 'We learn from our mistakes,' the editorial said, 'and one of our lessons is that to hate and harry the sinner to his grave is hardly in the American tradition.' Robert Kennedy was later heard to say somberly that he did not think that anyone now buried in Arlington would object to the holder of the Distinguished Service Cross lying there, so he could not see why veterans' organizations were so agitated about it."

On Thanksgiving Day, 1988, a friend of mine was in Washington with his wife and kids. Because his son was named after Bob, he asked for the grave site number and location at Arlington so he could take his children to the grave. He called to tell me that the marker had been vandalized and there was red paint splattered over the name and part of the inscription. He took pictures of the marker, and after I had the roll of film developed, I wrote to the superintendent of the cemetery. I also wrote to my own congressperson and I wrote to Senator Ted Kennedy. I sent Senator Kennedy and the congressman photos of the vandalized marker. I informed the superintendent how upset and indignant I was that such a thing could happen in a national cemetery. I had an immediate answer from Senator Kennedy, assuring me that the marker had been cleaned up and restored. I also had a letter from the superintendent of the cemetery apologizing for what hap-

---

William Z. Foster (1881–1961) led the great steel strike of 1919 and later served as national secretary of the Communist Party of America. In 1949 he was charged under the Smith Act, along with other top leaders of the CPA. His case was severed because of his ill health.

pened. But since then, I must tell you that once a year I have someone go by Arlington Cemetery to check out Bob's grave site to make sure it hasn't happened again.

That was the Arlington case. What a crime to have had to go to court for the simple act of burying a man who was an acknowledged hero in two of the Army's own official histories.[5] So when you think the McCarthy period ended in the middle fifties, forget it. It took a fight up to the beginning of 1969 for the right for his ashes to be interred in Arlington Cemetery.

[5] *Victory in Papua* (Washington, D.C.: Office of Chief of Military History, 1957) and *32d Infantry Division, World War II* (Madison, Wis.: Bureau of Purchases, 1957).

Sources

GENERAL SURVEYS

Barson, Michael. *"Better Dead Than Red!"* New York: Hyperion, 1992.

Belfrage, Cedric. *The American Inquisition: 1945–1960.* Indianapolis: Bobbs-Merrill, 1973. Reprint. New York: Thunder's Mouth Press, 1989.

Caute, David. *The Great Fear: The Anti-Communist Purge Under Truman and Eisenhower.* New York: Simon & Schuster, 1978.

Fried, Richard M. *Nightmare in Red: The McCarthy Era in Perspective.* New York: Oxford Univ. Press, 1990.

Kutler, Stanley I. *The American Inquisition: Justice and Injustice in the Cold War.* New York: Hill & Wang, 1982.

Latham, Earl. *The Communist Controversy in Washington: From the New Deal to McCarthy.* Cambridge: Harvard Univ. Press, 1966.

McWilliams, Carey. *Witch Hunt: The Revival of Heresy.* Boston: Little, Brown, 1950.

Schultz, Bud, and Ruth Schultz. *It Did Happen Here: Recollections of Political Repression in America.* Berkeley and Los Angeles: Univ. of California Press, 1989.

AMERICA AT MID-CENTURY

Diggins, John Patrick. *The Proud Decades: America in War and Peace, 1941–1960.* New York: Norton, 1988.

Gitlin, Todd. *The Sixties: Years of Hope, Days of Rage.* New York: Bantam, 1987.

Manchester, William. *The Glory and the Dream: A Narrative History of America, 1932–1972.* Boston: Little, Brown, 1974. Reprint. New York: Bantam, 1975.

May, Elaine Tyler. *Homeward Bound: American Families in the Cold War Era.* New York: Basic Books, 1988.

Oakley, J. Ronald. *God's Country: America in the Fifties.* New York: Dembner Books, 1986.

Stone, I. F. *The Truman Era: 1945–1952.* New York: Monthly Review Press, 1953. Reprint. Boston: Little, Brown, 1988.

———. *The Hidden History of the Korean War: 1950–1951.* New York: Monthly Review Press, 1952. Reprint. Boston: Little, Brown, 1988.

———. *The Haunted Fifties: 1953–1963.* Boston: Little, Brown, 1988.

———. *In a Time of Torment: 1961–1967.* Boston: Little, Brown, 1988.

ORIGINS OF THE COLD WAR

Barnet, Richard J. *The Rocket's Red Glare: War, Politics, and the American Presidency.* New York: Simon & Schuster, 1990.

Clemens, Diane Shaver. *Yalta.* New York: Oxford Univ. Press, 1970.

Department of State. *The China White Paper.* 2 vols. Stanford: Stanford Univ. Press, 1967.

Freeland, Richard M. *The Truman Doctrine and the Origins of McCarthyism: Foreign Policy, Domestic Politics, and Internal Security, 1946–1948.* New York: Schocken, 1974.

LaFeber, Walter. *America, Russia, and the Cold War, 1945–1975.* New York: Wiley, 1975.

Paterson, Thomas G. *Meeting the Communist Threat: Truman to Reagan.* New York: Oxford Univ. Press, 1988.

Williams, William Appleman. *Empire as a Way of Life.* New York: Oxford Univ. Press, 1980.

Yergin, Daniel. *Shattered Peace: The Origins of the Cold War and the National Security State.* Boston: Houghton Mifflin, 1978.

INSIDE THE WHITE HOUSE

Clifford, Clark, with Richard Holbrooke. *Counsel to the President: A Memoir.* New York: Random House, 1991. Reprint. New York: Anchor Books/Doubleday, 1992.

Cook, Blanche Wisen. *The Declassified Eisenhower: A Startling Reappraisal of the Eisenhower Presidency.* New York: Doubleday, 1981. Reprint. New York: Penguin, 1984.

McCullough, David. *Truman.* New York: Simon & Schuster, 1992.

LOYALTY AND SECURITY PROGRAMS

Beck, Carl. *Contempt of Congress: A Study of the Prosecutions Initiated by the Committee on Un-American Activities.* New York: Da Capo Press, 1974.

Bernstein, Carl. *Loyalties: A Son's Memoir.* New York: Simon & Schuster, 1989.

Bontecou, Eleanor. *The Federal Loyalty-Security Program.* Ithaca: Cornell University Press, 1953. Reprint. Westport, Conn.: Greenwood Press, 1974.

Brown, Ralph S., Jr. *Loyalty and Security: Employment Tests in the United States.* New Haven: Yale Univ. Press, 1958.

Congressional Record—Senate. Debate on Internal Security Act. September 11, 1950.

Jahoda, Marie, and Stuart W. Cook. "Security Measures and Freedom of Thought: An Exploratory Study of the Impact of Loyalty and Security Programs." *Yale Law Journal* 61, no. 3 (March 1952).

Newman, Robert P. *The Cold War Romance of Lillian Hellman and John Melby.* Chapel Hill: Univ. of North Carolina Press, 1989.

Rauh, Joseph L., Jr. "The Privilege Against Self-Incrimination from John Lilburne to Ollie North." *Constitutional Commentary* 5, no. 2 (Summer 1988).

———. "An Unabashed Liberal Looks at a Half-Century of the Supreme Court." *North Carolina Law Review* 69, no. 1 (November 1990).

———. "Informers, G-Men, and Free Men." *Progressive,* May 1950.

U.S. Congress. House. Committee on Un-American Activities. *Guide to Subversive Organizations and Publications.* 82nd Cong., 1st sess., 1951, and 87th Cong., 2nd sess., 1961.

———. *Hearings Regarding Communism in the United States Government.* Parts 1 and 2. 81st Cong., 2nd sess., 1950.

———. *Issues Presented by Air Reserve Center Training Manual.* 86th Cong., 2nd sess., 1960.

U.S. Congress. Senate. Report of the Subcommittee to Investigate the Administration of the Internal Security Act and Other Internal Security Laws to the Committee on the Judiciary. *Interlocking Subversion in Government Departments.* 83rd Cong., 1st sess., 1953.

———. *The New Drive Against the Anti-Communist Program.* 87th Cong., 1st sess., 1961.

Wilson, Ellen. "I Was a Security Risk." *New Leader,* May 3, 1954.

HISS CASE

Hiss, Alger. *Recollections of a Life.* New York: Seaver Books/Henry Holt, 1988.

Hiss, Tony. "My Father's Honor." *New Yorker,* November 16, 1992.

Klingsberg, Ethan. "The Noel Field Dossier: Case Closed on Alger Hiss?" *Nation,* November 8, 1993.

Margolick, David. "After 40 years, a Postscript on Hiss: Russian Official Calls Him Innocent." *New York Times,* October 29, 1992.

Navasky, Victor. "The Case Not Proved Against Alger Hiss." *Nation,* April 8, 1978.

Schmemann, Serge. "Russian General Says He was 'Not Properly Understood'." *New York Times,* December 17, 1992.

Schmidt, Maria. "A Historian's Report: The Hiss Dossier." *New Republic,* November 8, 1993.

Smith, John Chabot. *Alger Hiss: The True Story.* New York: Holt, Rinehart & Winston, 1976. Reprint. New York: Penguin, 1977.

Stone, I. F. "The 'Flimflam' in the Pumpkin Papers." *New York Times,* April 1, 1976.

Tanenhaus, Sam. "Hiss Case 'Smoking Gun'?" *New York Times,* October 15, 1993.

Weinstein, Allen. " 'Perjury,' Take Three." *New Republic,* April 29, 1978.

————. *Perjury: The Hiss-Chambers Case.* New York: Knopf, 1978.

ATOMIC ESPIONAGE

Anders, Roger M. "The Rosenberg Case Revisited: The Greenglass Testimony and the Protection of Atomic Secrets." *American Historical Review,* April 1978.

Dan, Uri, and Leo Standora. "KGB Claims It Has No Record of Rosenbergs." *New York Post,* November 11, 1991.

Langer, Elinor. "The Case of Morton Sobell: New Queries from the Defense." *Science,* September 1966.

Major, John. *The Oppenheimer Hearing.* Historic Trials Series, edited by J. P. Kenyon. New York: Stein & Day, 1971.

Meeropol, Robert and Michael. *We Are Your Sons: The Legacy of Ethel and Julius Rosenberg.* Boston: Houghton Mifflin, 1975.

Radosh, Ronald, and Joyce Milton. Review of *Invitation to an Inquest,* by Walter and Miriam Schneir. *New York Review of Books,* July 21, 1983.

Radosh, Ronald, and Joyce Milton. *The Rosenberg File: A Search for the Truth.* New York: Holt, Rinehart & Winston, 1983. Reprint. New York: Vintage, 1984.

Schmemann, Serge. "1st Soviet A-Bomb Built from U.S. Data, Russian Says." *New York Times,* January 14, 1993.

Schneir, Walter and Miriam. *Invitation to an Inquest.* New York: Doubleday, 1965. Reprint. New York: Pantheon, 1983.

————. Reply to review of Radosh and Milton. *New York Review of Books,* September 29, 1983.

U.S. Congress. House. Committee on Un-American Activities. *Hearings Regarding Communist Infiltration of Radiation Laboratory and Atom Bomb Project at the University of California, Berkeley, Calif.* 3 vols. 81st Cong., 1st sess., 1948 and 1949.

————. *Hearings Regarding Shipment of Atomic Material to the Soviet Union During World War II.* 81st Cong., 1st and 2nd sess., 1950.

————. *Report on Atomic Espionage (Nelson-Weinberg and Hiskey-Adams Cases).* September 29, 1949.

Williams, Robert Chadwell. *Klaus Fuchs: Atom Spy.* Cambridge: Harvard Univ. Press, 1987.

J. EDGAR HOOVER, JOE MCCARTHY, AND VARIOUS HOUNDS

Donner, Frank. *Protectors of Privilege: Red Squads and Police Repression in Urban America.* Berkeley and Los Angeles: Univ. of California Press, 1990.

Gentry, Curt. *J. Edgar Hoover: The Man and the Secrets.* New York: Norton, 1991.

Kahn, Albert E. *Matusow Affair: Memoir of a National Scandal.* Mt. Kisco, New York: Moyer Bell Limited, 1987.

Matusow, Allen J. *Joseph R. McCarthy.* Great Lives Observed, edited by Gerald Emanuel Stearn. Englewood Cliffs, N.J.: Prentice-Hall, 1970.

Matusow, Harvey. *False Witness.* New York: Cameron & Kahn, 1955.

Philbrick, Herbert. *I Led Three Lives: Citizen, "Communist," Counterspy.* New York: Grosset & Dunlap, 1952.

Reeves, Thomas C. *The Life and Times of Joe McCarthy.* New York: Stein & Day, 1982.

Rovere, Richard H. *Senator Joe McCarthy.* New York: Harcourt, Brace, 1959. Reprint. Cleveland: World Publishing, 1960.

Theoharis, Athan G., and John Stuart Cox. *The Boss: J. Edgar Hoover and the Great American Inquisition.* Philadelphia: Temple Univ. Press, 1988.

Von Hoffman, Nicholas. *Citizen Cohn.* New York: Doubleday, 1988.

THE COMMUNIST PARTY AND THE LEFT

Baer, Donald. "Leftists in the Wilderness." *U.S. News & World Report,* March 19, 1990.

Breindel, Eric M. "The Stalinist Follies." *Commentary,* October 1982.

Buhle, Mari Jo, Paul Buhle, and Dan Georgakas, eds. *Encyclopedia of the American Left.* Urbana and Chicago: Univ. of Illinois Press, 1992.

California. Fourth Report of the Senate Fact-Finding Committee on Un-American Activities. *Communist Front Organizations.* 1948.

Crossman, Richard, ed. *The God That Failed.* New York: Harper & Row, 1950. Reprint. New York: Bantam, 1952.

Draper, Theodore. *The Roots of American Communism.* New York: Viking, 1957.

———. *American Communism and Soviet Russia.* New York: Viking Penguin, 1960. Reprint. New York: Vintage, 1986.

Fast, Howard. *Being Red: A Memoir.* Boston: Houghton Mifflin, 1990. Reprint. New York: Dell, 1991.

Gornick, Vivian. *The Romance of American Communism.* New York: Basic Books, 1977.

Healey, Dorothy, and Maurice Isserman. *Dorothy Healey Remembers: A Life in the American Communist Party.* New York: Oxford Univ. Press, 1990.

Hoover, J. Edgar. *Masters of Deceit.* New York: Henry Holt, 1958. Reprint. New York: Pocket Books, 1959.

Isserman, Maurice. *Which Side Were You On? The American Communist Party During the Second World War.* Middletown, Conn.: Wesleyan Univ. Press, 1982.

———. *If I had a Hammer: The Death of the Old Left and the Birth of the New Left.* New York: Basic Books, 1987.

Kelley, Robin D. G. *Hammer and Hoe: Alabama Communists During the Great Depression.* Chapel Hill: Univ. of North Carolina Press, 1990.

Klehr, Harvey, and John Haynes. "The Comintern's Open Secrets." *American Spectator,* December 1992.

Klehr, Harvey. *The Heyday of American Communism: The Depression Decade.* New York: Basic Books, 1985.

Naison, Mark. *Communists in Harlem During the Depression.* Urbana: Univ. of Illinois Press, 1983. Reprint. New York: Grove, 1985.

Nelson, Steve. *The 13th Juror: The Inside Story of My Trial.* New York: Masses and Mainstream, 1955.

Raskin, Jonah. *Out of the Whale: Growing Up in the American Left.* New York: Links Books, 1974.

Richmond, Al. *A Long View from the Left: Memoirs of an American Revolutionary.* Boston: Houghton Mifflin, 1973.

Scales, Junius. *Cause at Heart: A Former Communist Remembers.* Athens: Univ. of Georgia Press, 1987.

Starobin, Joseph R. *American Communism in Crisis, 1943–1957.* Berkeley and Los Angeles: Univ. of California Press, 1975.

Turque, Bill. "The Party's Shaky Line." *Newsweek,* November 13, 1989.

U.S. Congress. House. Committee on Un-American Activities. *100 Things You Should Know About Communism.* Series: *—in the U.S.A., —and Religion, —and Education, —and Labor, —and Government,* and *Spotlight on Spies.* 82nd Cong., 1st sess., 1951.

———. *The Ideological Fallacies of Communism.* 85th Cong., 1st sess., 1957.

———. *Communist Target—Youth: Communist Infiltration and Agitation Tactics. A Report by J. Edgar Hoover.* July 1960.

———. *Structure and Organization of the Communist Party of the United States.* Parts 1 and 2. 87th Cong., 1st sess., 1961.

U.S. Congress. Senate. Subcommittee to Investigate the Administration of the Internal Security Act and Other Internal Security Laws of the Committee on the Judiciary. *A Handbook for Americans. The Communist Party: What It Is, How It Works.* 84th Cong., 2nd sess., 1956.

LABOR

"Assuring Fair Trial." *Washington Post and Times Herald,* June 5, 1957.

Bruce, Robert V. *1877: Year of Violence.* Indianapolis: Bobbs-Merrill, 1959. Reprint. Chicago: Quadrangle, 1970.

Emery, Lawrence. "High Court Tears the Top off Edgar's Pandora's Box." *National Guardian,* June 17, 1957.

Fink, Gary F., ed. *Biographical Dictionary of American Labor Leaders.* Westport, Conn: Greenwood Press, 1974.

Foner, Philip S. *History of the Labor Movement in the United States, 8 vols.* New York: International Publishers, 1947.

Foster, William Z. *Pages from a Worker's Life.* New York: International Publishers, 1939.

Frost, Richard H. *The Mooney Case.* Stanford: Stanford Univ. Press, 1968.

Ginger, Ann Fagan, and David Christiano. *The Cold War Against Labor.* 2 vols. Studies in Law and Social Change, no. 3. Berkeley: Meiklejohn Civil Liberties Institute, 1987.

Jencks, Virginia. "My Favorite." *March of Labor,* August 1954.

"The Jencks Case." *New York Times,* June 5, 1957.

"The Jencks Trial." *Frontier,* March 1954.

"Jencks v. United States." *Supreme Court Reporter.* 353 U.S. 657. 77 S.Ct. 1007.

Kerby, Elizabeth. "Violence in Silver City: Who Caused the Trouble?" *Frontier,* May 1953.

Larrowe, Charles P. *Harry Bridges: The Rise and Fall of Radical Labor in the U.S.* New York: Lawrence Hill, 1972.

Lipset, Seymour Martin. *Unions in Transition: Entering the Second Century.* San Francisco: ICS Press, 1986.

McKelway, St. Clair. "Some Fun with the FBI." *New Yorker,* October 11, 1941.

Moody, Kim. *An Injury to All: The Decline of American Unionism.* The Haymarket Series. New York: Verso Press, 1988.

Nelson, Bruce. *Workers on the Waterfront: Seamen, Longshoremen, and Unionism in the 1930s.* The Working Class in American History. Urbana and Chicago: Univ. of Illinois Press, 1988.

Quin, Mike. *The Big Strike.* New York: International Publishers, 1949.

Radosh, Ronald. *American Labor and United States Foreign Policy: The Cold War in the Unions from Gompers to Lovestone.* New York: Random House, 1969.

Rayback, Joseph G. *A History of American Labor*. New York: Macmillan, 1968.

Rehmus, Charles M., Doris B. McLaughlin, and Frederick H. Nesbitt. *Labor and American Politics: A Book of Readings*. Ann Arbor: Univ. of Michigan Press, 1978.

Stone, I. F. "The Jencks Decision Reopens the Matusow Case." *I. F. Stone's Weekly*, June 10, 1957.

U.S. Congress. Senate. Committee on Labor and Public Welfare. *Communist Domination of Unions and National Security*. 82nd Cong., 2nd sess., 1952.

"The Whole Truth." *Denver Post*. June 5, 1957.

HOLLYWOOD, ENTERTAINMENT, LITERATURE,
AND THE PRESS

Aronson, James. *The Press and the Cold War*. New York: Monthly Review Press, 1990.

Bayley, Edwin R. *Joe McCarthy and the Press*. Madison: Univ. of Wisconsin Press, 1981. Reprint. New York: Pantheon, 1982.

Bentley, Eric. *Thirty Years of Treason: Excerpts from Hearings Before the House Committee on Un-American Activities, 1938–1968*. New York: Viking, 1971. Reprint. New York: Viking Compass, 1973.

Bessie, Alvah. *Inquisition in Eden*. New York: Macmillan, 1965.

Boyle, Kay. *Words That Must Somehow Be Said: Selected Essays, 1927–1984*. Berkeley: North Point Press, 1985.

Brown, Jared. *Zero Mostel: A Biography*. New York: Atheneum, 1989.

Ceplair, Larry. "Who Wrote What? A Tale of a Blacklisted Screenwriter and His Front." *Journal*, August 1991.

Ceplair, Larry, and Steven Englund. *The Inquisition in Hollywood: Politics in the Film Community, 1930–1960*. Reprint (by arrangement with Anchor Press). Berkeley and Los Angeles: Univ. of California Press, 1979.

Cogley, John. *Report on Blacklisting*. 2 vols. The Fund for the Republic, 1956.

Dunaway, David. *How Can I Keep from Singing: Pete Seeger*. London: Harrap, 1985. Reprint. New York: Da Capo, 1990.

Friedrich, Otto. *City of Nets: A Portrait of Hollywood in the 1940s*. New York: Harper & Row, 1986.

Goodson, Mark. "If I'd Stood Up Earlier . . ." *New York Times Magazine*, January 13, 1991.

Halliwell, Leslie. *Halliwell's Film Guide*. 7th ed. New York: Harper & Row, 1989.

Hamilton, Ian. *Writers in Hollywood, 1915–1951*. New York: Harper & Row, 1990.

Katz, Ephraim. *The Film Encyclopedia*. New York: Harper & Row, 1979. Reprint. New York: Harper & Row, 1990.

Kazan, Elia. *A Life*. New York: Knopf, 1988.

Lardner, Ring, Jr. *The Lardners: My Family Remembered*. New York: Harper & Row, 1976.

Mathews, Jack. "Children of the Blacklist." *Los Angeles Times Magazine*, October 15, 1989.

Miller, Arthur. "The Year It Came Apart." *New York*, December 30, 1974—January 6, 1975.

Miller, Arthur. *Timebends*. New York: Harper & Row, 1988.

Mitgang, Herbert. *Dangerous Dossiers: Exposing the Secret War Against America's Greatest Authors*. New York: Donald Fine, 1988.

Moldea, Dan E. *Dark Victory: Ronald Reagan, MCA, and the Mob*. New York: Viking Penguin, 1986. Reprint. New York: Penguin, 1987.

Navasky, Victor S. *Naming Names*. New York: Viking, 1980. Reprint. New York: Penguin, 1981.

———. "Has 'Guilty by Suspicion' Missed the Point?" *New York Times*, March 31, 1991.

Roberts, Jerry. "Red-Faced: Old Cold War Films Are a Hoot." *Daily Breeze*, February 22, 1991.

Ross, Lillian. "Come in, Lassie!" *New Yorker*, February 21, 1948.

Slide, Anthony. "Hollywood's Fascist Follies." *Film Comment,* July–August 1991.

Smollett, Peter. "The Real-Life Cast of Guilty by Suspicion." *People's Weekly World,* April 20, 1991.

Spanier, Sandra Whipple. *Kay Boyle: Artist and Activist.* Edwardsville: Southern Illinois Univ. Press, 1986. Reprint. New York: Paragon House, 1988.

Sperber, A. M. *Murrow: His Life and Times.* New York: Freundlich, 1986.

Trumbo, Dalton. *Additional Dialogue: Letters of Dalton Trumbo, 1942–1962.* Edited by Helen Manfull. New York: Evans, 1970.

———. *The Time of the Toad: A Study of Inquisition in America.* New York: Harper & Row, 1972.

U.S. Congress. House. Committee on Un-American Activities. *Communist Infilitration of Hollywood Motion-Picture Industry.* Parts 1–7. 82nd Cong., 1st sess., 1951.

Vaughan, Robert. *Only Victims: A Study of Show Business Blacklisting.* New York: Putnam, 1972.

Willens, Doris. *Lonesome Traveler: The Life of Lee Hays.* New York: Norton, 1988. Reprint. Lincoln and London: Univ. of Nebraska Press, 1993.

EDUCATION

Cook, Stuart W. "Research on Anticipatory Ideological Compliance: Comment on Sargent and Harris." *Journal of Social Issues* 42, no. 1 (1986).

Davidson, Keay. "The Nobel Pursuits of Linus Pauling." *California,* February 1991.

Davis, Chandler. "The Purge." *A Century of Mathematics in America,* Part 1. Providence: American Mathematical Society.

Davis, Marian Rubins, and Horace Bancroft Davis. *Liberalism Is Not Enough.* Berkeley: Orca Press, n.d.

Rowe, Frank. *The Enemy Among Us: A Story of Witch-Hunting in the McCarthy Era.* Sacramento: Cougar Books, 1980.

Sargent, S. Stansfield. "Academic Freedom, Civil Liberties, and SPSSI." *Journal of Social Issues* 42, no. 1 (1986).

Schrecker, Ellen W. *No Ivory Tower: McCarthyism and the Universities.* New York: Oxford Univ. Press, 1986.

Smith, M. Brewster. "McCathyism: A Personal Account." *Journal of Social Issues* 42, no. 4 (1986).

CIVIL RIGHTS AND CIVIL LIBERTIES

Ardoin, Morris. "Dombrowski v. Pfister: An Incredible Impact on the Law." *Tulane Lawyer,* Fall 1991.

Braden, Anne. "The Civil Rights Movement and McCarthyism." *National Lawyers Guild Practitioner* 37, no. 4 (Fall 1980).

———. *House Un-American Activities Committee: Bulwark of Segregation.* Los Angeles: National Committee to Abolish the House Un-American Activities Committee, 1963.

Branch, Taylor. *Parting the Waters.* New York: Simon & Schuster, 1988.

Cox, Archibald. *The Court and the Constitution.* Boston: Houghton Mifflin, 1987.

Criley, Richard. *The FBI v. the First Amendment.* Los Angeles: First Amendment Foundation, 1990.

Dawley, Edward A. "Kinoy Contra Dixie." *National Lawyers Guild Practitioner* 47, no. 2 (Spring 1990).

Garrow, David J. *The FBI and Martin Luther King, Jr.* New York: Norton, 1981. Reprint. New York: Penguin, 1983.

Hand, Learned. "A Plea for Freedom of Dissent." *New York Times Magazine,* February 6, 1955.

Horne, Gerald. *Black & Red: W.E.B. Du Bois and the Afro-American Response to the Cold War, 1944–1963.* Albany: State Univ. of New York Press, 1986.

MacLeish, Archibald. "Must We Hate?" *Atlantic,* February 1963.

———. "The Conquest of America." 1949. Reprint, *Atlantic Monthly,* March 1980.

Simon, James F. *The Antagonists: Hugo Black, Felix Frankfurter, and Civil Liberties in Modern America.* New York: Simon & Schuster, 1989.

MISCELLANEOUS

Conquest, Robert. *The Great Terror: A Reassessment.* New York: Oxford Univ. Press, 1990.

Cortada, James W. *Historical Dictionary of the Spanish Civil War, 1936–1939.* Westport: Greenwood Press, 1982.

Diggins, John P. *Mussolini and Fascism: The View from America.* Reprint. Princeton: Princeton Univ. Press, 1975.

Hoar, Victor. *The Mackenzie-Papineau Battalion.* Copp Clark Publishing, 1969.

Hofstadter, Richard. *The Paranoid Style in American Politics.* Reprint. New York: Vintage, 1967.

Roth, Cecil. *The Spanish Inquisition.* Reprint. New York: Norton, 1964.

Seldes, George. *Facts and Fascism.* New York: In Fact, 1943.

Smith, Denis Mack. *Mussolini: A Biography.* Reprint. New York: Vintage, 1983.

Starkey, Marion L. *The Devil in Massachusetts: A Modern Inquiry into the Salem Witch Trials.* New York: Knopf, 1949. Reprint. Garden City: Dolphin/Doubleday, 1961.

Wade, Wyn Craig. *The Fiery Cross: The Ku Klux Klan in America.* New York: Simon & Schuster, 1986. Reprint. New York: Touchstone, 1988.

Williams, Evelyn. *Inadmissible Evidence.* New York: Lawrence Hill Books, 1993.

Index

Abbott, Carl, 536*n*
Acheson, Dean, 29, 34, 151
Action in the North Atlantic (film),
    256*n*
Adams, Frank, 357
Adams, James, 95
Addams, Jane, 474
Additional Dialogue (Trumbo), 65
Administrative Index, 96
Adventures of Robin Hood, The (TV show),
    264, 275
Agricultural Adjustment Administration
    (AAA), 147*n*
Alabama Christian Movement for Human
    Rights, 502
Aldrich Family, The (TV show), 316,
    320
Algren, Nelson, 319
Allan, Lewis, 53
Allen, Raymond, 421
Amerasia, 144, 159, 162
America First, 199*n*
American Association of University Professors,
    491–92
American Broadcasting Company (ABC), 324,
    369
American Business Consultants, 315
American Civil Liberties Union (ACLU), 42,
    44, 56, 355*n*, 474*n*, 490
  Arlington case and, 546
  Barnet and, 359–60
  FBI and, 132–33
  maritime workers and, 408
  Wilkinson and, 528*n*, 531, 532
American Communications Association (ACA),
    395, 396

American Federation of Labor (AFL), 59*n*,
    114, 220*n*, 375, 377, 378, 380, 382*n*,
    391–93, 413, 414, 423, 442
American Federation of Labor and Congress
    of Industrial Organizations
    (AFL-CIO), 61*n*, 233*n*
American Friends Service Committee, 523
American Jewish Congress, 490
American Labor Party, 44, 191
American Legion, 66, 74, 76, 79, 112, 153*n*,
    211*n*, 221*n*, 259, 260, 291, 305, 317,
    318, 324*n*, 340–41, 342*n*, 348, 368,
    372, 420, 531, 540, 543
  Americanization Committee of, 264, 275–76
American Negro Slave Revolts (Aptheker),
    453, 454
American Newspaper Guild, 318–19
American Peace Crusade, 509
Americans Battling Communism (ABC), 204,
    206, 208
American Security Council, 42
Americans for Democratic Action (ADA), 137,
    139
American Student Union, 444
American Veterans Committee, 420
American Youth for Democracy (AYD), 420
Anderson, Bill, 287
Anderson, Jack, 107
Anderson, Walter, 149*n*
Andrews, Dana, 117–18
Annunzio, Frank, 527
Appel, Donald T., 102, 346
Aptheker, Herbert, 451–55
Arens, Richard, 471
Arkansas Gazette, 498
Arlington case, 544–48

Arthur, Art, 119
Arvad, Inga, 81n
Associated Farmers of California, 465
Atomic Energy Act (1946), 185
Atomics, 175
Auden, W. H., 233
Audubon Society, 43
Auslander, Jacob, 157
Aware, Inc., 116n, 316, 324n, 341n, 342n

Bacall, Lauren, 64n, 261
Baez, Joan, 508
Bailey, Bill, 405–13
Baldwin, Roger N., 233n, 332
Barenblatt, Lloyd, 438–39
Barnet, Melvin, 355–61
Barr, Richard, 267
Barton (Marzani's friend), 152–53, 155
Baruch, Bernard, 36, 148n
Bates, Daisy, 497
Baxter (OSS officer), 152
Being Red (Fast), 299n
Bela, Nicholas, 258n
Belafonte, Harry, 321, 502n, 505n
Bell, Daniel, 232n
Bellow, Saul, 233n
Belmont, Alan, 96
Bennett, James V., 187, 533–34
Bennett, John C., 233n
Bentley, Arvilla, 100n, 106
Bentley, Elizabeth, 136, 140–41, 224
Berkeley, Martin, 120n, 166n, 265, 276, 289,
        291, 292, 308
Berle, Adolf, 147
Bernal, J. D., 517
Bernstein, Al, 141–43
Bernstein, Carl, 37
Bernstein, Leonard, 321, 325
Bernstein, Ted, 357
Bessie, Alvah, 258n
Best Years of Our Lives, The (film), 117–18
Better America Federation, 42
Biberman, Herbert, 258n, 259n, 263, 280, 298
Biddle, Francis, 94n
Billings, Warren, 188
Bioff, Willie, 113n, 256n, 283n
Birdsell (professor), 152–53
Bitter Heritage (Schlesinger), 547
Black, Arthur, 355
Black, Bob, 78–80
Black, Hugo, 151, 185n, 231, 455n, 488,
        489, 490, 532
blacklist, 64–65

black market and, 260
clearance men and, 316–17, 327–28
Ford Motor Co. and, 325
graylist and, 259, 266
Hollywood, 63n, 255–60
print media and, 319–20
radio and television industries and, 131n,
        315–16
ritual of informing and, 258–59
symbolic capitulation and, 66–67
Weavers and, 362, 368
Black Panthers, 43
Blake, Fay, 251–54
Bloch, Emanuel, 51, 186
Block, Hal, 320
Bogart, Humphrey, 64n, 261
Bohlen, Charles, 129
Bohm, David, 197n
Bonanno, Joseph, 93n
Bond, Ward, 297n
Book of Daniel, The (Doctorow), 49
Books at Sea program, 448
Bostick, Floyd, 385n
Boudin, Kathy, 53
Boudin, Lenny, 357
Boyle, Kay, 319, 331–37
Braden, Anne, 472–82
Braden, Carl, 472, 474, 475, 476, 480–81,
        482, 533, 539
Brando, Marlon, 341n–42n
Bransten, Louise, 449
Branton (attorney), 222n
Brave One, The (film), 63, 64
Brecht, Bertolt, 257n–58n
Bremen, 405–6
Brennan, William, 231, 532
Brewer, Roy, 112–22, 256, 257, 265, 283,
        297n, 300n, 342
Bridge on the River Kwai, The (film), 281n
Bridges, Harry, 58–63, 70, 120–21, 245n,
        300n, 377, 400, 403–4, 410–11, 519,
        520, 543
Bridges, Lloyd, 63, 274n, 302
Bridges, Robbie, 58–63
Bright, John, 65
Broken Lance (film), 294, 304
Brooklyn Eagle, 319, 355, 358
Brooks, Van Wyck, 233n
Browder, Earl, 200, 201
Brown, Archie, 241–42, 243, 246, 249,
        540–43
Brown, Betsy, 243
Brown, Douglas, 244

Brown, Hon, 243–46, 543
Brown, Stephanie, 244
Brown, Susie, 244
Brown, Vernon, 476–79
Browne, George, 113*n*, 256*n*, 283*n*
Brownell, Herbert, Jr., 83, 84, 100*n*, 108–12, 185*n*, 241, 353–54, 450*n*
Brownmiller, Susan, 453
Brown v. Board of Education, 473*n*, 488, 489, 492–93, 499*n*, 530
Bryson, Hugh, 404
Buchman, Sidney, 120*n*, 310*n*
Budenz, Louis, 136, 166*n*, 333
Burdett, Winston, 319, 355–56, 357, 358
Bureau of Internal Revenue, 202
Bureau of Security and Consular Affairs, 145
Burns, Hugh H., 70*n*, 398, 518
Burns Committee, 70, 424, 463, 518, 519
Burrows, Abe, 321, 324, 325
Bush, George, 44, 369
Butler, Hugo, 65
Byrnes, James F., 147

Caen, Herb, 218
Cagney, William, 287
Caine Mutiny, The (film), 294
Caldwell, Erskine, 130*n*, 181
Caldwell, Ira S., 181*n*
Calhern, Louis, 345–46
California Fact-Finding Committee on Un-American Activities, 333*n*
California Quarterly, 458
Cameron, Angus, 107, 319, 352–55
Canoga Park Herald, 460, 461
Cantor, Jay, 270, 271
Canwell, Albert, 469
Canwell Committee, 420–21
Capone, Al, 283*n*
Carey, James, 377
Carlson, Frank, 212*n*, 448
Carmichael, Ian, 330
Carmichael, Stokely, 470*n*
Carnegie Endowment for International Peace, 146
Casablanca (film), 272
Casals, Pablo, 233*n*
Case of the Ten Dollar a Week Robbery, The (Hall), 483
Castro, Fidel, 59, 441
Catholic War Veterans, 74, 321, 340–41, 342*n*, 372
Caute, David, 36, 128, 175
Cecil, Lester, 497

Central Intelligence Agency (CIA), 43, 60, 172, 422, 509, 519
Cercone (attorney), 208, 211
Cerf, Bennett, 139*n*, 355
Chadwick, Ike, 119
Chambers, Whittaker, 102*n*, 109*n*, 144, 146, 147–50
Chaney, Frances, 266–72
Chaplin, Charlie, 260, 305
Charny, George, 105*n*
Chayevsky, Paddy, 271
Chernin, Rose, 212*n*, 214, 223
Cherny, Robert, 60*n*
Chiang Kai-shek, 144, 145, 159, 160, 161, 164
Chicago Committee to Defend the Bill of Rights, 523–24
Chicago Tribune, 392
Chief: My Life in the LAPD (Gates), 536*n*
Childress, Alice, 453
Childs, Jack, 92*n*
Childs, Morris, 92, 95
China, People's Republic of, 130, 144–45, 158–60, 323, 344
China Daily News, 145*n*
China Lobby, 144–45, 158, 161, 162
Chinatown Anti-Communist League, 144*n*–45*n*
Chinatown purges, 144*n*–45*n*
Chisholm, Shirley, 505*n*
Christopher, Mayor, 542–43
Church, Frank, 94*n*
Church Committee, 94, 95
Churchill, Winston, 33, 147*n*, 154
Cincinnati Enquirer, 318*n*
Cincinnati Kid, The (film), 261, 264
Citizens Committee to Preserve American Freedom, 531*n*
Civil Rights Commission, 83
Civil Rights Congress (CRC), 76, 453*n*, 482
civil rights movement, 469–70, 487–88, 508, 521
civil service, 127–31
Civil Service Commission (CSC), 127, 128, 152, 153, 163
Clamage, Ed, 348–49
Clardy, Kit, 379
Clark, Bill, 334
Clark, Maurice, 302*n*
Clark, Tom, 38*n*, 83, 84, 128, 185*n*, 450*n*, 482*n*
clearwater campaign, 365
Clifford, Clark, 35, 37, 38*n*, 39, 139*n*

Clifford-Elsey Report, 38
Clift, Montgomery (Monty), 304
Clinton, Bill, 44
Clubb, O. Edmund, Jr., 159
Coast Guard, U.S., 404–5, 406, 407, 410, 417, 524
Cobb, Julie, 285
Cobb, Lee J., 120, 271, 274n, 285, 302
Coburn, Charles, 297n
Coburn, Nathaniel, 435n
Coe, Fred, 271
Cogley, John, 115–16, 315
Cohen, Mickey, 218
Cohen, Rabbi, 463
Cohn, Harry, 120n, 121, 310
Cohn, Roy, 98n, 101, 102, 104, 107–8, 123, 136, 275–76, 334–35, 348, 354
  Rosenberg case and, 185n, 188
COINTELPRO, 90–91, 443
Cold War, 24, 73n, 108, 154, 201, 226, 269, 274, 378, 384, 413, 416, 417–18, 438n, 456, 489, 506, 507–8, 526
Cole, Lester, 157, 258n, 259n, 263
Colin, Ralph, 321
Collier's, 130
Collins, Richard, 119–20, 258n, 274n, 276
Colodny, Robert, 440–43
Columbia Broadcasting System (CBS), 34n, 131, 316, 317, 319, 321–23, 325, 351, 546
Comden, Betty, 371
Commerce Department, U.S., 141
Committee for the First Amendment (CFA), 64, 118, 261
Committee on Offenses Against the Administration of Justice, 471
Committee of One Thousand, 333
Committee to Investigate Blacklisting in TVA, 351
Communist Commentary (radio program), 221n
Communist Control Act (1954), 19, 111n, 203, 241, 379–80
Communist Infiltration of the United States, 376
Communist Party, Greek, 34
Communist Party, Italian, 32n, 201n, 205n
Communist Party, U.S., 18, 27, 31, 36–37, 39, 43, 44, 54, 55n, 56, 63n, 66, 77, 125, 132, 241, 399
  categories of membership in, 121n,
  "cells" of, 68
  Chambers and, 150n

CIO and, 375, 377
civil rights movement and, 469–71
contributions of, 200
decline of, 203
FBI break-ins and, 84–87
FBI informants in, 82, 90n, 92–93
founding of, 199
Hitler-Stalin pact and, 113n, 199, 444
ideological purge in, 236–37
Khrushchev report and, 72–73, 203, 230, 411n, 522
labor schools and, 69, 291n, 423–24
legislation against, 202–3
loyalty program and, 40–41
maritime workers and, 402
OSS and, 154n
Rosenberg case and, 186
Scottsboro case and, 129n
Security Index and, 94–97
Smith Act indictments and, 201–4
Soviet Union and, 38, 109, 199, 295
Supreme Court and prosecution of, 111
Trumbo and, 67–68
underground of, see "five minutes to midnight" policy
during World War II, 200–201
Communists Within the Labor Movement, 376
Conference of Studio Unions (CSU), 112, 114, 256
Conference to Combat Communism, 341n
Congress, U.S., 24, 28, 43, 93, 109, 112, 130–31, 144, 154, 175, 204, 344, 400n
  Dixiecrats in, 507n
  FBI and, 94–95
  Gwinn Amendment and, 219n
  loyalty program and, 37–38
  McCarran Act and, 229
  Magnuson Act passed by, 404
  organized labor and, 378
  Public Law 733 passed by, 128
  Security Index and, 94–97
Congressional Committee on Atomic Energy, 179
Congress of Industrial Organizations (CIO), 59n, 114, 154, 200, 220n, 375–78, 380, 391, 394, 409, 423
  Communist Party and, 375, 377
  maritime workers and, 413–14
  Operation Dixie of, 413n, 482
Connelly, Philip, 212n, 218, 223

Connor, Eugene T. "Bull," 483
Conspirator (film), 259n
Constitution, U.S., 184, 213, 214, 404, 505, 526
    First Amendment of, 21, 63n, 64, 215, 218, 257, 259, 261, 279, 317, 354, 355, 374, 427, 436, 438n, 505, 522, 531–32
    Fifth Amendment of, 21, 40, 84, 136, 219, 220, 229n, 279, 284, 287, 290, 317, 318, 327, 338–39, 354–58
    Thirteenth Amendment of, 402
    Fourteenth Amendment of, 487n, 523
Consumer Reports, 130
Consumers Union, 130
Cook, Stuart, 130
Cooper, Gary, 257, 261, 297n
Coplon, Judith, 27
Corey, Evie, 285
Corey, Jeff, 284–88
Cornered (film), 296, 304
Cory, George, 302n
Cory, Giles, 521, 527–28
Corwin, Norman, 363
Coughlin, Charles Edward, 432
Council for a Democratic Far Eastern Policy, 508–9
Council for Pan-American Democracy, 508–9
Counsel to the President (Clifford), 38n
Counterattack, 259, 315–16
Cousins, Norman, 67, 514
Crawford, Joan, 293
Criley, Richard, 91, 521–28
Criley, Ted, 524
Crosley, George, *see* Chambers, Whittaker
Crossfire (film), 304
Crouch, Paul, 98, 488
Crucible, The (Miller), 317, 342–43
Crum, Bartley, 300
Cultural and Scientific Conference for World Peace, 340
Cunningham, Sarah, 347, 348
Curran, Joe, 377, 404, 414–16
Curtiz, Michael, 273n
Custodial Detention list, *see* Security Index
Cvetic, Matt, 98, 98n, 208–9

Daily Worker, 52, 99n, 113n, 122, 139–40n, 166n, 186, 202, 205, 247n, 323n, 357, 363, 372, 487, 522
Daily World, 461
Dallet, Joe, 195
Darkness at Noon (Koestler), 303

Da Silva, Howard, 259
Davies, John Paton, 159, 161
Davies, Joseph E., 273
Davis, Angela, 53, 505n
Davis, Benjamin, 201n
Davis, Chandler, 434–40
Davis, Elmer, 82
Davis, Horace B., 436n
Davis, Joan, 327
"Days of Rage," 91n
Deadline for Action (film), 154
Death of a Salesman (Miller), 340–41
de Beauvoir, Simone, 441
Debs, Eugene V., 253n, 380n, 507
De Caux, Len, 377
Dees, Ruby, 505n
Defenders, The (TV show), 272
Defense Department, U.S., 133, 419
Defiant Ones, The (film), 293
Delany, Hubert T., 492, 497
Dellinger, Dave, 509
Dellums, Ron, 505n
Democratic Front, 200
Democratic Party, U.S., 28, 84, 131, 146, 199, 344, 383, 506
Democratic Party of the Left (PDS), 205n
Democratic Socialists of America, 219
Dennis, Eugene, 54, 56–58, 201n
Dennis, Gene, 54–58
Depression, the, 23–24, 212
Devil and the Book, The (Trumbo), 68
Dewey, Thomas E., 74–75, 78, 111, 457
Dies, Martin, 17
Dies Committee, 17, 146
Dilworth, Nelson S., 466n
Dilworth Act (1953), 424, 466
Disney, Walt, 257, 297n
Dixiecrats, 503, 504, 506
Dixon, Maynard, 69
Dmytryk, Edward, 63n, 118–120, 258n, 259, 263, 265, 269–70, 276, 294–305
Dmytryk, Jean Porter, 269
Dobbs, Ben, 212n
Dodd, Chris, 221
Dodd, Thomas J., 17, 221, 512–13
Dodd Committee, 221
Dolson, James, 205, 209
Dombrowski, Jim, 488
Dondero, George, 161, 161n
Donovan, "Wild Bill," 153–54, 155, 157
Douglas, Melvin, 348
Douglas, Paul, 18n

Douglas, William O., 41, 50, 151, 156, 185*n*, 231, 303*n*, 490, 532
Doyle, Bernadette, 212*n*, 221
Doyle, Clyde, 310, 532
Draper, Theodore, 233*n*
Draper Project, 471
Dreiser, Theodore, 130*n*
Dubinsky, David, 234, 396
Du Bois, W. E. B., 303*n*, 434*n*, 453, 505*n*
Du Bridge, Lee Alvin, 427
Duclos, Jacques, 201*n*
Duffy, Adrian, 406
Duffy, Bill, 108
Dukakis, Michael, 44
Dulles, John Foster, 32, 145, 167
Dunne, Philip, 261
Du Pont, Irénée, 148*n*
Du Pont, Pierre, 148*n*
Durr, Clifford, 487
Durr, Virginia, 487–89
Dylan, Bob, 508

Eastland, James O., 17, 319, 441–42, 470–71, 488, 489, 496, 500, 504, 523
"Eight Fallacies of Nuclear Test Ban" (Dodd), 513
Einstein, Albert, 135, 157, 421–22, 462, 508, 510
Eisenberg, Frances, 459–64, 466, 468
Eisenhower, Dwight D., 28, 36*n*, 39, 40, 50, 84, 94, 108, 111, 112, 127, 129, 131, 513
  Hoover and, 83
  school desegregation and, 439*n*
elections:
  of 1920, 507
  of 1928, 39
  of 1936, 220*n*
  of 1946, 27, 37, 38*n*
  of 1948, 39, 377, 378, 414–15, 507–8
  of 1950, 124*n*
  of 1952, 105, 108, 124*n*, 139, 216*n*, 245
  of 1956, 495, 497
  of 1968, 91*n*
  of 1988, 44
Elitcher, Max, 182
Emergency Civil Liberties Committee, 40
Emergency Committee of Atomic Scientists, 510
Emerson, Faye, 323
End of Ideology, The (Bell), 232*n*
Engels, Friedrich, 208, 221, 500
English, Richard, 300

Ernst, Morris, 132–33, 133*n*
Espionage Act (1917), 160, 185*n*, 321*n*
Executive Order 9835, 36, 140*n*, 142
Executive Order 10241, 40, 140*n*
Executive Order 10450, 40, 94, 336*n*
Exodus (film), 66, 264, 280

Fact-Finding Committee on Un-American Activities, 449*n*
False Witness (Matusow), 100, 102*n*, 104*n*, 106, 107, 352
Farmer, Fyke, 185
Farmer, John, 43
Fast, Howard, 299, 420
Faubus, Orval, 494, 498
Faulk, John Henry, 116*n*, 324*n*
Faulkner, William, 229
Federal Bureau of Investigation (FBI), 25, 42, 43, 55, 70, 73*n*, 75*n*, 109, 128, 129, 139, 175, 198*n*, 201–2, 287–88, 293, 352–53, 356, 397, 442, 458, 508, 509, 538
  ACLU and 132–33
  Bridges and, 404
  COINTELPRO program of, 90–91, 110–12
  Communist underground and, 237–38
  Congress and, 94–95
  Criley and, 521–24, 526
  Custodial Detention (Security Index) of, 84, 94–97, 249*n*
  Domestic Intelligence Division of, 85, 96
  expanded power of, 81–82
  harassment of Reds and, 90–91
  Hiss case and, 147, 150, 150*n*
  HUAC and, 523, 524–25
  illegal break-ins by, 84–87, 159*n*
  Jencks and, 380, 384, 386
  maritime unions and, 404–8, 411
  Marzani case and, 152–55
  Matusow as double agent for, 97, 99, 107, 387*n*
  organized crime and, 93–94, 93*n*
  OSS and, 154
  public image of, 81
  Rosenberg case and, 180
  Sachs and, 394–95
  Scales and, 226–27
  Service case and, 159–60
  Shaftel and, 432–33, 435
  Sobell case and, 181, 182–183, 186–87, 190, 192, 193–94
  surveillance by, 87–88

T designation used by, 142–43
teachers and, 422
Top Hood program of, 93–94
Weavers and, 362, 369
Federal Bureau of Investigation, The
(Lowenthal), 139*n*
Federal Employees Loyalty Program, 112*n*,
128–30, 138, 163–64, 420
civil liberties and, 40–41
Congress and, 37–38
deaths resulting from, 42–43
Eisenhower administration and, 41
private industry and, 42
public and, 40, 41
security officers and, 82–83
State Department and, 41, 129
Truman's launching of, 36–40
Federation of Former Communists, 98
Fefer, Itzik, 230*n*
Feinberg Law (1949), 424
Fellowship of Reconciliation, 508
Ferencz, Benny, 333
Ferlinghetti, Lawrence, 508
Ferman, Irving, 133*n*
Fidelifax, Inc., 42
File 13, 316
Fine, Fred, 87
Finger of Guilt (film), 275
Finkelstein, Sidney, 453, 455
Firing Line, 259, 316
"five minutes to midnight" policy, 202, 215*n*,
236–38
Blake and, 251–54
Brown in, 241–42, 243
levels of, 237
Passen and, 249–51
Scales in, 239–40
Thompson and, 247–49
Flanner, Janet, 334, 336
Flynn, Elizabeth Gurley, 355
Ford, Henry, 199*n*–200*n*
Foreign Aid Administration, 174
Forer, Joe, 228
Fortune, 44, 379
Foster, William Z., 201, 236, 546, 547*n*
Fox, David, 197*n*
Fox, Ernest, 212*n*
France, 34, 100, 185–86
Francis, Arlene, 320
Franckenstein, Joseph von, 331, 333, 334–36
Franco, Francisco, 195*n*, 318*n*, 320
Frank, Jerome, 184*n*
Frankfurter, Felix, 139, 151

Freedom, 453*n*
Freedom of Information Act (1966), 104,
149, 187, 225, 249*n*, 293, 446, 528,
536
Freedomways, 505
Friedman, Max, 197*n*
Friedman, Milton, 501
Fuchs, Klaus, 27, 177–179, 439*n*
Fund for the Republic, 116

Gang, Martin, 274, 307–9, 310
Gangbusters (radio show), 267
Garfield, John, 43, 116–17, 260
Garland, Judy, 214
Garrett, Betty, 301
Gates, Daryl, 536*n*
Gates, John, 201*n*
Geber, Anthony, 170–74
Geer, Will, 259
Genovese, Vito, 93*n*
George, Tex, 416, 417
George II, King of Greece, 33
Germany, Nazi, 31, 101, 199, 200,
215*n*
Gilbert, Ronnie, 362, 367, 370–74
Gilford, Jack, 321
Give Us This Day (film), 305
God That Failed, The (Crossman), 303*n*
Go East Young Man (Douglas), 151
Goebbels, Josef, 256*n*
Goheen, Robert, 233
Gold, Ben, 375*n*–76*n*
Gold, Harry, 179, 439*n*
Goldberg, Harold, 348–49
Goldberg, Ruth, 455–58
Goldwyn, Sam, 258
Gompers, Samuel, 382*n*
Goodson, Mark, 320–26
Good War, The (Terkel), 23
Gordon, Max, 186
Gordon, Michael, 265, 302*n*
Gordon, Murray, 133
Goudsmit, S. A., 82
Gouzenko, Igor, 177*n*
Gray, Fred, 487
Graylist, 259, 266
Great Britain, 32–35
Greek crisis (1947), 32–36
Green, Adolph, 371
Green, Ann, 273, 274, 275
Green, Gilbert, 56, 87, 201*n*, 202*n*
Greenbaum, General, 336–37
Greene, Richard, 275

Greenglass, David, 48, 133, 178–79, 182n, 184n, 185, 187
Greenglass, Ruth, 48, 179n, 184n
Gregory, Yvonne, 453
Groves, Leslie, 188n
Grutzner, Charles, 356
Guardian, 52
Guilty of Treason (film), 259n
Guinier, Lani, 44
Guthrie, Woody, 76n, 79, 363
Gutride, Minnie, 425
Gwinn Amendment (1952), 219n

Hagen, Uta, 321
Hall, Gus, 201n, 202n
Hall, Sam, 247, 248, 482–87, 544
Hallinan, Vincent, 216, 245
Hallinan, Vivian, 216
Halliwell, Leslie, 208n
Hamby, Alonzo, 30
Hamilton, Scott, 475–76
Hammarskjöld, Dag, 514
Hammer, Al, 371
Hammett, Dashiell, 165n, 338n, 453
Hanford, Ben, 253n
Hansberry, Lorraine, 453
Harding, Ann, 273n
Hard Times (Dickens), 253–54
Harriman, Averell, 31, 167, 169
Harris, Dr., 196
Harris, M. Lafayette, 498
Hartford, Bruce, 397, 399
Hartford, Claire, 395–401
Hartford, Ken, 396–400
Hartle, Barbara, 231n
Hartnett, Vincent, 341n
Hatch Act (1939), 127
Havighurst, Robert, 523
Havoc, June, 261
Hawaii (film), 66
Hawkins, David, 197n
Hay, Harry, 236n
Hayden, Sterling, 274n
Haymarket Square riot, 75n, 546
Hays, Lee, 362, 363, 374
Healey, Dorothy, 212n, 214, 219–25
Health, Education and Welfare Department, U.S. (HEW), 427–28
Hearst, William Randolph, 300n, 466
Hecht, Selig, 177
Heilbroner, Robert, 233n
Heller, George, 351
Hellerman, Fred, 362, 367–70

Hellman, Lillian, 165–67, 168n, 302, 338–39
Hemingway, Ernest, 130n
Hendry, Whitey, 309
Hepburn, Katharine, 269
Herblock, 27n
Herbst, Josephine, 319
Hickenlooper, Bourke, 139
High Noon (film), 287
Hill, Gladman, 106
Hill, Joe, 355n
Hill, Russell, 267
Hiss, Alger, 27, 102n–3n, 109, 144–52, 258
History of the Civil War in the USSR, 222n
Hitler, Adolf, 113, 124n, 195n, 199, 444
Hitler-Stalin Nonaggression Pact (1939), 113n, 199, 444
Hobby, Oveta Culp, 427n
Hoffa, Jimmy, 59
Hoffman, Abbie, 509
Holcomb, Robert, 480n
Holiday, Billy, 53n
Holiday Song (radio show), 271
Holliday, Judy, 260, 321, 371
Holloway, David, 176n
Hollywood Nineteen, 257n, 258, 274, 333n
Hollywood Reporter, 66, 119n, 267, 268, 288
Hollywood Ten, 63, 63n, 64n, 65n, 114n, 118n, 257n, 258–59, 260, 268, 269, 276, 284, 370, 398, 532
Holmes, Oliver Wendell, 144
Holt, Henry, 139n
Home of the Brave (film), 284
Homolka, Oscar, 273n
Hook, Sidney, 233n
Hook, The (Miller), 120, 341–42
Hoover, J. Edgar, 18n, 28, 38n, 83, 86, 91, 96n, 97, 122, 123n, 133n, 138, 139, 145, 175, 187, 194, 234, 237, 380, 392–93, 442, 500, 523, 524, 536
  Cohn and, 101
  Custodial Detention list and, 249n
  Eisenhower and, 83
  Hiss and, 147–48
  homosexuality of, 101
  JFK blackmailed by, 81n, 147
  King and, 504n
  Matusow and, 97, 100–101, 107
  Nixon and, 83
  organized crime and, 93n
  OSS and, 153n, 154
  Palmer Raids and, 353n
  power of, 83
  public image of, 81

Rosenberg case and, 180, 185*n,* 187
Swearingen on, 93–94
wiretap directives and, 100*n*–111*n*
Hopkins, Harry, 533
Hopper, Hedda, 297
Horton, Myles, 488
House Committee on Appropriations, 110*n,*
    161*n*
House Committee on Education and Labor,
    385, 425
House Committee on Un-American Activities
    (HUAC), 36*n,* 43, 63*n,* 64, 99*n,*
    109*n,* 112, 114, 120*n,* 128, 139*n,*
    194, 196*n*–97*n,* 198*n,* 220, 225, 279,
    379, 387, 390*n,* 397, 443, 477, 494
  abolition of 526–27
  atomic secrets hearings of, 175, 176
  Broadway theater hearings of, 317, 318
  Canal Zone and, 392
  civil rights movement and, 470–72,
    502
  FBI and, 523, 524–25
  Garfield and, 116
  graylist of, 259, 266
  Hellman and, 167, 338–39
  Hiss case and, 102*n,* 146, 148
  history of, 17
  Hollywood allies of, 255–57, 299–300
  Hollywood hearings of, *see* Hollywood
    Nineteen; Hollywood Ten
  Nixon and, 175
  Oxnam and, 352*n*
  peace movement and, 507–9
  renaming of, 526
  Rusk and, 169
  Shaftel and, 429, 435, 436–37
  teachers and, 419, 420, 422, 423
  Weavers and, 362, 371, 374
  Wilkinson and, 531–32
House I Live In, The (film), 448–49
"House I Live In, The" (song), 53, 337*n*
House in the Country, A (radio show), 267
Houseman, John, 312, 314
House of Representatives, U.S., 161, 262,
    526–27
Housing Administration Act, 219*n*
Howe, Irving, 233*n*
Hoyer, Louis, 424
Hruska, Roman Lee, 523
Hughes, Howard, 278
Hughes, Langston, 130*n*
Hungary, 170–71, 174, 203, 230, 288, 411*n*
Hunter, Ian, 65, 264

Hurley, Patrick, 161
Huston, John, 64*n,* 261
Huston, Walter, 273*n,* 515

Ichord, Richard H., 17
I Led Three Lives (TV show), 68, 98
I Married a Communist (film), 259*n*
Immigration and Nationality
    (McCarran-Walter) Act (1952), 18–19,
    43–44, 202–3
Industrial Workers of the World (IWW),
    355*n,* 380*n*
Institute for the Study of Nonviolence, 508
Interior Department, U.S., 43, 143
Internal Security (McCarran) Act (1950), 17,
    18, 94*n,* 202, 223, 224, 229, 249*n,*
    394–95, 450*n,* 453*n*–54*n,* 525,
    527
International Alliance of Theatrical Stage
    Employees (IATSE), 112, 114, 256,
    283
International Longshoremen's and
    Warehousemen's Union (ILWU), 58,
    61*n,* 242, 403–4, 406, 410, 449*n*
International Mine, Mill and Smelter Workers
    Union, 103, 280, 37 , 380–81, 387*n,*
    388
International Monetary Fund, 10\
International Publishers, 104, 452, 455
Isaacs, Stan, 450
Italy, 34, 204, 215*n,* 375*n*
Ivanhoe (film), 55
Ivanov, Peter, 198*n*
I've Got a Secret (TV show), 320, 321
I Was a Communist for the FBI (TV series),
    98, 208–9, 259*n*

Jack (security officer), 122–23
Jackson, Donald, 281, 286, 310–11, 385
Jackson, Jesse, 505*n*
Jackson, Robert H., 110*n*
Jaffe, Philip, 159–60
Jaffe, Sam, 350
Jahoda, Marie, 130
Japan, 153*n,* 161, 177, 402
Japanese-American Citizens League, 525
Jarrico, Paul, 119*n,* 259*n,* 276–84, 326
Jefferson, Thomas, 287
Jencks, Clinton, 100*n,* 103–4, 280, 281,
    354–55, 380–90
Jencks, Virginia, 280
Jenkins, Becky, 69–73, 518, 520
Jenkins, Dave, 69, 447–51, 516, 520

Jenkins, Edith, 515–20
Jenkins, Margie, 71
Jenner, William E., 17, 445
Jerome, V. J., 132
Jewish Anti-Fascist Committee, 230n
Jewish Board of Guardians, 51
Jewish Restitution Committee, 333
Jimmie Higgins (Sinclair), 253n
Johnson, Haynes, 44n
Johnson, Laurence A., 324–25, 350
Johnson, Lyndon, 489
Johnson, Manning, 471
Joint Anti-Fascist Refugee Committee, 157, 320, 348, 440, 442, 443
Joliot-Curie, Madame, 510–11, 517
Jones, Dorothy, 257n
Jones, Howard P., 174
Jones, Joseph, 34
Jones, Roger, 169
Josephson, Leon, 436
Journal American, 134, 326, 342n
Justice Department, U.S., 39, 84, 94n, 97–98, 101n–2n, 109n, 110n, 116n, 151, 154n, 162n, 178; 179, 237, 352, 404, 434n, 443, 471, 505, 508
    labor movement and, 378–79
    labor schools and, 423
    Matusow and, 353–55
    Smith Act prosecutions by, 201–2

Kael, Pauline, 276
Kahn, Albert, 107, 352, 354
Kahn, Gordon, 65, 258n
Karesh, Joseph, 214
Katzenbach, Nicholas, 231, 234
Kaufman, Irving R., 179, 185, 185n
Kaye, Danny, 261
Kazan, Elia, 120–21, 341–42
Keeler, Christine, 504n
Keeley, Miss, 71
Kelley, Clarence, 96
Kempton, Murray, 192
Kennedy, Edward M. "Ted," 547
Kennedy, John F., 59, 169, 531
    civil rights movement and, 503–4, 505
    Hoover's blackmailing of, 81n, 147
    Sobell and, 193
Kennedy, Joseph, Sr., 200n
Kennedy, Robert F., 59, 193, 547
    Gladys Scales and, 234
Kenny, Robert, 279, 286
Kent, Rockwell, 264–65

Kepler, Roy, 508
Kerr, Jean, 105, 105n
KGB, 151
Khrushchev, Nikita, 68, 96, 288, 505
    Stalin denunciation by, 72–73, 203, 230, 276, 411n, 522
Kibre, Jeff, 113–14, 113n
Kilgallen, Dorothy, 320
King, Martin Luther, Jr., 59, 233, 471, 472, 500, 503–4, 508, 532, 534
Kinoy, Arthur, 481
Klein, Lawrence, 435–36
Knight, Frances, 512n
Knopf, Alfred, 355
Koch, Howard, 258n, 272–76
Kochler, Dan, 449
Koenig, Lester, 118
Koestler, Arthur, 303
Korean War, 42, 71, 73n, 104, 180, 206, 258, 263, 268–69, 386, 404, 406, 417, 440, 486, 508, 517n
KPFK, 221, 223
Ku Klux Klan, 471–72, 483, 486, 487, 502, 506
Kundera, Milan, 23
Kuntsler, William, 481
Kuntz (Sobell's attorney), 186, 191
Kuomintang Party (KMT), 144, 159, 161, 164
Kushner, Sam, 88

labor schools, 69, 291n, 423–24
Labor's Nonpartisan League, 220
Labor Youth League (LYL), 73, 420
La Guardia, Fiorello, 414
Lambert, Carl, 212n
Lampell, Millard, 363
Lancaster, Burt, 260
Lane, Myles, 179
Lang, David, 326
Lannon, Al, 414n
Lardner, David, 266–67, 270, 272
Lardner, Jim, 267
Lardner, John, 270
Lardner, Ring, Jr., 63n, 65, 67, 157, 258n, 259n, 260–66, 267, 268, 269, 270, 272, 276, 370
Lardner, Silvia, 268
Larsen, Emannuel, 159–60
Las Vegas Story, The (film), 278
Lattimore, Owen, 162, 303n
Laura (film), 305
Lautner, John, 222, 228

Law of the Soviet State, The (Vishinsky), 104, 107
Lawrence, Ernest, 197*n*
Lawrence, Marc, 284*n*, 285
Lawrence of Arabia (film), 281*n*
Lawrenson, Jack, 414*n*
Lawson, John Howard, 113–14, 258*n*, 259*n*, 262–63, 287, 296, 297, 312, 398
Lay, Huston, 334*n*–35*n*
Lee, Anna, 323–24
Lee, Gypsy Rose, 321, 348*n*
Lee, Robert E., 161*n*
Lees, Robert, 259
Legal Education Advisory Committee, 471
Legion Magazine, 259, 260
Lenin, V. I., 138, 157, 208, 215, 217, 221, 235, 397, 481
Leonard, Sheldon, 328
Leontiev, Wassily W., 134
Le Sueur, Meridel, 319
Leventhal, Harold, 368–69
Levison, Stanley, 472
Lewis (attorney), 208
Lewis, John L., 59, 63
Liberator, 321*n*
Life, 214, 498, 515
Lightfoot, Claude, 88–89, 91, 92, 97
Lima, Albert, 212*n*
Lindbergh, Charles, 200*n*
Linschitz, Henry, 188*n*
Lippmann, Walter, 36
Lloyd, David, 139–40
Loeb, Louis, 356, 357, 359
Loeb, Philip, 43, 350–51
Lomanitz, Giovanni R., 197*n*
Long View From the Left, A (Richmond), 223*n*
Lorch, Alice, 496–97
Lorch, Grace, 490, 495–96
Lorch, Lee, 489–99
Los Angeles Times, 428, 531*n*
Losey, Joe, 275
Lowenfels, Walter, 374
Lowenthal, John, 152*n*
Lowenthal, Max, 139
loyalty oaths, 24–25, 42, 154, 321–22, 419, 424, 426, 440, 462
Loyalty Review Board, 129, 158, 163
Luce, Claire Boothe, 214
Luckel Act (1953), 424
Lumet, Sidney, 350
Lundeberg, Harry, 60*n*

MacArthur, Douglas, 445*n*, 545
McCarey, Leo, 99*n*
McCarran, Pat, 17, 319
McCarran (Internal Security) Act (1950), 17, 18, 94*n*, 202, 223, 224, 229, 249*n*, 394–95, 450*n*, 453*n*–54*n*, 525, 527
McCarran-Walter (Immigration and Nationality) Act (1952), 18–19, 43–44, 202–3
McCarthy, Joseph R., 18, 24, 40, 41, 97, 101, 106*n*, 108, 109, 111, 123, 139*n*, 158, 167, 234*n*, 263, 319, 353, 367*n*, 383, 401, 417, 471, 472, 514
   career of, 27–28
   Manheim case and, 136–37
   Matusow and, 97, 99, 105–6
   Nixon and, 23, 28*n*
   State Department and, 28, 40, 161–62
   Tydings Committee and, 162
   Wheeling speech of, 145, 161–62
"McCarthyism," 27*n*
   defined, 28
McClellan, John L., 18, 353
McCullough, David, 29–30
McElroy, Robert, 413*n*
McGrath (HUAC attorney), 392–93
McGrath, J. Howard, 27
McGrath, Tom, 319
McGuire, Father, 167
McInerney, James, 159*n*
McKenzie, Howard, 415*n*–16*n*
MacLeish, Archibald, 24
McLeod, Scott, 41, 128, 145, 167, 173
Macmillan, Harold, 504*n*
McNeil, W. H., 33
McSurely, Al, 480
McSurely, Margaret, 480
Mafia, 93, 303, 526, 527
Magnuson (Screening) Act (1950), 404, 405, 406, 524*n*
Mailer, Norman, 53
Malin, Patrick, 360
Maltz, Albert, 65, 119*n*, 258*n*, 266, 295–97, 299*n*, 330
Mandel, Benjamin, 102
Manheim, Carl, 134
Manheim, Jerry, 131–37, 131*n*
Manheim, Sylvia, 131, 132, 134, 135–36
Mann, Thomas, 157
Mannix, Eddie, 291, 292, 311
Mao Tse-tung, 144, 160*n*, 481
March on Washington for Integrated Schools, 502

Margolis, Ben, 217n, 220, 279, 281
Marine Engineers Union, 404
Marine Firemen, Oilers and Watertenders
    Union, 404
Marine Workers Industrial Union (MWIU),
    405, 406
Marion, Paul, 284
Markert, Clement, 435n
Marsh, Reginald, 130n
Marshall, Burke, 503
Marshall, Daniel, 185, 185n
Marshall, George C., 36, 155
Marshall Plan, 414, 416
Marty (film), 271
Marx, Karl, 138, 208, 221, 222, 235, 397,
    481, 500
Marxist Commentary (radio program), 221n
Marzani, Carl, 144, 152–58
Mason, Edward, 155
Masses, The, 320, 321n
Masters, Mates and Pilots Union, 404
Mathes, William C., 221
Mathews, J. B., 318n, 471
Mattachine Society, 236n
Matthiessen, F. O., 43, 422
Matusow, Harvey Job, 97–108, 109–10, 352
    as FBI double agent, 97, 99, 107, 387n
    Hoover and, 97, 100–101, 107
    HUAC and, 368
    Jencks and, 385–87
    Justice Department and, 353–55
    McCarthy and, 97, 99, 105–6
    Supreme Court and, 387n
    teachers' blacklist and, 425
    Weavers and, 367–68, 372
May, Alan Nunn, 177n
May Day parades, 75–76
Mayer, Louis B., 261, 311
Mazzei, Joseph, 211
Meany, George, 234
media, 24, 42, 175, 258
    blacklist and, 319–20
    red-baiting by, 43, 318
    security program and, 130–31
Medina, Harold, 111
Meeropol, Abel, 51–53
Meeropol, Ann, 51–52
Meeropol, Michael, 50n, 51, 53
Meeropol, Robert, 47–54
Meet the Press, 140, 148n, 323
Meiklejohn, Alexander, 531, 539
Melby, John, 165–69

Melson, Inez, 312, 314
Memoirs (Truman), 35, 37
Menjou, Adolphe, 257, 261, 297
Meredith, James, 505
Metaxis, John, 33n
Meyer, Howard, 184n, 187
Meyers, Blackie, 414
Miami Daily News, 318n
"Midnight Special, The" (song), 364
Milestone, Lewis, 258n
Miller, Arthur, 43, 53, 120–22, 302, 303n,
    317, 340–45
Mills, Saul, 154
Minority of One, 515
Mission to Moscow (film) 256n, 273, 276
Modern Times (film), 305
Monroe, Marilyn, 312, 343
Montgomery, Judge, 206–8, 209
Montgomery, Robert, 257, 261
Mooney, Tom, 188, 447
Moore, Garry, 322, 325
Moore, Harry T., 506
Morgan, Henry, 322–23
Morley, Karen, 259
Morris, Mr., 445
Morse, Wayne Lyman, 512
Mosk, Ed, 278
Mostel, Zero, 59
Motion Picture Alliance for the Preservation of
    American Ideals (MPAPAI), 112, 115,
    255, 297n
Motion Picture Industry Council, 119, 300n
"Moving Forward" (Maltz), 297n
Moy, Eugene, 145n
Mr. District Attorney (radio show), 267
Muir, Jean, 316
Mundt, Karl, 175
Murder My Sweet (film), 296, 304
Murphy (writer), 119
Murphy, Charles, 139–40, 139n
Murphy, Frank, 58, 404
Murphy, George, 257
Murray, James, 198n
Murray, Philip, 377, 394, 415n, 482n
Murrow, Edward R., 337
Musmanno, Michael Angelo, 204–5,
    208
Mussolini, Benito, 195n, 402
My Son John (film), 99, 259n

Nagy, Imre, 539n
Nash, John, 275

Nashville Tennessean, 493

Nation, 41, 191*n*

National Association for the Advancement of Colored People (NAACP), 42, 471, 490, 492, 497, 502, 506

National Association of Manufacturers (NAM), 18, 376, 378

National Broadcasting Company (NBC), 362

National Catholic Welfare, 167

National Committee Against Repressive Legislation, 525

National Committee for a Sane Nuclear Policy, 514

National Committee to Abolish HUAC, 91*n,* 521, 525, 528, 533

National Committee to Secure Justice in the Rosenberg Case, 192, 192*n*

National Guardian, 191*n,* 349

National Labor Relations Board (NLRB), 256, 378, 379

National Lawyers Guild, 300*n*

National Liberation Front (EAM), 33–34

National Maritime Union, 403, 404, 413, 414, 415, 416, 447, 500

National Student League, 515

Nature of the Chemical Bond, The (Pauling), 511

Navasky, Victor, 313

Navy Department, U.S., 82

Nazi Party, U.S., 66, 472

Nehru, Jawaharlal, 511–12

Nellor, Ed, 161*n*

Nelson, Margaret, 196

Nelson, Steve, 176–77, 195–98, 204–12, 478

New Deal, 30, 128, 144, 146, 147, 175, 233, 274, 344, 375, 376, 378, 452, 515

New Masses, 130, 132, 297

New Orleans Tribune, 500–501

New Republic, The, 41, 191*n*

News Leader, 499*n*

Newsweek, 268

New York *Daily News,* 52, 193, 360

New Yorker, 276, 319, 331, 335–36

New York Herald Tribune, 129, 130, 318, 332, 336*n*

New York Mirror, 187, 360

New York Newspaper Guild, 359

New York Post, 52, 106, 107, 134, 234, 319, 353, 358

New York Society for Prevention of Cruelty to Children, 51*n*

New York Times, 52, 102, 106, 107, 108, 110*n,* 134, 175, 234, 282, 288, 319, 339, 355, 358–61, 431, 435, 438, 441, 456, 480*n,* 491, 492, 495, 496, 512, 522, 545

New York World-Telegram, 342, 363

Nickerson, Mark, 435*n*

Niebuhr, Reinhold, 233, 534

Nitti, Frank, 256*n,* 283*n*

Nixon, Richard M., 23, 28, 59, 84, 94, 144, 369, 466

  Hiss case and, 102*n,* 148, 150–51

  Hoover and, 83

  HUAC and, 175

  McCarthy and, 23, 28*n*

Nizer, Louis, 116–17

Nofziger, Lyn, 460, 461, 466*n*

Now, Robert, 43, 415*n*

nuclear freeze movement, 43

Nye, Gerald P., 148*n*

Nye Committee, 148

Obenhouse, Victor, 523, 525

O'Brien, Jack, 325–26

O'Dell, Jack, 413–18, 472, 500–506

O'Dwyer, Thomas J., 529–30

Office of Naval Intelligence (ONI), 153, 160

Office of Strategic Services (OSS), 127, 152, 153, 162

  Hoover and, 153*n,* 154

  U.S. Communist Party and, 154*n*

Office of War Information, 162

O'Herlihy, Dan, 285

Olson, Governor, 447*n*

Onda, Andy, 205, 209

Only the Valiant (film), 287

On the Waterfront (film), 341*n*–42*n*

Open Door policy, 159

Operation Abolition (film), 543

Operation Correction (film), 543*n*

Operation Dixie, 413, 482

Operation Mind, 435

Oppenheimer, Frank, 196

Oppenheimer, J. Robert, 168, 176, 196–97, 421–22, 488

Oppenheimer, Kitty, 195–96, 197

"Ordinary Spring, An" (Koch), 275

Ornitz, Samuel, 258*n*

O'Shea, Danny, 323

O'Toole, Tara, 44

Owen, Richard, 151

Oxnam, G. Bromley, 107, 352, 443

Pacifica Radio Network, 221, 508
Palazzi, Paul, 415n–16n
Palmer, A. Mitchell, 353n
Palmer Raids, 353
Panama Canal Zone, 390–95
Panken, Jacob, 51n
Parker, Chief (LAPD), 530
Parks, Larry, 258n, 270, 278, 301, 313
Parks, Rosa, 470, 479, 480, 487
Parkinson, Thomas, 43, 422
Parsons, Bishop, 450
Partisan Review, 458
Passen, Joe, 249–51
Patterson, William L., 454
Pauling, Linus, 287, 426–28, 508, 509–15
Paxton, Johnny, 296
Peace Information Center, 434n, 509
peace movement, 507–9
Pearson, Drew, 107, 352
Peekskill Evening Star, 74, 75
Peekskill riots, 74–80, 362, 364, 368, 372
    Black and, 78–80
    injuries in, 75, 77n
    Robeson and, 74–79
    Silber and, 75–78
Pegler, Westbrook, 318n
Pennock, William, 203
People's Artists, Inc., 75, 76, 373
People's Education and Press Association,
    247
People's Folksay, 78
People's Liberation Army (ELAS), 33–34
People's Songs, 373
People's World, 121–22, 197, 222, 461
Pepper, George, 65
Perlin, Marshall, 188n
Perlo, Victor, 455
Philbrick, Herbert, 68n, 98, 318
Philco Playhouse (radio show), 270–71
Photoplay, 64n
Pichel, Irving, 258n
Pidgeon, Walter, 281
Pieces, The (Manheim), 131
Pittsburgh Courier, 492
Pittsburgh Press, 208, 441
Place in the Sun, A (film), 304
Plessy v. Ferguson, 530
Poindexter, John M., 155
Political Economy (Leontiev), 134, 135
Polk, George, 34n
Port Security Program, 405
"Possible Resurrection of the Communist
    International, Resumption of Extreme

Leftist Activities, Possible Effect on
    United States" (State Department), 38
Potash, Irving, 201n
Preminger, Otto, 264
President's Temporary Commission on
    Employee Loyalty, 128
Pressman, Lee, 377, 393–94
Price, Bill, 360
Profumo, John, 504
Progressive Labor Party, 67
Progressive Party, U.S., 507
Prokofiev, Sergey, 306n
Public Law 733 (1950), 128
Pumpkin Papers, 102, 149–50

Quayle, Dan, 369
Quill, Mike, 377
Quinn, Anthony, 350

Radosh, Ronald, 180n
Raft, George, 294
Raintree County (film), 294, 304
Raksin, David, 305–14
Rand, Ayn, 261, 273
Randolph, A. Philip, 233, 502n
Randolph, John, 345–51
Rank, J. Arthur, 275, 298, 305
Rankin, John, 256, 469, 470–71
Ratliff, Thomas, 480n, 481–82
Rauh, Joseph, 136–41, 338–39, 344
Ray, Tommy, 414n
Reagan, Ronald, 43, 119, 155, 257, 261, 265,
    300
Rebel, The (TV show), 321
Red Channels, 259, 272, 315–16, 320, 322,
    323, 324, 325, 351n, 367
Red Planet Mars (film), 259n
Reed, Stanley F., 151
Rein, David, 228, 229
Remington, William, 43, 131, 140–41
Republican Party, U.S., 39, 40, 144–45, 146,
    147, 199, 344, 383
    China issue and, 158n
Reserve Index, 95
Reuben, William, 191n
Reuther, Walter, 59
Revueltas, Rosaura, 281–82
Rice, Charles Owen, 443
Rich, Robert, 63
Richmond, Al, 212n, 214, 215n, 218, 223
Riefenstahl, Leni, 257n
Riesel, Victor, 117, 316, 318n, 392
Riess, Bernard, 446

Roberson, Mason, 280

Roberts, Holland, 448

Roberts, Marguerite, 289, 290, 291, 292, 294

Robeson, Paul, 53*n*, 181, 280, 303*n*, 325, 333, 337, 362, 372, 396, 414, 420, 435, 451, 453*n*, 460–61, 505*n*, 515–16

   Peekskill riots and, 74–79

   Scales and, 231

Robinson, Edward G., 64*n*

Roemer, Bill, 93

Rogers, Ginger, 301*n*

Rogers, Lela, 301*n*

Roman (juror), 210–11

Roosevelt, Eleanor, 146, 187, 233*n*, 456, 472, 488

Roosevelt, Franklin D., 28–31, 33, 41, 110, 112, 127, 144, 147, 220*n*, 256, 273, 274, 344, 375, 459, 533

Roosevelt, James, 526

Rosenberg, Ethel, 47, 133*n*, 177–88, 190, 191–92, 350, 439*n*

Rosenberg, Julius, 47, 133*n*, 177–88, 190, 191–92, 350, 439*n*

Rosenberg, Meta, 274*n*

Rosenberg Fund for Children, 47, 53

Ross, Harold W., 335–36

Rosselson, Leon, 366

Rossen, Robert, 258*n*

Roth, Andrew, 160, 160*n*

Rubin, Jerry, 509

Rukeyser, Muriel, 423

Rumania, 33, 36, 62, 170

Rushmore, Howard, 318*n*

Rusk, Dean, 167*n*, 169

Russell (HUAC investigator), 307, 309

Russell, Bertrand, 194, 508

Russell, Harold, 117–18

Rustin, Bayard, 502*n*

Ruthven, Madeleine, 307*n*

Ryan, Joe, 342

Sacco, Nicola, 188, 188*n*

Sachs, Joe, 390–95

Sackler, Arthur M., 360

Saillant, Louis, 519

Sailors Union of the Pacific, 60*n*

Salt, Waldo, 67, 258*n*

Salt of the Earth (film), 276, 280–82, 384–85

Sandperl, Ira, 508

Sanford, John, 289–94, 319

San Francisco Chronicle, 542

San Francisco Examiner, 218, 449, 466

San Francisco General Strike (1934), 389

Sartre, Jean-Paul, 441

Satterthwaite, Joe, 168

Saturday Evening Post, 119, 130, 300

Saturday Review of Literature, 354

Saunders, Butch, 215*n*

Saypol (attorney), 181*n*, 188

Sayre, Francis, 149

Scales, Gladys, 228, 233–34

Scales, Junius, 193*n*, 226–35, 239–40, 470

Schafer, Jack, 360

Schary, Dore, 258, 290–91, 300*n*, 329

Schine, David, 123, 334–35

Schlesinger, Arthur, Jr., 547

Schlesinger, Hyman, 206

Schmidt, Godfrey, 348

Schnaubelt, Rudolph, 546*n*

Schneiderman, William, 212*n*

School for Scoundrels (film), 330

Schulberg, Budd, 265–66, 341*n*–42*n*

Schumach, Murray, 288

Schumlun, Herman, 348

Science and History (Bernal), 517

Science and Society, 442

Scientific American, 191*n*

"Scientist X," 177, 195, 197*n*

Scott, Adrian, 258*n*, 295, 296, 297, 314

Scott, Hazel, 321

Scottsboro Defense Fund, 129

Screen Actors Guild, 257*n*, 281, 288

Screen Cartoonists Guild, 257

Screening (Magnuson) Act, 404, 405, 406, 524*n*

Screen Writers Guild, 68, 14, 278

Seabury, Samuel, 430*n*

Seabury Committee, 430

Security Index, 84, 94–97, 249*n*

Seeger, Pete, 76*n*, 78–79, 99, 362, 363–67, 369, 373*n*, 508, 535, 539

Seeger, Toshi, 80, 365, 539

Selsam, Howard, 452

Senate, U.S., 28, 103, 139, 162

Senate Committee on Government Operations, Permanent Subcommittee on Investigations of, 18

Senate Foreign Relations Committee, 145, 162

Senate Internal Security Subcommittee (SISS), 17, 319, 352, 353, 355, 387, 423, 425, 429, 441, 443, 488, 496, 500, 502, 509, 512, 523, 527

Senate (continued)
  civil rights movement and, 470–72
  Smith and, 444, 445
  Weavers and, 364
Senate Select Committee on Intelligence
    Activities, 94n
Sennett, William, 86, 88, 91, 95
Serpico (film), 350
Serreo, Rudolfo, 415n
Service, John Stewart, 158–65, 168
Severeid, Eric, 423
Shaftel, Oscar, 429–34
Sharp, Malcolm, 192
Shawn, William, 335–36
Sherwood, William, 43, 422
Shipley, Ruth, 154n, 512
Shirer, William, 337
Shively Newsweek, 474
Shlakman, Vera, 429
Shostakovich, Dmitry, 306n, 517
Shuttlesworth, Fred, 502
Sierra Club, 43
Silber, Irwin, 75–78
Silver City Daily Press, 383
Sim, Alastair, 330
Sinatra, Frank, 448–49
Sinclair, Upton, 253n
Sing Out!, 76, 364, 373n
Sipes, John, 334n
Slack, Alfred, 439
Smith, Al, 39
Smith, Ferdinand, 404, 413, 414–16
Smith, M. Brewster, 444–47
Smith, McNeil, 231–32
Smith Act (1940), 18, 39, 54, 55, 68, 85,
    87n, 98n, 104, 105n, 156, 186n,
    201, 205, 211, 221, 229, 230–31,
    237, 242, 247, 387, 451, 452n, 478,
    506
Smith Act Families Defense Fund, 56
Sobell, Helen, 189–94
Sobell, Morton, 178, 181–88, 190, 193
Sobell, Sidney, 189, 190
Socialist Party, 67n
Socialist Study Club, 131–32
Socialist Workers Party, 67n, 201n
Socialist Workers Party v. Attorneys General,
    110n
Sokolsky, George, 318n
Sondergaard, Gale, 317–18
Song of Russia (film), 119n, 256n, 261
Sons of the American Revolution, 424
Sontag, Susan, 59

Sorrell, Herbert, 114, 256
Southern Christian Leadership Conference
    (SCLC), 472, 500, 503, 532
Southern Conference Educational Fund
    (SCEF), 472, 479–80, 481, 532
Southern Conference for Human Welfare, 472
Southern Mountain Project, 480
Southern News Almanac, 247n
Southern Worker, 247
Soviet Union, 24, 34, 35, 55n, 92n, 112,
    132n, 144, 175, 176, 177, 178, 179,
    180, 200, 236, 332, 364, 444, 511
  Bridges' views of, 61–62
  Great Purge trials in, 104n
  Hungarian Revolution and, 203, 288, 411n
  onset of Cold War and, 24
  U.S. Communist Party and, 38, 109, 199,
    295
  World War II aftermath and, 31–32
Spain, 127, 152, 195–96, 318n, 320
Spanish Civil War, 127, 152, 195, 425, 452
Spartacus (film), 66, 280, 330
Spector, Frank, 212n, 223
Spellman, Francis, 101
Stachel, Jacob, 201n
Stack, Joe, 403, 414
Stalin, Joseph, 31, 32, 33, 44, 71n, 72n,
    124n, 132n, 147n, 201n, 203, 406,
    444, 522
Stanford, Sally, 60
Stapleton, Maureen, 271
Star Chamber hearings, 287, 387
Stars and Stripes, 336n
Starvus, Loretta, 212–19
Stassen, Harold, 111
State Department, U.S., 27, 32, 38, 333, 337,
    508
  China issue and, 158, 164
  China White Paper of, 161, 164, 165
  Conference for Peace and, 340n
  Greek crisis and, 34
  Hiss case and, 144–45
  homosexuals and, 123, 124
  loyalty program and, 41, 129
  McCarthy and, 28, 40, 161–62
  Miller and, 343
  OSS and, 153
  Panama and, 393
  passport denial and, 265n, 279, 393, 435,
    511–12
  security officers in, 82, 122–26
  security program and, 144–46
  Service and, 160, 161, 162–64

Stauffer, Samuel, 41
Stein, Art, 142
Steinbeck, John, 340, 354
Steinberg (attorney), 206
Steinberg, Harry, 212n, 223
Steinmetz Club, 181
Sterling, Wallace, 421
Stevenson, Adlai, 151
Stimson, Henry, 29
Stockholm Peace Petition, 434, 486
Stone, I. F., 30, 233n
Stookey, Paul, 364n, 508
Strack, Celeste, 465
"Strange Fruit" (song), 53
Student Peace Union, 508
Students for a Democratic Society (SDS), 43,
    91n
Subversive Activities Control Board (SACB),
    17–18, 379–80, 387, 423, 450n, 509
Sullivan, Ed, 316
Sullivan, William, 83
Sulzberger, Arthur Hays, 357n, 358, 360
Supreme Court, U.S., 84, 104, 110n, 131,
    211, 241, 376n, 388n, 394, 490,
    512n, 521, 531
  Barenblatt decision of, 438–39
  Bridges case and, 58, 404
  Brown decision of, 473, 492–93, 499n,
    502
  Communist Party prosecution and, 111,
    215n, 217–19, 221, 223–24
  Hiss case and, 151
  Hollywood Ten and, 263
  Jencks case and, 104n, 387, 389
  Lightfoot case and, 88n
  maritime workers and, 402
  Marzani case and, 156
  Matusow and, 387n
  Nelson case and, 478, 481
  passport issue and, 264–65, 279
  poll tax and, 487n
  Remington case and, 141
  Rosenberg case and, 50
  Scales case and, 231
  Service case and, 158, 163
  Smith Act and, 97, 237
  Taft-Hartley Act and, 380
Swearingen, M. Wesley, 84–97, 249n
  on harassment of Reds, 90–91
  on Hoover, 93–94
  on illegal break-ins, 84–87
  on informants, 92–93
  Lightfoot arrest and, 88–89

  on Security Index, 94–97
  on surveillance, 87–88
Syracuse Herald-Journal, 102n
Szago, Stephen, 75
Szluk, Peter, 122–26

Taft-Hartley Act (1947), 18, 39, 202,
    375n–76n, 378, 380, 383, 388, 396
Tarloff, Frank, 326–31
Tavenner, Frank S., 309
Taylor, Robert, 55, 257, 261, 297n
Taylor, Telford, 229–30, 231, 232n
Teachers' Defense Committee, 463
Teachers Union of New York, 425
Teamsters Union, 59n
Tender Comrades (film), 301n
Tenney, Jack B., 220–21, 449n, 450, 459,
    460
Tenney Committee, 449–50, 459n, 466
Terkel, Studs, 23–24
Terry and the Pirates (radio show), 267
Thau, Ben, 291, 292
Theobald, John Jacob, 105, 431n
Thomas, Bob, 288
Thomas, Danny, 328
Thomas, J. Parnell, 17, 157, 257, 261–62, 263
Thomas, Norman, 233, 234
Thomas, Stephen, 43, 422
Thompson, Robert, 43, 201n, 202n, 203–4,
    247, 544–48
Thompson, Sylvia, 9, 202n, 247–49, 482–87,
    544–48
Thurmond, J. Strom, 501, 504, 534
Time, 106, 107, 164, 268, 282, 389, 439n
Timebends (Miller), 120n
Tito, Marshall, (Josip Broz), 161
Tolin, Ernest, 213n
Tolson, Clyde, 85, 85n
Tomara, Sonia, 336n
To Tell the Truth (TV show), 320
Townshend, Pauline, 326
Trachtenberg, Alexander, 104–5, 107–8,
    333n, 354, 355, 452
Trading with the Enemy Act, 145n
Trafficante, Santos, 93n
Travers, Mary, 364n, 508
Travis, Maurice, 377, 388
Treasury Department, U.S., 450n
Trotsky, Leon, 67n, 132n, 235, 287, 481
Truman, Harry S., 17, 24, 27, 28, 84, 112,
    139–40, 147, 163, 175, 405, 445n,
    456, 461–62
  anticommunism of, 32–33

Truman (*continued*)
   background and personality of, 29–30
   Baylor speech of, 35–36
   China Lobby and, 145*n*
   civil rights movement and, 503*n*,
      505–6
   foreign policy of, 37–39
   Greek crisis and, 34–36
   labor movement and, 376–78
   loyalty program launched by, 36–40
   OSS and, 153
   presidential succession of, 28–31
   White's promotion and, 109*n*
Truman Doctrine, 31, 32, 34–35, 37, 377,
      508–9
Trumbo, Chris, 63–69
Trumbo, Dalton, 63–68, 258*n*, 262–63, 264,
      266, 270, 280, 295–96, 301*n*, 314,
      326
Twain, Mark, 507
Tydings, Millard, 145, 162*n*
Tydings Committee, 162

Unemployment Councils, 375*n*
Unfriendly Nineteen, 119*n*
United Electrical Workers, 154
United Mine Workers, 59*n*
United Nations, 130, 146, 147, 287, 414,
      461, 514
United Press (UP), 288
United Public Workers of America, 44,
      141–42, 390, 391, 394
United States v. Stack, 218
Untermeyer, Louis, 320, 321
Untouchables, The (TV show), 288
Urey, Harold, 192

Vandenberg, Arthur, 35
Van Dorn, Daisy, 222*n*
Vanech, A. Devitt, 128
Van Siesteran, Urban, 106
Vanzetti, Bartolomeo, 188
Varkiza Agreement (1945), 33–34
Veterans Administration, 129*n*
Veterans of Foreign Wars, 39–40, 74, 79,
      318, 531
Vietnam War, 60, 508, 509
View From the Bridge, A (Miller), 340
Vincent, John Carter, 159
Vinson, Frederick M., 185*n*
Vishinsky, Andrei, 104
Volkogonov, Dmitri, 151

Volpe, Joe, 168
Vorhaus, Bernard, 302*n*

Wade, Andrew, 472–73, 476, 479
Wade, Charlotte, 477
Wadleigh, Henry Julian, 149
Wagner, Robert, 342
Wagner Act (1935), 375*n*, 382
Walcott, Derek, 505*n*
Walker, Alice, 505*n*
Walker, Jimmy, 430*n*
Walker, Robert, 99
Wallace, Henry, 39, 41, 371, 377, 405, 415,
      420, 425, 452, 457–58, 507–8
Wallach, Eli, 271
Wall Street Journal, 84
Walsh, Edmund, 139
Walsh, Richard F., 117, 117*n*, 118
Walter, Francis E., 17, 343*n*, 471
Walters Committee, 225
Warner, Harry, 273
Warner, Jack, 257, 261, 272, 304
War of the Worlds (radio show), 272
Warren, Earl, 231, 286, 499*n*, 531, 532
Washington Bookshop, 143
Washington Confidential, 124*n*
Washington Daily News, 547
Washington Post, 27*n*, 139, 186*n*, 496,
      513
Washington Star, 83, 193
"Wasn't That a Time" (song), 374
Wayne, John, 297
Weathermen, 91
Weavers, 99, 362–74, 508
Webster, William H., 526
Wechsler, James, 234, 358
Wedemeyer, Albert, 164
Weekly Domestic Intelligence Summary, 373*n*
Weinberg, Joseph, 176, 196–97, 197*n*
Weinstein, Hannah, 264
Welles, Orson, 272, 312*n*, 423
West, Don, 102*n*
Western Research Foundation, 42
Wexley, John, 296
What Makes Sammy Run? (Schulberg), 265*n*
"What Shall We Ask of Writers?" (Maltz),
      297*n*
What's My Line? (TV show), 320, 321, 322,
      323
Wheeling Intelligencer, 27
Wherry, Kenneth, 124*n*, 158*n*
White, E. B., 335

White, Harry Dexter, 43, 109
White, Katherine, 335–36
White, Theodore, 146
White, Thomas, 466
White Citizens' Councils, 471–72, 502
Whitmore, James, 346–47
Why Are They Attacking My Teacher?, 463
Wicker, Ireene, 315*n*
Wilde, Cornell, 262
Wilkerson, Doxey, 452
Wilkinson, Frank, 349, 464–66, 521, 526,
 528–37, 538, 539
Wilkinson, Jean, 460, 464–68, 537–40
Wilkinson, Jo, 537
Wilkinson, Tony, 537
Williams, Aubrey, 488, 533–34
Williams, Edward Bennett, 275–76
Williams, Evelyn, 51*n*
Williamson, John, 201*n*
Willis, Edwin, 17, 471, 540, 541, 542
Wilson, Charles, 376
Wilson, Edmund, 233*n*
Wilson, Michael, 280, 281, 330
Winchell, Walter, 101
Winston, Henry, 201*n*, 202*n*
Winter, Carl, 201*n*
Woman of the Year (film), 260
Women's International League of Peace and
 Freedom, 474, 476
Women Strike for Peace, 509
Wood, John S., 17, 286, 287
Wood, Sam, 115*n*, 255, 297
Woodhouse, C. M., 33

Woodward, C. Vann, 233*n*
World Bank, 109*n*
World Peace Congress, 434*n*, 486*n*, 516–17
"World Turned Upside Down, The" (song),
 366
World War I, 127, 155, 419, 507
World War II, 121, 376, 420, 508, 545
 fading memory of, 23–24
 Greek crisis and, 33
 Soviet Union and, 31–32
 U.S. Communist Party during, 200–201
Wright, Alexander, 211*n*
Wright, Frank Lloyd, 423
Wright, Henry, 456
Wyler, William, 117*n*, 118

Yalta Conference (1945), 28, 147
Yarrow, Peter, 364*n*, 508
Yates, Oleta O'Connor, 212*n*, 216, 218,
 242
Yergin, Daniel, 29
Yippies, 509
Young Communist League, 73*n*, 178–79,
 181, 216, 234*n*, 249, 444, 465, 515,
 522
Young Lions, The (film), 294, 304
Young People's Socialist League, 116*n*, 133
Young Progressives, 420
Yugoslavia, 36, 61

Zanuck, Darryl, 262
Zoll, Allen, 445*n*
Zubilin, Vassili, 197–98